LATER ITALIAN PAINTINGS
IN
THE NATIONAL GALLERY OF IRELAND
THE SEVENTEENTH, EIGHTEENTH AND NINETEENTH CENTURIES

LATER ITALIAN PAINTINGS
IN
THE NATIONAL GALLERY OF IRELAND
THE SEVENTEENTH, EIGHTEENTH AND NINETEENTH CENTURIES

MICHAEL WYNNE

THE NATIONAL GALLERY OF IRELAND 1986

British Library Cataloguing in Publication Data
National Gallery of Ireland.
    Later Italian paintings in the National
    Gallery of Ireland: the seventeenth, eighteenth
    and nineteenth centuries.
    1. Painting, Italian — Catalogs   2. Painting,
    Modern — 17th-18th centuries — Italy —
    Catalogs   3. Painting, Modern — 19th century
    — Italy — Catalogs
    I. Title II. Wynne, Michael
    759.5'074   ND616

    ISBN 0-903162-32-6
    ISBN 0-903162-33-4 Pbk

First published, 1986, by the National Gallery of Ireland, Dublin 2.

© Michael Wynne and the National Gallery of Ireland, 1986.

Edited by Elizabeth Mayes
Photography by Michael Olohan
Design, origination and print production by Printset & Design Ltd., Dublin.
Printed in Ireland by Criterion Press Ltd.

COVER: detail of *The shepherdess Spako with the infant Cyrus* by G. B. Castiglione (cat. no. 994).

CONTENTS

FOREWORD

THE ITALIAN *seicento* pictures in the National Gallery of Ireland are among the glories of the whole Collection. From the early years of the nineteenth century until relatively recently such pictures were rather frowned upon by *cognoscenti*, neglected by scholars, and ignored by collectors, including Galleries. Through curious circumstances, documented in the Introduction, Dublin has a remarkably fine collection of Italian pictures dating from this period, although, in fact, they were not always thought of as such. One of my predecessors Thomas Bodkin, in his Preface to a selective catalogue of the Gallery's pictures published in 1932, found many of these paintings 'remarkable for their area rather than their authenticity', excluded them from the Catalogue, and regretted that they had been purchased 'in haste and with more enthusiasm than discretion'. In fairness, many of the pictures so dismissed by Bodkin had become very darkened with time and were in need of cleaning; and he could not possibly have assessed them better even if his taste had encouraged him to do so. Nor would Bodkin have been alone in decrying such paintings at that time.

In the late 1960's and 1970's, however, an extensive cleaning programme was put in hand, carried out largely by the Istituto Centrale del Restauro of Rome and it was revealed that Dublin had a highly important collection of Italian seventeenth-century pictures; indeed one of the finest anywhere outside of Italy. Since that time a number of the paintings have been shown in international exhibitions: exhibitions which have demonstrated a new appreciation of the Italian seventeenth century. The Dublin Collection of later Italian pictures is not, however, confined solely to the *seicento*; and the eighteenth-century paintings are also choice. Regretably Canaletto is represented only by one modest canvas, but his Roman contemporary Panini is shown through a set of very fine *capricci* and a superb documentary picture of *A fête in the Piazza Navona*. Nor is the representation of G. B. Tiepolo strong; but from Venice there are two typical works by Pellegrini of good quality and a delightful Sebastiano Ricci. The 'country house' origins of part of the Collection is documented by a group of portraits by Pompeo Batoni.

For many years Michael Wynne has researched aspects of the Collection. His was the discovery that the *St. John in the Wilderness* after Titian was in fact a documented copy by Gian Antonio Guardi. He has also published the rare paintings by Piscelli, investigated the Milltown Collection and delved into the provenance of the paintings from the collection of Cardinal Fesch which are now in Dublin. Here the fruits of his researches are gathered together in one volume which is the first detailed catalogue of the entire collection ever to be published: and all the paintings are illustrated, together with comparative photographs of preparatory drawings, related paintings and X-rays. His text is a mine of information on later Italian painting in general and the Collection in the National Gallery of Ireland in particular; and his Catalogue will be valued by visitors to the Gallery and by scholars for many years to come.

HOMAN POTTERTON
Director, The National Gallery of Ireland
September 1986

AUTHOR'S ACKNOWLEDGEMENTS

In compiling a catalogue even of modest size it is inevitable that one seeks the advice, assistance, and answers to specific questions from a wide circle of colleagues and friends. Therefore it is a pleasant duty to thank sincerely Keith Andrews, Michael Archer, Walter Balzano, Satia and Robert Bernen, Piero Bigongiari, Didier Bodart, Allan Braham, Hugh Brigstocke, Christopher Brown, Giuseppe Cantelli, Giovanni Carandente, Anica Cevc, Marco Chiarini, Andrew Ciechanowiecki, the late Anthony M. Clark, Hilde Claussen, Hans Max Cramer, Francesca Flores D'Arcais, Andrea Emiliani, Gerhard Ewald, Cecil Gould, Dieter Graf, Mina Gregori, David and Gerti Halliday, Larissa Haskell, François Heim, Rupert Hodge, the late Nicola Ivanoff, the late Stefan Kozakiewicz, Alastair Laing, Kenneth Martin-Leake, Denis Mahon, Jennifer Montagu, Paolo and Laura Mora, the late Antonio Morassi, Mary Newcome-Schleier, the late Benedict Nicolson, A.V.B. Norman, Harald Olsen, Giovanna de Orléans-Borbòn, Ruth R. Philbrick, Terisio Pignatti, Wolfgang Prohaska, Stefania Mason Rinaldi, Aldo Rizzi, Pierre Rosenberg, John Rowlands, Francis Russell, Erich Schleier, Antoine Schnapper, David Scrase, John Somerville, John Spike, Nicola Spinosa, Christine Staderini, John Sunderland, Laura Tagliaferro, Anthony Thompson, Nicholas Turner, Giovanni Urbani, Francesco Valcanover, Clovis Whitfield, Reginald Williams, and Federico Zeri. Several other persons who made specific contributions are mentioned in the text. From those whose names have been omitted inadvertently, either here or in the text, I ask pardon.

The Courtauld Institute of Art, with its Witt Library, in London, The Biblioteca Hertziana, in Rome, and the Kunsthistoriches Institut, in Florence, helped advance work on the catalogue in a very significant way. I gladly thank the Directors and staff of these institutions.

My colleagues at the National Gallery of Ireland have contributed discussions on attributions and condition; the Librarian and her staff have gone to a lot of trouble to find elusive publications. I do not think that any of my colleagues will take it amiss if I thank particularly Sergio Benedetti, Restorer, who has a very special interest in Italian seventeenth century painting. The Director has given the project wholehearted support throughout.

The typing and retyping of the text has been undertaken with patience and perseverance by Mrs. Valerie Dunning. The indexes have been compiled by Nicole Arnould. Elizabeth Mayes ably assisted with proof-reading. Tony Moroney, with interest and skill, did the typesetting, while the overall production of the catalogue was in the capable hands of Colm Hanley.

Francis Haskell read the penultimate drafts of fifty-five of the entries, those relatingly mainly to the Venetian, North Italian, Neapolitan, and some of the Roman Schools. He made some very valid criticisms, indicated ways to further comprehension, and in general improved the quality of many of the entries. To him the writer owes a special debt of personal gratitude; to him the National Gallery of Ireland is indebted, as are all those who will use the catalogue. The remaining deficiencies and inadequacies are, of course, the sole responsibility of the writer.

INTRODUCTION

The nucleus of the collection of Italian Seicento and Settecento paintings presented in this catalogue was due to an enlightened and magnanimous initial purchase. The National Gallery of Ireland was established by Act of Parliament in 1854; the first building was opened to the public in 1864. In the interval the Board of Governors and Guardians was active. A Roman dealer Alessandro Aducci offered a collection of paintings to the embryonic Dublin Gallery in 1855, paintings which he had acquired at the sales of the famous collection of Cardinal Fesch,[1] Archbishop of Lyons, Primate of the Gauls (1763-1839), who died in exile in Rome.

Monies had been voted for the construction of the Gallery, but no provision was made for suitable items to hang therein. Aducci's offer was investigated by Maziere Brady, Lord Chancellor of Ireland, one of the most active members of the Board, frequently taking the chair (the Chairman being elected on an *ad hoc* basis). The Lord Chancellor entered into communication with Mrs Jameson, and Robert Macpherson, another dealer in Rome. While there is no known record in the Gallery about Mrs. Jameson, one may fairly suppose that she was the well-known English nineteenth century art historian. Mrs. Anna Jameson was actually born in Dublin in 1794, but lived most of her life in England with frequent travels abroad.

On 15 September 1856, less than a year since Aducci's overture, Maziere Brady made a proposal to the Board that thirteen of Aducci's paintings be purchased for the Gallery, out of funds which he would provide, without any interest charges, until such time as the Board obtained monies from which the advance could be repaid. The paintings would remain as collateral. The Lord Chancellor's proposal was passed.

Less than two months later, on 3 November 1856, the Lord Chancellor came forward with a further proposition. Through Macpherson's agency three more of Aducci's paintings were added, bringing the total to sixteen, at a sum of £1,700, which sum was to include export duty payable to the Papal Government. Of these paintings, one apparently never reached the National Gallery of Ireland.[2] At this November meeting in 1856 the Lord Chancellor made a further proposal analogous to the previous one. He sought and obtained permission to purchase five paintings belonging to Macpherson and a further selection chosen by Macpherson, presumably from other dealers, and including four redeemable from the Monte di Pietà, the official papal pawnbroking establishment. The Lord Chancellor's total outlay was £3,333 for thirty-nine paintings (including £150 commission to Macpherson for his trouble).

It is interesting to look first at the paintings which came from Aducci (formerly Fesch Collection). These included a very fine full-length portrait by Andrea Celesti (no. 1925), two magnificent examples of the work of Giovanni Lanfranco (nos. 67 and 72), a Pier Francesco Mola (no. 1893), a fine late Palma Giovane (no. 68), a large Antonio Maria Panico (no. 89), a magnificent altarpiece by Giulio Cesare Procaccini (no. 1820), a rare if rather dull altarpiece by Francesco Pascucci (no. 1918), a Roman School, 17th century *Nativity*

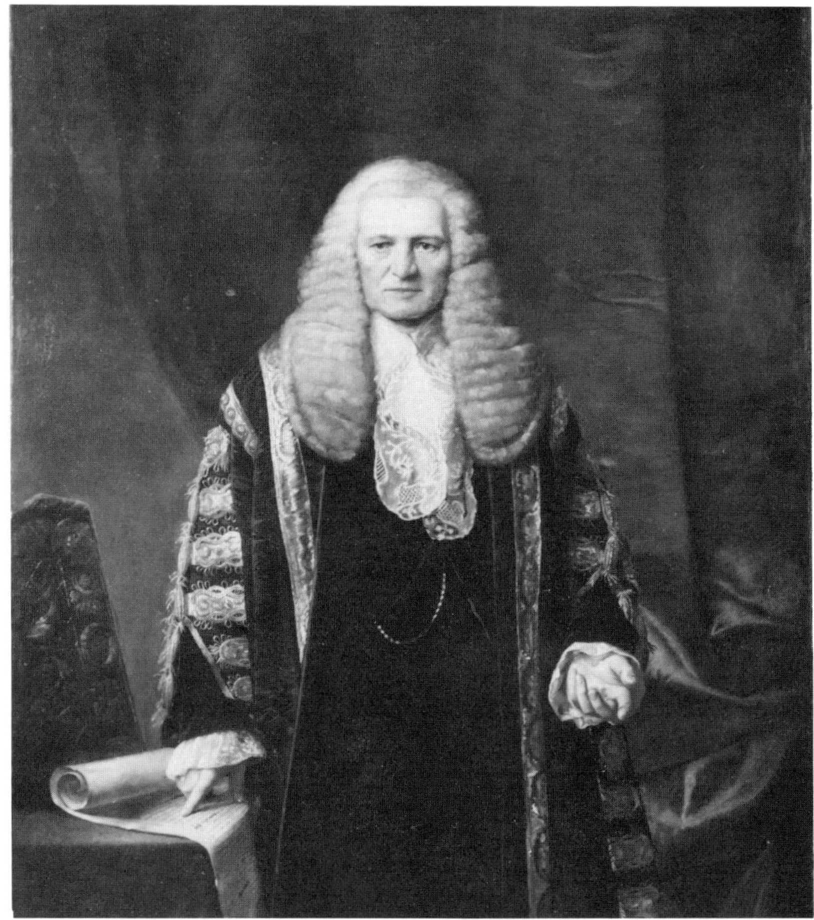

SIR MAZIERE BRADY (1796-1871). *Detail of a portrait by Thomas Jones (coll. National Gallery of Ireland).* Brady, who was Lord Chancellor of Ireland, was one of the most active among the first Governors of the National Gallery of Ireland. From his own personal funds he advanced a substantial interest-free loan to secure the purchase of thirty-nine paintings for the Gallery in 1856. Most of these were Italian seventeenth-century pictures and they form the nucleus of the collection described in this catalogue.

(no. 1911), a good example of the work of Ignazio Stern (no. 1739), and a landscape attributed to Giovanni Battista Viola (no. 1977). Thus, of the fifteen paintings obtained from Aducci which actually arrived in the newly built National Gallery of Ireland, eleven fall within the scope of this catalogue and all eleven are permanently exhibited — with occasional temporary rotation. Of the remaining four, three are excellent altarpieces of the French seventeenth and very early eighteenth centuries, and hang permanently, again apart from occasional rotation. Consequently, from the Aducci selection there is only one inferior work.

As mentioned earlier Macpherson obtained four paintings 'pledged in the Monte di Pietà for £280 and bought for £300'.[3] Of these, three are included in the present catalogue, namely, the large Padovanino, the similarly large Pietro della Vecchia, and the painting, *Love triumphant*, attributed to Riminaldi. The fourth picture, an excellent Palmezzano, is outside the scope of this catalogue.

These two sources account for approximately half the paintings of the original block purchase through Macpherson. The other twenty pictures either belonged to Macpherson

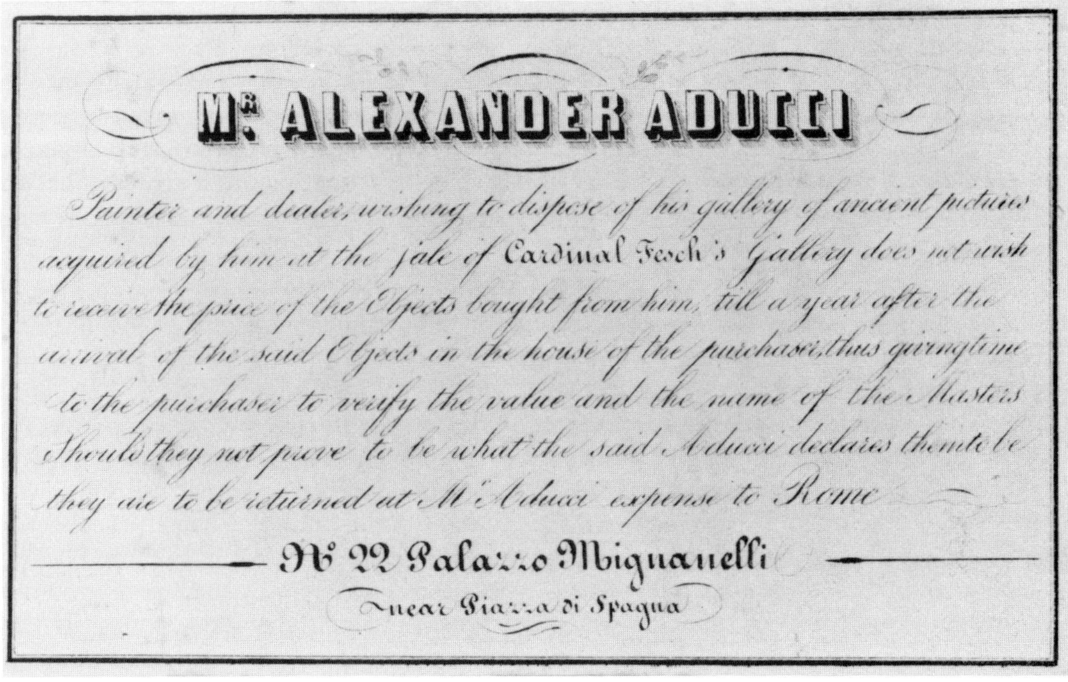

THE TRADE CARD OF THE ROMAN PICTURE-DEALER, ALESSANDRO ADUCCI.
Aducci acquired a number of paintings at the sales of the famous collection of Cardinal Fesch and subsequently sold several of these to the National Gallery of Ireland.

or were selected by him. The overall quality is much inferior to the groups already mentioned (but one must give Macpherson credit for the choice of those at the Monte di Pietà). Relevant to this catalogue are Maratti's large *Europa and the bull,* and the picture attributed to Paolo Pagani; Macpherson also obtained the fine Salvator Rosa. Outside the scope of this catalogue are two or three excellent paintings, but the balance are rather indifferent, including a number of acknowledged copies, offered as such.

From the Gallery archives, it is recorded that Aducci offered more paintings than those acquired; it is worth considering this unaccepted portion.

Aducci's offer also included four more Lanfrancos, in fact the two pairs which flanked the two actually acquired when the paintings were completed in 1625 for the Blessed Sacrament Chapel of the Basilica of St. Paul's-without-the-Walls in Rome. The offer also proposed a fine Nicolas Regnier which is now in the Ferens Art Gallery, Kingston-upon-Hull; a fine Gerard Seghers, now in the collection of the Earl of Mansfield; a *Supper at Emmaus,* attributed to Filippo Tarchiani, now in the Los Angeles County Museum of Art; a Valentin de Boulogne in the Galleria Nazionale d'Arte Antica, Palazzo Corsini, Rome, and a substantial altarpiece by Marco Palmezzano, now in the collection of the Marquess of Northampton. Two other paintings, attributed to Cavedone and Jouvenet, which can not be traced at present, completed Aducci's offer.[4]

One cannot but think that, by eliminating eleven of the paintings submitted by Aducci, Macpherson could sell Dublin some of his own stock and by selecting others more directly could ask for a higher commission or fee. On the other hand, one must allow for the possibility that Macpherson genuinely believed that he was making a more varied collection for a new Gallery, even if it meant including four known copies. Unfortunately, however, for Dublin Macpherson's own selection, apart from the four pictures obtained at the Monte di Pietà, did not match in quality the eleven other paintings offered initially by Aducci, but not purchased.

Disregarding the 'what might have been', the purchase for the new National Gallery of Ireland was quite remarkable. At a time when the major Galleries and private collectors, in the field of Italian painting, were acquiring works by the great painters of the Quattrocento and Cinquecento the Dublin Board saw fit to acquire, with the borrowed money, not a handful of paintings from those centuries, but thirty-nine paintings covering a wide field, but with a strong emphasis on the Seicento including some excellent French pictures of the same century. It would be facile to say that the initial purchase was motivated by the large size of many of the pictures. For the building which was to open in 1864 the members of the Board would have been in a very strong position to borrow paintings from private owners. Following Aducci's initial offer, the Lord Chancellor, from the meagre documentation available, consulted at least Mrs. Jameson, and brought in the assistance of a non-Italian dealer. In general one gets the impression that the Board made a deliberate decision to proceed as it did.

Later it became quite fashionable to sneer at the quality of the pictures in the initial purchase, but for several decades now Dublin's relative richness, for a non-Italian Gallery, in Italian Seicento painting has been fully appreciated. There is a certain parallel with the Dutch Collection. With a very modest purchase fund, the Gallery's second Director, Henry Doyle, between 1869 and 1892, built up the Dutch School, which today is known as much for its excellent examples of the work of lesser known painters as for good works by the foremost Dutch artists.

Apart from the remarkable and courageous Aducci/Macpherson purchase already described, the Gallery has always been active in the salesrooms, both in Ireland and England. Indeed it has gone to venues in continental Europe. A Sassoferrato was bought at the Count Koucheleff Besborodko Sale in Paris in 1869; the superb Bellotto views of Dresden were purchased at the Naryschkin Sale in Paris in 1883. Private treaty sales in Rome in 1864 brought the Gallery Preti's *Beheading of St. John the Baptist*, and the splendid Bolognese School *St. John the Baptist*. A private purchase in Milan in 1873 was the fine Sassoferrato of the *Virgin and Child*.

Private benefaction, so remarkable throughout the entire history of the Gallery, may also be seen in the limited number of paintings catalogued here. Sir Henry Page Turner Barron, Bt., presented a splendid Vignali, and a good example of another Florentine artist of the Seicento, Furini. The Duke of Leinster presented an important *St. Sebastian* by Luca Giordano. Mr. J. Orpin of Dublin presented *Bathsheba*, a quintessential Pellegrini. An excellent Batoni of Pope Pius VI was given by Robert Tighe, Q.C., in 1885, exactly one hundred years after the election of that Pontiff. Bartholomew Watkins, London, presented

St. Sebastian, now attributed to the Neapolitan, Filippo Vitale. Sir Hugh Lane's outstanding generosity lay mainly in paintings of other schools and other centuries; nonetheless he gave the Gallery its only Magnasco and an excellent Strozzi. Tantalizing is the absence of knowledge of how these paintings reached these off-shore islands.

The outstanding gift with regard to the paintings catalogued here was the Milltown Gift of 1902. The sixth Earl of Milltown was succeeded by his brother Henry, who died unmarried on 24 March 1891. At this point the title became dormant, with little likelihood of a claimant. Geraldine Evelyn, widow of the sixth Earl, apparently was proud of the collection at her beautiful home, Russborough, county Wicklow (now the seat of the Alfred Beit Foundation), conceived the idea of giving the entire contents to the National Gallery of Ireland, and to house this a large extension to the Gallery was built and opened to the public in March 1903.[5] The actual Deed of Gift was executed by the Countess of Milltown on 30 July 1902.

From the paintings included in the Milltown Gift it is possible to reconstitute the acquisitions of one of the more important Irish eighteenth century Grand Tourists.[6]

The archives or papers of the Milltown family, if they still exist, have not been found in searches by several scholars. However, we know that in the early 1740s work had begun on the beautiful villa, Russborough, county Wicklow, to the designs of Richard Castle (or Cassels).[7] The patron was Joseph Leeson, later to become 1st Earl of Milltown, the source of whose wealth was a family brewery. With his country seat launched, Leeson left for Rome, and in 1744 sat for his portrait to Batoni. Clearly Leeson enjoyed his Italian sojourn, for we find him back in Rome, this time with his son and heir, in 1750. In 1751 the latter was also painted by Batoni.

Even from secondary sources there is little documentation of actual transactions. The earliest known list of the Milltown Collection is that published by Neale in 1826.[8] However, two visits to Rome and Italy by the builder of the splendid country seat, Russborough, must account for the majority of the Italian paintings prior to the 1750s in the Milltown Collection.

From contemporary Italian painters Leeson acquired four Batoni portraits, and, almost certainly from the artist, four Paninis which are signed and dated 1740. Also available at the time were the one Coccorante, the one Masucci, and the two Piscellis. One must not forget the presence in Rome of Vernet, from whom, in 1745, he commissioned a full size copy of Salvator Rosa's *Death of Atilius Regulus*, which was then in the Colonna gallery.[9] On his second visit to Rome Leeson acquired four oval marines by Vernet, which were not included in the Gift to the Gallery, but which were subsequently bought by Sir Alfred Beit, Bt., and now hang at Russborough.[10] From Vernet's account book we know that the artist also sold Leeson four rectangular paintings of 'imperial' size;[11] these have not been identified to date.

In these islands it has already been noted how Grand Tourists bought originals or copies of the major Bolognese artists of the seventeenth century; Leeson, unfortunately, only seems to have obtained copies: one after Annibale Carracci, one after Domenichino, six after Guercino, and three after Reni. He did buy seventeenth century originals, but by

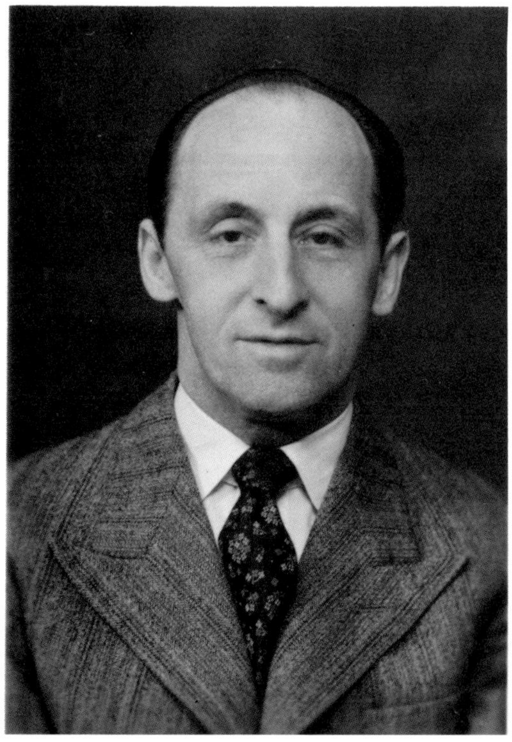

DR. GEORGE FURLONG, DIRECTOR OF THE NATIONAL GALLERY OF IRELAND, 1935-50. With very limited purchase funds at his disposal, Furlong added a number of very beautiful and unusual Italian pictures to the Collection including the paintings by Castiglione, Crespi, Gentileschi, Passeri, Pensionante del Saraceni, Ricci and Tiepolo described in this catalogue.

less esteemed masters, paintings by or attributed to: Bassetti, Chimenti da Empoli, Ferri, Giordano, Langetti, Lauri, Pagani, Rosa da Tivoli, Salvator Rosa, Troppa and Turchi.

One group of paintings is quite remarkable for a collector from either Great Britain or Ireland. This consists of works by Florentine seventeenth century painters almost all of importance to scholars of that school, in which, only the last few decades has witnessed a rebirth of interest. It is difficult to conceive that Leeson himself saw the merit of these canvases, one Cesare Dandini, three Ficherellis, two Furinis, one Lorenzo Lippi, and a possible Mehus. The choice of these was probably due to an Irish medical doctor who lived in Florence, but whose main occupation, from the little that is known of him, appears to have been that of an agent, not only of fine works of art, but also of cheese and wine, and other Italian produce.[12] Dr. Tyrrell acted for other notable Irish Grand Tourists, but to date no other *cache* of Florentine paintings of that period has been found. One can not, however, rule out the possibility that even small groups of such were incorrectly catalogued in the ever increasing sales of the contents of Irish country houses, which began early in the present century, and, alas, still flourish.

How may one be so convinced that the paintings mentioned in the foregoing paragraphs were the acquisitions of Joseph Leeson, 1st Earl of Milltown? Clearly a man of wealth, he built Russborough, visited Italy at least twice, and in the late 1770s bought a town house in Dublin, at 17 St. Stephen's Green.[13] Russborough required furnishings of quality, and got such in terms of paintings and furniture; this was undoubtedly the work of the first Lord Milltown, who lived until 1783. His heir, also Joseph, was described by Croft as an 'incorrigible simpleton', and other nasty things by other satirical authors. Surveying the entire Deed of Gift of the Milltown Collection, it is evident that there was another major purchase period, towards the middle of the nineteenth century, strong in furniture and objets d'art, weak in paintings, apart from family portraiture.

The account given here to date brings the collection up to World War I. After that, the area under review did not attract much attention, but under the directorship of George Furlong (1935-1950) several very interesting purchases were made including a fine Gentileschi in 1936; an excellent pair of Bazzanis also in 1936; a painting which later revealed an authentic signature of Giovanni Battista Passeri in 1937; a really splendid and large Castiglione, also in 1937; a good Crespi in 1940, and an excellent Sebastiano Ricci, in 1942. After that Italian Seicento and Settecento paintings have been added when, so to speak, the opportunity presented itself close to home. Thus a Dolci was acquired in 1951, a Benedetto Veli in 1961, an Orazio De Ferrari in 1978, and a *Portrait of a young man of the Branconio family from L'Áquila*, by an artist as yet unidentified, in 1983.

1. M. Wynne, in *Gazette des Beaux-Arts*, vol. 89 (January 1977), pp. 1-8.
2. *Ibid.*, p. 5.
3. *Ibid.*, p. 2.
4. M. Wynne in *The J. Paul Getty Museum Journal*, vol. 5 (1977), pp. 101-04.
5. H. Potterton in Introduction to *National Gallery of Ireland. Illustrated Summary Catalogue of Paintings* (Dublin 1981), p. xxv.
6. M. Wynne in *Apollo*, vol. 99 (February 1974), pp. 104-11.
7. *The Georgian Society Records of Eighteenth-Century Domestic Architecture and Decoration in Dublin*, vol. 5 (Dublin 1913), p. 68.
8. J. P. Neale, *Views of the Seats of Noblemen and Gentlemen in the United Kingdom*, 2nd Series, vol. 3 (London 1826), n.p.
9. M. Wynne in *The Burlington Magazine*, vol. 113 (September 1971), p. 543.
10. *Ibid.*
11. *Ibid.*
12. C. O'Connor in *Studies*, vol. 69 (Summer 1980), pp. 137-44.
13. *The Georgian Society Records of Eighteenth-Century Domestic Architecture and Decoration in Dublin*, vol. 2 (Dublin 1910), pp. 47-48.

NOTE ON USING THE CATALOGUE

CONDITION REPORTS

The condition reports begin with a brief statement. In making these the standpoint or principle adopted makes allowances for the fact that the vast majority of the paintings in the catalogue are at least two hundred years old. The main descriptions used are:

Excellent — Painting in remarkably well preserved condition, especially allowing for its age. This category includes those pictures which are in really pristine condition, for example, the pair of Bellottos, the Solimena *Winter*, the Tiepolo sketch, etc.

Very good — Painting in very good condition, even though it may have suffered some damage over the years, especially localized damage at edges, minor tears, small areas of paint loss, etc.

Good — Painting which has suffered more considerable areas of paint loss, or larger cuts, or flattening of impasto due to a bad relining, or abrasions due to some bad restoration in the past. Nonetheless, such works still represent well the artist by whom they were painted.

Poor — Painting which has suffered serious damage.

For some of the pictures it is impossible to give a short statement; for example, due to the necessity for a thorough cleaning and restoration any judgement would be imprudent. In such cases the condition report may read: ''Covered by a thick layer of heavily discoloured varnish''.

SUBJECT MATTER

The subject matter of the paintings has been described briefly, except for well known iconographical images such as *The Nativity of Christ, Adam and Eve,* and so forth.

Where quotations from the Scriptures are given, these have been taken from the Douay Version. Either this Version or the Authorized Version of King James I would have been the principal translations in English of the Bible available to English-speaking collectors throughout the seventeenth and eighteenth centuries.

MILLTOWN GIFT PAINTINGS

Frequently in this catalogue, under Provenance, one reads ''Milltown Collection by 1826''. This refers to the earliest list of Milltown paintings known at present, namely the one in J. P. Neale, *Views of the Seats of Noblemen and Gentlemen in the United Kingdom,* 2nd Series, Vol. 3 (London 1826), no pagination.

İACOPO ȦMIGONI, Venice 1675—1752 Madrid

Firmly established as a painter in his native Venice, Amigoni subsequently worked in Rome, Munich and London. Back in Venice by 1739, he shortly went to Madrid where he was fully employed until his death.

After AMIGONI

1688   The birth of Adonis (Fig. 1).

Oil on canvas, 1.22 × 1.52 m.

CONDITION: apparently good, under a heavy layer of discoloured varnish.

PROVENANCE: a small Belfast auction, where purchased by Anthony Thompson, Belfast, from whom purchased, 1959, for £180.

Adonis was born of the incestuous relationship between his mother and his grandfather. Because of her unorthodox behaviour Adonis's mother was changed into a tree. Adonis was delivered through a fissure in the tree, assisted by the goddess of childbirth and her attendant nymphs. (Ovid).

This composition is known through a painting of much freer treatment destroyed during the Second World War, which was at the Gymnasium zum Grauen Kloster, Berlin.[1] In details there are many differences; for example, the vessels at the left hand side of the painting, the cushion or pillow in the bottom left foreground. The Dublin painting has an extra figure in front of the woman carrying a basket on her head. The group of trees to the left hand side of the canvas is different in both paintings. There are many other minor differences. Unfortunately Voss does not give the dimensions of the painting now destroyed, but from photographs one gets the impression that it was probably smaller than no. 1688.

Even more relevant to no. 1688 is a painting of the same subject in a private collection in Ireland, whose measurements (1.23 × 1.53 m. (sight)) make it identical, to all intents and purposes, in size to the Dublin canvas. Moreover, it is extremely difficult to find any but the slightest details which make it different to no. 1688. This painting in a private collection abounds in pastel shades of purple and blue, yellow and pale red, and a considerable amount of white, precisely the colours which one would expect from Amigoni. While some of the anatomical passages seem slightly crude, this deficiency is compensated for by the spirited free handling of paint with rapid brushstrokes, again a characteristic of Amigoni.

Dublin's no. 1688 is a copy from the privately owned Amigoni. The provenance of both is so hopelessly inadequate that it is impossible to say when and where the copy was made. For the Gallery's painting it is highly unlikely that any further provenance will emerge. For the privately owned Amigoni, its history can be traced somewhat further back, but not anywhere near Amigoni's lifetime. It is conceivable that some further provenance will be found for the latter painting.

The Gallery's painting is very competently executed. It has a feature which is rather foreign to Amigoni; almost all the mouths of the figures are rather tight and almost ugly. This is quite unlike the style of the author of so many decorative schemes on canvas or fresco. There is also a firmness of line throughout, and a lack of bravura that seems to push it away from Amigoni's own work. Yet the copy is not arid; it is competent and confident.

Pallucchini published two paintings, formerly on the London art market, but now in a private collection in Pordenone; these are *Clorinda and Zephyr,* and *Hercules and Omphale.*[2] The Venetian scholar assigns the two paintings to Amigoni's London sojourn, 1729-39, on the grounds that Amigoni in London mitigated his full-blown rococo style, treating figures in a more polished fashion, and cooling his palette. This is a rather dangerous hypothesis when one recalls some of the portraits executed in London by Amigoni. It is true that the two paintings now in Pordenone might be more appealing to a patron more puritanical than the Bavarian Wittelsbachs.

Synthesizing Amigoni's late works, Wittkower writes: 'His later manner degenerated into a languid and melodramatic classicizing Rococo, a trend paralleled in the works of other artists not only in Italy but also in France and England.'[3] Such a conclusion is not backed up by a series of authentic examples. Gualdaroni, writing about Amigoni's work for the Bourbon court, illustrates several works not seen by the writer.[4] In them there appears to be no hardening of line or decadence of treatment. A similar conclusion is to be drawn from the Amigonis published by Fernandez.[5]

Amigoni's most classical works, as known to the writer, are the portraits of *Charles III* and *Queen Maria Amalia,* and another pair, *Ferdinand VI* and *Queen Maria Barbara,* all formerly in the collection of the Marchese Zacchia-Rondanini, in Bologna.

Two of Amigoni's finest works in Spain are now in the Faculty of Medicine at Barcelona University, *The finding of the cup in Benjamin's sack* and *Joseph received by the Pharaoh.* In neither of these does one find what might be described as an academic rigidity which permeates the Dublin canvas. Griseri, in surveying the last phase of Amigoni's career, does not find any Roman academic influence in it, but rather the *barocchetto,* which, in common with other Italian artists, he adopted at a time when Roman and French paintings heralding the neoclassical phase were beginning to find favour.[6]

In another Irish private collection is a very interesting painting (oil on canvas, 1.00 × 1.235 m.: sight) of the same subject as no. 1688. It has several differences in foreground details, but the rather special difference is the introduction of a page attendant as the figure most distant in the left background. This painting does not have the hard linear quality of the Gallery's no. 1688. It would appear to be a version of the larger painting in the Irish private collection from which no. 1688 is so clearly derived. Unfortunately, again there is no helpful provenance (Fig. 2).

1. H. Voss in *Jahrbuch der Königlich Preuszischen Kunstsammlungen,* vol. 39 (1918), p.159.
2. R. Pallucchini in *Arte Veneta,* vol. 25 (1971), pp.168-69; figs. 212 and 213.
3. R. Wittkower, *Art and Architecture in Italy: 1600-1750* (3rd ed., Harmondsworth 1973), p.317.

4. R. Gualdaroni in *Archivo Español de Arte* (1974), pp.129-47.
5. J.U. Fernandez, *La Pintura Italiana del Siglo XVIII en España* (Valladolid 1977), pls. 1-7.
6. A. Griseri in *Paragone,* no. 123 (1960), pp.21-26.

ANDREA APPIANI, Milan 1754-1817 Milan

Appiani was taught by Carlo Maria de Giudici. He worked as a decorative painter in Florence, Rome and Naples. By 1801 he was in Paris, and found favour with Napoleon, who made him a court painter, and gave him the Légion d'honneur. *He did numerous portraits of Napoleon.*

Circle of APPIANI

1189 Bonaparte as a general of the army of the Revolution (Fig. 3).

Oil on canvas, 0.38 × 0.33 m.

CONDITION: good; covered with a coat of yellowed varnish.

PROVENANCE: Milltown Collection; Milltown Gift, 1902.

The quality of this painting is not sufficiently high to be worthy of a secure attribution to Appiani, who did several very important portraits of Napoleon in various sizes.

No. 1189 is very similar to a painting (0.99 × 0.80 m.) sold from the estate of the late Margret Louise van Alen Brug at Christie's, 5 December 1969, lot 53 (bt. Duke). The main differences are that, in the salesroom picture, the background is light, the figure is slightly longer and the breeches are dark. A virtually identical, perhaps even the same, painting (38½ × 31¼ ins. or 0.978 × 0.793 m.) was at Sotheby's, 30 July 1947, lot 80. When in the Milltown Collection, no. 1189 was given to Gérard.

These paintings date from the last few years of the eighteenth century, during the Italian Campaign.

MARCANTONIO BASSETTI, Verona 1586-1630 Verona

Having studied in his native city under Felice Brusasorzi, Bassetti went to Venice. About the age of thirty he went down to Rome, and among his works there were some frescos for the Sala Regia in the Quirinal Palace. About 1620 he went back to Verona. He is well known for his portraits; he was considerably influenced by the great masters of Venice of the previous century.

1031 Portrait of an elderly man (Fig. 4).

Oil on canvas, 0.85 × 0.68 m.

CONDITION: excellent. Restored Summer 1968.

PROVENANCE: Milltown Collection; Milltown Gift, 1902.

Tentatively attributed to Titian in the manuscript catalogue, it was described as 'Italian School' in the 1956 catalogue, and as by Turchi in the 1971 and 1981 catalogues. Cleaning opened the way to various hypotheses. The name of Turchi was proposed by Federico Zeri,[1] Rolf Kultzen suggested looking in the direction of Marcantonio Bassetti,[2] another Veronese artist. This is indeed a very convincing hypothesis when one looks at Bassetti's *Portrait of an old man with a book* (0.888 × 0.73 m.), in the Museo di Castelvecchio, Verona,[3] or *Portrait of an old man with a glove* (0.70 × 0.645 m.), in the same museum.[4]

No. 1031 has that intense gaze of the sitter found in the two portraits in Verona. There are similarities, too, in the plain background, in the precise, tightly painted details of hair, visual features, and attributes. Another painting in the Verona museum, *Christ and the tribute money,* has a portrait head of a man, immediately to the left of Christ, which again is very closely related to no. 1031.

Bassetti's *Portrait of an old man with a book* is dated 1626, and a date about this time would be appropriate for the Dublin portrait.

1. Verbal communication.
2. Written communication, July 1981.
3. A.C. Ottani, in exhibition catalogue, *Cinquant' Anni di Pittura Veronese 1580-1630* (Palazzo della Gran Guardia, Verona, 1974), no. 126, fig. 152 (no. 66 in the Museo di Castelvecchio inventory). *Cf.* also R. Pallucchini, *La Pittura Veneziana del Seicento* (Milan 1981), vol. 1, p. 125, and vol. 2, pp. 581-82, figs. 344-45.
4. *Ibid.,* no. 111, fig. 135 (no. 7 in the Museo di Castelvecchio inventory). *Cf.* also R. Pallucchini, *La Pittura Veneziana del Seicento* (Milan 1981), vol. 1, p. 123, and vol. 2, p. 582, fig. 341.

POMPEO GIROLAMO BATONI, Lucca 1708-1787 Rome

Born in Lucca, Batoni went to Rome, in 1727, before he was twenty years of age. He was attracted towards the antique, and this influenced him to such an extent that his mature work could virtually be called neoclassical. He painted altarpieces and history pictures. He is still best known for his many fine portraits of visitors to Rome, many of which show the sitters in classical settings either real or contrived.

109 Pope Pius VI (Fig. 5).
(Giovanni Angelo Braschi, 1717-1799, Pope from 1775)

Oil on canvas, 1.37 × 0.99 m.
INSCRIBED: *Alla Santità di Ntò Sig^re / Papa Pio VI* (on document held by the Pontiff)
CONDITION: the painting is in excellent condition, apart from two small abrasions. One is close to the bottom edge of the canvas, across the side of the chair and the Pontiff's soutane. The second is very slight, above the Pontiff's head, close to the top edge of the canvas.

PROVENANCE: Robert Tighe, J.P., Q.C., Dublin,[1] by whom presented, 1875.

Over a white soutane, the Pontiff is wearing a lace rocchetto (a type of surplice worn by bishops), a mozzetta (an episcopal cape), and a stole. On top of the books, in front of the clock, is his camauro (a cap reserved for use only by Popes). The main supports of the back of the chair, on which the Pope is seated, are carved at the finials with the crest of his family, the Braschi, surmounted with papal symbols, tiara and keys. Michael Archer and several of his colleagues in the Victoria and Albert Museum's Department of Ceramics studied a black and white photograph of the painting with a view to establishing the origins of the polychrome clock. They could not propose a definitive answer, but all agreed that it was not Italian porcelain. They considered it to be possibly Meissen, but knew of no Meissen model corresponding to it. They also wondered if it might not be a carved wooden case.

There are versions of this portrait in the Museo di Roma, Rome[2]; the Galleria Sabauda, Turin[3]; the Pinacoteca Vaticana, Vatican City[4]; and a version with a statue of Minerva in place of the clock in the National Museum, Warsaw.[5]

The versions in the Museo di Roma and the Galleria Sabauda are both signed and dated 1775, the year of the Pontiff's accession. It is to be presumed that the other versions were painted in the same year or shortly afterwards. Consequently they are works of the artist's mature period. While accepting no. 109 as autograph, the late Anthony M. Clark suggested that the vestments were by another hand.[6]

1. Robert Tighe came from the branch of the family that lived at South Hill, Delvin, county Westmeath. He was called to the Bar in the Michaelmas Term of 1829; later he became a J.P., Q.C., and then Assistant Barrister for the county of Limerick. Born in 1806, he died in 1881. *Cf.* his memorial for admission to the Bar in the King's Inns Library, Dublin 7, and *The Irish Law Times*, vol. 15 (1881), p.471. Unfortunately there is no record known at present of how or where Mr. Tighe acquired the Batoni portrait.
2. G. Incisa Della Rocchetta, 'Il Ritratto di Pio VI del Batoni al Museo di Roma', *Bollettino dei Musei Comunali di Roma*, vol. IV (1957), pp.1-4; exhibition catalogue, *Mostra di Pompeo Batoni* (Lucca 1967), no. 54. This version was not accepted as autograph by the late Anthony M. Clark: A. M. Clark (ed. by E.P. Bowron), *Pompeo Batoni* (Oxford 1985), p.339, no. 391.
3. E. Emmerling, *Pompeo Batoni, sein Leben und Werk* (Darmstadt 1932), p.106, no. 46; N. Gabrielli, *Galleria Sabauda. Maestri Italiani* (Torino 1971), p.70 and fig. 438.
4. *Cf.* G. Incisa Della Rocchetta, *op. cit.*, p.4.
5. T.S. Jaroszewski, in *Bulletin du Musée National de Varsowie*, vol. VII (1966), p. 105. This version was not accepted as autograph by the late Anthony M. Clark: A.M. Clark, *loc. cit.*
6. A.M. Clark, *op. cit.*, p. 340, no. 393.

701 Joseph Leeson, afterwards 1st Earl of Milltown, 1711-1783 (Fig. 7).

Oil on canvas, 1.37 × 1.02 m.

SIGNED: *Pompeo.Batoni.Pinse.Roma.1744*

CONDITION: excellent. The painting has a few very small areas of damage which were treated during restoration in August 1970. In 1982 restorer Sergio Benedetti noticed traces of letters in front of the artist's surname. Further judicious cleaning revealed the artist's first name: *Pompeo*. This intervention, with the removal of the later (but yet very old) signature, revealed a small lacuna in the place of the last two digits of the date. Because of the antiquity of the later signature and date, and because Joseph Leeson was known to have been in Rome in 1744, the last two digits *44* were reinstated.

PROVENANCE: commissioned from the artist by Joseph Leeson, subsequently 1st Earl of Milltown; Milltown Collection; Milltown Gift 1902.

EXHIBITED: 1982 Kenwood, London *Pompeo Batoni and his British Patrons* (Iveagh Bequest, Kenwood), no. 1.

The Leeson family from whom the sitter is descended came from Northamptonshire. One of their number came to Ireland as a soldier during the reign of Charles I (1625-49), and settled in the country. Joseph Leeson portrayed here was a member of, at least, the fourth generation of a Dublin brewing family. He represented the borough of Rathcormac (Rathcormick), county Cork, in Parliament for several years. In 1756 he was created Baron Russborough, of county Wicklow; in 1760 he was made Viscount Russborough, of Russellstown, county Wicklow; in 1763 he was elevated as Earl of Milltown, county Dublin; and in 1770 he was made a Privy Councillor.

Leeson began the construction of his country house, Russborough, county Wicklow, in 1741, to the designs of Richard Castle; the house was nearing completion in 1748. Russborough is one of Ireland's most elegant country mansions, and is constructed with the best materials throughout. Fully restored to its pristine condition by Sir Alfred Beit, Bt., who bought it in 1951, it is now the seat of the Alfred Beit Foundation.

Leeson had a fine town house, no. 17, St. Stephen's Green, now occupied by the Kildare Street and University Club. This house was built in the late 1770s.

In this portrait Joseph Leeson is wearing a fur-lined indoor coat. This item of clothing is found in many of Batoni's portraits, including that of Joseph Leeson's son (no. 702 *infra*). Many people are unaware that Rome in winter can be very cold. While snow and ice are rare, a piercing cold wind comes from the east and down from the Appenines.

This portrait was painted during Joseph Leeson's first visit to Rome, and must be among the earliest acquisitions of the Milltown Collection.[1] As far as is known it is the earliest portrait by Batoni of any sitter from Great Britain or Ireland,[2] although a portrait of Arthur Rowley, destroyed by fire at Summerhill, county Meath, in 1922, was reputedly painted in 1740.[3]

The Gallery possesses a copy of no. 701 (oil on panel, 0.377 × 0.319 m.: cat. no. 1648). It is not a work of high quality. It was probably painted by an Irish artist after no. 701 was brought home.

1. M. Wynne, 'The Milltowns as Patrons', *Apollo*, vol. 99, (February 1974), pp. 104 ff.
2. J. Steegman in *The Burlington Magazine*, vol. 88, (March 1946), pp. 55 ff. A. M. Clark (ed. by E. P. Bowron), *Pompeo Batoni* (Oxford 1985), pp. 233-34, no. 87.
3. *Cf.* F. Russell in exhibition catalogue, by E. P. Bowron, *Pompeo Batoni and his British Patrons* (Iveagh Bequest, Kenwood, London, 1982), p. 94.

702 Joseph Leeson, afterwards 2nd Earl of Milltown, 1730-1801 (Fig. 8).

Oil on canvas, 0.99 × 0.73 m.

SIGNED: *P.B. 1751*

CONDITION: excellent. There is a small area of damage on Leeson's left arm. Restored 1981.

PROVENANCE: commissioned from the artist by Joseph Leeson, subsequently 1st Earl of Milltown; Milltown Collection; Milltown Gift, 1902.

EXHIBITED: 1960-61, Paris, *La peinture italienne au XVIIIe siècle* (Petit Palais), no. 57.

The sitter here depicted was the eldest son and heir of Joseph Leeson, of no. 701 preceding. By his contemporaries he was not considered very intelligent. He represented the borough of Thomastown, county Kilkenny, from 1757 to 1760. He inherited his father's property and titles in 1783. In this portrait he is shown wearing a furlined coat similar to that described in no. 701 preceding. Sir Herbert Croft, in *The Abbey of Kilkhampton* (1780), called the future 2nd Earl of Milltown an 'incorrigible simpleton'.

Joseph Leeson, later 1st Earl of Milltown, returned to Rome for a second visit in 1750. On this occasion he was accompanied by his son and his nephew, Joseph Henry, of Straffan, county Kildare.[1] During this visit Joseph Leeson the younger was portrayed in this three-quarter length by the artist of his father's portrait, Batoni.[2]

The Gallery possesses a copy of no. 702 (oil on canvas, 0.43 × 0.35: cat. no. 909). It is an indifferent work, and was probably painted in Ireland after the original was brought home. Another comparable copy is in an Irish private collection.

1. M. Wynne, 'The Milltowns as Patrons', *Apollo*, vol. 99 (February 1974), pp. 104 ff.

2. A. M. Clark (ed. by E. P. Bowron), *Pompeo Batoni* (Oxford 1985), p. 250, no. 146.

703 Portrait of a lady, possibly Anne Leeson, subsequently 1st Countess of Milltown, as Diana (Fig. 9).

Oil on canvas: 0.47 × 0.36 m. (painted surface)

SIGNED: *P.B. 1751*

CONDITION: excellent. Restored 1984.

PROVENANCE: commissioned from the artist by Joseph Leeson, subsequently 1st Earl of Milltown; Milltown Collection; Milltown Gift, 1902.

The sitter may be Anne, second wife of Joseph Leeson, whose first wife had died in 1731. Anne was a daughter of Nathaniel Preston of Swainstown, county Meath, and married Leeson in 1738. She is portrayed as Diana, the goddess of hunting. This is clear because of the crescent-shaped moon on her head. In this picture, the attributes of a huntress are quite evident, the bow and dead animal, the quiver of arrows, and the hunting dogs. Diana was proud of her virginity, as recorded by Ovid. Consequently, it is slightly ironical that Joseph Leeson, who had children by his second wife Anne, should have had her portrayed here as Diana the virgin huntress. It was not unusual to have people portrayed in the guise of gods and goddesses, saints and other historical personages. In the same year as no. 703 was painted, Batoni painted Sarah (Lethieullier), Lady Fetherstonhaugh as Diana, in the portrait now at Uppark, Sussex.[1]

On his second visit to Rome in the early 1750's, Joseph Leeson, subsequently 1st Earl of Milltown, could have brought with him a miniature or drawing of his second wife,

Anne.[2] Joseph commissioned two small whole-lengths of ladies from Batoni, one catalogued here, the second, in the guise of a shepherdess, in the collection of Sir Denis Mahon.[3] (Fig. 10). The latter is also initialed and dated 1751, and the two paintings are so similar in feeling that they must have been painted at the same time. Sir Denis Mahon's painting was formerly in the Milltown Collection.[4] The Gallery possesses a copy of no. 703 (oil on panel 0.463 × 0.332 m.: cat. no. 1650). It is a very competent copy, but not of the quality of a Batoni. Most probably it was executed by an Irish artist after no. 703 was brought home. As yet uncleaned, it would appear to be an eighteenth century work.

1. J. Steegman in *The Burlington Magazine*, vol. 88 (March 1946), p. 59, no. 6.
2. M. Wynne, 'The Milltowns as Patrons', *Apollo,* vol. 99 (February 1974), pp. 104 ff.
3. Exhibition catalogue, *Mostra di Pompeo Batoni,* Lucca 1967, no. 31.
4. J. P. Neale, *Views of the Seats of Noblemen and Gentlemen in the United Kingdom,* 2nd series, vol. 3 (London 1826), no pagination. Both the Mahon Collection painting and Dublin's no. 703 are fully discussed in A. M. Clark (ed. by E. P. Bowron), *Pompeo Batoni* (Oxford 1985), pp. 250-51, nos. 149 and 148 respectively.

Attributed to BATONI

704 **Venus and Cupid** (Fig. 6).

Oil on canvas, 0.54 × 0.69 m.

CONDITION: excellent.

PROVENANCE: Milltown Collection, by 1826; Milltown Gift, 1902.

EXHIBITED: 1960 London *Italian Art and Britain* (Royal Academy), no. 128.

COPY: there is a copy of identical size in an Irish private collection; it was probably executed in the early nineteenth century. Unfortunately there is no useful provenance for it.

This canvas depicts a playful moment between Cupid, god of love, and his mother, Venus. Cupid's traditional accoutrements are a torch, a bow, and a quiver of arrows. (Calepinus). In this scene Venus holds her son's torch.

This delightful small painting has a very long traditional attribution to Pompeo Batoni. The one major dissenting opinion is that of Anthony Clark, but unfortunately his premature death prevented him from coming to study the painting in reality, and substantiating his attribution of it to Andrea Procaccini (1671-1734).[1] Easel paintings by this artist are not common; no painting by him was included in the immense exhibition of *Il Settecento a Roma*, in Rome, in 1959.

The draperies in no. 704 have an angular disposition, without appearing geometric. In Batoni's *Hagar in the wilderness*, in the Galleria Nazionale, Rome, signed and dated 1776, a very similar approach to the painting of cloths is to be observed.[2]

The bunch of flowers in no. 704 is very distinctive; extremely similar bunches are to be found in several Batonis, for example, in: *Marchesa Spinelli in Merenda* (formerly in the Conti Merenda Collection in Forlì), in which the flowers are held in a jug instead of an urn, vessels treated, with regard to definition and highlights, in very like fashion; *Lady Headfort and a child* (Christie's, 29 November 1968, lot 47), in which the Viscountess is seated by a table, covered with a very simple cloth, as in no. 704, on which there is a

8

jug of flowers; *Mr. and Mrs. Thomas Barrett-Lennard with their daughter, Barbara Ann Barrett* (Collection Sir Richard Barrett-Lennard, Bt.), a painting dated 1750 in which the little girl Barbara holds a bunch of flowers.[3] In all these the flowers are virtually interchangeable.

In *The angel at the tomb of Christ when the Holy Women arrive* (Stuttgart), a painting dated 1747, the treatment of the angel's wings is stylistically very close to that of Cupid's wings in no. 704.

1. In correspondence, March 1970. Edgar Peters Bowron, on the basis of a photograph, supports Clark's attribution to Andrea Procaccini: in correspondence, August 1979. The publication of the magnificent monograph on Batoni does nothing to elucidate the recondite attribution:

A.M. Clark (ed. by E.P. Bowron) *Pompeo Batoni* (Oxford 1985), p. 372.
2. Exhibition catalogue, *Il Settecento a Roma* (Palazzo delle Esposizioni, Rome 1959), no. 52.
3. *Ibid.*, no. 33.

GIUSEPPE BAZZANI, Mantua 1690-1769 Mantua

Bazzani developed a personal style of quality and distinction. Various critics have pointed to various possible sources of inspiration, but Bazzani's individuality remains paramount; this is all the more significant because of the fact that the artist worked virtually exclusively in his native city and surrounding countryside. Bazzani's output was chiefly confined to religious subjects, although he did execute some notable history paintings.

982   Christ meets his Mother (Fig. 11)

Oil on canvas, 1.16 × 0.875 m. (oval, made up to a rectangle of the same dimensions).

CONDITION: excellent. All around the original oval, however, there is a narrow band of repainting where it has been built up to form a rectangle. There is also a small area of damage below the right hand foot of the soldier at the left hand side. Restored June 1971.

PROVENANCE: sale, Drouot's, Paris, date unknown, where attributed to Tiepolo and bought by W. E. Duits, London, from whom purchased, 1936, for £250, with no. 983.

EXHIBITED: 1934 Amsterdam *Italiaansche Kunst in Nederlandsch Bezit* (Stedelijk Museum), no. 28. (Lent by W. E. Duits, Dealer, Amsterdam); 1960 Coventry *Loan Exhibition* (Herbert Art Gallery and Museum), no. 1.

This painting and its pendant (no. 983 following) were purchased in Paris by Duits along with two others now in the Royal Gallery of Copenhagen.[1] N. Ivanoff dates this Dublin painting and its companion (following entry) to *circa* 1750,[2] comparing them with *The rest on the flight into Egypt* and *The adoration of the Magi*, both in the Accademia, Venice. H. Olsen proposes a dating to the 1740s,[3] while C. T. Perina merely says about the middle of the century.[4]

It is possible that no. 982, and no. 983 following, were from a Stations of the Cross series, being the Fourth Station, and the Thirteenth Station, respectively. The Stations of the

Cross, sometimes known as the Way of the Cross, or *Via Crucis,* was a practice of devotion which became particularly widespread in eighteenth century Italy, promoted by, among others, St. Leonard of Porto Maurizio, 1677-1751, an exceptional preacher.[5] The two paintings, now in the Royal Gallery of Copenhagen, which have virtually the same dimensions as no. 982 and no. 983 (original ovals *c.* 1.15 × *c.* 0.87 m., and *c.* 1.15 × *c.* 0.86 m.)[6] are of subjects which are not found in the Stations of the Cross, namely *The massacre of the Innocents* and *Suffer little children to come unto Me.* The two paintings in the Accademia in Venice are smaller in size than nos. 982 and 983, and again are of subjects not related to the Stations of the Cross, namely *The adoration of the Magi* and *The rest on the flight into Egypt.*[7]

Bazzani did a *Via Crucis* (Stations of the Cross), for the church of St Barnaba, Mantua.[8] Ivanoff regards them as early works.[9] The canvases are rectangular. The painter also did some drawings for a further set of Stations of the Cross, which are dated 1747, and are now in the Palazzo d'Arco, Mantua.[10] These drawings are rectangular. Ivanoff knew other paintings which might possibly have been from sets of the *Via Crucis;* these were single subjects,[11] or, at most, two subjects from such a series.[12] Perhaps the painting most closely connected with the Dublin pair, in treatment, form, and subject, is *The Entombment,* no. 958 in the Museum der Bildenden Künste zu Leipzig. Its measurements are somewhat smaller, (1.055 × 0.80 m. (oval)), which makes one hesitant about declaring it the Fourteenth Station of a set which also included the Dublin pair.

It is worth mentioning that Bazzani frequently used the oval form of canvas.[13]

1. L. Swane, 'To billeder af Giuseppe Bazzani', *Saertryk of Kenst Museest Aerskrift,* vol. 22 (1935), pp. 13ff. *Cf.* also N. Ivanoff, exhibition catalogue, *Bazzani,* (Mantova 1950), p. 69 and fig. 48.

2. In correspondence, September 1977.

3. H. Olsen, *Italian Paintings and Sculpture in Denmark* (Copenhagen 1961), pp. 39-40.

4. C. T. Perina, *Giuseppe Bazzani* (Florence 1970), p. 63.

5. L. Réau, *L'Iconographie Chrétienne,* Part 3 *Iconographie des Saints,* vol. 2 (Paris 1958), p. 802.

6. *Royal Museum of Fine Arts. Catalogue of Old Foreign Paintings* (Copenhagen 1981), p. 17, no. 38, and p. 18, no. 39.

7. S. M. Marconi, *Gallerie dell' Accademia di Venezia. Opere d'Arte dei Secoli XVII, XVIII, XIX* (Rome 1970), p. 136, nos. 302 and 303; dimensions 1.04 × 0.78 m.

8. N. Ivanoff, *op. cit.,* p. 43, nos. 1-14.

9. *Ibid.*

10. *Ibid.,* p. 47, no. 27, and p. 48, nos 33, 34, 35 and 36.

11. *Ibid., passim.*

12. *Ibid., passim,* but *praesertim,* p. 74.

13. C. T. Perina, *op. cit., passim.*

983   The descent from the Cross (Fig. 12).

Oil on canvas, 1.165 × 0.867 m. (oval, made up to rectangle of the same dimensions).

CONDITION: excellent. All around the original oval, however, there is a narrow band of repainting where it has been built up to form a rectangle. Restored June 1971.

PROVENANCE: sale, Drouot's, Paris, date unknown, where attributed to Tiepolo and bought by W. E. Duits, London, from whom purchased, 1936, for £250, with no. 982.

EXHIBITED: 1934 Amsterdam *Italiaansche Kunst in Nederlandsch Bezit* (Stedelijk Museum), no. 28. (Lent by W. E. Duits, Dealer, Amsterdam).

Purchased in Paris by Duits along with two paintings now in the Royal Gallery of Copenhagen.[1] See note about dating of no. 983 in previous entry. For the possibility of this being one of a series of paintings forming a *Via Crucis* (the Stations of the Cross), see also previous entry no. 982.

1. L. Swane, 'To billeder af Giuseppe Bazzani', *Saertryk of Kenst Museest Aerskrift*, vol. 22 (1935), pp. 13ff. *Cf.* also N. Ivanoff, exhibition catalogue, *Bazzani*, (Mantova 1950), p. 69 and fig. 49.

BERNARDO BELLOTTO, Venice 1720-1780 Warsaw

Bellotto trained under his uncle, Canaletto. Like his uncle he became known as a view painter. Having visited and painted in several Italian cities, he emigrated, and is definitely recorded as being in Dresden in 1748, where he became a court painter to the Elector of Saxony. He made short visits to Vienna and Munich, and finally left Dresden for Warsaw in 1767. The King of Poland, Stanislaus Poniatowski, gave him many commissions. Outside of Italy, but particularly in Poland, Bellotto was also known as Canaletto, which has frequently given rise to confusion between the work of uncle and nephew, although their styles are quite distinctive.

181 Dresden from the right bank of the Elbe above the Augustus Bridge (Fig. 13).

Oil on canvas, 0.515 × 0.84 m.

CONDITION: excellent. The painting was restored in June 1968, and in 1984. There were only a few small areas of paint loss.

PROVENANCE: M. B. Naryschkine sale, Paris, 5 April 1883, lot 2, where purchased, for £379, with no. 182.

EXHIBITED: 1911 London *Venetian Painting of the Eighteenth Century* (Burlington Fine Arts Club), no. 21; 1954-55 London *European Masters of the Eighteenth Century* (Royal Academy), no. 302; 1985 London *Masterpieces from The National Gallery of Ireland* (National Gallery), no. 8.

VERSIONS: Dresden, State Art Collections, Gallery of Old Master Paintings;[1] Raleigh, North Carolina Museum of Art;[2] Atherton, California, private collection.[3]

The differences between the various versions are very slight. The Dublin version shows more of the view than the others, and is therefore closer to the engraving, which is Bellotto's own work.[4] The principal buildings are that of the Protestant Church of the Virgin, with its dome completed to the designs of George Bähr (1726-43).[5] In front of it are the gallery and terrace of the most influential Count Brühl. The Augustus Bridge was constructed to the designs of Daniel Pöppelmann (1727-31).[6] The church with the tower and spire is the Catholic Court Church, designed by the Roman architect, Gaetano Chiaveri (1689-1770), who had already worked at St. Petersbourg and Warsaw. The building of the church commenced in 1738 and was completed just before this painting was executed.[7] Earlier versions show scaffolding on the tower, for example that in Dresden dated 1748.[8]

Kozakiewicz dates this painting to about 1750.[9] Bellotto had arrived in Dresden in 1747.

1. S. Kozakiewicz, *Bernardo Bellotto* (Recklinghausen 1972), vol. 2, p. 107, no. 40.
2. *Ibid.*, pp. 107-08, no. 141.
3. *Ibid.*, pp. 108 and 115, no. 143.
4. *Ibid.*, p. 115, no. 144.
5. E. Hempel, *Baroque Art and Architecture in Central Europe* (Harmondsworth 1965), pp. 196-98.
6. *Gemäldegalerie Alte Meister Dresden* (Dresden 1979), p. 103, no. 606.
7. Hempel, *op. cit.*, pp. 198-99.
8. *Gemäldegalerie Alte Meister Dresden* (Dresden 1979), p. 103, no. 606.
9. Kozakiewicz, *op. cit.*, p. 108, no. 142.

182 Dresden from the right bank of the Elbe below the Augustus Bridge (Fig. 14).

Oil on canvas, 0.515 × 0.84 m.

SIGNED: *Bernard Bellotto dit Canaletto Peintre du Roi.*

CONDITION: excellent. The painting was restored in June 1968, and in 1984. There were only a few small areas of paint loss.

PROVENANCE: M. B. Naryschkine sale, Paris, 5 April 1883, lot 3, where purchased, for £379, with no. 181.

EXHIBITED: 1911 London *Venetian Painting of the Eighteenth Century* (Burlington Fine Arts Club), no. 17; 1985 London *Masterpieces from The National Gallery of Ireland* (National Gallery), no. 9.

VERSIONS: Dresden, State Art Collections, Gallery of Old Master Painters;[1] Madrid, collection Marques De Deleitosa;[2] Dresden, same Gallery.[3]

The difference between the versions listed above are very slight. No. 182 shows more of the view than the others, and is therefore closer to the engraving, which is Bellotto's own work.[4] The tower of the Catholic Court Church, on the right in this view, was just completed before this painting was executed. The architect of the church was the Italian, Gaetano Chiaveri, (1689-1770). Construction commenced in 1738.[5] The impressive bridge, the Augustus Bridge, was designed by Daniel Pöppelmann and built 1727-31.[6] Beyond the bridge, one can clearly see the Protestant Church of the Virgin, whose dome was constructed 1726-43 to the designs of George Bähr.[7] Kozakiewicz dates this painting to about 1750.[8]

1. S. Kozakiewicz, *Bernardo Bellotto* (Recklinghausen 1972), vol. 2, pp. 115-16, no. 146.
2. *Ibid.*, p. 116, no. 147.
3. *Ibid.*, pp. 116-21, no. 149.
4. *Ibid.*, p. 121, no. 150.
5. E. Hempel, *Baroque Art and Architecture in Central Europe* (Harmondsworth 1965), pp. 198-89.
6. *Gemäldegalerie Alte Meister Dresden* (Dresden 1979), p. 103, no. 606.
7. Hempel, *op. cit.*, pp. 196-98.
8. Kozakiewicz, *op. cit.*, p. 116, no. 148.

After BELLOTTO

1960   View of Pirna on the Elbe with the Sonnenstein fortress (Fig. 15).

Oil on canvas, 0.72 × 1.23 m.
CONDITION: the painting has been damaged around the edges. Also evident are areas of damage throughout the picture.

PROVENANCE: Robert Clouston, Dublin, by whom presented, 1855.

PROTOTYPE: Gallery of Old Master Paintings, Dresden.

This canvas is derived from Bellotto's famous view in the Staatliche Kunstsammlungen, Gemäldegalerie Alte Meister, Dresden,[1] inv. nr. 626. This was engraved by Bellotto himself.[2]

As Pirna is a small town about ten miles south east of Dresden, Bellotto visited it frequently; Kozakiewicz dates to 1753-56[3] the genuine Bellotto from which this canvas is directly copied.

1. S. Kozakiewicz, *Bernardo Bellotto*
(Recklinghausen 1972), vol. 2, p. 173, no. 217.
2. *Ibid.*, p. 174, no. 219.
3. *Ibid.*, p. 173, no. 217.

BOLOGNESE SCHOOL, 17th Century

71   Saint John the Baptist in the wilderness (Fig. 17).

Oil on canvas, 1.23 × 0.97 m.

CONDITION: excellent. Restored 1971.

PROVENANCE: reportedly from the collection of the Marchese Campana, Rome;[1] purchased in Rome, from an unrecorded source, 1864, for £75.

EXHIBITED: 1984 New Orleans *Treasures of the Vatican* (New Orleans Vatican Pavilion at the 1984 Louisiana World Exposition), no. 42.

This painting is certainly in the tradition of the Guido Reni School. Both Sir Denis Mahon and Stephen Pepper, during visits to the Gallery, firmly put forward the name of Simone Cantarini. This attribution was not accepted by Andrea Emiliani, also on a visit to the Gallery, who tentatively suggested that it was an early work by G. A. Burrini.

Accordingly, it would seem prudent to wait for further studies and opinions by the Bolognese experts before ascribing the painting firmly to a particular artist.

Following its acquisition the painting was catalogued as by Guercino down to and including the 1898 catalogue. Then it was dropped, until being given to Reni in the 1963 catalogue, and to Cantarini in both the 1971 and 1981 editions.

1. National Gallery of Ireland Archives.

BOLOGNESE SCHOOL, 18th Century

1967 Lucretia stabbing herself (Fig. 16).

Oil on canvas, 0.88 × 0.74 m.

CONDITION: the painting has suffered damage around all four sides. It is covered with oxidized varnish.

PROVENANCE: Sir Henry Page Turner Barron, Bt., by whom presented, 1878.

This canvas is not seventeenth century. When received at the Gallery it was attributed to Sirani. It is likely that it is based on a composition by a Bolognese artist, not yet identified. It was probably executed in the mid-eighteenth century.

ANTONIO CANAL, called CANALETTO, Venice 1697-1768 Venice

Giovanni Antonio Canal, known as Canaletto, was born in Venice; early in his career he became known as a view painter, and his works were eagerly sought. He made a number of visits to England; this, combined with the activities of British agents in Venice, made sure that many of his best works found their way into British collections.

286 Saint Mark's Square, Venice, with the Doge's Palace, the Campanile, and the Procuratie Nuove (Fig. 18).

Oil on canvas, 0.46 × 0.77 m.

CONDITION: excellent. Restored 1968.

PROVENANCE: J. Newington Hughes sale, Christie's, 15 April, 1848, lot 138, bt. Farrer; Charles Cope sale Christie's, 8 June 1872, lot 36, bought by Nieuwenhuys; C. Beckett Denison, London, sale, Christie's, 13 June 1885, lot 857, where purchased, for 170 guineas.

VERSIONS: London Art Market, 1938; formerly with Sabin, London; formerly with Leggatt, London; Cyril Humphris, London, 1971.

The view is taken from the north side and shows the very south of the front of St. Mark's basilica, with the Doge's palace beyond. To the west is the Campanile and then the Procuratie Nuove.

No. 286 has always been accepted as a genuine Canaletto by leading specialists of later Venetian painting.

This view is dated by Constable[1] to the period after Canaletto's final return from England to Venice in 1756. Puppi[2] is more precise and attributes it to the years 1756-57.

1. W. G. Constable, *Canaletto* (Oxford 1976), vol. 2, p. 207, no. 49.
2. L. Puppi in D. Bindman and L. Puppi, *The* *Complete Paintings of Canaletto* (London 1970), p. 121, no. 340A.

After CANALETTO

705 The Grand Canal with the Church of the Salute, and the Customs House, from Campo Santa Maria Zobenigo (Fig. 19).

Oil on canvas, 0.59 × 0.96 m.

CONDITION: very good. Restored October-November 1968.

PROVENANCE: Milltown Collection; Milltown Gift, 1902.

This work of slightly coarse execution should be compared with the similar view by Canaletto formerly in the Craven Collection, Hamstead Marshall, Berkshire, England,[1] and sold Sotheby's, 29 November 1961, lot 41, bt. Weitzner.[2]

No. 705 was previously described as 'After Bellotto', in the 1963 and 1971 catalogues, and as 'Studio of Canaletto' in the 1981 catalogue.

1. L. Puppi in D. Bindman and L. Puppi, *The Complete Paintings of Canaletto* (London 1970), p. 103, no. 134.

2. W. G. Constable, *Canaletto* (Oxford 1976), vol. 2, p. 273, no. 180.

After CANALETTO

1043 The Grand Canal with the Church of the Carità towards the harbour of St. Mark's (Fig. 20).

Oil on canvas, 0.59 × 0.96 m.

CONDITION: very good. Restored October-November 1968.

PROVENANCE: Milltown Collection; Milltown Gift, 1902.

VERSIONS (AUTHENTIC): estate of the late Elwood B. Hosmer, Montreal; Kimbell Art Foundation, Fort Worth, Texas; H.M. The Queen, Windsor Castle; private collection, Lombardy.[1] Constable also lists six school pieces.[2]

This school work of slightly coarse execution should be compared with the similar view by Canaletto in a U.S.A. private collection.[3] Constable lists several authentic versions.

No. 1043 was previously described as 'After Bellotto', in the 1963 and 1971 catalogue, and as 'Studio of Canaletto' in the 1981 catalogue.

1. W. G. Constable, *Canaletto* (Oxford 1976), vol. 2, pp. 280-82.
2. *Ibid.*, pp. 282-83.

3. L. Puppi in D. Bindman and L. Puppi, *The Complete Paintings of Canaletto* (London 1970), p. 93, no. 41.

GIOVANNI BATTISTA CANEVARI, Genoa 1789-1876 Rome

Canevari was a distinguished nineteenth century portrait painter, who, as well as executing canvases on traditional sizes, also worked in miniature. He painted many visitors to Rome, and also sent works to the Royal Academy.

4169   Colonel Richard Wogan Talbot, 2nd Baron Talbot of Malahide, and Baron Furnival of Malahide, c.1766-1849 (Fig. 21).

Oil on canvas, 1.36 × 0.99 m.

SIGNED: *Canevari/Roma/1840*

CONDITION: very good.

PROVENANCE: Talbot family, Malahide Castle, county Dublin; the Hon. Rose Talbot, Malahide Castle, from whom purchased, 1976.

Richard Wogan was the eldest son of Richard Talbot of Malahide Castle, county Dublin, by his wife Margaret, eldest daughter of James O'Reilly, of Ballinlough Castle, county Westmeath. Richard's mother, for many years a widow, was created Baroness Talbot of Malahide, in the Irish peerage, in 1831. Her son, Richard Wogan, was born about 1766. He was M.P. for county Dublin in 1790-91, when the election was declared void. He served in the army for some years, being captured at Ostend in 1798; he rose to the rank of Colonel.

In 1834 he succeeded, following his mother's death, as 2nd Baron; in 1836 he was appointed to the Privy Council of Ireland; in 1839 he was given a U.K. peerage as Baron Furnival of Malahide.

Lord Talbot married twice, but, as he had no sons alive at the time of his death, was succeeded by his younger brother, James.

ALESSANDRO CAPALTI, Rome 1807-1868 Rome

Capalti trained in Rome under Tommaso Minardi. He did decorative schemes, historical subjects, but is remembered principally as a portrait painter. He painted Romans and foreigners alike, and sent a few works to exhibitions of the Royal Academy.

406   The Most Reverend John MacHale, Archbishop of Tuam (1791-1881) (Fig. 22).

Oil on canvas, 1.37 × 0.98 m.

SIGNED: indistinctly.

INSCRIBED: *A Monsignore / J . . . . . MacHale / A . . . . . di Tuam*

CONDITION: very good.

PROVENANCE: Monsignor MacHale, Paris, by whom presented, 1890.

John MacHale was born at Tubbernavine, county Mayo, in the diocese of Killala. His initial education was at one of the hedge-schools, then the sole means of education for Catholic peasant children; on wet days master and pupils endeavoured to find a disused barn.

Later he was sent to a school in Castlebar, and when he was sixteen the Bishop of Killala sent him to St Patrick's College, Maynooth, a Catholic seminary founded by George III in 1795. There he had a brilliant academic career, being appointed a lecturer in theology while only a sub-deacon. He was ordained a priest in 1814 and was retained as a lecturer in theology, being nominated professor in 1820.

In 1825 MacHale was consecrated Bishop of Maronia *(in partibus infidelium)*, to act as coadjutor to the Bishop of Killala. It would be difficult to find a more zealous priest and prelate, visiting and preaching in every part of the diocese. Very much aware of the deprivations of the Catholic population, especially in poorer areas, he was very active on a national basis in the campaign for Catholic Emancipation, as well as for reforms in land tenure, the abolition of rack-renting and the usury of seed merchants. From his days as a Maynooth professor, he had a wide circle of friends and acquaintances, the Duke of Leinster and Daniel O'Connell being particularly close friends.

In 1830 he went with a deputation of Mayo gentlemen to the Prime Minister, Earl Grey, and attended the coronation of William IV.

In 1834 he was appointed Archbishop of Tuam, much to the annoyance of some members of the establishment. He was the first prelate since the Reformation who had received his entire education in Ireland. He continued to work ceaselessly, both within his diocese, and on a national level. He improved vastly the educational facilities within his diocese, did everything possible to alleviate poverty, and was particularly kind to his clergy.

At meetings of the bishops, through publications and preaching, he strove ardently for the reforms which were so obviously needed and seen to be needed even by many English politicians. Outspoken and direct, he was christened 'the Lion of St Jarlath's' (after the patron saint of his diocese and of his cathedral). While campaigning for reforms, he always acknowledged help, for example the despatch from England of cargoes of food during the famine years.

Despite his advanced years, in 1869 he went to Rome for the Vatican Council. He was opposed to the definition of papal infallibility as a dogma of faith, not on doctrinal grounds but because he considered the timing inopportune. However, he fully accepted the dogma on its definition. At home in his diocese he continued his work and his writing. In 1877 he was given a coadjutor bishop; after a short illness he died in 1881, aged ninety.

In this threequarter-length portrait the prelate is shown in episcopal attire, wearing a rochet and mozzetta over a soutane; from his neck is suspended an archiepiscopal pectoral cross.

The portrait was painted in Rome in 1855, when the Archbishop was on an *ad limina* visit.

CARLO INNOCENZO CARLONE, Scaria near Como 1686-1776 Como

The son of a sculptor, Carlo Carlone studied painting under Giulio Quaglia in Como. He worked in Venice and Rome, and later in many centres in Germany and Austria, and at Prague. His frescos are as well known as his oil paintings.

1640 The Annunciation (Fig. 23).

Oil on canvas, 0.56 × 0.40 m.

CONDITION: very good. Restored July 1973; there were some small paint losses, in horizontal lines, as if the canvas had been rolled up at some time.

PROVENANCE: Monsignor Shine, by whom bequeathed to Miss Kathleen Farrelly, from whom purchased, 1961, for £50.

EXHIBITED: 1973 Münster *Johann Conrad Schlaun, 1695-1773* (Landesmuseum), special supplementary exhibit.

This sketch was identified by Hilde Claussen[1] as being a study for the left-hand altarpiece in the Church of Saint Clement, Münster, Westphalia. Although the altarpiece itself was destroyed during World War II and no complete photograph existed of it, the hypothesis was sustainable. The architect of the Church was Johann Conrad Schlaun, 1695-1773, who worked on this building and the adjoining monastery-hospital from 1745-53.[2]

The left-hand altarpiece of the delightful church of Saint Clement was normally raised up out of view, except for a small strip of the bottom edge, to allow the faithful a view into the facsimile Holy House of Loreto which was built onto the church at this point.

A letter from the architect to Clemens August von Wittelsbach, Elector and Archbishop of Cologne, and Bishop of Münster, dated 13 July 1749,[3] contained drawings of the three altars of the church. That for the left-hand altar showed an iron-grilled window in exactly the position which such a window occupies in the Dublin sketch. The window in the outline drawing and Dublin painting echoes the window of the House of Loreto itself. In all other respects the proportions of the Dublin sketch are correct for the destroyed altarpiece, including the photographic evidence for the lower edge of the lost painting. (Fig. 24).

The Dublin sketch should be dated consequently to late 1749 or early 1750.

1. H. Claussen 'Carlo Carlone's Bozzetto for a destroyed Altar-piece in the Church of St. Clement, Münster', *The Burlington Magazine*, vol. 117 (February 1975), pp. 109-10.
2. K. Noehles, 'Die Clemenskirche und das Hospital der Bermherzingen Brüder in Münster', *Johann Conrad Schlaun 1695-1773.*

Schlaunstudie, vol. 1 (Greven 1973), pp. 125-57.
3. Staatsarchiv Münster: Fürstentum Münster Kabinettsregistratur P XXII A Nr. 6. *Cf.* also H. Claussen, 'Zwei Altargemälde Carlo Carlones für die Clemenskirche in Münster', *Westfalen* Band 53 (1975), pp. 159-73.

GIOVANNI BENEDETTO CASTIGLIONE, Genoa *c.*1610-*c.*1665 Mantua

A native of Genoa, Castiglione studied there under Giovanni Battista Poggi and Giovanni Andrea De Ferrari. Not being satisfied with his success in his native city, Castiglione went to Rome where he worked for a picture dealer called Pellegrino Peri. Following an introduction to the Duke of Mantua he was appointed a court painter, moved to Mantua in 1651, where he lived until his death. Apart from working for the Duke, he undertook commissions for other members of the Gonzaga family, and other patrons.

994 The shepherdess Spako with the infant Cyrus (Fig. 25).

Oil on canvas, 2.34 × 2.265 m.

CONDITION: the canvas has two horizontal seams, the first about 30 cms. from the top, the second about 1.30 m. from the top. The painting is in very good condition. It has not been restored recently.

PROVENANCE: Dukes of Mantua;[1] the 9th Earl of Lincoln (subsequently 2nd Duke of Newcastle-under-Line) by 1765; Dukes of Newcastle-under-Line; by descent to the Earl of Lincoln, heir to 8th Duke of Newcastle-under-Line, at whose sale, Christie's, 4 June 1937, lot 19, purchased for £378.

EXHIBITED: 1857 Manchester *Art Treasures Exhibition*, no. 834 (lent by the Duke of Newcastle); 1985 London *Masterpieces from the National Gallery of Ireland* (National Gallery), no. 6.

Even by the time Herodotus (*c.* 484-425 B.C.) wrote his famous *History*, the story of the early life of Cyrus had become entangled in legends. Herodotus gives four accounts, but chooses one as being the most probable. This is followed here. Cyrus was born to Mandane, a daughter of Astyages, king of Media, (evidently by a god). Because of an oracle, which foretold that Cyrus would overthrow his grandfather, the infant was given to a shepherd to be abandoned on a mountainside. The shepherd and his wife (whose name Spako means 'bitch') had lost their own child and decided to rear Cyrus in place of their recently dead son. Because of the literal meaning of the shepherd's wife's name, the myth grew that Cyrus was suckled by a dog. It is useful to recall that a dog was a sacred animal for the Persians.

The theme, like the *Finding of Romulus and Remus*, has a biblical parallel in the *Finding of Moses*; in all three a great future leader has been cast out as an infant and subsequently recovered. Castiglione's literary contemporaries certainly sought out such parallels between pagan and biblical literature, and Ann Percy has pointed out in the case of another subject that Castiglione may well have 'consciously pursued this type of intellectualising syncretism'.[2]

Cyrus grew up indeed to be a great leader, conqueror, and founder of the Persian Empire. Much of his success was due to the fact that he respected the traditions of the various peoples who made up the Empire, such as the Jews, the Medes, the Greeks, the Babylonians, and so forth. Cyrus died in 528 B.C.

The Dublin painting is regarded as one of the finest and most beautiful works by Castiglione. As it was in Mantua in 1705 (see 'Provenance') and relates to the *Deucalion and Pyrrha*, dated 1655, now in Berlin, it seems very likely that it was painted during Castiglione's Mantua years, 1651-59, and as a specific commission. The statue of a man in no. 994 is almost identical to that in the *Deucalion and Pyrrha* at the Bodemuseum, Berlin.

G. B. Castiglione painted the subject on at least one other occasion, the canvas now in the vestibule of the Palazzo Durazzo-Pallavicini, Genoa.[3] A copy of this painting was at a Christie's sale on 27 June 1969, lot 38 (0.97 × 1.32 m.).[4]

His son, Francesco, also executed the same theme,[5] in a painting whose present whereabouts is unknown, and two drawings for it.[6]

Another Cyrus painting is that which was at Houghton Hall, Norfolk, in the eighteenth century and given to G. B. Castiglione. U. Meroni suggested that this painting might now be Dublin's no. 994. That is not possible because the measurements given in his source as '2 feet 4 inches ½ high, by 3 feet 6 inches ¼ wide' are not only incorrect but the wrong proportion for no. 994.[7] The ex-Houghton Hall painting is now supposed to be the one in the Hermitage and attributed to Vassallo. The painting in the Musée des Beaux-Arts at Lyons is a more expansive composition though smaller in size than the Dublin canvas.[8] Most historians regard it as having been painted after Castiglione's death.

A drawing in the Royal Library at Windsor is probably a first idea for part of the Dublin painting[9] (Fig. 26). A drawing of a bust in the Accademia, Venice,[10] is preparatory to Castiglione's etching of 1648 *The Genius of Castiglione*. This is similar to the bust on top of a grass-topped pedestal in no. 994.[11] A very important drawing including the complete composition (as a horizontal rather than a square format) is Inv. T. 120 A (193 × 269 mm.) in brown ink, belonging to the Musée de Dijon (Fig. 27).

No. 994 was engraved by John Boydell on the basis of a drawing by Richard Earlom. Boydell published his engraving on the 1st May 1765. The Gallery has an impression of this print, cat. no. 11,943. It shows the composition in reverse (Fig. 28).

1. N.a., but U. Meroni (ed.), *Fonti per la storia della Pittura. I Serie Documentaria. Lettere e altri documenti intorno alla Storia della Pittura. Giovanni Benedetto Castiglione detto il Grechetto, Giovanni Francesco Castiglione, Salvatore Castiglione* (Genoa 1971), p. 108, no. I (year 1705).
2. A. Percy, *Giovanni Benedetto Castiglione* (Exhibition catalogue), Philadelphia Museum of Art, 1971, p. 126.
3. G. Delogu, *Giovan Battista Castiglione detto il Grechetto* (Bologna 1928), pl. 18. P. Torriti, *La Galleria del Palazzo Durazzo Pallavicini a Genova* (Genoa 1967), p. 28, fig. 20, p. 30, fig. 21, p. 300, n. 12.
4. *Apollo*, vol. 89 (June 1969), ill. p. xix: Christie's, 27 June 1969, lot 38.
5. A. Percy, *op. cit.*, p. 43, fig. 36.
6. *Ibid.*, p. 129, no. 118, and Sotheby's, 28 March 1968, lot 70, as by Giovanni Benedetto.

Cf. The Burlington Magazine, vol. 110 (March 1968) ill. p. viii.
7. U. Meroni (ed.) *Fonti per la Storia della Pittura e della scultura antica. VIII Serie documentaria. Lettere e altri documenti intorno alla Storia della Pittura. Giovanni Benedetto Castiglione detto il Grechetto, Salvator Rosa, Gian Lorenzo Bernini* (Monzambano 1978), p. 54: this is a citation from Horace Walpole's *Aedes Walpolianae . . .* (London 1747), p. 77, and an interpretation of it.
8. R. Jullian in *Bulletin des Musées Lyonnais* (1956), pp. 25-38.
9. A. Blunt, *The Drawings of G. B. Castiglione and Stefano Della Bella in the Collection of Her Majesty the Queen of Windsor Castle* (London 1954), p. 40, no. 183.
10. Delogu, *op. cit.*, pl. 35.
11. Blunt, *op. cit.*, p. 33, fig. 15.

ANDREA CELESTI, Venice 1637-1712 Toscolana

Celesti studied with the Venetian, Matteo Ponzone; he was influenced by several artists including Francesco Maffei. He received numerous commissions for church altarpieces, and historical paintings. He is also known to have done portraits. His work appears to be entirely in Venice, the Veneto, and Lombardy.

1925 Imaginary portrait of Count Alberto Alberti of Baone (Fig. 29).

Oil on canvas, 2.06 × 1.40 m.

INSCRIBED: *Albertus De Comitibus / Alberti Filius / Consylvarum Ecclesiam / Proprio aere Construxit / Dotavitque / Et Familiae suae Ius Patronatus reliquit / Idem arrepto Vexllo / Cives ad Libertatem vocavit / Expulso Vrbe Imperiali Vicario / Ideoque Pater Patriae dictus / Mox Consul / Inde post decennium / Praetor creatus est / ANNO D. / MCLXXIV.* (Albert, son of the Counts Alberti, built and endowed with his own money the church of Conselve; he left to his family the right to the patronage of it. The same man, having taken up the standard, called the citizens to freedom; having expelled from the town the Emperor's representative he was called founder of the homeland, later Consul; then after a decade he was made Praetor. 1174 A.D.).

CONDITION: very good. Restored 1977-79. The two narrow lateral strips of added canvas appear to be original. At the base, however, a very narrow strip of canvas, not more than 5 cms. wide, is a much later addition.

PROVENANCE: Cardinal Fesch, Rome; Alessandro Aducci, Rome,[1] from whom purchased, 1856. One of sixteen paintings acquired for £1,700.

EXHIBITED: 1979 London *Venetian Seventeenth Century Painting* (National Gallery), no. 46.

This full length portrait shows a man dressed in armour; in his right hand he clasps a standard. At the bottom right is a helmet. According to A. V. B. Norman, Master of the Armouries at the Tower of London, the armour is fanciful with some attempt at antiquarianism shown by the besagew (the disk) on the left shoulder, the mail skirt, and the mail sabatons (shoes).

On the basis of the inscription the Count Alberto is undoubtedly a member of the family of the Counts of Baone (in which family the name Alberto is repeatedly found). In 1174 the Counts of Baone also had castles at Pernumia and Conselve. The church referred to in the inscription is to be associated with this last property, a small town 17.5 kilometres east of Este. The church referred to must be that known as the Chiesa Arcipretale of San Lorenzo, first publicly recorded under that dedication in a document dated 27th February 1026, written by Orso, bishop of Padua.[2] The reconstruction of the church by Count Alberto da Baone, and its endowment by him, is well documented, and the consensus of opinion on the date of this patronage is 1194.[3]

The family of the Counts of Baone lost their power and possessions at the very end of the twelfth century. Who then, after an interval of five hundred years commissioned this portrait, and for what location was it destined? Clearly it did not stay too long in its original setting. Were other paintings associated with it?

In the Slovenian Academy of Science and Art, Ljubljana, are two similar full length portraits of men in armour.[4] Could they originally have formed part of a series with the Dublin canvas? Another possible candidate for such a series is a *Capitano de mar* described as 'mediocrissimo' and bearing a plaque *Comes Albertus*,[5] in the Palazzo Conti, Padua.

Celesti was working near Brescia from 1688 to 1700, and a date of 1690 or shortly after has been suggested for the Dublin canvas.[6]

1. M. Wynne in *Gazette des Beaux-Arts,* vol. 89 (January 1977), pp. 2-3.
2. Cited in n.a. (but, in fact, I. Daniele), *La Diocesi di Padova* (Padova 1973), p. 224.
3. Bernardinus Scardeonius, *De Antiquitate Urbis Patavii, claris civibus Patavinis* (Basilear 1560), *Lib. III, Classis XIII,* p. 298, in which the church is described as dedicated to St. Andrew; Jacobus Salomonius, (referring back to Scardeonius) in *Agri Patavini Inscriptiones Sacra, et Prophanae* (ed. of Jacobus Philippus Tomasinus, Patavii 1696), p. 359, corrects the dedication to St. Laurence, and gives 1194 as the date of Count Alberto's reconstruction. This is accepted by Daniele (note 2 above). For these references, and photocopies of them, the writer is indebted to Professor Francesca Flores d'Arcais.
4. A. Rizzi in *Arte Veneta,* vol. 24 (1970), pp. 233-34.
5. A. M. Mucchi and C. Della Croce, *Il Pittore Andrea Celesti* (Milan 1954), p. 76.
6. M. Wynne in *The Burlingron Magazine,* vol. 121 (October 1979), pp. 654-55.

ACKNOWLEDGEMENT: The first clue to the present reasonable amount of knowledge about no. 1925 was provided by Sergio Benedetti, Restorer at the National Gallery of Ireland, when he identified the tiny town of Conselve out of 'Consylvarum'.

IACOPO CHIMENTI DA EMPOLI, Empoli or Florence *c.* 1551-1640 Florence

Chimenti studied under Maso da San Friano; he was greatly influenced by the work of Pontormo and del Sarto, whose works he frequently copied in his youth. He appears to have received numerous commissions for use in churches, and it is by his religious subject paintings that he is best remembered. He also painted portraits and some still life. Among his pupils was Felice Ficherelli.

Studio of CHIMENTI

1068 Adoration of the shepherds (Fig. 30).

Oil on canvas, 1.12 × 0.98 m.

CONDITION: good. Requires cleaning and conservation.

PROVENANCE: Milltown Collection by 1826; Milltown Gift, 1902.

McCorquodale regards no. 1068 as a studio variant of the painting of the same subject in the City Museum and Art Gallery, Plymouth.[1] The latter has been dated 1570-80 on the basis of the dating of the Uffizi preparatory drawing (no. 9281) by Anna Forlani.[2]

The Dublin picture is considerably larger than the Plymouth one and there are several notable differences. No. 1068 has no cherubs; it has three shepherds instead of two; St. Joseph is seen more in profile; the Christ Child lies vertically on the canvas plane instead of horizontally. No. 1068 has not been cleaned so that it is difficult to assess its quality adequately. However, given the differences between it and the Plymouth painting, one may legitimately ask if no. 1068 does not relate to another commission. Giuseppe Cantelli considers no. 1068 to be autograph,[3] but the compiler would prefer to wait for its restoration before giving it this accolade.

In the Uffizi there is a drawing (no. 9327 F) in which the major figure could be a preparatory sketch for the shepherd on the extreme right hand side of no. 1068. That drawing has been dated to 1618-28.[4] The posture of the Virgin, the placing of the Christ child, and the figure of the shepherd closest for the viewer are to be found in another Uffizi drawing (no. 992 F). This is a squared drawing for an *Adoration of the shepherds* of a different composition.

1. Exhibition catalogue, *Painting in Florence 1600-1700* (Royal Academy, London, and Fitzwilliam Museum, Cambridge, 1979), no. 6.
2. Exhibition catalogue, *Mostra di Disegni di Iacopo da Empoli* (Uffizi, Florence, 1962), no. 2.

3. G. Cantelli, *Repertorio della Pittura Fiorentina del Seicento* (Fiesole 1983), p. 42.
4. Exhibition catalogue, *Mostra di Disegni di Iacopo da Empoli* (Uffizi, Florence, 1962), no. 66.

Studio of CHIMENTI

1671   Susanna and the Elders (Fig. 31).

Oil on canvas, 0.72 × 0.98 m.

CONDITION: apparently good. Requires cleaning and restoration.

PROVENANCE: Milltown Collection by 1826; Milltown Gift, 1902.

No. 1671 does not appear to have the quality of an autograph Chimenti; nor is a prototype of the painting known at present. There are, however, many features which make one think of this artist, to whom it was given in the 1826 Milltown inventory and in the 1963 catalogue. This was changed to 'Studio of Chimenti' in the 1971 and 1981 concise catalogues.

The head of the Elder to the left hand side of no. 1671 reminds one of the head of Abraham in Chimenti's *The sacrifice of Isaac* in the Uffizi,[1] and the head of Noah in *The drunkeness of Noah*, another Chimenti in the Uffizi.[2] The gesticulating hands and arms in no. 1671 recall particularly similar passages in the latter. Alternatively, because of the generic nature of the subject and composition, no. 1671 could derive from some Bolognese prototype.

1. *Gli Uffizi. Catalogo Generale* (Florence 1979), p. 258, no. P577.

2. *Ibid.*, no. 576.

LEONARDO COCCORANTE, Naples 1680-1750 Naples

Little is known about Coccorante's life. He was patronized by the Bourbon court in Naples, and by many private collectors. He painted some real views, but is best known for his imaginary scenes with ruins, storms and shipwrecks.

1744   Coast scene with ruins and shipwrecks (Fig. 32).

Oil on canvas, 0.69 × 0.99 m.

CONDITION: very good. Restored June-July 1970. There were some minor paint losses.

PROVENANCE: Milltown Collection; Milltown Gift, 1902.

No. 1744 has a turbulent sky with striking contrasts of light and shade. Typical, too, of Coccorante are the contrast in the lighting of the ruins, ornamental urns, and several people dashing around the foreground with no evident purpose. The handling of the storm-driven waves and the foundering ships are very like similar passages in signed or documented works. An appropriately comparative signed work was exhibited recently in Naples.[1]

The painting was given to Vernet, until attributed to Coccorante in the 1981 catalogue. The reattribution was first proposed by Sergio Benedetti, verbally.

1. Exhibition catalogue, *Civiltà del' 700 a Napoli 1734-1799* (Naples 1979-1980), no. 71b. (on loan from the Kress Foundation to the Lowe Art Museum, University of Miami, Coral Gables).

GIUSEPPE MARIA CRESPI, Bologna 1665-1747 Bologna

Having studied in his native city, and having been influenced by some of the major artists' works of the first half of the seventeenth century to be seen there, Crespi travelled extensively in the northern part of Italy. Settling in Bologna, Crespi painted an extensive oeuvre, developing a very personal style. Some of his compositions were so successful that he had to execute several versions. Crespi had some pupils, including Pietro Longhi.

1020   The massacre of the Innocents (Fig. 33).

Oil on canvas, 1.31 × 1.80 m.

CONDITION: very good. Restored June 1968. There were some minor paint losses.

PROVENANCE: private collection England; Robert Frank, England, by whom sold to Alfred Scharf, from whom purchased, 1940, for £670.

EXHIBITED: 1951 London and Birmingham *Eighteenth Century Venice* (Whitechapel Art Gallery and City Museum and Art Gallery), no. 31; 1979 Bologna *L'Arte del Settecento Emiliano: La Pittura: L'Accademia Clementina* (Palazzi del Podestà e di Re Enzo), no. 29.

Crespi painted this subject several times and the Dublin painting is considered a late one by Scharf.[1] In the catalogue of the 1979 exhibition at Bologna, Eugenio Riccòmini, confirming notes available to him prepared by Mira Pajes Merriman, dated the painting to 1720-25. By then Riccòmini knew of ten different renderings of the same subject painted over a wide span of years. Mira Pajes Merriman herself leaves the date of the Dublin painting more open: 1720-30.[2]

1. A Scharf, 'A *Massacre of the Innocents* by G.M. Crespi', The Burlington Magazine, vol. 77 (July 1940), pp. 34.

2. M. Pajes Merriman, *Giuseppe Maria Crespi* (Milan 1980), p. 246, no. 39.

CESARE DANDINI, Florence 1596-1656 Florence

Trained initially by Francesco Curradi, Dandini subsequently studied under Domenico Passignano. After some years he began to work on his own, and, it would appear, was successful; he was commissioned to execute several paintings by Don Lorenzo de' Medici. The painters Ottaviano and Vincenzo Dandini were Cesare's brothers, while Pietro was his nephew.

1683 Moses driving away the shepherds (Fig. 34).

Oil on canvas, 2.06 × 2.72 m.

CONDITION: excellent. Restored 1970. An old intervention had completely painted out the camel and its attendant (in the background, to the left).

PROVENANCE: possibly Michel' Agnolo Venturi, Florence,[1] in the seventeenth century; Milltown Collection by 1826;[2] Milltown Gift, 1902.

EXHIBITED: 1979 London and Cambridge *Painting in Florence 1600-1700* (Royal Academy and Fitzwilliam Museum), no. 10.

In *Exodus*, ch. 2, vs. 16-17, one reads how the seven daughters of Jethro, priest of Midian, came to a well to draw water, but were driven away by shepherds. Moses, who had fled into Midian to escape Pharoah, protected them and was given Jethro's daughter Zipporah in marriage.

Studies on Dandini are not advanced enough yet to enable one to date precisely the Dublin canvas, but Evelina Borea regards it as a high point in Florentine painting of the Seicento.[3] Charles McCorquodale endorses this and tentatively suggests a date in the period 1635-45.[4]

A somewhat coarse version, with richer costume and exaggerated facial expressions, was formerly in a Florentine private collection.[5]

1. F. Baldinucci, *Delle Notizie de' Professori del Disegno, ecc.*, vol. 15 (D. M. Manni's edition, Florence 1772), p. 125.
2. M. Wynne in *Apollo,* vol. 99 (February 1974), pp. 107-08.
3. Exhibition catalogue, *La Quadreria di Don*

Lorenzo de' Medici (Villa Medicea di Poggio a Caiano, 1977), p. 27.
4. 1979 exhibition catalogue, no. 10.
5. As by Vincenzo Dandini: G. Cantelli, *Repertorio della Pittura Fiorentina del Seicento* (Fiesole 1983), p. 63.

GIACINTO DIANO, Pozzuoli 1731-1804 Naples

Diano worked in the Naples studio of Francesco de Mura for a number of years. Firmly established, he did numerous decorative schemes for churches and other important buildings in Naples, Pozzuoli, and Lanciano. Into de Mura's style he added some classical ideas.

357   The dedication of the Temple at Jerusalem (Fig. 35)

Oil on canvas, 0.77 × 1.42 m.

CONDITION: the painting is in very good condition, but its true beauty is obscured by discoloured varnish. There is a vertical seam in the canvas about 34 to 35 cms. from the right hand side.

PROVENANCE: purchased at an auction in Dublin, (about November) 1859. One of three pictures acquired for £35.

Israel reached the height of its glory when the twelve tribes were united under three kings, Saul, David and Solomon. Solomon, the tenth son of David, was anointed king through the influence of his mother, Bathsheba. He reigned in the tenth century B.C.[1] Solomon realized the wishes of his father, namely to build a temple to house the Ark of the Covenant. The building began about 960 B.C.[2]

This *bozzetto* was identified by Oreste Ferrari, following a suggestion by Ferdinando Bologna, as a sketch for Diano's fresco in the ceiling of the sacristy of Sant' Agostino alla Zecca, Naples,[3] a work executed in 1776. When purchased, no. 357 was called a De Vos. In the catalogues of the Gallery from that of 1879 to the edition of 1885 it was called a G. B. Tiepolo. After that it was dropped until the 1904 edition when it was called a G. B. Castiglione. This remained its appellation until the 1956 catalogue, in which it was correctly given to Diano.

No. 357 contains a self-portrait of the artist; this is the figure in the middle ground, slightly right of centre, with arms and hand outstretched, and head turned towards the viewer. Another example of the inclusion of a self-portrait by Diano in one of his works is the figure at the extreme left foreground in the *bozzetto, Scene from the life of S. Giovanni di Dio,* which belongs to Mr. Roy Fisher, New York (Fig. 36). This sketch is for one of the frescos executed by Diano in the Ospedale di S. Maria della Pace, Naples, in 1764.[4]

Until the 1956 catalogue the title of the picture was *Elijah invoking, by prayer, the Sacred Fire from Heaven.*

1. Biblical scholars differ on the precise years of the reign of King Solomon.
2. *The Third Book of Kings,* chapters 5-7, details the construction of the temple, which took seven years to build. Chapter 8 narrates the actual dedication ceremony.
3. In correspondence, May 1956; subsequently published by N. Spinosa 'La Pittura Napoletana da Carlo a Ferdinando IV di Borbone' in *Storia di Napoli,* vol. 8 (Napoli 1971), p. 541, n. III. *Cf.* also N. Spinosa in exhibition catalogue *Civiltà del '700 a Napoli 1734-1799* (Naples 1979-80), p. 143, fig. 12, for the fresco. In the same catalogue, no. 138 is an entry for the Dublin sketch, but in fact the painting was not brought to Naples.
4. In correspondence from Mr. Fisher, September 1982; Mr. Fisher's *bozzetto* was first recognized as a Diano by Erich Schleier, and correlated with the fresco in Naples by Nicola Spinosa.

CARLO DOLCI, Florence 1616-1686 Florence

Dolci trained partly in the studio of Vignali; in Florence Dolci was successful, and scarcely ever left his own city. His works, notably religious works, were much sought by Italians and visitors alike. However, he ought also be remembered as a fine portraitist.

1229 St. Agnes (Fig. 37).

Oil on canvas, 0.64 × 0.53 m. (octagonal)

CONDITION: very good.

PROVENANCE: Lord Baltimore; Sir Richard Glyn, Bt., from whom acquired by C. Marshall Spink, London, from whom purchased, 1951, for £185.

Agnes, a martyr for Christianity in pagan Rome, is portrayed with a lamb because her name, as well as her innocence, reminded people of the Latin word *agnus*, a lamb, also a symbol of Christ: *Ecce Agnus Dei* (Behold the Lamb of God).

For no. 1229 a date in the 1660s is suggested, by which time Dolci had moved away more definitely from the style of his mentor, Vignali, and before he adopted very crisp and polished treatment of faces, draperies and objects.[1] Dolci frequently painted half-lengths in octagonal format.[2] While basically accepting no. 1229's autograph status, Cantelli hints at collaboration by the master's pupil, Bartolomeo Mancini.[3]

1. *Cf.* G. Heinz in *Jahrbuch der Kunsthistorischen Sammlungen in Wien*, Band 56 (1960) pp. 197-234. C. Del Bravo in *Paragone*, vol. 14, no. 163 (1963), pp. 32-41.
2. *Cf.* G. Heinz, *loc. cit.* A good example of the half-length in octagonal format is the portrait of St. Charles Borromeo in the Pitti Palace, Florence (no. 275).
3. G. Cantelli, *Repertorio della Pittura Fiorentina del Seicento* (Fiesole 1983), p. 73.

DOMENICO ZAMPIERI, called DOMENICHINO, Bologna 1581-1641 Naples

Domenico Zampieri, known as Domenichino, was a pupil in the Bolognese studio of Ludovico Carracci; about 1602 he went down to Rome to assist Annibale Carracci. Subsequently in Rome he received some important commissions, particularly for frescos, for the Abbey of Grottaferrata, the church of San Luigi dei Francesi, in Rome itself, and the Villa Aldobrandini at Frascati. He returned to Bologna briefly, and the last twenty years of his life were divided between Rome and Naples. He was elected President of the Roman Accademia di San Luca in 1628.

Attributed to DOMENICHINO

70 **St. Cecilia** (after Raphael) (Fig. 38).

Oil on canvas, 2.34 × 1.47 m.

CONDITION: very good. Restored September 1983. There was some slight contraction of the paint in a few areas of dark blue-green.

PROVENANCE: (?) Conte Serbelloni. Passavant refers to this copy as being in the collection of Bozzotti, a goldsmith in Milan,[1] from whom purchased in 1836, by the 6th Viscount Powerscourt, of Powerscourt House, Enniskerry, county Wicklow; 7th Viscount Powerscourt, by whom presented, 1866.

EXHIBITED: 1983-84 Bologna *L'Estasi di Santa Cecilia di Raffaello da Urbino nella Pinacoteca Nazionale di Bologna* (Pinacoteca Nazionale), no. 22.

This copy of the famous Raphael in the Pinacoteca at Bologna[2] has traditionally been attributed to Domenichino. Such an attribution is difficult either to reject or substantiate, but the picture was certainly painted in the early 1600s. Curiously, Spear, who knows the Dublin collection at first hand, in his major monograph on Domenichino,[3] makes no reference to no. 70, despite its age and its long traditional attribution to Domenichino. Even allowing for the fact that the prototype is the famous Raphael at Bologna, there is another factor that might have warranted its consideration within an exhaustive study of Domenichino. The decoration of the Polet Chapel in San Luigi dei Francesi, Rome, was carried out by Domenichino, except for the altarpiece, which is in fact another copy of the same famous Raphael at Bologna.[4] The copy in this case is by another great Bolognese artist, Guido Reni.

1. J. D. Passavant, *Raphael D'Urbin*, vol. 2 (Paris 1860), p. 150. Antonio Bozzotti's label was on the back of the stretcher, and has now been put in the Gallery's archives. Bozzotti gives one address for the Galleria and a different one after his own name as Orefice; it would seem reasonable to presume that he had indulged in

some diversification of his business interests.
2. O. Fischel, *Raphael*, vol. 2 (London 1948), pl. 244.
3. R. E. Spear, *Domenichino* (New Haven and London 1982).
4. Spear, *op. cit.*, pp. 178 ff.

After DOMENICHINO

1083 **Expulsion of Adam and Eve** (Fig. 39).

Oil on canvas, 1.23 × 1.75 m.

CONDITION: very good.

PROVENANCE: Milltown Collection by 1826; Milltown Gift, 1902.

This is a copy of the well known painting in a private collection in Rio de Janeiro.[1] The original had previously been in the Barberini collection in Rome, and before that again in the Colonna collection, at the Palazzo Colonna, Rome. The Dublin copy, which is full-size, was probably painted from the original when it belonged to the Colonna family, in the eighteenth century.

Spear says that 'the Dublin copy reveals no trace of Domenichino's hand.'[2] Spear's title for the painting is *The rebuke of Adam and Eve*.[3]

1. R. E. Spear, *Domenichino* (New Haven and London 1982), p. 264.

2. Spear, *op. cit.*, p. 265.
3. Spear, *op. cit.*, p. 264.

After DOMENICHINO (Fig. 40)
1885 The last communion of St. Jerome

Oil on canvas, 3.925 × 2.415 m.

CONDITION: difficult to assess because of the obfuscation due to darkened varnish.

PROVENANCE: unknown.

This canvas is a copy of the well known painting in the Pinacoteca Vaticana. Spear, in his major monograph on Domenichino,[1] makes no reference to the Dublin copy.

1. R. E. Spear, *Domenichino* (New Haven and London 1982).

ORAZIO DE FERRARI, Voltri in Liguria 1605-1657 Genoa

A member of a family in which there were numerous painters, Orazio De Ferrari studied in Genoa under Andrea Ansaldo. He was very successful in obtaining commissions, both in oils and in fresco, in Genoa; he also enjoyed the patronage of the princely family of Monaco.

4302 The incredulity of St. Thomas (Fig. 41).

Oil on canvas, 1.89 × 1.28 m.

CONDITION: very good. Restored 1980-81. There were some minor paint losses and abrasions. On the reverse of the old Neapolitan lining canvas there were two wax seals; one with the Bourbon royal heraldic achievement undoubtedly licenced the picture's export from the Kingdom of the Two Sicilies; the second is a family crest.

PROVENANCE: Monsignor Shine; Monsignor Boylan, Dun Laoghaire, county Dublin, by whom presented to the Sisters of St. Michael's Hospital, Dun Laoghaire, County Dublin, from whom purchased, 1978, for £5,000.

EXHIBITED: 1984 New Orleans *Treasures of the Vatican* (New Orleans Vatican Pavilion at the 1984 Louisiana World Exposition), no. 45.

Following the Resurrection of Christ, the apostle St. Thomas was not among the first to see him. He did not believe the story told to him by some of his fellow-disciples, saying he would only believe when he had seen the wounds in Christ's hands and feet, and placed his hand in the wound in Christ's side caused by the piercing lance of Longinus. Shortly afterwards St. Thomas was in a group when Christ entered; St. Thomas fell on his knees exclaiming, 'My Lord and my God'; now St. Thomas clearly believed, but Christ insisted that Thomas should carry out the proof he had demanded (*John* ch. 20, vs. 19-29). This incident gave Thomas the description of Doubting Thomas. The painting discussed here shows the encounter between St. Thomas and Christ. In the middle ground the figure at the right hand side is most probably St. John, while that next to him is almost certainly St. Peter. No suggestion can be made for the person whose head emerges from the background.

The attribution of this painting to Orazio De Ferrari was first proposed, verbally, by Sergio Benedetti in 1980, and, on the basis of a photograph was supported by Mary Newcome Schleier.[1] In 1969 in Genoa an important exhibition was held which surveyed this period of Genoese painting. In that exhibition there were four works by Orazio De Ferrari in which there are passages which are very useful for comparison with Dublin's no. 4302. The face of Christ is of similar physiognomy to that in an *Ecce Homo* exhibited from a private Genoese collection.[2] The latter picture also has a second prominent figure similar to St. Thomas in no. 4302. The modelling is alike in both, and the two paintings also have a figure barely emerging from the dark background. Compare also the background figures with those in two other paintings included in the 1969 exhibition at Genoa.[3] The presumed figure of St. Peter in no. 4302 is extremely like that of the figure on the outside right hand side of another painting exhibited in 1969.[4] The presumed figure of St. John in no. 4302 is similar to that of the Apostle immediately on Christ's left hand side in *The Last Supper* in the church of San Siro, Genoa.

A date in the 1640s is suggested, because of the more subdued chiaroscuro than that manifested in later works. Quite independently, Mary Newcome Schleier has proposed a similar dating, comparing no. 4302 with *St. Augustine washing Christ's feet*, in the Accademia Ligustica, Genoa.[5]

1. In correspondence, December 1981.
2. *Mostra dei Pittori Genovesi a Genova nel '600 e nel '700*, (Palazzo Bianco, Genoa 1969), no. 19.
3. *Ibid.*, nos. 20 and 21.
4. *Ibid.*, no. 22.
5. In correspondence, December 1981.

CIRO FERRI, Rome 1634-1689 Rome

Ferri is probably the best known pupil of Pietro da Cortona. Pope Alexander VII and the Borghese gave him several commissions. He went up to Florence to complete frescos, left unfinished by Pietro da Cortona, for the Grand Duke Cosimo III.

1670   Expulsion of Hagar (Fig. 42).

Oil on canvas, 1.36 × 0.97 m.

CONDITION: very good. Restored 1970. There were some minor paint losses.

PROVENANCE: Milltown Collection by 1826; Milltown Gift, 1902.

When Isaac, Sarah's son, was born, Ishmael, son of Abraham by Hagar, Sarah's Egyptian maid-servant, began to mock his younger brother. Consequently, Sarah asked Abraham to banish both Ishmael and Hagar *(Genesis,* ch. 21, vs. 9-21). This painting shows Abraham pointing the way out to Hagar and Ishmael. In the middle ground, towards the top of the picture, Sarah looks out of the window of her house.

Formerly attributed to G. B. Castiglione,[1] but soon afterwards to Italian School,[2] no. 1670 was first given to Ferri by Federico Zeri.[3] The painting is a very clear example of Ferri's dependence on the style of his master, Pietro da Cortona.

The model of Hagar appears to be identical with that of Jacob's betrothed in the *Marriage of Jacob* by Ferri at Corsham Court, Wiltshire. There is a version of the Dublin picture at Kedleston Hall, Derbyshire, in the state dining room, which is virtually identical in size. In the Moravska Galerie, Brno, Czechoslovakia, is a drawing of the same subject by Ferri, but differently composed (Fig. 43).

1. National Gallery of Ireland Archives.
2. 1963 Concise Catalogue.
3. Verbal communication — on a visit to the Gallery: this attribution was adopted for the 1971 Catalogue, and later that of 1981.

DOMENICO FETTI, Rome 1588/89-1623 Venice

The Florentine painter Cigoli was in Rome when Fetti joined his studio. The Gonzaga family gave Fetti many commissions, and when he became attached to their court at Mantua the Duke sent him on various missions to acquire paintings for the ducal collection. Fetti was immensely impressed by the great works of Veronese and his Venetian contemporaries which he saw on these missions. The works of Peter Paul Rubens, too, made an impact. Fetti painted fine portraits, but is best known by his small paintings, many of which were illustrations of parables of the New Testament. These parable paintings were so popular that Fetti had to do several versions of many of them.

Studio of FETTI

898   The parable of the lord of the vineyard (Fig. 44).

Oil on panel, 0.62 × 0.39 m.

CONDITION: excellent. Restored Summer 1968.

PROVENANCE: W. J. McCoy, Belfast, 1927, from whom purchased by Thomas Bodkin, by whom presented, 1927.

EXHIBITED: 1957 Manchester *Art Treasures Centenary. European Old Masters* (City Art Gallery), no. 146; 1979 London *Venetian Seventeenth Century Painting* (National Gallery), no. 15.

VERSIONS: Dresden; Marquess of Exeter; Pamela Askew; Castlevecchio Museum, Verona; Capitoline Museum, Rome; Palazzo Pitti, Florence; Mrs. Alfred du Pont, Florida; A. Staring, The Hague; formerly collection Sir Andrew Fountaine, Christie's, 1 December 1978, lot 31; Duc de Tallyrand, Rome.

Jesus told his disciples of the owner of a vineyard who paid his labourers an equal wage per day regardless of the length of time they had worked. When those who had worked longest complained, the lord of the vineyard replied, 'so shall the last be first and the first last' (*Matthew,* ch. 20, vs. 1-16).

The lord of the vineyard is seated and remonstrates with an old labourer whose deportment and torn clothes suggest that he has worked all day. To the right are young labourers whose fine clothes in good state indicate that they have not worked too long.

Although there are at least eleven versions of this painting, Pamela Askew only considers the version in Dresden to be certainly and entirely painted by Fetti himself.[1] She does not rate the Dublin version very highly,[2] but could only have seen it prior to cleaning. Jennifer Fletcher, who saw the painting after cleaning, endorses Pamela Askew's verdict that it is 'a not very distinguished replica'.[3]

Fetti's parable paintings, because of the number of versions, and variations in quality, pose problems of attribution. A painting such as that catalogued here may, in the opinion of the writer, be still considered as possibly autograph; otherwise it is by a very close imitator. It has been dated by Potterton to late 1621 or early 1622.[4]

1. P. Askew in *Art Bulletin,* vol. 43 (1961), p. 39.
2. *Ibid.,* p. 44, no. 8c.

3. J. Fletcher in *The Burlington Magazine,* vol. 121 (October 1979), p. 665.
4. 1979 London exhibition catalogue, no. 15.

FELICE FICHERELLI, sometimes called IL RIPOSO,
San Gimignano *c.* 1605-1669 Florence

Ficherelli came to Florence as a youth and studied under Iacopo Chimenti da Empoli; later he was influenced by Giovanni Biliverti and Francesco Furini. It was undoubtedly from the latter that he developed his interest in languid ladies, lugubrious luminosity, and morbid subject-matter, especially in paintings for private collectors. His works for churches demonstrate his apprenticeship to Chimenti.

1070   The sacrifice of Isaac (Fig. 45).

Oil on canvas, 0.685 × 0.985 m.

CONDITION: very good, although covered with a layer of darkened varnish.

PROVENANCE: Milltown Collection by 1826; Milltown Gift, 1902.

This painting is very close in design and feeling to the larger vertical canvas of the same subject in the collection of Mina Gregori, Florence.[1]

A date of *circa* 1640 is suggested. Much work remains to be done before Ficherelli's chronology can be firmly established.

1. G. Cantelli, *Repertorio della Pittura Fiorentina del Seicento* (Fiesole 1983), p. 78.

1707   St. Mary Magdalen (Fig. 46).

Oil on canvas, 1.17 × 0.86 m.

CONDITION: excellent. Restored February-March 1975.

PROVENANCE: Milltown Collection by 1826; Milltown Gift, 1902.

This painting may be compared with other *Magdalens* by Ficherelli.[1] The Dublin *Magdalen* seems to have been painted from the same model as that for the half-length formerly in the Serristori Collection and now in the Piero Bigongiari Collection,[2] Florence.

A date of *circa* 1640 is tentatively suggested because in no. 1707 one sees the beginnings of Ficherelli's interest in the languid tenebrist morbidity of his later paintings for private collections.

1. G. Cantelli in *Antichità Viva*, anno X, no. 4 (July-August 1971), p. 6, fig. 12.
2. M. Gregori, in *Apollo*, vol. 100 (September 1974), p. 226, fig. 22. Cf. G. Cantelli, *Repertorio della Pittura Fiorentina del Seicento* (Fiesole 1983), pls. 335-36.

1746   Lot and his daughters (Fig. 47).

Oil on canvas, 1.59 × 1.76 m.

CONDITION: very good. Restored July 1978-January 1979. There were some minor paint losses.

PROVENANCE: Milltown Collection by 1826; Milltown Gift, 1902.

EXHIBITED: 1979 London and Cambridge *Painting in Florence 1600-1700.* (Royal Academy and Fitzwilliam Museum), no. 26. Catalogue by Charles McCorquodale.

After the destruction of Sodom and Gomorrah, Lot and his two daughters went up into the mountains. Believing that no one but they remained alive, to ensure the preservation of the human race, Lot's daughters first made their father drunk and then committed incest with him. Each bore a son, Moab and Ammon (*Genesis*, ch. 19).

Between the two girls is a distant view with a city on fire, presumably Sodom. Behind the right arm of the daughter on the right hand side, is a white figure, presumably Lot's wife turned into a pillar of salt, because she disobeyed the heavenly instruction not to look back as the angel led the family to safety. *Lot and his daughters* is a subject frequently met with in Florentine seventeenth century painting.

In this painting there is much of the spirit, and quite a lot of the action, of the *Judith and Holofernes* formerly in the collection of Marchese Dottore Gian Francesco Giaquili Ferrini.[1] Moreover the profile of the head, shoulder, and left arm of the daughter to the right hand side of the picture compares closely to the same anatomical passage of Stratonice in *Antiochus and Stratonice* in the collection of the Marchese Carlo Lotteringhi della Stufa, Florence.[2]

McCorquodale argues well a date of *circa* 1650.[3]

1. Exhibited 1960, Florence, *Tesori Segreti delle Case Fiorentine*, no. 92.
2. G. Cantelli in *Antichità Viva*, anno X, no. 4 (July-August 1971), p. 12.

3. Catalogue of 1979 exhibition mentioned above, no. 26. *Cf.* also G. Cantelli, *Repertorio della Pittura Fiorentina del Seicento* (Fiesole 1983), p. 79.

FRANCESCO FIERAVINO, sometimes called IL MALTESE,
Malta — fl. 1640-1660 Rome

This little known painter specialized in still-life painting, particularly with fruit, flowers and rugs, clocks, armour, musical instruments and sweets. He appears to have come to Rome in the middle of the seventeenth century, but only rarely does his name occur in the early inventories of old Roman collections. Many paintings attributed to Fieravino may not be by him.

Attributed to FIERAVINO

1014 Still life with musical instruments (Fig. 48).

Oil on canvas, 0.94 × 1.17 m.

CONDITION: very good.

PROVENANCE: Miss H. M. Reid, Dublin, by whom bequeathed, 1939.

Traditionally given to Bartolomeo Bettera, it was first suggested, verbally, by Harald Olsen that it might be the work of Il Maltese. In signed works by Bettera[1] there is a formality of composition that is almost geometrical. The lines of musical instruments, the folds of rugs or table coverings are crisp and clear. By comparison when one looks at *Quaedam Sensuum Instrumenta*, a painting by Il Maltese engraved by L. Coelemans in 1704,[2] the composition is more informal. The rug is ruffled, and the musical instruments, flowers, and a mirror are more casually arranged. This style appears in other works attributed to Il Maltese, who would appear to be a much more appropriate painter for no. 1014.[3]

1. For example paintings nos. 846 and 847 in the Accademia Carrara, Bergamo; Christie's, 21 April 1967, lot 85; Christie's, 20 March 1964, lot 39.
2. There is an impression of this print in the Witt Collection, London.
3. For the most up-to-date scholarly synthesis on Fieravino *cf.* L. Salerno, *La natura morta italiana 1560-1805* (Rome 1984), *praesertim* pp. 183-87.

FLORENTINE SCHOOL, 17th century

4096 Crowd at city gates (Fig. 49).

Oil on *paesina* stone, 0.16 × 0.27 m. (rounded ends)

CONDITION: very good.

PROVENANCE: unknown.

The city is indicated by the natural configurations of the *paesina* stone. A crowd is processing out from the city led by a king who is escorted by soldiers.

This decorative plaque most probably was inserted into a piece of furniture.

FRANCESCO FURINI, Florence 1603-1646 Florence

Furini's best known masters were Giovanni Biliverti and Matteo Rosselli; during a visit to Rome in 1623-24 he worked with Giovanni da San Giovanni. Apart from brief excursions from his native city, all his short painterly life was spent in Florence.

368 Charity (Fig. 52).

Oil on canvas, 0.75 × 0.58 m.

CONDITION: very good. There is a slit across the forehead and down into the sitter's left eye.

PROVENANCE: Sir Henry Page Turner Barron, Bt., by whom presented, 1878.

The figure of a lady holding a coin is a not uncommon manner of depicting *Charity* in seventeenth century Italian paintings.

This allegory is considered a good example of the artist's later work by Giuseppe Cantelli.[1] An oval canvas of *Abundance* by Furini, which was with Antichità Piselli, Florence, in 1978, may be compared stylistically and for mood with no. 368.

1. In correspondence, October 1973; and in G. Cantelli, *Repertorio della Pittura Fiorentina del* *Seicento* (Fiesole 1983), p. 89, and pl. 447.

1679   St. Mary Magdalen (Fig. 50).

Oil on parchment, 0.415 × 0.345 m.

CONDITION: very good. Restored 1970. The painting with its parchment support was transferred on to deacidified Saunders paper. This in turn was affixed to Purlboard faced on both sides with sheets of Perspex.

PROVENANCE: Milltown Collection by 1826; Milltown Gift, 1902.

Giuseppe Cantelli is reluctant to accept this painting as autograph,[1] but it is difficult to suggest another artist, especially as in technique and handling it is so like no. 1716, below, which Cantelli does accept. Moreover, it comes from the same collection, and has exactly the same measurements; in addition, it too is painted on parchment. Could it possibly be a picture which Furini painted for Marchese Giulio Vitelli in the 1640s: '. . . una simil figura [piccola figura], cioè Santa Maria Maddalena nel deserto.'[2]?

1. In correspondence, October 1973. More recently in his *Repertorio della Pittura Fiorentina del Seicento* (Fiesole 1983), p. 104 and pl. 520, he attributes it firmly to Furini's pupil Vincenzo Mannozzi (d. 1657). The compiler is not convinced by the juxtapositions used to underpin this conclusion, noting particularly Mannozzi's sweeter facial types.
2. F. Baldinucci, *Delle Notizie de' Professori del Disegno, ecc.*, vol. 16 (D. M. Manni's edition, Florence 1773), pp. 14-15.

1716   Crucifixion of a female saint (Fig. 51).

Oil on parchment, laid on panel, 0.415 × 0.345 m.

CONDITION: very good. Covered with darkened varnish.

PROVENANCE: Milltown Collection by 1826; Milltown Gift, 1902.

Giuseppe Cantelli accepts this as an autograph work,[1] as do Mina Gregori[2] and Walter Balzano.[3] No. 1716 is a pendant to no. 1679 preceding.

Could this painting possibly be a picture painted in the 1640s for Marchese Giulio Vitelli: '. . . una Santa Martire Crocifissa ad una antenna, piccola figura'?[4]

1. On examining a photograph, October 1973, and November 1977. *Cf.* G. Cantelli, *Repertorio della Pittura Fiorentina del Seicento* (Fiesole 1983), p. 89 and pl. 454.
2. On examining a photograph, November 1977.

3. During a visit to Dublin, 1978.
4. F. Baldinucci, *Delle Notizie de' Professori del Disegno, ecc.*, vol. 16 (D. M. Manni's edition, Florence 1773), pp. 14-15.

Attributed to FURINI

1658 Hylas and the nymphs (Fig. 53).

Oil on canvas, 1.17 × 1.57 m.

CONDITION: covered with layers of darkened varnish.

PROVENANCE: Milltown Collection by 1826; Milltown Gift, 1902.

Hylas, son of Theiodamas, King of the Dryopes, who was killed by Heracles, was spared by the victor who took him as a page. Heracles took Hylas with him on the voyage of the Argonauts as far as the landing at Cios. There Hylas went to get water, found a spring, and then was pulled into the water by nymphs who fell in love with him. By the nymphs he was spirited away and never found again.

This is a smaller version of the painting in the Galleria Palatina, Florence, no. 3562 (2.30 × 2.61 m.). As it has not been cleaned for a long time, it is difficult to decide whether or not it is by Furini himself, and, if not, how close is its relationship to the larger autograph painting in Florence. No. 1658 would appear to be of seventeenth century workmanship; and its proportions differ somewhat from the major work in the Galleria Palatina.

ORAZIO GENTILESCHI, Pisa 1563-1639 London

Born in Pisa, a son to the goldsmith, Giovanni Battista Lomi, Orazio initially studied painting with his elder brother, Aurelio Lomi, and with his uncle Bacci Lomi. In 1576 or 1578 Orazio moved to Rome, staying with a maternal uncle, Captain Gentileschi, whose family name he adopted. He is first recorded as a painter when working under the direction of Cesare Nebbia in the Biblioteca Sistina, in the Vatican, in 1588-89. He continued to paint in a not very notable way, until he saw some of Caravaggio's work. From about 1605 his own personal style emerged and he painted some very distinguished canvases. He painted some murals in 1611 in the papal Quirinal Palace, and more in 1611-12, with Agostino Tassi, in Scipio Borghese's Casino delle Muse on the Quirinal hill. He then went to work in Fabriano and Florence; invited to Genoa, he painted several large canvases;

from Genoa he was called to Turin to work for the Duke of Savoy; having returned to Genoa to work for the Sauli and Doria families, he was invited to Paris by Maria de' Medici, in 1624. In 1625 he was invited to London by Charles I to be a court painter, and remained there until his death in 1639. Several of Gentileschi's works remain in the Royal Collections to this day.

980   David and Goliath (Fig. 54).

Oil on canvas, 1.855 × 1.36 m.

CONDITION: excellent. There were some minor paint losses around the edges, and a few others elsewhere.

PROVENANCE: a small sweet shop in Limehouse, London, whence purchased by Tomás Harris, London, from whom purchased, 1936,[1] for £1,400.

EXHIBITED: 1951 Milan *Mostra del Caravaggio e dei Caravaggeschi* (Palazzo Reale), no. 108; 1985 London *Masterpieces from The National Gallery of Ireland* (National Gallery), no. 4.

The story of David and Goliath is told in Chapter 17 of the *First Book of Samuel.* Goliath was one of the great warriors of the Philistines. He challenged to fight any man from the troops of the Israelites. King Saul and his senior advisers were terrified. David came forward, and went out to meet Goliath, armed with his sling and five stones. With the first stone he knocked Goliath to the ground, having hit him in the middle of the forehead. David ran forward, took Goliath's sword, and then cut off Goliath's head. The Philistines, dismayed, fled.

The attribution to Gentileschi is unequivocal. Longhi suggests a date at the beginning of the second decade of the seventeenth century,[2] which seems eminently reasonable given the striking Caravaggesque qualities of the painting. Could one even suggest a slightly earlier date, as Wittkower writes that it 'must have been created in Rome at an early period of his career'[3]? Both of these would agree with Emiliani's date of *c.* 1610.[4] Bissell, in his major monograph on Gentileschi, places it within the years *c.*1605-10.[5]

No. 980 has no direct prototype in the known works of Caravaggio. In the Prado there is a painting of David and Goliath at a point in the story where Goliath's head has been quite definitely severed. The autograph status of the painting in the Prado has been debated at length.[6]

Gentileschi, a Tuscan artist, who had been working industriously in Rome for roughly a quarter of a century, produced in the early years of the seventeenth century a relatively small number of exciting works which bore witness to the impact which Caravaggio made on the Roman artistic scene. While not utterly Caravaggesque, especially in excluding the extreme tenebrist qualities of many Caravaggios, these works of Gentileschi are among his finest, and were to have a bearing on his future development. Dublin's *David and Goliath* is a particularly good example of the important paintings which he executed in the first decade of the seventeenth century. They are all powerful pictorial images, and frequently present a profound psychological penetration of the subject portrayed. Invariably the subjects are those associated with the ideals of the Counter Reformation, to show the triumph of good over evil.

1. Bissell, *loc. cit.*, states that the painting belonged to Vitale Bloch prior to its acquisition by Tomás Harris; this can scarcely be true, since the provenance as indicated here is substantiated by a later letter written by Harris from Camp de Mar, Mallorca, Spain, dated 24 November 1956, which is preserved in the Gallery's archives. In this he recalls how he was persuaded by his brother-in-law to go and look at the painting in the small sweet shop in Limehouse. The invoice to the Gallery was issued by Tomás Harris, Ltd., and receipt for payment for the painting was issued by the same firm. The purchase took place in 1936, and not in 1932, as stated by Bissell. However, Bloch is involved in the attempt to sell the painting to Dublin. Other letters in the Gallery's archives show that Bloch was offering the painting for sale as if it were his own, at the same period as Harris was doing likewise! The precise financial arrangements between the two men may never be known fully. An interesting footnote to emerge from all the correspondence is that both Kenneth Clark and Vitale Bloch at one time were considering the painting to be possibly by Caravaggio, on the basis of an old inscription on the reverse of the canvas, no longer visible since the painting's relining. Had the Caravaggio theory prevailed, the painting might have gone to the National Gallery, London, which still has no Gentileschi. Nonetheless, Clark, in a letter dated 27 January 1936 to George Furlong, then Director at the National Gallery of Ireland, supported him in his endeavours to secure the Gentileschi for Dublin (National Gallery of Ireland Archives).

2. R. Longhi, in *Proporzioni*, vol. 1 (1943), p. 22.
3. R. Wittkower, *Art and Architecture in Italy 1600-1750* (Harmondsworth 1973, 3rd ed.), p. 43.
4. A. Emiliani in *Paragone*, no. 103 (July 1958), p. 43.
5. R. W. Bissell, *Orazio Gentileschi and the Poetic Tradition in Caravaggesque Painting* (University Park and London 1981), p. 146.
6. For a recent account of this painting see the magistral entry by Mina Gregori in the exhibition catalogue, *The Age of Caravaggio* (Metropolitan Museum of Art, New York, and Museo Nazionale di Capodimonte, Naples), pp. 268-70.

CORRADO GIAQUINTO, Molfetta 1703-1766 Naples

Giaquinto studied in Naples; among his mentors was Francesco Solimena. At the age of twenty he came to Rome and collaborated there, and in Turin, with Sebastiano Conca. One of Giaquinto's most important works in Rome is the ceiling of the Church of Santa Croce in Gerusalemme, executed in 1744. He arrived in Madrid in 1753, and executed many important decorative schemes for King Ferdinand VI, at the Palacio Real, Madrid, the royal complex at El Escorial, and at the royal palace of Aranjuez. When King Charles III invited Mengs to work in Spain, in 1761, Giaquinto returned to Italy.

542 (?) The glorification of Marcantonio II Colonna, hero of Lepanto (Fig. 55).

Oil on canvas, 0.61 × 0.97 m.

CONDITION: very good. Restored 1980-86. The *inquadratura*, before cleaning, appeared to be complete. It proved, however, to be about two-thirds due to a later intervention. The top left hand quarter is original, as is a section at the bottom centre; another small area of original *inquadratura* is at the centre of the right hand side. It was quite normal for an artist executing a *bozzetto* for a ceiling fresco to indicate only the treatment of the surrounding borders. All non-original paint was removed. Paint losses were not severe, being mainly confined to lines which would suggest that, at some time, the sketch was folded up.

PROVENANCE: J. P. O'Reilly, Dublin, from whom purchased, 1902, for £10.

The identification of the subject of this *bozzetto* is not one which springs to mind immediately. Early thoughts would tend to direct the search towards a warrior saint who has served Christianity in a very special way. The writer has investigated several such saints with unconvincing conclusions.

The scene portrays Mother Church seated and holding a substantial cross, beckoning a warrior holding a spear to take the prominent empty seat beside her. Above Mother Church is the Dove representing the Holy Spirit, while at her feet a cherub holds a papal tiara. The half-kneeling warrior has already doffed his helmet, abandoned to the care of two other cherubs, while behind him is clearly a senior comrade at arms. To the left of the latter another figure holds a flag bearing a Maltese cross, for centuries the emblem of the crusaders of Christianity. At the bottom of the composition is a stricken Turk, clutching a flag whose principal feature, the crescent, is the perennial symbol of the Christian Church's main adversary for centuries, Islam. This overthrown soldier is further threatened by a belligerent putto who holds a three-pronged spear. At the extreme left and right of the picture are pairs of Virtues: Justice with a sword beside Fortitude with a lion, on the left; on the right are Prudence with books and Temperance with pitcher and basin. There is one small item that is not easy to explain: this is the double crown which an angel holds above the chair awaiting the victor. Most probably it indicates the iron crown of the Holy Roman Empire.

The scene as described is most appropriate for a glorification of Marcantonio II Colonna. Colonna was one of the commanders-in-chief under Don John of Austria when the Christians achieved a notable victory over the Turks at the Battle of Lepanto in October 1571.

For the symbol of Mother Church in no. 542, it is useful to see a virtually identical treatment by Corrado Giaquinto in *The triumph of Religion and the Church* which adorns the principal staircase of the Royal Palace in Madrid.[1]

Eduard Safarik, of the Colonna Collection Administration, does not see sufficient specific elements in the *bozzetto* to identify the subject as proposed by the writer; however, he does not rule out the possibility entirely. Neither does he know of the existence of a ceiling worked up from no. 542.[2]

There is one serious reservation about the suggested subject matter of no. 542. Nowhere is there any naval symbolism — and Lepanto was a decidedly marine engagement. What other victory over Islam would be worthy of such a glorification? An outstanding one was that led by John Sobieski, King of Poland, called in by the Emperor Leopold, who had fled Vienna in 1683, and drove the Sultan's immense battalions away from the capital of the Holy Roman Emperor. Who, however, would have commissioned such a tribute to Sobieski's achievement? The Emperor was known to have been jealous of his ally's prowess. Perhaps, the glorification is of the Emperor some sixty years after the battle which saved his position, while he himself was miles away from the dangers of the Grand Vizier's troops.

Another possibility is that the *bozzetto* is for a *Glorification of St. James,* to be executed in Spain; but many Santiago iconographical attributes are absent.

Bought as a work by Sebastiano Ricci, and catalogued thus, the attribution cannot be sustained. In the 1971 catalogue it was Attributed to Ricci, while in 1981 edition it was described as Italian School, pending further investigation.

The most convincing attribution is Corrado Giaquinto, in his later period. In the City Art Museum, St. Louis, U.S.A., is a *bozzetto, The Emperor Constantine being presented by the Virgin to the Holy Trinity.* This work is not dated, but most probably belongs to the 1740s. There are certain comparisons which one can make with no. 542. Constantine has removed his crown and helmet; there is a comparable progression in the movement of the action; the Archangel Michael trampling on the infidels finds an echo in the overthrown Turk in no. 542.

Stylistically comparable to the Dublin sketch are the works which Giaquinto executed in the 1740s in the church of Santa Croce in Gerusalemme, Rome.

An attribution to Giaquinto in a later decade is also very possible. One has only to look at the *Allegorical Compositions* in the Casita del Príncipe at El Escorial, outside Madrid,[3] or the Italian's decorations of the principal staircase and the chapel in the Royal Palace at Madrid.

One can safely propose that no. 542 is by Giaquinto, and that it is a late work. One can still hope that the fresco was executed, and that the ceiling will be rediscovered.

1. J. U. Fernandez, *La Pintura Italiana del Siglo XVIII en España* (Valladolid 1977), p. 125, and pl. XIII, fig. 1.
2. In correspondence, September 1985.

3. M. D'Orsi, *Corrado Giaquinto* (Rome 1958), p. 146, nos. 274-75, and figs. 132-33: these are datable to 1759-60.

LUCA GIORDANO, Naples 1634-1705 Naples

Giordano received his initial tuition from his painter father, Antonio; in his native city he was influenced by a variety of artists, but particularly by the Spaniard, Jusepe de Ribera. Giordano was successful in many places; a particularly noteworthy commission was the fresco decoration of the Palazzo Medici-Riccardi in Florence; he painted in Spain for ten years from 1692 until 1702, having been invited there by King Charles II.

79 St. Sebastian tended by St. Irene (Fig. 56).

Oil on canvas, 1.52 × 1.27 m.

CONDITION: apparently excellent. Requires cleaning.

PROVENANCE: 3rd Duke of Leinster, by whom presented, 1868.

Sebastian was an officer in the army of the Roman Emperor, Diocletian (third century). When the Emperor discovered that Sebastian was a Christian he had him bound to a stake in the middle of a field and 'archers shot at him until he looked like a hedgehog. Then thinking him dead they abandoned him'.[1] A Christian woman, Irene, came to bury him; she found him alive and nursed him back to full health. When the Emperor next saw Sebastian, he had him beaten to death, this time effectively.

No. 79 was first attributed to Giordano by Langton Douglas, having been given to Caravaggio in the Gallery's catalogues from 1875 to 1920 inclusive. The Giordano attribution was fully accepted by Ferrari and Scavizzi.[2] Sir Denis Mahon inclines to the view that the painting is by Massimo Stanzione (verbal communication).

Mayer also accepted it and inserted it in that group of paintings inspired by Ribera, a group that includes *The taking down from the cross of St. Andrew*, and *Death of Seneca* in the Alte Pinakothek, Munich.[3] Consequently, a date in the early 1650s would seem appropriate.

There is a version of this work in the Musée des Beaux-Arts, Poitiers, on loan from a private collection. Another version, fully attributed to Giordano, was with Sotheby's, 8 December 1976, lot 40 (1.56 × 1.23 m.). Yet another version is in a private German collection. In autumn 1985 Colnaghi, New York, exhibited a version with some significant differences in detail, but very close in composition and size (1.57 × 1.25 m.).[4]

1. Translated from Jacques de Voragine, *La Légende Dorée* (translation by T. de Wyzewa: Paris 1913), p. 96.
2. O. Ferrari and G. Scavizzi, *Luca Giordano,* vol. 2 (Naples 1966), p. 11.

3. A. L. Mayer, *Jusepe de Ribera* (Leipzig 1923), p. 145.
4. *European Paintings 1550-1800* (Colnaghi, New York, 1985), no. 7.

1069   St. John the Baptist preaching in the wilderness (Fig. 57).

Oil on canvas, 1.84 × 1.285 m.

CONDITION: good. Restored Summer 1978.

PROVENANCE: Milltown Collection by 1826; Milltown Gift, 1902.

Apparently this work was not known to Ferrari and Scavizzi.[1] Despite its somewhat worn condition, it can be considered autograph, and, by comparison with the altarpiece of the same subject, but of different composition, in the Church of San Giovanni Battista, Naples,[2] it may be dated to the late 1680s.

Fairly closely related to no. 1069 is the *modello* formerly in the Eric Young Collection.[3] A version, oil on canvas, 1.80 × 1.37 m., was in a private collection in Ireland.[4]

1. O. Ferrari and G. Scavizzi, *Luca Giordano,* 3 vols. (Naples 1966).
2. *Ibid.,* vol. 2, p. 142, and vol. 3, pl. 273.
3. Sold at Christie's, 30 November 1973, lot

110. Subsequently with Heim Gallery (London) Ltd.; exhibited there in 1975, *Paintings by Luca Giordano,* no. 14.
4. Sold at Sotheby's, 13 February 1985, lot 106.

1988 Aesop (Fig. 58).

Oil on canvas, 1.22 × 0. 96 m.

CONDITION: very good. There were minor paint losses, especially in the background and along the lower edge. Restored June-July 1970.

PROVENANCE: purchased, Dublin, 1857, for £13 (name of vendor not noted).

Aesop was famed as a storyteller; he lived as a slave on the island of Samos in the sixth century B.C. He died there in 564 B.C.

This painting is not catalogued by Ferrari and Scavizzi.[1] However, it is undoubtedly an autograph Giordano. In the Gallery's catalogues for 1864, 1867, 1871 and 1874 it was given to Caravaggio. Thereafter, enigmatically, it was omitted until its reinsertion in the 1971 edition as Italian School. In the 1981 catalogue it was included as a Giordano.

Giordano painted numerous figures of 'Philosophers' of similar composition and proportions.[2] They belong to his earlier phase of influence by Ribera. A date in the early 1650s would be appropriate.

A version of this picture was in the Munoz de Ortiz sale, Lepke Gallery, Berlin, 12 December 1911, lot 68, (measurements 1.10 × 0.85 m.) attributed to Ribera. Another version is in the monastery of San Lorenzo, El Escorial, Spain (1.23 × 0.97 m.). Attributed previously to Ribera, Spinosa suggests Luca Giordano in his early period, perhaps working from an original composition by Ribera.[3]

1. O. Ferrari and G. Scavizzi, *Luca Giordano*, 3 vols. (Naples 1966).
2. For example those in the Louvre, nos. 1726-29; *cf.* Ferrari and Scavizzi, *op. cit.*, vol. 2, p. 23, and Vol. 3, pls. 538-41. *Cf.* also a half-length figure of an *Astronomer* or *Mathematician* (unpublished) which was with Ars Studio S.A.S., Brescia (in 1983).
3. N. Spinosa, *L'opera completa del Ribera* (Milan 1978), p. 138, no. 394.

Circle of GIORDANO

4006 Adam and Eve, with Cain and Abel (Fig. 59).

Oil on canvas, 0.76 × 0.64 m.

CONDITION: apparently good beneath a thick layer of discoloured varnish. An old relining has increased the original size of the painting by a small amount, which cannot be measured precisely at present.

PROVENANCE: Milltown Collection by 1826; Milltown Gift, 1902.

According to the book of *Genesis*, Cain and Abel were the first two children of Adam and Eve;[1] there is no way of ascertaining that the children in this painting are the first-born; the title of the picture is a traditional one.

The painting is given to Luca Giordano in the oldest known inventory of the Milltown Collection (1826). This is retained in the Deed of Gift (1902). The painting was overlooked by the compilers of the Gallery catalogues until that of 1971, where it appears as Giordano in the numerical index with the tiresome omission of the text entry. In the 1981 catalogue the attribution is changed to 'After Pietro da Cortona'. No. 4006 cannot be designated as a genuine Giordano, especially in its present condition. The existence of more than one seventeenth century version of the composition *(vide infra)* would make one suppose that a prototype exists, or existed. Compositionally Giordano seems the most likely author of the type; it reflects his mature style, certainly that of the late 1660s, but possibly even later.

Firmly given to Luca Giordano, a version of no. 4006 was recorded in a private collection in Milan, in 1951.[2] Entitled *The First Family*, no dimensions were noted, but the composition and proportions relate it to the Dublin painting.

Another version of no. 4006 is in the Musée des Beaux-Arts, Angers, France,[3] and recently it has been attributed, albeit tentatively, to Paolo de Matteis, by Marco Chiarini.[4]

1. *Genesis,* ch. 4, vs. 1-2.
2. *Emporium,* vol. 114 (December 1951), p. 263; ill., p. 260.
3. Inv. 319. J. 1881. Oil on canvas, 0.74 × 0.62 m.
4. In *La Revue du Louvre et des Musées de France* (1983), pp. 2-3 (fig. 4).

FRANCESCO GUARDI, Venice 1712-1793 Venice

The son of a painter, Francesco Guardi initially worked with his brother Giovanni Antonio on figurative subjects; later he successfully diversified into view painting and also executed many capricci, *which were imaginary scenes redolent with Venetian elements.*

92 The Doge wedding the Adriatic (Fig. 60).

Oil on canvas, 0.39 × 0.57 m.

CONDITION: very good. Restored Summer 1968.

PROVENANCE: Edward Wright Anderson, sale, Christie's, 7 May 1864, lot 39, where purchased for 19 guineas.

To the right is the promontory of the Lido; to the left is the fortress of St. Andrew. These constitute the mouth of the canal which joins the lagoon to the open sea. The foreground is a creation of the artist for compositional purposes. In the centre is the gilded state barge, Il Bucintoro, in which each year, on Ascension Day, the Doge and his suite went out to the mouth of the Lido. The Doge threw a gold ring, blessed by the Patriarch of Venice, into the sea as a symbol of Venetian dominance of the sea. The ceremony commemorated Venice's defence of the Papacy against Frederick Barbarossa in 1178. It was in that year that Pope Alexander III gave a gold ring to the Doge.

The attribution of this work has never been questioned.

The only other version known is that formerly in a private collection in Paris.[1] A closely related drawing, but with a slightly more extensive landscape to the right, is in the Royal

Library at Turin.[2] (Fig. 61) Another drawing of similar subject matter, but much more sketchy, passed through Christie's on 29 June 1962, lot 43 (bought by Kroedle).

The painting is regarded as quite late by Morassi.[3] Fritz Heinemann dated it to about 1780.[4]

The subject was certainly of some interest, because it was repeated on a number of occasions by Francesco's son, Giacomo, a much less talented artist. An example, by Giacomo is to be found in Trieste. It is a wash drawing.[5]

1. A. Morassi, in *Arte Veneta*, 1952, fig. 98.
2. A. Bertini, *I Disegni Italiani della Biblioteca Reale di Torino* (Rome 1958), p. 77, no. 645 (inv. no. 15963).
3. A. Morassi, *Guardi* (Venice 1973), p. 365, cat. 291.

4. In correspondence, following a visit to Dublin, in 1975.
5. Exhibition catalogue, *Pitture, designi e stampe del '700 dalle collezioni dei Civici Musei di Storia ed Arte di Trieste* (Museo Sartorio, Trieste, 1972), p. 39, no. 12, and pl. 12.

Style of GUARDI

819 Imaginary landscape (Fig. 62).

Oil on oval poplar panel, 0.275 × 0.22 m.

REVERSE: there is a red seal and an old label on which is written *Canaletto 161ⁿ*. On the timber itself is written (?) *Hamilton*. The significance of these has not been established. The painting is not to be found in the catalogue of the famous Hamilton Palace sale, 1882.

CONDITION: very good.

PROVENANCE: Captain R. Langton Douglas, from whom purchased, 1918, for £231.

Guardi executed several paintings known as *capricci*: they are composed of various elements of landscape and buildings, real or imaginary.

This picture has not been accepted as authentic by certain specialists, notably Morassi,[1] and Fritz Heinemann,[2] who said it was by a late imitator. The painting lacks the sparkling freshness of Guardi's autograph *capricci* known to the writer.

Morassi relates this work to portion of a larger painting in a private collection in Brescia.[3]

1. A. Morassi, *Guardi* (Venice 1973), p. 462, cat. 816.
2. In correspondence, following a visit to

Dublin in 1975.
3. A. Morassi, *loc. cit.*

GIOVANNI ANTONIO GUARDI, Venice 1698-1760 Venice

Giovanni Antonio was the elder brother of the much more famous Francesco Guardi. He is not particularly well known as an artist in his own right; yet he was the principal of a flourishing Venetian studio in which Francesco, fourteen years younger, was first an apprentice and then collaborator on many important commissions. Much later Francesco developed his metier *as a view-painter and the author of* capricci, *which led to his fame internationally.*

63 St. John the Baptist in the wilderness (after Titian) (Fig. 63).

Oil on canvas, 1.64 × 1.26 m.

CONDITION: excellent. Restored January-March 1979.

PROVENANCE: Marshal Johann Matthias von der Schulenburg, Venice, by whom commissioned, 1738; the Ven. Charles Thorp, D.D., Archdeacon of Durham, sale, 6-7 May 1863, lot 173 (as Titian), where purchased for 28 guineas.

This painting was commissioned by Marshal Johann Matthias von der Schulenburg in Venice from Giovanni Antonio Guardi who painted it between November 1738 (or a little earlier) and February 1739.[1] It is a copy of Titian's famous painting of the same subject which was then in the church of Santa Maria Maggiore, Venice, and is now in the Accademia.[2] Guardi's copy is not much smaller in size than the Titian. It is wider in proportion than the Titian, whose dimensions are 2.01 × 1.34 m. Marshal von der Schulenburg, 1661-1747, was a noted collector of both contemporary painters, and also of commissioned copies of old masters. His gallery was very extensive. Before his death many of his paintings were sent back to Germany and later were divided among members of his family.

No. 63 was bequeathed to the Marshal's nephew, Colonel Frederick Adolph von der Schulenburg, and was sent to Germany with the twelfth consignment, on 24 March 1741, as noted in *Quadri Mediocri Estratti per Commando di S. Ecc.za . . .*, which is drawn from the Inventory of the Gallery of Marshal J. M. von der Schulenburg at Venice, 30 June 1741.[3]

None of the known inventories of collections of members of the Marshal's family in Germany includes no. 63. Nor can it be reconciled with any of the paintings sold by Christie's, 12-13 April, 1775, sent for auction by Count Schulenberg [*sic*] de Zell, Hehlen (on the Weser).

Undoubtedly the painting was known as a Guardi copy of a famous Titian by the Marshal's immediate heirs. Then it disappeared until its inclusion in the sale of the collection of the Venerable Charles Thorp, D.D., Archdeacon of Durham, as by Titian, when it was bought for the National Gallery of Ireland.[4]

George F. Mulvany, R.H.A., the first Director of the National Gallery of Ireland, who bought no. 63 at the Thorp sale, was under no illusion that he had acquired a large Titian for twenty-eight guineas. In the very first catalogue of the Gallery, published in 1864 to coincide with the opening of a suitable building for an institution founded in 1854, Mulvany gave the picture to Salvator Rosa (after Titian). This attribution was retained, as the varnish darkened, for more than a century. When the painting was restored, in January-March 1979, Andrew O'Connor and Sergio Benedetti, in the Department of Conservation, were adamant that the fabric of the painting was eighteenth century, and not seventeenth century. The present writer investigated the matter and came forward with the current attribution,[5] which Francesco Valcanover has endorsed.[6]

Puzzling, however, is the provenance given by Mulvany in the 1864 catalogue, and retained in subsequent editions in which any detailed account of the paintings was given. Before noting that it was purchased at Archdeacon Thorp's sale, he writes: 'This picture was brought from Italy by Greffiers Fagel, by whom it was sold in 1742, to the Heckering family'. A painting sent from Venice to Germany in March 1741, for which there is documentary evidence, could scarcely have been exported from Italy and resold in 1742.

Alice Binion, an authority on the von der Schulenburg Collection, has made a suggestion which might explain Mulvany's undocumented statement. Perhaps no. 63, while billed for shipment to Berlin on 24 March 1741, was never actually loaded. A significant number of von der Schulenburg pictures were stolen or just disappeared before actual shipments from Venice.[7]

1. A. Morassi in *Emporium,* vol. 131 (April 1960) pp. 154-55 and p. 164, n. 9.
2. S. M. Marconi, *Gallerie dell' Accademia di Venezia. Opere d'Arte del secolo XVI* (Rome 1962), pp. 259-60.
3. Morassi, *loc. cit.,* p. 151, figs. 7 and 8 (these are reproductions from the original manuscript, F1 and F2). Professor Morassi was given access to all known surviving manuscripts of the von der Schulenburg family.

4. See 'Provenance'.
5. *National Gallery of Ireland News Review,* no. 3 (April-July 1980), p. 6.
6. In correspondence. Subsequently published: F. Valcanover, in G. Buccellati and L. Speroni (edd.), *The Shape of the Past. Studies in Honor of Franklin D. Murphy* (Los Angeles 1982), pp. 287-88.
7. In correspondence, September 1985.

GIOVANNI FRANCESCO BARBIERI, called GUERCINO,
Cento, near Bologna 1591-1666 Bologna

Giovanni Francesco Barbieri, known as Guercino, initially worked in his home town, Bologna, and Ferrara. In the early 1620s he went down to Rome at the invitation of Pope Gregory XV. Perhaps the most famous work of his Roman sojourn is the decoration of the charming Casino Ludovisi. He returned to his native province and had considerable influence on many young artists of the Bolognese School.

192 St. Joseph with the Christ Child (Fig. 64).

Oil on canvas, 0.99 × 0.77 m. (oval).

CONDITION: very good. There were minor paint losses around the edge. Restored July 1966-January 1967.

PROVENANCE: 24th Lord de Clifford sale, Christie's, 29 July 1882, lot 55, where purchased for 16 guineas.

EXHIBITED: 1968 Bologna *Il Guercino* (Palazzo del l'Archiginnasio), no. 69.

This painting was commissioned for the Ferri chapel, the third on the right hand side, in the Church of San Giovanni in Monte, Bologna,[1] and paid for on 30 October 1637 and

30 May 1638, by Signor Giovanni Battista Ferri. Sir Denis Mahon, in the exhibition catalogue mentioned above, suggests that the flower held by the Christ Child was painted by Guercino's brother, Paolo Antonio Barbieri. It is not known at what date the Dublin painting was removed from its Bolognese setting.

The *St. Joseph with the Christ Child,* which was on a side wall of the chapel, had a pendant, *St. Jerome.* The latter was also removed. Both have been replaced by copies, that of the Dublin picture being post-Second World War, as the pre-1939 copy was destroyed. The original of *St. Jerome* has not yet been found.

1. C. C. Malvasia, *Le Pitture di Bologna* (Bologna 1686), p. 288.

After GUERCINO

483 Virgin and Child with Saints Joseph, Augustine, Louis, Francis, and a young donor; also two musical angels (Fig. 65).

Oil on canvas, 3.35 × 1.92 m.

CONDITION: very good. Restored July-August 1970.

PROVENANCE: (?) Count Bolza, Dresden; the Baring family, Stratton, England, by 1838;[1] Francis Baring, by whom presented, 1898.

EXHIBITED: 1839 London *British Institution,* no. 1 (lent by Sir Thomas Baring, Bt.); *cf.* T. Smith, *Recollections of the British Institution* (London 1860), p. 186.

This is a copy of the painting in the Musée d'Art Ancien at Brussels (inv. no. 198), which is fully described by Sir Denis Mahon in his catalogue entry for the 1968 Guercino exhibition at Bologna.[2] The original was painted for the church of St. Augustine at Cento. It was plundered by the French in 1796 and soon afterwards exhibited at the Louvre. In 1802 it was sent to the new museum in Brussels. Its measurements are 3.09 × 1.92 m.

It is not possible to be very precise about the dating of the Dublin copy, but it is undoubtedly eighteenth century.

1. Mentioned in G. F. Waagen, *Works of Art and Artists in England,* Vol. 3, (London 1838), p. 38.

2. Exhibition catalogue, *Il Guercino* (Bologna 1968) no. 19.

After GUERCINO

1323 The triumph of David (Fig. 66).

Oil on canvas, 1.34 × 1.75 m.

CONDITION: very good.

PROVENANCE: Milltown Collection; Milltown Gift, 1902.

The painting was first catalogued in the manuscript catalogue as by Guercino. On the basis of a photograph Berenson said that it was a Guercino.[1] Frederico Zeri, on a visit, said that it was Neapolitan, but the writer cannot agree with that.

Guercino received two payments for a *Triumph of David*, on 11 December 1636, and 10 August 1637, totalling 236 scudi, from Cardinal Colonna.[2] The painting was still in the Galleria Colonna at Rome in 1783.[3] Consequently it was available for copying for a long time. Sir Denis Mahon believes that Cardinal Colonna's painting is that of the same composition as no. 1323 at Burghley House, in Lincolnshire. In March 1983 he was able to revisit Burghley, and, partially because of relatively recent cleaning, he was further convinced that the painting bought by Lord Exeter in 1847 was the missing original.[4]

Dublin's no. 1323 was most probably executed in the late seventeenth century, when the original was available for study in Rome.

1. National Gallery of Ireland archives.
2. Information kindly communicated, from the original Guercino manuscripts, by Sir Denis Mahon.
3. *Catalogo dei Quadri, e Pitture esistenti nel Palazzo dell'eccellentissima Casa Colonna in Roma* (Rome 1783), p. 30, no. 183.
4. The writer is indebted not only to Sir Denis Mahon, but also to Lady Victoria Leatham, who, with John Somerville, arranged the further study of the painting at Burghley (verbal and written communications: March-April 1983).

After GUERCINO

1659 Day (Fig. 67).

Oil on canvas, 0.78 × 1.02 m.

CONDITION: good. There are some minor paint losses, especially close to the top.

PROVENANCE: Milltown Collection by 1826, Milltown Gift, 1902.

This is a copy of a detail from the frescos in the Casino Ludovisi, Rome.[1] The original does not have the cherubs, nor the trees, in the left corner.

This copy is probably mid-eighteenth century in date.

1. N. B. Grimaldi, *Il Guercino* (Bologna 1968), pl. 125.

After GUERCINO

1668 St. Agatha (Fig. 69).

Oil on canvas, 1.09 × 0.99 m.

CONDITION: very good.

PROVENANCE: Milltown Collection by 1826; Milltown Gift, 1902.

Saint Agatha was a noble Christian virgin from Catania. The Roman governor of Sicily fell in love with her and asked her to sacrifice to pagan gods. She was put to various tests, but remained constant. The governor had her breasts cut off before she was martyred by being roasted over burning coals. In most depictions of her Agatha is shown holding a plate on which she carries her cut off breasts. In this image it would appear that the artist has placed flowers over or instead of the breasts.

Because of the flowers some observers have suggested that no. 1668 shows St. Dorothy. This is most unlikely since the typical iconography of St. Dorothy, based on the account of her life in the *Acta Sanctorum,* shows her with a basket containing three roses and three apples.

Guercino painted a half-length of St. Agatha for the Principe di Massa, and was paid for it on 15 March 1654 (60 ducats = 75 scudi). The payment was made on behalf of the prince by Pietro Antonio Davia.[1]

Sir Denis Mahon does not consider no. 1668 to be autograph,[2] although it would appear to be of seventeenth century fabric. Consequently, the Principe di Massa's painting is still missing.

A small version of the same model, but called *St. Lucy,* after Guercino, measuring only 0.23 × 0.18 m., is in the Pinacoteca at Forlì (noted verbally by Sergio Benedetti). Appropriately she carries her eyes on a small *tazza.*[3]

1. *Diario Barbieri:* quoted in N. B. Grimaldi, *Il Guercino* (Bologna 1968), p. 110.
2. Verbal communication.

3. G. Viroli, *La Pinacoteca Civica di Forlì* (Forlì 1980), p. 250.

After GUERCINO
1682 Night (Fig. 68)

Oil on canvas, 0.71 × 0.99 m.

CONDITION: difficult to assess accurately under layers of oxidized varnish.

PROVENANCE: Milltown Collection by 1826; Milltown Gift, 1902.

Very recently Sergio Benedetti drew the writer's attention to the fact that this painting attributed to a Follower of A. Carracci in the 1981 catalogue was in fact a copy, with alterations compositionally, from *Night* in the celebrated fresco suite in the Casino Ludovisi, Rome.[1]

Consequently, this copy belongs serially with no. 1659 preceding, and no. 1686 following, all three coming from the Milltown Collection.

1. Verbal communication. *Cf.* N. B. Grimaldi, *Il Guercino* (Bologna 1968), pl. 126.

After GUERCINO

1686 Aurora (Fig. 70).

Oil on canvas, 1.00 × 1.37 m.

CONDITION: good. There are some minor paint losses, especially at the right hand side.

PROVENANCE: Milltown Collection by 1826; Milltown Gift, 1902.

This is a copy with some slight alterations of the famous fresco in the Casino Ludovisi, Rome.[1] The copy appears to be of mid-eighteenth century execution.

1. N. B. Grimaldi, *Il Guercino* (Bologna 1968), pl. 123.

After GUERCINO

1692 Angel leading Innocence to heaven (Fig. 71)

Oil on canvas, 0.64 × 0.48 m.

CONDITION: difficult to assess accurately before restoration.

PROVENANCE: Milltown Collection by 1826; Milltown Gift, 1902.

This is a copy of a picture in the Galleria Colonna, Rome.[1] The copy is probably datable to the mid-eighteenth century.

1. N. B. Grimaldi, *Il Guercino* (Bologna 1968), pl. 118. E. A. Safarik, *Catalogo Sommario della* *Galleria Colonna in Roma. Dipinti* (Rome 1981), pp. 71-72, no. 83.

ITALIAN SCHOOL (*circa* 1610)

4468 Portrait of a young man of the Branconio family (Fig. 72);

Oil on canvas, 1.68 × 1.05 m.

CONDITION: very good.

PROVENANCE: the Hon. Mrs. Aileen Plunket, Luttrellstown Castle, Clonsilla, county Dublin, sale (conducted by Christie's), 27 September 1983, lot 477, where purchased for IR£23,000 (Shaw Fund).

EXHIBITED: 1984 Dublin, *National Gallery of Ireland. Acquisitions 1982-83* (National Gallery of Ireland), no. 10.

The heraldic shield in the top left hand corner of the painting has been identified, by Alberto Laudi, as that used by the Branconio family of L'Áquila, capital of the Abruzzi, in the seventeenth century. Through Laudi's researches and Harald Olsen's kind communications, we know that it is the shield carved on the base of the altar in the Branconio family chapel in the church of San Silvestro in L'Áquila.[1]

In the early sixteenth century, when the Medici Pope, Leo X, reigned (1513-1521), Giovanni Battista Branconio of L'Áquila was the Pope's Chamberlain. For Branconio Raphael designed a *palazzo,* as Fischel has written, 'at the entrance from the Borgo to Piazza San Pietro, ... The palace was demolished; it had to make way for Bernini's colonnades.'[2] The close link with the Medici may account for the fact that the upper half of the heraldic shield in the painting is in fact the upper half of the Medici shield. Such heraldic achievements are not unknown in Italian heraldry.

The destruction of Raphael's splendid palace (known through drawings) for Giovanni Battista did not end the presence in Rome of the Branconio family. In a manuscript in the Vatican Library there is a list of Roman nobles, an official document of the pontificate of Innocent X, dated 6 February 1653, and entitled *Nota dei gentilhuomini di tutti li Rioni di Roma posti per ordine d'alfabeto con la loro età fatto l'anno 1653;* in this, one Antonio Branconio, aged 29, is recorded as living in the *rione* (district) of Trevi. The family is not represented in a much later official list of nobles recognized in *Urbem Romam,* dated 4 January 1746, in the reign of Benedict XIV.

Aileen Ribeiro has remarked upon the extremely interesting sleeveless cassock worn by the young man in our portrait; he wears Venetian breeches, fastened by typical garters. The ruff collar, she maintains, may be dated, at the very latest, to the early 1620s.[3]

In the catalogue of the sale in which the painting was purchased, Christie's, without any qualification whatsoever, gave the portrait to the painter Carlo Ceresa (1609-1679), an artist from Bergamo who, it would appear, never left that city or its hinterland.[4] This attribution is understandable because of the similarity to a *Ritratto di gentiluomo con due bambini* in a private collection in Bergamo,[5] which shows precise treatment of lips and mouth, bright open eyes and trim fringes, characteristics found in no. 4468. Another privately owned painting, *Ritratto di famiglia a tavola,* features a youth depicted with comparable physiognomy.[6] Ruggeri, who publishes these pictures, does not accept the Dublin painting,[7] nor does Luisa Vertova who wrote the catalogue for an exhibition devoted to Ceresa in the autumn of 1983, in Bergamo.[8] Indeed the evidence of the costume makes such an attribution untenable.

The hand of the unidentified painter is clearly a distinctive one, the date about 1610, and the young man portrayed is a member of the Branconio family, some of whom were at this time living in Rome and others in L'Áquila.

All the scholars who have been so helpful in researching this work comment on the quality of the painting, which also has areas of interest for specialists.

In dating the painting to about 1610, one is taking into account the fact that the typical sixteenth century Renaissance portrait compositions (except perhaps for some very late ones) have been left behind. The informal formal pose is attractive. The use of a large drape on the right hand side heralds the great portraitists of the Van Dyck period; the manner in which it is used here is somewhat unsophisticated. Indeed it is this lack of sophistication which gives to the painting much of its charm. Idiosyncracies such as the elongated fingers, and the curious transition from light to shade in the face, will surely lead to the identification of the artist. Whether painting in Rome, or even possibly in

L'Áquila, the artist has not been affected by the descent on Rome of the Bolognese School, starting with Annibale Carracci and his team for the famous decoration of the Palazzo Farnese, or by the dramatic impact of Caravaggio. The artist, who must remain anonymous for the moment, has an integrity and personality of his own.

1. In correspondence, November 1983 and February 1984.
2. O. Fischel, *Raphael*, (London 1948), vol. 1, p. 163.
3. In correspondence, January 1984.
4. U. Ruggeri, *Carlo Ceresa. Dipinti e disegni* (Bergamo 1979), *passim*.
5. Ruggeri, *op. cit.*, p. 30, fig. 22.
6. Ruggeri, *op. cit.*, p. 41, fig. 30.

7. In correspondence, January 1984.
8. In correspondence, January 1984. *Cf.* L. Vertova, exhibition catalogue, *Carlo Ceresa un pittore bergamasco nel '600* (Bergamo, various locations, 1983). Also unable to accept the attribution to Ceresa is M. Gregori (author of the appropriate entry in *Dizionario Biografico degli Italiani*), in correspondence, September 1984.

ITALIAN SCHOOL, 17th Century

1074 Bacchanalian boys and satyrs (Fig. 75).

Oil on canvas, 0.38 × 0.99 m.

CONDITION: very good. Covered with a layer of yellowed varnish.

PROVENANCE: Milltown Collection; Milltown Gift, 1902.

No. 1074 and its pendant, no. 1075, were entered in the manuscript catalogue, and then in the 1956 catalogue, as by the Cavaliere d'Arpino; this is an attribution which can not be sustained. Federico Zeri[1] suggested that this painting and its pendant were Neapolitan, and as such they were designated in the 1971 and 1981 catalogues. This is a possible search area. In the famous *Triumph of Galatea*, by Luca Giordano, in the Pitti Palace, Florence (no. 2218), putti play in the bottom left hand corner; the colour of the sea, the putti's rosy cheeks, and part of the background are similar to the same components in no. 1074. The modelling of the figures, however, is not strong enough.

Michael Levey, on the basis of photographs, suggested searching in or around Genoa.[2] From the time of Luca Cambiaso, at least, putti played an important role in Genoese painting. One has only to look at paintings such as his *Venus chastising Cupid*, in the Palazzo Rosso, Genoa, or *The Holy Family with St. John the Baptist and angels*, in the Accademia Ligustica di Belle Arti, Genoa, to see that infants and putti were an important feature of the work of this influential Genoese master.

Having looked at dozens of paintings by such Genoese seventeenth century artists as Domenico Piola, Pellegro Piola, Guidobono, Valeri, Malò, and Vassallo, the writer was unable to link positively the name of any of these artists with no. 1074 and its pendant.

Mary Newcome, on the basis of photographs, suggested very tentatively, Pietro Paolo Raggi.[3] The *corpus* of this artist's work is so slight that it would be imprudent to give the Dublin paintings to him.

For the moment, the paintings must be left anonymous.

One day an artist's name will emerge; the paintings have a very distinctive style, and it is imperative to see them in reality in order to realize why none of the various artists' names mentioned above can be linked to them.

The virtually sculptural quality of the figures, the strong transitions from light to shade, and the dark blue in the backgrounds are all features to be found in masters of the Genoese School, and among the followers of Luca Giordano. Even when all these characteristics are to be seen in more or less similar fashion in works of some of the artists mentioned, they never have the same strength throughout, and the colouring is not quite the same.

Because of their proportions and size, no. 1074 and no. 1075 were most probably overdoors.

1. During a visit to the Gallery. 3. In December 1981.
2. In August 1981.

1075 Young satyrs and boys at play (Fig. 76).

Oil on canvas, 0.38 × 0.99 m.

CONDITION: very good. Covered with a layer of yellowed varnish.

PROVENANCE: Milltown Collection; Milltown Gift, 1902.

For discussion see previous entry, no. 1074.

4159 Peter Talbot, Archbishop of Dublin, 1620-1680 (Fig. 73).

Oil on canvas, 0.72 × 0.62 m.

CONDITION: good.

PROVENANCE: Talbot family; the Hon. Rose Talbot, Malahide Castle, county Dublin, from whom purchased, 1976.

EXHIBITED: 1872 *Dublin Exhibition of Arts, Industries and Manufactures* (Earlsfort Terrace), *Loan Portrait Gallery*, no no., but p. 132 (as by Reilly).

It is most unlikely that the name of the artist will ever be found. The date of the portrait should be *circa* 1660.[1]

Peter Talbot was a son of Sir William Talbot, first Baronet, of Carton, county Kildare; he was an older brother of the future Duke of Tyrconnell. He was received into the Jesuits in Portugal; after studies in philosophy and theology he was ordained a priest in Rome. He returned to Portugal and later moved to Antwerp, where he taught moral theology. He left the Society of Jesus in 1659, and was consecrated Archbishop of Dublin at Ghent, on 2nd May 1669.[2] He is also remembered for the fact that he endeavoured to have Dublin recognized as the primatial see of Ireland, instead of Armagh, when St. Oliver Plunkett was Archbishop and Primate of all Ireland. In 1673 the Roman Catholic bishops and priests were ordered to leave the country. Archbishop Talbot went to Paris. In 1676 he came to England, under the protection of James, Duke of York. In 1678 he returned to Dublin; shortly afterwards he was imprisoned, being suspected of complicity in the Popish Plot. He died in gaol.

1. This agrees with Sir Oliver Millar's opinion, written in his typescript catalogue, *The Pictures at Malahide Castle,* an unpublished work consulted by its author's gracious permission.

2. Information kindly supplied by Father John Keegan, Secretary to His Grace the Archbishop of Dublin (1981).

4337 Shield: Head of Medusa (convex side) with Battle scenes (concave side) (Fig. 74).

Oil on canvas (convex side); gold leaf, incised, on canvas (concave side); laid on poplar wood shield, diameter 0.585 m.

CONDITION: most probably very good. This extremely interesting work of art will be fully restored by Sergio Benedetti.

PROVENANCE: unknown.

Medusa was one of the Gorgons, monsters of the underworld. Once renowned for her beauty, she was raped by Neptune in a temple of Minerva and the goddess, in her wrath, changed Medusa's hair into snakes and declared that all who looked upon her would turn to stone. Later Perseus, having got winged sandals from Mercury and a sword and shield from Minerva, cut off Medusa's head while she was asleep and used it to turn his enemies to stone. Eventually Minerva put the head on her own shield.

No. 4337 is directly inspired by the *Shield: Head of Medusa* (oil on canvas, laid on poplar wood, diameter 0.555 m.) which Caravaggio painted, in 1596, according to Marini,[1] an object presented by Cardinal Del Monte to Ferdinand I, Grand Duke of Tuscany. It is now in the Uffizi Gallery, Florence.

I. I. D. Eaves, Keeper of Armour, The Armouries, H.M. Tower of London, says that painted shields such as no. 4337 were almost certainly made for parade or pageant.[2]

In the armour collection of the Glasgow Museums and Art Galleries is a comparable shield, the convex side of which is painted with a curiously long-haired head of a cherub (scarcely Medusa).[3]

A very important shield, *Rotella di Gala,* is in the Museo Civico, Palazzo Madama, Turin. It depicts, on the convex side, Giovanni Maria della Rovere besieging Pesaro on the orders of Pope Julius II, 1512, and, on the concave side, mythological scenes in grey, white, and gilt. It is the work of Polidoro Caldara, known as Polidoro da Caravaggio, 1492-1543.

Until much more research has been done on such painted parade shields it will not be possible even to begin to suggest names of artists. In the meantime Caravaggio's shield now in the Uffizi remains a very special example.

Depictions of the head of Medusa go back to an early date in Italian art. For example, an inlaid marble *Head of Medusa*, datable to the late second century, A.D., was found in the Mithraeum at S. Prisca, on the Aventine hill in Rome. The use of the head of Medusa on a shield did not stop with Caravaggio and his followers. There is one in Sebastien Bourdon's *Liberation of Andromeda*, in the Alte Pinakothek, Munich.[4] Another example is that in the fresco of *Turnus and Aeneas* in Schleissheim Castle, near Munich, painted by Amigoni *circa* 1723.[5] Yet another head of Medusa adorns the breastplate of Fortitude in Giaquinto's *Fortitude and Vigilance,* in the Royal Palace at Caserta,[6] datable to 1752-62. Hugh Douglas Hamilton, who spent about twelve years in Rome, painted a *Head of Medusa* in oils, in the 1790s.[7] This he exhibited at the Hibernian Society of Artists in 1804. These examples are only a handful of literally hundreds which are known, and are mentioned solely to indicate the continued popularity of the theme.

1. M. Marini, *Io Michelangelo da Caravaggio* (Rome 1974), p. 116, no. 21, and pp. 363-64, no. 21.
2. In correspondence, November 1982.
3. Inv. no. A 7627 f. *Cf.* H. Adamson in *Scottish Art Review,* special no., vol. 15 (no. 2), pp. 23-26.
4. Alte Pinakothek, no. 1290.
5. In the Grosser Saal at Schleissheim.
6. M. D'Orsi, *Corrado Giaquinto* (Rome 1958), p. 147 and fig. 149.
7. *The Hibernian Magazine* (May 1810), p. 272.

ITALIAN SCHOOL, 18th Century

1084 Pope Benedict XIII (Fig. 77).
(Pietro Francesco Orsini, 1649-1730. Pope from 1724).

Oil on canvas, 0.57 × 0.50 m.

CONDITION: covered with layers of darkened varnish.

PROVENANCE: Milltown Collection; Milltown Gift, 1902.

The identity of the sitter is based on a commemorative medallion by Antonio Travani II,[1] and on a reproduction.[2] The pontiff wears a mozzetta, a stole, and the camauro, a cap reserved for use by popes alone.

Pietro Francesco Orsini was a member of the Roman Orsini — Gravina family. At the age of sixteen he entered the Dominican Order, in Venice, against the wishes of his parents. He took the names Vincenzo Maria. He was made a cardinal in 1672. In 1675 he was consecrated Archbishop of Manfredonia. In 1680 he was translated to the see of Cesena, and, in 1686, to that of Benevento. He was an exemplary pastor, and personally led a frugal life. Against his own wishes he was elected Pope, in 1724. As Pope he strove to make all the clergy, including cardinals, lead a simple life.

The picture is of very modest quality, and it would be very difficult to suggest the name of an artist for it.

1. Private collection, Northern Ireland.
2. C. Castiglioni, *Storia dei Papi*, vol. 2 (Torino 1957), p. 527. Reproduction of an engraving by F. Zucchi, 1692-1764.

ITALIAN SCHOOL, *circa* 1800

1239 Head of a saint (Fig. 78).

Oil on canvas, 0.59 × 0.47 m.

CONDITION: **very good.**

PROVENANCE: Rev. Patrick Gorry, Monasterevin, county Kildare, from whom purchased, 1952, for £50.

This slight work may have been done by a student painter. Generically it derives from the classical school of the early seventeenth century in Bologna and Rome.

EBERHARD KEIL, sometimes called MONSÙ BERNARDO, Helsingør 1624-1687 Rome

After initial studies in Copenhagen, Keil in 1642 went down to Amsterdam to work in Rembrandt's studio. Some ten years later he went to Italy sojourning initially in various cities, including Bergamo, Venice and Milan. He arrived in Rome in 1656 and remained there for the rest of his life. He executed some ecclesiastical commissions, but devoted himself principally to genre subjects, frequently working on a large scale.

4092 The embroidery shop (Fig. 79).

Oil on canvas, 1.53 × 1.85 m.

CONDITION: **excellent.**

PROVENANCE: the Hon. Mr. Justice James A. Murnaghan, Dublin; by inheritance to his widow, Mrs. Alice Murnaghan, from whom purchased, 1974, for £2,500.

The attribution to Keil of this painting is purely on stylistic grounds which scarcely leave any possible room for doubt. Very useful comparative paintings are *Family group in an interior* (0.99 × 1.37 m.) in the Museum Boymans — van Beuningen, Rotterdam (inv. no. 2626), *L'éducation en famille* (0.96 × 1.35 m.) in the Musées d'Art et d'Histoire, Chambéry (inv. no. 998), and *Lace making* (1.22 × 1.83 m.) in Prague Castle (inv. no. 035). In the last of these the figures of the two girls actually engaged in making lace compare closely with their counterparts in the Dublin painting.

Since no detailed work has been done on Keil's genre work in Rome, it is difficult to suggest a precise date for no. 4092. It was Keil who developed this type of painting in Rome some time after his arrival there in 1656; the work was well received and his paintings generated a demand for this genre; moreover, several Italian painters adapted his manner and continued this mode of painting well into the eighteenth century.

GIOVANNI LANFRANCO, Parma 1582-1647 Rome

Lanfranco studied with Agostino Carracci; at the age of twenty he went down to Rome to work with Annibale Carracci's team. Subsequently he worked in Parma, Piacenza and Rome. Most of his principal commissions were in Rome.

67 The Last Supper (Fig. 80).

Oil on canvas, 2.29 × 4.26 m.

CONDITION: excellent. There were minor paint losses around the edges. Restored Summer 1968.

PROVENANCE: Blessed Sacrament Chapel of Abbey Basilica of St. Paul's-without-the-Walls, Rome; removed from its original setting by 1668; possibly Benedictine Abbey of San Callisto, Rome, in the eighteenth century; Cardinal Fesch sale, Rome, 1845, lot 584, bt. Alessandro Aducci; Aducci, from whom purchased, 1856. One of sixteen pictures acquired for £1,700.[1]

Before discussing details of this picture it is useful to describe the circumstances of its commissioning, which apply equally to the following entry, no. 72 which is the pendant to *The Last Supper*. Both paintings come from what is now the Cappella del Coro in the Abbey Basilica of Saint Paul's-without-the-Walls, Rome. In the early seventeenth century a commission was given for its total redecoration as the Blessed Sacrament Chapel. The vault was frescoed by the Florentine artist, Anastasio Fontebuoni.[2] There remained for Lanfranco the walls, a small lunette over the door, two lunettes over the central portions of the side walls, and an altarpiece. The arrangement of the paintings was as follows. On entering the chapel, to the left of the door , on the back wall, was *Elias in the cave is brought bread by a raven*, a canvas now in the Musée Cantini, Marseille. Then first on the left side wall came *The explorers from Cana*, now in the J. Paul Getty Museum, Malibu, California. Next, this entry, *The Last Supper*, approximately double the length of the preceding pictures and about the same height. Above this painting was a fresco lunette, also by Lanfranco, depicting *The fall of manna*. The last painting on the left hand side was *The widow of Sarepta brings food to Elias*, now in the J. Paul Getty Museum, Malibu. Entering the chapel and turning right, one had immediately on the back wall, *Elias asks the widow of Sarepta for food*, now belonging to the Musées de Poitiers. On the right hand side wall first came *The fall of quails*, now in the Nunes Collection, Rome. Then there was the second Dublin painting, the subject of the following entry, *The multiplication of loaves and fishes*, over which was placed the large lunette depicting, in fresco, *Moses and the serpent of bronze*. Both this fresco and *The fall of manna* from the opposite wall are preserved, though somewhat worn, in a room of the Abbey of Saint Paul's itself. The last painting on the right hand side was *Elias and the angel*, now in the Rijksmuseum, Amsterdam. The altarpiece was suited to its position, around the tabernacle, with a glory, cherubs and angels. Its present location is unknown, as is that of *Charity*, the fresco which surmounted the entrance on the inside.

In 1856 when this painting and its pendant, *The multiplication of loaves and fishes*, were offered to the National Gallery of Ireland, the other four canvases from the two lateral walls were also offered, but only the two larger paintings were bought. It would have been quite splendid had the two entire side walls been acquired.

The baroque in Italy is frequently an animated defence of dogmas of the Church of Rome which were challenged by the Reformation. This is particularly true of the doctrine of the Eucharist in which the question of the Real Presence was severely attacked. Consequently, much effort and genius was expended on the construction of special chapels and altars for the Blessed Sacrament; one thinks of the Blessed Sacrament chapel in Saint Peter's, decorated by Bernini, or of the flamboyant altars of the Gesù and Sant'Ignazio. The Blessed Sacrament Chapel of Saint Paul's-without-the-Walls belongs to this category.

Apart from *The multiplication of loaves and fishes*, a New Testament foreshadowing of the Eucharist, and *The Last Supper*, the institution of the sacrament, the inspiration for Lanfranco's paintings at Saint Paul's is taken from the Old Testament. The episodes represented are types or anticipative symbols of the Eucharist. Four of them are taken from the biblical account of the life of Elias and refer to the extraordinary way in which he was nourished: firstly, while praying in the desert, by a raven (1 *Kings*, ch. 17, vs. 1-7); secondly, by the widow of Sarepta, on the instructions of Jahweh (1 *Kings*, ch. 17, vs. 8-24); thirdly, while sleeping in the shade of a juniper tree, by an angel (1 *Kings*, ch. 19). *The fall of quails* (*Exodus*, ch. 16, vs. 13) refers to the miraculous feeding of the followers of Moses, while *The explorers from Cana* (cf. *Numbers*, ch. 13, vs. 22-28) is a symbol of plenty in the Promised Land, and thus of the Eucharist as one of its future fruits. Over *The multiplication of loaves and fishes* was a lunette in fresco of *Moses and the serpent of bronze*, an Old Testament figure of Christ the Saviour on Calvary (source of the Eucharist), while over *The Last Supper* was a corresponding lunette showing *The fall of manna* (*Exodus* ch. 16, vs. 14-15), another type of the Christian Eucharist. The two main paintings of the series, under the lunettes, were the only ones which represented the New Testament climax of the vital promises of Old Testament types.

Apart from *Moses and the serpent of bronze*, many of the paintings in the series contain overtones of the sacrificial aspect of religion. It is most striking, however, that the central emphasis throughout is the sacramental element. Lanfranco was not only influenced by the live issues of the day. He was, in fact, prepared to give his wholehearted support to the theologians of Rome in their defence of the Real Presence by clearly demonstrating in these works that the Eucharist was to be regarded as much as a sacrament as a sacrifice.

Lanfranco most probably received his commission for this chapel of the Blessed Sacrament when Paolo Scotti was Abbot at Saint Paul's, 1621-1623.[3] Abbot Scotti was a relative of Orazio Scotti in whose house in Piacenza Lanfranco had been a page. Lanfranco may have begun studies for this extensive work, but it was apparently far from complete when Pope Urban VIII paid an Apostolic Visit on 10th November, 1624.[4] The chapel, however, was complete in 1625 which was a Holy or Jubilee Year.[5] The works of Lanfranco, at least all the canvases, were removed from their setting sometime before 1668, allegedly because they were damaged. When the two large Dublin canvases were cleaned in 1968, they were found to be in excellent condition, apart from minor damages along the edges. Some of the smaller canvases had suffered more. The chapel in Rome was altered several times, but even today could take back all the Lanfranco paintings.

There are two recorded drawings for this painting. The first, a black and white chalk drawing of the hands, arms and draperies of Christ is in the Museo di Capodimonte, Naples, no. 420 (233 × 307 mm.)[6] (Fig. 82). The second is a black and white chalk drawing on grey-brown paper for the Apostle on the extreme left and is preserved in the Royal Library at Windsor, no. 5692 (355 × 229 mm.)[7] (Fig. 83).

There are also two known copies of the entire composition: the first is from the Studio of Domenico Piola and is a small study in oils on canvas in the Palazzo Bianco, Genoa: inv. no. 1755 (1.075 × 1.70 m.).[8] A not full-size copy, eighteenth century in date, is in the sacristy of the Church of San Martino, Fermo.[9]

1. M. Wynne in *Gazette des Beaux-Arts,* vol. 89 (January 1977), pp. 1-7.
2. G. Baglione, *Le Vite de' Pittori, . . .* (Rome 1642), p. 163. The subject in the vault was Abraham and Melchisedek.
3. I. Schuster, *La Basilica ed il Monastero di S. Paolo fuori le Mura* (Torino 1934), p. 242.
4. Vatican Secret Archives: Misc. Arm VII, vol. III. *Acta Sacrae Visitationis Apostolicae S.D.N. Urbani VIII,* fol. 69.
5. G. Baglione, *Le Nove Chiese di Roma* (Rome 1639), p. 64 f.
6. E. Schleier in *Arte Antica e Moderna,* no. 31/32 (1965), p. 345 and fig. 151a; p. 355, n. 129.
7. *Ibid.,* p. 345 and fig. 151d; p. 355, n. 131.
8. E. Schleier, in *Arte Antica e Moderna,* no. 29 (1965), p. 77, n. 26.
9. *Ibid.*

72 Multiplication of loaves and fishes (Fig. 81).

Oil on canvas, 2.29 × 4.26 m.

CONDITION: excellent. There were some minor paint losses around the edges. Restored Summer 1968.

PROVENANCE: Blessed Sacrament Chapel of Abbey Basilica of St. Paul's-without-the-Walls, Rome; removed from its original setting by 1668; possibly Benedictine Abbey of San Callisto, Rome, in the eighteenth century; Cardinal Fesch sale, Rome, 1845, lot 585, where purchased by Alessandro Aducci; Aducci, from whom purchased 1856. One of sixteen paintings acquired for £1,700.[1]

Details of the commissioning of this painting from Giovanni Lanfranco and of the siting of all the paintings in the Blessed Sacrament Chapel of the Abbey Basilica of St. Paul's-without-the-Walls, Rome, are given under the preceding entry, no. 67, which is the pendant to this picture.

Two drawings which are studies for this painting are recorded. In the Museo di Capodimonte, Naples, drawing no. 336 (422 × 236 mm.), on grey-green paper has a black and white chalk study of the large figure of Christ.[2] (Fig. 84) On the *verso* of this sheet is a study for the young man bending down from the top left-hand corner.[3] (Fig. 85) The second drawing is also in the Museo di Capodimonte, Naples, no. 493 (272 × 220 mm.). On the *verso* of this sheet of blue paper is a black and white chalk sketch for one of the more prominent figures on the hillock.[4] (Fig. 86)

A somewhat simplified copy, by Lanfranco himself, in oils of the entire painting is in a Florentine private collection, and was published by Boschetto.[5]

1. M. Wynne in *Gazette des Beaux-Arts*, vol. 89 (January 1977), pp. 1-7.
2. E. Schleier in *Arte Antica e Moderna*, no. 30-31 (1965), p. 346 and fig. 151c; p. 355, n. 134.
3. *Ibid.*, p. 346 and fig. 151e.
4. *Ibid.*, p. 346 and fig.152a; p. 355, n. 136.
5. A. Boschetto in *Paragone*, no. 29 (1952), pp. 19-20.

GIOVANNI BATTISTA LANGETTI, Genoa (?)1635-1676 Venice

Very little is known about the early training of Langetti, and there are also wildly conflicting accounts of his date of birth. The one adopted here is based on documents concerning his death. While still young, Langetti went down to Rome and worked in the studio of Pietro da Cortona. Langetti was influenced to a certain degree by the Caravaggist movement; he also showed a marked interest in anatomy. Sometime before 1660 Langetti settled in Venice.

4002   St. Sebastian (Fig. 88).

Oil on parchment, 0.35 × 0.25 m.

CONDITION: very good. There were small paint losses around the edges, and some throughout the picture. Restored 1970. The parchment was removed from the wooden panel on which it had been mounted. A support of Purlboard sandwiched between Perspex was prepared. To this was attached deacidified Saunders paper on which the parchment was mounted.

PROVENANCE: Milltown Collection; Milltown Gift, 1902

The saint is dramatically posed against what might be a piece of decorated leather, but the decoration has no structural role. It probably was regarded merely as an appropriate background.

No. 4002 was attributed to Furini, doubtless because of its similar size to the small Furinis which came to the Gallery with the Milltown Gift. Cleaning revealed a marked difference. Terisio Pignatti and Walter Balzano were the first to suggest an attribution to Langetti.[1] This is very plausible when one considers Langetti's interest in anatomy as manifested in such works as *Hercules* in the collection of Walter Mio, Udine; *The Good Samaritan* in the Harrach Gallery, Vienna;[2] *The Good Samaritan* which was with Heim, Paris, in 1955,[3] or *The Good Samaritan* in the Holburne of Menstrie Museum, Bath. While none of these has the intimate quality of the tiny, rather dashing Dublin sketch, they do support the attribution by their vivid anatomical passages. Fiocco, as early as 1922, signalled Langetti's *eroi muscolosi*,[4] citing the *St. Jerome* in the Brass Collection, Venice;[5] Archimedes and his murderer in *The slaying of Archimedes* (Palazzo Widmann-Foscari, Venice),[6] and *Apollo and Marsyas* in Dresden.[7] Another interesting comparison may be made with the torso of Isaac in *Isaac blessing Jacob*, in a private collection in Treviso.[8] Two further parallels of 'muscular heroes', from private collections in Genoa, were exhibited in 1969, *Archimedes with allegorical figures of War and Peace*,[9] and *Milo of Croton*.[10] These characteristics, and some of the paintings already referred to, are included in Pallucchini's masterly survey of the Venetian Seicento.[11]

Perhaps the painting closest to no. 4002 is the *St. Sebastian* in the Hermitage.[12] The intense pose, the study of muscular structure and tension, and the somewhat gaping mouth of no. 4002 are echoed in the Hermitage *St. Sebastian*. Also to be noted are the strong diagonals in both of these paintings, and indeed in most of Langetti's works.

No date is being suggested. Much work has to be done yet to establish a chronology of the works of this short-lived artist.

1. In correspondence, September 1978, and verbally, respectively.
2. *L'Arte,* vol. 32 (September-December, 1929), p. 270, fig. 6.
3. *The Burlington Magazine,* vol. 97 (August 1955), advertisement.
4. G. Fiocco in *Dedalo,* year 3 (1922), p. 282.
5. *Ibid.,* p. 286; ill. opp. p. 275.
6. *Ibid.,* p. 282; ill. p. 281.
7. *Ibid.,* pp. 282-86; ill. p. 285. This painting was destroyed during the Second World War.

8. R. Pallucchini in *Bollettino d'Arte,* vol. 28 (1934), p. 254, fig. 4.
9. Exhibition catalogue: *Mostra di Pittori Genovesi a Genova nel '600 e nel '700* (Palazzo Bianco, Genoa, 1969), no. 123.
10. *Ibid.,* no. 124.
11. R. Pallucchini, *La Pittura Veneziana del Seicento* (Milan 1981), vol. 1, pp. 243-50; vol. 2, figs. 777-806.
12. *Ibidem,* vol. 1, p. 248; vol. 2, fig. 794.

FILIPPO LAURI, Rome 1623-1694 Rome

Lauri studied painting under Angelo Caroselli. He is known above all for his easel paintings in which one sees the influence of Francesco Albani and Claude Lorrain. He did, however, execute a number of commissions for altarpieces.

989 Rebecca at the well (Fig. 87).

Oil on canvas, 0.32 × 0.57 m.

CONDITION: apparently good under a thick layer of discoloured varnish.

PROVENANCE: Milltown Collection by 1826; Milltown Gift, 1902.

At the left of the picture is Rebecca beside the well head, with, behind her, some young women. To the right of Rebecca is Eliezer, Abraham's servant, who is giving a gift to Rebecca. Eliezer had been sent into Mesopotamia to find a wife for Abraham's son Isaac, and chose Rebecca following their chance encounter at the well. (*Genesis*, ch. 24).

The painting has been given to Lauri since first noted in the Milltown Collection, in 1826.

Stylistically no. 989 has the characteristics of a Lauri subject painting, the group of figures well composed with the landscape structured in the classical tradition. A useful comparison may be made with *Noah leaving the ark* by Lauri in the Colonna Gallery, Rome.[1]

A date of *circa* 1650 seems appropriate.

1. E. A. Safarik, *Catalogo Sommario della Galleria Colonna in Roma. Dipinti* (Rome 1981), pp. 80-81, no. 101.

LORENZO LIPPI, Florence 1606-1665 Florence

Lippi studied under Matteo Rosselli; he was also much influenced by the works of Santi di Tito. He enjoyed considerable patronage from different members of the Medici family including Claudia de' Medici, Archduchess of Austria, for whom he worked at Innsbruck, around 1643. Salvator Rosa spend some time in Tuscany between 1640 and 1649, and was particularly friendly with Lippi.

1747 Medoro and Angelica (Fig. 89).

Oil on canvas, 1.73 × 2.38 m.

CONDITION: excellent. Restored June-July 1970.

PROVENANCE: (?) Marchese Mattias Maria Bartolommei, Florence;[1] Milltown Collection by 1826; Milltown Gift, 1902.

EXHIBITED: 1979 London and Cambridge *Painting in Florence 1600-1700* (Royal Academy and The Fitzwilliam Museum), no. 31. Catalogue by Charles McCorquodale.

This painting illustrates a passage from the nineteenth Canto of Ariosto's *Orlando Furioso*. Medoro, who reclines at the left hand side of the picture, was a follower of the Moorish leader Dardinello and was wounded in the battle before Paris. Angelica, who stands in the centre of the painting, found him and went off to collect various herbs, which are in the basket which she holds. Angelica had learned the skill of curing with herbs in India, and, with her memory of this, cured Medoro. The couple fell in love and were married. In the very top left hand corner is a cupid with bow and arrow. In the very bottom left hand corner are Medoro's sword and head-dress. To the right of Angelica a landscape leads back, and in it one can see the horse which Angelica requisitioned, standing by its owner, and beyond the bodies of two dead men, presumably companions of Medoro.

No. 1747 was published as the work of Vignali by Bigongiari,[2] and by the present writer,[3] in 1974. This attribution was upheld by Miles Chappell in 1977.[4] However, in the 1979 exhibition catalogue cited above, McCorquodale argues well the attribution to Lippi, suggesting further that it may be one of two paintings with stories from *Orlando Furioso* commissioned from Lippi by Marchese Mattias Maria Bartolommei of Florence. The similarity between the work of Vignali and Lippi, at times, was clearly demonstrated at the 1979 exhibition when one could turn round and compare this painting with no. 55, *Hagar and the angel*, signed with Vignali's monogram and dated 1632. Among those who endorsed McCorquodale's attribution were Claudio Pizzorusso,[5] Chiara D'Afflitto,[6] and Giuseppe Cantelli.[7] Previously Mina Gregori had proposed Lippi (verbally 1975).

McCorquodale suggested a date in the early 1640s, observing a similarity of landscape in no. 1747 with that in *Christ and the woman of Samaria* in the Kunsthistorisches Museum, Vienna (no. 264), signed and dated 1644. D'Afflitto, on the other hand, proposed a date in the early 1630s.[8] The writer would support the latter suggestion.

A distinctive feature in the paintings of Lippi is the very long neck which he gives to the principal protagonists. The Samaritan woman in the painting in Vienna, referred to in the preceding paragraph, has a singularly long neck; other examples are to be found in Lippi's work in the Cappella Ardinghelli, in the church of San Gaetano, Florence, and in his painting of *Samson and Delila*, in the Nationalmuseum, Stockholm (no. 2402).

1. F. Baldinucci, *Notizie de' Professori del Disegno,* . . . (D. M. Manni's edition), vol. 18, (Florence 1773), p. 14.
2. P. Bigongiari, *Il Seicento Fiorentino tra Galileo e il 'Recitar Cantando'* (Milan 1974), p. 43.
3. M. Wynne in *Apollo*, vol. 99 (February 1974), p. 108.
4. M. Chappell in *The Art Bulletin*, vol. 59 (September 1977), p. 437.
5. C. Pizzorusso in *Antologia di Belle Arti*, nos. 9-12 (December 1979), p. 173.
6. C. D'Afflitto in *Paragone*, no. 353 (July 1979), p. 67.
7. G. Cantelli, *Repertorio della Pittura Fiorentina del Seicento* (Fiesole 1983), p. 97.
8. C. D'Afflitto, *loc. cit.*

JOHANN LISS (or JAN LYS), Oldenburg 1597-1631 Verona

Born in the north of Germany, Liss trained in the Low Countries. He worked in Paris, and was quite definitely in Venice in 1621. He went to Rome for a while, and returned to Venice only to become a victim of a plague which struck the city in 1629/30. Liss's altarpiece of St. Jerome in the Venetian church of San Nicolò da Tolentino became very famous, and was copied much. Despite his short life, the bravura of Liss's style had an important influence on later Venetian painting.

After LISS

981 The vision of St. Jerome (Fig. 90).

Oil on canvas, 1.12 × 0.90 m.

CONDITION: excellent. Restored 1970.

PROVENANCE: bought from an antique dealer in Leeds by Monsignor J. Shine, Dublin, from whom purchased, 1936, for £500.

EXHIBITED: 1938 London, *Exhibition of 17th Century Art in Europe* (Royal Academy) no. 302; 1975-76 Augsburg and Cleveland, *Johann Liss* (Rathaus and Cleveland Museum of Art), no. 40.

This is a version after the altarpiece in the Church of San Nicolò da Tolentino, Venice. Its measurements are almost exactly half of those of the altarpiece. Steinbart believed no. 981 to be the *bozzetto* which secured for Liss the commission,[1] and therefore autograph. Pallucchini regarded it as a replica after the altarpiece,[2] as did Zykan;[3] De Logu was of the same opinion.[4] Mariacher dismissed it as a minor replica.[5] In the Gallery's own concise catalogues of 1963 and 1971, and in the *Illustrated Summary Catalogue of Paintings,* 1981, it was given to Liss, notwithstanding suggestions that its date of execution might well be eighteenth century. The painting is of extremely high quality executed with freedom and vitality in rich impasto. The question of authorship was deliberately left open by Ann Tzeutschler Lurie in her entry for the 1975-76 exhibition *(vide supra),* especially as she had never seen the painting itself. Following that exhibition the earlier suggestions of eighteenth century fabric were endorsed by many observers. The problem was to find an artist. While several critics saw it as Venetian, there was a very strong lobby for Jean-Honoré Fragonard. The strength behind the Fragonard proposal is supported by the fact that he did an etching of the altarpiece about 1761.[6] The question remains as tantalizing as ever. One can only hope that some documentary evidence will come to light to solve the problem of the authorship of this high quality painting.

The altarpiece at San Nicolò has been copied in whole or in part many times, and in various sizes. These copies are variously considered autograph or mere later copies. As they have been fully discussed in the 1975-76 exhibition catalogue (no. 39), it is not proposed to discuss them here again; since then only one further version has become known to the writer, namely a canvas measuring 1.05×0.83 m. in a private collection in Mexico (1977). To judge from the photograph it does have some quality. Compositionally it seems cut on both sides by comparison with no. 981, but this may be due to photography. The great popularity of Liss's altarpiece must be due to a very large extent to the painting's *avant-garde* quality, an anticipation of Venetian eighteenth century art.

1. K. Steinbart, *Johann Liss, der Maler aus Holstein* (Berlin 1940) pp. 135, 137, *passim,* and 161.
2. In exhibition catalogue, *Cinque Secoli di Pittura Veneta* (Venice 1945), p. 104.
3. J. Zykan, 'Berichte' *Österreichische Zeitschrift fur Denkmalpflege,* vol. I-II (1947-48), p. 190.
4. G. DeLogu, *Pittura Veneziana dal XIV al XVII secolo* (Bergamo 1958), p. 277.
5. In exhibition catalogue, *Arte a Venezia dal medioevo al Settecento* (Venice 1971), p. 72.
6. *Cf.* entry E 103 in catalogue of 1975-76 exhibition referred to above.

ALESSANDRO LONGHI, Venice 1733-1813 Venice

Alessandro studied with Nogari, as well as under his celebrated father, Pietro Longhi. Alessandro is chiefly remembered as a portraitist. He also made engravings, some of them after his father's works.

Attributed to LONGHI

1814   Portrait of a lady holding a fan (Fig. 91).

Oil on canvas, 0.527 × 0.428 m.

CONDITION: good. Restored Summer 1968. The painting had suffered from earlier abrasions.

PROVENANCE: an Irish private collection, from which purchased, 1967, for £300.

This painting has not been accepted as an autograph Alessandro Longhi by a number of critics including the late Benedict Nicolson.[1] Weak as it may be, partly due to its state of preservation, its quality is just as high as the half-length (of the same sitter?) in the Castello Sforzesco, Milan,[2] which is labelled Alessandro Longhi; and a painting advertised for sale in 1929[3] would appear to be equally weak and stylistically unattractive. At this point one must ask the question whether these portraits, including Dublin's no.1814, are really the work of Alessandro Longhi himself. While it is difficult to answer with an unequivocal negative, a very high degree of doubt must remain. Alessandro Longhi is the painter of some very beautiful portraits, of elegance and quality. It suffices to refer to the *Portrait of a lady* in the Pitti Palace.[4]

One of Alessandro Longhi's stylistic idiosyncracies is the slightly lumpy handling of flesh, even in passages of his best works. This characteristic is visible in the picture catalogued here, in the juncture of the thumb and first finger of the lady's right hand.

1. *The Burlington Magazine,* vol. 110 (November 1968), p. 596.
2. Museo d'Arte Antica, Castello Sforzesco, Milan, no. 77.

3. Advertisement by J. Leger and Son, London, in *Pantheon* (July 1929).
4. *Portrait of a lady* in the Pitti Palace, Florence: Inv. 1890, no. 3573.

PIETRO LONGHI, Venice *c.* 1701-1785 Venice

Longhi's real family name was Falca; he trained as a painter under Balestra, and later at Bologna with Crespi. About the age of forty he began to paint a type of genre or conversation piece, for which he is best remembered. In these one notes often a fairly strong sense of satirical observation of the Venetian society of his time.

952   The artist painting a lady's portrait (Fig. 92).

Oil on canvas, 0.61 × 0.50 m.

CONDITION: excellent. Restored 1968. On the stretcher is a label bearing the number *163*; its significance can not be established.

PROVENANCE: Captain R. Langton Douglas, London, from whom purchased, 1932, for £450.

The painting is absolutely autograph, and has been repeatedly published by Pignatti.[1] A version exists in a private Venetian collection.[2] Pignatti considers that these versions, both of a vertical axis, are slightly later than that on a horizontal axis which is in the Ca' Rezzonico, Venice,[3] datable to 1740-45. A version of the horizontal composition is in a private collection in London.[4]

In the Museo Correr, Venice, are preparatory drawings for the figure of the artist and of the male sitter (nos. 437 and 439).[5] Pignatti is of the opinion that the drawings relate primarily to the painting in the Ca' Rezzonico.[6]

1. T. Pignatti, *Pietro Longhi* (Venice 1968), p. 87; *id., L'opera completa di Pietro Longhi* (Milan 1974), p. 88, no. 36.
2. T. Pignatti, *L'opera completa di Pietro Longhi* (Milan 1974), p. 88, no. 37.
3. *Ibid.*, p. 88, no. 35.

4. *Ibid.*, p. 87, no. 34.
5. V. Moschini, *Pietro Longhi* (Milan 1956), pl. 76 and pl. 154.
6. T. Pignatti, *Pietro Longhi. Dal disegno alla pittura* (Venice 1975), pl. 4b and pl. 4a.

ALESSANDRO MAGNASCO, sometimes called IL LISSANDRINO, Genoa 1667-1749 Genoa

Having studied with his father, Stefano, until the latter's death, Magnasco removed to Milan to perfect his talents under the Venetian, Abbiati. On his own, however, Magnasco developed a very personal and effective style, which was particularly suited to narrative and genre subjects. After an extended stay away from home, including some years in Florence, Magnasco settled in Genoa in 1735.

678 Landscape with washerwomen (Fig. 93).

Oil on canvas, 1.04 × 0.83 m.

CONDITION: rather thin with numerous small areas of paint loss. Restored August 1970.

PROVENANCE: Sir Hugh Lane, by whom presented, 1914.

Fausta Franchini, in her thesis on Magnasco for the University of Genoa, dates the Dublin picture to after 1725, on stylistic grounds.[1] In many ways no. 678 bears close comparison, both in composition and details, with the painting of the same title, but of much larger dimensions, in the Museo e Gallerie Nazionali, Naples, inv. no. 199.[2] Another comparable painting is *Landscape with friars and pilgrims* in the Brera, Milan, dated by Morassi to the decade 1720-30.[3] Geiger, in his major monograph on Magnasco, catalogues as autograph no. 678, but does not suggest a date.[4] Another painting, very close in style and composition, is in the Seilern Collection.[5] The Seilern painting is in excellent condition, and is a striking example of how Magnasco made good use of a red-earth ground colour by allowing it to surface prominently in many places.

1. Communicated by letter, June 1967.
2. H. Dürst, *Alessandro Magnasco* (Teufen 1966), p. 187, pl. 35.
3. Exhibition catalogue, *Mostra del Magnasco* (Palazzo Bianco, Genoa, 1949) p. 31, no. 25 and

pl. 30.
4. B. Geiger, *Magnasco* (Bergamo 1949), p. 83 and pl. 77.
5. H. Braham, *The Princes Gate Collection* (London 1981), p. 26, no. 39.

CARLO MARATTI, Camerano 1625-1713 Rome

Maratti studied painting in Rome in the studio of Andrea Sacchi; he became very successful and well known, and in turn trained a number of disciples. Predominant in Maratti's work are religious commissions, but he also did historical and mythological subjects, as well as very successful portraits.

81 Europa and the bull (Jupiter) (Fig. 94).

Oil on canvas, 2.48 × 4.24 m.

CONDITION: very good, there were some paint losses in the foreground, and some very small ones elsewhere. Restored June 1967-June 1968.

PROVENANCE: (?) Lebrun sale, Paris, September 1806; R. Macpherson, Rome, from whom purchased, 1856. One of twenty-three paintings acquired for £1,483.

Jupiter fell in love with Europa, daughter of a king. Desirous of abducting her, he disguised himself as a white bull and mingled with a herd in the field where Europa was playing with her friends. Making himself very tame in the eyes of Europa, Jupiter eventually induced the King's daughter to sit on his back. Thereupon Jupiter made off into the sea. He brought Europa to Crete, and there was born to them the hero King Minos.

The attribution of the painting to Maratti is the traditional one and has been maintained by leading authorities. Rudolph suggested that the flowers in this picture were painted by Carlo Van Vogelaer, and that, if this hypothesis was correct, the painting was the one painted by Maratti for Cardinal Savelli.[1]

Amalia Mezzetti dates this painting between 1680 and 1685, and suggests that it may have been the *Giove ed Europa* painted, according to Bellori,[2] for the artist's friend Cardinal Paolo Savelli. However, on reading Bellori, one has good reason to doubt the suggestion, 'Nel l'altro Quadro rappresentasi Europa sedente sopra il Toro, il quale entrato nel mare s'allontana dal Lido. La Regia Fanciulla impaurita al periglio, con una mano s'attiene al corno del Toro, con l'altra accenna, e chiama le Compagne, che non lungi sopra un Prato colgono fiori, e tessonvi ghirlande; . . .'[3] First of all it is quite clear in the Dublin picture that the bull is on dry land; that he is not moving, but in fact very sedentary. Neither does Europa seem scared; nor does she hold on to either of the bull's horns, but plays with the garland of flowers on the bull's head. The whole atmosphere of tranquillity which permeates the picture, and especially the calm face of Europa, leads one to discount the proposition that it was the painting done for Cardinal Savelli. Nor is it likely to be the copy of the Cardinal's painting commissioned by Sigr. Don Gio. Batta Spinelli, Duca di Seminara, after the Cardinal's death, from Maratti.[4]

In the print room of the Kunstmuseum of Düsseldorf there are two sheets by Maratti with studies for the Dublin picture (FP 13749 and FP 7545).[5] FP 13749 (verso) is a study for Europa seated on the bull, and a cupid (Fig. 95), while FP 13749 (recto) is a study for one of Europa's attendants (Fig. 96). FP 7545 (recto) is a study for the head of one of the three female figures on the left (Fig. 97).

1. S. Rudolph in *Antichità Viva,* anno XVIII, no. 2, (1979), p. 15.
2. A. Mezzetti in *Rivista del l'Istituto Nazionale d'Archeologia e Storia dell'Arte,* nuova serie — anno 4 (1955), p. 322. no. 35.
3. M. Piacentini (ed), *Giovan Pietro Bellori; Vite di Guido Reni, Andrea Sacchi e Carlo Maratti* (Roma 1942), p. 127.
4. *Ibid.,* note 2.
5. A. S. Harris and E. Schaar, *Die Handzeichnungen von Andrea Sacchi und Carlo Maratta.* (Kataloge des Kunstmuseums Düsseldorf, Düsseldorf 1967), p. 126, nos. 339-40.

Studio of MARATTI

1703   The Virgin and Child, with St. Elizabeth, St. John the Baptist, and an angel (Fig. 98).

Oil on canvas, 0.76 × 0.63 m.

DATED: *1705.*

CONDITION: excellent.

PROVENANCE: Milltown Collection; Milltown Gift, 1902.

PROTOTYPE: the Hermitage, Leningrad.

VERSION: a version of no. 1703, or of its prototype in Leningrad, was catalogued by Sotheby's in their New York sale of 20 January 1983, lot 22, as Circle of Lorenzo Masucci (oil on canvas, 0.735 × 0.57 m.).

This painting was fully given to Maratti in the 1963 catalogue; in the concise catalogues of 1971 and 1981 it was included as 'After Maratti'. It would seem more just, on account of its competent handling and date, to regard it as a studio work. It is directly based on the painting by Maratti in the Hermitage, Leningrad, no. 1500.

After MARATTI

298   Father Luke Wadding, O.F.M., 1588-1657 (Fig. 99).

Oil on canvas, 0.66 × 0.51 m.

INSCRIBED: *F. Lvcas Wadingvs*

CONDITION: good.

PROVENANCE: Signor Rotondo, Newcastle, England, from whom purchased, 1889, for £50.

EXHIBITED: 1965 Belfast *Great Irish Men and Women* (Ulster Museum), no. 229.

PROTOTYPE: Sotheby's, 8 July 1981, lot 21.

Luke Wadding was born in Waterford in 1588. He was educated abroad, becoming a Franciscan in 1605. He went to Rome in the retinue of the Spanish Ambassador in 1618. Here he spent the rest of his life. He was respected for his great humility and learning. He warmly supported the cause of the Irish Catholics in 1641, and through his influence Rinuccini was sent to Ireland as Nuncio by Innocent X in 1642. He wrote many books, of which the most important is the monumental history of his order, *Annales Minorum Ordinum Franciscanorum.* He founded the College of Saint Isidore in Rome, in 1625. He died in Rome in 1657, and was buried at Saint Isidore's. Wadding is wearing the Franciscan habit.

Acquired as by Ribera, this fairly soon changed to 'Attributed to Ribera'. It is only in recent years that the attribution has been changed to 'After Maratti'. It is clear that the picture is not by the master himself because of its quality, and as early as 1955 it was noted as a copy after a lost original by Mezzetti.[1]

In 1980 Nicholas Turner saw what he believed to be the original Maratti in a private collection in London. From a photograph his conclusion appears to be correct. The painting subsequently came up for sale at Sotheby's, 8 July 1981, lot 21. The original portrait may be dated to about 1653 when Maratti was doing some work for the Franciscans at St. Isidore's,[2] in Rome. No. 298 is derived from this.

Another copy, similar to no. 298, and at least as good in quality, belongs to the Franciscans in Ireland and is kept at their House of Higher Studies, Dun Mhuire, Killiney, county Dublin. It was brought to Ireland from St. Isidore's, Rome, in 1870. The original was engraved by Stephen Picart in 1658.[3]

1. A. Mezzetti in *Rivista dell' Istituto Nazionale d'Archeologia e Storia dell'Arte*, nuova serie — anno 4 (1955), p. 348, no. 170.

2. *Ibid.*

3. *Ibid.* and *op. cit.*, p. 292, fig. 42.

MICHELE MARIESCHI, Venice 1710-1743 Venice

Possibly Marieschi trained under the Venetian painter Gaspare Diziani. For a short while Marieschi worked for the Elector of Saxony at Dresden. At the age of twenty-five he was back in Venice, practising as a view painter, and as such is best remembered through his series of some twenty-one etchings. Given his short life, his oeuvre is not extensive, but in oil paintings his style is quite distinct from that of Carlevaris, Canaletto, or Francesco Guardi, although he is closest to the latter, who was almost an exact contemporary. Aesthetically his paintings are not of the quality of Guardi's.

473 Piazza San Marco, Venice (Fig. 100).

Oil on canvas, 0.55 × 0.83 m.

CONDITION: very good. Restored September 1968.

PROVENANCE: purchased in 1902. No source for the vendor is recorded in either the manuscript catalogue, or the Minutes of the Board of Governors and Guardians.

EXHIBITED: 1911 London *Venetian Painting of the Eighteenth Century* (Burlington Fine Arts Club), no. 23.

This is a view of the Piazza looking south. On the left is the facade of St. Mark's basilica, then, to the right, a glimpse of the Grand Canal, then the Campanile, the range of the Procuratie Nuove, as well as part of the West side.

No. 473 has always been considered absolutely autograph,[1] and there is no reason to doubt the attribution.

The painting was almost certainly executed in the late 1730s.

Versions of no. 473 include one with the Koetser Gallery, London, in 1946; a painting which Mitchell Galleries, Duke Street, St. James's, London, had in 1948;[2] another with the Galleria Lorenzelli, Bergamo, in 1966; and one with the Brod Gallery, London, in 1969.[3] The Koetser Gallery version and that with the Galleria Lorenzelli may be one and the same painting. The other versions have several differences in details and staffage. The view, in general, was etched by Marieschi himself in his series *Magnificentiores selectioresque urbis Venetiarum prospectus quos olim Michael Marieschi venetus pictor et architectus in plerisque tabulis dipinxit* (Venice 1741). None of the versions known to the writer is the precise basis for the engraving.

1. For example, G. Delogu, *Pittori veneti minori del Settecento* (Venice 1930), p. 111.

2. *Apollo*, vol. 48 (November 1948), ill. in colour on front cover.
3. *Apollo*, vol. 89 (April 1969), advertisement.

AGOSTINO MASUCCI, Rome 1691-1758 Rome

Masucci was one of Carlo Maratti's most loyal pupils in terms of both quality and style. He painted many works for Roman churches. He also did some excellent portraits.

1040 Mystic marriage of St. Catherine (Fig. 101).

Oil on canvas, 0.65 × 0.50 m.

CONDITION: excellent. There were some very small areas of paint loss. Restored 1977-1986.

PROVENANCE: Milltown Collection by 1826; Milltown Gift, 1902.

Heretofore the painting was called Italian School.[1] When cleaning it Sergio Benedetti suggested the name of Masucci, one of Maratti's closest followers, who carried his personal interpretation of the Marattesque principles right down into the middle of the eighteenth century.

Benedetti's attribution is well supported by two paintings in the Roman church of S. Maria in via Lata. Both of them are oval. One, *The Annunciation*, is on the first altar of the right hand side aisle; the second, *The adoration of the Magi*, is the last painting in the right hand aisle. The face of the Virgin in no. 1040 is virtually identical to that in *The adoration of the Magi*. Masucci's paintings of figures show very delicate long fingers, such as those visible in no. 1040. His profiles are elegant.

A close relationship between Masucci and his master, Maratti, in terms of colour, can be seen by comparing no. 1040 and the two paintings in S. Maria in via Lata, Rome, with *The Virgin of the Annunciation* and *The Angel of the Annunciation*, two Marattis of approximately the same size as no. 1040 in the Galleria Nazionale di Palazzo Spinola, Genoa.[2]

Anthony Clark tentatively dates the paintings in S. Maria in via Lata to *circa* 1716-17.[3] Clark has an interesting observation of Masucci's position in Rome of the eighteenth century: 'Masucci's investment in the Rococo was only skin deep, with the grace and pretty surface handling put upon compositions clearer and colder than those of any of his teachers. The early *Adoration of the Kings* in S. Maria in via Lata is a brilliant essay in latter-day Marattism, exceptionally careful, delicate, gracious and rich. The opulence is not pictorial but technical, not grandiose and Baroque (or even purely Rococo) but academic and draughtsmanly, with some appeal to the pre-Baroque. A late-Baroque painting in the gentle early-Rococo mode, this work is an attempt at pure academic authority, and the authority supersedes the given style.'[4]

Other useful comparisons are *The Annunciation* on the high altar of the Church of the Annunciation, Veroli, and the *Virgin and Child* in the Galleria Pallavicini, Rome, although the latter lacks the precise tight outlines of the other Masuccis mentioned.

No. 1040 may well have been available for sale on either of the two visits made to Rome by Joseph Leeson, later 1st Earl of Milltown, the first being in the mid-1740s, the second in the early 1750s.

1. National Gallery of Ireland Catalogues, 1971 and 1981.
2. P. Rotondi, *La Galleria Nazionale di Palazzo Spinola a Genova* (Milan 1967), p. 128, ill. p. 126; p. 128, ill. p. 127.
3. A. M. Clark, *Studies in Roman Eighteenth-Century Painting* (Washington, D.C., 1981), p. 91.
4. *Ibid.*, p. 96.

LIVIO MEHUS, Oudenarde 1630-1691 Florence

In 1640 Mehus came to Milan with his parents. Later he studied painting with Giuliano Periccioli and Pietro da Cortona in Florence. After sojourns in various places he eventually became a court painter for the Medicis in Florence.

Attributed to MEHUS

1661 St. Sebastian (Fig. 102).

Oil on canvas, 1.47 × 1.00 m.

CONDITION: covered by heavy layers of discoloured varnish.

PROVENANCE: Milltown Collection by 1826; Milltown Gift, 1902.

Sebastian was an officer in the army of the Roman Emperor, Diocletian (third century). When the Emperor discovered that Sebastian was a Christian he had him bound to a stake in the middle of a field and 'archers shot at him until he looked like a hedgehog. Then thinking him dead they abandoned him'.[1] A Christian woman, Irene, came to bury him; she found him alive and nursed him back to full health. When the Emperor next saw Sebastian, he had him beaten to death, this time effectively.

Given to Van Dyck in the Milltown inventory of 1826, and in the Deed of Gift of the Milltown Collection, in 1902, no. 1661 was curiously not included in any of the Gallery's catalogues until the concise one of 1971, where it was entered as 'After Van Dyck'; the 1981 Illustrated Summary Catalogue retained that description.

Pierre Rosenberg, on a visit to the Gallery, suggested Livio Mehus. Given the condition of the painting it is not possible to be very positive, but the suggestion is very worthwhile, all the more welcome because the Gallery staff and Larsen[2] had rejected the Van Dyck label.

The figure of St. Sebastian may be compared with that of Isaac in Mehus's *Sacrifice of Isaac* in the Depositi delle Gallerie Fiorentine.[3] The head of St. Sebastian in no. 1661 points towards Mehus as well. One half is in shadow through compositional *chiaroscuro*, while the upper half of the left hand side of the face is cast into shade by the saint's hair. In each of three well established Mehus paintings, *Genius of Painting*,[4] *Genius of Sculpture*,[5] and *Allegory of Music*[6] one of the figures is wearing a dark floppy hat which ensures that a substantial portion of the upper head is cast into shade. In the first it is a young painter, in the second it is a young sculptor, while in the last it is a painter standing behind a keyboard instrument. In all three the face is a self-portrait of Mehus. While it would be a little incongruous to expect St. Sebastian to wear a hat at the moment of his martyrdom, the dramatic *chiaroscuro* of the three Genius or Allegory pictures is effected by other means. The St. Sebastian may also be a self-portrait and datable to the 1650s.

Mina Gregori, on the basis of a photograph, could not accept an attribution to Mehus; she felt that the answer might be found in the Genoese post-Van Dyck school.[7]

Pending cleaning and restoration one must be a little cautious. However, it is worth commenting that the majority of Dublin's good Florentine seventeenth century pictures came with the Milltown Gift. Thus, the addition of a work by the Flemish-born Medici court painter would be in keeping with a significant part of the Milltown Collection.

1. Translated from Jacques de Voragine, *La Légende Dorée* (translation by T. de Wyzewa: Paris 1913), p. 96.
2. E. Larsen, *L'opera completa di Van Dyck, 1626-1641* (Milan 1980), A29.
3. G. Cantelli, *Repertorio della Pittura Fiorentina del Seicento* (Fiesole 1983), p. 111 and pls. 573-74.
4. Formerly Contini-Bonacossi Collection;

G. Ewald in *The Burlington Magazine*, vol. 116 (July 1974), pp. 392-93.
5. Pitti Palace, Florence: inv. 1890, no. 5337; G. Ewald, *loc. cit.*
6. At Knole; F. Russell in *National Trust Studies 1980* (London 1979), pp. 147-49.
7. In correspondence, January 1984.

Anton Raphaël Mengs, Aussig 1728-1779 Rome

Born in Aussig, in Bohemia, Mengs studied under his painter father and in Rome. In 1745 he was appointed a court painter to the Elector of Saxony, at Dresden. From 1747, however, he settled in Rome, but made significant and prolonged visits to Madrid. In Rome, with Batoni, and later his brother-in-law, Anton von Maron, he was one of the most sought after portraitists of the Grand Tourists. In Rome, too, he was one of the pioneers of the emerging Neoclassical movement, his extensive Parnassus *in the Villa Albani being one of the landmarks of that development.*

4458   Thomas Conolly, 1738-1803 (Fig. 103).

Oil on canvas, 1.35 × 0.98 m.

SIGNED: *Ant. Raf. M. . . Sassone*

CONDITION: very good. There were small paint losses throughout the canvas. Restored 1983.

PROVENANCE: presumably commissioned by the sitter in Rome, *circa* 1757-58, either this painting or the other signed version was seen by Horace Walpole in the house of the sitter's mother, Lady Anne Conolly, Grosvenor Square, London;[1] the Conolly family, Castletown, County Kildare; by descent to the 6th Lord Carew, Castletown, from whom purchased by the Hon. Desmond Guinness, Leixlip Castle, county Kildare, *circa* 1966, from whom purchased for the Gallery, April 1983, for £15,000.

EXHIBITED: 1984 Dublin *National Gallery of Ireland. Acquisitions 1982-83* (National Gallery of Ireland), no. 15.

VERSION: Christie's, 29 November 1974, lot 13, when bought by the late David Carritt, London.

Thomas Conolly was son of William Conolly, M.P., and grandnephew of William Conolly, Speaker of the Irish House of Commons, and builder of Castletown, a great mansion in County Kildare.

The sitter of this portrait was in Rome in the late 1750s, like so many other young Irishmen and Englishmen, finishing their education in a very agreeable fashion. The painting must have been executed when Conolly was about nineteen years of age, since we know that he was back at home in the second half of 1758, when he met, became engaged to, and married, on the 30th December 1758, Lady Louisa Lennox, sister of the Duchess of Leinster, who was staying at Carton, the adjoining fine estate which belonged to the Leinsters.[2] Conolly himself was M.P. for several years.

Mengs was clearly quite proud of the fact that he had been made an official court painter to the Elector of Saxony at Dresden, adding, in this instance, *Sassone* (Saxon) to his signature. In Rome Mengs was becoming quite a rival for Batoni in the painting of portraits of the Grand Tourists, although his long absences left plenty of custom for his rival from Lucca. Already a substantial number of sitters from these islands who had their portraits painted by Mengs has been found and documented.[3] Some sitters solved the problem of choosing by sitting to both Batoni and Mengs. Conolly, however, clearly made a deliberate decision, since a signed variant passed through the salesrooms relatively recently.[4]

At the bottom of the painting, behind the sitter, is a sculptured relief showing three figures; these represent Calliope, Urania, and Melpomene, three of the nine Muses; the figures were taken directly from the side of a sarcophagus which was in the Capitoline Museum, when Mengs painted this portrait; the sarcophagus is now in the Louvre, Paris.

Conolly's likeness is particularly well documented for an Irish sitter. For example, he was painted in 1764 by Sir Joshua Reynolds, in a half-length, now in the collection of Sir Alfred Beit, Bt., at Russborough, county Wicklow;[5] in 1768 he was included in *The*

Castletown Hunt, a large frieze-like pastel in black and white chalks, by Robert Healy;[6] in 1771 Hunter painted him in one of his highly distinctive small whole-length oils, which, in 1970, belonged to the Trustees of Mr and Mrs Julian Byng's Marriage Settlement;[7] in 1780 he was, of course, included by Francis Wheatley in his *Irish House of Commons,* now at Lotherton Hall, which is administered by Leeds City Art Galleries;[8] later R. Bull exhibited a miniature of him at the Royal Academy in 1796 (present whereabouts untraced); finally there is an amusing plaster bust of him incorporated into the stucco decoration of the main staircase of his own mansion, almost certainly the work of Filippo Lafranchini done in 1765.[9] Rarely has the physiognomy of an Irishman been so carefully recorded down through the decades of his manhood.

1. F. W. Hilles and P. B. Daghlian (edd.), H. Walpole, *Anecdotes of Painting in England,* vol. 5 (Yale 1937), p. 52.
2. B. Fitzgerald, *Lady Louisa Conolly 1743-1821. An Anglo-Irish Biography* (London and New York 1950), pp. 16-17.
3. F. Russell, 'The British Portraits of Anton Raphael Mengs' in *National Trust Studies 1979* (London 1978), pp. 9-19.
4. Originally in the collection of the Earl of Clancarty, this version was sold at Christie's, 29 November 1974, lot 13. The ex-Clancarty version most probably came into that family's possession when Henrietta Staples, Thomas Conolly's niece, married Richard de la Poer Trench, second Earl of Clancarty. After the death of their mother the young Staples girls lived almost entirely with their uncle and aunt at Castletown: B. Fitzgerald, *op. cit.,* p. 73.
5. A. Graves and W. V. Cronin, *A History of the Works of Sir Joshua Reynolds,* Vol. 1 (London 1899), p. 190.
6. D. Guinness and W. Ryan, *Irish Houses and Castles* (London 1971), p. 206. This pastel is now in the private collection of Paul Mellon, K.B.E., Upperville, Virginia.
7. Exhibition catalogue, A. Crookshank and The Knight of Glin, *Irish Portraits 1660-1860* (Dublin, London and Belfast, 1969-70), p. 46, no. 45.
8. M. Webster, *Francis Wheatley* (London 1970), p. 128, no. 33.
9. C. Palumbo-Fossati, *Gli stuccatori ticinesi Lafranchini in Inghilterra e in Irlanda nel secolo XVIII* (Lugano 1982), p. 79.

Attributed to MENGS

120 The Transfiguration (after Raphael) (Fig. 104)

Oil on canvas, 4.11 × 2.74. m.

CONDITION: apparently very good under heavy coats of discoloured varnish. The painting was taken down from exhibition in 1914 and placed in the stores.[1]

PROVENANCE: 'It was purchased by the Earl of Bristol in Rome more than one hundred years ago.'[2] Purchased in London in 1864.[3]

The painting is a life-size copy of Raphael's famous painting in the Pinacoteca Vaticana.[4] Mengs admired, in particular, three Italian painters, Raphael, Titian and Correggio. He was referred to as 'an idolator of Raphael' by Cumberland.[5] He painted several subject pictures for English patrons,[6] and also executed many portraits of English and Irish Grand Tourists.[7] With regard to no. 120 it is important to note that he was commissioned, in 1752, by Lord Northumberland to paint a life-size copy of Raphael's *School of Athens.*[8] This picture, signed and dated 1755, is now in the Victoria and Albert Museum,[9] and has been cleaned recently.

The documentation for no. 120 (see 'Provenance') leaves much to be desired with regard to precise information. If, however, what is stated is true, there is considerable reason for believing that no. 120 was a commissioned copy, and that Mengs was the artist.

1. National Gallery of Ireland Archives.
2. *National Gallery of Ireland Catalogue* (Dublin 1867), p. 87 (no source given).
3. No name of vendor given in Director's Annual Report for 1864: National Gallery of Ireland Archives.
4. Panel, 4.05 × 2.78 m. *Cf.* L. Dussler, *Raphael. A Critical Catalogue of his Pictures, Wall-Paintings and Tapestries* (London and New York 1971), pp. 52-54.
5. Quoted in J. N. D'Azara, *The Works of*

Antony Raphael Mengs, Vol. 1 (London 1796), p. 62.
6. J. N. D'Azara, *op. cit.*, vol. 1, reverse of Preface, p. 5.
7. F. Russell in *National Trust Studies 1979* (London 1978), pp. 9-19.
8. J. N. D'Azara, *op. cit.*, Vol. 1, pp. 12-13.
9. C. M. Kauffmann, *Victoria and Albert Museum. Catalogue of Foreign Paintings*, vol. 1, *Before 1800* (London 1973), pp. 188-90.

PIER FRANCESCO MOLA, Coldrerio, near Lugano 1612-1666 Rome

As an infant, Mola was brought to Rome by his parents who settled there. Among his artistic mentors was Cesare (Cavaliere) d'Arpino. Mola made a number of visits outside Rome, including a sojourn in Venice where he was very impressed by the great masters of the Venetian Cinquecento, and another sojourn in Bologna, where he was strongly influenced by Guercino, and the works of Albani. Basically, however, his career is as a painter in Rome, and he was elected President of the Accademia di San Luca in 1662.

1893 St. Joseph's dream (Fig. 105).

Oil on canvas, 1.915 × 1.595 m.

CONDITION: very good. The painting was restored in July 1969. Paint losses were minimal.

PROVENANCE: Cardinal Fesch sale, 1845, lot 1016;[1] Alessandro Aducci, Rome, from whom purchased 1856. One of sixteen paintings acquired for £1,700.

'. . . an angel of the Lord appeared in sleep to Joseph, saying, Arise, and take the child and his mother, and fly into Egypt: and be there until I shall tell thee. For it will come to pass that Herod will seek the child to destroy him.' (*Matthew*, ch. 2, vs. 13.)

The angel in no. 1893 may be compared with that in *The angel appearing to Hagar and Ishmael*, by Mola in the Galleria Colonna, Rome.[2] In both paintings the angel's wings' spatial effect is accentuated by the introduction of a swirling piece of drapery. Both paintings show a typical Mola device, the placing of an aura of light behind the wings and drapery, to emphasize their effect. Hagar's reclining pose is compositionally close to that of St. Joseph in no. 1893. Allowing for the fact that the Colonna painting has not been cleaned recently, the brown of Hagar's cloak must be rather close to that of St. Joseph.

In the church of S. Carlo al Corso, Rome, is a fine painting by Mola, *St. Barnabas preaching*.[3] The face of the first person to the right of St. Barnabas is virtually identical with the St. Joseph in no. 1893.

A drawing of an angel in the Nationalmuseum, Stockholm,[4] is worth mentioning as it shows the artist's approach to the depiction of these celestial beings.

Richard Cocke, on the basis of a photograph, does not accept the Dublin painting as autograph.[5] The painting was unknown to him when he was preparing his monograph.[6]

Arslan dates the Colonna painting to 1640-50,[7] while Cocke places it decidedly later: 1655-59.[8] Rudolf dates it precisely to 1647.[9] The comparison between the Colonna painting and the Dublin one is the most convincing argument for the authenticity of no. 1893.

Richard Cocke has kindly drawn the writer's attention to a drawing in the British Museum (1946-7-13-720), executed in red chalk, pen and ink. On the verso of this sheet are sketches for both a *Rest on the flight into Egypt* and a *St. Joseph's dream*;[10] it is conceivable that these very slight sketches are in some way connected with the genesis of no. 1893 (Fig. 106).

1. M. Wynne in *Gazette des Beaux-Arts*, vol. 89 (January 1977), p. 4.
2. E. A. Safarik, *Catalogo Sommario della Galleria Colonna in Roma: Dipinti* (Roma 1981), pp. 93-94, no. 123.
3. G. Drago and L. Salerno, *Ss. Ambrogio e Carlo al Corso* (Rome 1967), pp. 122-23.
4. Exhibition catalogue, *Italienska Barockteckningar* (Nationalmuseum, Stockholm, 1965), no. 106.
5. In correspondence, January 1977.
6. R. Cocke, *Pier Francesco Mola* (Oxford 1972).
7. W. Arslan in *Bolletino d'Arte*, N.S., vol. 8 (1928), p. 59.
8. R. Cocke, *op. cit.*, p. 55.
9. S. Rudolf in *Arte Illustrata*, vol. 5, no. 50 (1972), p. 348.
10. R. Cocke, *op. cit.*, p. 47, no. 12, and pl. 177.

BARTOLOMEO NAZARI, Clusone near Bergamo 1699-1758 Milan

Nazari studied in Venice under Vittore Ghislandi, and later in Rome under Francesco Trevisani. He settled in Venice where he developed a successful career as a portraitist.

261 Major General Christopher Nugent (d. 1742) (Fig. 108).

Oil on canvas, 0.74 × 0.58 m.

CONDITION: very good.

PROVENANCE: purchased, London, 1886, for £150.

The sitter, fifth son of John Nugent of Upper Killasonna, county Longford, and grandson of the Earl of Westmeath, was one of six brothers who served in the army of Charles II (reigned 1665-1700) in Spain. Christopher Nugent was subsequently in the service of the Venetian Republic for twenty-six years; he was given command of a regiment sixteen years before his death; subsequently he was made Governor of Corfu, then Peschiari, and finally Verona where he died in 1742.[1]

No. 261 had been accepted as a Pietro Longhi by Brosch.[2] Terisio Pignatti questioned this traditional attribution, feeling that the portrait was too formal; he wondered if it might not be by Bartolomeo Nazari.[3] Pignatti's reattribution is indeed convincing. Two signed Nazaris in England are useful for comparison. The background architectural treatment in both the portrait of Carlo Broschi (Il Farinelli)[4] and in that of Samuel Egerton[5] is very similar to the manner in which it is handled in no. 261. The parquet in no. 261 is treated like the paving in the portrait of Samuel Egerton. Although no. 261 is much smaller than the two portraits in England, the fashion in which the dress is painted is comparable. Nazari's portraits have a stylishness found throughout European court portraiture of the period, a characteristic lacking in Longhi's very personal and anecdotal style.

A date in the late 1730s is proposed for no. 261.

1. J. Lodge (revised by M. Archdall), *The Peerage of Ireland*, vol. 1 (Dublin 1789), p. 229.
2. L. Brosch, ''Pietro Longhi'' in Thieme-Becker, *Allgemeines Lexikon …*, vol. 23 (Leipzig 1929), p. 357.
3. T. Pignatti, *Pietro Longhi* (Venice 1968), p. 132.

4. Royal College of Music, London, 1734.
5. Tatton Park (National Trust), Cheshire: datable to 1732. *Cf.* exhibition catalogue, *Italian Art in Britain* (Royal Academy, London 1960), no. 207; and exhibition catalogue, *Souvenirs of the Grand Tour* (Wildenstein, London 1982), no. 36.

MARIO NUZZI, also known as MARIO DE' FIORI,
Penna *c.* 1603-1673 Rome

Nuzzi specialized in the painting of flowers, and much of his work consisted in collaborating with other painters in, for example, surrounding with garlands of flowers images of the Virgin and Child. He also painted still-life pictures with flowers, fruit and game. Among the artists with whom he worked was Carlo Maratti.

262 A lady, surrounded by a garland of flowers (Fig. 109).

Oil on canvas, 1.13 × 0.83 m.

CONDITION: very good.

PROVENANCE: anon. sale, Christie's, 12 December 1885, lot 76, where purchased for 9½ guineas.

This is a very typical example of the work of Nuzzi, also known as Mario dei Fiori (of the flowers). Nuzzi painted numerous images of the Virgin, of saints, of mythological gods, and portraits of people, surrounding all of them with splendid garlands of flowers. Many examples of his work are to be found in Roman churches. Particularly well known are the painted mirrors in the Saloon of the Galleria Colonna, Rome, where putti by Maratti are surrounded by Nuzzi's garlands of flowers.

ALESSANDRO VAROTARI called PADOVANINO,
Padua 1588-1648 Venice

Born in Padua, the son of a painter, Padovanino probably studied under Damiano Mazza. By 1614 he had settled in Venice, from which city he moved but little. Padovanino had a great admiration for the work of Titian, and may be regarded artistically as a lineal descendant of this great master. Padovanino occupies a rather special place in Venetian painting; he may be considered as unadventurous and out of step with the developments of some of his contemporaries. However, his interpretation of Titian, and his transmission of that master's art was to become a cornerstone for many of the leading Venetian artists of the second half of the seventeenth century.

87 Penelope bringing the bow of Odysseus to her suitors (Fig. 110).

Oil on canvas, 1.96 × 2.36 m.

CONDITION: excellent. Restored February-July 1975.

PROVENANCE: Monte di Pietà, Rome, whence acquired by Robert Macpherson, Rome, from whom purchased, 1856.[1] One of twenty-three paintings acquired for £1,483.

EXHIBITED: 1979 London *Venetian Seventeenth Century Painting* (National Gallery), no. 4.

The subject is very well described in the catalogue to Homan Potterton's exhibition at the National Gallery, London, in 1979, *Venetian Seventeenth Century Painting*: 'The picture was referred to as *Meleager* when it was in the Monte di Pietà in Rome in 1856, and at the National Gallery of Ireland it has always been called *Artemis appearing to Œneus*. The true subject was identified by Elizabeth McGrath as Penelope bringing the bow of Odysseus to her suitors (Homer, *Odyssey*, 21): when Odysseus had not returned after twenty years, his wife Penelope, prompted by Athene, went to her suitors and said, ''Hear me, ye proud wooers, who have beset this house to eat and drink ever without end since its master had long been gone. . . . I will set before you the great bow of divine Odysseus, and whosoever shall most easily string the bow in his hands and shoot an arrow through all twelve axes, with him will I go.'' The figure on the left may be intended to represent Odysseus's son Telemachus, and that in the centre Antinous, the chief of Penelope's suitors; axes appear in the foreground.'[2]

The attribution to Padovanino was on the picture when it came to Dublin in 1856, and there never has been any reason to doubt it.

Potterton has suggested a date in the 1620s, after the artist's return to Venice by 1615, and more particularly because of the similarity of the figure of Penelope to that of Roxana in *Eumanes and Roxana* which is in the Hermitage, Leningrad, which is datable about 1620.[3] This suggestion for no. 87 seems reasonable.

1. M. Wynne in *Gazette des Beaux-Arts*, vol. 89 (January 1977), p. 2.
2. H. Potterton, exhibition catalogue, *Venetian Seventeenth Century Painting* (National Gallery, London, 1979), p. 55. *Cf.* C. Valone in *Arte Veneta*, vol. 36 (1982), p. 161.
3. H. Potterton, *loc. cit.*

PAOLO PAGANI, Castello Valsolda 1661-1716 Milan

Pagani had a flourishing practice and studio in Venice; his main commissions were ecclesiastical. Later in Milan he painted frescos and altarpieces, and also did easel paintings for private collections.

Attributed to PAGANI

1086 Death of Lucretia (Fig. 111).

Oil on canvas, 0.97 × 1.35 m.

CONDITION: excellent. There were some very minor paint losses. Restored Summer 1968.

PROVENANCE: Milltown Collection; Milltown Gift, 1902.

Lucretia, the wife of a Roman nobleman, was raped by Sextus, son of the tyrant, Tarquin the Proud. Having written to her father and husband, she took her own life. This picture shows her, to the right hand side, reclining, with the dagger plunged deeply into the middle of her chest. On the left are two soldiers, perhaps Brutus and Collatinus, who swore revenge.

Cleaning made quite clear that the original attribution to Pietro da Cortona could not be sustained; subsequently it was put into the 1971 and 1981 catalogues as Attributed to Pagani. The painting has a rich impasto and strong colouring which suggest this master. In the Villa Bruzzo at Sant' Erasmo, Genoa, there is a painting, signed *Paganus*, depicting *Cimon in prison suckled by his daughter, Pero*.[1] The anatomical passages of this correspond very closely to those in no. 1086; moreover, the Cimon painting is remarkable for its strong purple-red, aquamarine, and silvery white.

The absence of further comparable works by Pagani of absolutely unequivocal authenticity make it imperative that the attribution of no. 1086 to this artist is decidedly qualified.

1. M. Bonzi in *L'Arte*, N.S. Vol. 6 (1935), pp. 219-221, and fig. 1.

IACOPO NEGRETTI PALMA, known as PALMA GIOVANE, Venice *c.*1548-1628 Venice

Palma Giovane was so called to distinguish him from his painter grand-uncle Palma Vecchio. Having worked in Urbino and Rome, Palma Giovane returned to Venice and went into Titian's studio. On his own, especially after the death of Titian in 1576, Palma received a large number of public commissions. He was a rapid worker and left behind him an extensive number of altarpieces as well as paintings for civic buildings.

68 Madonna and Child with saints and angels (Fig. 107).

Oil on canvas, 2.26 × 1.27 m. (arched top).

CONDITION: very good. There were numerous tiny paint losses. Restored between June 1975 and December 1980. To the original painting there had been added narrow strips to both sides and around the arched top. As these were clearly later, they were removed, and the painting was brought back to its original size.

PROVENANCE: ? Sanudo family, Venice; Cardinal Fesch sale, bt. Alessandro Aducci, Rome, from whom purchased, 1856.[1] One of sixteen paintings acquired for £1,700.

On the right is (?) St. George, in the centre St. Clare holding the sacred host of the Eucharist in a monstrance, and on the left an unknown saint wearing a chasuble and tonsure. Apart from St. Clare, the other saints are described as (?) St. Fermo and a Dominican, by N. Ivanoff and P. Zampetti.[2]

The attribution is the traditional one, and in recent years has been upheld by several leading specialists of Venetian painting of the period.

No. 68 has been dated around 1565/70 by Fritz Heinemann.[3] Much more convincing is Stefania Mason Rinaldi's proposal of the second decade of the seventeenth century,[4] thereby confirming in print her earlier suggestion of 'about 1620'.[5]

1. M. Wynne in *Gazette des Beaux-Arts,* vol. 89 (January 1977), pp. 2 and 5.
2. In *I Pittori Bergamaschi dal XIII al XIX Secolo. Il Cinquecento,* vol. III (Bergamo 1979), p. 537, no. 61.
3. In correspondence, August 1975.
4. S. M. Rinaldi in *Apollo,* vol. 110 (November 1979), p. 399.
5. In correspondence, January 1976.

GIOVANNI PAOLO PANINI, Piacenza *c.*1691-*c.*1765 Rome

After initial studies in his home city, Panini settled in Rome in 1711. He became undoubtedly the leading view painter in Rome in his time, with an unerring eye in the delineation of architectural elements, which suggests that he had training as an architectural draughtsman. He executed decorative schemes and series of events which were directly commissioned. He also painted many views and capricci *(imaginary compositions with various elements from monuments both old and new) which were readily available for supply to Grand Tourists.*

95 Fête in the Piazza Navona, Rome; to celebrate the birth of a Dauphin in France, 1729 (Fig. 112).

Oil on canvas, 1.09 × 2.46 m.

SIGNED: *I.P. Panini 1731*

CONDITION: very good. Restored 1968. There were many paint losses, but these were exaggerated by the fact that a previous restorer had restored the lacunae and overpainted considerable areas around them.

PROVENANCE: Cardinal Melchior de Polignac, by whom commissioned; the de Polignac family, from whom acquired by the 3rd Lord Ashburton; 4th Lord Ashburton sale, Christie's, 3 June 1871, lot 31, where purchased for 610 guineas.

EXHIBITED: 1882 London *Old Master Exhibition* (Burlington House), no. 209; 1911 Rome *La vita degli stranieri a Roma. Royal Commission International Exhibition, British Historical Section* (Castel Sant' Angelo); 1954/55 London *European Masters of the 18th Century* (Royal Academy) no. 368.

On 4 September 1729, a son and heir (known as a Dauphin) was born to Louis XV of France. In Rome the King's Ambassador, Cardinal Melchior de Polignac, arranged for the following November several celebrations, both religious and secular. The culminating festive occasion was a fireworks display in Piazza Navona. For the celebrations the Ambassador commissioned Pier Leone Ghezzi to decorate the Piazza with arches, trophies, and columns evocative of the time when it was the site of the stadium or circus of Domitian. The Ambassador commissioned from Panini a large painting of Piazza Navona with the preparations well advanced. This painting was given by Cardinal de Polignac to his King, and it subsequently became part of the foundation collection of the Louvre.[1] Most probably before parting with the original 1729 version, the Cardinal commissioned the Dublin version of 1731, which is virtually identical in size with that in the Louvre today. The Dublin canvas is not a laboured copy and between it and the Paris first version there are numerous minor variations, especially in the figures.[2] Some of the figures are quite scintillating with dresses worthy of a Watteau of the highest quality.

In the foreground of the canvas, almost at the centre, prominent in a group of people is a man dressed in black and wearing a black tricorne hat. He clearly wears the French order of the Holy Spirit. This man is the French Ambassador.

Somewhat behind this group, and to the viewer's right, is another with two children. The latter are Charles Edward (Bonnie Prince Charlie) and Henry (subsequently Cardinal, Duke of York), with their father James III, the Old Pretender. The exiled Stuarts were living in Rome at this time.

Other personalities may be identified, notably, to the left of the Stuart group, a pair representing Panini himself, and, most probably, Ghezzi.

The authenticity of no. 95 has never been questioned.

The only other known version is that primary one of 1729 in the Louvre, referred to above. The Arts Institute of Chicago has a small sketch in oils (Fig. 113) for a group of figures in the centre foreground (no. 33.914), most probably executed before either of the complete pictures.[3] A preparatory drawing is in the de Polés Collection in Paris.[3]

Another preparatory drawing for part of the painting is in the Berlin Print Room (no. 17532).[5] Yet another is in a private collection in Parma.[6] These studies are equally applicable to the Louvre and Dublin versions. However, it was the Dublin version, which has more figures, that was engraved by C. N. Cochin in 1735, and later by Tilly and Smeeton.

1. F. Arisi, *Gian Paolo Panini* (Piacenza 1961), p. 138, no. 78.
2. *Ibid.*, p. 143, no. 85.
3. *Ibid.*, p. 138, no. 77.
4. *Ibid.*, p. 139, no. 78.
5. *Ibid.*,
6. *Ibid.*

725 The Colosseum and the Arch of Constantine (Fig. 114).

Oil on canvas, 0.73 × 0.99 m.

SIGNED: *I.P. Panini Romae 1740*

CONDITION: excellent. Restored May 1970.

PROVENANCE: this and the three following works by Panini were most probably purchased in Rome by Joseph Leeson, subsequently 1st Earl of Milltown, in 1744; Milltown Collection; Milltown Gift, 1902.

This scene was portrayed several times by Panini and on more than one occasion it was a pendant to a view of the Roman Forum.[1] The prominent statue being admired on the left is a representation of the Borghese gladiator,[2] the marble statue now in the Louvre.

1. F. Arisi, *Gian Paolo Panini* (Piacenza 1961), pp. 162-63, no. 138.
2. F. Haskell and N. Penny, *Taste and the Antique* (New Haven and London 1981), *praesertim* pp. 221-24.

726 The Roman Forum (Fig. 115).

Oil on canvas, 0.73 × 0.99 m.

SIGNED: *I. P. Panini 1740.*

CONDITION: excellent. Restored February 1970.

PROVENANCE: see preceding entry. Milltown Collection; Milltown Gift, 1902.

The descriptive view of the Roman Forum looking from North to South is combined with a certain introduction of elements of the classical ideal. Included is a representation of the famous marble Borghese vase, now in the Louvre, to which handles have been added.[1] The three large columns to the left of the vase are the remains of the Temple of Castor and Pollux. Panini painted several views of the Forum.[2]

1. F. Haskell and N. Penny, *Taste and the Antique* (New Haven and London 1981), *praesertim* pp. 314-15.
2. F. Arisi, *Gian Paolo Panini* (Piacenza 1961), p. 162, no. 137.

727 Roman ruins with fifteen figures (Fig. 116).

Oil on canvas, 0.73 × 0.99 m.

SIGNED: *I.P. Panini 1740*

CONDITION: excellent. Restored February 1970.

PROVENANCE: see entry on no. 725 preceding. Milltown Collection; Milltown Gift, 1902.

In his lifetime Panini was already famous for paintings combining a number of identifiable Roman buildings or monuments.[1] In this typical and high quality example the two outstanding features are the round temple of Vesta and the pyramid of Cestius.

It is not possible to prove that the figures in such works were intended to do more than people the scenes. On occasion attempts have been made to give them a religious or historical significance, but such attempts have not been convincing.

1. F. Arisi, *Gian Paolo Panini* (Piacenza 1961), pp. 167-68, no. 153.

728 Roman ruins with eleven figures. (Fig. 117).

Oil on canvas, 0.73 × 0.99 m.

SIGNED: I.P. Panini 1740

CONDITION: excellent. Restored February 1970.

PROVENANCE: See entry on no. 725 preceding. Milltown Collection; Milltown Gift, 1902.

This is another of Panini's typically free compositions, but differs from the preceding example in so far as the main architectural feature has not been identified nor has the imposing vase with the relief of dancing maidens, which Panini included in other paintings.[1]

1. F. Arisi, *Gian Paolo Panini* (Piacenza 1961), p. 168, no. 154.

Style of PANINI

1531 Ruins with figures (Fig. 118).

Oil on canvas, 0.71 × 0.98 m.

CONDITION: moderate.

PROVENANCE: Sir A. Chester Beatty, Dublin, by whom presented, 1954.

This picture does not have the quality of a genuine Panini, but is similar in style to some of his early work, when he painted in a manner close to Giovanni Ghisolfi.

FRANCESCO PASCUCCI, *fl.* 1787-1803.

Very little is known about Pascucci who reputedly was a Roman. His principal works are two altarpieces in the Cathedral of Livorno and another now in the National Gallery of Ireland. The Musée de Draguignan, in the Var, France, has a portrait by Pascucci of M. Fauchet, the Prefect who was responsible for the founding of the library and the museum at Draguignan.

1918 Adoration of the shepherds (Fig. 122).

Oil on walnut panel, 2.73 × 1.80 m.

SIGNED: *Fran. Pascucci 17..*

CONDITION: excellent. Restored June-July 1971. There were some very minor paint losses.

PROVENANCE: In Parma (?). Cardinal Fesch, at whose sale, Rome, 1843 (there was no catalogue for this portion of the Fesch sale); bought by Alessandro Aducci, Rome, from whom acquired 1856. One of sixteen paintings purchased for £1,700.

This painting was sold to the Gallery as a Rondani[1] and was so attributed in the early catalogues of the Gallery. The change to Pascucci was made following the discovery of a signature in the course of cleaning, in 1971.

It is not possible to suggest a precise date for this painting because so little is known about the artist and his works.

1. National Gallery of Ireland Archives. *Cf.* M. Wynne in *Paragone*, no. 297 (November 1974), pp. 56-58, and *Id.* in *Gazette des Beaux-Arts*, vol. 89 (January 1977), pp. 2 & 5.

LORENZO PASINELLI, Bologna 1629-1700 Bologna

Pasinelli studied under Simone Cantarini and, later, under Flaminio Torri. By the age of thirty he was certainly working on his own. He worked in Mantua, Turin and Rome, but for very short periods.

1335 The Muse of Sculpture (Fig. 120).

Oil on canvas, 0.93 × 0.735 m.

CONDITION: excellent.

PROVENANCE: acquired in Rome, from an undisclosed source, by Robert Macpherson, from whom purchased, 1856, one of twenty-three paintings bought for £1,483.[1]

Acquired as a work by Peruzzi, it was catalogued as such in catalogues down to and including the 1874 edition. It was omitted from the 1879 and subsequent editions, until its reinstatement in the 1971 and 1981 catalogues as Italian School. Federico Zeri, visiting the Gallery in 1973, attributed no. 1335 to the Neapolitan School, and more particularly to Conca. This is quite unacceptable; the solution must be found in the Bolognese School. The name of Lorenzo Pasinelli can be put forward with reasonable confidence. In 1959 Peter Claas of London had a Pasinelli, *Cupid being disarmed by Diana's nymphs.*[2] In this the head of the figure plucking an arrow from Cupid's quiver is seen in profile. The model for this could well be the same as that for *The Muse of Sculpture*. The hair of both figures referred to is tied in a very like fashion. In addition, the cherub or putto being carved by Sculpture is handled in a manner very close to Cupid in the Claas picture, especially if one allows for the difference between the representation of an animate and inanimate figure.

Another painting which is helpful in supporting the attribution of no. 1335 to Pasinelli is *Judith meeting Holofernes*, in the collection of Count Girolamo De Bosdari, Bologna.[3] The grip with which Holofernes holds his baton, and the modelling of the hand and fingers is stylistically very similar to the way in which Sculpture grips her hammer.

Further support for the attribution to Pasinelli of no. 1335 is to be found by examining Roli's engraving after Pasinelli's (?) *Pittura* (a print drawn to the writer's attention by David Scrase). The profile of the allegorical figure in the print (she holds no painter's attributes) shows a bold line like that in no. 1335. Similar in both works is the manner in which the hair is gathered. There is an impression of the print in the British Museum (1874-8-8-737) (Fig. 119).

Chromatically there is a very useful comparison to be found in an altarpiece in the Basilica of San Petronio, Bologna. It hangs on the right hand wall in the chapel off the right aisle used for the reservation of the Blessed Sacrament (1983), and depicts *St. Anthony raising to life a man dead and buried*. In the centre there are passages of grey and blue-grey comparable to those colours used in no. 1335.

On the basis of Roli's account of the development of Pasinelli's work, and of his biography, a date in the 1680s would be plausible.[4]

1. M. Wynne, in *Gazette des Beaux-Arts*, vol. 89 (January 1977), p. 2.
2. Exhibition catalogue, *Maestri della Pittura del Seicento Emiliano* (Palazzo dell'Archiginnasio, Bologna, 1959), no. 77. The painting was subsequently acquired by Brinsley Ford, London. D. C. Miller, in *The Burlington Magazine*, vol. 101 (March 1959), pp. 106-09; p. 104, fig. 27.

3. Exhibition catalogue cited, no. 74. D. C. Miller, in *The Burlington Magazine*, vol. 101 (June 1959), p. 211; p. 208, fig. 8.
4. R. Roli, *Pittura Bolognese 1650-1800. Dal Cignani ai Gandolfi* (Bologna 1977), pp. 93-94; 284-85.

Attributed to PASINELLI
1740 Albunea, the Tiburtine Sibyl (Fig. 121).

Oil on canvas, 0.94 × 0.74 m.

INSCRIBED ON SCROLL: *NASCETUR DE VIRGINE* (He shall be born from a virgin).

CONDITION: very good. The paint is beginning to lift; consequently restoration is required.

PROVENANCE: acquired in Rome, from an undisclosed source, by Robert Macpherson, from whom purchased, 1856. One of 23 paintings bought for £1,483.[1]

A sibyl was a prophetic female in classical times. At first there was only one, associated with various locations at different times. She became pluralized. The influence of Jewish and Christian interpolations of Sibylline books, combined with the prophecy of the Cumaean Sibyl in Virgil's fourth *Eclogue* to give to all the sibyls a position in Christian literature and art somewhat similar to that accorded to the prophets of the Old Testament.

The fourth *Eclogue,* written in 40 B.C., looked forward to the birth of a child coincident with a new era which would fulfil the yearning of many nations for peace and happiness. Many Christian writers subsequently interpreted this writing as a prophecy of the birth of Christ, without attempting to have it inserted in the canon of Sacred Scripture. While not quite as widely known as Virgil's fourth *Eclogue,* but nonetheless extensively narrated was the revelation of Albunea, the Tiburtine Sibyl (of Tivoli, 18 miles east-north-east of Rome). To her is attributed the foretelling of the virgin birth of someone very special. Such Christian interpretations of passages of pagan literature are analogous to the adaptations of pagan feasts in the early days of Christianity. The most famous of the latter is the fixing of Christmas on the day of celebration of the pagan *Natalis solis invicti* (the [re]birth of the invincible sun.)

The same Sibyl is the subject of a half-length oil by Elisabetta Sirani (signed and dated 1660) in the Pinacoteca Nazionale, Bologna. In this a cherub holds a scroll with the same Latin inscription as in No. 1740.

Acquired as a work by Peruzzi, it was catalogued as such in catalogues down to and including the 1874 edition. It was omitted from the 1879 edition and following editions, until its reinstatement in the 1963 edition, again as a Peruzzi. In the 1971 and 1981 editions it was inserted as Italian School. An attribution to Lorenzo Pasinelli is proposed here, on the basis of comparison with a number of paintings reliably attributed to that Bolognese master. In 1968 the Heim Gallery, London, exhibited a small painting of *Apollo.*[2] There are between this and no. 1740 slightly comparable facial characteristics, but very strong links in the fashion in which the areas of light cede to shade. These are particularly noticeable in the handling of the right arm of Apollo and that of both arms in no. 1740. Drapery is treated in closely resembling manner in both paintings.

In a private collection in Bologna is an allegory of *Astronomy.*[3] This painting is stronger in chiaroscuro than no. 1740, but the transition from light to shade in the modelling is very comparable. Both paintings share a slightly cavalier approach to the handling of drapery, except where the artist is apparently concerned, in both of these paintings, in the headdress.

The draperies of no. 1740 compare very closely with those of the *Madonna* in the Liechtenstein Collection at Vaduz.[4] In this, as in the preceding comparison, one notices how Pasinelli usually gives a very narrow cuff to the sleeves, and a narrow white highlight around the neck of the upper garment, which sometimes reveals an undergarment.

Yet another similar work of Pasinelli is *The Sibyl* at the Fitzwilliam Museum, Cambridge.[5]

This painting, which should respond well to cleaning, while of very simple composition shows clearly the characteristics of Pasinelli's work as mentioned above. It seems clear that Pasinelli painted numerous allegories and sibyls. For example, a fine *Sibilla* (0.72 × 0.59 m.) was advertised in the March 1973 issue of *The Burlington Magazine,* by the Galleria del Caminetto, Bologna; *A Sibyl,* apparently of rather indifferent quality, was sold at Christie's, 18 May 1979, lot 141; also showing the artist's interest in this type of subject matter is the red chalk drawing, *Allegory of Poetry,* after Pasinelli, in the Royal Library, Windsor Castle, No. 0253.[6]

Sir Denis Mahon is of the opinion that no. 1740 should be located in the Roman School,[7] but that is difficult to sustain. Andrea Emiliani accepts the work as Bolognese, suggesting that it comes from the circle of Giuseppe Marchesi (1699-1771).[8] In the *Genre scene* by Marchesi, in a pivate collection in Rome,[9] the head of the central female figure and the head-dress of the man on the right hand side bear comparison with no. 1740. In *Solomon worshipping idols* in the Morini Collection, Bologna,[10] a work datable to *circa* 1730, the head of the female figure on the extreme right hand side is closely comparable to no. 1740.

Locating no. 1740 in the circle of Marchesi would make the painting at least about thirty years later than situating it among the late works of Pasinelli. Perhaps complete restoration of the picture will help towards a more precise attribution. In the meantime one may leave it closer to Pasinelli.

A date in the 1680's is tentatively proposed. The *Magdalen* pendant to the Liechtenstein *Madonna* is signed and dated 1685.

1. M. Wynne in *Gazette des Beaux-Arts*, vol. 89 (January 1977), p. 2.
2. Exhibition catalogue 1968 London *Baroque Paintings, Sketches and Sculptures for the Collector* (Heim Gallery), no. 19.
3. R. Roli, *Pittura Bolognese 1650-1800. Dal Cignani ai Gandolfi* (Bologna 1977), p. 94, fig. 97a.
4. R. Roli, *op. cit.*, p. 94, fig. 93b.
5. J. W. Goodison and G. H. Robertson, *Fitzwilliam Museum Cambridge. Catalogue of Paintings*, vol. 2, *Italian Schools* (Cambridge 1967), p. 128, no. 137.
6. O. Kurz, *Bolognese Drawings of the XVII and XVIII Centuries . . . at Windsor Castle* (London 1955), no. 333.
7. In correspondence, April 1982.
8. In correspondence, September 1982.
9. R. Roli, *op. cit.*, fig. 256a.
10. R. Roli, *op. cit.*, fig. 254a.

ALBERTO PASINI, Busseto 1826-1899 Cavoretto

Pasini studied at the Academy of Fine Arts in Parma, the nearest centre to his place of birth. He specialized in lithography, and published an illustrated book on the architecture and history of Parma and the surrounding area. In 1851 he went to Paris where he took lessons from Cicéri, Isabey and Rousseau.

Having been introduced to the diplomat Prosper Bourré, Pasini was invited to accompany him on his official mission to the Shah of Persia, where his role was to explain France's position in the Crimea. Setting out in March 1855, the journey took Pasini through Egypt, Saudi Arabia, and the South Yemen. Pasini spent a year and a half in Teheran, and was in the Shah's entourage during many journeys within Persia; the Shah acquired several of Pasini's works. The artist returned to Paris late in 1856; he exhibited many oriental scenes at the Salons.

In 1868 Pasini paid an extended visit to Constantinople, returning in 1869. In 1873 the artist visited Asia Minor, Syria, and the Lebanon. In 1879, and again in 1883, he travelled in Spain in the company of the French orientalist, J.-L. Gérôme.

Having achieved success, and a certain financial independence, he acquired a villa near Turin at Cavoretto; he divided his time between this and Paris, before finally settling at Cavoretto where he took a direct interest in the agricultural aspect of his property as well as continuing to paint.

4269CB   An Arab soldier seated by a doorway (Fig. 123).

Oil on canvas, 0.41 × 0.34 m.

SIGNED: *A. Pasini.*

CONDITION: excellent.

PROVENANCE: Sir Alfred Chester Beatty, by whom presented to the Irish nation, 1950. Deposited at the National Gallery of Ireland by the Government.

Unfortunately it has not been possible, to date, to locate this scene precisely. It does, however, demonstrate clearly the artist's abiding interest in architectural detail and subtle lighting effects. It is also clear how Pasini recorded accurately local dress, and, in this case, the soldier's weaponry.

Since Pasini executed so many of his paintings from studies made during his travels after his return to his studio, it is not possible to suggest a date for no. 4269CB.

4271CB   An eastern scene (Fig. 124).

Oil on canvas, 0.22 × 0.16 m.

SIGNED: *A. Pasini 1888*

CONDITION: excellent.

PROVENANCE: Sir Alfred Chester Beatty, by whom presented to the Irish nation, 1950. Deposited at the National Gallery of Ireland by the Government.

To date, the subject of this delightful little picture has not been precisely located; there are in it, however, sufficient distinctive features to make one hopeful that the precise place shown will be identified before too long.

Pasini's preoccupation with recording accurately architectural features and local lighting effects is abundantly clear.

Given the late date of the picture, it is almost certain that the artist executed this work during his active retirement, from a sketch taken during one of his visits to the Orient.

GIOVANNI BATTISTA PASSERI, Rome *c.*1610-1679 Rome

This artist is known to more people as the author of a work on the lives of seventeenth century artists in Rome than as a painter. A follower of Domenichino, and indeed his successor as President of the Academy of St. Luke, Passeri painted portraits, still-life and religious paintings, as well as historical ones. Late in life he took holy orders, and was attached to the church of S. Maria in via Lata.

993   Party feasting in a garden (Fig. 126).

Oil on canvas, 0.76 × 0.615 m.

SIGNED: *Io: Baptista Passarus Rom Facie. a.*

CONDITION: very good. Restored 1983 (Fig. 125).

PROVENANCE: Messrs Sabin Ltd., London; Messrs P. & D. Colnaghi Ltd., London, from whom purchased, 1937, for £170.

EXHIBITED: 1958 Belfast *Loan Collection from The National Gallery of Ireland* (Belfast Museum and Art Gallery); 1985 London *Masterpieces from The National Gallery of Ireland* (National Gallery), no. 7.

The bacchic fountain figure on the right hand side, the urn looming up in the background to the right of centre, and the statue of a man at the left hand side, were all revealed in the 1983 restoration. None of the sculptures appears to represent a well-known piece. The most likely reason for their having been over-painted is the fact that they do not improve the picture's composition. In fact they lead towards a slight feeling of clutter.

Inscribed on the pedestal of the statue on the left hand side: *DMS* which stand for *Dis Manibus Sacrum* (sacred to the gods of the underworld). The end of the table faces the viewer and on its carved support is a shield decorated with flowers and bearing the motto *cadun./etremanent* (they fall and yet remain). When writing about the painting Anne Crookshank suggested that this inscription might refer to the flowers, but on balance felt that, despite its rather insignificant position, it should be related to the *DMS* before Passeri's signature.[1] The serious expression on the faces of those feasting, noted by Crookshank, would seem to be at odds with the concept of a meal out of doors, and the use of musical instruments. The full meaning of the subject remains elusive. It may lie somewhere along the lines of a family ceremonial banquet in memory of a deceased relative.

Sergio Benedetti, verbally, made an interesting suggestion that some of the words which Passeri used in his life of Pietro Testa might well be applicable to Passeri's own painting (and indeed to the Suida Manning Collection picture referred to below): 'My opinion would be that in the depiction of stories or narratives, either religious or non-religious, one should never introduce personal poetical concepts, in order to avoid confusing the general public; such additions might be permitted, however, in the treatment of fables or idealizations.' (a free translation from Passeri).[2] The picture catalogued here may fall into the latter category.

Purchased as an Italian seventeenth century painting, no firm attribution was proposed until Anne Crookshank read the inscription style signature correctly when the picture was on loan to the Belfast Museum and Art Gallery (now the Ulster Museum) in 1958.[3] Her reading was confirmed by infra-red photography.

The Dublin Passeri remains at present his only known signed work in oils. It served as the basis for the firm attribution to him of a somewhat larger painting, *Musical party in a garden* (oil on canvas, 0.736 × 0.990 m.), in the Robert and Bertina Suida Manning Collection, New York.[4] As in the Dublin painting, the setting in the Suida Manning Collection painting is festive and out of doors. The latter shows several people playing musical instruments in the garden of a villa. Conspicuous among those not playing a musical instrument is a gentleman at the extreme right hand side of the painting (dressed in the same style as the elegant male figures in no. 993) with his right hand outstretched pointing to the activities taking place. The walls are studded with classical reliefs. There is a classical statue in the centre, there are other classical pedestals, and further statuary, the visible leg of the key-board instruments is carved with a pair of crouching figures back to back; in short the painting makes a cogent statement, whose exact meaning can not be explained at present. This is a quality which it shares with the Dublin canvas, being perhaps more enigmatic with the introduction of classical attire for some of the figures. Spike says of the New York picture: 'As a more ambitious conception, this *Musical party in a garden* affords us our first good glimpse into the artistic career of Passeri.'[5] The composition is more extensive, and the canvas about sixty percent larger, but there is no change in quality. Surely that 'first good glimpse . . .' came when Crookshank detected the signature on the Dublin painting.[6]

Very recently, Zeri published three additions to the tiny known *oeuvre* of Passeri.[7]

1. A. Crookshank in *The Burlington Magazine,* Vol. 106 (April 1964), pp. 179-80.
2. G. B. Passeri, *Vite De' Pittori, Scultori, ed Architetti che anno lavorato in Roma, Morti dal 1641 fino al 1673* (Rome 1772), p. 184.
3. Crookshank, *loc. cit.*
4. J. T. Spike, Exhibition catalogue, *Italian Baroque Paintings from New York Private Collections* (The Art Museum, Princeton University, 1980), no. 31.
5. *Ibid.*
6. Crookshank, *loc. cit.*
7. F. Zeri, in *Paragone,* no. 427 (September 1985), pp. 41-46.

GIOVANNI ANTONIO PELLEGRINI, Venice 1675-1741 Venice

Pellegrini studied with Paolo Pagani, but was also clearly influenced by other painters like Sebastiano Ricci. In 1704 he married Rosalba Carriera's sister. Pellegrini made working visits to England twice, and also executed commissions in Düsseldorf, the Low Countries, and Paris. His Rococo style anticipates the work of Tiepolo.

467 Bathsheba (Fig. 127).

Oil on canvas, 1.27 × 1.013 m.

CONDITION: excellent.

PROVENANCE:John Orpin, Dublin, by whom presented, 1897.

One evening King David was walking on the roof of his palace when he saw a beautiful woman washing herself. On enquiry he found out that she was the daughter of Eliam, and the wife of Uriah the Hittite. He sent messengers to fetch her and they became lovers. Bathsheba bore David a son, who died, and later, after David had arranged for her husband to be killed on the battle-field, another son, Solomon. In this painting Bathsheba is shown at her toilet, with a young girl holding a mirror and a young black page holding an urn. Looking over the parapet of the building behind, on the left, is the tiny figure of King David. (2 *Samuel* ch. 11, vs. 2 ff.).

First catalogued as School of Tiepolo, it continued to be so attributed in the catalogues until the 1963 edition. It was recognized as a Pellegrini as least as early as the late 1940s.[1]

The picture has been convincingly dated to the earlier part of Pellegrini's first English visit *c.*1708-11, by Eric Young.[2]

A Pellegrini of *Bathsheba* in the Luigi Rocchetti Collection, Rome, is quite like no. 467; compositionally it is reversed, and the black page holds the mirror instead of the young girl attendant.[3] Also similar is the *Bathsheba* in the collection of Roger Lazzarelli, Geneva. This is composed in the same direction as no. 467; the black page holds the mirror, but a third attendant is introduced, namely a girl behind Bathsheba carrying a basket of flowers.

1. National Gallery of Ireland Archives.
2. E. Young in *Apollo*, vol. 89 (March 1969), pp. 197-98.
3. *The Connoisseur*, Vol. 142, (August 1958), p. 4, and ill. p. 5, fig. 5. In this the title 'The Toilet of Venus' is incorrectly used. Eric Young in *Apollo, loc. cit.*, describes it correctly.

1938   Susanna and the Elders (Fig. 128).

Oil on canvas, 1.225 × 1.043 m.

CONDITION: very good. Restored November 1969-April 1970. There were some areas of paint loss, especially around the edges. More paint loss was found above Susanna's head, and in the bottom right hand corner.

PROVENANCE: Viscount Harberton. In 1859, John James (Pomeroy), 5th Viscount Harberton, 1790-1862, loaned his collection of paintings to the Irish Institution, giving his permission to have them exhibited. The Institution included many of them in their Winter Exhibition, held at the premises of the Royal Hibernian Academy. In the catalogue of that exhibition there is no painting described which could be correlated with no. 1938. An old label bearing Harberton's name, the Institution's name and the number 40, was attached to the old stretcher of no. 1938. No. 40 in the 1859 exhibition was: N. Maes, *Portrait of a Little Girl with Flowers*. Presumably all Lord Harberton's loans to the Irish Institution were given a number, even if some of them were not exhibited. As yet, it has not been possible to ascertain when this Pellegrini, no. 1938, came to the Gallery from the Harberton Collection.

Susanna was the beautiful wife of Joachim, a prominent man in Babylon. One hot day while she was washing herself in the garden two Elders, who had hidden themselves, came forward and tried to seduce her. She refused, and cried out so that her handmaids came out to her aid. (Deuterocanonical book: *Susanna: Daniel*, ch. 13).

The attribution to Pellegrini is quite clear.

Despite the lack of detailed knowledge about the painting's provenance, stylistically it is reasonable to suggest a date similar to no. 467 above, namely *c.*1708-11. It differs chromatically from no. 467 with its extensive areas of silvery white and the highlights on the Elders' garments, as well as the tree trunk. There is even more of this light colour than in the *Rebecca at the well*, in the National Gallery, London (no. 6332).

On 18 June 1982, as lot 49 (oil on canvas, 1.345 × 1.06 m.), Christie's, New York, auctioned a replica of no. 1938, as a Pellegrini. However, to judge from a photograph, the laboured facture makes it most unlikely that this is an original work by the artist.

On 29 May 1929, Wertheim, Berlin, sold the collection of Joseph Cremer of Dortmund. Lot 138 was a *Susanna and the Elders* by Pellegrini (oil on canvas, 1.10 × 0.92 m.). Its present location is unknown to the writer. A photograph suggests that it would be very interesting to be able to compare this painting more closely with no. 1938, since compositionally it is almost a mirror image, with variations.

Attributed to PELLEGRINI

1999 Allegory of Justice (Fig. 129).

Oil on canvas, 1.055 × 0.89 m.

CONDITION: the painting is covered with heavy layers of darkened varnish, and requires cleaning and conservation.

PROVENANCE: unknown.

The painting represents a complex allegory around Justice, who has the traditional attributes of a sword and scales, and is blindfolded. Standing on the left is Prudence, with snake and mirror. Standing on the right is Truth, holding a sun in her right hand at which she gazes, and holding an open book in her left hand.[1] The figure kneeling at the right hand side, holding a branch of what appears to be fir, poses a problem; what does she personify? Quite clearly the painting does not represent the cardinal virtues. On the other hand the dominance of Justice among virtues is not surprising, since Justice is often regarded as regulating the working of all other virtues.

The painting was not included in any of the Gallery's catalogues until those of 1971 and 1981 in which it was inserted as French School, following a suggestion by Pierre Rosenberg, on a visit to the Gallery. On a more recent visit he agreed with the growing consensus of opinion that it should be considered Venetian. In its present condition it is difficult to be very precise about an attribution; however because of the style and texture of the paint it may prove to be an early work by Pellegrini.

1. Truth was identified by Jennifer Montagu, who also, with colleagues at the Warburg Institute, endeavoured to elucidate the fourth enigmatic personage.

PENSIONANTE DEL SARACENI, active in Rome 1610-1620

This artist's name is the creation of Roberto Longhi,[1] who wished to group together a small number of paintings which had common characteristics, but for whom no actual name could be found. As the sobriquet indicates, the artist is supposed to have been a lodger in Saraceni's house but there is absolutely no proof of this.[2]. There is now a general consensus that Pensionante del Saraceni was French, because of nuances of the French approach to Caravaggism.[3] This is not surprising, since Saraceni is known to have been a francophile. Endorsing Ottani Cavina's opinion Nicolson and Wright have written of the Pensionante that ''He is a close follower of Caravaggio, probably active in Rome in the second and third decades of the seventeenth century, and possibly French. . . .''[4] The curious thing is that more than forty years since Longhi's study a mere six paintings (of one a couple of versions) are known.[5]

1178   St. Peter denying Christ (Fig. 135).

Oil on canvas, 1.044 m. × 1.33 m.

CONDITION: very good. Restored 1984. A strip, measuring between 3.5 and 4.5 cm, along the top edge of the painting had been added in the course of a much earlier restoration.

PROVENANCE: the Marquess of Sligo, Westport House, county Mayo; Lord Terence Morris Browne, Westport House, county Mayo; Lady Isabel Mary Peryonnet Browne, Mount Browne, Guildford, Surrey; F.A. Drey, London, from whom purchased, 1948, for £350.

EXHIBITED: 1985 London *Masterpieces from the National Gallery of Ireland* (National Gallery), no. 5.

After the arrest of Christ, while he was being questioned in the high priest's house, St Peter and some of the apostles stood outside in the hall. A maid recognized St. Peter and went over to him. She challenged him as being one of Christ's followers. St. Peter denied this. *(Luke,* ch. 22, vs. 54 ff).

Nicolson and Wright,[6] and Rosenberg[7] originally described the subject as being Job mocked by his wife, but the current consensus of scholars, including Rosenberg himself,[8] is that the title used above is correct.

First entered in the manuscript catalogue of the Gallery as Attributed to Caravaggio, it remained so described until the 1971 catalogue. It was Benedict Nicolson who first suggested Pensionante del Saraceni, during a visit to Dublin in September 1968.

After due consideration, and having inspected the picture, Rosenberg believes that no. 1178 'is merely a very good workshop replica.'[9] It may seem a little strange that an obscure artist, although decidedly an artist of quality, whose known *oeuvre* amounts to six works and one autograph replica, should have had a workshop.

The autograph prototypes of no. 1178 are considered to be that in the Pinacoteca Vaticana, and the canvas recently acquired by the Musée de la Chartreuse, Douai (formerly in the Count Terzi collection Rome, and later with Paul Rosenberg and Co., New York, in 1981).[10]

Before relegating no. 1178 to the status of 'merely a very good workshop replica' one should have another good hard look at it. In the first place St. Peter's right shoulder reveals a small piece of white undergarment which is not to be found in either the Vatican or Douai versions; Peter's waist-band differs considerably in detail from the treatment of that area in the two accepted autograph versions, especially where it is gathered at his right side, at the point closest to the viewer. St. Peter's left hand is vibrantly painted, with details significantly different to the other two versions, notably the index finger. Even before the strip was added at the top edge, in the Dublin painting the maid-servant's head-dress was complete, unlike its truncation in the other two versions; additionally the Dublin picture has more space to the right of the maid-servant. These features combined with

94

the fresh handling and spontaneity of no. 1178, all the more evident since the 1984 restoration, compel one to reject its categorization as 'merely a very good workshop replica' and propose that it is in fact an autograph version in its own right.

About a version formerly in the Rivera Schreiber collection, now known only through a photograph in the Witt Library, London, no useful comment may be made at this point. Less important versions, probably copies, are those recorded in a private collection in Rome (in 1948), and in the Galleria Quixote, Madrid (in 1965).

1. R. Longhi, in *Proporzioni*, vol. 1 (1943), pp. 5 ff.
2. A. Ottani Cavina, *Carlo Saraceni* (Milan 1968), p. 49.
3. P. Rosenberg in exhibition catalogue, *The Age of Caravaggio* (Metropolitan Museum of Art, New York, and Museo Nazionale di Capodimonte, Naples, 1985), p. 167: this is the most authoritative *status quaestionis* on the Pensionante, to date.
4. B. Nicolson and C. Wright, *Georges de La Tour* (London 1974), p. 33.
5. P. Rosenberg, *loc. cit.*
6. B. Nicolson and C. Wright, *loc. cit.*
7. P. Rosenberg in exhibition catalogue, *France in the Golden Age; Seventeenth-Century French Paintings in American Collections* (Metropolitan Museum of Art, New York, 1982), p. 298.
8. P. Rosenberg, in *The Age of Caravaggio, loc. cit.*
9. *Ibid.*
10. P. Rosenberg in *La Revue du Louvre et des Musées de France*, (1983), p.355.

GIOVANNI BATTISTA PIAZZETTA, Venice 1683-1754 Venice

Piazzetta studied to be a painter under Antonio Molinari and the Bolognese artist Giuseppe Maria Crespi. Back in Venice he received many commissions for work in churches. He also did a small number of non-religious subject paintings, a number of portraits, and many book illustrations. Many of his works are characterized by a rich impasto and a delight in chiaroscuro.

Studio of PIAZZETTA

656 A pastoral outing (Fig. 130).

Oil on canvas, 2.10 m. × 1.50 m.

CONDITION: good. Restored June-July 1971. The surface impasto had been rather flattened due, doubtlessly, to an earlier relining.

PROVENANCE: Marchesi Guidi di Faenza sale, Sangiorgio, Rome, 21 27 April 1902, lot 414; Sir Hugh Lane, by whom presented, 1914.

EXHIBITED: 1918 Dublin *Exhibition of Pictures by Old Masters given and bequeathed to the National Gallery of Ireland by the late Sir Hugh Lane* (National Gallery of Ireland), no. 12; 1930 London *Italian Art* (Burlington) House), no. 134. 1935 Paris *Exposition de l'art Italien de Cimabue à Tiepolo* (Petit Palais), no. 363.

VERSION: a smaller derived version is in the Luciano Temerelli Collection, Vicenza.[1]

The subject matter of the primary version of this painting in Cologne, and of the comparable decorative painting, *Pastoral*, in the Art Institute of Chicago, has been interpreted in different ways. In recent times the subject of this painting was described as *Idyll on the shore*.[2] No sea shore is visible. White and Sewter[3] see in this composition a deliberate essay in class distinction, with the young cow herd in the foreground cynically gesturing towards the aristocratic lady and her companion behind him. Jones[4] goes further, and maintains that the composition has an overtly erotic meaning. Ruggeri[5] quite rightly rejects these interpretations, because of the lack of supporting arguments, and the absence of such readings in the work of Piazzetta. It is useful to recall that the painting which is now in Chicago was quite simply called *Pastorale* when paid for by Marshal Johann Matthias von der Schulenburg, who commissioned it. The payments were made in three amounts in 1740. Similar precise information is not available for the *Idyll on the shore,* or, more correctly, *A pastoral outing.* This, however, also belonged to the Marshal. The paintings did not remain long with the heirs of von der Schulenburg, since both were consigned for sale to Christie's, in London, and auctioned 12 April 1775, lots 41 and 42. Both were quite simply described then as *A group of Italian peasants finely disposed.* While this may not be very precise, nowhere in the early literature is there any indication of a satirical or erotic meaning behind the compositions.

The authenticity of the Dublin painting was clearly believed by its donor, Sir Hugh Lane; this was maintained, at least by a certain body of opinion, until 1930 and later, as exemplified by the exhibitions *(vide supra)* in which it was included.

The Cologne version, as far as can be ascertained at present, was first considered autograph by W. Bombe, in 1918, while still in the collection of Dr. Richard von Schnitzler, in Cologne.[6] This view was supported by A.E. Brinckmann in 1923,[7] and by O.H. Försters in 1930.[8] Thereafter it was constantly considered autograph by the great body of scholars. It was only in 1949 that it was purchased from von Schnitzler's heirs for the Wallraf-Richartz Museum in Cologne (no. 2806).[9] The emphasis placed on the Cologne painting naturally coincided with a closer scrutiny of the Dublin canvas; it had come from the Guidi de Faenza Collection. From the same collection had come a copy of the Chicago *Pastoral.*[10] The consensus of opinion is that the two paintings from the Guidi di Faenza collection were painted in the studio of Piazzetta, or by one of his close followers. This results in the fact that the Cologne and Chicago paintings may be considered as truly autograph, even though neither of them can be traced back historically to the sale from the Schulenburg Collection in London in 1775.

Having regard to the number of painters who studied under Piazzetta, and especially to those, including Maggiotto, who were extremely influenced by their master's style, it would seem inopportune to assign the Dublin painting to any one hand. Having examined carefully the condition of the Dublin painting, making a precise attribution is even more hazardous. Piazzetta himself may well have worked on it.

Von der Schulenburg's commission for this subject was almost certainly executed in 1744-45, and the most likely time for the commissioning of a second version is undoubtedly soon after the completion of the first.

1. M.A. Bulgarelli in *Arte Veneta,* vol. 27 (1973), p.234, n.7.

2. W. Bombe, 'Die Sammlung Dr. Richard von Schnitzler in Köln' in *Cicerone,* vol. 10 (1918), p.39f.

3. D.M. White and A.C. Sewter in *The Connoisseur,* vol. 143 (March 1959), pp. 96-100.

4. L. Jones, *The Paintings of Giovanni Battista Piazzetta,* Vol. 2 (1983), pp. 47-49.

5. U. Ruggeri in the exhibition catalogue,

Giambattista Piazzetta. Il suo tempo, la sua scuola (Venice 1983), p.103.
6. W. Bombe, *loc. cit.*
7. A.E. Brinckmann, *Kunst des Barocks und Rokokos* (Berlin-Neubabelsberg 1923), p.117.
8. O.H. Försters in *Pantheon,* vol. 6 (1930), p. 450.

9. B. Klesse, *Katalog der Italienischen, Französischen und Spanischen Gemälde bis 1800 im Wallraf-Richartz Museum* (Köln 1973), pp. 94-99.
10. R. Pallucchini and A. Mariuz, *L'opera completa del Piazzetta* (Milan 1982), no. 96.

ANDREA PISCELLI, *fl.* early 18th century

None of the usual reference works mention this artist; further investigations have, so far, proved in vain. One may reasonably suggest that Piscelli was a Roman because of the letter 'R' which follows his signature.

1093   Lake scene with figures (Fig. 131).

Oil on canvas, 0.44 m × 0.92 m

CONDITION: very good. There is a tear in the canvas, about the centre, vertically, which will be repaired.
PROVENANCE: Milltown Collection; Milltown Gift, 1902.

First entered in the manuscript catalogue as Ascribed to Henry Fuseli. Cleaning of the pendant, no. 1094 following, which is signed *Andrea Piscelli R.,* revealed the correct attribution to Piscelli. Despite extensive enquiries, no information about Piscelli has been found yet. The 'R' after the artist's signature may indicate that he was a Roman.[1]

This painting belongs to the type of coastal scene known through the works of Vernet, Lacroix and Bonavia. The atmosphere of no. 1093 is one of tranquillity, with calm water and fishermen going about their business.

1. M. Wynne in *Paragone,* no. 395 (January 1983), pp. 40-41.

1094   Coast scene with shipwreck (Fig. 132).

Oil on canvas, 0.44 × 0.92 m.

SIGNED: Andrea Piscelli R.
CONDITION: excellent. Restored June 1977.
PROVENANCE: Milltown Collection; Milltown Gift, 1902.

First entered in the manuscript catalogue as Ascribed to Henry Fuseli, cleaning revealed the signature of Piscelli.[1]

This is the pendant to no. 1093 preceding. In contrast to its companion, no. 1094 has an atmosphere of turbulence with the stormy sea, flashing lightning, and foundering ships.

1. M. Wynne in *Paragone,* no. 395 (January 1983), pp. 40-41.

MATTIA PRETI, Taverna in Calabria 1613-1699 Valletta

Still in his teens Preti went to Rome, and from there travelled extensively throughout northern Italy. It is very difficult to get precise details of these travels or to find dated works. By the 1640s he was back in Rome where a number of documented commissions are to be found, mostly frescos in churches. In the mid-1650s he went to Naples, and about 1660 removed to Malta where he remained for the rest of his life. His works best known are those which manifest a strong interest in chiaroscuro, and dark tonalities.

366   The beheading of St. John the Baptist (Fig. 133).

Oil on canvas, 1.35 m. × 0. 97 m.

CONDITION: excellent; restored 1968.

PROVENANCE: the Marchese Cambiaso, Genoa;[1] purchased in Rome, 1864, for £100.

St. John, already bound, still manages to hold the shaft of his cross, around which is tied the ribbon with the letters *E.A.D.E.*, which are merely an abbreviation of his primary proclamation: 'Ecce Agnus Dei; ecce . . .' (Behold the Lamb of God; behold . . .) The figure to the left behind St. John is presumably one of Herod's courtiers, clerical or lay. He is wearing a head-dress with stripes, a type that recurs frequently in Preti's paintings, for example in *Christ raising Lazarus* in the Pinacoteca at Naples,[2] or *Christ and the Canaanite woman* in the Museo Nazionale at Palermo.[3]

This picture came to the Gallery as a Caravaggio and under this name was catalogued until 1971. In some of the previous catalogues it had been modified to School of Caravaggio. The attribution to Preti is absolutely convincing.

It is not easy to date no. 366 with precision. Undoubtedly it is a work of his maturity. It was probably painted during his years in Naples before he went to Malta in 1660. The clear chiaroscouro and the handling of the executioner's armour, both find an echo in Preti's painting of *The martyrdom of St. Catherine* in the Church of S. Pietro a Maiella, Naples, which Taschetta is inclined to believe was painted in Naples and not sent back from Malta.[4] However, the tranquillity, the clarity, the dignity, and the plain background of the Dublin painting are attributes not readily found in Preti's *oeuvre*. The rather different painting of *Two philosophers* in the Pinacoteca Capitolina, Rome, does have some of these qualities,[5] as does *The liberation of St. Peter*, in Vienna.[6] John T. Spike proposes a somewhat earlier date of *circa* 1640, grouping it with such works as *St. Catherine of Alexandria visited in prison by the Empress* in the Dayton Art Institute, Ohio, and *The Crucifixion of St. Peter*, in the Musée, Grenoble.[7]

1. Note in the National Gallery of Ireland archives. This is a possibility, because Mariana Starke in *Information and Directions for Travellers on the Continent* (6th ed., London, 1828), p. 112, records that in The Third Saloon of the Palazzo del Sig. Gaetano Cambiaso, Genoa, there was a *Decapitation of St. John the Baptist* by Guercino.

The attributions of paintings in private collections at that period were very often incorrect. Many paintings from the Cambiaso Gallery, Genoa, were sold at an auction held in Paris, 16-17 January 1829, by M. Potrelle, but no item in the catalogue of that sale can be reconciled with no. 336.

2. C. F. Taschetta, *Mattia Preti. Contributi alla conoscenza del Cavalier Calabrese* (Brindisi, n.d., but probably 1961), pl. 22.
3. *Ibid.*, pl. 37.
4. *Ibid.*, pp. 66-67; pls. 53, 55.

5. *Ibid.*, pl. 65.
6. B. Chimirri and A. Frangipane, *Mattia Preti detto Il Cavaliere Calabrese* (Milian 1914), pl. 16.
7. In letter, November 1981.

Attributed to PRETI

1912 St. Ambrose (Fig. 134).

Oil on canvas, 1.345 × 1.005 m.

CONDITION: good. Apart from minor paint losses there were only two more sizeable ones: to the left of the mitre, and above the books. Restored February – May 1970. It was found that narrow strips had been added to the top and two sides.

PROVENANCE: said to have been formerly the property of Madame Letitia Bonaparte Wyse;[1] Dowager Marchioness of Ormonde sale 1860, where purchased, for £12. (Sale catalogue not recorded).

St. Ambrose was Archbishop of Milan in the second half of the fourth century. He is one of the four Doctors of the Church. Iconographically no. 1912 is typical. St. Ambrose is seated at a desk wearing an episcopal mitre and cope. His scholarship is indicated by the books and papers in front of him.

Described in the archives of the Gallery as Attributed to Giovanni Lanfranco, it does not appear in any of the published catalogues until that of 1971, in which it is given to Mattia Preti. The attribution to Mattia Preti is not ill founded, especially when one considers the texture of both the paint and the canvas. The Preti attribution is sustained by Carandente and Zeri.[2] Pierre Rosenberg maintains that this and several other versions are copies after a lost orginal by Vignon.[3]

That original Vignon may be the *St. Ambrose* (1.33 × 0.97 m.), one of a set of the Four Doctors of the Church, which appeared at Colnaghi's, London, in 1985, and surely from the brush of Vignon with his particularly sparkling handling of paint, especially in the panache of the draperies.

It is useful to recall that Vignon was in Rome intermittently between 1617 and 1624; that he was influenced by the prevalent Caravaggesque spirit; that he was open to the demands of Counter-Reformation patrons, which included depicting the Four Doctors of the Church who epitomized the learning, scholarship, and truth of early Christianity in the Western Church.

John T. Spike regards no. 1912 as an early copy after what he considers to be an original Preti (1.325 × 0.975 m.), which apparently was on the Rome art market some years ago. The present location is unknown, but a photograph is in the archives of the National Gallery of Art, Washington.[4]

No. 1912 is very close to Preti himself, and may indeed be by him; it is of seventeenth century fabric. A date in the late 1630s is most likely. Spike agrees with such a dating for the original Preti.[5]

Other versions recorded are: in the church of Saint Jacques du Haut Pas, Paris; in a private collection in Florence; at the Heim Gallery, London (in 1971); in the Museo del Castello

Sforzesco, Milan; in a private collection in Montecompatri. A very grand portrait of St. Ambrose, signed and dated 1623 by Vignon, but not the prototype for no. 1912, is in the Minneapolis Institute of Arts (no. 68. 43).[6]

It is very likely that a picture such as no. 1912 was one of a set of four, the Doctors of the Church. Saints Augustine and Jerome by Vignon are to be found in the Abbey Museum at Cava dei Tirreni.[7] Saints Ambrose, Jerome and Augustine, also by Vignon, are to be found in the church of San Pedro Màrtir,[8] Toledo.

1. Note in National Gallery of Ireland Archives.
2. On visits to the gallery.
3. On a visit to the gallery.
4. In a letter, November 1981.
5. In a letter, November 1981.
6. P. Rosenberg in *Bulletin of the Minneapolis Institute of Arts,* vol. 58 (1968), pp. 7-16.
7. A. Brejon de Lavergnée and J.P. Cuzin in *La Revue du Louvre et des Musées de France,* no. 1 (1974), p. 26 and figs. 2-3.
8. Exhibition catalogue *Caravaggio y el Naturalismo Español* (Sala de Armas de Los Reales Alcazares, Seville, 1973), nos. 55-57, where no artist is suggested. However, see the catalogue, by A. Brejon de Lavergnée and J. P. Cuzin of the exhibition *1 Caravaggeschi Francesi* (Accademia di Francia, Villa Medici, Rome, 1974), p. 247. *cf.* P. Rosenberg, exhibition catalogue, *France in the Golden Age. Seventeenth Century French Paintings in American Collections* (Metropolitan Museum of Art, New York, 1982), p. 332.

GIULIO CESARE PROCACCINI, Bologna 1574-1625 Milan

Giulio Cesare is one of the most prominent exponents of the Baroque style in Lombardy. Based in Milan, such was his reputation that he had little need to travel, receiving a constant flow of commissions in his own city, and some for other northern cities.

1820 St. Charles Borromeo in glory with the Archangel Michael (Fig. 136).

Oil on canvas, 3.85 × 2.52 m.

CONDITION: excellent. Restored Summer 1967 – Summer 1968. Paint losses were minimal and almost entirely confined to the edges. The altarpiece is made up of two principal pieces of canvas sewn together on a vertical axis. To both vertical edges are sewn narrow bands of canvas (original), each about 15 cm. wide.

PROVENANCE: Church of San Carlo al Corso, Rome, by 1628;[1] Church of Santa Maria In Traspontina, Rome, by 1663,[2] whence sold to Carlo Maratti (1625-1713) in 1673.[3] Cardinal Fesch sale, Rome, 1845, lot 982; Alessandro Aducci, Rome, from whom purchased, 1856. One of sixteen paintings acquired for £1,700.[4]

EXHIBITED: 1974 Birmingham *Lombard Paintings c.1595-c.1630* (City Museums and Art Gallery), p. 191.

In the upper portion of this painting, St. Charles Borromeo (1538-1584), clad in archiepiscopal vestments is being escorted into heaven by cherubs. The pallium which St. Charles in wearing around his neck is reserved for use by archbishops (and the Pope). St. Charles holds his crozier, while cherubs are entrusted with his cardinal's hat and his motto, a crowned inscription *Humilitas*. Below this scene is the Archangel Michael, clad like a soldier, and holding in his right hand a pair of scales. Almost certainly this is intended to mean that the Archangel has found the soul of the deceased Archbishop of Milan worthy of entry into heaven. More cherubs watch from the left. The Archangel tramples on Satan and the sword which he carries in his left hand pierces one of the devil's wings. Such was the esteem in which the deceased archbishop was held that he was canonized as early as 1610, a mere twenty-five years after his death.

Charles Borromeo was born of noble family, in Arona, on Lake Maggiore, in 1538. In 1559 his maternal uncle, Pope Pius IV, called him to Rome, where he was created a Cardinal deacon, and appointed Secretary of State, at the age of twenty-one. He had not taken holy orders; at that time, and for several centuries later, it was quite normal to have lay people, including lay Cardinals, in the Papal Service. Charles Borromeo was the Pope's special representative at the final session of the Council of Trent, 1562-1563. Shortly afterwards he took Holy Orders, and in 1565 was appointed Archbishop of Milan following the death of his uncle. He was an exemplary churchman, active in the pastoral care of those who lived in his diocese; he visited the poor and the sick. His personal life-style was simple and ascetic. He devoted much time to reorganizing the diocese and implementing the decrees of the Council of Trent. He died in 1584, at the age of forty-six, and was canonized in 1610.

The reason for the inclusion of the Archangel Michael may be explained in various ways.[5] St. Charles may have had a particular devotion to the Archangel; the cult of the Archangel was wide-spread in Lombardy at that time; the man who commissioned the painting may have chosen the subject.

However, the action of the Archangel in weighing the soul of the Saint, as he enters the glory of Heaven, is a particularly noteworthy feature. Much Italian painting of religious subjects which followed the Council of Trent, in the late sixteenth century and early seventeenth century, reflected the Council's teaching. In this instance there is a clear portrayal of the fact that grace alone does not of itself necessarily justify salvation.[6] The good works of a man or woman were an important factor in his or her ultimate destiny. This was a clear decision against the doctrine of Justification by Faith alone, propounded by, among others, Martin Luther.[7] At this point it is also very well worth remembering that, towards the closing of the same Council of Trent, during the twenty-fifth session (3rd and 4th December, 1563), the Church of Rome endorsed yet again its belief in the value of works of sacred art.[8] This was also incorporated into the Tridentine Profession of Faith (13th November, 1564).[9] From the earliest times the church believed in the value of images of Christ, the Virgin, and the Saints; in the eighth century it had to call an Oecumenical Council (the second Council of Nicaea) to condemn Iconoclasm.[10]

While in the manuscript archives of the Gallery no. 1820 was given to Camillo Procaccini, the first edition of the new Gallery's catalogue, that of 1864, attributed the painting to Giulio Cesare. Under this correct name it appears in the 1867, 1871, and 1874 editions. Thereafter the picture is omitted until its reinstatement in the 1971 catalogue. Curiously in a book on the National Gallery of Ireland, published in 1968, the painting was given to Camillo Procaccini,[11] an attribution not used in any of the Gallery's earlier publications. The attribution to Giulio Cesare Procaccini is beyond dispute.

The first documentary evidence of the painting's position in Rome, to be found to date, is in a letter from Antonio Mariani, writing from Rome, on 24th October, 1628, to Cardinal

Federico Borromeo.[12] In this Mariani, a painter, refers to a painting of St. Charles and St. Michael that was then in the Church of San Carlo al Corso. It was placed there by Gasparo Mola, according to Mariani, after it had been refused elsewhere, at an unspecified location. Gasparo Mola came down to Rome from Lombardy, by 1625, to work in the papal service, as Director of the Pontifical Mint. He was an armourer.[13] When Mola made his will in 1631 he implied that the painting was his personal property.[14] In 1640, before his death on 27th January of that year, Mola made a new will, in which he bequeathed the painting to San Carlo al Corso.[15] The next firm fact is that the painting was in the first chapel, on the left hand side, of the church of S. Maria in Traspontina, in 1663.[16] One does not know, so far, whether or not Mola had made yet another will. He had not much time to do so, but it is a possibility which must be considered. The painting had an appropriateness for the church of S. Maria in Traspontina, which belonged to the Carmelite Order of which St. Charles had been Cardinal Protector.[17] The church was linked to Castel Sant' Angelo, which was so called because of its dedication to the Archangel Michael. Castel Sant' Angelo was serviced by the Carmelites of S. Maria in Traspontina. Thus there is an added appropriateness for finding no. 1820 in a church which had been under the protection of Charles Borromeo, and which served the spiritual needs of the soldiers stationed in a fortress protected by the Archangel Michael. In March 1673 the Carmelite fathers of the Traspontina decided to sell the Procaccini for 300 scudi and to have it replaced by a smaller copy of it. Carlo Maratti took up the offer to buy the Procaccini, and to paint a smaller copy of it.[18] The sale was approved by Cardinal Albizzi, on 20th March 1673, on behalf of the Sacred Congregation of the Council.[19] Maratti's copy was moved into the monastery at some later date. It has been restored and now hangs in the Sacristy of the Church.[20]

The Procaccini has been studied in recent years by several writers, who do not agree on its dating, apart from the fact that it is a late work. Peter Cannon-Brookes has suggested a date of *circa* 1618.[21] Hugh Brigstocke makes a case for a somewhat later date, 1624-25.[22] Patricia McKenna, on stylistic grounds places the altarpiece *circa* 1619.[23] Brigstocke's late dating is based to a large extent of the involvement of one Gasparo Mola (whose role has been discussed above) with the painting. It will be very interesting to see his further considered opinion in his forthcoming monograph on the artist. The earlier dating by both Cannon-Brookes and McKenna is largely based on stylistic comparison with *Constantine receiving the instruments of the Passion*,[24] a painting signed and dated 1620. Brigstocke's later dating relies heavily on the involvement of Gasparo Mola, but this only provides a *terminus ante quem*. To clinch the precise date one must await the discovery of a particular commission, or a letter from the artist, or a letter from the patron, or some analagous evidence. Gasparo Mola was not necessarily the first proprietor of the altarpiece. At present there is no evidence to prove that he commissioned it; initially in Rome he may have been merely an agent of the patron.

1. Letter cited in note 12 below.
2. Reference cited at note 16 below.
3. Documents cited at notes 18 and 19 below.
4. M. Wynne in *Gazette des Beaux-Arts*, vol 89 (January 1977), pp. 2, 5-6.
5. P. McKenna in *Studies*, vol. 69 (1980), p. 217.
6. H. Denzinger, *et alii, Enchiridion Symbolorum Definitionum et Declarationum de rebus fidei et morum* (31st ed., Barcelona, Freiburg and Rome, 1960), nos. 809, 822.
7. *Ibid.*, nos. 802, 809.
8. *Ibid.*, nos. 986, 987.
9. *Ibid.*, no. 998.
10. *Ibid.*, nos. 302-04.

11. J. White, *National Gallery of Ireland* (London 1968), p. 21; fig. 17; p. 219.

12. Milan: Ambrosiana Library: Lib. Borr. L. IV-7; published by L. Beltrami in his preface to L. Gasselli's translation of Federico Borromeo's *Musaeum* (1909).

13. C. Buttin, in *Gazette des Beaux-Arts*, vol. 66, 1st. Sem. (1924), pp. 104-06; *cf.* also A. Bertolotti, *Antonio Moro, Gaspare Mola, e Gaspare Morone Mola, incisori alla Zecca di Roma* (Milan 1877).

14. Cited by A. Bertolotti, *Artisti Lombardi a Roma*, vol. 2 (Milan 1881), p. 204.

15. *Ibid.*, p. 210.

16. G. B. Mola, *Breve racconto delle miglior opere d'Architettura, Scultura et Pittura fatte in Roma, descritta da Giovanni Battista Mola l'anno 1663* (ed. K. Noehles), (Berlin 1966), p. 115.

17. P. M. F. A. Mastelloni, *La Traspontina: Notizie Historiche* (Naples 1717), p. 105.

18. *Corporazioni Religiose Maschili. Archivio dei Carmelitani Calzati in S. Maria in Traspontina: Busta 4. Inventario 25 II, no. 2. Notizie di Funzioni Ecclesiastich. spettanti alla Chies della Traspa: dall'Anno 1609 al 1761*, fol. 39 (Archivio di Stato di Roma, Palazzo della Sapienza).

19. *Ms. cit.*, fol. 40 *v*: 20th March 1673. Curiously, Carandente, and Cannon-Brookes, do not give this as the date of Cardinal Albizzi's permission to sell the Procaccini and a less important work of art. Although the date differs by only a matter of days, one may as well give the precise date which is eminently clear in the manuscript of the Cardinal's letter of authority. The date given by Carandente and Cannon-Brookes is that on which senior Curia officials forwarded the Carmelites's petition to Cardinal Albizzi for his consideration and decision.

20. G. Carandente, in *Attività della Soprintendenza alle Gallerie del Lazio: XII Settimana dei Musei* (Rome 1969), pp. 33-34, no. 31.

21. Exhibition catalogue: *Lombard Paintings c.1595-c.1630* (Birmingham City Museums and Art Gallery 1974), p. 191.

22. H. Brigstocke in *The Burlington Magazine*, vol. 118 (April 1976), p. 198; *Id.* in *Jahrbuch der Berliner Museum*, vol. 18 (1976), p. 90, n. 40; *Id.* in *Revue de l'Art*, no. 48 (1980), p. 33, where the writer makes a stylistic comparison between no. 1820 and *The death of Abel*, in the Accademia Albertina, Turin, which is monogrammed and dated 1623 (*Ibid.* p. 30, fig. 3).

23. P. McKenna in *Studies*, vol. 69 (1980), pp. 220 and 224.

24. Museo del Castello Sforzesco, Milan.

POSTSCRIPT: In his history of the church of S. Maria in Traspontina, C. Catena, *Traspontina. Guida storica e artistica* (Rome 1956), Father Catena, continuously basing his statements on the Archives of the Church, now in the Archivio di Stato di Roma, refers to an Inventory of 1626, in which he finds that the Procaccini was at that time in the Traspontina. The enumeration of the Archives has changed since they were used by Father Catena. The writer only had a limited time in the Archivio di Stato, but was able, nonetheless, to examine several manuscripts containing material relating to a period of years which included 1626. No reference to the Procaccini was found. Hopefully someone else will have more luck. It is indeed most probable that Father Catena saw a document connecting the Procaccini with the Church of the Traspontina in 1626, given the detailed nature of his book.

GUIDO RENI, Calvenzano 1575-1642 Bologna

Reni studied under Denys Calvaert, and, from either 1594 or 1595, in the Carracci school also at Bologna. For quite some years he appears to have divided his time between Bologna and Rome. The famous Aurora fresco, commissioned by Cardinal Scipione Borghese, for his casino, was executed in 1614. After that he was principally based in Bologna, visiting some of the north Italian cities. Gradually he appears to have settled in Bologna, and particularly during the later part of his life had many pupils and a flourishing studio.

After RENI

118   Virgin and Child with the protector saints of the city of Bologna (Fig. 137).

Oil on copper, 0.61 × 0.36 m.

CONDITION: **very good.**

PROVENANCE: Prince Lucien Bonaparte; Thomas Kibble sale, Christie's, 5 June 1886, lot 109; anonymous collection, Christie's, 29 June 1889, lot 106, where purchased apparently after the sale, as it is marked as ''withdrawn'', with five other paintings, in the annotated copy of the catalogue at the Courtauld Institute of Art, London. Bought in London for £50.

This is a small replica of the large silk banner in the Pinacoteca Nazionale at Bologna. The latter was commissioned by the City's Senate after the plague of 1630 and carried in processions each year, until some time in the eighteenth century. The saints depicted are Ignatius of Loyola, Petronius, Procolus, Francis of Assisi, Francis Xavier, Dominic and Florianus. Curiously in no. 118 St. Procolus is omitted. Commissioned as the *pallione per il voto*, the great silk banner is known as the *Pala della Peste*.

The small copper is seventeenth century, but it is very difficult to support an attribution to Cantarini, made without any apparent evidence, in a monograph on Reni.[1] Pepper notes its existence, but prudently offers no attribution;[2] he does not link it with the ex-Prince Lucien Bonaparte copy.[3]

1. E. Baccheschi, *L'opera completa di Guido Reni* (Milan 1971), p. 118, no. 149.
2. D. S. Pepper, *Guido Reni. A Complete*

Catalogue of his Works with an Introductory Text (Oxford 1984), p. 266, no. 135.
3. *Ibid.*

After RENI

1065   The Virgin sewing, or The Virgin of the Annunciation (Fig. 138).

Oil on canvas, 1.42 × 1.11 m.

CONDITION: **very good.**

PROVENANCE: Milltown Collection by 1826; Milltown Gift, 1902.

Two cherubs hold a ribbon on which are painted appropriate quotations: *VOCAVIT IS QUI VOCAT EAM A PRINCIPIO* and *VIRGO CONCIPIET ET PARIET FILIVM.* ('He who calls her called her from all eternity' and 'a virgin shall conceive and bear a son').

The alternative title of this painting, which is frequently used, *The Virgin of the Annunciation*, is based on the iconography suggested by the passage in the New Testament apocryphal text the *Book of James.*[1]

This painting is based on the fresco of 1610 by Guido Reni in the Cappella dell'Annunciata in the papal Palazzo del Quirinale, Rome. No. 1065 is a seventeenth century work but it is not possible to suggest an artist. Baccheschi attributes the canvas to Cantarini,[2] but this can not be substantiated. Pepper quite understandably does not attempt to offer an attribution.[3]

1. Since the sixteenth century this text has also been known in Europe as the *Protevangelium*: see Chapters 10-11.
2. E. Baccheschi, *L'opera completa di Guido Reni* (Milan 1971), p. 92, no. 52.
3. D. S. Pepper, *Guido Reni. A Complete Catalogue of his Works with an Introductory Text* (Oxford 1984), p. 225.

After RENI

1334 **St. Jerome** (Fig. 139).

Oil on canvas, 0.74 × 0.62 m.

CONDITION: **poor.**

PROVENANCE: W. Anthony, by whom presented, London, 1854.

The painting seems to be a poor derivative from the half-length *St. Jerome* in the Gemäldegalerie, Dresden.[1]

No. 1334 is early nineteenth century in fabric.

1. D. S. Pepper, *Guido Reni. A Complete Catalogue of his Works with an Introductory Text* (Oxford 1984), p. 274, no. 160, where no reference is made to no. 1334.

After RENI

1695 **The crucifixion of St. Peter** (Fig. 140).

Oil on canvas, 0.62 × 0.49 m.

CONDITION: **poor.**

PROVENANCE: Milltown Collection by 1826; Milltown Gift, 1902.

This is a diminutive copy after the famous arch-topped altarpiece originally in St. Peter's, Rome, and now in the Pinacoteca Vaticana.[1]

No. 1695 is late seventeenth century or early eighteenth century in fabric.

1. M. von Boehn, *Guido Reni* (Bielefeld and Leipzig 1925), fig. 8; D. S. Pepper, *Guido Reni. A Complete Catalogue of his Works with an* *Introductory Text* (Oxford 1984), pp. 215-16, no. 17, where no reference is made to no. 1695.

After RENI

1908 **Rape of Europa** (Fig. 141).

Oil on canvas, 1.82 × 2.38 m.

CONDITION: good.

PROVENANCE: Milltown Collection; Milltown Gift, 1902.

According to Malvasia Reni executed three versions of this subject.[1] Not one of these commissioned works can be traced today with absolute certainty. In the Mahon Collection,

London, there is a canvas that is firmly believed to be authentic. It shows only Europa and the Bull (Jupiter).[2] Likewise depicting the two essential figures is a painting in a Swiss private collection.[3]

No. 1908 is by an unidentified seventeenth century painter and most probably shows what one of Reni's original compositions looked like. Pepper does not mention the Dublin canvas at all, but in his discussion of the Mahon Collection *Rape of Europa* refers to a 'very different composition, but which has been attributed to Reni.'[4] This is the painting which is at Sanssouci, Potsdam, and measures 1.94 × 2.50 m. Kurz considered the latter to be a copy of a lost original by Reni,[5] but Pepper believes it to be 'a work by Francesco Gessi of *c.* 1620 which may reflect a composition of Reni's.'[6]

Dublin's no. 1908 and the canvas at Potsdam are, apart from very minor details, identical. The measurements, too, are remarkably close. While neither painting may be by Reni himself, both are by artists (or *an* artist) working very close to that great master. The history of neither painting is adequate. Pepper records the Potsdam canvas as having been purchased from the collection of Count von Plettenberg in 1755-56; the Dublin painting was most probably acquired by Joseph Leeson (later 1st Earl of Milltown) in Italy by the early 1750s (at the latest), but, as with all the Milltown pictures of this sort, this is only a very reasonable conjecture based on sound circumstantial evidence.

1. One for the King of England (Charles I); one for the Duke of Guastalla, and one for the King of Poland and Sweden (Wladislaus IV): C. C. Malvasia, *The Life of Guido Reni* (Trans. by C. and R. Enggass, University Park and London 1980), pp. 71, 84, 111.
2. E. Baccheschi, *L'Opera completa di Guido Reni* (Milan 1971), p. 108, no. 164; D. S. Pepper, *Guido Reni. A Complete Catalogue of his Works*

with an Introductory Text (Oxford 1984), p. 285, no. 184.
3. D. S. Pepper, *op. cit.,* p. 275, no. 164.
4. D. S. Pepper, *op. cit.,* p. 285.
5. O. Kurz, *Bolognese Drawings of the XVII and XVIII Centuries at Windsor Castle* (London 1955), p. 127, no. 389.
6. D. S. Pepper, *op. cit.,* p. 285.

NICCOLÒ RENIERI (NICOLAS REGNIER),
Maubeuge 1591-1667 Venice

Renieri trained as a painter in Antwerp; about 1615 he came down to Rome, where he was considerably influenced by the Caravaggist movement; about a decade later he settled in Venice, where he was successful. He is particularly remembered by his paintings of languid ladies, notably Mary Magdalen; he took a special interest in rich fabrics, and precious staffage such as alabaster jars and boxes. The Venetian painters Carpioni, Negri, Ruschi and Molinari, were almost certainly influenced by him.

363 St. Mary Magdalen (Fig. 142).

Oil on canvas, 1.205 × 0.99 m.

CONDITION: excellent. Restored May-July, 1978. There were small paint losses along both sides and at the base.

PROVENANCE: George Perkins, Kent, sale, Christie's, 14 June 1890, lot 38, bought for 38 guineas.

Mary Magdalen was a living example of Christ's forgiveness. Having repented of her worldly and sinful ways, she became one of Christ's most beloved followers. Indeed Christ also extended his particular friendship to Mary's brother and sister, Lazarus and Martha. Down through the centuries painters have depicted Mary Magdalen in penitential pose. The jar in the top left-hand corner of this painting reminds us that it was Mary who brought an alabaster jar of precious unguent, with which she anointed Christ's feet at the feast in the house of Simon the Pharisee. (*Mark*, ch. 14, vs. 3, and *John*, ch. 11, vs. 2).

The attribution of no. 363, at the time of purchase, was to Carlo Dolci, but there is no doubt about the correctness of its transfer to the *oeuvre* of Renieri. No. 363 was given to Elizabetta Sirani, from date of acquisition up to and including the 1956 catalogue.

Other versions exist in a private collection, Prague (1971), and in the Palazzo Durazzo Pallavicini, Genoa.[1] The same model and composition are to be seen in the extended full-length version that belongs to the City Museums and Art Gallery, Birmingham.[2] A small copy related to no. 363 is in the reserve collections of the Soprintendenza ai Beni Artistici e Storici per le Provincie di Firenze e Pistoia.[3] Renieri also painted St. Mary Magdalen in a somewhat different compositional arrangement; rather similar, for example, is the half-length *Mary Magdalen* in the Martin von Wagner-Museum, University of Würzburg (inv. no. 7761), Würzburg.

1. P. Torriti, *La Galleria del Palazzo Durazzo Pallavicini a Genova* (Genoa 1967), pp. 112-13, fig. 95, and p. 304, n. 57.
2. Exhibition catalogue, *Venetian Seventeenth Century Painting* by H. Potterton (National Gallery, London 1979), pp. 106-7, no. 30.
3. Exhibition catalogue, *Pittura francese nelle collezioni publiche fiorentine* by P. Rosenberg (Florence 1977), p. 225, no. 70.

Sebastiano Ricci, Cividale di Belluno 1659-1734 Venice

Trained under Mazzoni and Cevelli in Venice, he later studied with Giovanni del Sole in Bologna. He worked in many Italian cities and sojourned in England between 1712 and 1716. He eventually settled in Venice. Ricci is a key figure between the Baroque and Rococo styles.

1099   King Hieron II of Syracuse calls on Archimedes to fortify the city (Fig. 143).

Oil on canvas, 1.04 × 0.84 m.

CONDITION: excellent. Restored 1970.

PROVENANCE: Talbot Collection, Margam Castle, Port Talbot, Glamorgan, Wales; Dr. A. Scharf, London, from whom purchased in 1942, for £320.

On the left King Hieron II rides on horseback holding a standard. Syracuse was under attack from the Romans led by the Consul, Marcellus. Archimedes (*c.*287-212 B.C.), the great inventor and mathematician, sits by a rock. The picture shows the king soliciting the inventor's help. Archimedes did indeed devise several machines to be used against the Romans.[1]

The painting is certainly by Ricci.

Daniels convincingly suggests a late dating, in the 1720s.[2]

There are other known versions, but the Dublin example is considered the best.[3] The other versions are in the Ulster Museum, Belfast, Northern Ireland;[4] in the collection of Mrs. M. S. de Slowak, Montevideo, Uruguay;[5] a version which may be by Joseph Goupy, and the version in the Cecil Higgins Art Gallery, Bedford, England.[6]

One of the versions was engraved by Joseph Goupy, in reverse. The inscription on the print mentions that it was taken from a painting in his own collection. The Department of Prints and Drawings of the British Museum has an impression of the print (1871-1-14-152).

1. N. G. L. Hammond and H. H. Scullard, *The Oxford Classical Dictionary* (Oxford 1972), p. 98.
2. J. Daniels, *Sebastiano Ricci* (Hove 1976), p. 26.
3. *Ibid.*
4. *Ibid.*, p. 4.
5. *Ibid.*, p. 76.
6. *Ibid.*, pp. 104, 156.

ORAZIO RIMINALDI, Pisa 1586-1630/31 Pisa

After initial studies with Aurelio Lomi, Riminaldi went down to Rome to work in the studio of Gentileschi. He soon returned to his native city where he received most of his commissions. He died in a plague.

Attributed to RIMINALDI

1235 Victorious Earthly Love (Fig. 144).

Oil on canvas, 1.78 × 1.22 m.

CONDITION: excellent. Restored June 1968. The drapery covering Cupid's genitals, being non-original, was removed. There were very minor paint losses around the edges. A number, *133* appears on the back of the old relining. At present its significance can not be determined.

PROVENANCE: Monte di Pietà, Rome, (as *Cupid* by Caravaggio) from which purchased by Robert Macpherson, Rome,[1] from whom acquired 1856. One of twenty-three paintings purchased for £1,483.

EXHIBITED: 1969 Bordeaux *L'art et la musique* (Galerie des Beaux-Arts), no. 58.

Victorious Earthly Love derives from the famous Caravaggio painting now in the Staatliche Museen, Berlin-Dahlem, which counterpointed the missing *Divine Love Conquering Profane Love*, also by Caravaggio. *Victorious Earthly Love* is an allegory of the power of love to control or destroy the achievements of the world, a secular counterpart of *Vanitas vanitatum* (Vanity of vanities).[2]

The painting was acquired for the Gallery in Rome in 1856. It was described as a Caravaggio and so catalogued in the 1864, 1867, 1871 and 1874 editions of the catalogue. Thereafter it was omitted, for no known reason, until the 1956 catalogue, in which and in subsequent catalogues it was attributed to Riminaldi. Moir has expressed reservations about the latter attribution,[3] without making an alternative proposal. The name of Rutilio Manetti has been suggested, but to date the evidence to support this is not very convincing. For the moment then Attributed to Riminaldi is retained; and for those who think that the head is not like Riminaldi's work, one has only to draw attention to the artist's documented fresco in the Duomo at Pisa, and particularly to some of the cherubic heads there.[4] No. 1235 bears very close comparison with *Amore artefice* in the Pitti Palace, Florence, one of Riminaldi's most celebrated works.

1. M. Wynne in *Gazette des Beaux-Arts,* vol. 89 (January 1977), p. 2.
2. M. Marini, *Io Michelangelo da Caravaggio* (Rome 1974), p. 396, no. 46, where the nuances

of different interpretations are given.
3. A. Moir, *Caravaggio and his Copyists* (New York 1976), pp. 128-30, no. 208 xi.
4. *Cf. Paragone,* no. 269 (July 1972), pl. 57.

Circle of RIMINALDI, circa 1620

1667 Cain and Abel (Fig. 145).

Oil on canvas, 2.00 × 1.475 m.

CONDITION: excellent. Restored February-December 1978. An old restoration had altered the position of Abel's left hand; the original position has been retained. The painting is on a canvas composed of two parts, with a seam running horizontally across at the level, approximately, of Abel's left hand.

PROVENANCE: Milltown Collection by 1826; Milltown Gift, 1902.

Catalogued hitherto as a Giordano, it became quite clear after cleaning that such an attribution could not be sustained. The painting has perplexed several specialists in the field of Italian Seicento painting. Several artists have been suggested but only in a tentative way. Giovanni Baglione (1571/2-1645/55) is one of them. In his *Entombment,*[1] signed and dated 1616, there are distinct similarities between the anatomical passages of the dead Christ, and the male attendant in front of Mary Magdalen, and the figures of Cain and Abel in no. 1667. The mouth of the male attendant also bears comparison. For features such as mouth, eyebrows and hair one can consider the *St. John the Baptist seated* at Hampton Court Palace.[2] Neither of these has the extreme chiaroscuro of no. 1667, but perhaps it was the horrific aspect of the incident that provoked such a dramatic result. Another artist to be considered is Riminaldi who did at least three paintings of the same subject: one in the Museum at Valetta;[3] one in the Schönborn Collection, Pommerstelden;[4] a third in the Uffizi, Florence.[5] Of the three the most gruesome is that in the Schönborn Collection, which, unfortunately, the present writer only knows through a photograph. In this painting there are sharp contrasts of light and shade. Mina Gregori has studied Riminaldi's contacts with the Roman artistic scene,[6] but on seeing a photograph of no. 1667 was not disposed to call it an autograph Riminaldi. She did consider it a work which was very close to Riminaldi.[7] Another artist to be considered is Biagio (or Michele) Manzoni. Since Longhi's study of 1957,[8] and Corbara's additional note,[9] not much more has been learned about him. In none of the Manzoni paintings illustrated[10] is the chiaroscuro as dramatic as in no. 1667, even though two of the scenes portrayed are of martyrdom. In the *Martyrdom of Saint Sebastian* in a private collection in Paris[11] the contrast of light and shade is fairly pronounced. The wrinkles on the Saint's forehead[12] may be compared with those on Abel's neck or on the back of his right hand shoulder. However, the overall evidence is not sufficient to warrant an attribution to this Caravaggesque painter from Faenza.

The subject of Cain and Abel is one that occurs very frequently in Italian painting of the first half of the seventeenth century. In cataloguing the *Cain and Abel* at Edinburgh, Brigstocke surveyed an array of works of that subject;[13] his work underlines the difficulty of the terrain, and for the Edinburgh painting no firm attribution was proposed. Since then the publication of generically comparable paintings, or further studies on some of the works known to Brigstocke, have not led to clear conclusions.[14]

For the present, therefore, it would appear prudent to leave no. 1667 in the Circle of Riminaldi, and suggest a date of *circa* 1620.

1. Christie's, 16 June 1967, lot 139. The painting is now in the Bob Jones University Art Gallery, Greenville, U.S.A.
2. M. Levey, *Later Italian Paintings in the Royal Collection* (London 1964), no. 353.
3. *Paragone*, no. 269 (July 1972) pl. 43.
4. *Ibid.*, pl. 47.
5. *Ibid.*, pl. 50.
6. *Ibid.*, pp. 35-66.
7. Verbal communication, February 1982.
8. R. Longhi in *Paragone*, no. 89 (May 1957) pp. 42-45.

9. A. Corbara, *ibid.*, pp. 45-47.
10. *Ibid.*, pls. 27-34.
11. *Ibid.*, pl. 31.
12. *Ibid.*, pl. 32.
13. H. Brigstocke, *Italian and Spanish Paintings in the National Gallery of Scotland* (Edinburgh 1978), pp. 88-90.
14. For example, the rather unconvincing attribution to Manfredi of the Vienna painting: K. Garas in *Acta Historiae Artium Academiae Scientiarum Hungaricae*, vol. 26 (1980), p. 273; ill. p. 271, fig. 7.

ROMAN SCHOOL, 2nd half of the 17th century

1911 The Holy Family with several Carmelite monks (Fig. 155).

Oil on canvas, 2.79 × 2.00 m.

CONDITION: good. Restored June-August 1970. There were considerable small paint losses throughout the picture, especially in the lowest quarter.

PROVENANCE: possibly Church of San Pancrazio, Rome; Cardinal Fesch sale, 1843; bt. Alessandro Aducci, Rome, from whom purchased 1856.[1] One of sixteen paintings acquired for £1,700.

The Carmelite monk holding the Christ Child may be the Venerable Francesco del Bambino Gesù, 1544-1606.[2]

The painting was formerly attributed to Placido Costanzi, an attribution which is not acceptable. According to Alessandro Aducci,[3] the Roman dealer, the painting came from the church of San Pancrazio. That church was renovated extensively in 1673[4] and perhaps this painting was installed in it then. San Pancrazio was sacked in 1798,[5] and, if the painting had been there, and if it had survived that incursion, it might have been sold subsequently to Cardinal Fesch.

At least thirty specialists of Roman Seicento painting have seen the picture itself, or a photograph of it. The writer has pursued several channels. All in all no name can be even tentatively proposed for the artist.

A date of *circa* 1673 seems appropriate.

1. M. Wynne in *Gazette des Beaux-Arts*, vol. 89 (January 1977), pp. 3-4.
2. Verbal communication from Father Annibale Gabriele Saggi, a Carmelite father in Rome, at San Martino ai Monti, 1974.

3. National Gallery of Ireland Archives.
4. Paulinus A.S. Bartholomaeo, C.D., *De Basilica S. Pancratii M. Christi Disquisitio* (Rome 1803), p. 21.
5. *Ibid.*, p. 48.

SALVATOR ROSA, Arenella, near Naples 1615-1673 Rome

Rosa studied in his native city with Francesco Fracanzano, but was also influenced by Giuseppe Ribera and Aniello Falcone. He removed to Rome in 1635. His landscapes, portraits and battle scenes were eagerly sought. He lived in Florence from 1640 until 1649; during this period he visited Siena and Pisa. His paintings with groups of bandits are virtually a genre of their own.

96 Landscape with the baptism of Christ in the Jordan (Fig. 146).

Oil on canvas, 1.47 × 2.21 m.

CONDITION: excellent. Restored July 1969. There were minor paint losses.

PROVENANCE: Robert Macpherson, Rome, from whom purchased, 1856. One of twenty-three paintings acquired for £1,483.[1]

Christ was baptized in the river Jordan by St. John the Baptist, his Precursor. All four Gospels narrate this episode and describe the descent of the Holy Spirit on Christ as being manifested outwardly by the appearance of a dove coming down from heaven.

This painting has been fully accepted by Luigi Salerno[2] as autograph. In the Glasgow Art Gallery there is a similar painting of the subject, but with more figures (inv. no. 2987).[3]

A date in the early 1650s would seem appropriate.

1. M. Wynne in *Gazette des Beaux-Arts*, vol. 89 (January 1977), p. 2.
2. L. Salerno, *Salvator Rosa* (Milan 1963), p. 141;

L. Salerno, *L'opera completa di Salvator Rosa* (Milan 1975), p. 95, no. 125.
3. *Ibid.*, p. 95, no. 121.

School of ROSA

738 Mountain landscape (Fig. 147).

Oil on canvas, 0.74 × 0.97 m.

CONDITION: good.

PROVENANCE: Milltown Collection by 1826; Milltown Gift, 1902.

The painting does not have the crisp vitality of a work by Salvator Rosa himself.

School of ROSA

739 Mountain landscape (Fig. 148).

Oil on canvas, 0.74 × 0.97 m.

CONDITION: good.

PROVENANCE: Milltown Collection by 1826; Milltown Gift, 1902.

Like its pendant, no. 738 preceding, it does not have the vitality of a genuine Rosa.

PHILIPP PETER ROOS, called ROSA DA TIVOLI,
Frankfurt-am-Main 1657-1706 Rome

Pupil of his father, Johann Heinrich, Philipp very early attracted attention. With an allowance from the ruling family of Hesse he went to Rome. He established himself in Tivoli (hence the name by which he is generally known) and devoted his attention to depicting animals with accuracy and in a natural landscape. He remained there for the rest of his life and maintained his primary interest in animal painting.

1664 Landscape with cattle (Fig. 149).

Oil on canvas, 1.00 × 1.37 m.

CONDITION: very good.

PROVENANCE: Milltown Collection (probably by 1826); Milltown Gift, 1902.

Roos came to Italy from his native Hesse at an early stage, with an allowance from the Landgrave, and established himself at Tivoli. As his style did not vary greatly it is difficult to suggest a precise date for this painting.

1666 Landscape with cattle and sheep (Fig. 150).

Oil on canvas, 1.00 × 1.37 m.

CONDITION: very good. Restored December 1970-January 1971.

PROVENANCE: Milltown Collection (probably by 1826); Milltown Gift, 1902.

This is a pair to no. 1664 preceding and equally difficult to date.

GIOVANNI BATTISTA SALVI, called SASSOFERRATO,
Sassoferrato 1609-1685 Rome or Florence

Giovanni Battista Salvi is known as Sassoferrato, after the name of his birthplace in the Marches. He was trained by his father. He went to Rome and was much influenced by the work of Raphael and Annibale Carracci. A classical mode dominates his work which is very difficult to date because of the fact that, having found his fundamental style, he did not vary from it. He is known mainly for his religious work, which he executed principally in Rome and Umbria.

93 The Madonna and Child seated in clouds (Fig. 152).

Oil on canvas, 1.04 × 0.75 m.

CONDITION: excellent. Restored June 1968. There were some very minor paint losses.

PROVENANCE: Signor Bastini, Milan, from whom purchased, 1873, for £150.

This painting is clearly based on the central group of Raphael's *Madonna da Foligno* in the Pinacoteca Vaticana,[1] which was engraved by Marcantonio Raimondi. Sassoferrato used the engraving, in which Raphael's composition is reversed.[2]

Another much smaller, but apparently authentic, Sassoferrato based on the same famous Raphael is to be found in the Museo Poldi-Pezzoli, Milan (no. 475: oil on copper, 0.22 × 0.16 m.). The latter does not have cherubs in the top left and right hand corners.

1. O. Fischel, *Raphael* (London 1948), Vol. 1,
pp. 133-134; Vol. 2, pl. 146.
2. Bartsch 47.

After SASSOFERRATO

83 Mater Dolorosa (Fig. 151).

Oil on canvas, 0.48 × 0.37 m.

CONDITION: very good.

INSCRIBED: bottom left, with an inventory number: *37*. It has not been possible to find the inventory to which this number refers.

PROVENANCE: Count Koucheleff Besborodko sale, Paris, 5 June 1869, lot 32, for £80.

This is an old copy after a Sassoferrato, of which there are numerous versions considered to be autograph, for example: Venice, S. Maria della Salute (in Sacristy); Chatsworth, Derbyshire, collection of the Duke of Devonshire.

FRANCESCO SOLIMENA, Canale di Serino 1657-1747 Barra di Napoli

Solimena studied with his father, Angelo; by 1674 he was in Naples, where the works of Mattia Preti and Giovanni Lanfranco had a profound influence on him. He became one of Naples's leading Baroque painters, received abundant commissions and reached international fame.

626   Winter: A man warming his hands at a brazier (Fig. 153).

Oil on panel, 0.62 × 1.07 m.

CONDITION: excellent. Restored August 1970. There were very minor paint losses.

PROVENANCE: private collection, sold Christie's, 1 December 1906, lot 48; A. H. Buttery, London, by whom presented, 1911.

EXHIBITED: 1913-14 London *Spanish Old Masters* (Grafton Gallery), no. 38 (as Spanish School *c.* 1620).

Undoubtedly the subject is intended to portray Winter. Perhaps there were three other similar works depicting the other seasons, but none has been traced so far. They would have made very fine overdoors.

Exhibited (see above) as a work of the Spanish School, it was then catalogued as Italian School (1956 catalogue). It was first attributed to Solimena by Frederico Zeri, on a visit to the Gallery, the attribution used in the 1971 and 1981 catalogues.

The solid qualities of the figure of *Winter* and the firm contrast of light and shade compare with those found in rather early works by Solimena, for example the altarpiece of *St Francis de Sales, St. Francis of Assisi and St. Anthony of Padua with angels* in the church of S. Nicola alla Carità, Naples, dated by Bologna to shortly after 1681.[1] The figure in the background of *Winter* is handled in a manner similar to those in the fresco, *The Conversion of St. Paul*, in the sacristy of the church of San Paolo Maggiore, Naples, signed and dated 1689.[2] A date in the 1680s is proposed for *Winter*. A bottle trimmed with raffia, although not identical to that in no. 626, appears in *Natura Morta con Fiori, Libri e un Teschio* in the Romano Collection, Rome.[3] Unfortunately, this work is not dated.

1. F. Bologna, *Francesco Solimena* (Naples 1958), p. 58.
2. *Ibid.*, p. 182.

3. Exhibition catalogue, *La Natura Morta Italiana* (Palazzo Reale, Naples, 1964), no. 105.

1107 St. Simplicius (Fig. 154).

Oil on canvas, 1.27 × 0.86 m.

CONDITION: very good. Restored Summer 1968. There were some small areas of paint loss throughout the painting in a very random distribution.

PROVENANCE: Mrs. Creed Meredith, Dublin, by whom presented, 1943.

Within a painted oval is the three-quarter length figure of the saint. He clutches his cloak with his left hand, while his right elbow is firmly planted on a column, which allows him to point upwards and outwards. There are cherubs behind his head.

Traditionally this painting was called *St. Paul.* Recently Sergio Benedetti queried the lack of Pauline attributes, and, verbally, suggested that the subject was St. Simplicius. The latter saint was a martyr beheaded in Rome in the 3rd century, under Diocletian. He is the patron of sculptors and stonemasons. His symbol is a column[1] which is very evident in this picture. A column frequently appears in paintings of St. Paul, but in such cases it is usually broken off in a jagged fashion.

On stylistic grounds the attribution to Solimena can be maintained. It had been attributed to Ribera, for a short while after acquisition.

The version referred to below was dated by Bologna to about 1690.[2] A similar date may be proposed for no. 1107.

In the church of San Filippo Neri, Vicenza, hanging over a door on the left hand side of the presbyterium, is a similar painting by Solimena, described as St. Paul (1.00 × 0.70).[3]

1. L. Réau, *Iconographie de l'Art Chrétien,* vol. 3, *Iconographie des Saints* (Paris 1959), p. 1228.
2. F. Bologna, *Francesco Solimena* (Naples 1958), p. 277.

3. E. Arslan, *Catalogo delle cose d'Arte e di Antichità d'Italia: Vicenza, I, Le Chiese* (Roma 1956), p. 91, no. 504.

IGNAZ STERN, frequently known as IGNAZIO STELLA,
Mariahilf 1680-1748 Rome

Following a brief period of tuition in Ingolstadt, this young Bavarian artist came down to Bologna where he studied under Carlo Cignani. He was in Rome by 1700. Among his works in that city are the ceiling of the sacristy of San Paolino alla Regola, the ceiling of the Parisano chapel in San Marcello, four lunettes in Sant'Anna dei Palafrenieri, the altarpiece of St John Nepomucene in Santa Maria in Campo Santo. He also worked for the churches of Santa Prassede, Santa Maria del Pascolo, and San Giovanni in Laterano.

As well as ecclesiastical commissions, Stern painted decorative works, and may be included among the Bamboccianti of this period.

Ignaz had a son Ludovico (1709-1777), who was born in Rome and spent his entire life there as a successful painter of portraits, flowerpieces and historical scenes.

In Italy Stern is usually known as Stella — an exact translation of his name, which means ''star''.

1739 Cupid chastised (Fig. 156).

Oil on canvas, 1.75 × 1.26 m.

CONDITION: very good. Restored Autumn 1971. There were some very minor areas of paint loss.

PROVENANCE: Cardinal Fesch. Probably no. 460 in 1844 Fesch sale catalogue (unattributed);[1] Alessandro Aducci, Rome, from whom purchased, 1856. One of sixteen paintings acquired for £1,700.

Cupid was punished by both Venus and Minerva on account of the mischief his arrows created.

From the date of acquisition, down to and including the 1971 catalogue, this picture was given to Prud'hon. After cleaning, the attribution to Stern was proposed by Pierre Rosenberg[2] and supported by the late Anthony M. Clark.[3] This opinion is endorsed by examination of a set of the four seasons which were with Leger, London, in 1958. One was signed and dated 1723. The face of Spring is very close to that of Venus while the child held by Spring has a face very similar to that of Cupid in no. 1739. In both cases the faces of Spring and the child she holds are more firmly modelled that those of Venus and Cupid. However, in *The Adoration of the Shepherds*, which was sold at Christie's, 8 October 1976, lot 52, a painting signed and dated 1737, the principal figures are handled in a freer fashion, similar to no. 1739.

Consequently, a date in the last decade of the artist's life would appear to be appropriate.

1. M. Wynne in *Gazette des Beaux-Arts,* vol. 89 (January 1977), pp. 2 and 6.

2. On a visit to the Gallery, December 1971.
3. In correspondence, January 1972.

BERNARDO STROZZI, Genoa 1581-1644 Venice

Trained as a painter and educated for the priesthood in the Capuchin order, Strozzi was allowed leave his order, but remain a priest, to take care of his mother. He painted extensively in and around Genoa. When his mother died in 1630 there was some question of his returning to his friary; apparently he chose to join the Canons Regular of the Lateran, and it was about this time that he transferred to Venice. He remained known, however, as 'il prete genovese' (the Genoese priest).

781 Portrait of a gentleman (Fig. 159).

Oil on canvas, 1.38 × 1.07 m.

CONDITION: good. Partially restored May-July 1969. There are some very thin passages in this picture; also areas of overpainting remain.

PROVENANCE: Sir Hugh Lane, by whom bequeathed, 1918.

EXHIBITED: 1918 Dublin *Exhibition of Pictures by Old Masters given and bequeathed to the National Gallery of Ireland by The Late Sir Hugh Lane* (National Gallery of Ireland), no. 7; 1925 London *Annual Exhibition of the Magnasco Society* (at Agnew & Sons).

This portrait is assigned to Strozzi's Venetian period, an opinion upheld by Mortari[1] who compares it with the portrait in the Von Schnitzler Collection, Klinken,[2] Mecklenburg. Very similar in the treatment of the face is the *Portrait of Cardinal Federico Correr* in the Museo Correr, Venice.[3] Cardinal Federico Correr was made Patriarch of Venice in 1632. The portrait was most likely painted soon afterwards. A date in the mid 1630s would be very appropriate for no. 781.

Drawings, studies for both hands in no. 781, are in the Baderou Collection in the Musée des Beaux-Arts, Rouen (nos. 975-4-859 and 975-4-860).[4] (Figs. 157 and 158).

1. L. Mortari, *Bernardo Strozzi* (Rome 1966), p. 104.
2. *Ibid.*, p. 140.
3. *Ibid.*, p. 182.
4. Information kindly communicated by Mary Newcome Schleier, September 1983. The photographs of the drawings were subsequently kindly sent from the Musée des Beaux-Arts, Rouen, by Marie Jeune.

856 Spring and Summer (Fig. 161).

Oil on canvas, 0.72 × 1.28 m.

CONDITION: good. Restored Summer 1972 and Spring 1986. Minor spots of paint loss were found throughout. An old relining had damaged the true rich impasto of this fine painting. An X-radiograph, taken in Spring 1986, confirmed a major *pentimento:* Spring's left arm and hand were originally raised above her left shoulder (Fig. 160).

On the back of the old lining canvas, and on the stretcher, are red wax seals bearing a double 'A', in monogram, undoubtedly the seal of Alessandro Aducci, the Roman dealer (*Cf.* PROVENANCE).

PROVENANCE: Alessandro Aducci, Rome, by whom sold to Richard, 6th Viscount Powerscourt, of Powerscourt, county Wicklow, Ireland, 1836;[1] Messrs Harris and Sinclair, Dublin (as from Powerscourt Collection), from whom purchased, 1924, for £350.

EXHIBITED: 1950-51 London, *Holbein and Other Masters* (Royal Academy), no. 402; 1959 Venice *La Pittura del Seicento a Venezia* (Ca' Pesaro), no. 81; 1979 London *Venetian Seventeenth Century Painting* (National Gallery), no. 26; 1986 Genoa *Il Giardino di Flora*, Loggia della Mercanzia, no. 4.

Two half-length ladies hold the attributes of their respective seasons; on the left is Summer, holding a sack of fruit with sprigs of corn in her hair; on the right is Spring, holding flowers in both hands, her hair decorated with more flowers.

The attribution to Strozzi is quite secure.

Strozzi worked in Venice from 1631. There is a consensus about the dating of this work. The catalogue of the 1959 exhibition at Venice says that it belongs to the artist's last phase, while Potterton, in the catalogue of the 1979 exhibition in London, places it at the end of the 1630s. By this time Strozzi had fully absorbed all the lessons of Venetian colouring and light. Moreover, there is an exceptionally rich use of impasto. Potterton correctly links it stylistically to *The personification of Fame* in the London National Gallery.

One would suppose that no. 856 had a pendant depicting Autumn and Winter, but if such ever existed it has not yet come to light. They would have made splendid overdoors.

Mortari relates a drawing of a female head in the Suida Manning Collection, New York[2] to the small Annunciation painting in the Museum of Fine Arts, Budapest; the drawing shows a slightly down-turned head, whereas the Virgin's head in the Budapest painting is upturned. The drawing is in fact much closer to the head of Summer in no. 856, (as suggested by Potterton in the catalogue of the 1979 exhibition) with its serious countenance. However, no strict connection can really be claimed, because the face of Summer is facing to the right while that in the drawing is facing to the left.

1. Information recorded by the purchaser's son: Viscount Powerscourt, K.P., P.C., *A Description and History of Powerscourt* (London 1903), p. 53. In 1903, the picture was at Powerscourt, hanging in the Drawing Room over the door leading into the Saloon. According to Lord Powerscourt the ladies personifying Spring and Summer were supposed to represent two ladies of the Borghese family!

2. L. Mortari, *Bernardo Strozzi* (Rome 1966), fig. 475.

AGOSTINO TASSI, Rome *c.* 1580-1644 Rome

In the mid-1590s Tassi left Rome and worked in Florence, Livorno and Genoa. In 1612 he was involved in a lawsuit with Artemisia Gentileschi, and was imprisoned for a while. Thereafter he appears to have remained in Rome, where he received many commissions. For several years in the 1620s Claude Lorrain was his pupil.

School of TASSI

1751 Coast scene (Fig. 170).

Oil on canvas, 0.39 × 0.62 m.

CONDITION: moderate. Restored June 1968. The paint layer is rather thin.

PROVENANCE: Milltown Collection (probably by 1826, as by Voughs); Milltown Gift, 1902.

Having regard to the condition of the painting, it does not seem to have ever had the quality of a Tassi.

School of TASSI

1752 Coast scene (Fig. 171).

Oil on canvas, 0.39 × 0.62 m.

CONDITION: moderate. Restored June 1968. The paint layer is rather thin.

PROVENANCE: Milltown Collection (probably by 1826, as by Voughs); Milltown Gift, 1902.

A pair to the preceding, no. 1751, this painting does not seem to have ever had the quality of a Tassi.

GIOVANNI BATTISTA TIEPOLO, Venice 1696-1770 Madrid

Tiepolo's early life as a painter in Venice was greatly influenced by the work of both Sebastiano Ricci and Giovanni Battista Piazzetta. He became arguably the greatest exponent of the Rococo style in Italy, particularly in fresco. His work is to be found throughout the Veneto. Some of his finest achievements are to be found abroad, for example, in the Residenz at Würzburg; in 1762 he went to Spain to work for the court, endowing it with an impressive heritage before his death in Madrid.

353 Allegory of the Immaculate Conception and of Redemption (Fig. 162).

Oil on paper, laid on canvas, 0.587 × 0.45 m.

CONDITION: excellent. Restored August 1968.

PROVENANCE:the Right Hon. G.A.F. Cavendish Bentinck sale, Christie's, 13 July 1891, and following days, lot 771, where purchased for 50 guineas.

EXHIBITED: 1960 Coventry *Loan Exhibition* (Herbert Art Gallery and Museum), no. 43. 1985 London *Masterpieces from The National Gallery of Ireland* (National Gallery), no. 10.

God the Father appears amid the clouds, surrounded by angels. To the top left is the dove representing the Holy Spirit. Almost centrally is the Virgin, kneeling, with stars forming a halo and the moon below her feet.[1] Also below her is a terrestrial globe on which crawls a serpent with an apple in its mouth. Iconographically this may be considered an Allegory of the Immaculate Conception and an Allegory of Redemption.

Biblical scholars are at pains to point out that the woman of the Apocalypse[2] is not really an appropriate basis for an image of the Immaculate Conception; they cannot, however, deny that this is the image that was in use for centuries. Exegesis, therefore, does not eliminate a traditional iconography. Perhaps the most abundant use of the image was in seventeenth century Spain, where literally hundreds of paintings were executed by Murillo, Zurbarán, Cano, Valdés Leal and many less well known painters. The crescent shape of the moon is rooted in the imagery of the pagan goddess, the virgin huntress, Diana.

The allegory of Redemption is quite clear. Following the sin of Adam, the Lord said to the serpent: 'I will put enmity between you and the woman, and between your seed and her seed; ...'[3] The serpent holds in his mouth an apple, the traditional image of the fruit of the tree which Adam had been forbidden to touch or eat.[4] The mirror held by a cherub just above the serpent's head may well be a reference to one of the medieval descriptions of the Virgin: *Speculum sine macula* (the mirror without blemish). Less likely is the possibility of it being a symbol of *vanitas*, or worldliness, since the cherub is holding it in a rather threatening fashion in front of the serpent. The palm tree stricken down is a symbol of fallen mankind. A palm tree is used in such imagery because 'The righteous flourish like the palm tree, ...'[5]. The pillar on the left hand side is most probably a reference to another title for the Virgin found in medieval hymnology: *turris Davidica*[6] (the tower of David). Normally the tower is like the tower of an ancient castle, with windows looking out on all sides, and less like the obelisk shape which it has in this painting. Specialists of oriental languages have not been able to read what appears to be a precise inscription on the structure. One cannot rule out the possibility of the structure being meant to depict the tower of Baris, mentioned in the sixth chapter of *Speculum Humanae Salvationis,* where it symbolizes the unassailable purity of the Virgin (suggested, verbally, by Satia Bernen).

Obelisks are found in many of Tiepolo's compositions, but it is useful to note two very prominent ones in late works. One is to be found in his fresco of 1762-64 for the Throne Room of the Royal Palace, Madrid, *Glory of the Spanish monarchy.* In this the obelisk stands for princely glory.[7] Another important work, a painting executed between 1762 and 1770, for the imperial court at St. Petersbourg, *Monument to the glory of heroes* is composed around an obelisk. The painting is missing but its composition is known through Lorenzo Tiepolo's engraving.[8] The concept of glory or honour represented by an obelisk is found in Ripa's *Iconologia.*[9] In no. 353 the expression of honour or glory applied to the Virgin is very appropriate: *Tu gloria Hierusalem* (You are the glory of Jerusalem).[10] Consequently, one must allow for the possibility of this attribute, in this painting, which, after all, is not far from the concept of 'the tower of David'.

The powerful dual allegory of the Immaculate Conception fused with that of Redemption is not unique in the work of Tiepolo. For example, it occurs with some minor changes in the altarpiece which Tiepolo painted for the church of the Franciscan Friary of St. Paschal Babylon at Aranjuez, a favourite summer retreat of the Spanish Royal Family in the eighteenth century.[11] The altarpiece is now in the Prado.[12] The *bozzetto* for this altarpiece is very like Dublin's no. 353. It is part of Count Seilern's collection[13] in the Courtauld Institute Galleries, London, through the generosity of the Count's bequest. It is known as the Princes Gate Collection.

No. 353 is an excellent example of a Tiepolo *bozzetto.* There is no record known, at present, of a larger canvas, for which it might have been a preliminary sketch.

Recently Catherine Whistler made an interesting hypothesis.[14] When his work at Aranjuez was completed, Tiepolo was commissioned by Charles III, on 2 September 1769, to execute the frescos of the dome of the collegiate chapel of St. Ildefonso, at La Granja. Since by the time of Tiepolo's death the stucco adornment of the dome was not complete, the painter could not have prepared detailed *modelli.* Whistler's suggestion is that no. 353 might have been a sketch out of which one part of the fresco decoration could have been elaborated.

Morassi dates no. 353 *circa* 1760-70[15] which is very acceptable, because the painting in the Prado, referred to above, is datable to 1767-69.[16] Pallucchini proposes a date of 1766-70.[17]

Tiepolo painted the Immaculate Conception on very few occasions. The earliest recorded was for the Church of Aracoeli in Vicenza (*circa* 1735); this altarpiece is now in the Museo Civico there, while the *modelletto* for it is in the Musée de Picardie, Amiens.[18] In 1759 he painted an altarpiece on this theme for the Oratorio della Purità, Udine.[19] Neither of these relates closely to Dublin's no. 353. The only other work is the altarpiece referred to already, painted for Aranjuez, but now in the Prado, together with its *bozzetto,* now in the Princes Gate Collection at the Courtauld Institute Galleries.

There is, however, a tantalizing reference to a *bozzetto* in a letter published by Francis Haskell;[20] this may or may not be either the Princes Gate Collection *bozzetto* or Dublin's no. 353; if not either of these, it refers to a work as yet unidentified. In 1804 the famous sculptor Antonio Canova wrote from Rome to Pietro Edwards, Inspector-General of the Venetian public collections, asking him to procure for him a *modello* by Tiepolo and some views of his native city. With difficulty, and with the help of the architect Selva, Edwards found Canova an *Immaculate Conception*.[21] In his letter Edwards says that the work does not date from the period of Tiepolo's 'maggior energia', remarks that a certain finicky quality in the treatment of the large number of cherubs betrays the hand of Domenico ('la sovervchia minuzzaglia di tanti cherubini sia in parte una introduzione posteriore di Domenico'). Nonetheless, Edwards underlines the dignity of the work 'per una certa elevatezza di pensiero dantesco.' Neither the Princes Gate Collection *bozzetto* nor Dublin's no. 353 betrays two hands at work; the known provenance of either leaves a short space of time for ownership by Canova; of the two perhaps Dublin's no. 353 would have a higher claim to that 'certa elevatezza di pensierso dantesco.' If either of these works were the *Immaculate Conception* found by Pietro Edwards, he would have had to be mistaken in seeing the intervention of Domenico in the completion of the *modello*.

1. *The Apocalypse of St. John*, ch. 12, vs. 1.
2. *Ibid.*
3. *Genesis*, ch. 3, vs. 15.
4. *Genesis*, ch. 2, vs. 15-17.
5. *Psalm 92*, vs. 12-15.
6. *Litaniae deiparae Virginis ex Sacra Scriptura depromptae quae in alma domo lauretana omnibus diebus Sabatthi, Vigiliarum et Festorum decantari solent* in C. Bernardino, *Trattato sopra l'historia della Santa Chiesa et Casa della gloriosa Madonna Maria Vergine di Loreto* (Macerata 1576), pp. 103 ff, *ad versum*. See also *Song of Solomon*, ch. 4, vs. 4.
7. L. Jones in *Apollo*, vol. 114 (October 1981), p. 223; p. 224, fig. 6; p. 225, fig. 10.
8. A. Rizzi, exhibition catalogue, *Mostra del Tiepolo. Disegni e acqueforti* (Villa Manin di Passariano, Udine, 1971), no. 98.
9. C. Ripa, *Iconologia, overo Descrittione d'Imagini delle Virtù, Vitij, Affetti, Passioni humane, Corpi celesti, Mondo e sue parti* (Padua 1611), pp. 204.
10. *Missale Romanum: Festa In Conceptione Immaculata Beatae Mariae Virginis, Graduale,* adopting for the Virgin the words of *The Book of Judith*, 15, 10 (Rome, Tournai, Paris 1951), p. 510.
11. M. Wynne in *Archivo Español de Arte*, vol. 53 (July-September 1980), pp. 382-84.
12. *Museo del Prado. Catalogo de las Pinturas* (Madrid 1963), p. 675, inv. no. 363.
13. A. Seilern, *Italian Paintings and Drawings at 56, Princes Gate London SW7: Addenda* (London 1969), p. 29, no. 342.
14. C. Whistler, in *Apollo*, vol. 121 (March 1985), pp. 172-73.
15. A. Morassi, *A Complete Catalogue of the Paintings of G. B. Tiepolo* (London 1962), p. 11.
16. H. Braham, *The Princes Gate Collection* (London 1981), p. 75; p. 77, no. 112, pl. 16.
17. A. Pallucchini, *L'Opera completa di Giambattista Tiepolo* (Milan 1968), no. 287.
18. A. Pallucchini, *op. cit.*, no. 108 and no. 108a.
19. A. Pallucchini, *op. cit.*, no. 259.
20. F. Haskell in *Journal of the Warburg and Courtauld Institutes*, vol. 23 (1960), pp. 256 ff.
21. Letter from Pietro Edwards to Canova, dated 23 June 1804, preserved in the Seminario Patriarchale, Venice, MS 788.10, of which the relevant passages are quoted in the original Italian by Haskell, *loc. cit.*, p. 276.

1111 Christ in the House of Simon the Pharisee (after Veronese) (Fig. 163).

Oil on canvas, 1.45 × 1.585 m.

CONDITION: this painting is covered with a layer of heavily discoloured varnish; it is possible to see many small areas and tiny spots of old retouching, which detract from the appearance of the picture; nonetheless it is reasonable to suggest that restoration would reveal a work of high quality.

PROVENANCE: probably Conte Francesco Algarotti, Venice; by descent, 1764, to his brother, Conte Bonomo Algarotti; by descent, 1776, to his daughter, Contessa Maria Algarotti Corniani; Miss Colchester, Walcot, Pyrford, Surrey; Sir Thomas Barlow, KBE, London; F. A. Drey, London, from whom purchased in 1943 for £1,200.

EXHIBITED: 1938 Chicago *Loan Exhibition of Paintings, Drawings and Prints by the two Tiepolos* (Art Institute of Chicago), no. 2.

While Christ was eating in the house of Simon the Pharisee, a woman, known to be an adulteress, approached Him, washed his feet with her tears, dried them with her hair, and then anointed them with precious unguent. This caused scandal, but Christ rebuked Simon, and said '. . . I say to thee: Many sins are forgiven her because she hath loved much.' (*Luke*, ch. 7). The woman has been identified in subsequent legend as Mary Magdalen.

This painting is a copy with alterations in format and detail of the famous Veronese now in the Galleria Sabauda, Turin.[1] In the eighteenth century it hung in the *palazzo* of the Durazzo family in Genoa. No. 1111 is not a slavish copy of the Veronese. Perhaps the most striking difference is to be found in the very centre of the canvas, along the row of people in the foreground who constitute the story of the picture. Beside the dog emerging from under the tablecloth of the supper table, the author of no. 1111 has introduced a striking vase or urn; almost immediately above this vase, perched on the cornice of the elaborate architectural setting, approximately one-third of the distance from the top of the canvas, the decorative bird in no. 1111 has a long elegant tail quite distinctively different to the bird in the similar position in the original Veronese; the head of Christ in no. 1111 is in an almost vertical position rather than the more reclining posture in the Veronese; the architectural coulisse on the right hand side of the painting shows many details which differ from the Veronese; and there are further differences.
The Veronese was engraved while still in the Durazzo collection by Giovanni Volpato, in a print dated at Rome 1772.[2] This shows many differences of detail either with reference to the Veronese or to no. 1111; most significantly the sizeable vase introduced into the Dublin painting is not there.

Following the death in 1776 of Conte Bonomo Algarotti, his only daughter and heiress, Contessa Algarotti Corniani, found a manuscript catalogue of her father's collection of pictures, which he had caused to be made. Since it appeared to her that it had been her father's intentions to publish this brief work, she had it published in Italian,[3] in French,[4] and probably in German. The generally accepted date of publication is 1779, even though neither the Italian nor French editions bear a date.

Bonomo Algarotti's collection was basically that of his late brother, the patron and agent Conte Francesco Algarotti, who had died in 1764; again it is generally accepted that Bonomo only added a few works to his brother's collection.

Writing as early as 1806, G. A. Moschini states that the catalogue was prepared by G. A. Selva;[5] Morassi believes that the catalogue was the work of Francesco Algarotti.[6]

The Algarotti catalogue contains several works given to Giovanni Battista Tiepolo, and among those is:
'Convito in Casa del Fariseo, con la Maddalena che unge i piedi al Redentore

In tela, alto p. 4, onc. 1, l. p. 4, onc. 11.

(Copia bellissima dell'originale di Paolo Veronese che si conserva in Genova nel Palazzo dei Nobili Signori Conti Durazzo , e che si vede incisa da Giovanni Volpato nella Scola Italiana pubblicata in Roma.)'[7]

It is worth noting that the French edition of the catalogue observes that the measurements used are 'pieds de Paris',[8] also known as 'pieds de roi'.

This entry corresponds with Dublin's no. 1111, and when the measurements are converted into current metric usage the agreement is remarkable: Algarotti catalogue, 1.326 × 1.597 m.; actual, 1.345 × 1.585 m.

The entry in the Algarotti catalogue which immediately follows that of the *Convito in Casa del Fariseo*, which corresponds with Dublin's no. 1111, is of another Tiepolo after Veronese, namely the *Rape of Europa*. This painting, in the Sir Steven Runciman Collection, was fully discussed by Michael Levey and accepted as a thoroughly autograph Giovanni Battista Tiepolo.[9] In an extremely useful Appendix to that article Levey discusses briefly other paintings formerly in the Algarotti collection. With reference to *Convito in Casa del Fariseo* Levey writes: 'It seems to be the picture now in the National Gallery of Ireland, Dublin: 1956 cat., pp. 68-69, where it is suggested (plausibly) that the execution is Domenico Tiepolo's.'[10] The catalogue referred to was written by Thomas McGreevy,[11] whose opinion is correctly quoted.

The main issue to be resolved is whether no. 1111 is by Giovanni Battista or Giandomenico Tiepolo. It is fully accepted as a Giovanni Battista by Morassi,[12] and by Anna Pallucchini.[13] Additionally, it is not included as a Giandomenico by Mariuz.[14]

Morassi supports his argument by writing ''It is probably to this canvas that Tiepolo's letter to Algarotti refers (16th March, 1761), in which he writes that the *'Cena'* was almost finished. Another probable reference to the picture is in a letter of 4th April, 1761, where it is mentioned as finished.''[15]

In the letter of 16 March 1761 Tiepolo specifically mentions ''Il quadro poscia della Cena'',[16] while in that of 4 April 1761 reference is to two works, one finished, and one not yet begun; but no title is given for either.[17] However, the finished picture might well be the *Cena*, and both letters could pertain to Dublin's no. 1111.

It may seem somewhat strange that both patron and painter, Algarotti and Tiepolo, were still interested in copying Veronese at this late date, especially Tiepolo who was so very busy. But there is ample evidence scattered throughout the correspondence to confirm Tiepolo's continued admiration for his illustrious fellow-Venetian predecessor. For example, on 4 March 1760, Algarotti wrote from Bologna to Tiepolo asking him about the little copy of Veronese's *Cena dei Servi* then at Versailles (now in the Louvre), which he had asked him to overpaint.[18] Almost two years later Tiepolo, on 9 January 1762, wrote to Algarotti saying that he had not begun work on *la sua Cena*, due to pressure of work.[19] On 16 January 1762, Algarotti wrote to his brother, Bonomo Algarotti, advising him of the situation in regard to the copy of the *Cena dei Servi*, but asking him to ensure that Tiepolo would finish 'l'altro quadro copia di Paolo che aveva in mano.'[20]

It is also worth bearing in mind that Algarotti's working relationship was with Giovanni Battista Tiepolo rather than with his son Giandomenico, who showed no special interest in copying Veronese.

The authorship of no. 1111 can only be resolved at present by the evidence of the painting itself. Peering closely through the dirty varnish, making allowance for many small discoloured retouchings, one can still see some brilliant passages of brushwork and innovative detail. Considering also that the picture is closely based on a Veronese, one ought to conclude, for the present at least, that it is the work of Giovanni Battista Tiepolo.

1. N. Gabrielli, *Galleria Sabauda. Maestri Italiani* (Turin 1971), pp. 254-55.
2. There is an impression of this engraving in the Witt Collection, Courtauld Institute of Art, London.
3. *Catalogo dei Quadri, dei Disegni e dei Libri che trattano dell'arte del Disegno della Galleria del fu Sig. signor Conte Algarotti in Venezia:* published in P. Molmenti, *G. B. Tiepolo. La sua Vita e le sue Opere* (Milan 1909).
4. *Catalogue des Tableaux, des Desseins, et des Livres qui traitent de l'art du dessein, de la galerie du feu Comte Algarotti à Venise.*
5. G. A. Moschini, *Della Letteratura Veneziana* . . ., vol. 2 (Venice 1806), p. 106.
6. A. Morassi, *A Complete Catalogue of the Paintings of G. B. Tiepolo* (London 1962), p. 72.
7. *Catalogo dei Quadri, dei Disegni* . . . (*op. cit.*), p. xxv.
8. *Catalogue des Tableaux, des Desseins* . . . (*op. cit.*), p. xxv.
9. M. Levey in *The Burlington Magazine*, vol. 102 (June 1960), pp. 250-57.
10. M. Levey, *op. cit.*, p. 257, Appendix no. 11.
11. T. McGreevy, *National Gallery of Ireland. Catalogue of Pictures of the Italian Schools* (Dublin 1956), pp. 68-69.
12. A. Morassi, *op. cit.*, p. 11.
13. A. Pallucchini, *L'opera completa di Giambattista Tiepolo* (Milan 1968), no. 275.
14. A. Mariuz, *Giandomenico Tiepolo* (Venice 1971).
15. A. Morassi, *loc. cit.*
16. Letter preserved in the Museo Civico, Bassano, and published by B. Passamani, exhibition catalogue, *Acqueforti, disegni, lettere di G. B. Tiepolo* (Museo Civico, Bassano, 1970), pp. 76-77.
17. Letter preserved in a private collection, and published by A. Baudi Di Vesme in 'Paralipomeni Tiepoleschi' in *Scritti Varii* . . . *in onore di Rodolfo Renier* (Turin 1912), p. 312.
18. Published in *Opere del Conte Algarotti*, vol. 6, *Raccolta di Lettere sopra la Pittura e Architettura* (Livorno 1765), p. 95.
19. Letter preserved in the Civic Library, Turin, and published by A. Baudi Di Vesme, *op. cit.*, p. 313.
20. Letter preserved in the Royal Library, Turin, and published by A. Baudi Di Vesme, *op. cit.*, p. 312.
Note: The writer would like to thank Catherine Whistler, Oxford, and Elisa Gribaudi Rossi, Turin, for obtaining photocopies of material not available in Dublin.

GIROLAMO TROPPA, Rochetta Sabina *c.*1636-*c.*1706 Rome

Very little is known about this competent artist who worked in a style close to that of Carlo Maratti, and may well have been one of his pupils.

Attributed to TROPPA

1669 The adoration of the shepherds (Fig. 166).

Oil on canvas, 1.55 × 1.22 m.

SIGNED: with monogram: *TR*

CONDITION: excellent. Restored June 1968. There were very small areas of paint loss.

PROVENANCE: Milltown Collection by 1826; Milltown Gift 1902.

No. 1669 was attributed to Maratti in the Manuscript Catalogue, but the cleaning of the picture, with revelation of the monogram, led to several suggestions. To date the most likely name is that of Girolamo Troppa, which was used in both the 1971 and 1981 catalogues.

In the Gallery at Christ Church, Oxford, there is an *Allegory of Painting* (1.337 × 0.983 m.), which, while of a totally different scale in the figures, does have similarities in the anatomical passages and facial physiognomy.[1] The Oxford picture is signed: *Gmo Troppa.* More relevant to no. 1669 is the large altarpiece *The Virgin and Child with Saints Benedict and Scholastica* (2.45 × 1.78 m.) in the Church of S. Maria del Popolo, Cittàducale.[2] This painting is signed and dated 1692, by Troppa. There are cherubs in both upper corners of the Cittàducale altarpiece, and indeed two more between the two saints towards the bottom. Even though the Cittàducale altarpiece has not been cleaned recently it is reasonable to conclude that it and no. 1669 were painted by the same follower of Maratti. Perhaps even more closely related to no. 1669 is *The Virgin and Child with St. Francis,* by Troppa, in the third chapel of the right hand aisle of the Church of SS. Ambrogio e Carlo al Corso, Rome.[3] Here one notes an azurite blue and a rose colour in the Virgin's clothes, and what one might call an aura of light beneath the Virgin and Child. While not cleaned recently, this painting in Rome does manifest the sweet treatment which is so distinctive in no. 1669. The areas of light appearing in the background, and at the base of the pillar in the Rome painting also have affinities with no. 1669, which by comparison with documented works of the artist one may attribute to Troppa.

No. 1669 is a very late seventeenth century painting, perhaps *circa* 1690.

1. J. Byam Shaw, *Paintings by Old Masters at Christ Church, Oxford* (London 1967), p. 91, no. 153.
2. C. Verani in *L'Arte,* N.S. Vol. 26 (1961), pp. 300 ff.
3. G. Drago and L. Salerno, *Ss. Ambrogio e Carlo al Corso* (Rome 1967), p. 65.

ALESSANDRO TURCHI, sometimes called L'ORBETTO,
Verona 1578-1649 Rome

Turchi studied in his native city with Felice Brusasorzi; in the second decade of the seventeenth century he went down to Rome where he would have found the well established Carlo Saraceni, a celebrated son of Venice. With his fellow-Veronese painters, Marcantonio Bassetti and Pasquale Ottino, Turchi received a constant flow of commissions. As a group, the Veronese trio tended to look back to Raphael and the Carracci, rather than develop the mainstream of Baroque and Carravaggesque art.

1653   An angel leading Lot and his daughters out of Sodom (Fig. 164).

Oil on canvas, 0.69 × 0.96 m.

CONDITION: very good. Restored November 1969-April 1970. There were some small areas of paint loss.

PROVENANCE: Milltown Collection by 1826; Milltown Gift, 1902.

Before destroying Sodom, God sent angels to lead Lot, his wife, and daughters to safety. The angels warned them not to look back, but, as *Genesis*, ch. 19, tells, Lot's wife looked back and was turned into a pillar of salt. In no. 1653 the artist only shows one angel. Lot and one of his daughters carry large bundles, while the second daughter bears an urn. In the distance, on the right, can be seen the destroyed city, and the white figure of Lot's wife.

This painting was given to a follower of Guercino in the Manuscript Catalogue, but cleaning made other suggestions more tenable. An attribution to Turchi is most convincing, and this was used in the 1971 and 1981 catalogues.

In *The Flood* in the Molinari — Pradelli Collection, Bologna,[1] very prominent is a bundle just like those carried by Lot and one of his daughters in no. 1653. In *Lot and his daughters* in the Staatliche Kunstsammlungen, Gemäldegalerie, Dresden, on the ground is an urn very similar to that carried by one of Lot's daughters in no. 1653. Apart from this Dresden picture other depictions of the theme are known. Like the Dresden one they portray Lot's daughters plying their father with wine. One was with Viancini, Venice, in 1968;[2] another was with the Leger Galleries, London, in 1964.[3] The figures in no. 1653 are handled in a manner similar to those in the painting belonging to Viancini referred to above, or indeed those in *The Flood* likewise already cited. The angel in no. 1653 is very similar to that in the painting of *St. Agatha and St. Peter*, especially when one allows for the dramatic chiaroscuro in the latter picture, which is in the Galleria Nazionale d'Arte Antica, Rome.[4] This painting is also small (0.31 × 0.45 m.). Another comparable angel, from the point of view of stance and profile, is in *The flight into Egypt*, in the Prado, Madrid.[5] The chromatic range in no. 1653, and some compositional features, are extremely like the two large Turchis in the Alte Pinakothek, Munich, *The fury of Hercules* and *Hercules and Omphale*.[6] Drawings for the two Munich pictures are known,[7] but to date none has come to the writer's notice for no. 1653.

No. 1653 most probably dates from after Turchi's transfer to Rome which took place about 1614/15. A date *circa* 1620 would seem appropriate.

1. Exhibition catalogue, *Cinquant'Anni di Pittura Veronese 1580-1630* (Palazzo della Gran Guardia, Verona, 1974), no. 98.
2. *Apollo*, vol. 88 (December 1968), advertisement.
3. *The Burlington Magazine*, vol. 106 (June 1964), supplement.
4. See: exhibition catalogue: *La Pittura del Seicento a Venezia* (Ca' Pesaro, Venice, 1959), no. 35, and plate.

5. R. Pallucchini, *La Pittura Veneziana del Seicento*, Vol. 2 (Milan 1981), p. 574, fig. 323.
6. R. Kultzen, *Alte Pinakothek München. Katalog V. Italienische Malerei* (Munich 1975), pp. 131-132, nos. 490 and 496.
7. E. Schleier in *Master Drawings*, vol. 9 (1971), pp. 143-44, 148, and pl. 21 (formerly with B. Lenz, Prague); pp. 143-44, 148, and pl. 20 (Collection Freiherr Reinhard von König-Fachsenfeld, Fachsenfeld, Stuttgart).

PIETRO MUTTONI, called PIETRO DELLA VECCHIA,
Venice 1603-1678 Venice

Pietro della Vecchia studied with Padovanino, and this influence determined his love for the art of sixteenth century Venetian painting. Because he looked back so much, many critics consider him retardataire, but, building on the base of his illustrious predecessors, he introduced a truly Baroque element, but was not greatly influenced by the style of those Venetian artists returning from Rome with a distinct Caravaggesque style. It would appear that Pietro della Vecchia did not leave his native city, and he married a daughter of Niccolò Renieri, the painter from the Low Countries who arrived in Venice via Rome.

94 "Timoclea brought before Alexander" (Fig. 165).

Oil on canvas, 1.88 × 2.38 m.

CONDITION: excellent. Restored Summer 1968. The paint losses found were very minor.

PROVENANCE: Monte di Pietà, Rome, whence acquired through Robert Macpherson, Rome, 1856.[1] One of twenty-three paintings purchased for £1,483.

EXHIBITED: 1979 London *Venetian Seventeenth Century Painting* (National Gallery), no. 33.

The title of the picture is the traditional one, which, for the moment, is retained so as to avoid confusion. When the painting was exhibited in London, in 1979, Jennifer Fletcher quite correctly challenged the title of the subject matter,[2] but did not proffer an alternative one. Since then no convincing title has been found for the scene depicted.

Acquired as a work of Della Vecchia, the attribution has not changed. Recently Potterton[3] compared it with the artist's *Alexander and Diogenes*[4] which is in a private collection in Venice. For the latter Ivanoff proposed a date of *circa* 1653;[4] consequently a date in the 1650s would be appropriate for no. 94.

1. M. Wynne in *Gazette des Beaux-Arts*, vol. 89 (January 1977), p. 2.
2. J. Fletcher in *The Burlington Magazine*, vol. 121 (October 1979), p. 666.
3. In catalogue of 1979 London exhibition, no. 33.

4. Exhibition catalogue: *La Pittura del Seicento a Venezia* (Venice 1959), no. 105.
5. N. Ivanoff in *Emporium* (1944-45), p. 92.

BENEDETTO VELI, Florence 1564-1639 Florence

Biographically little is known about this painter who worked in a conservative late Mannerist style. His works are to be found in and around Florence.

1638   The mystic marriage of St. Catherine (Fig. 167).

Oil on canvas, 1.87 × 1.27 m.

SIGNED: *Beneds Veli Ping. Flor. 1610.*

CONDITION: very good.

PROVENANCE: Monsignor Shine, Dublin; by bequest to Miss K. Farrelly, from whom purchased, 1961, for £350.

Works by this artist are rare. The style of no. 1638 is curious indeed, as it does not appear to fit into any of the approaches to painting developing around 1610. It is a late, rather personal form of mild Mannerism.

Perhaps Veli's best known achievement is the series of wall paintings depicting the life of S. Atto in the Badia di San Michele di Passignano, Tavarnelle Val di Pesa, south of Florence. These are dated 1609. Also there, is the *Assumption.*

No. 1638 by Veli, and his better known works, give veracity to the conclusion of Wittkower: 'The Italian city-states and provincial centres looked back to an old tradition of local schools of painting. These schools lived on into the seventeenth century, preserving some of their native characteristics. In contrast to the previous two centuries, however, their importance was slight compared with Rome's dominating position.'[1]

1. R. Wittkower, *Art and Architecture in Italy 1600 to 1750* (Harmondsworth, 1975 reprint), p. 91.

IACOPO VIGNALI, Pratovecchio 1592-1664 Florence

Like Lorenzo Lippi, Vignali studied under Matteo Rosselli. Later he developed a very personal style of his own, which does owe much to several of his Florentine contemporaries. Vignali received abundant commissions for churches in and around Florence. Carlo Dolci was one of his pupils.

183   St. Cecilia (Fig. 169).

Oil on canvas, 1.40 × 1.45 m.

CONDITION: very good. Restored 1985. In the course of the cleaning and restoration carried out in 1985 notable later overpainting was removed. This concerned particularly the head of St. Cecilia, and the appearance of the heads of the two angels. St. Cecilia's head had been tilted back with upward gaze; her mouth was made to appear smaller and open in song; a veil flowed from the band of pearls which hold her hair at the back. The heads of the two angels were altered less radically; their pose was not altered; by endowing both of them with a more abundant crop of dark curly hair, the flowers which they wore as decoration in their hair and the pearl ear-rings were covered up. In addition the necklaces which they both wear were painted out. Thus, it would appear that a later owner ordered the overpainting in an attempt to make the picture less worldly in impact, and more "holy" according to an interpretation of piety prevalent in several schools of Italian Seicento painting, notably the Bolognese (Fig. 168).

PROVENANCE: Sir Henry Page Turner Barron, Bt., by whom presented, 1878.

St. Cecilia came from a wealthy Roman family. Secretly she was a Christian; immediately after her marriage she inspired her husband Valerian to become a Christian also. He and his brother Tiburtius became martyrs. Then Cecilia was sentenced to beheading. After three blows of the axe Cecilia was still alive and the law forbade further blows. Cecilia lingered on for several days half-alive, half-dead. Her house became a church. *(Golden Legend)*

St. Cecilia is the patroness of music.

The traditional attribution of this painting to the Bolognese artist, Carlo Cignani, survived unchallenged for more than a century from the time of its gift, perhaps largely because it had not been hung in the Gallery for a very long time. The writer questioned its location in the Bolognese School, and in this was supported by Sergio Benedetti. After a certain amount of investigation in the Florentine School the writer went to Florence, with a tentative attribution to Rosselli. In February 1982 Gerhard Ewald, Mina Gregori, and Giuseppe Cantelli all examined a good black and white photograph of the painting. Each of these three specialists of the Florentine Seicento, without any prompting, or any opportunity of discussing the painting together, said that it was a major work by Iacopo Vignali. Cantelli subsequently published his positive attribution.[1]

At Sotheby's, Florence, on 21 October 1970, lot 73, a large Vignali of *Christ at the pool of Bethsaida* was sold, under the title *Probatica piscina*. In this painting the face of a small kneeling figure in the foreground to the right of Christ resembled very closely that of St. Cecilia in no. 183.

In Vignali's very large *Triumph of David*, in the Bob Jones University Collection, at Greenville, U.S.A., the head of the girl in the background, immediately to the left of David, is virtually identical with that of St. Cecilia in no. 183.

A facial resemblance for the angels in no. 183 is to be found in the attendant holding the crown in Vignali's *Baptism of Constantine,* in the Pitti Palace.

A short journey to the south of Florence, about 18 kilometres, to the Chiesa della Misericordia, San Casciano in Val di Pesa, with the well studied Vignalis,[2] will convince anyone of the correctness of the opinion expressed by the three specialists of the Florentine Seicento. In *The Holy Family with attendant angels,* the wing of the large angel in the foreground is treated in a manner almost identical with that of the left hand angel in the Dublin painting. In addition, the compositional grouping of the angels in the Chiesa della Misericordia painting, while obviously not the same as that in no. 183, nonetheless has a very comparable construction.

The classical decoration on the musical instrument is found in many Florentine paintings of the period, the closest known to the writer being that in *Lady playing a musical instrument,* in the Ginori Lisci Collection, Florence, a work usually attributed to Matteo Rosselli, Vignali's teacher.

The harpsichord shown in no. 183 is a typical Italian instrument which one would expect to find in use when the picture was painted. It rests on a table rather than on its own legs. The lute being played by one of the angels is a theorboed lute, 'having six lower bass strings off the fingerboard and attached to a second pegbox (not visible here), and twelve pegs representing six double courses on the main pegbox.'[3]

1. G. Cantelli, *Repertorio della Pittura Fiorentina del Seicento* (Fiesole 1983), p. 144.
2. C. del Bravo, in *Paragone*, no. 135 (March 1961), p. 33, p. 41, n. 13. S. B. Bartolozzi, *Vita di Iacopo Vignali pittor fiorentino* (Florence 1753)

only mentions the other Vignali in this church, *The Circumcision* (p. XIII).
3. B. Boydell, *Music and Paintings in the National Gallery of Ireland* (National Gallery of Ireland, Dublin 1985), pp. 54-55.

GIOVANNI BATTISTA VIOLA, Bologna 1576-1662 Rome

Viola was trained by Annibale Carracci. He specialized in painting landscapes. He decorated the interiors of many Roman palaces, the figures being inserted by his fellow citizen Francesco Albani.

Attributed to VIOLA

1977 Landscape with Jacob wrestling with the angel (Fig. 173).

Oil on canvas, 1.69 × 2.13 m.

CONDITION: good. Restored Summer 1978. There were paint losses throughout the picture in a random fashion.

PROVENANCE: Cardinal Fesch; probably his sale, 1845, no. 1308 (unattributed); Alessandro Aducci, Rome, from whom purchased 1856.[1] One of sixteen pictures acquired for £1,700.

The painting was acquired as a work by Viola and catalogued thus in early catalogues, down to and including that of 1887. Thereafter it was omitted, until its reinstatement in the 1971 edition.

Works stylistically close to no. 1977 are: the landscape frescos in the Stanza dei Paesi in the Casino dell' Aurora, at the Villa Ludovisi, Rome, especially when one allows for the difference in medium; a *Landscape with cavaliers* in the Budapest Museum of Fine Arts;[2] and a *Landscape* in the Galleria Borghese, Rome, (inv. no. 1623). There is no proof that these works are definitely by Viola, but the attributions are reasonable.

1. M. Wynne in *Gazette des Beaux-Arts*, vol. 89 (January 1977), pp. 2, 6.
2. *Bulletin du Musée Hongrois des Beaux-Arts*, nos. 32-33 (1969), fig. 91.

FILIPPO VITALE, (?) Naples 1589-1650 Naples

Very little is known about the life and work of Vitale. A fellow Neapolitan painter, Carlo Sellito, was godfather to Vitale's son Carlo. Vitale's oeuvre *is based on one signed work, and another monogrammed one; consequently attributions to him must invariably be tentative.*

Attributed to VITALE

1377   St. Sebastian (Fig. 172).

Oil on canvas, 1.80 × 1.305 m.

CONDITION: very good. Restored 1983.

PROVENANCE: Bartholomew Watkins, London, by whom presented, 1854.

Having been pierced by arrows, St. Sebastian has slipped downwards so that his knees project forward. In the background, on the right hand side, St. Irene and companions are coming to tend the severely wounded saint.

From its acquisition this painting was catalogued as a Ribera, down to and including the 1874 edition, after which it was omitted. Reinstated in the 1963 catalogue, it was attributed to Ribera. In 1955 Raffaelo Causa proposed an attribution to Vitale;[1] about the same time Ferdinando Bologna made a similar suggestion.[2] Nicola Spinosa, on the other hand, more recently left the painting unattributed because it was in need of cleaning.[3] Paola Giusti adopted[4] the short *oeuvre* catalogue prepared by Bologna, accepting his attribution. It is worth taking seriously the suggested attribution to Vitale. The painting, *The martyrdom of St. Sebastian,* in the sacristy of the Church of S. Maria degli Angioli alle Croci, Naples, which may be by Vitale, does show some relationship with no. 1377. Similar are the stubby toes; similar are the closely folded draperies; further, the agonized position of the figure of St. Sebastian in Dublin is not matched by a dramatic treatment of strained muscles. The Naples St. Sebastian is also in a tortured pose not fully expressed by the anatomical depiction. The pain of both is expressed in the flung back heads. A fully signed work by Vitale is the *Pietà* in the Church of S. Maria Regina Coeli, Naples. The stubby toes of Christ, St. Mary Magdalen, and other figures compare with that idiosyncracy in no. 1377. The treatment of draperies is similar.

Another artist who should be seriously considered in connection with no. 1377 is Andrea Vaccaro (1605-1670). This artist's *St. Januarius* and *St. Rosalia of Palermo* (the former of which is signed with Vaccaro's monogram) in the Prado are distinguished by the dramatically upturned eyes and open mouth; comparable also is no. 1760 in the Hermitage, *Mary Magdalen,* which is monogrammed, as is the *St. Cecilia,* which, in 1927, was in the collection of A. L. Nicholson, London. More recently a monogrammed *St. Agatha* came on the art market (Sotheby's, 9 March 1983, lot 39).

No. 1377 must date to the 1630s.

Until more fully authenticated works by Vitale are published, it would be imprudent to be categorical about the attribution.

1. In correspondence, August 1955.
2. In *Opere d'arte nel Salernitano dal XII al XVIII secolo* (Naples 1955), p. 64, note 2. The writer is grateful to Wolfgang Prohaska, Vienna, who kindly gave him a photocopy of the relevant portion of this publication, not readily found in the Western Isles.

3. N. Spinosa, *L'opera completa del Ribera* (Milan 1978), p. 138, no. 388.
4. In exhibition catalogue, C. Whitfield and J. Martineau (edd.), *Painting in Naples 1606-1705. From Caravaggio to Giordano* (Royal Academy, London, 1982), p. 263.

NUMERICAL INDEX

Index of pictures by numerical order of catalogue number

542	Giaquinto	*(?) The glorification of Marcantonio II Colonna*
626	Solimena	*Winter*
656	Studio of Piazzetta	*A pastoral outing*
678	Magnasco	*Landscape with washerwomen*
701	Batoni	*Joseph Leeson, afterwards 1st Earl of Milltown*
702	Batoni	*Joseph Leeson, afterwards 2nd Earl of Milltown*
703	Batoni	*Portrait of a lady, possibly Anne Leeson, as Diana*
704	Attrib. to Batoni	*Venus and Cupid*
705	After Canaletto	*The Grand Canal with the Church of the Salute*
725	Panini	*The Colosseum and the Arch of Constantine*
726	Panini	*The Roman Forum*
727	Panini	*Roman ruins with fifteen figures*
728	Panini	*Roman ruins with eleven figures*
738	School of Rosa	*Mountain landscape*
739	School of Rosa	*Mountain landscape*
781	Strozzi	*Portrait of a gentleman*
819	Style of Francesco Guardi	*Imaginary landscape*
856	Strozzi	*Spring and Summer*
898	Studio of Fetti	*The parable of the lord of the vineyard*
952	Longhi, Pietro	*The artist painting a lady's portrait*
980	Gentileschi	*David and Goliath*
981	After Liss	*The vision of St Jerome*
982	Bazzani	*Christ meets His Mother*
983	Bazzani	*Descent from the Cross*
989	Lauri	*Rebecca at the well*
993	Passeri	*A party feasting in a garden*
994	Castiglione	*The shepherdess Spako with the infant Cyrus*
1014	Attrib. to Fieravino	*Still life with musical instruments*
1020	Crespi	*Massacre of the Innocents*
1031	Bassetti	*Portrait of an elderly man*
1040	Masucci	*Mystic marriage of St Catherine*
1043	After Canaletto	*The Grand Canal with the Church of the Carità*
1065	After Reni	*The Virgin sewing*
1068	Studio of Chimenti	*Adoration of the shepherds*
1069	Giordano	*St John the Baptist preaching in the wilderness*
1070	Ficherelli	*The sacrifice of Isaac*
1074	Italian School, 17th C.	*Bacchanalian boys and satyrs*
1075	Italian School, 17th C.	*Young boys and satyrs at play*
1083	After Domenichino	*Expulsion of Adam and Eve*
1084	Italian School, 18th C.	*Pope Benedict XIII*

1086	Attrib. to Pagani	*Death of Lucretia*
1093	Piscelli	*Lake scene with figures*
1094	Piscelli	*Coast scene with shipwreck*
1099	Ricci, Sebastiano	*King Hieron II of Syracuse*
1107	Solimena	*St Simplicius*
1111	Tiepolo, Giovanni Battista	*Christ in the house of Simon the Pharisee*
1178	Pensionante del Saraceni	*St Peter denying Christ*
1189	Circle of Appiani	*Bonaparte as a general in the army of the Revolution*
1229	Dolci	*St Agnes*
1235	Attrib. to Riminaldi	*Victorious Earthly Love*
1239	Italian School, *circa* 1800	*Head of a saint*
1323	After Guercino	*The triumph of David*
1334	After Reni	*St Jerome*
1335	Pasinelli	*The Muse of Sculpture*
1377	Attrib. to Vitale	*St Sebastian*
1531	Style of Panini	*Ruins with figures*
1638	Veli	*Mystic marriage of St. Catherine*
1640	Carlone, Carlo Innocenzo	*The Annunciation*
1653	Turchi	*An angel leading Lot and his daughters*
1658	Furini	*Hylas and the nymphs*
1659	After Guercino	*Day*
1661	Attrib. to Mehus	*St Sebastian*
1664	Rosa da Tivoli	*Landscape with cattle*
1666	Rosa da Tivoli	*Landscape with cattle and sheep*
1667	Circle of Riminaldi	*Cain and Abel*
1668	After Guercino	*St Agatha*
1669	Attrib. to Troppa	*Adoration of the shepherds*
1670	Ferri	*Expulsion of Hagar*
1671	Studio of Chimenti	*Susanna and the Elders*
1679	Furini	*St Mary Magdalen*
1682	After Guercino	*Night*
1683	Dandini, Cesare	*Moses driving away the shepherds*
1686	After Guercino	*Aurora*
1688	After Amigoni	*Birth of Adonis*
1692	After Guercino	*An angel leading Innocence to Heaven*
1695	After Reni	*Crucifixion of St Peter*
1703	Studio of Maratti	*Virgin and Child with saints*
1707	Ficherelli	*St Mary Magdalen*
1716	Furini	*Crucifixion of a female saint*
1739	Stern or Stella	*Cupid chastised*
1740	Attrib. to Pasinelli	*Albunea, the Tiburtine Sibyl*
1744	Coccorante	*Coast scene with ruins and shipwrecks*

1746	Ficherelli	*Lot and his daughters*
1747	Lippi, Lorenzo	*Medoro and Angelica*
1751	School of Tassi	*Coast scene*
1752	School of Tassi	*Coast scene*
1814	Attrib. to Alessandro Longhi	*Portrait of a lady holding a fan*
1820	Procaccini, Giulio Cesare	*St Charles Borromeo*
1885	After Domenichino	*Last communion of St Jerome*
1893	Mola	*St Joseph's dream*
1908	After Reni	*Rape of Europa*
1911	Roman School, 2nd half of 17th C.	*The Holy Family with monks*
1912	Attrib. to Preti	*St Ambrose*
1918	Pascucci	*Adoration of the shepherds*
1925	Celesti	*Imaginary portrait of Count Alberto Alberti*
1938	Pellegrini	*Susanna and the Elders*
1960	After Bellotto	*Pirna on the Elbe, with Sonnenstein*
1967	Bolognese School, 18th C.	*Lucretia stabbing herself*
1977	Attrib. to Viola	*Landscape with Jacob and the angel*
1988	Giordano	*Aesop*
1999	Attrib. to Pellegrini	*Allegory of Justice*
4002	Langetti	*St. Sebastian*
4006	Circle of Giordano	*Adam and Eve, with Cain and Abel*
4092	Keil, Eberhard	*The embroidery shop*
4096	Florentine School, 17th C.	*Crowd at city gates*
4159	Italian School, 17th C.	*Peter Talbot, Archbishop of Dublin*
4169	Canevari, Giovanni Battista	*Col. Richard Wogan, 2nd Baron Talbot of Malahide*
4269 **CB**	Pasini	*An Arab soldier seated by a doorway*
4271 **CB**	Pasini	*An eastern scene*
4302	Ferrari, Orazio De	*The incredulity of St Thomas*
4337	Italian School, 17th C.	*Shield: Head of Medusa*
4458	Mengs	*Thomas Conolly*
4468	Italian School, *circa* 1610	*Portrait of a young man of the Branconio family*

CHANGES OF ATTRIBUTION

Since the National Gallery of Ireland, *Illustrated Summary Catalogue of Paintings* (1981)

(An asterisk indicates that a painting which was previously catalogued as Italian of the centuries covered, is not included in this catalogue)

PREVIOUS ATTRIBUTION	CAT. NO.	REVISED ATTRIBUTION
Bettera	1014	Attrib. to Francesco Fieravino
Cantarini	71	Bolognese School, 17th C.
After Carracci	1682	After Guercino
Cignani	183	Iacopo Vignali
*After Domenichino	1910	Probably Lodovico Cardi da Cigoli
After Van Dyck	1661	Attrib. to Livio Mehus
French School, 17th C.	1999	Attrib. to Pellegrini
Style of Furini	1967	Bolognese School, 18th C.
Furini	4002	Giovanni Battista Langetti
Italian School, 16th C.	1335	Lorenzo Pasinelli
Italian School, 17th C.	1040	Agostino Masucci
Italian School, 17th C.	1667	Circle of Riminaldi
Italian School, 17th C.	1740	Attrib. to Lorenzo Pasinelli
*Italian School, 17th C.	4004	Probably Flemish
*Italian School, 17th C.	4048	French School, 17th C.
Italian School, 18th C.	542	Corrado Giaquinto
*Italian School, 18th C.	1693	To be attributed
Longhi	261	Bartolomeo Nazari
Neapolitan School, 17th C.	1074	Italian School, 17th C.
Neapolitan School, 17th C.	1075	Italian School, 17th C.
After Padovanino	1338	After Titian
After Pietro da Cortona	4006	Circle of Giordano
After Reni	1239	Italian School, *circa* 1800
Attrib. to Ribera	1377	Attrib. to Filippo Vitale
Turchi	1031	Marcantonio Bassetti
After Vignon	1912	Attrib. to Mattia Preti

INDEX OF PREVIOUS OWNERS

INDEX OF DONORS

*indicates a bequest.

Portrait Index

Topographical Index

INDEX OF RELIGIOUS SUBJECTS

INDEX OF IDENTIFIED SAINTS AND ANGELS

INDEX OF HISTORICAL AND MYTHOLOGICAL SUBJECTS

BIBLIOGRAPHY OF THE NATIONAL GALLERY OF IRELAND, CATALOGUES OF PAINTINGS

Date	Compiler
1864	G. F. Mulvany
1867	G. F. Mulvany, reprint with update addendum
1868	G. F. Mulvany, reprint with update addendum
1871	G. F. Mulvany, reprint with update addendum
1874	G. F. Mulvany, reprint with update addendum
1875	H. E. Doyle
1879	H. E. Doyle
1882	H. E. Doyle
1884	H. E. Doyle, minor changes
1885	H. E. Doyle, minor changes
1886 (?)	H. E. Doyle, minor changes
1887	H. E. Doyle, minor changes
1890	H. E. Doyle
1898	Walter Armstrong
1904	Walter Armstrong
1908	Walter Armstrong
1914	Walter Armstrong
1920	Langton Douglas (selective)
1928	Thomas Bodkin, editing Lucius O'Callaghan (selective)
1932	Thomas Bodkin, editing Lucius O'Callaghan, reprint
1956	Thomas McGreevy, *Catalogue of Pictures of the Italian Schools* (selective)
1963	Thomas McGreevy, Check list (selective)
1971	Michael Wynne, Check list (complete)
1981	Curatorial team, *Illustrated Summary Catalogue of Paintings* (complete, with every painting illustrated)
1981	Michael Wynne, *Recent Acquisitions 1980-1981*
1982	Homan Potterton and Michael Wynne, *Acquisitions 1981-82*
1984	Adrian Le Harivel and Michael Wynne, *Acquisitions 1982-83*
1986	Adrian Le Harivel and Michael Wynne, *Acquisitions 1984-86*

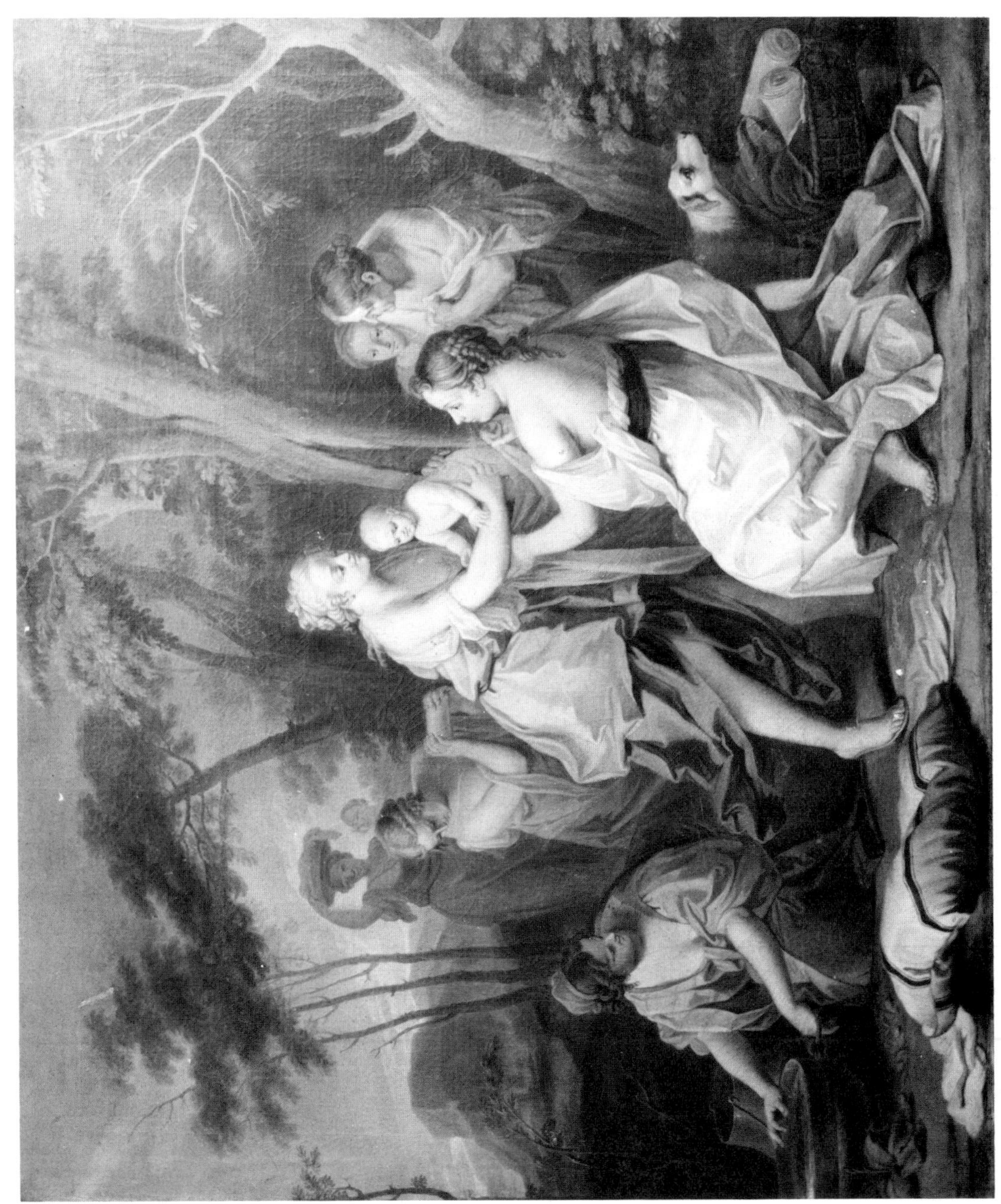

FIG. 1 After Amigoni, *The birth of Adonis* (cat. no. 1688).

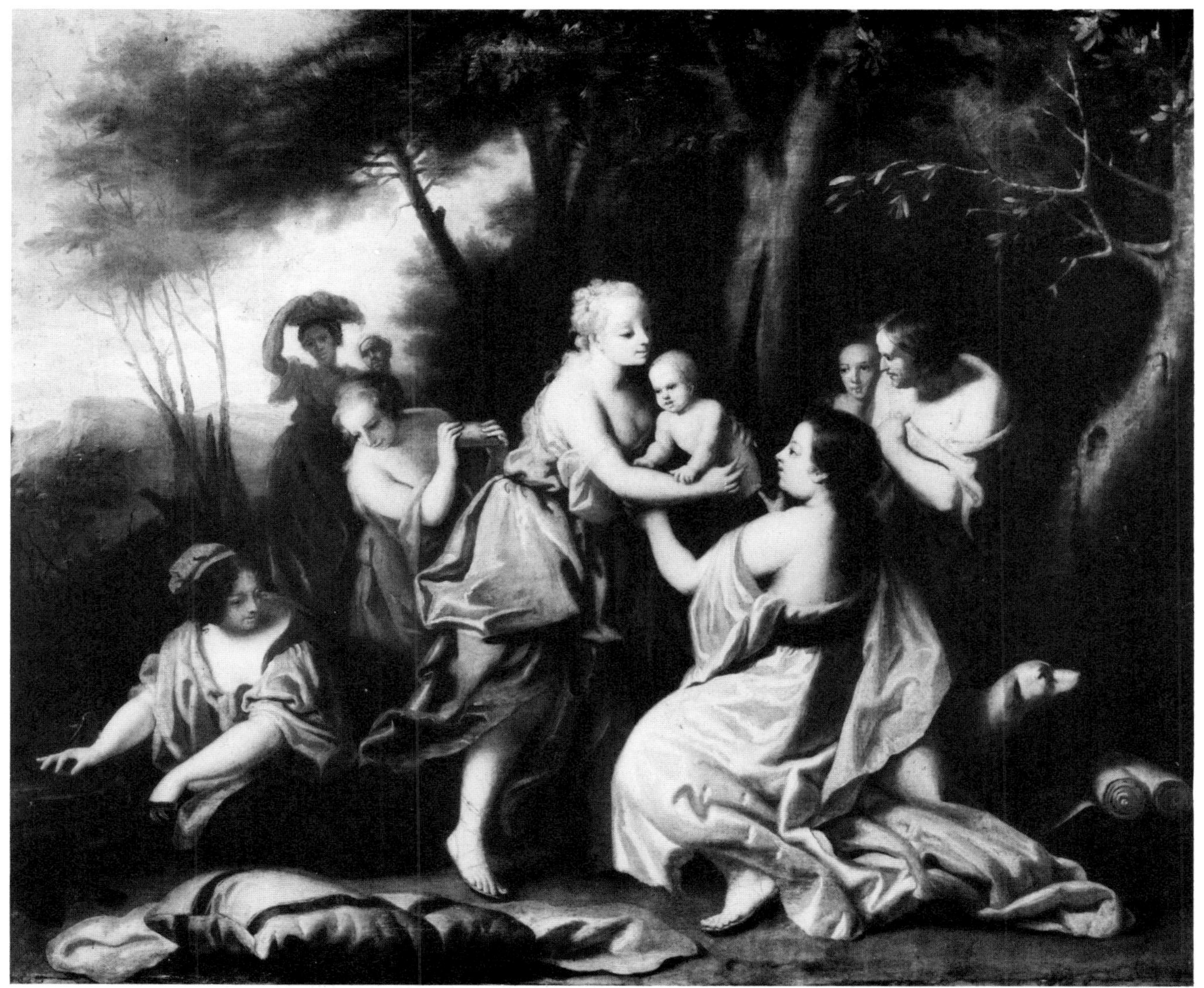

FIG. 2 Iacopo Amigoni, *The birth of Adonis*. Private Collection, Dublin.

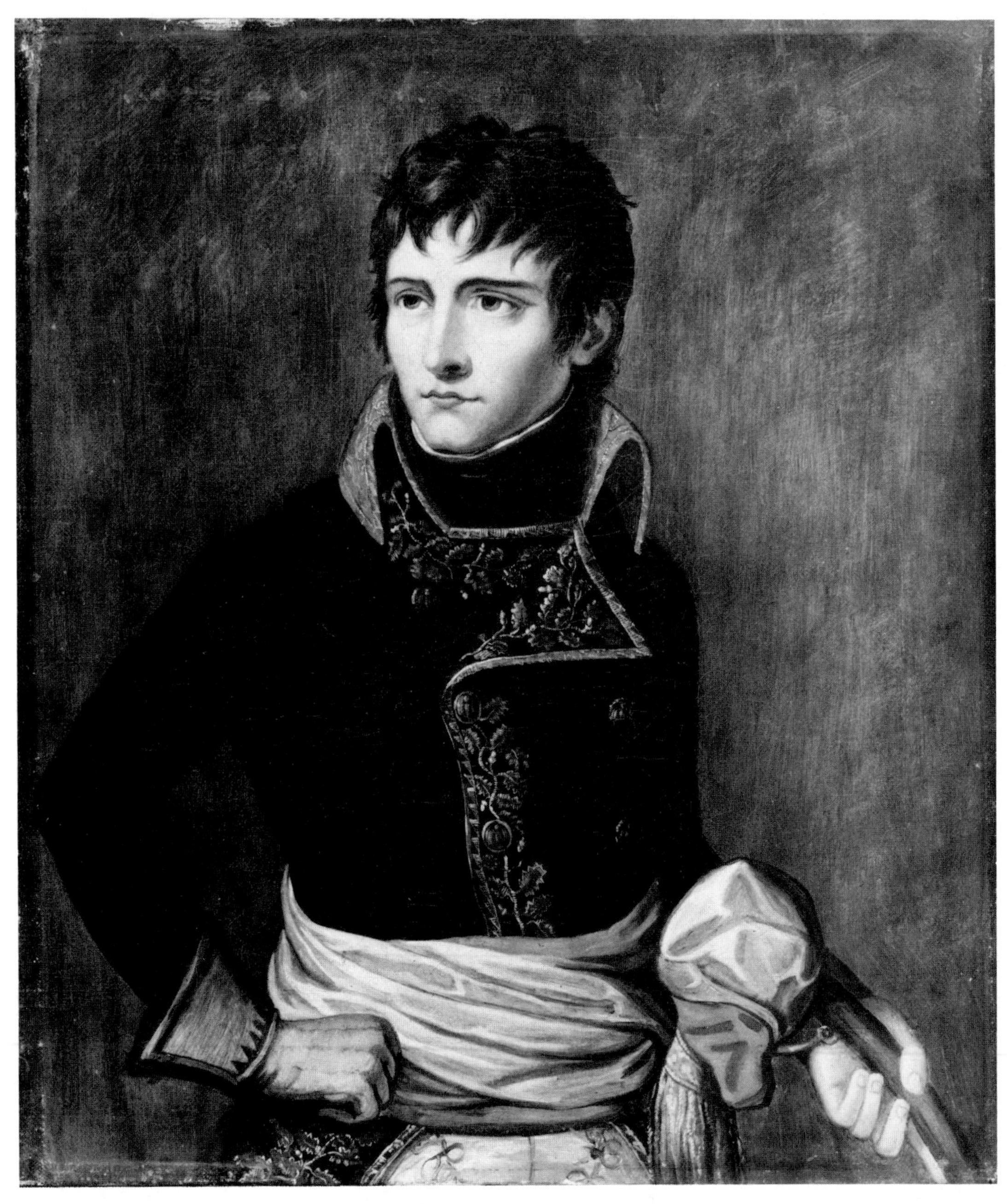

Fig. 3 Circle of Appiani, *Bonaparte as a general of the army of the Revolution* (cat. no. 1189).

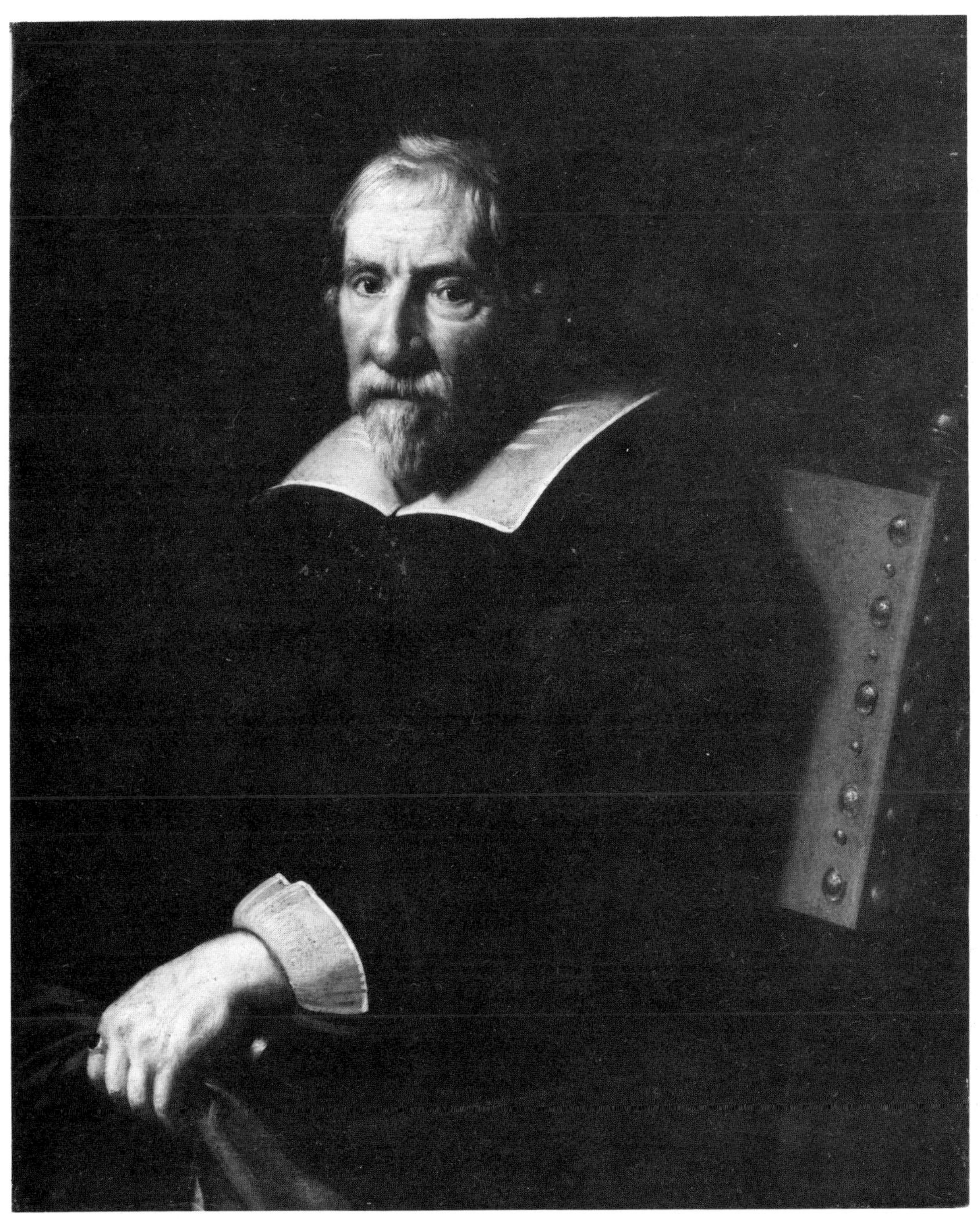

FIG. 4 Marcantonio Bassetti, *Portrait of an elderly man* (cat. no. 1031).

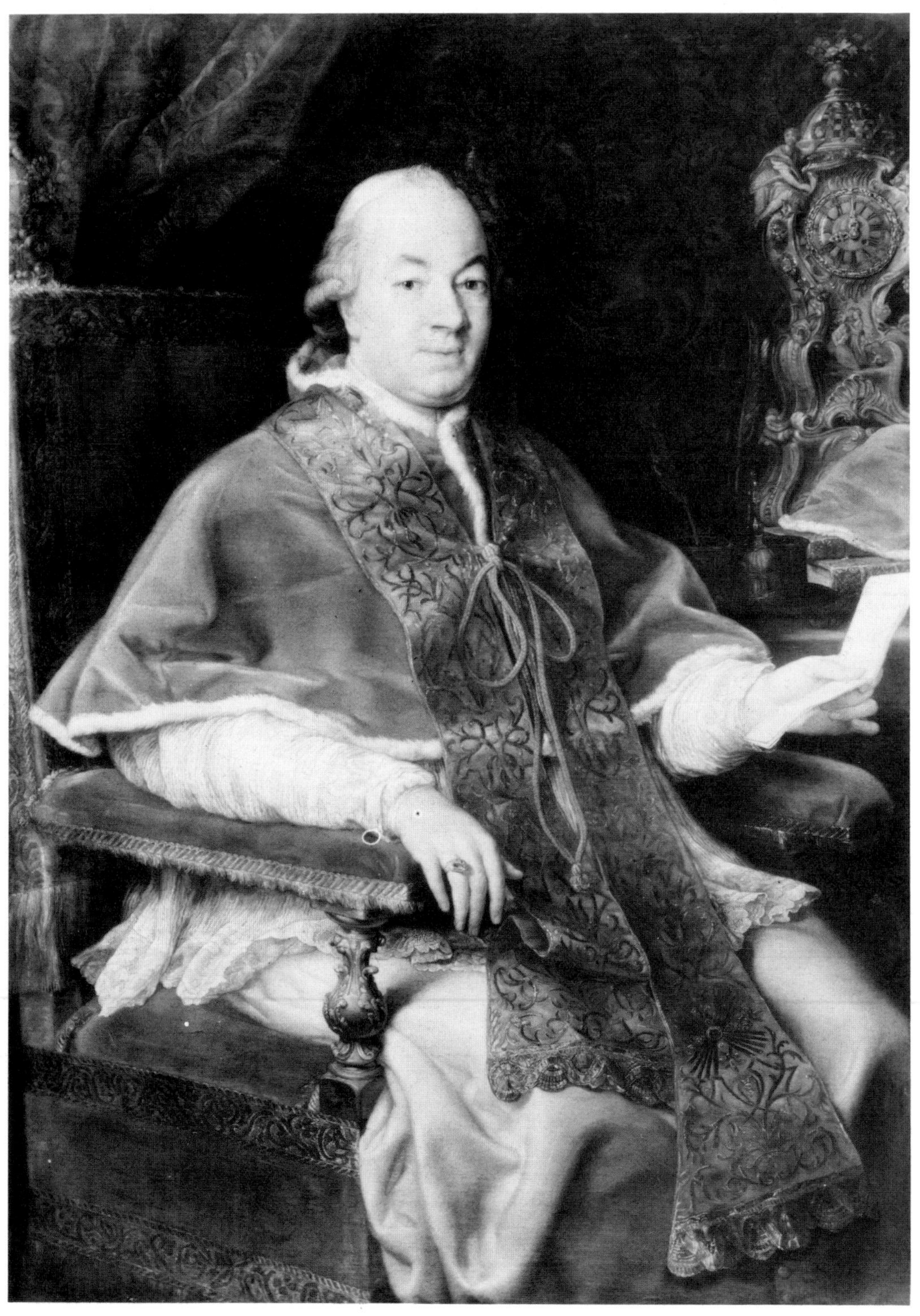

FIG. 5 Pompeo Girolamo Batoni, *Pope Pius VI* (cat. no. 109).

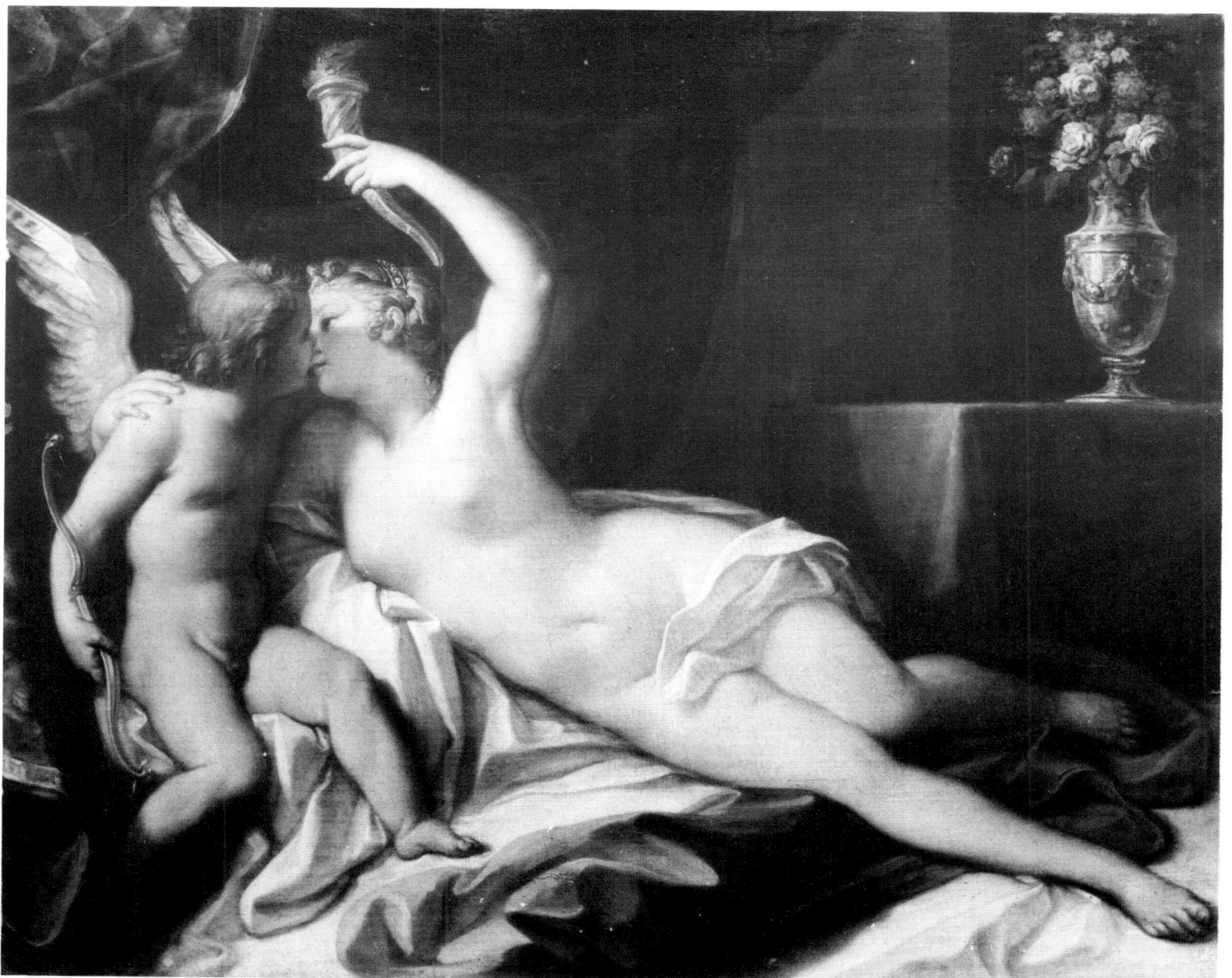

FIG. 6 Attributed to Batoni, *Venus and Cupid* (cat. no. 704).

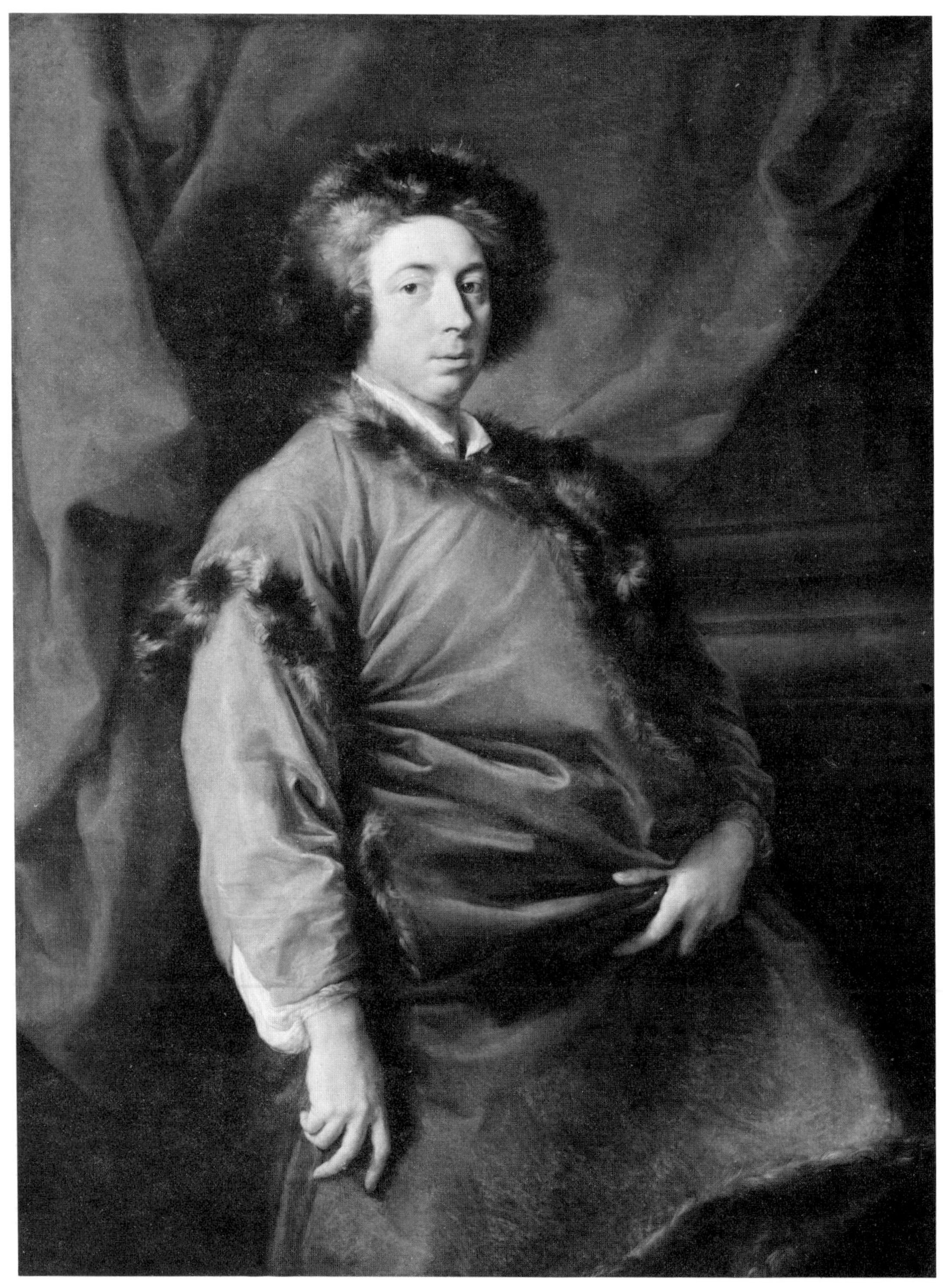

FIG. 7   Pompeo Girolamo Batoni, *Joseph Leeson, afterwards 1st Earl of Milltown, 1711-1783* (cat. no. 701).

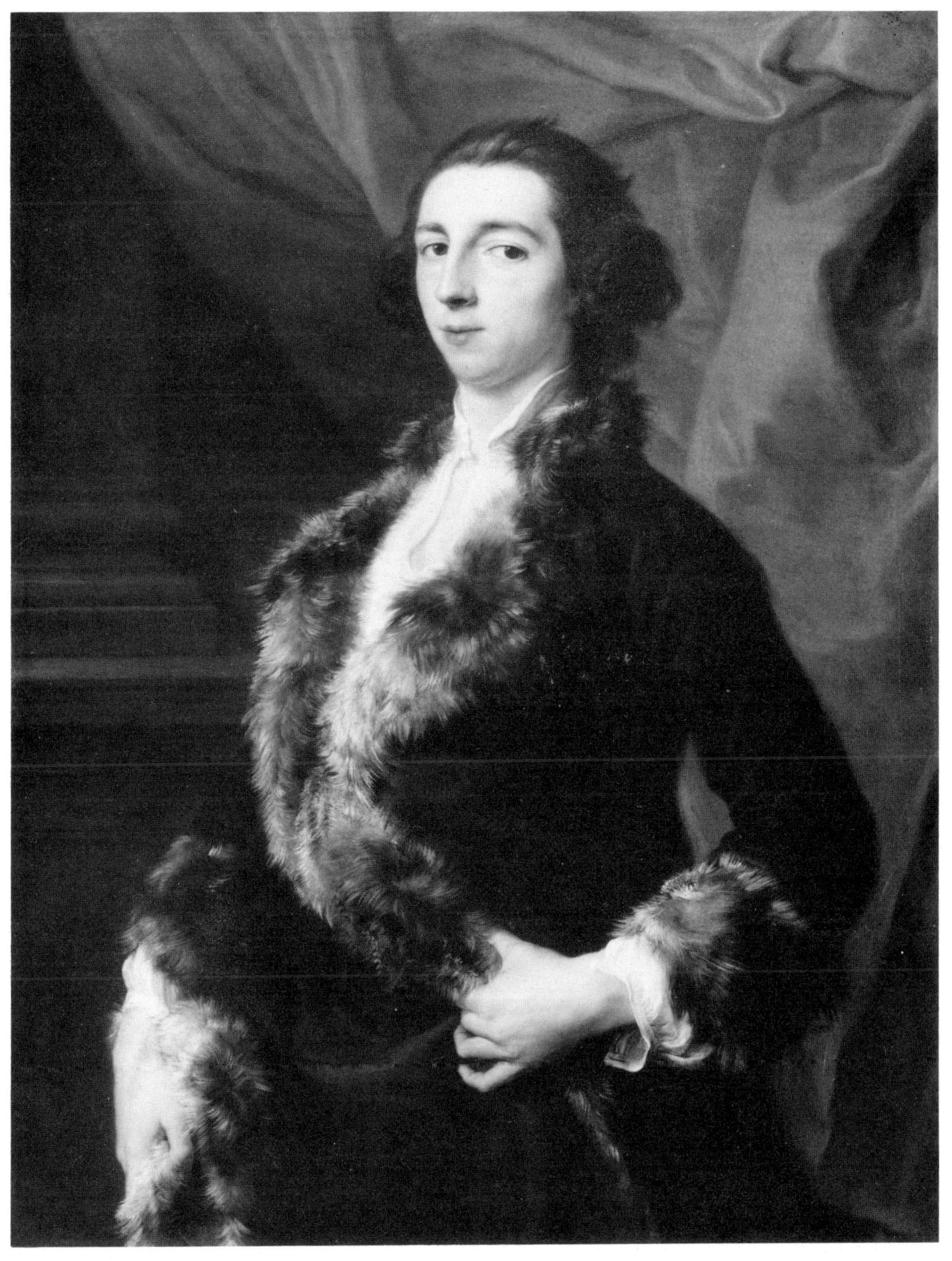

FIG. 8 Pompeo Girolamo Batoni, *Joseph Leeson, afterwards 2nd Earl of Milltown, 1730-1801* (cat. no. 702).

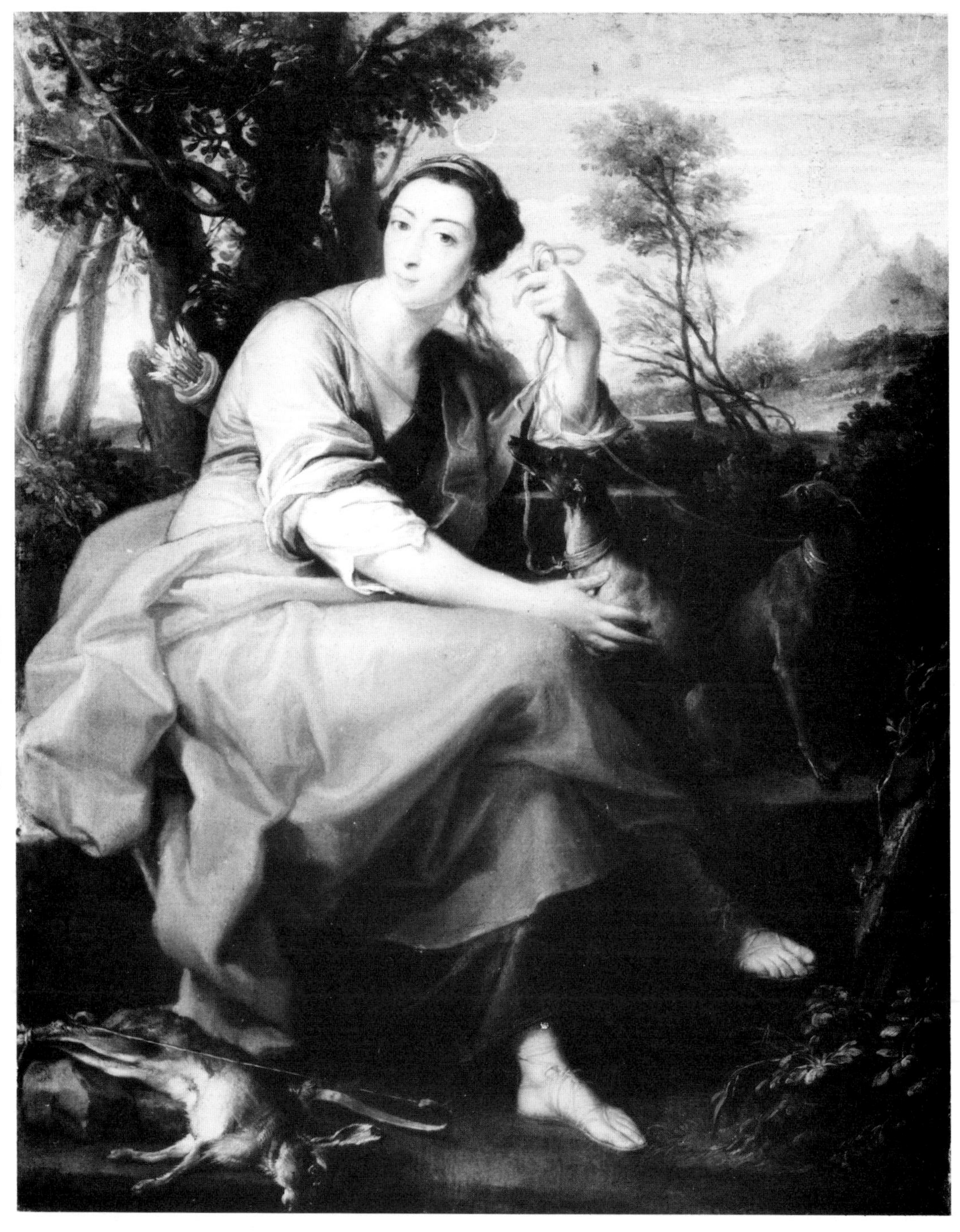

FIG. 9 Pompeo Girolamo Batoni, *Portrait of a lady, possibly Anne Leeson, subsequently 1st Countess of Milltown, as Diana* (cat. no. 703).

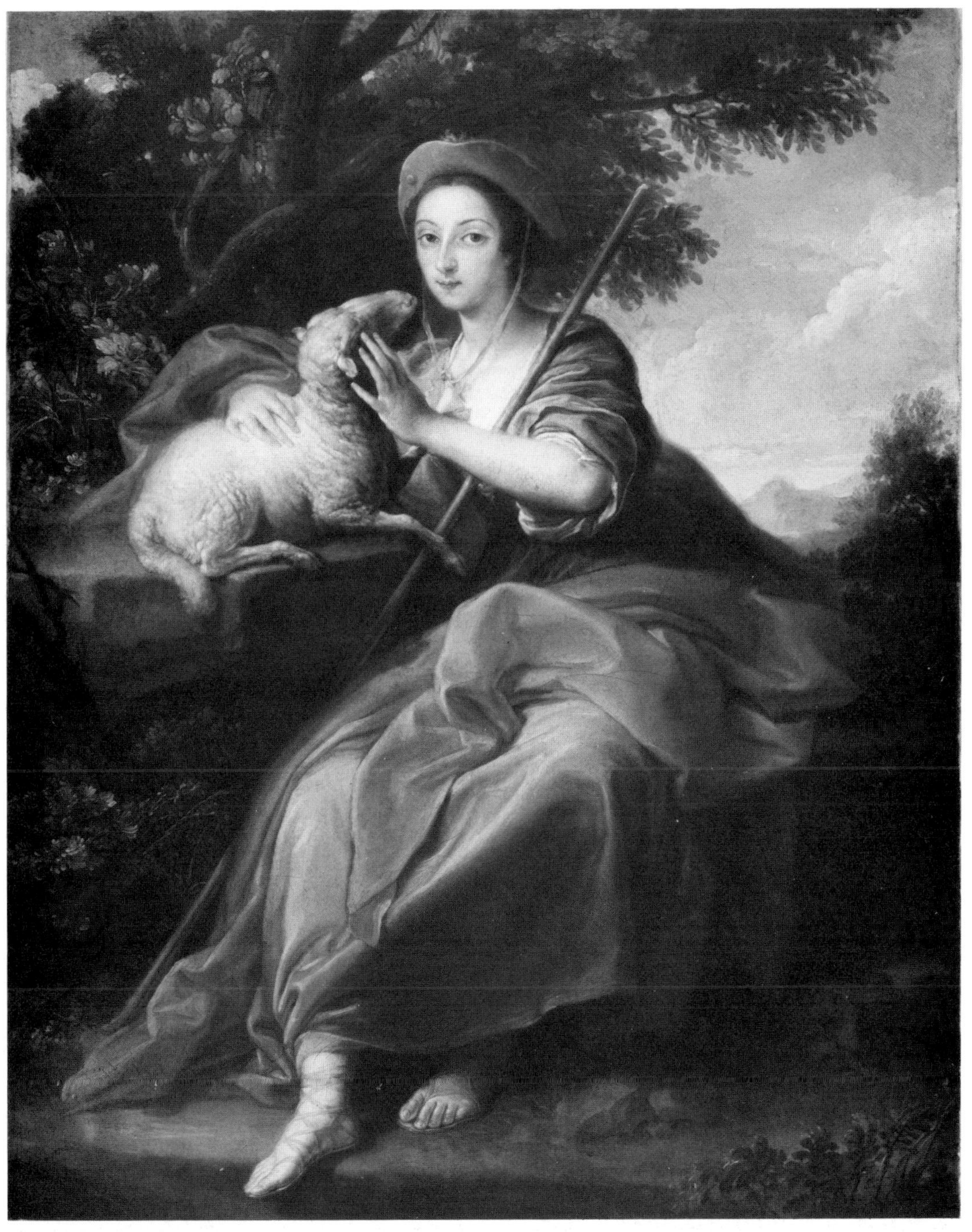

Fig. 10 Pompeo Girolamo Batoni, *Portrait of a lady, possibly a member of the Leeson family, as a shepherdess.* Oil on canvas, 0.47 × 0.36 m. (painted surface). Collection Sir Denis Mahon, London..

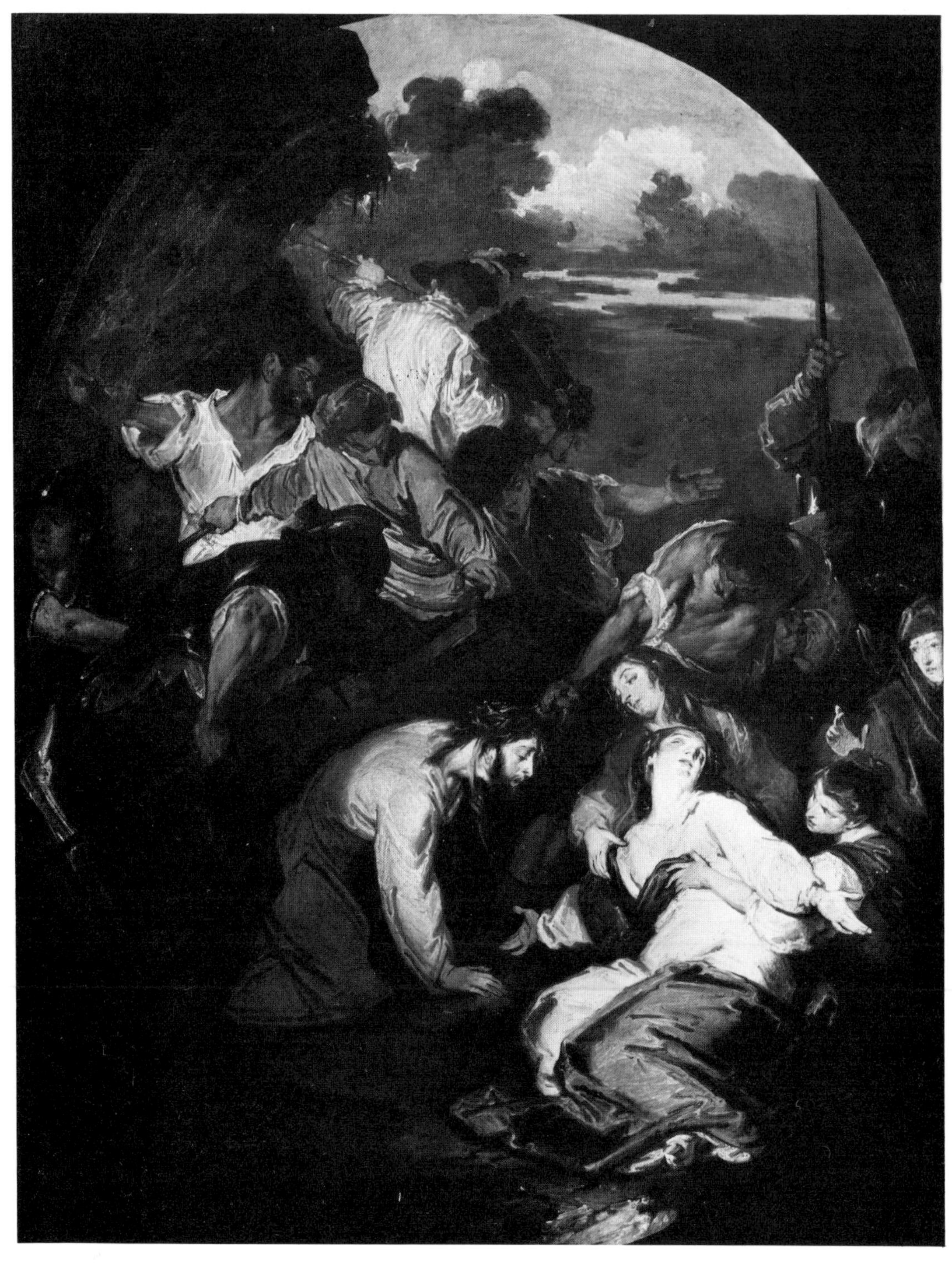

Fig. 11 Giuseppe Bazzani, *Christ meets his Mother* (cat. no. 982).

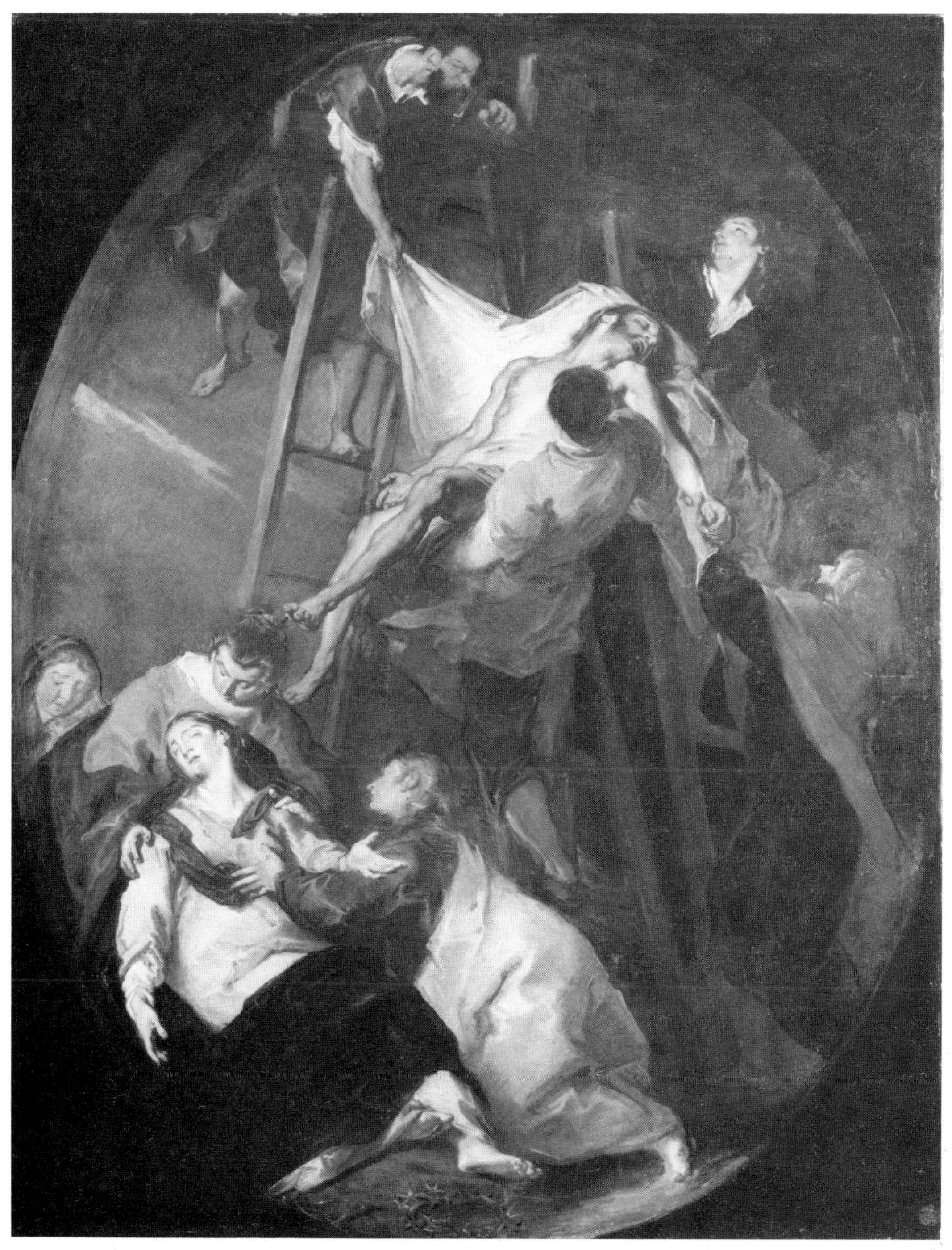

Fig. 12   Giuseppe Bazzani, *The descent from the Cross* (cat. no. 983).

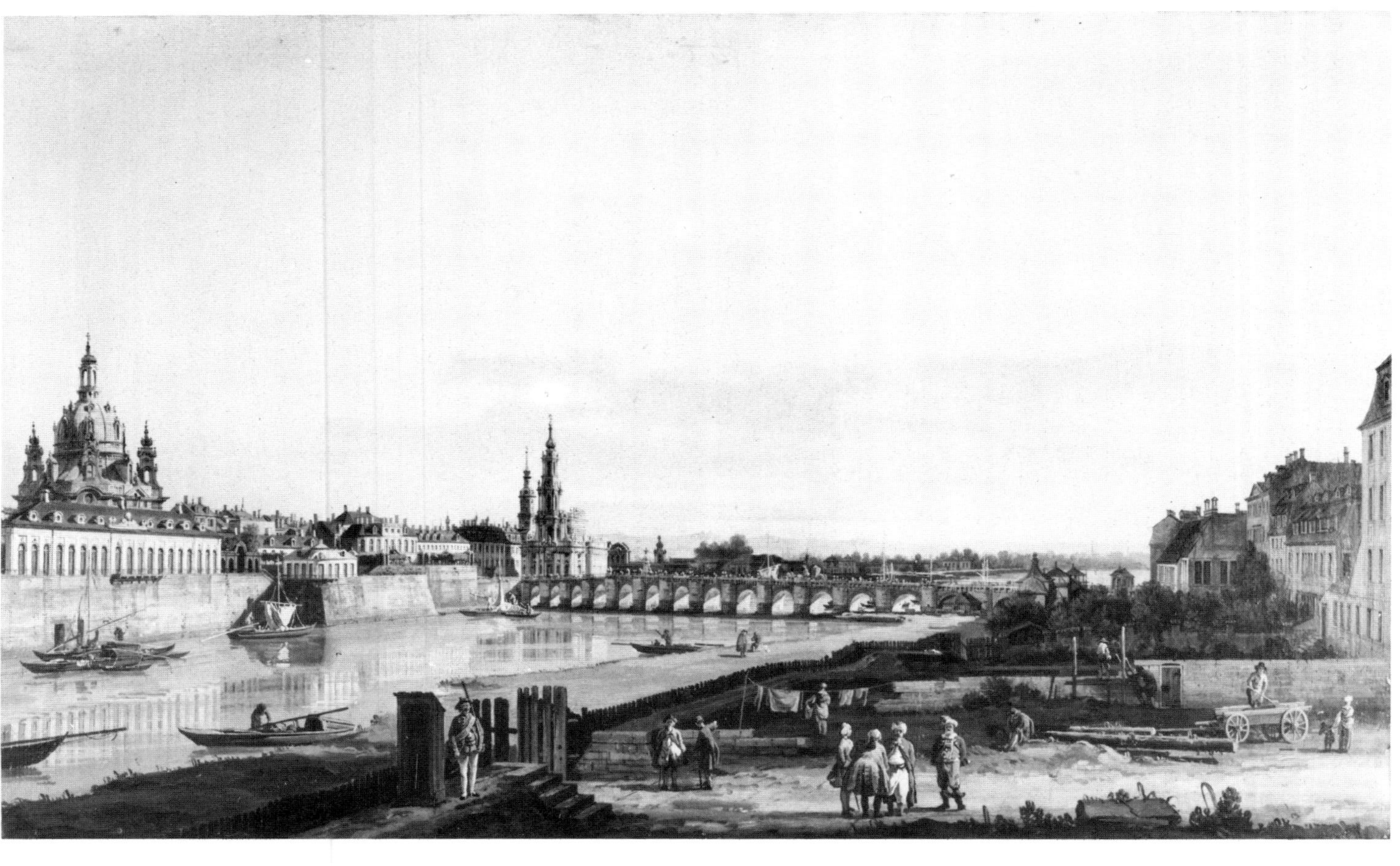

FIG. 13   Bernardo Bellotto, *Dresden from the right bank of the Elbe above the Augustus bridge* (cat. no. 181).

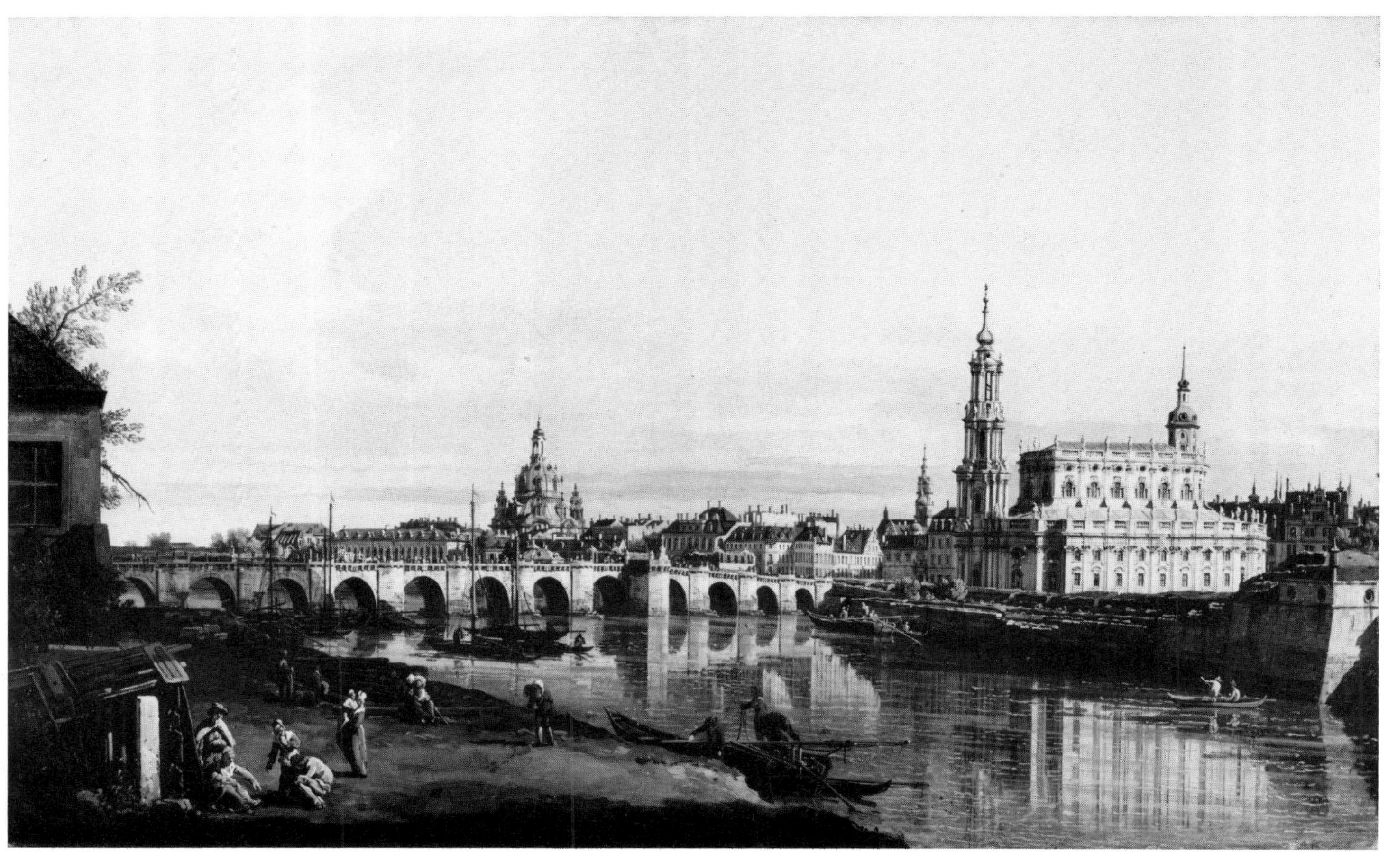

FIG. 14 Bernardo Bellotto, *Dresden from the right bank of the Elbe below the Augustus bridge* (cat. no. 182).

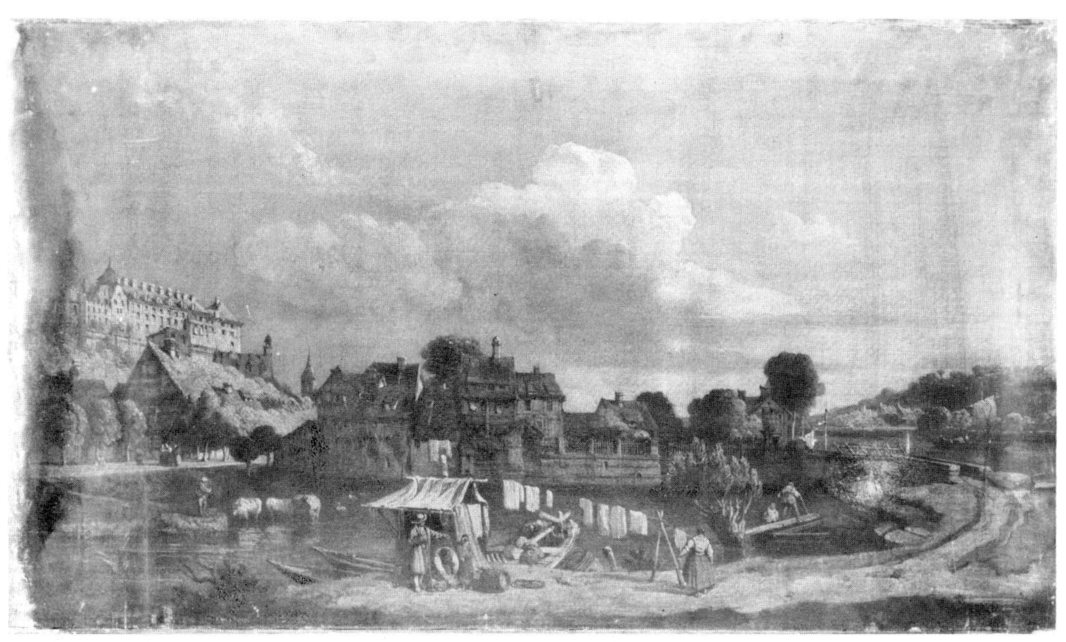

FIG. 15   After Bellotto, *View of Pirna on the Elbe with the Sonnenstein fortress* (cat. no. 1960).

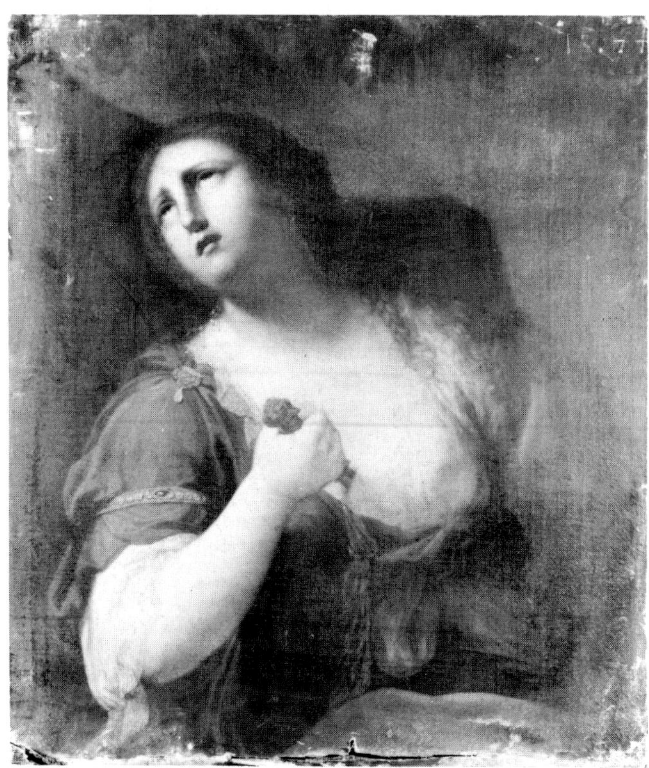

FIG. 17   Bolognese School, 18th Century, *Lucretia stabbing herself* (cat. no. 1967).

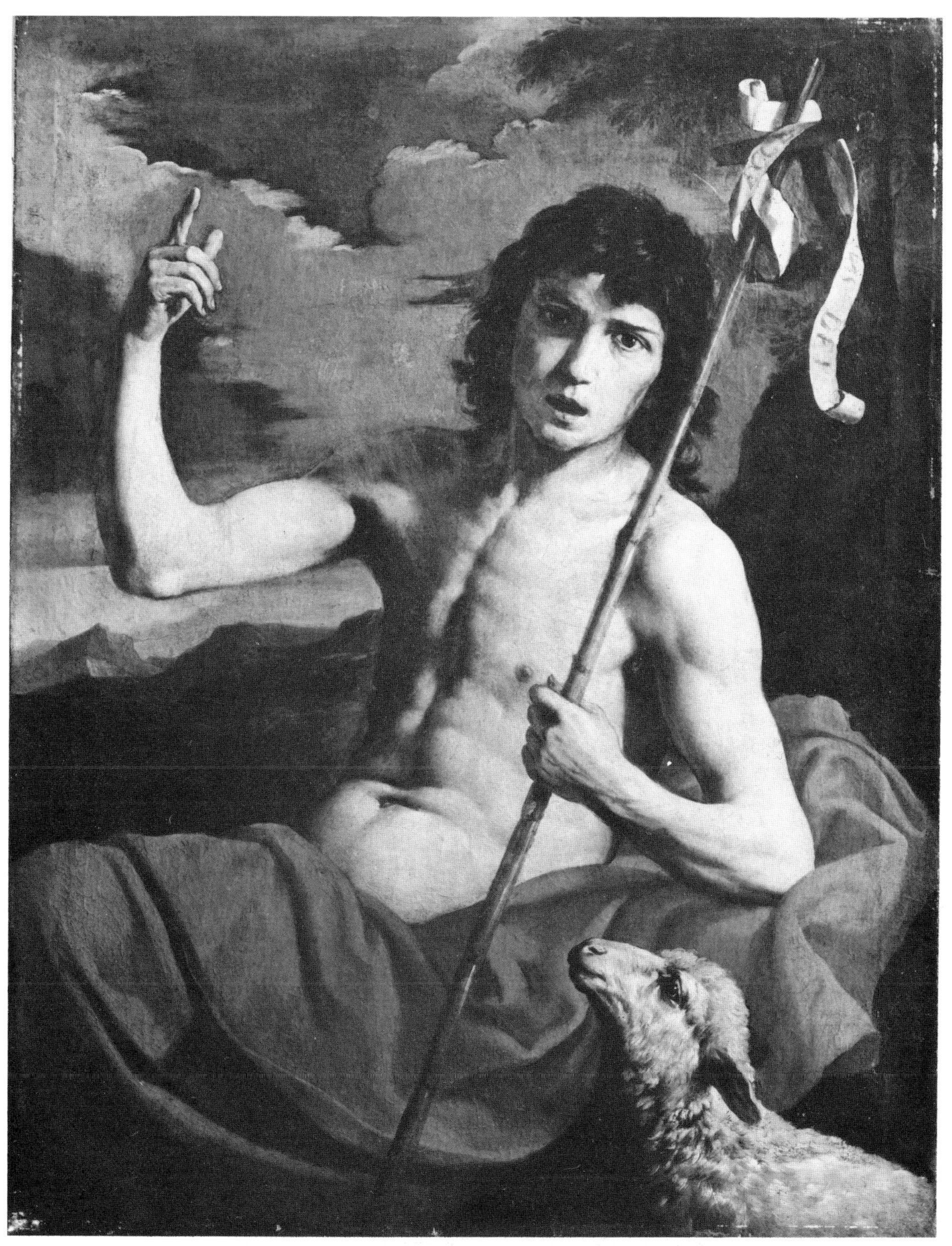

FIG. 16 Bolognese School, 17th Century, *St. John the Baptist in the wilderness*
(cat. no. 71).

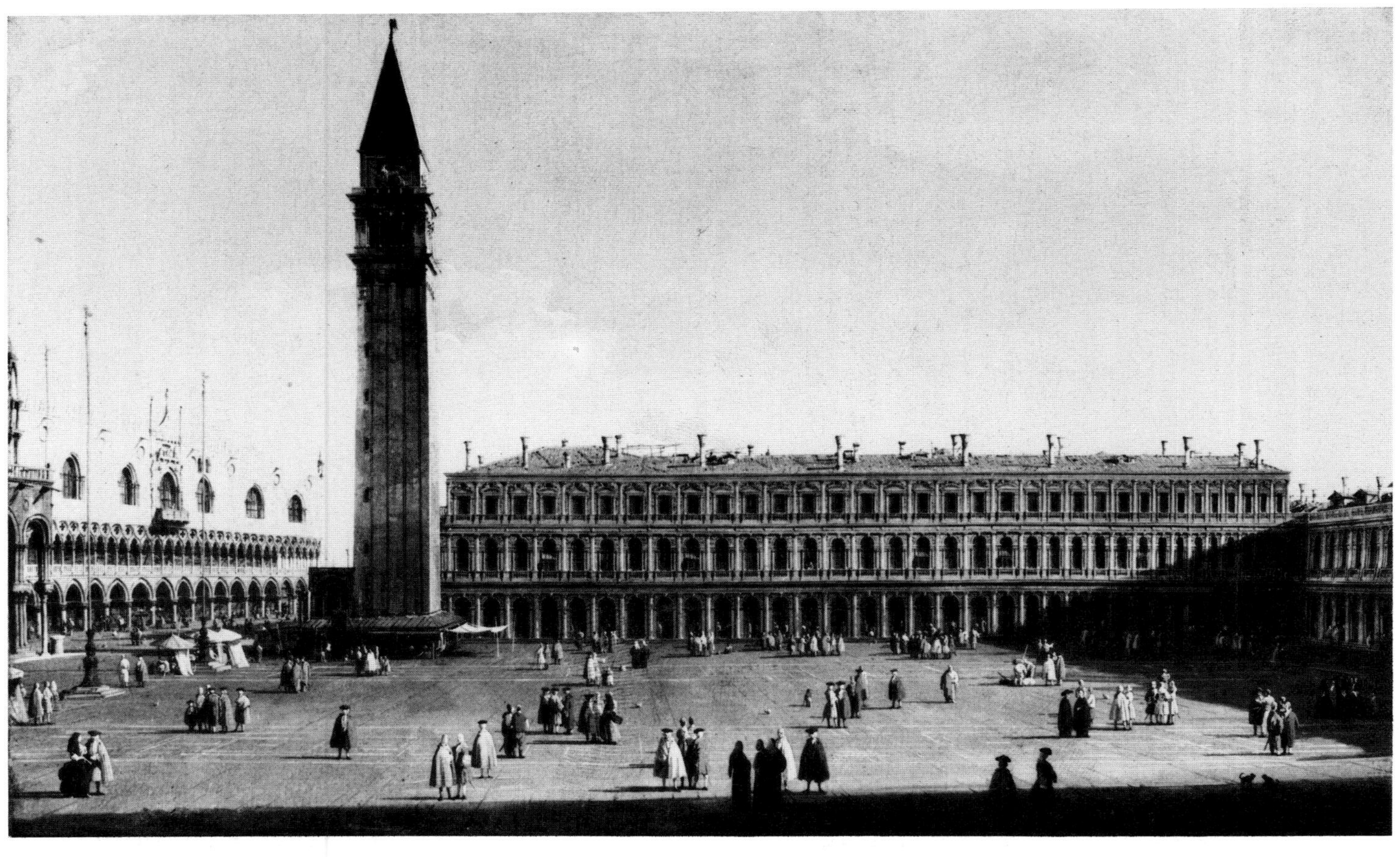

Fig. 18 Canaletto, *St. Mark's Square, Venice, with the Doge's Palace, the Campanile, and the Procuratie Nuove* (cat. no. 286).

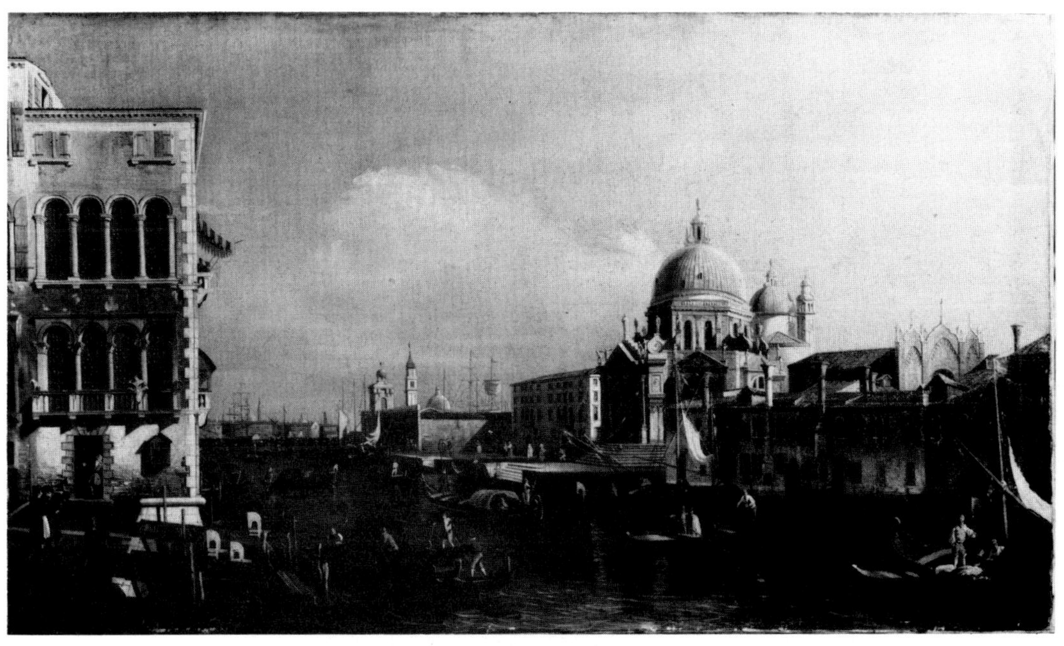

FIG. 19   After Canaletto, *The Grand Canal with the Church of the Salute and the Customs House, from Campo Santa Maria Zobenigo* (cat. no. 705).

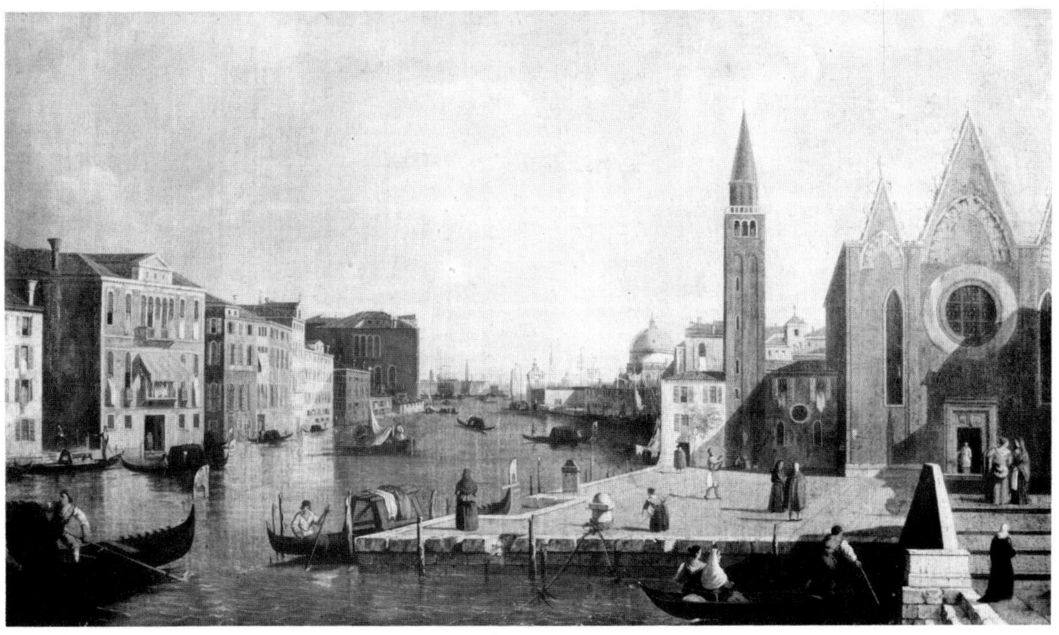

FIG. 20   After Canaletto, *The Grand Canal with the Church of the Carità towards the harbour of St. Mark's* (cat. no. 1043).

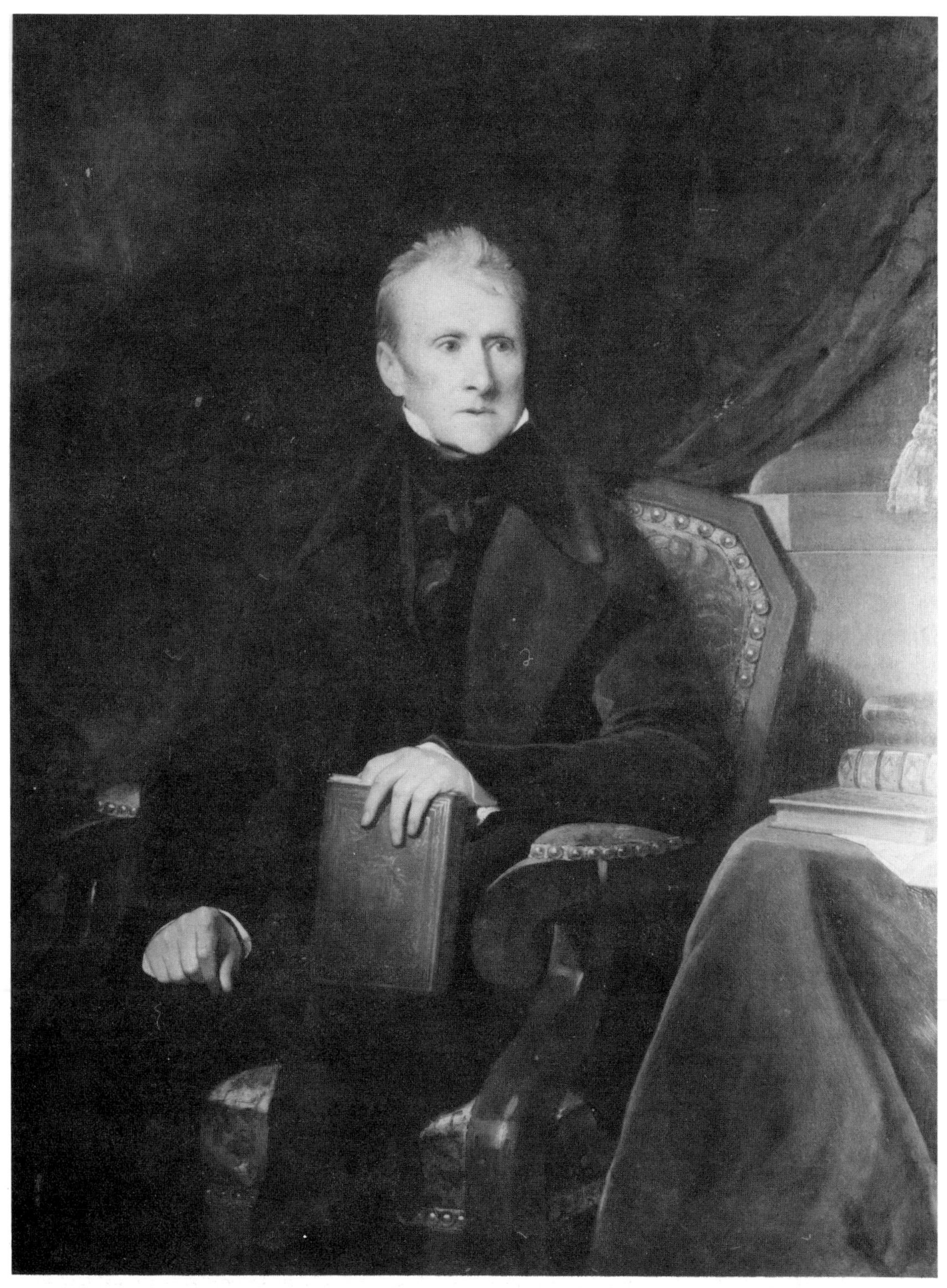

FIG. 21 Giovanni Battista Canevari, *Colonel Richard Wogan Talbot, 2nd Baron Talbot of Malahide, and Baron Furnival of Malahide, c.1766-1849* (cat. no. 4169).

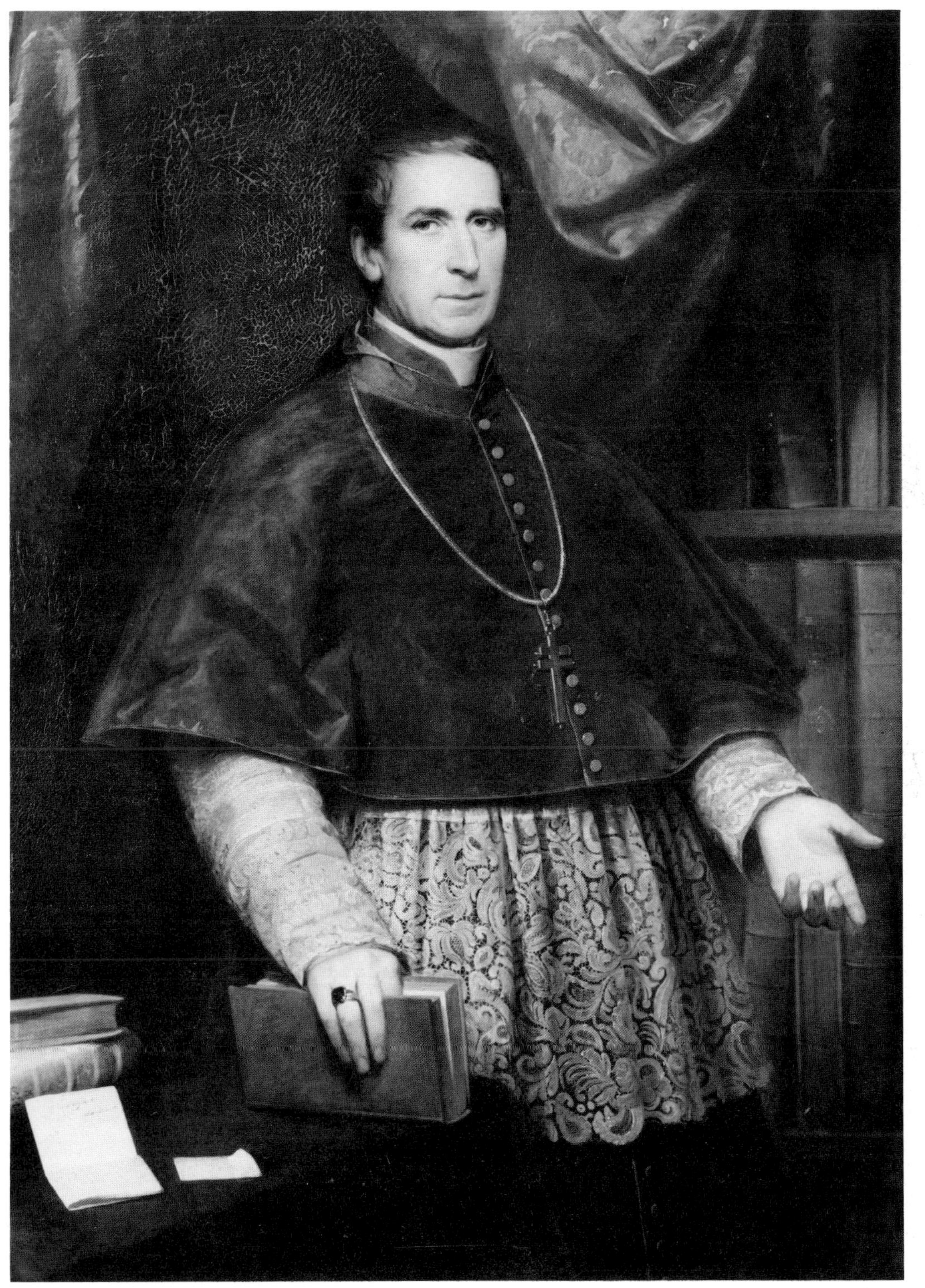

FIG. 22   Alessandro Capalti, *The Most Reverend John MacHale, Archbishop of Tuam, 1791-1881* (cat. no. 406).

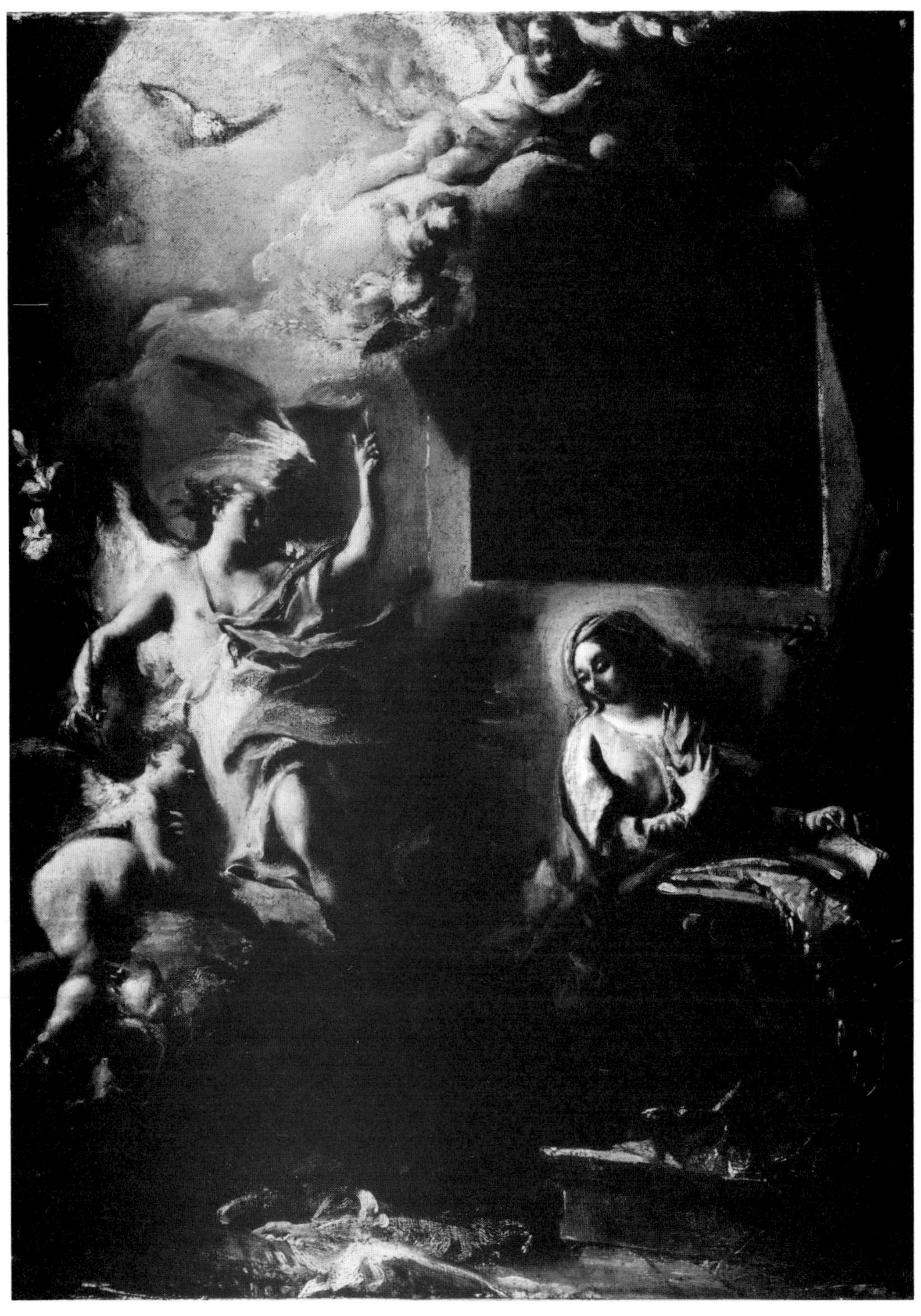

FIG. 23   Carlo Innocenzo Carlone, *The Annunciation* (cat. no. 1640).

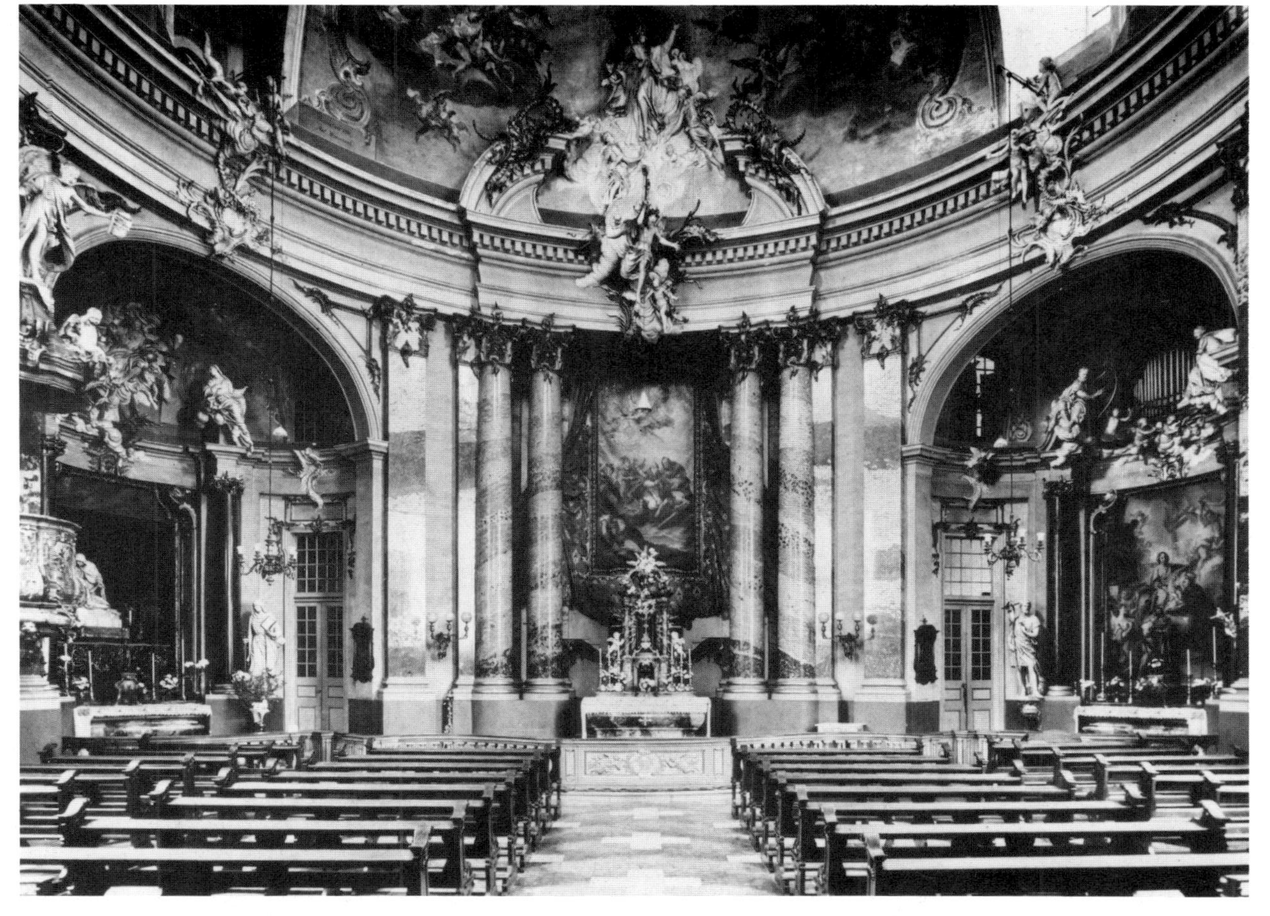

FIG. 24 A photograph of the interior of the church of St. Clement, Münster, Westphalia, built to
the designs of Johann Conrad Schlaun.
No. 1640 was a *bozzetto* for the altarpiece of the left hand altar. In 1973-74 no. 1640 was used as the basis for the
execution of the large altarpiece there today, the original having been destroyed in World War II. (Photograph by
courtesy of Dr. Hilde Claussen and Westfälisches Amt fur Denkmalpflege).

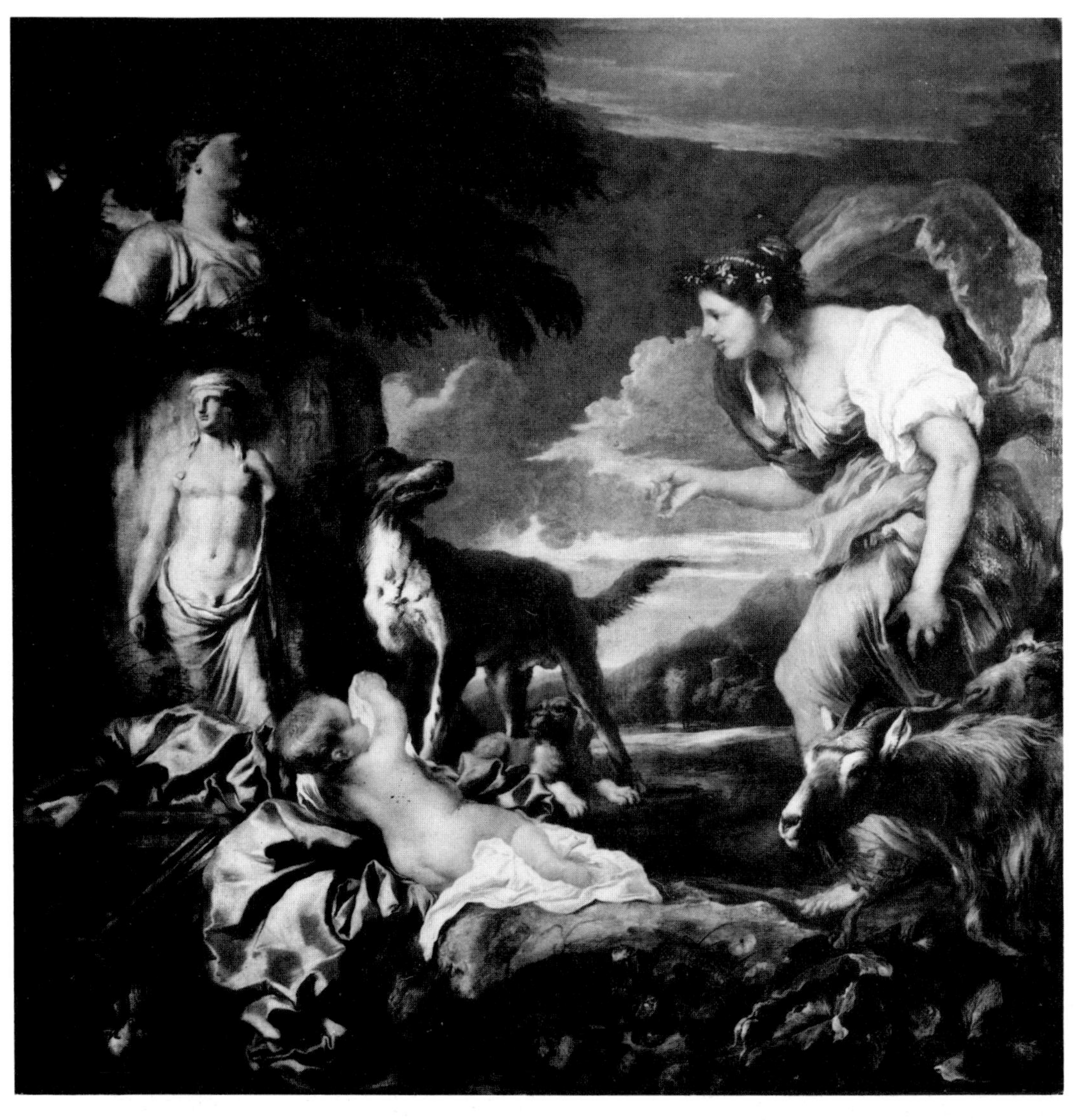

Fig. 25 Giovanni Benedetto Castiglione, *The shepherdess Spako with the infant Cyrus* (cat. no. 994).

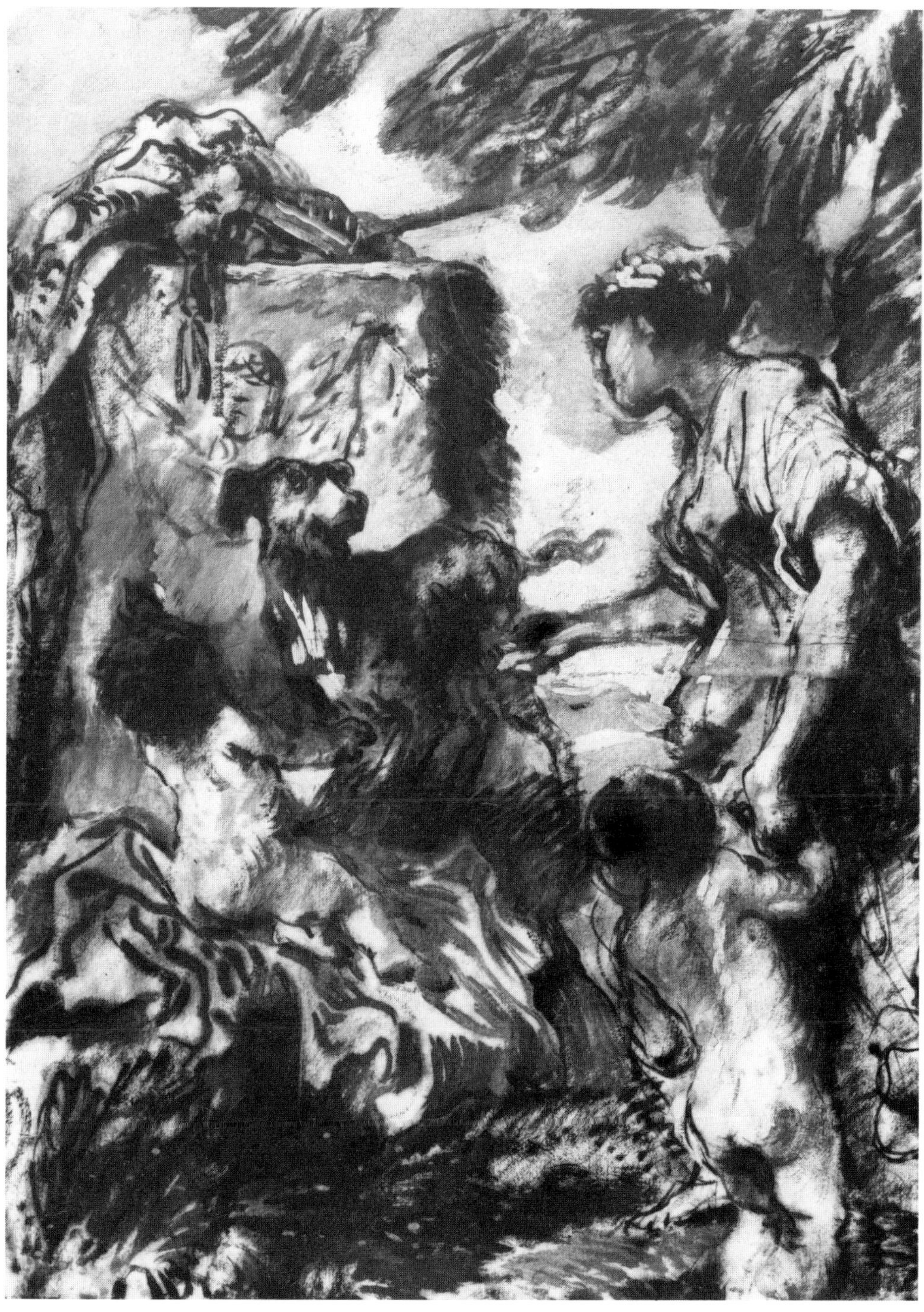

FIG. 26   Giovanni Benedetto Castiglione, *The shepherdess Spako with the infant Cyrus.* Brown and red oil, heightened with blue opaque pigment, on paper, 345 × 240 mm. The Royal Library, Windsor Castle. Reproduced by gracious permission of Her Majesty Queen Elizabeth II.

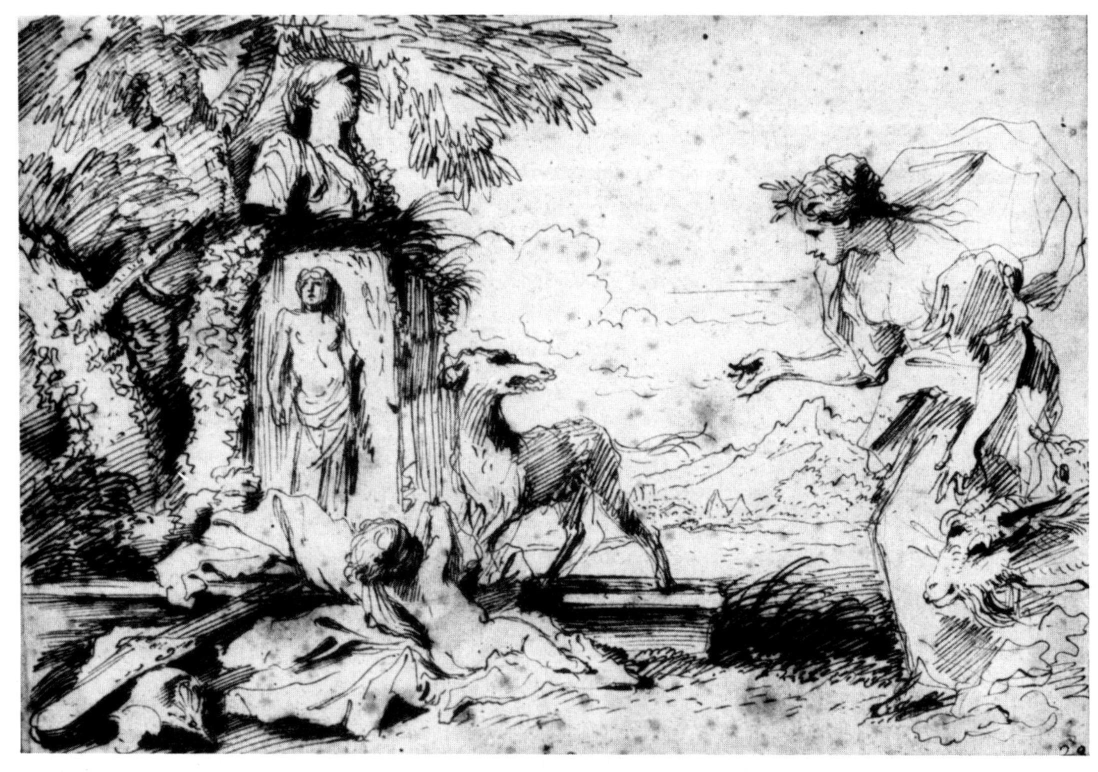

Fig. 27.   Giovanni Benedetto Castiglione, *The shepherdess Spako with the infant Cyrus.*
Brown ink on paper, 193 × 269 mm. Musée de Dijon, Dijon, France.

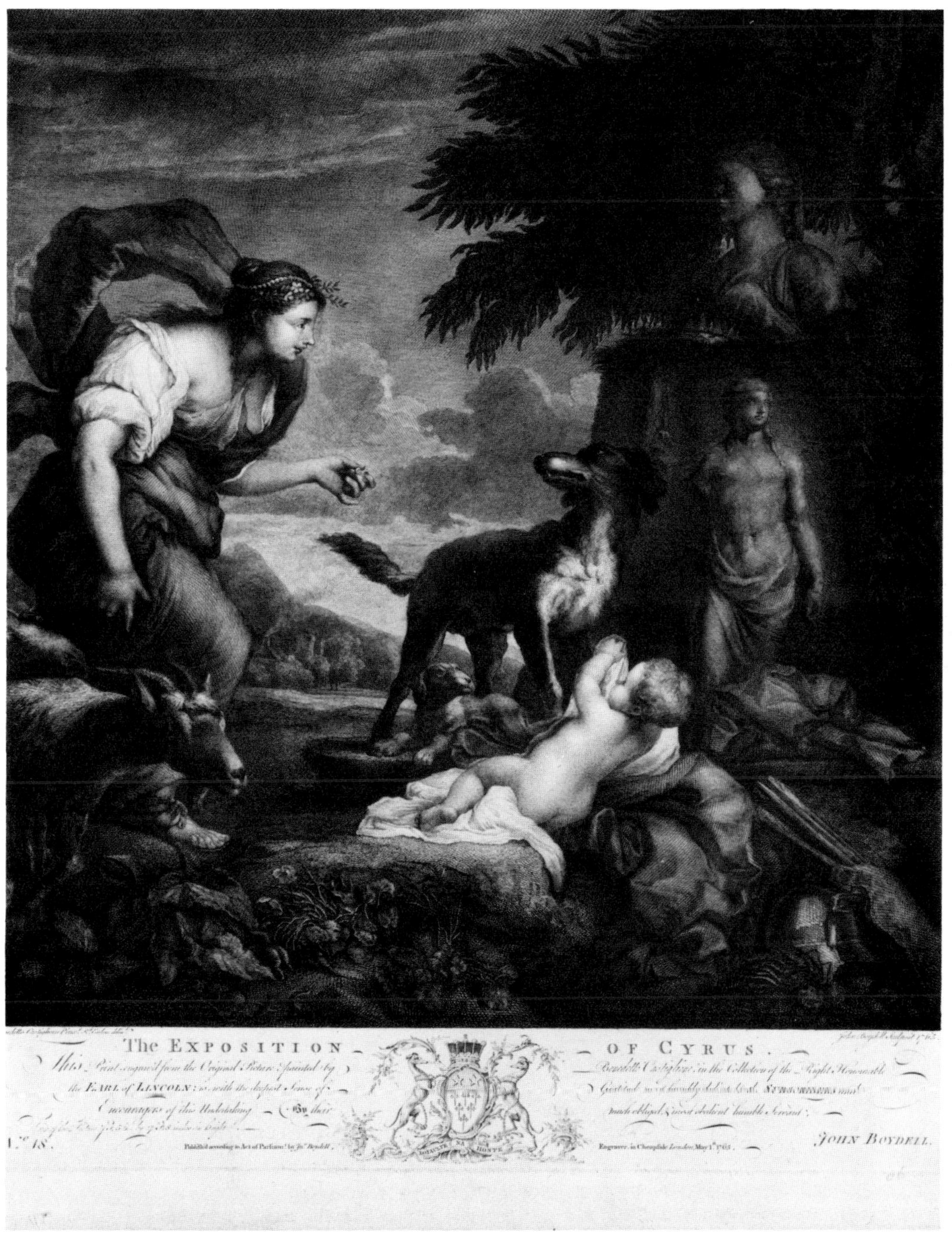

FIG. 28   John Boydell after Richard Earlom after Castiglione, *The exposition of Cyrus*
Line engraving, 516 × 408 mm. (plate size: trimmed at sides). Published
1 May 1765. National Gallery of Ireland, cat. no. 11,943.

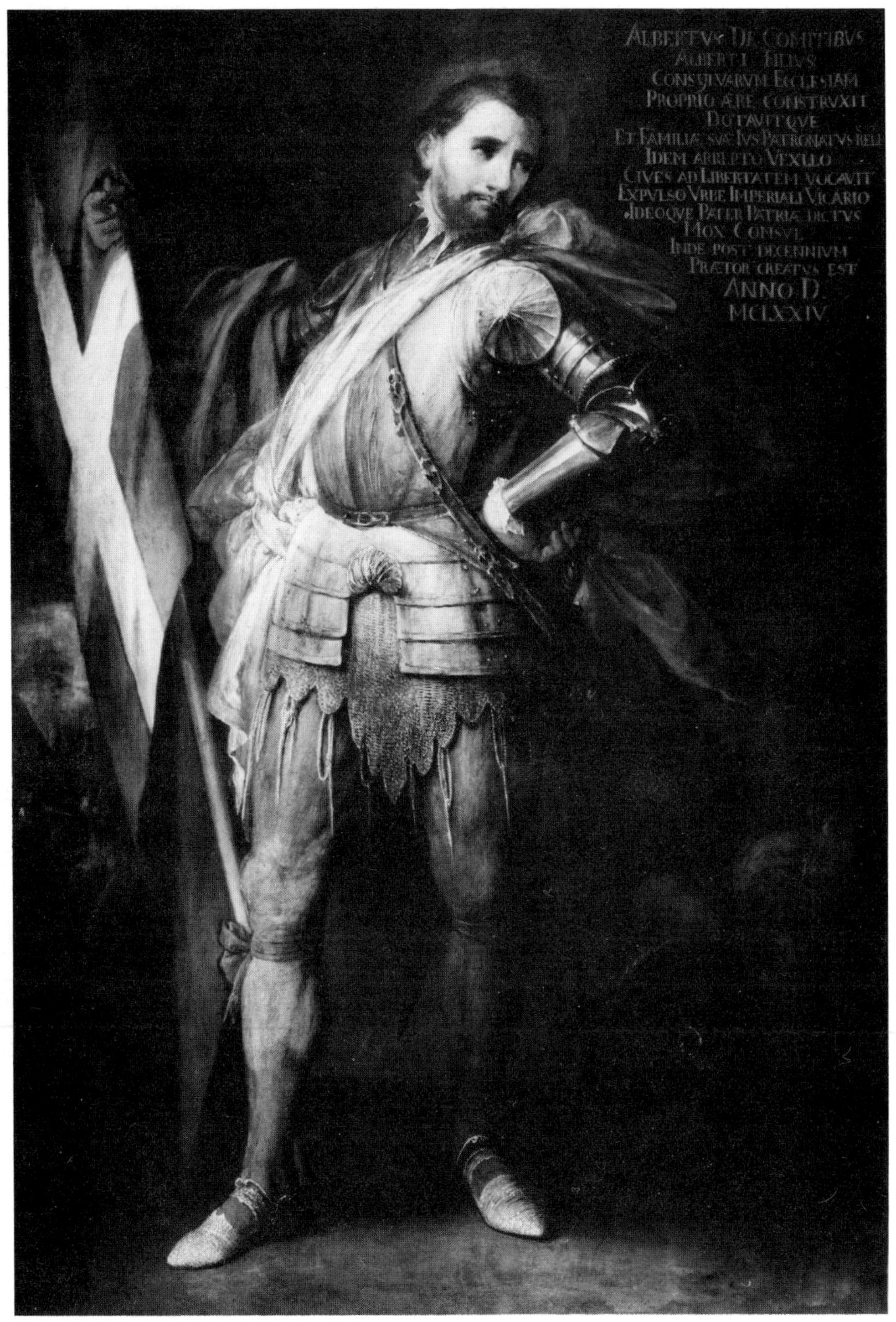

Fig. 29   Andrea Celesti, *Imaginary portrait of Count Alberto Alberti of Baone* (cat. no. 1925).

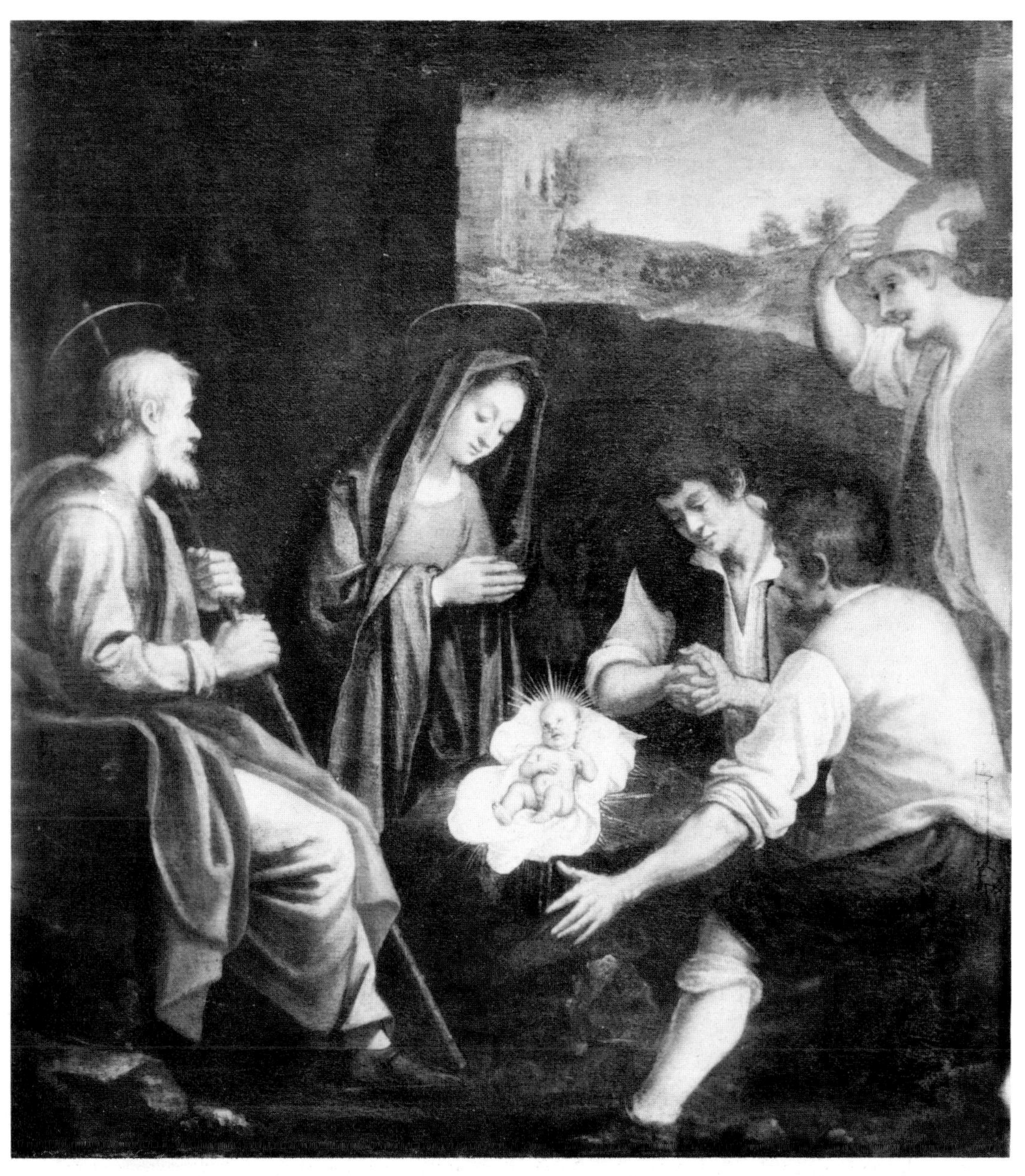

Fig. 30 Studio of Jacopo Chimenti da Empoli, *Adoration of the shepherds* (cat. no. 1068).

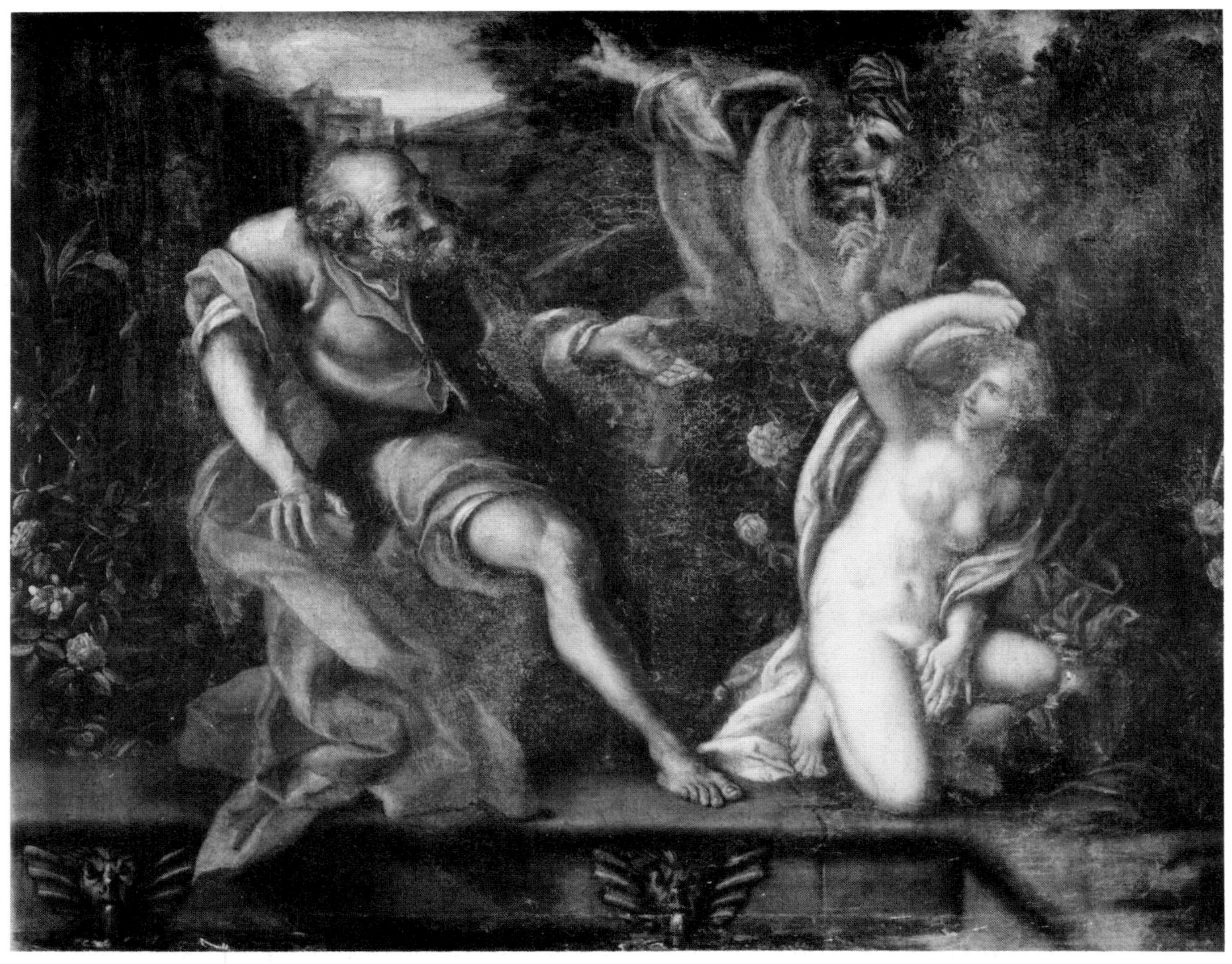

FIG. 31 Studio of Jacopo Chimenti da Empoli, *Susanna and the Elders* (cat. no. 1671).

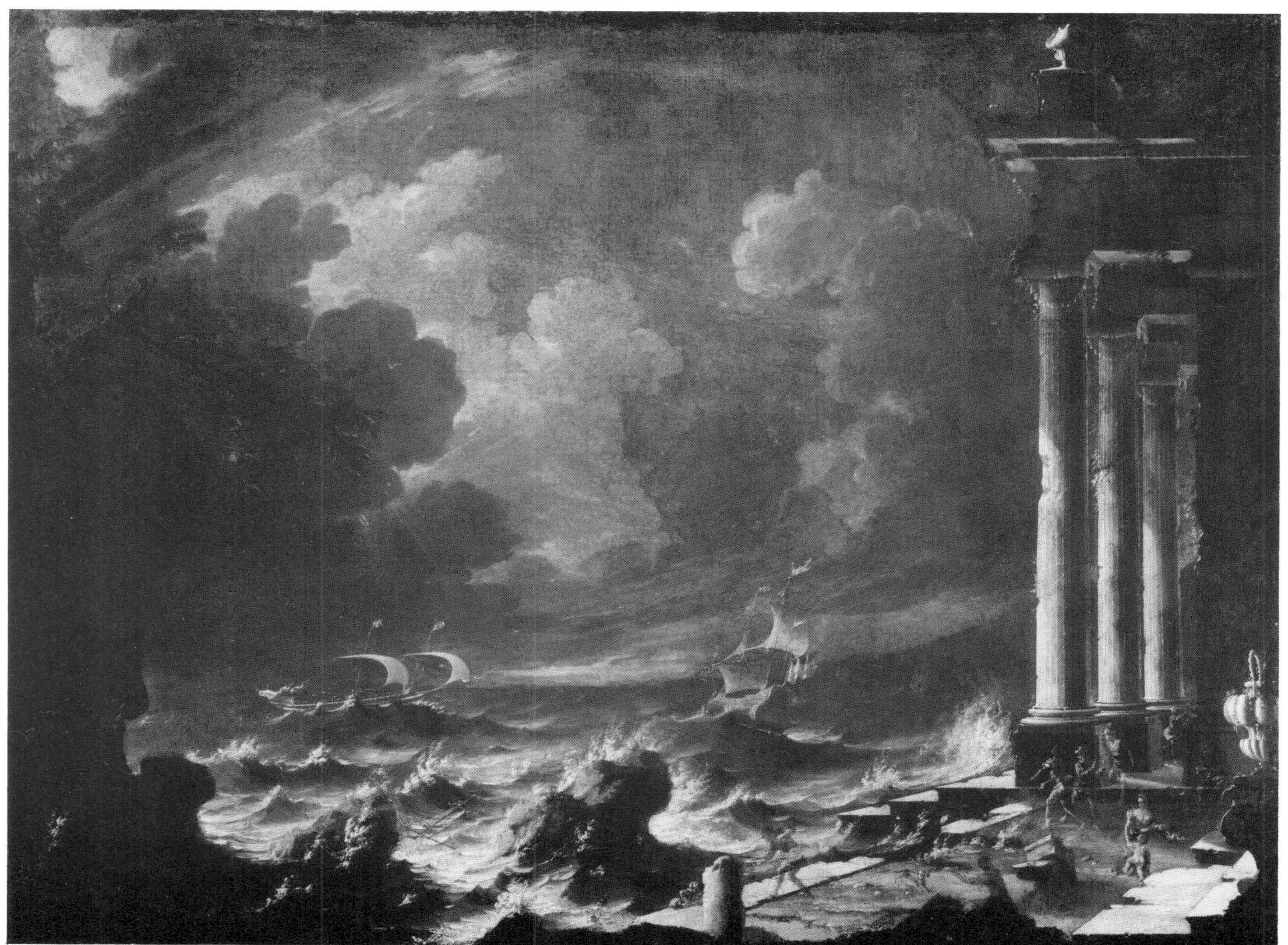

Fig. 32 Leonardo Coccorante, *Coast scene with ruins and shipwrecks* (cat. no. 1744).

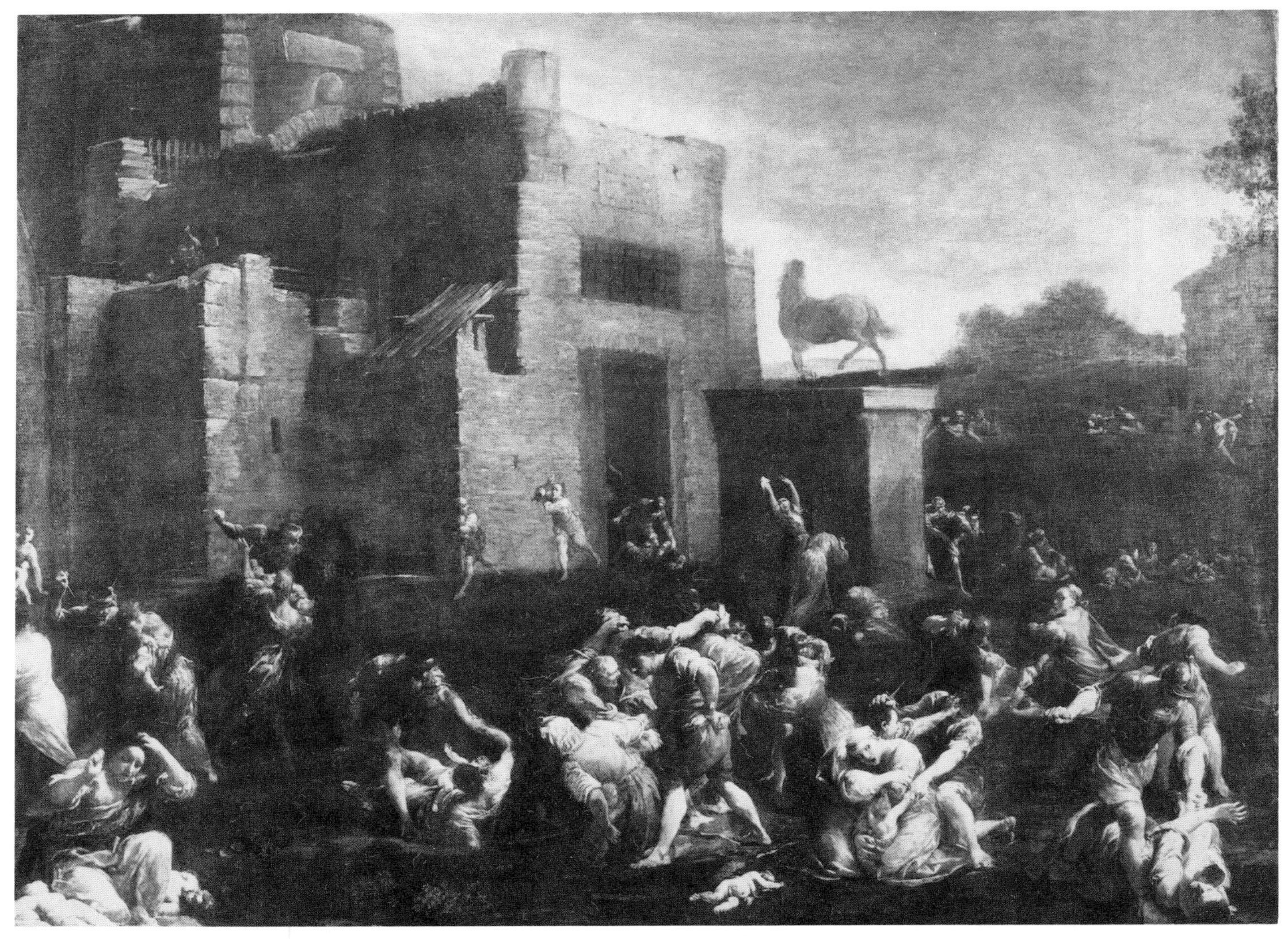

FIG. 33 Giuseppe Maria Crespi, *The massacre of the Innocents* (cat. no. 1020).

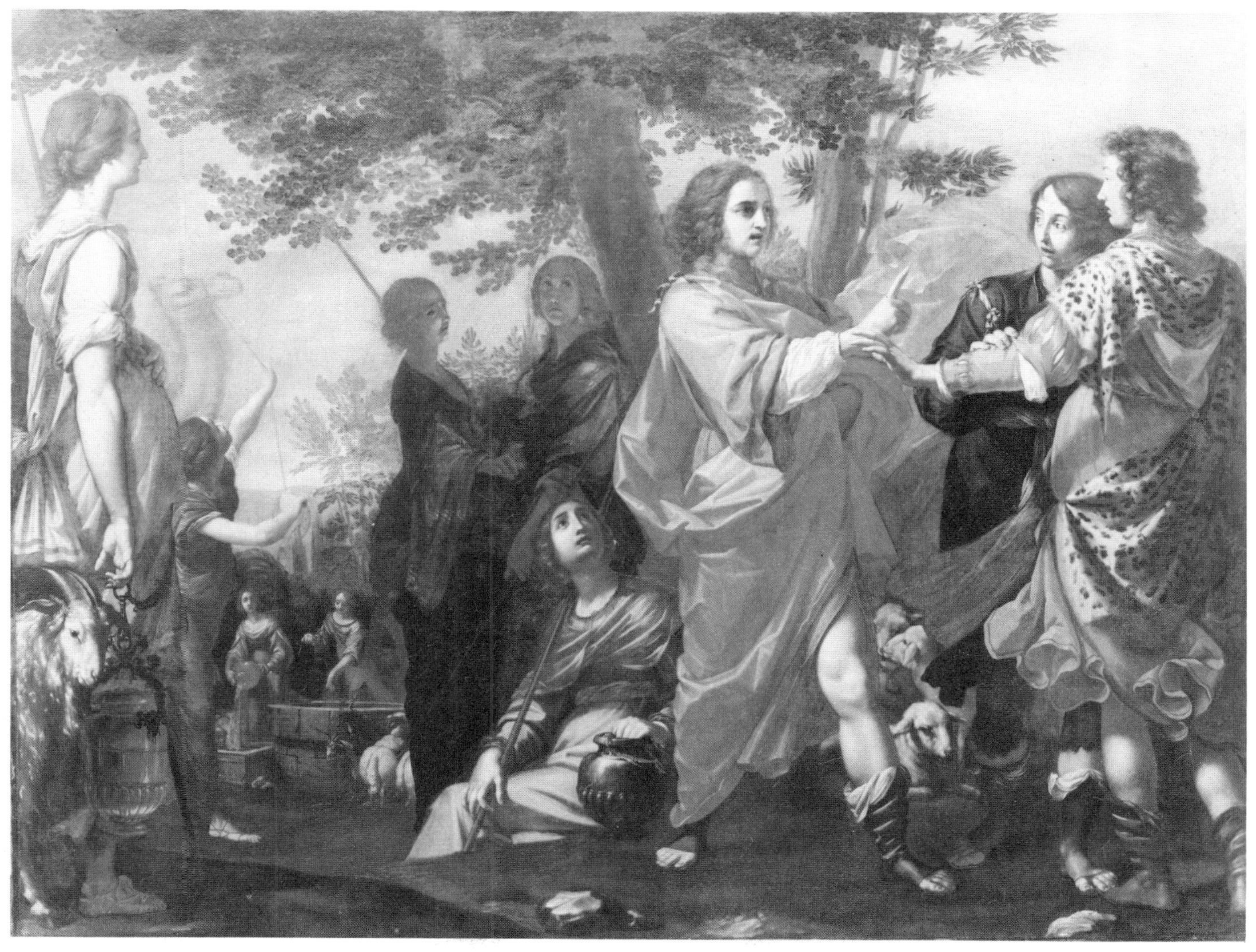

Fig. 34 Cesare Dandini, *Moses driving away the shepherds* (cat. no. 1683).

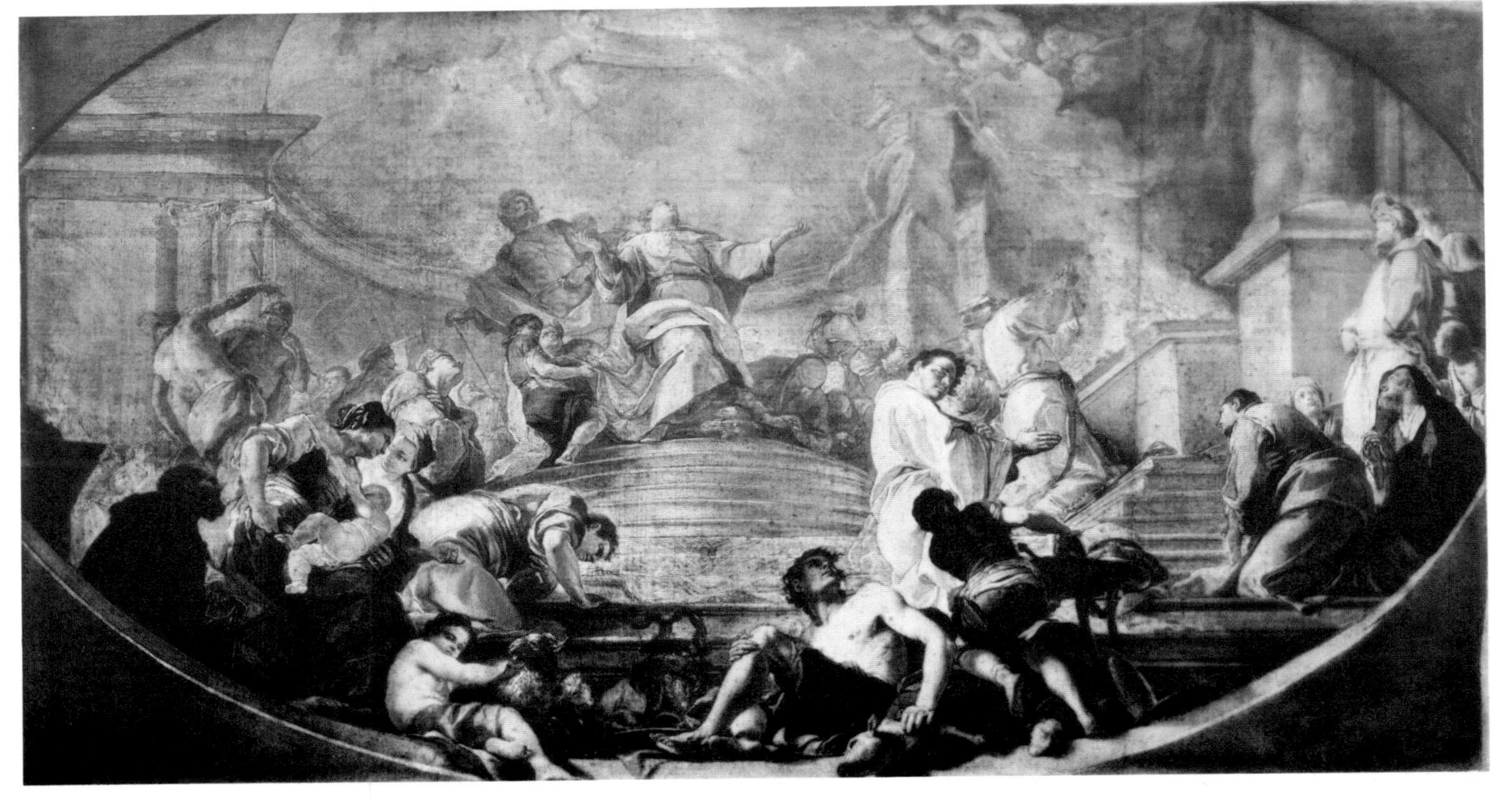

Fig. 35   Giacinto Diano, *The dedication of the Temple at Jerusalem* (cat. no. 357).

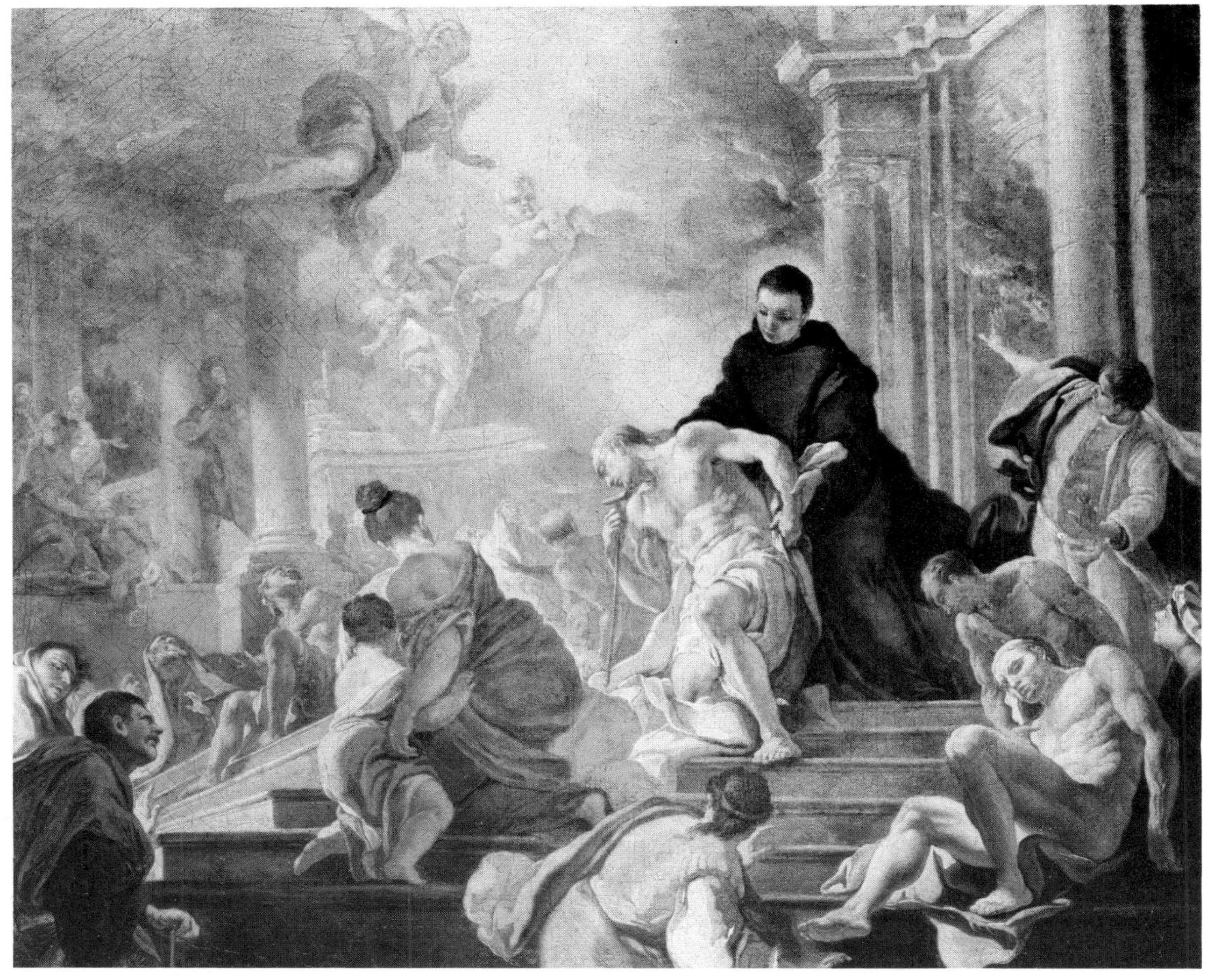

FIG. 36 Giacinto Diano, *Scene from the life of S. Giovanni di Dio.*
Oil on canvas, 0.51 × 0.635 m. Collection Mr. Roy Fisher, New York.

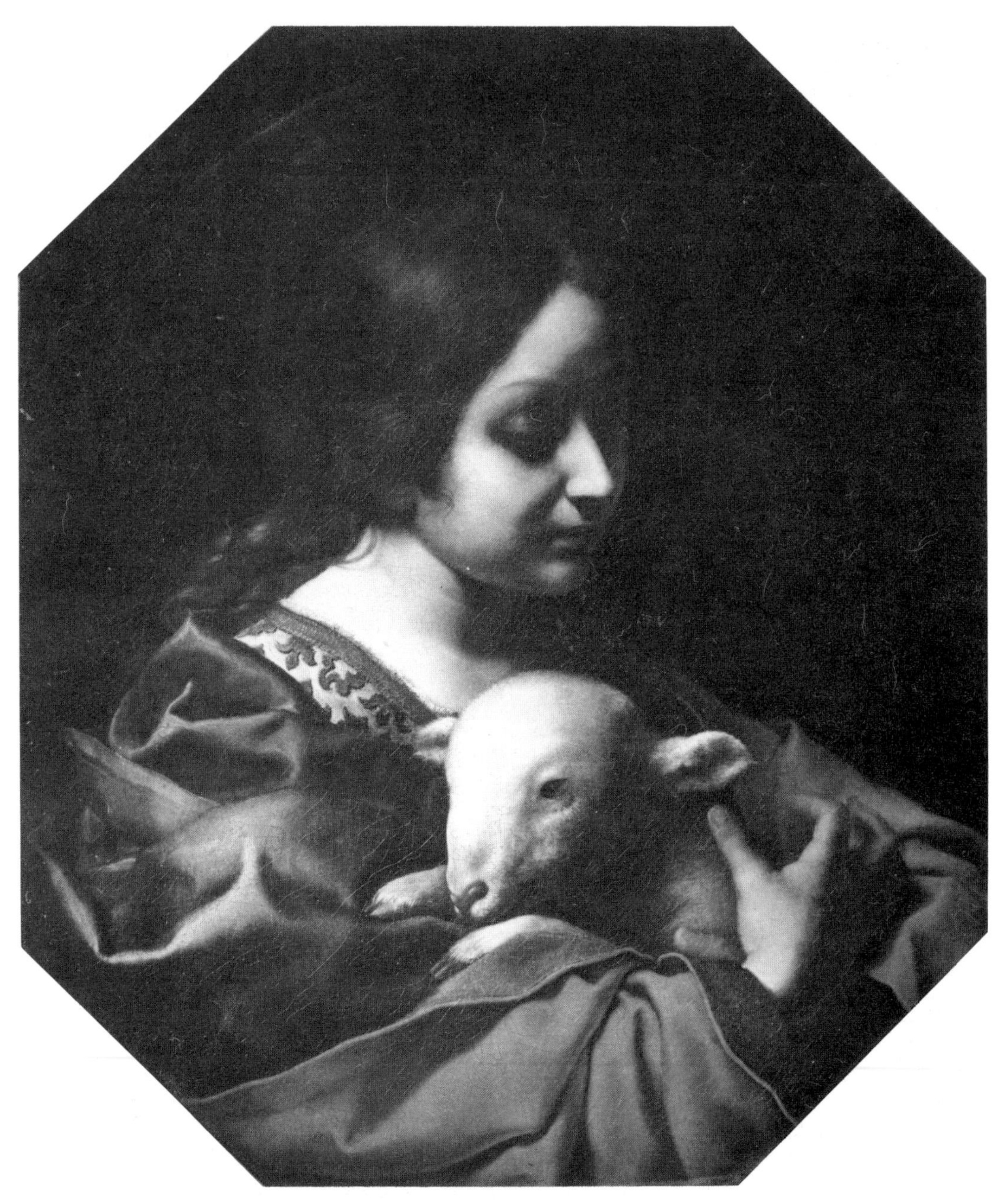

FIG. 37 Carlo Dolci, *St Agnes* (cat. no. 1229).

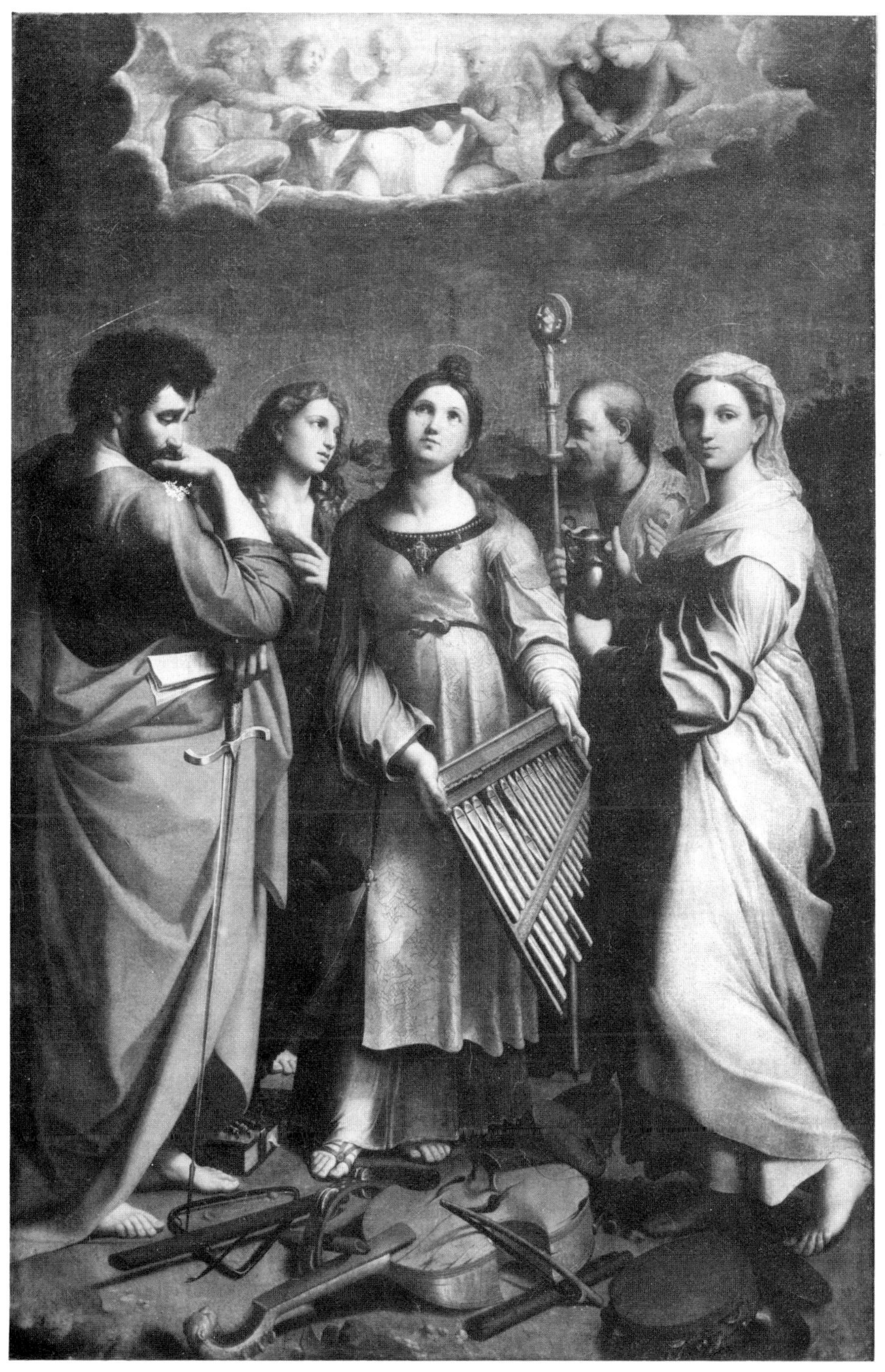

FIG. 38 Attributed to Domenichino, *St. Cecilia* (after Raphael) (cat. no. 70).

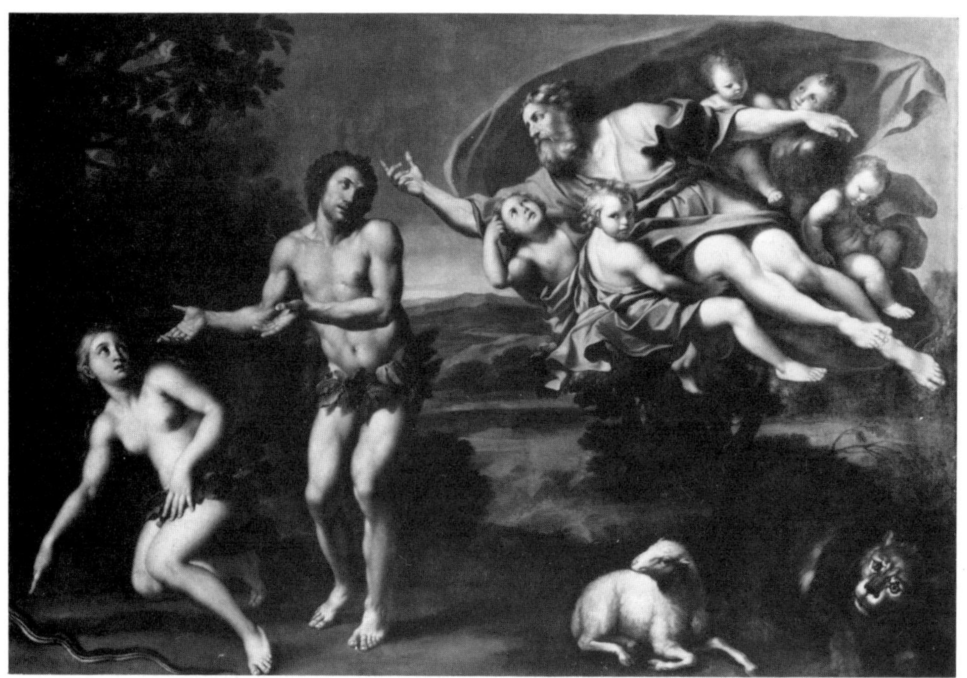

FIG. 39   After Domenichino, *Expulsion of Adam and Eve* (cat. no. 1083).

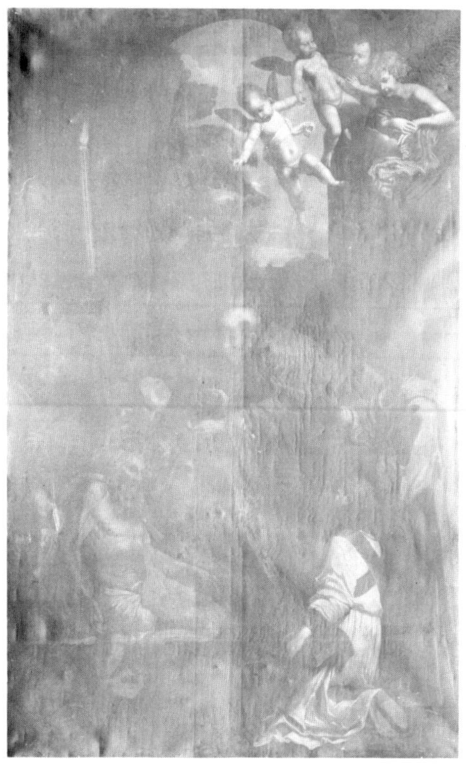

FIG. 40   After Domenichino, *The last communion of St. Jerome* (cat. no. 1885).

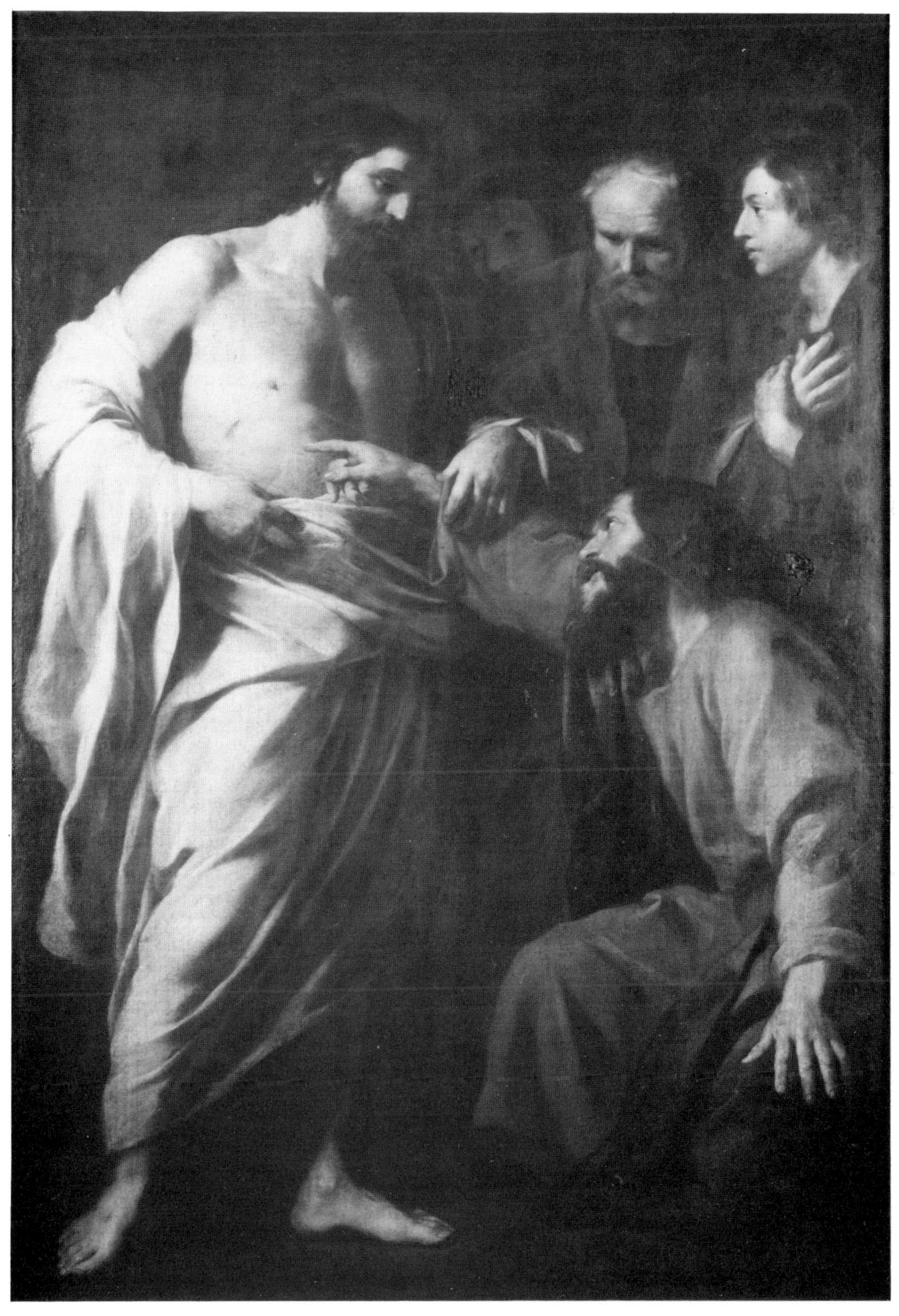

Fig. 41 Orazio De Ferrari, *The incredulity of St. Thomas* (cat. no. 4302).

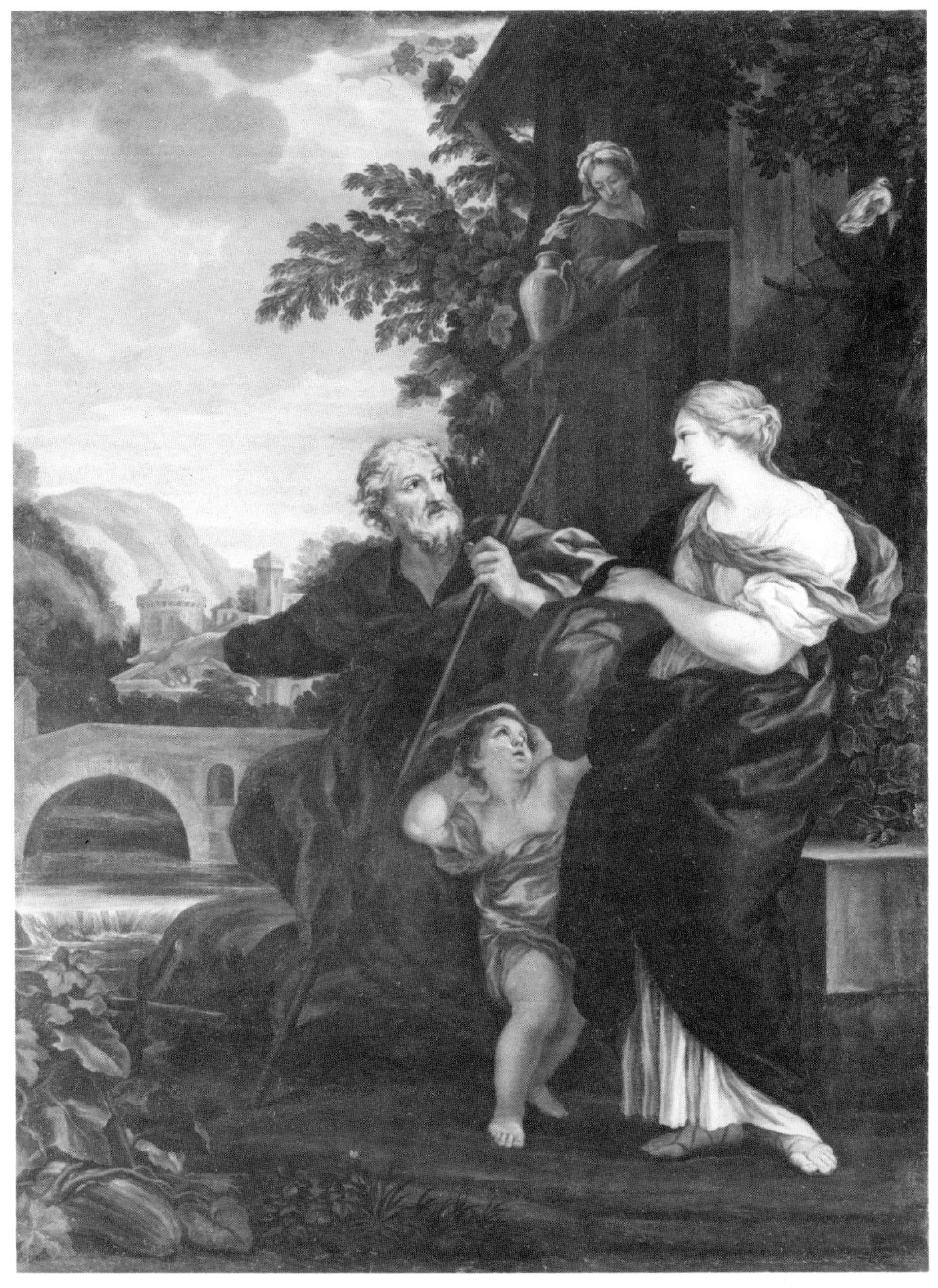

FIG. 42   Ciro Ferri, *The expulsion of Hagar* (cat. no. 1670).

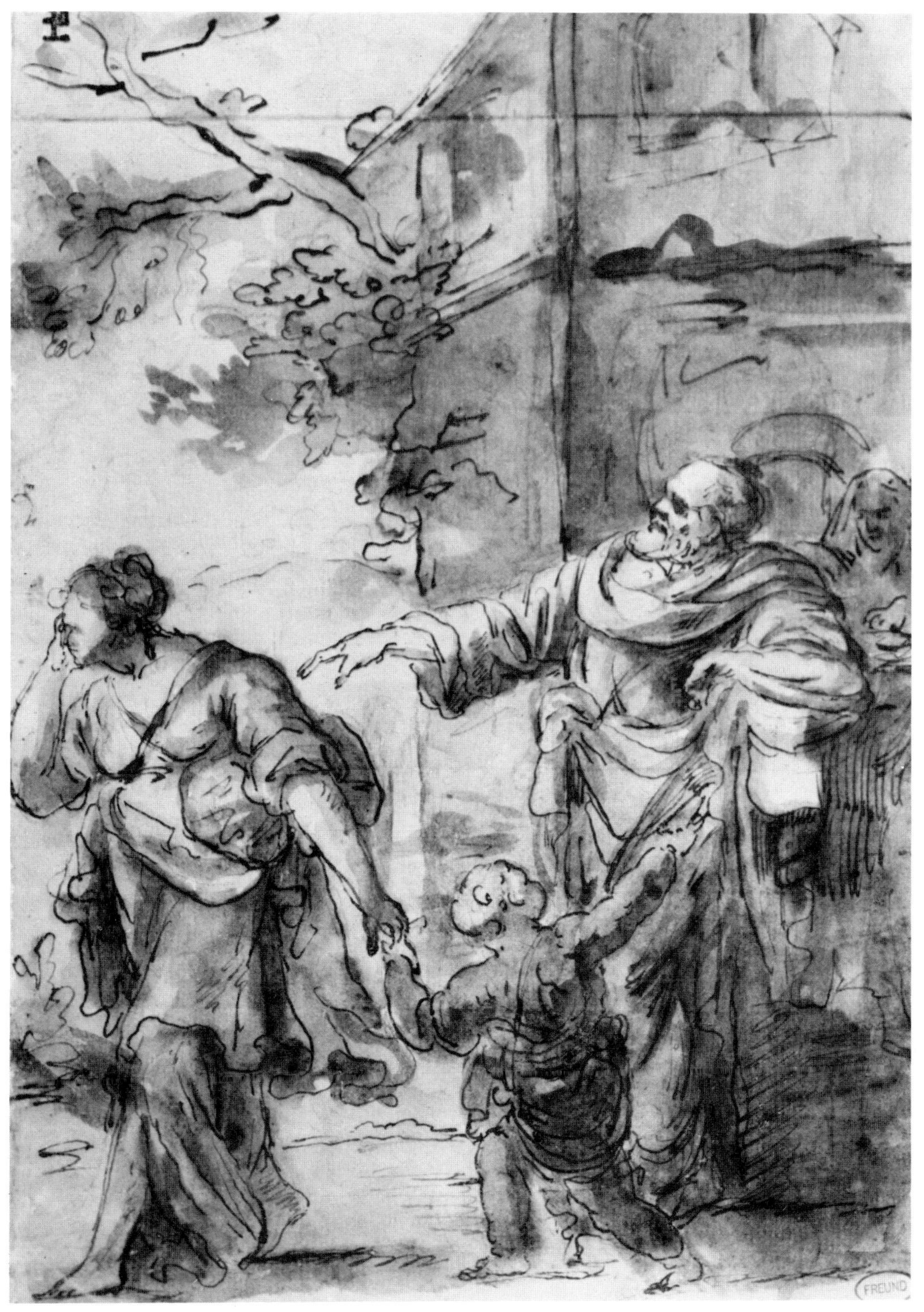

FIG. 43   Ciro Ferri, *The expulsion of Hagar*, Moravská Galerie, Brno, Czechoslovakia.

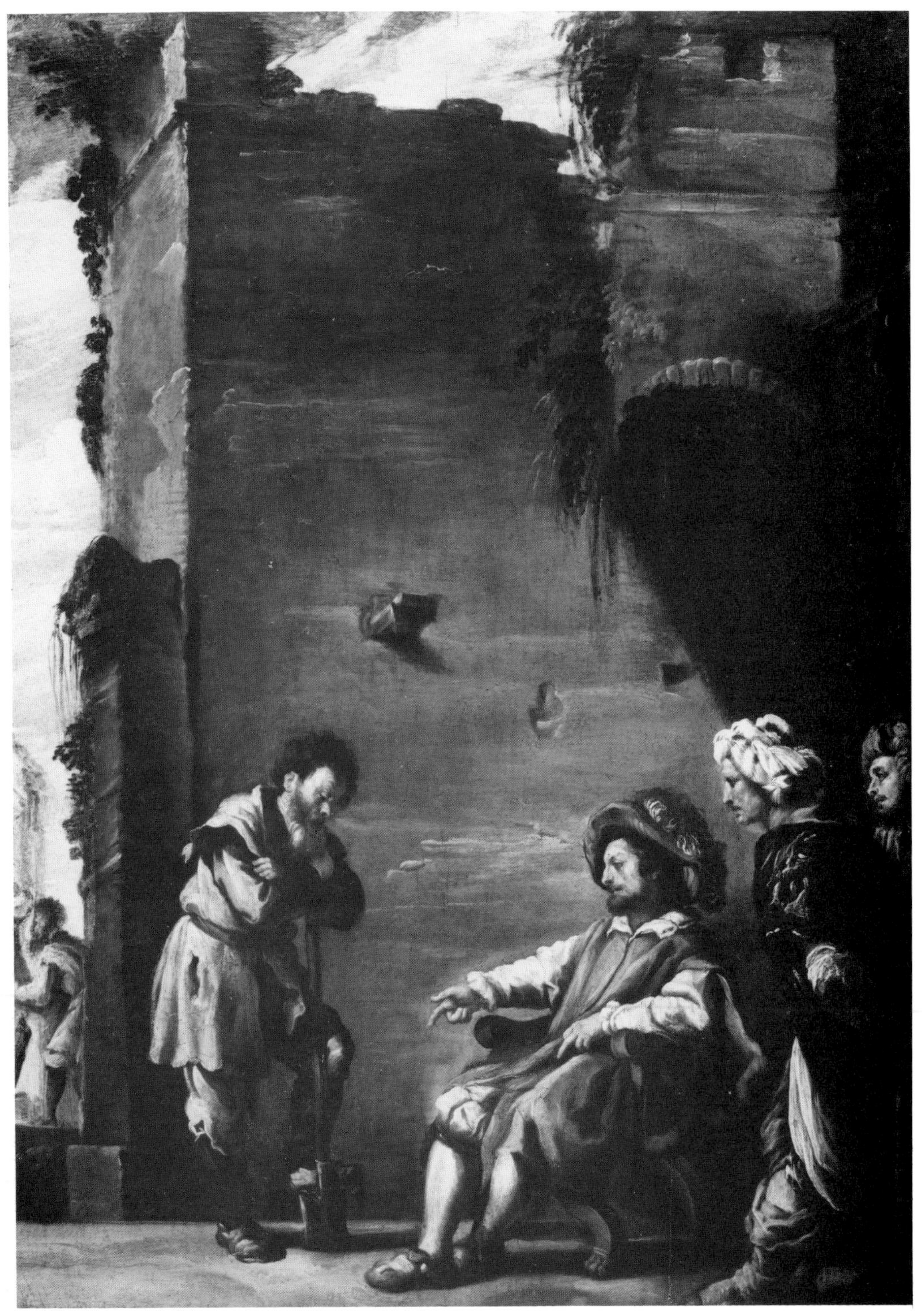

FIG. **44** Studio of Domenico Fetti, *The parable of the lord of the vineyard* (cat. no. 898).

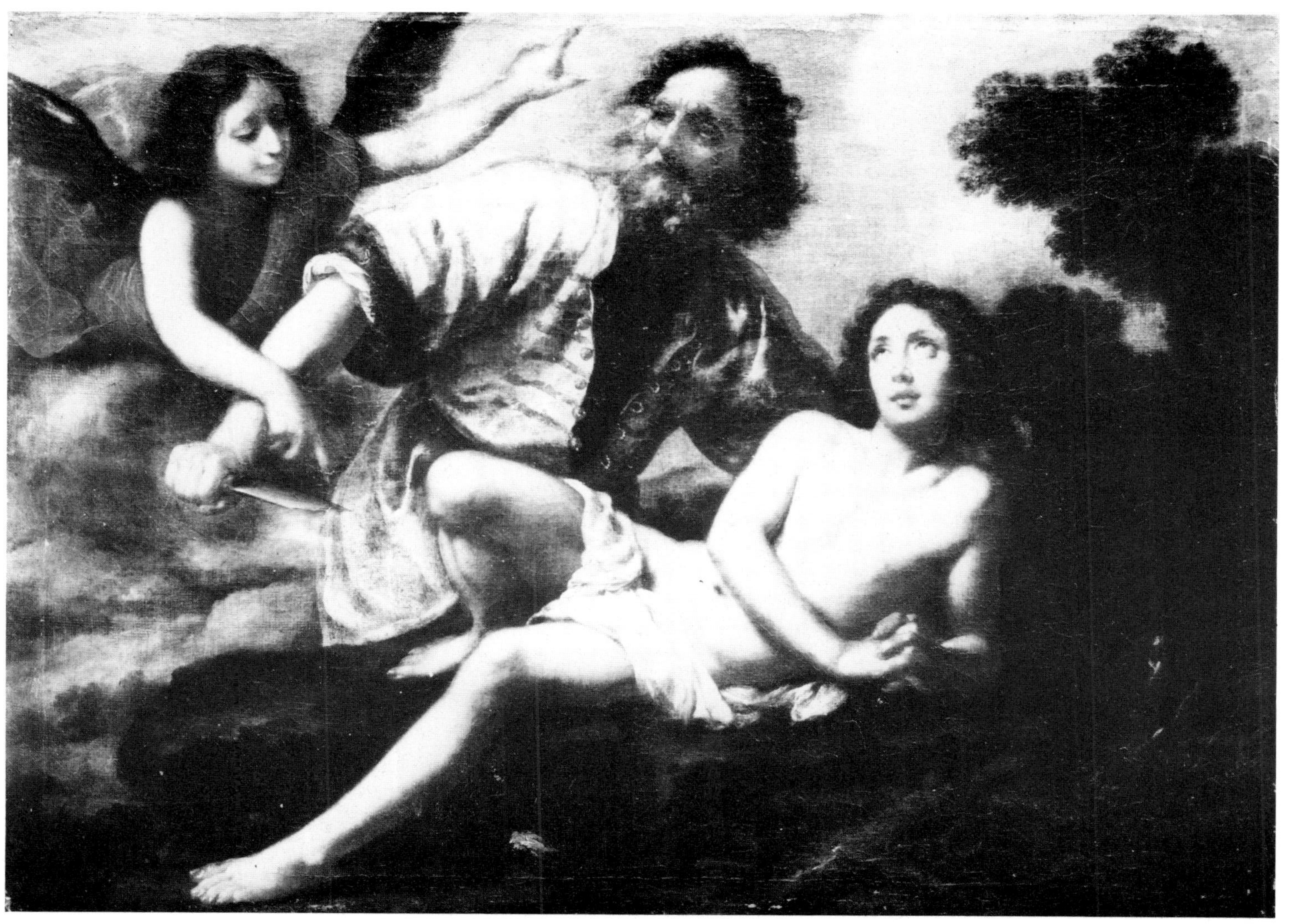

FIG. 45 Felice Ficherelli, *The sacrifice of Isaac* (cat. no. 1070).

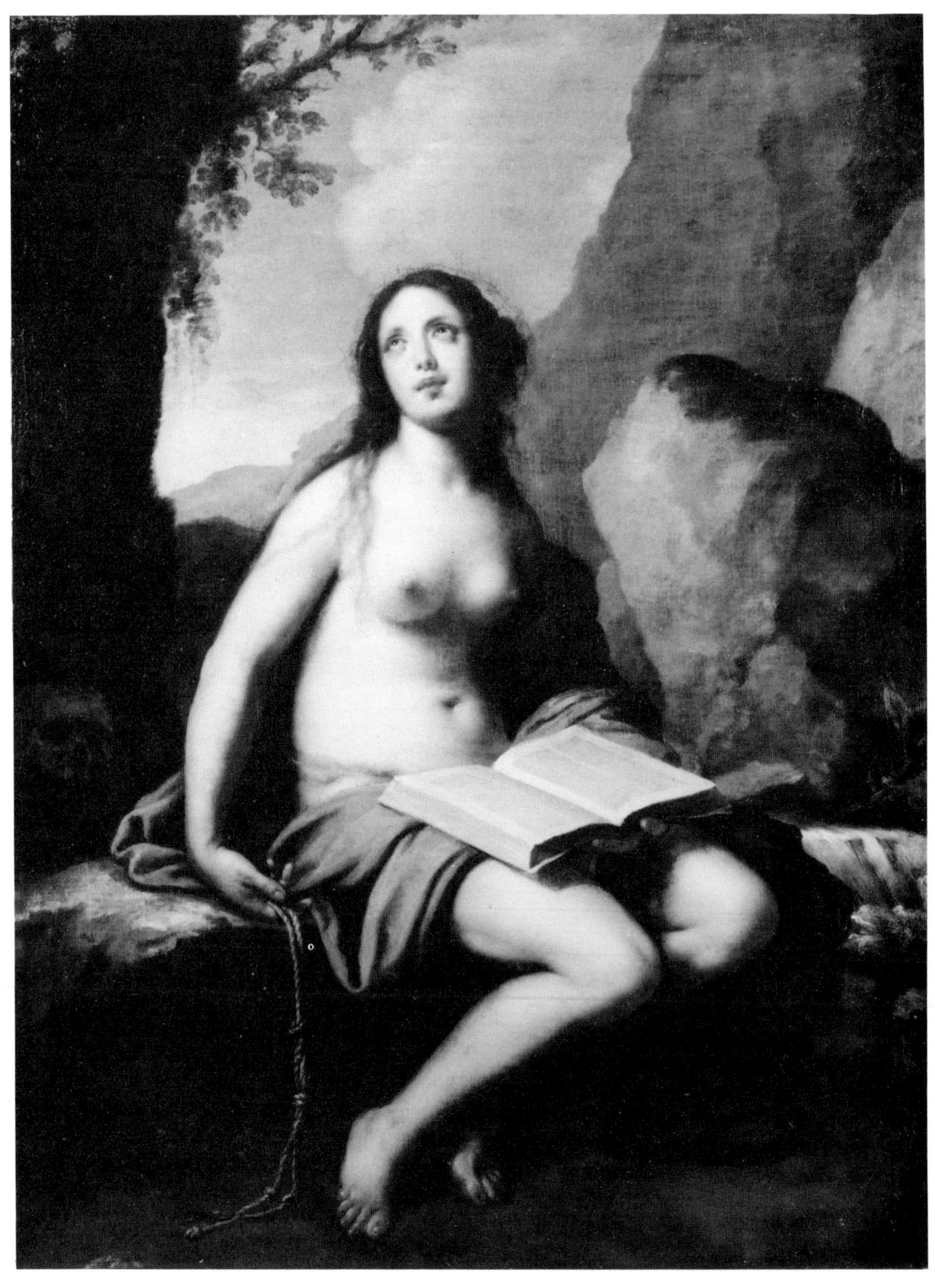

Fig. 46   Felice Ficherelli, *St. Mary Magdalen* (cat. no. 1707).

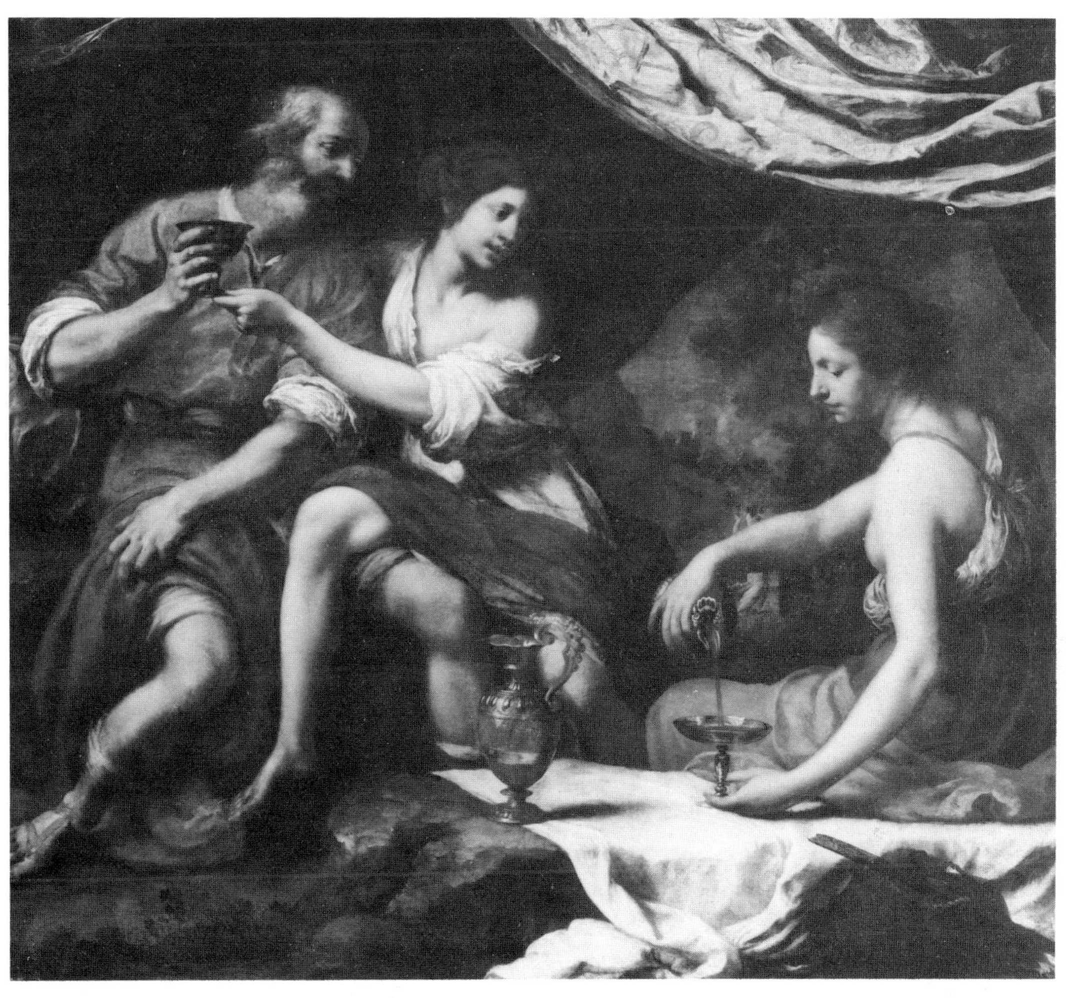

FIG. 47   Felice Ficherelli, *Lot and his daughters* (cat. no. 1746).

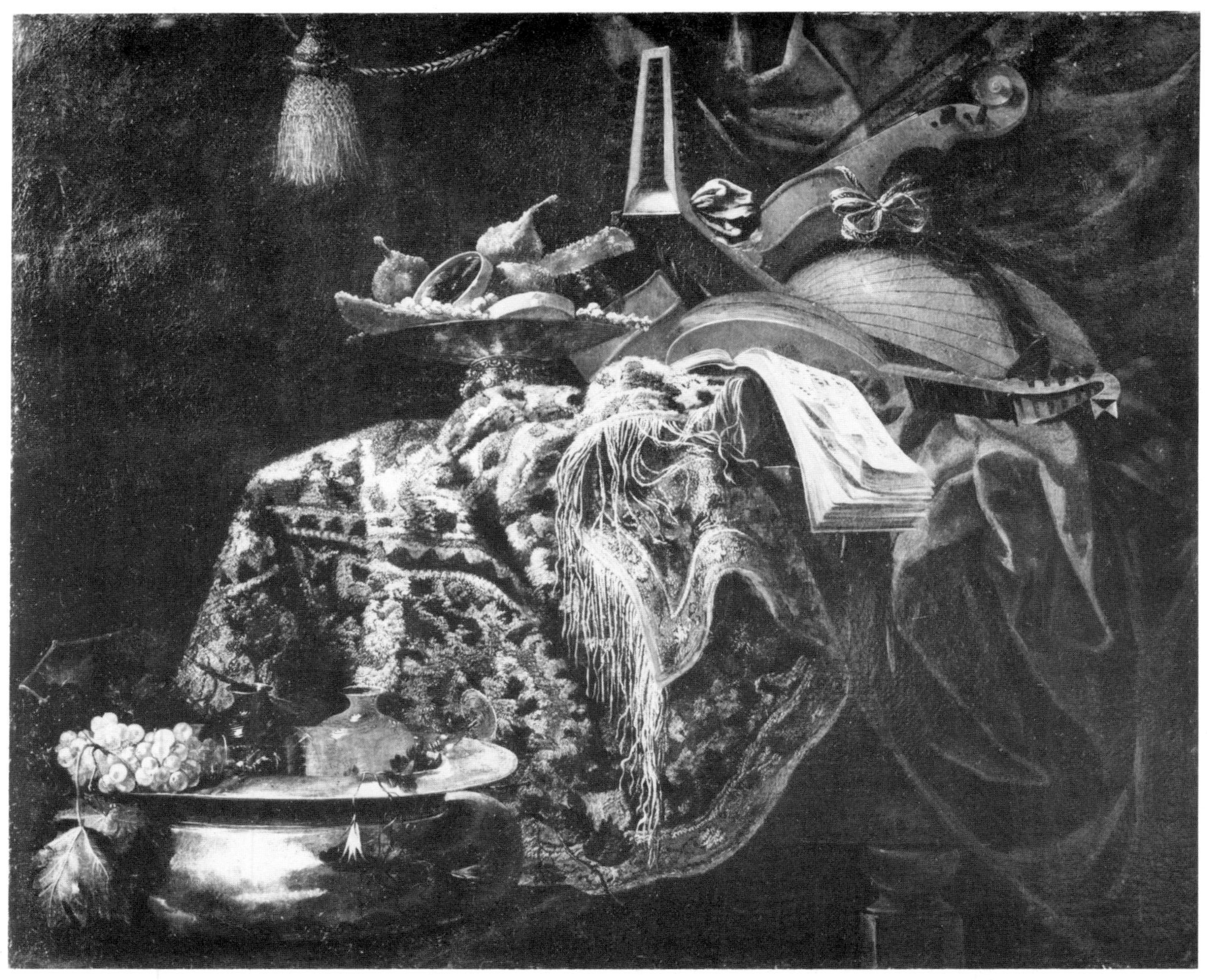

FIG. 48   Attributed to Fieravino, *Still life with musical instruments* (cat. no. 1014).

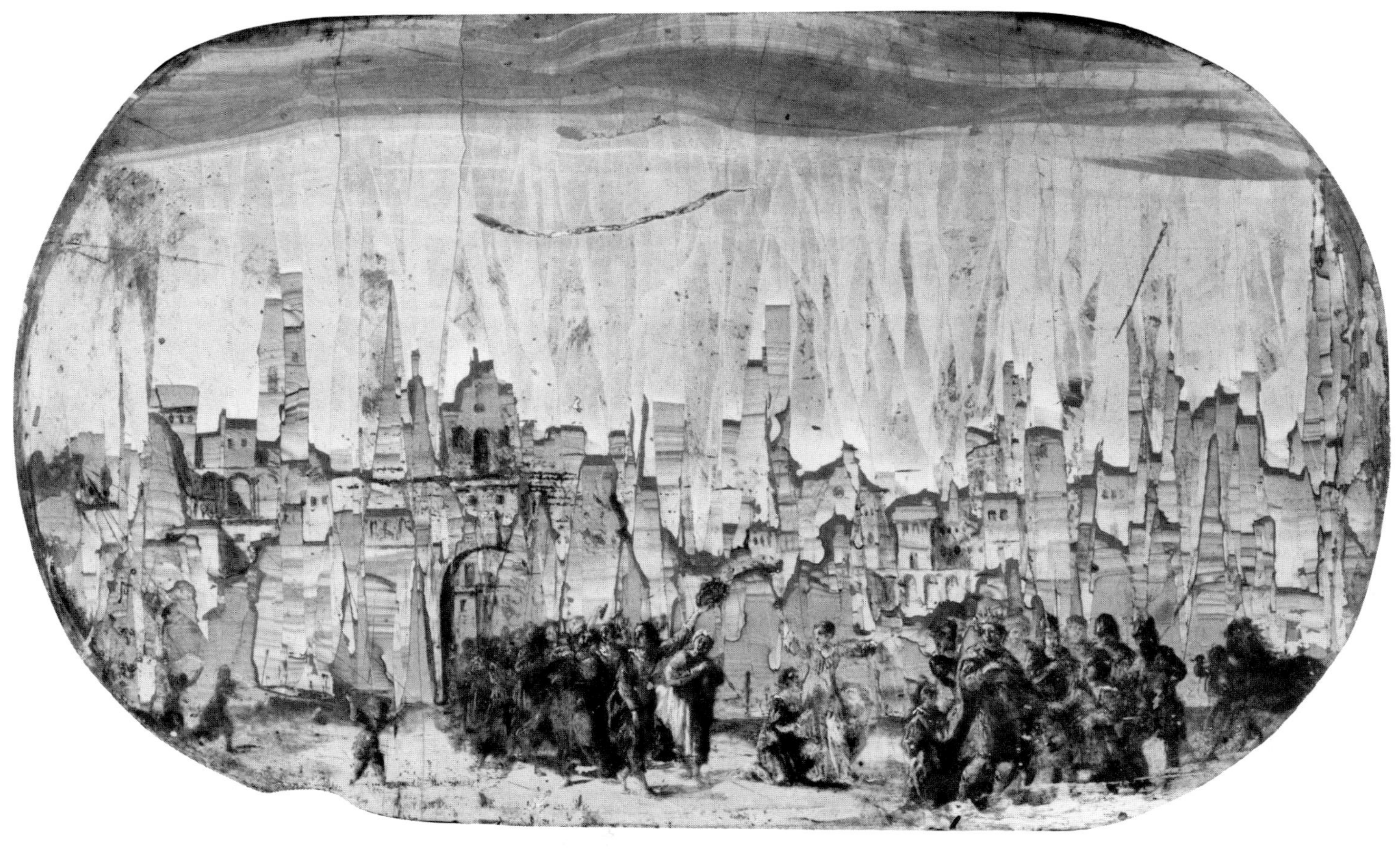

Fig. 49 Florentine School, 17th century, *Crowd at city gates* (cat. no. 4096).

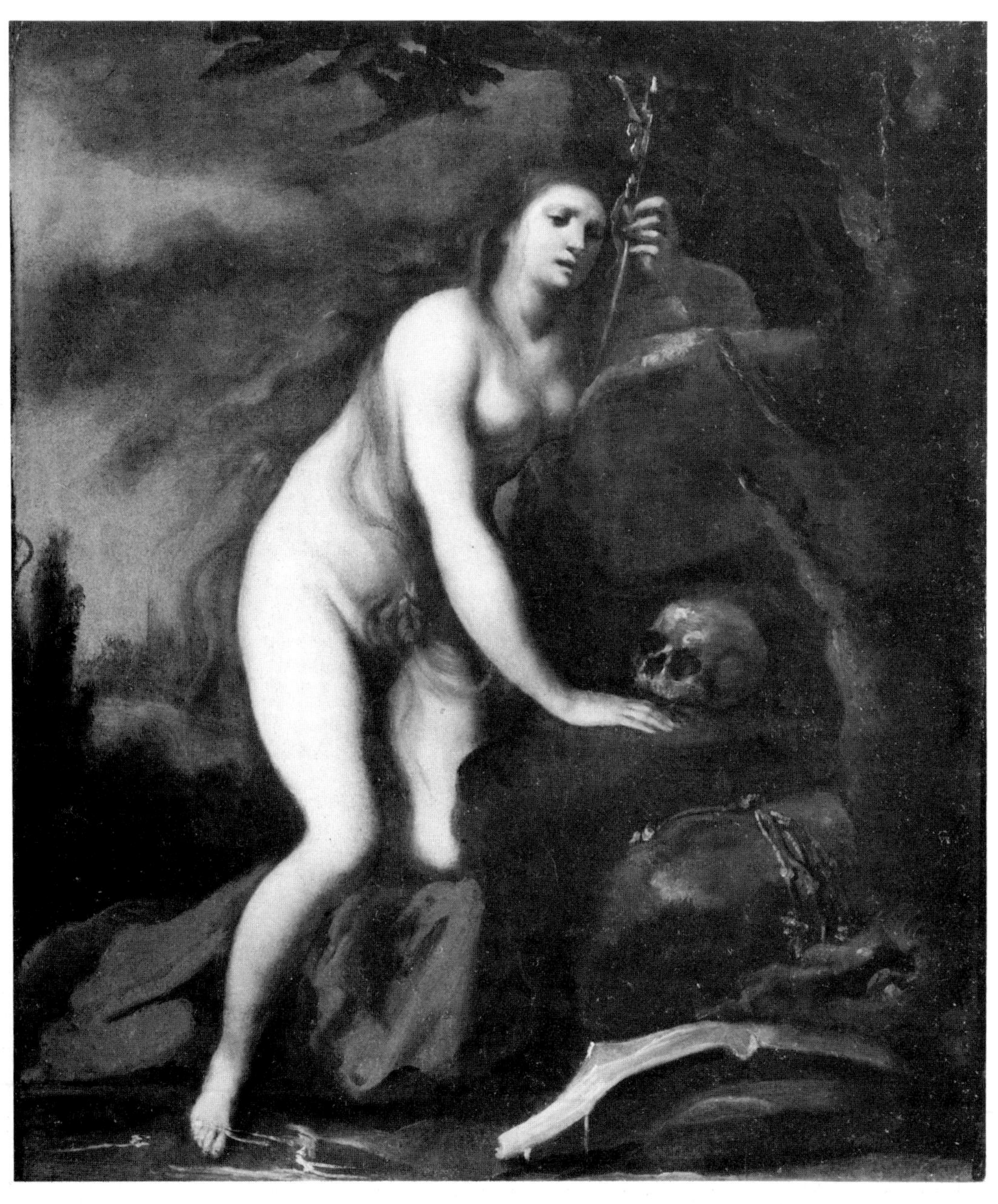

Fig. 50   Francesco Furini, *St. Mary Magdalen* (cat. no. 1679).

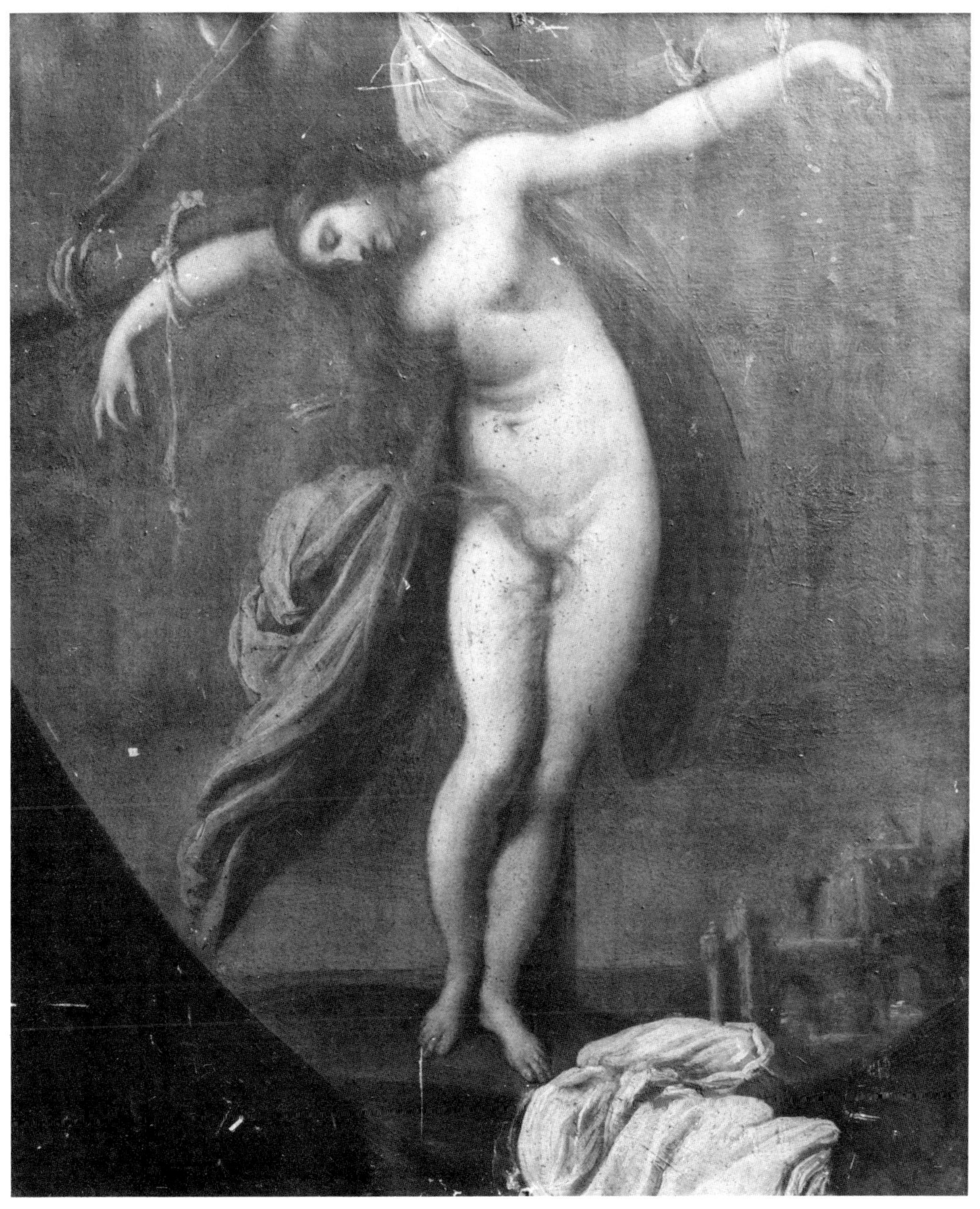

Fig. 51 Francesco Furini, *Crucifixion of a female saint* (cat. no. 1716).

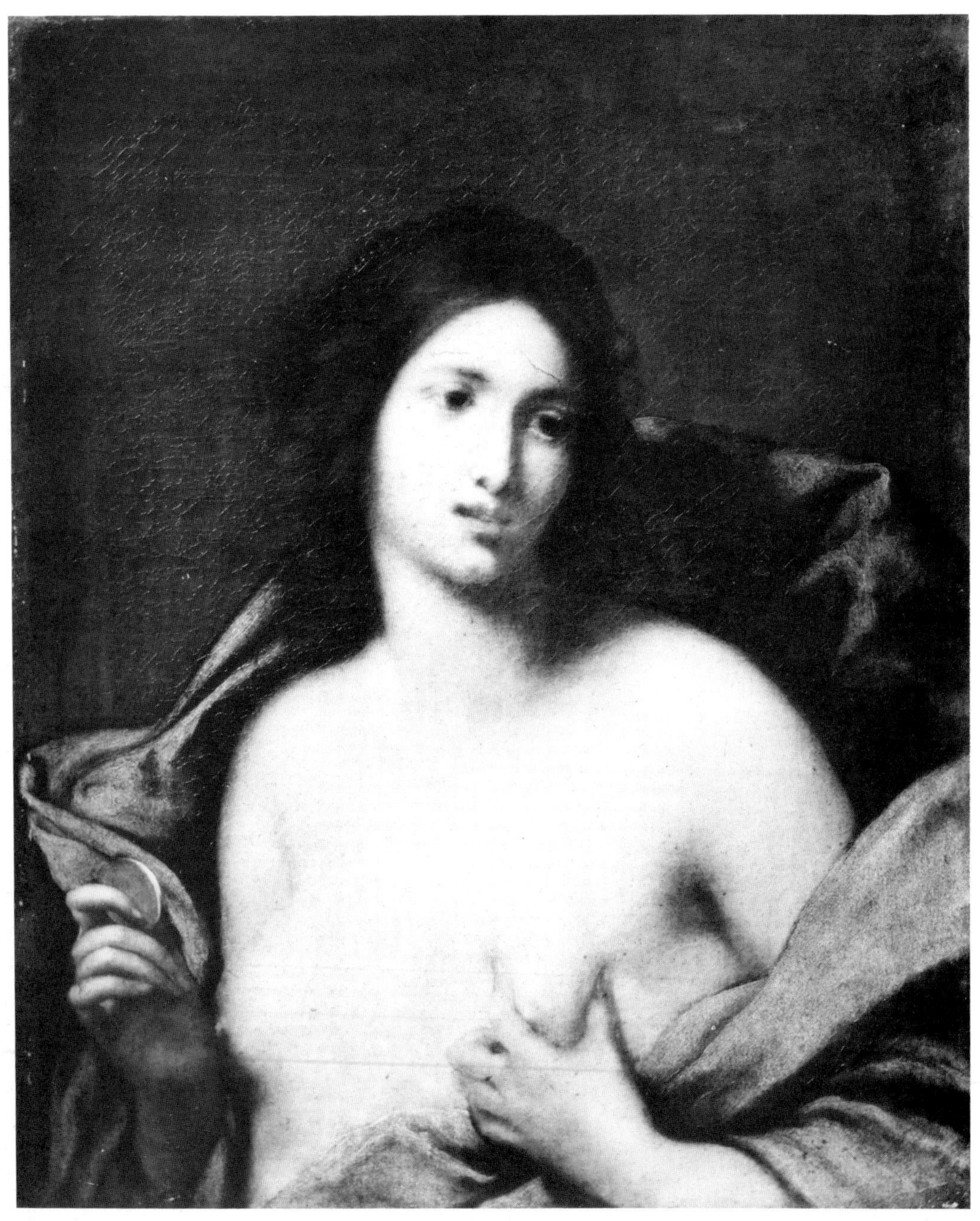

FIG. 52   Francesco Furini, *Charity* (cat. no. 368).

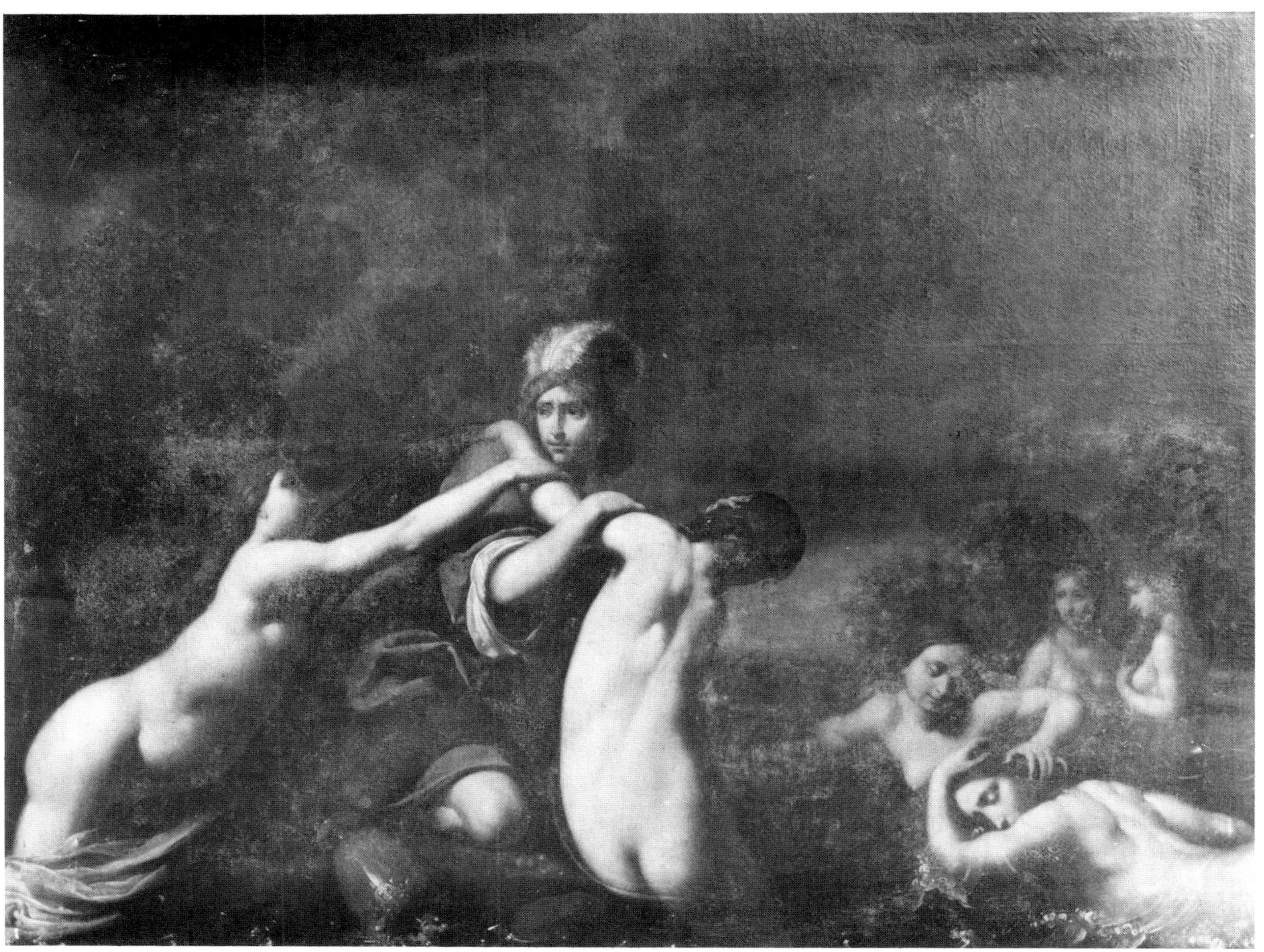

Fig. 53   Attributed to Furini, *Hylas and the nymphs* (cat. no. 1658).

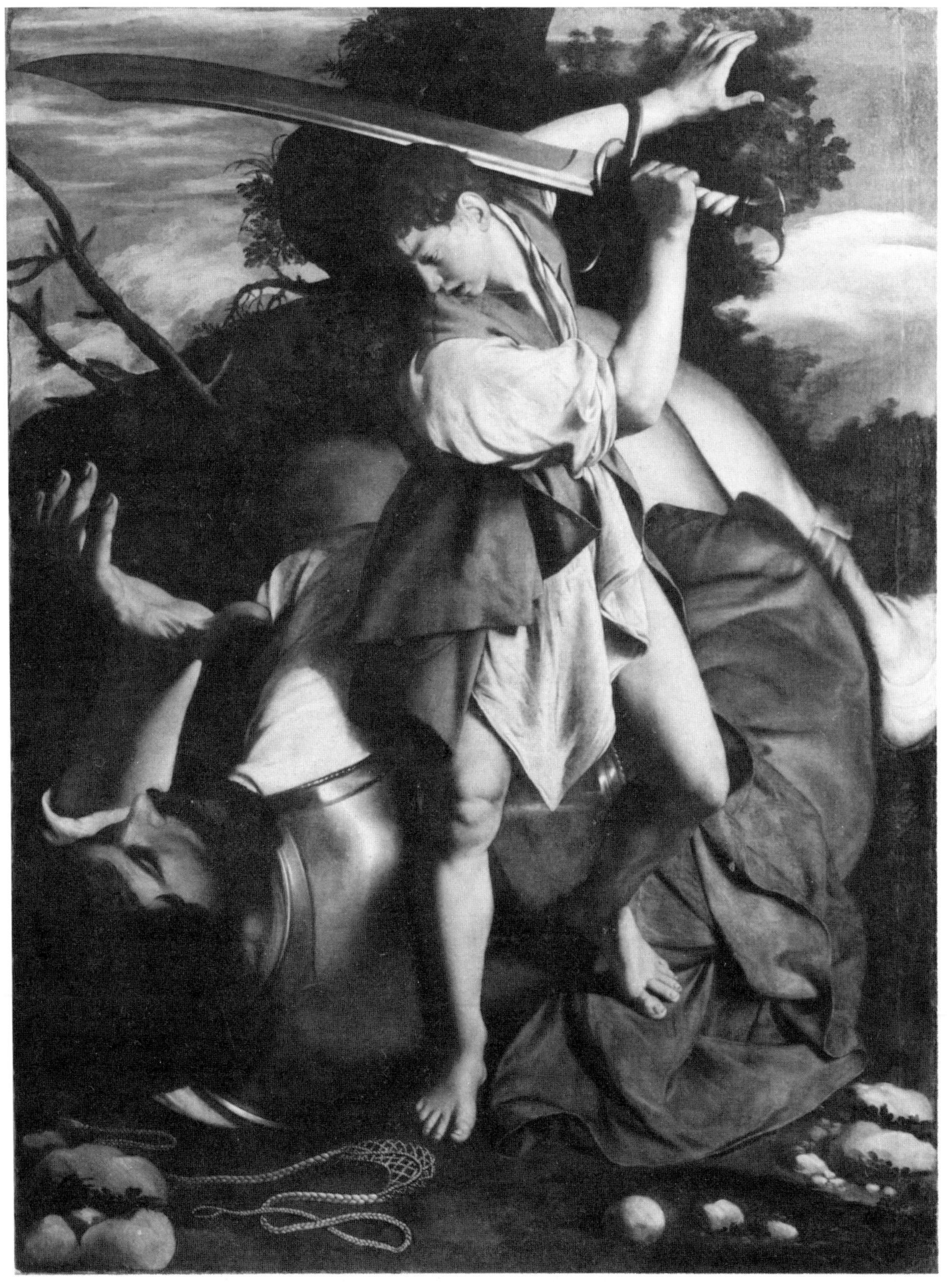

FIG. 54   Orazio Gentileschi, *David and Goliath* (cat. no. 980).

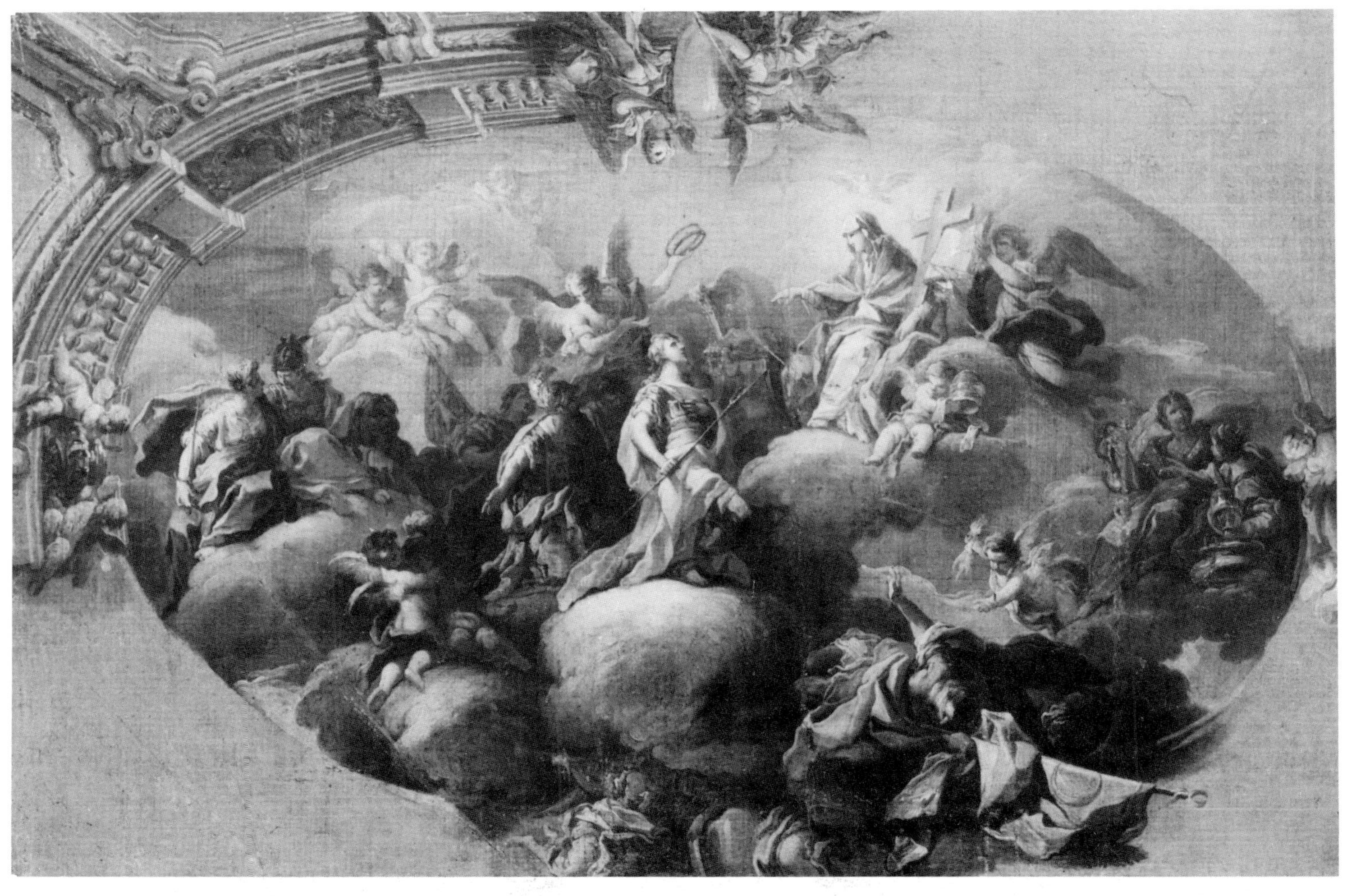

Fig. 55 Corrado Giaquinto, (?) *The glorification of Marcantonio II Colonna, hero of Lepanto* (cat. no. 542).

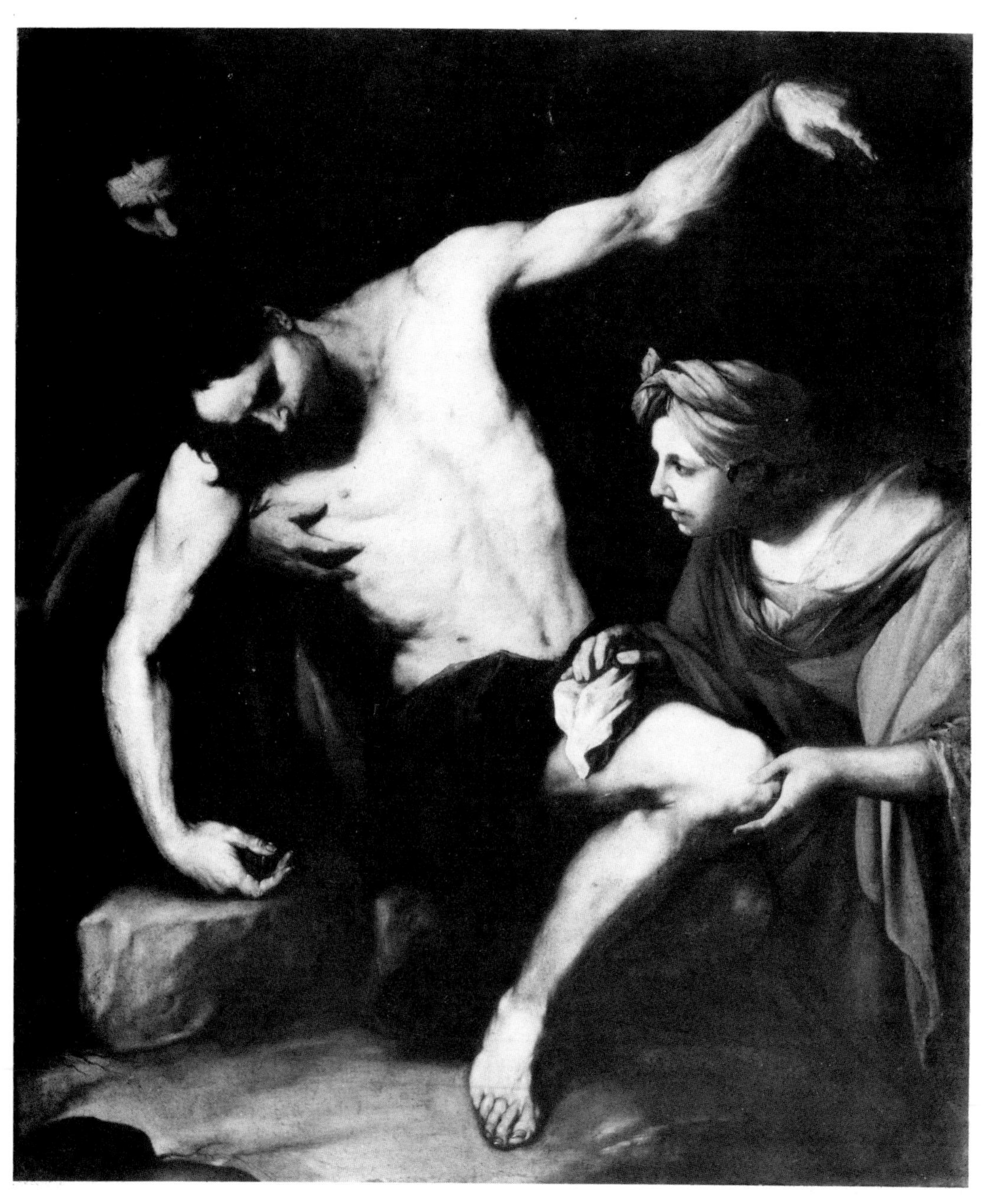

FIG. 56 Luca Giordano, *St. Sebastian tended by St. Irene* (cat. no. 79).

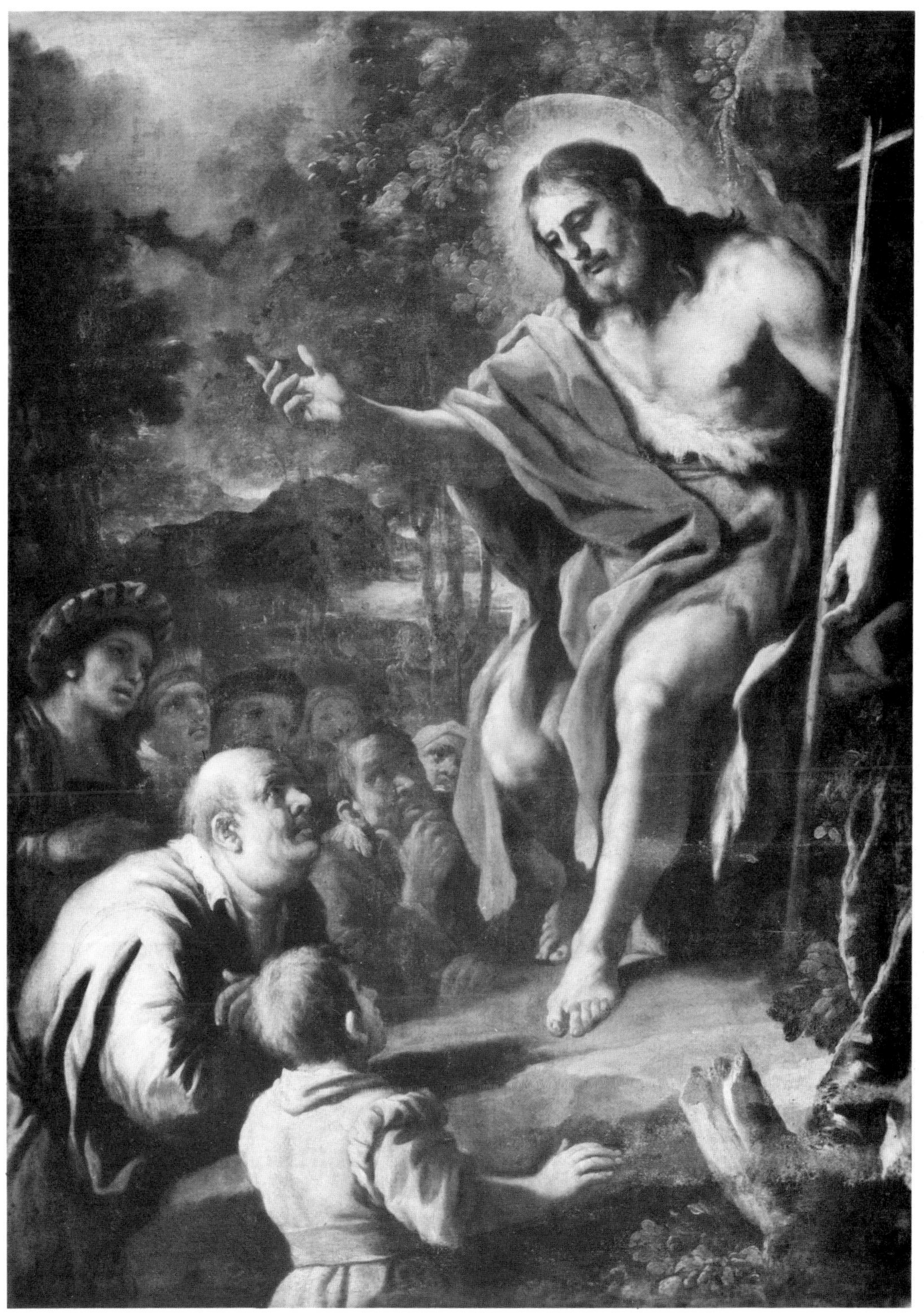

FIG. 57 Luca Giordano, *St. John the Baptist preaching in the wilderness* (cat. no. 1069).

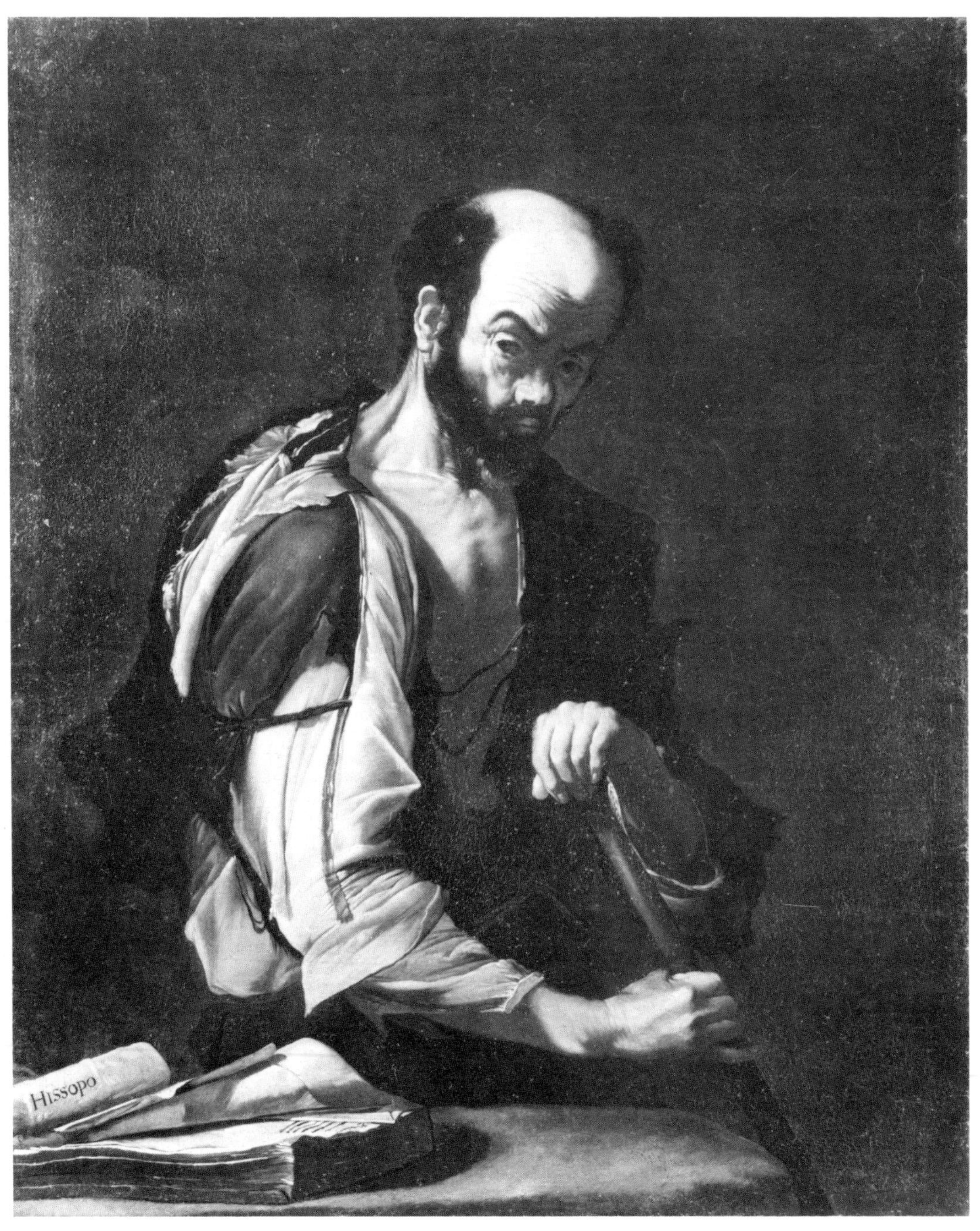

Fig. 58 Luca Giordano, *Aesop* (cat. no. 1988).

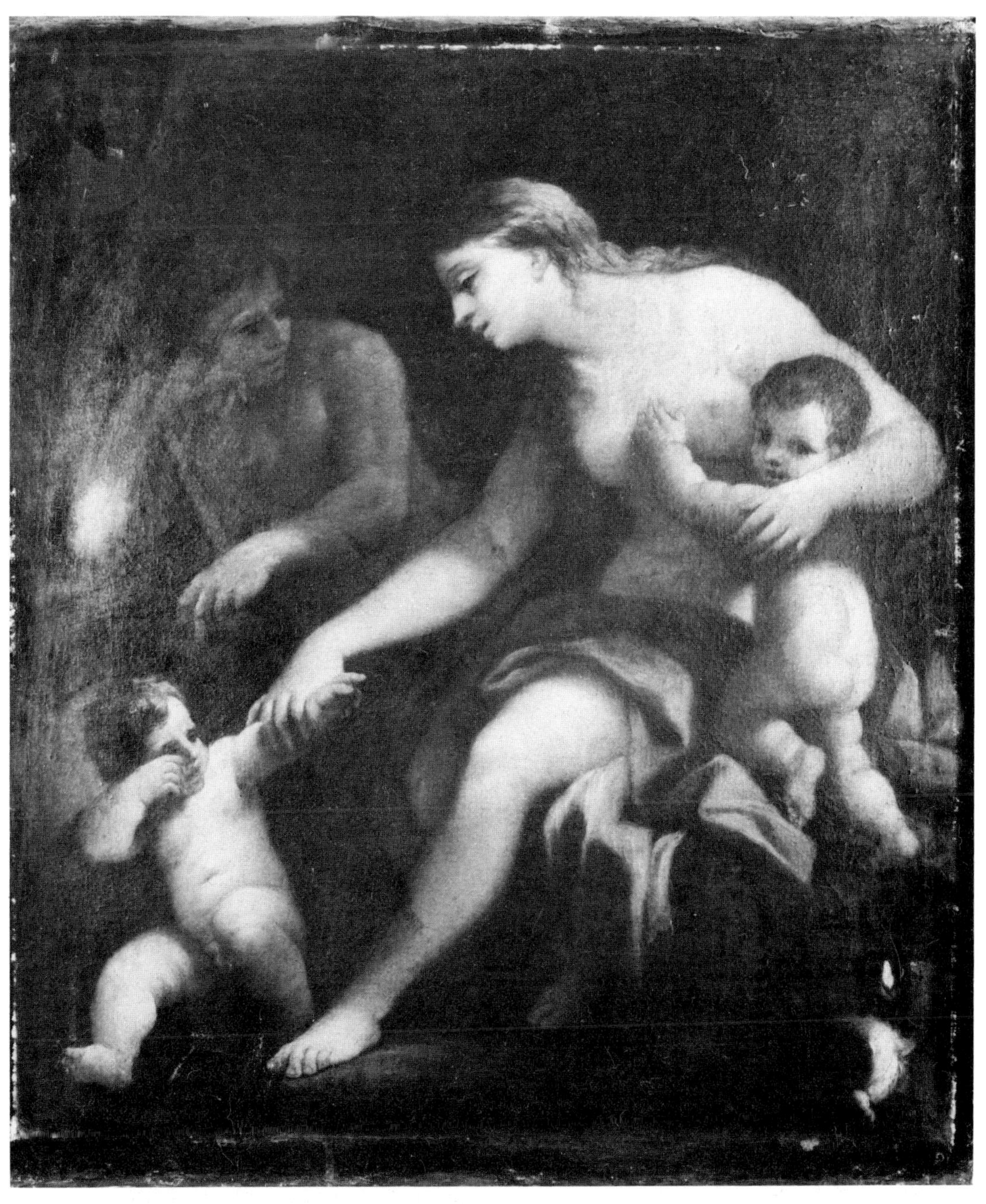

Fig. 59 Circle of Giordano, *Adam and Eve, with Cain and Abel* (cat. no. 4006).

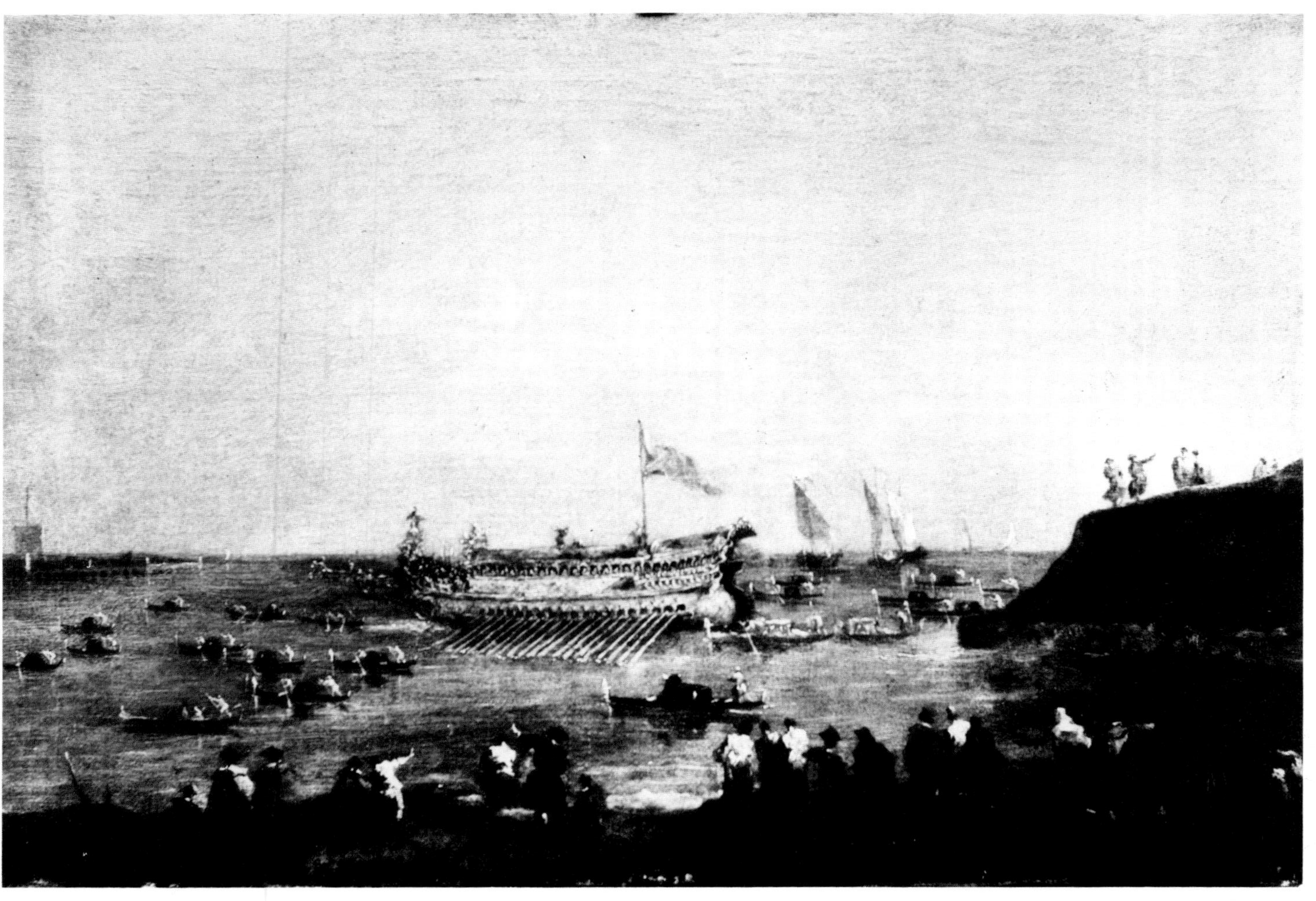

Fig. 60 Francesco Guardi, *The Doge wedding the Adriatic* (cat. no. 92).

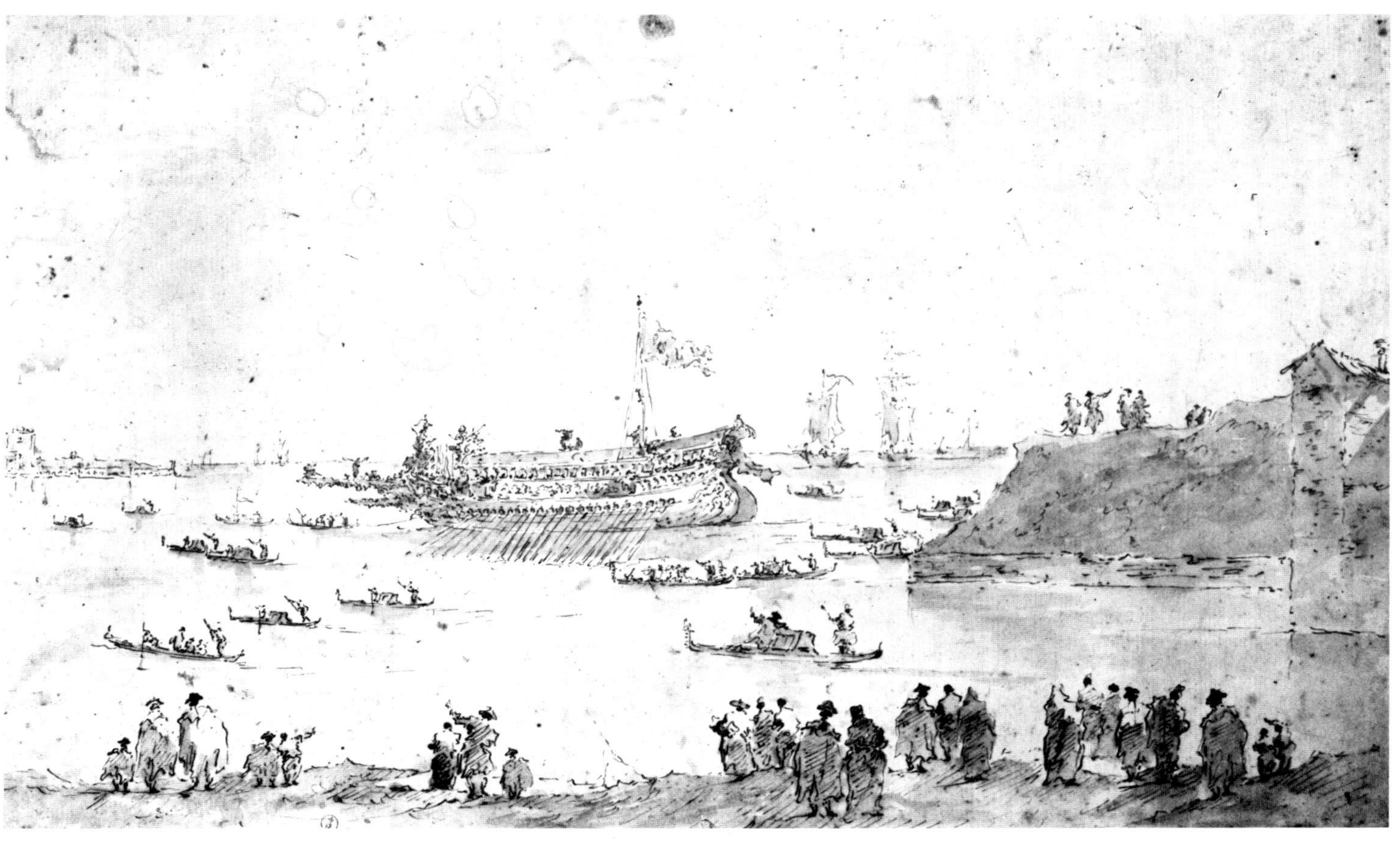

Fig. 61 Francesco Guardi, *The Bucintoro in front of the Lido*, Pen and ink and wash on paper, 300 × 505 mm. Biblioteca Reale, Turin.

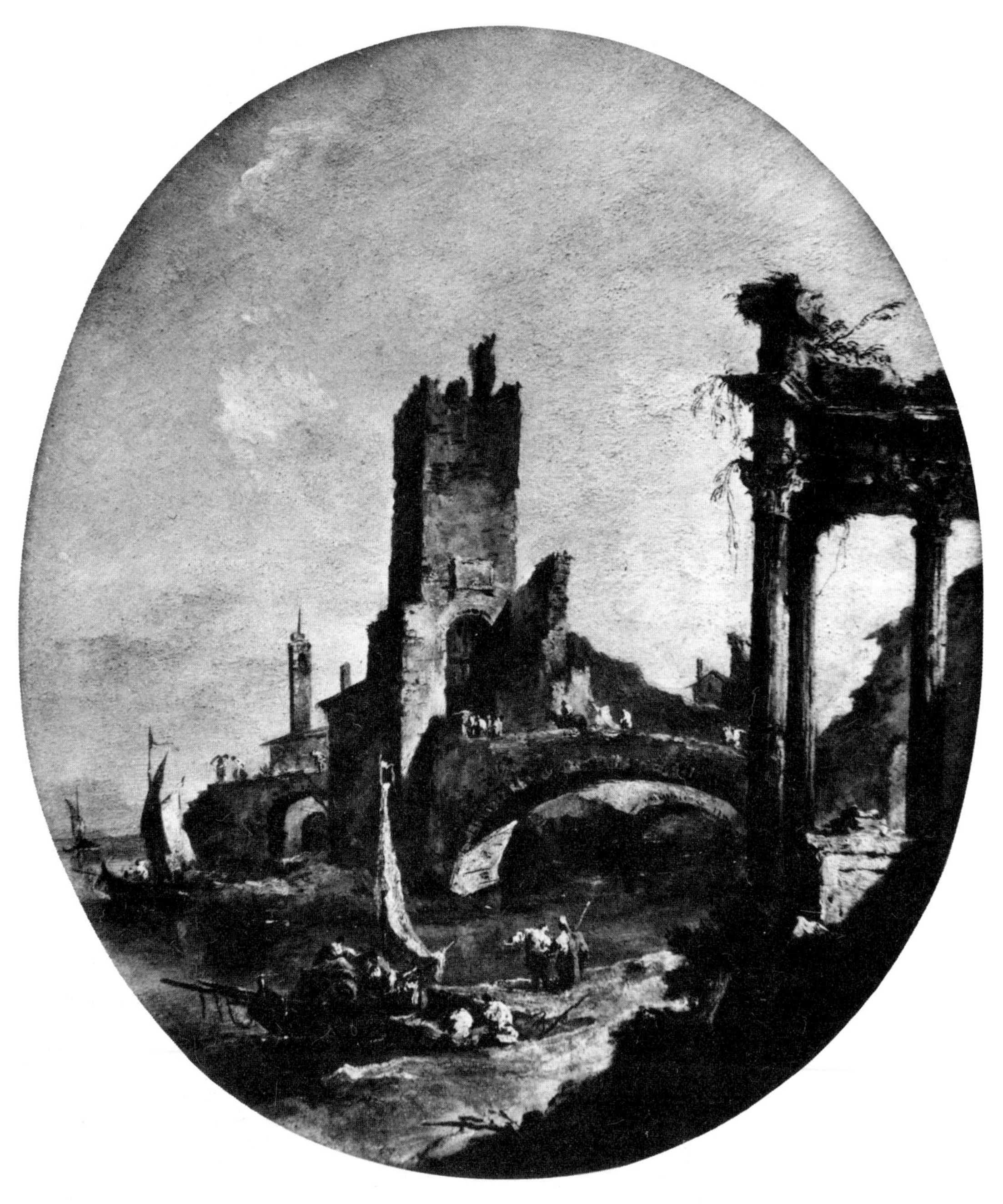

FIG. 62 Style of Guardi, *Imaginary landscape* (cat. no. 819).

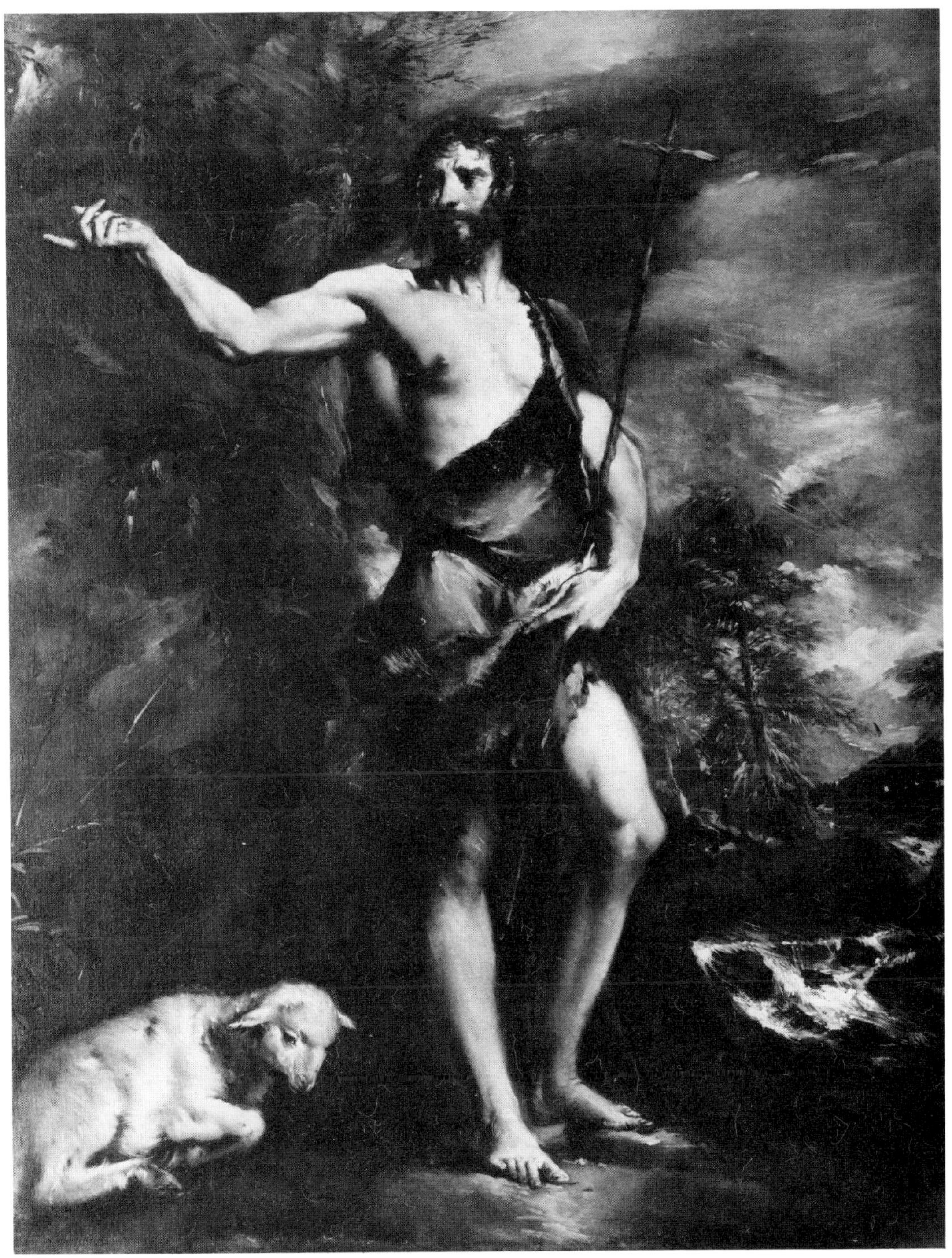

Fig. 63 Giovanni Antonio Guardi, *St. John the Baptist in the wilderness* (after Titian) (cat. no. 63).

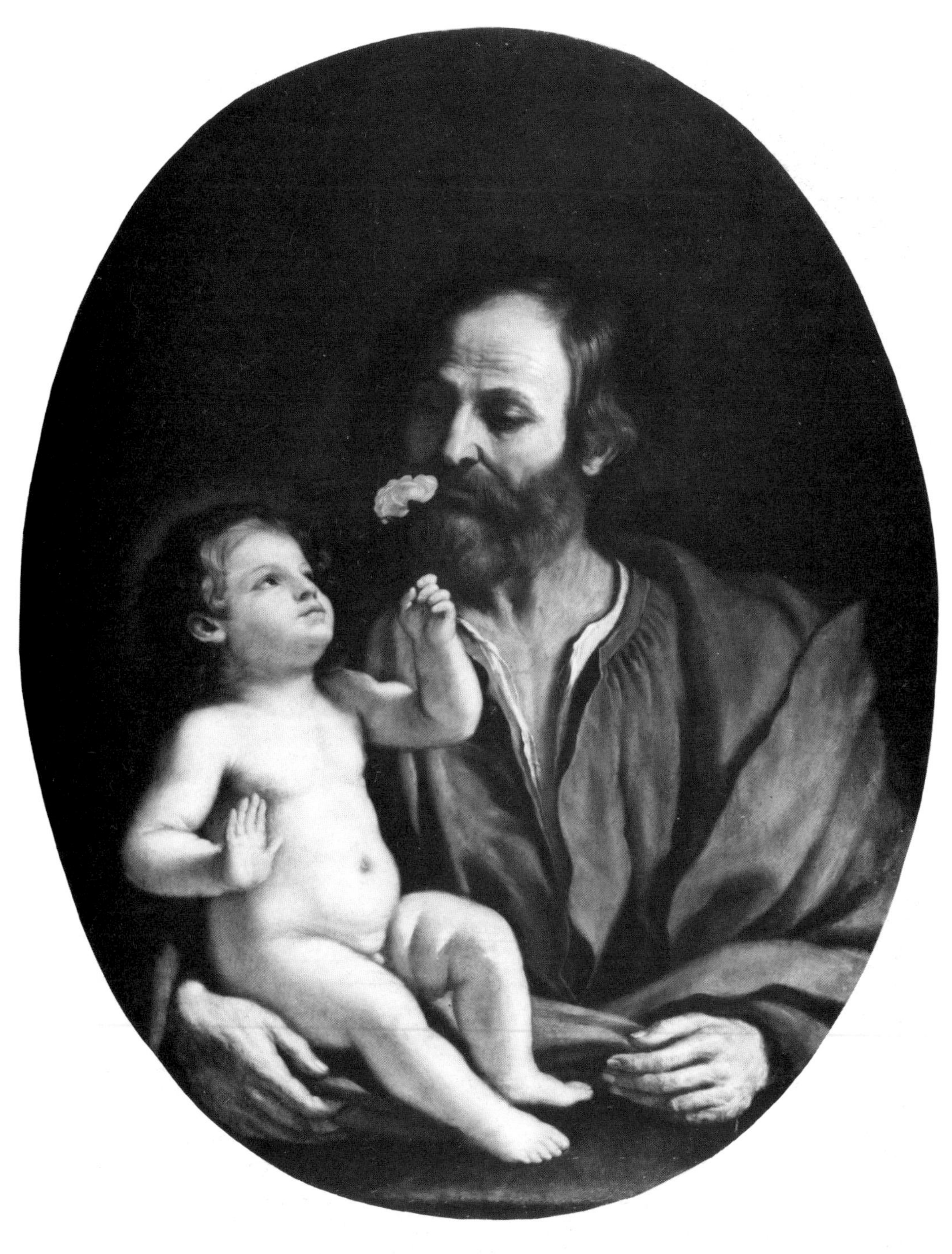

Fɪɢ. 64 Guercino, *St. Joseph with the Christ Child* (cat. no. 192).

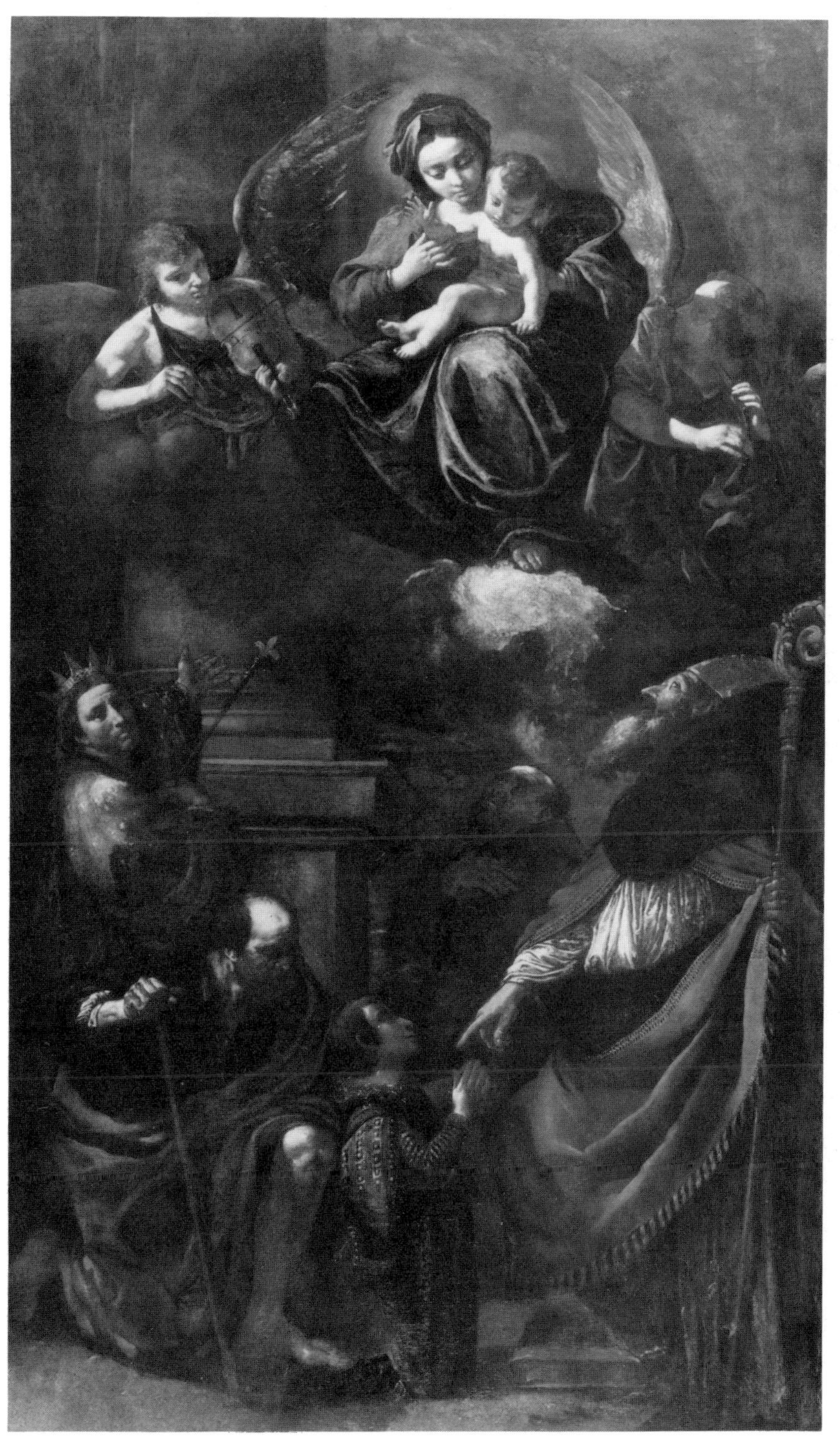

FIG. 65　After Guercino, *Virgin and Child with Saints Joseph, Augustine, Louis, Francis, and a young donor* (cat. no. 483).

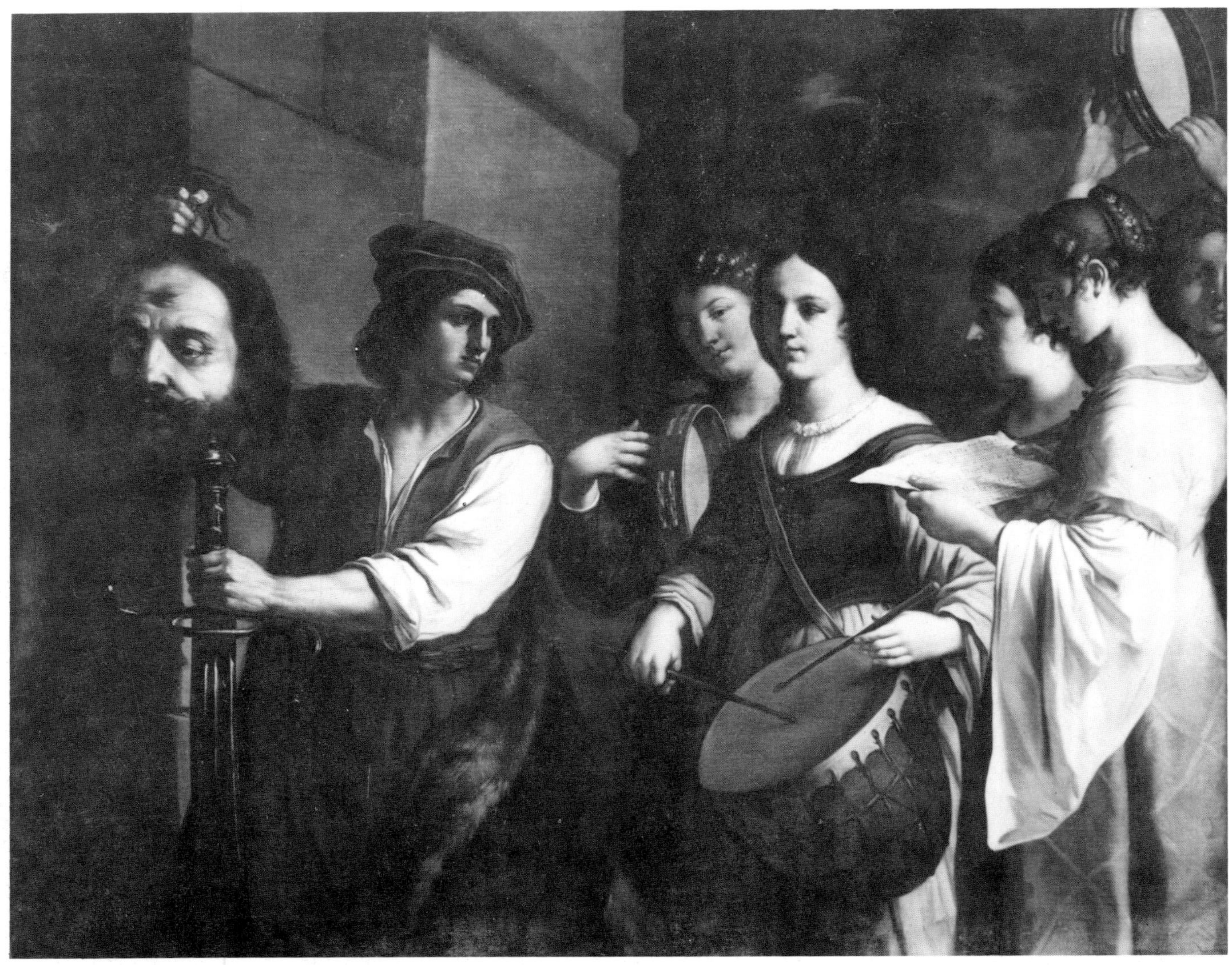

FIG. 66   After Guercino, *The triumph of David* (cat. no. 1323).

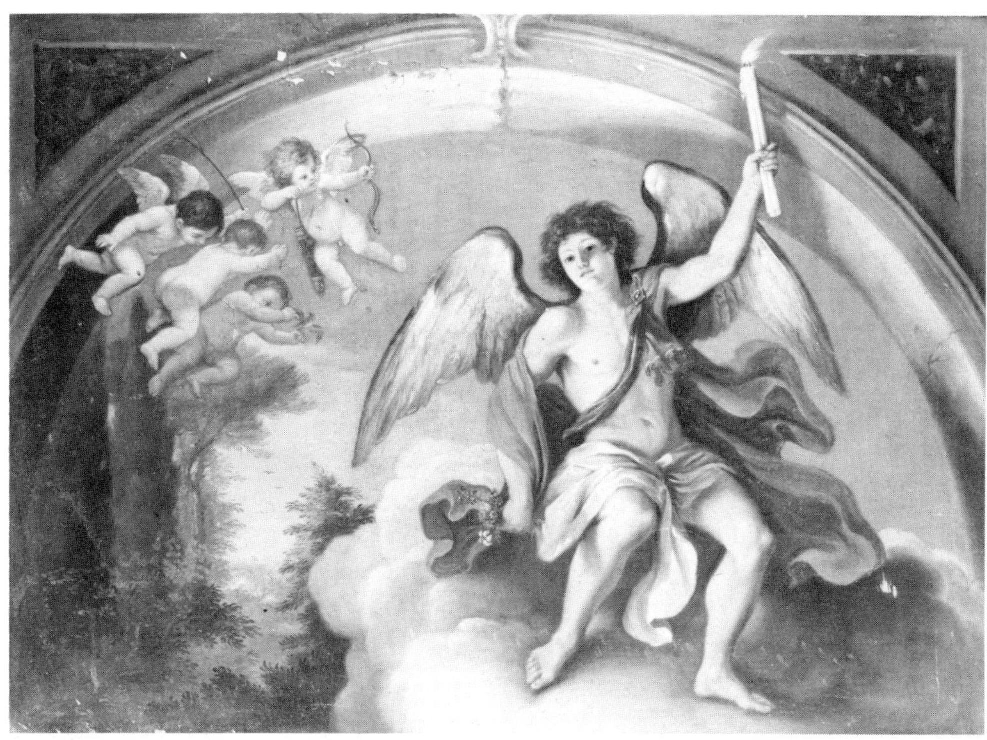

FIG. 67   After Guercino, *Day* (cat. no. 1659).

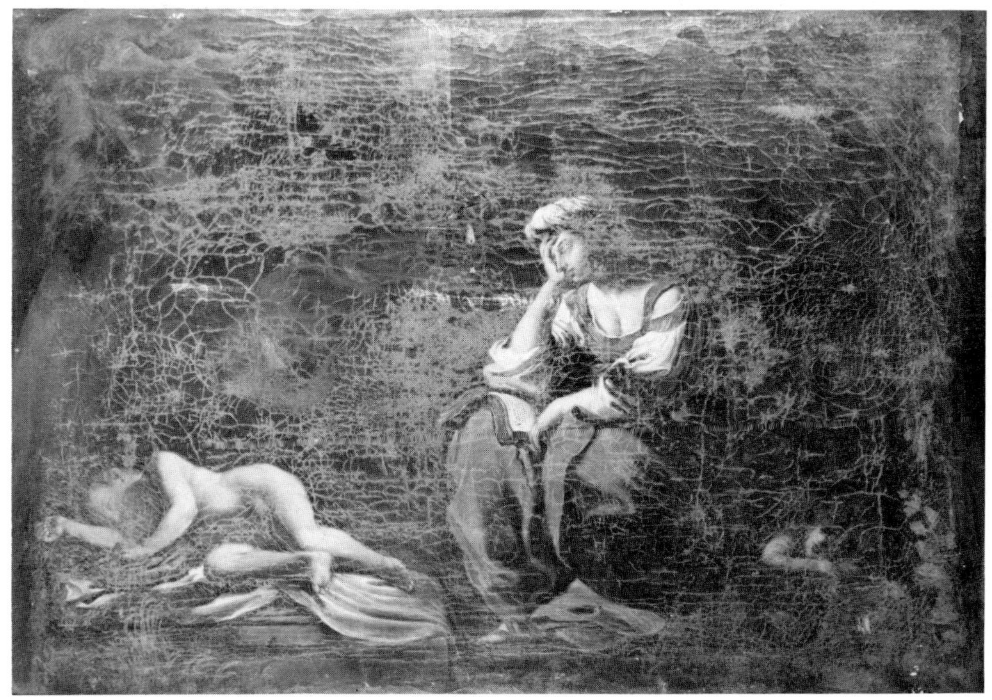

FIG. 68   After Guercino, *Night* (cat. no. 1682).

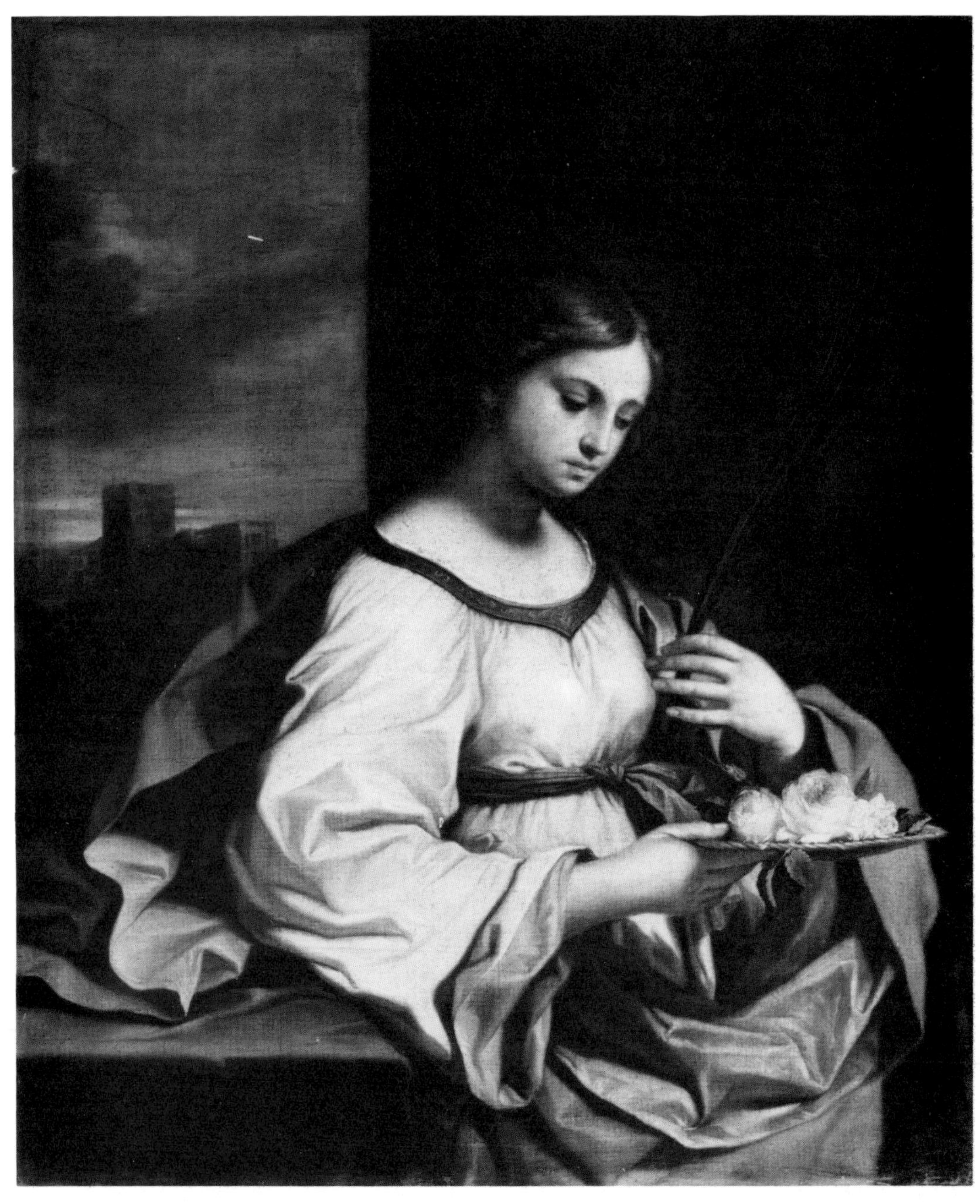

FIG. 69 After Guercino, *St. Agatha* (cat. no. 1668).

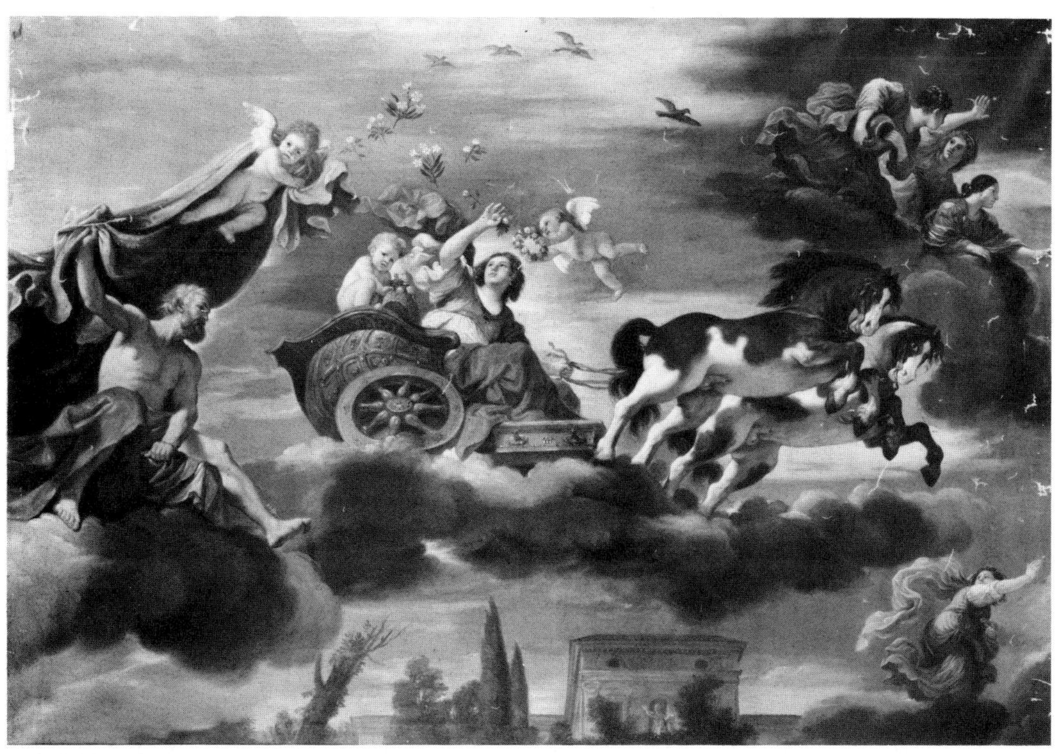

FIG. 70   After Guercino, *Aurora* (cat. no. 1686).

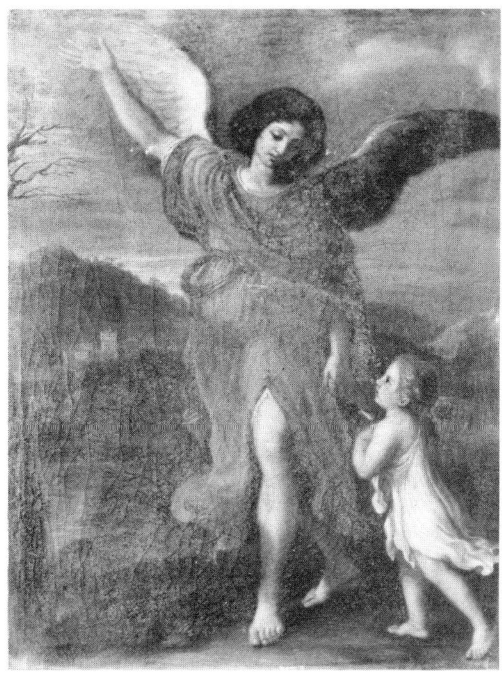

FIG. 71   After Guercino, *Angel leading Innocence to heaven* (cat. no. 1692).

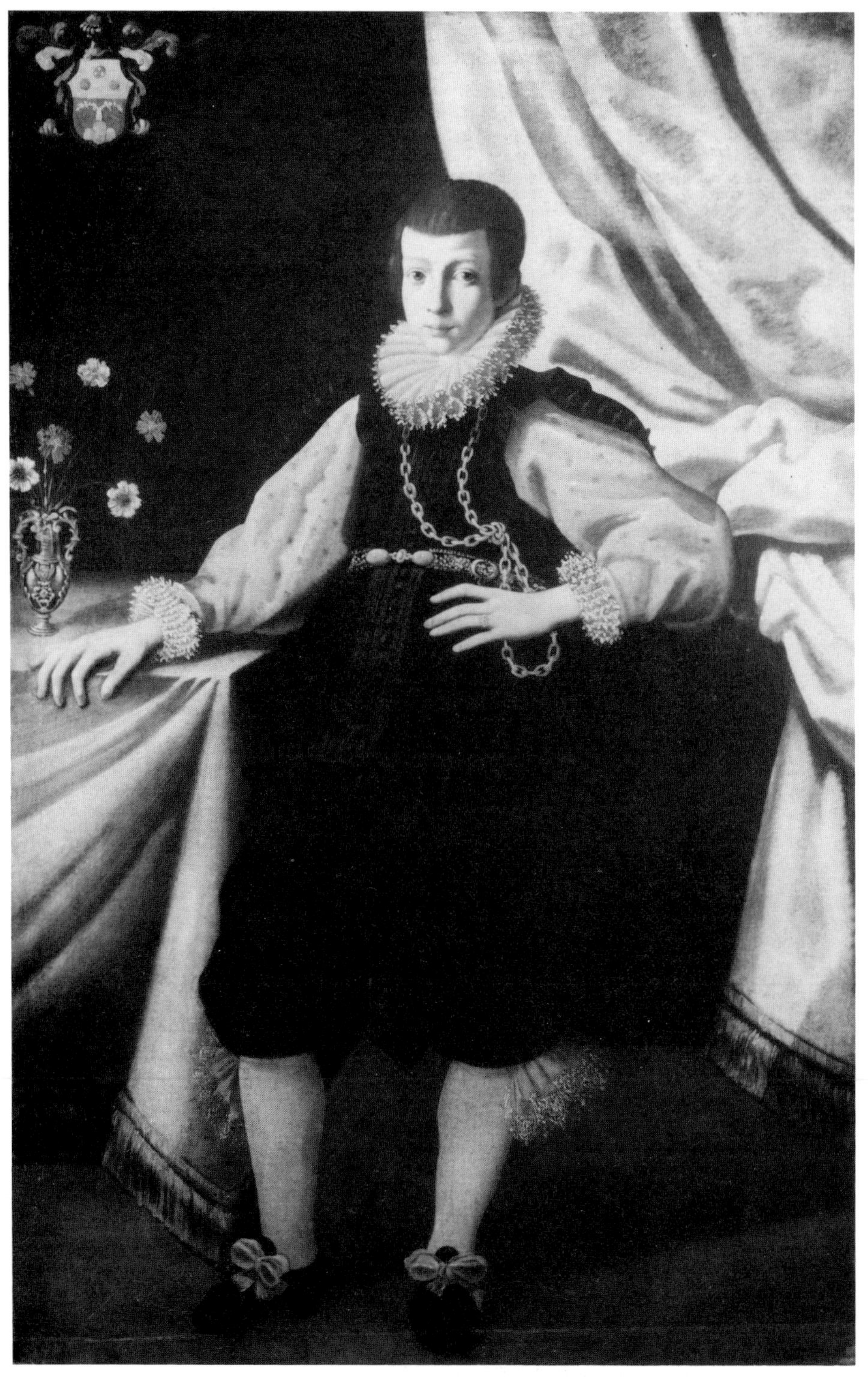

FIG. 72   Italian School, *circa* 1610, *Portrait of a young man of the Branconio family* (cat. no. 4468).

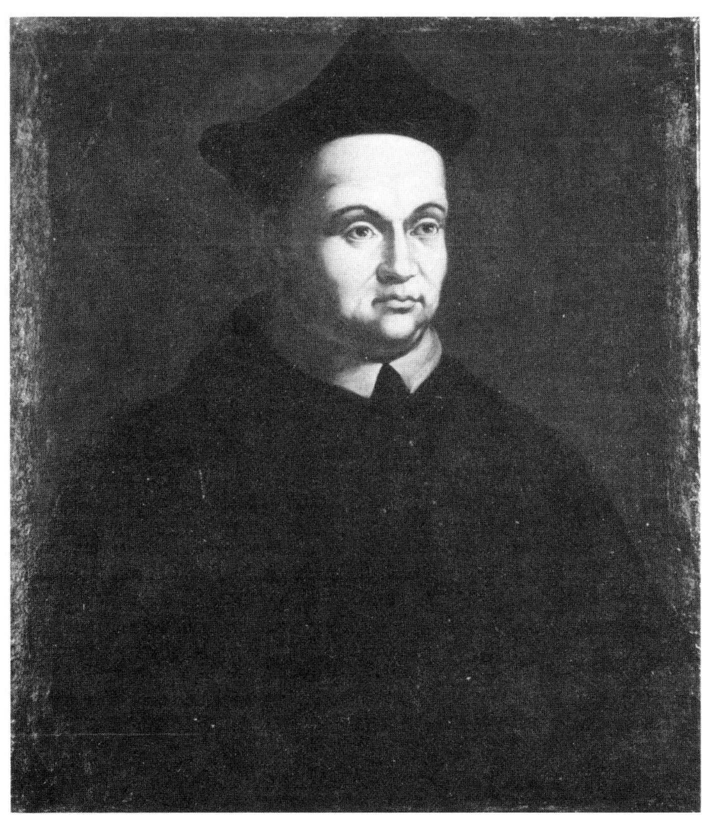

Fig. 73   Italian School,
17th century,
Peter Talbot,
Archbishop of Dublin,
1620-1680
(cat. no. 4159).

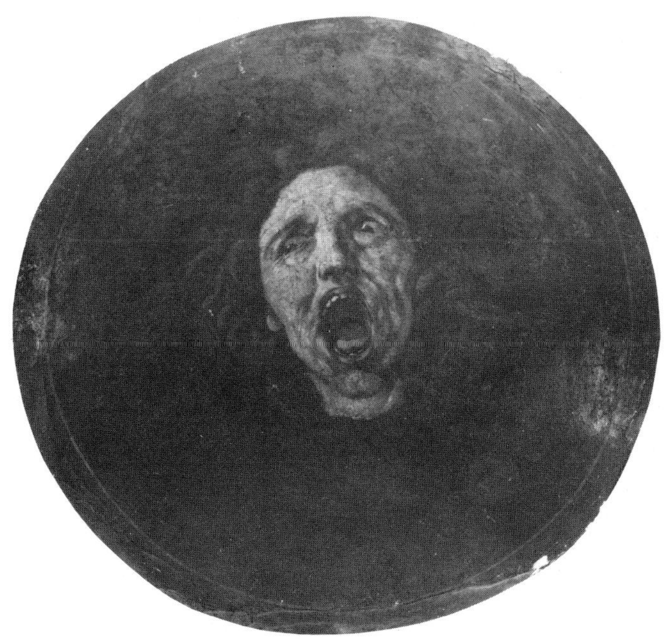

Fig. 74   Italian School, 17th century, *Shield: Head of Medusa* (cat. no. 4337).

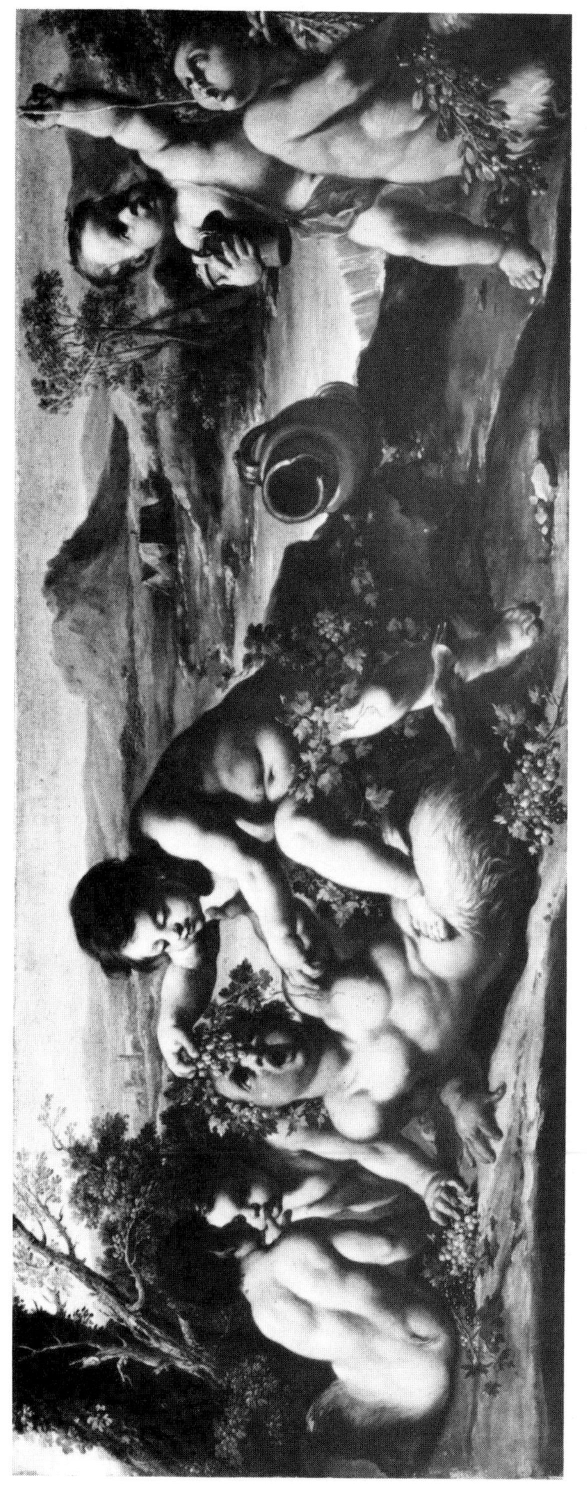

Fig. 75 Italian School, 17th century, *Bacchanalian boys and satyrs* (cat. no. 1074).

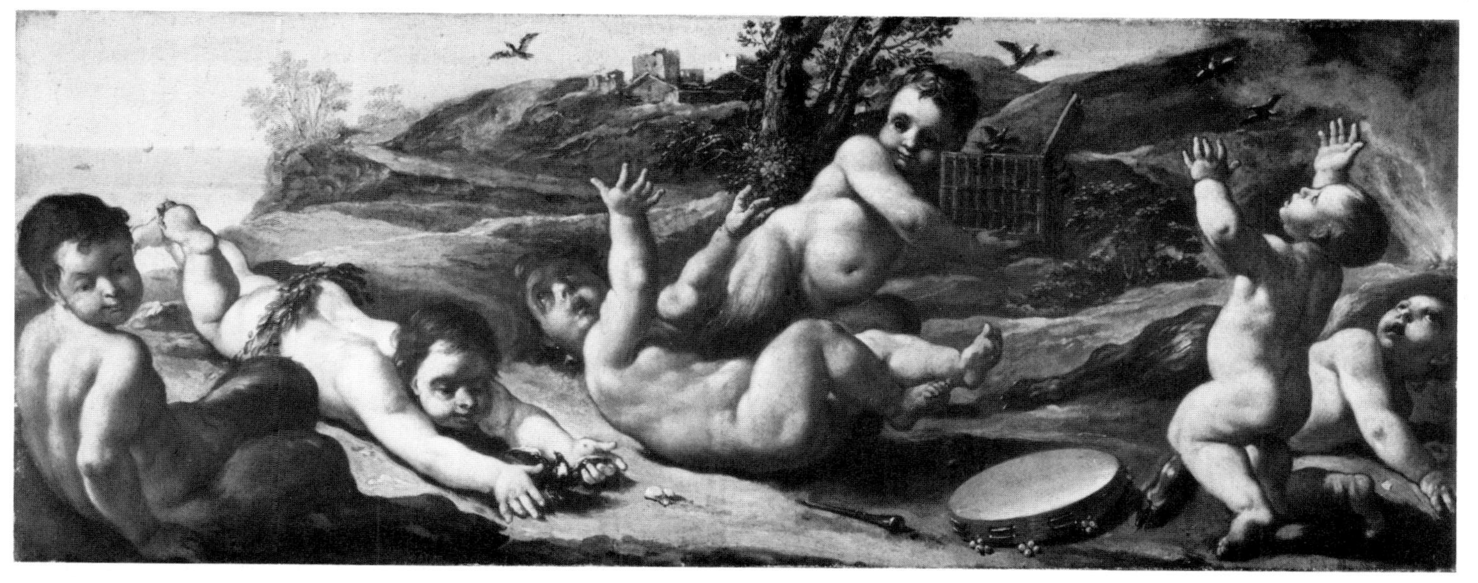

FIG. 76 Italian School, 17th century, *Young satyrs and boys at play* (cat. no. 1075).

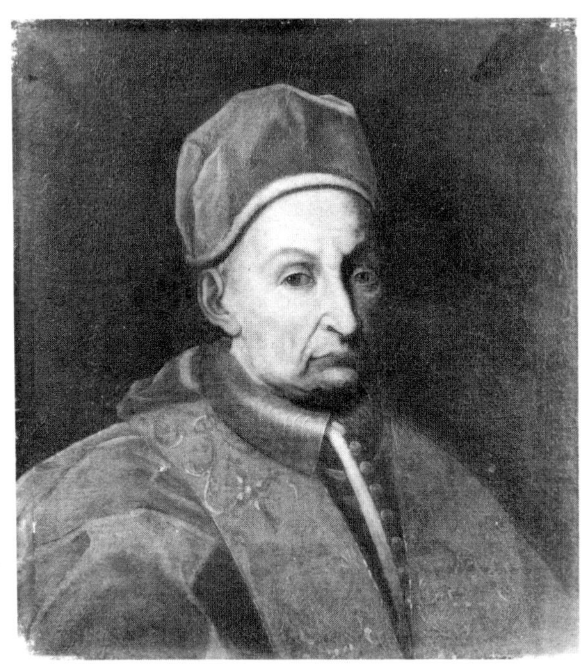

Fig. 77   Italian School, 18th century,
Pope Benedict XIII (cat. no. 1084).

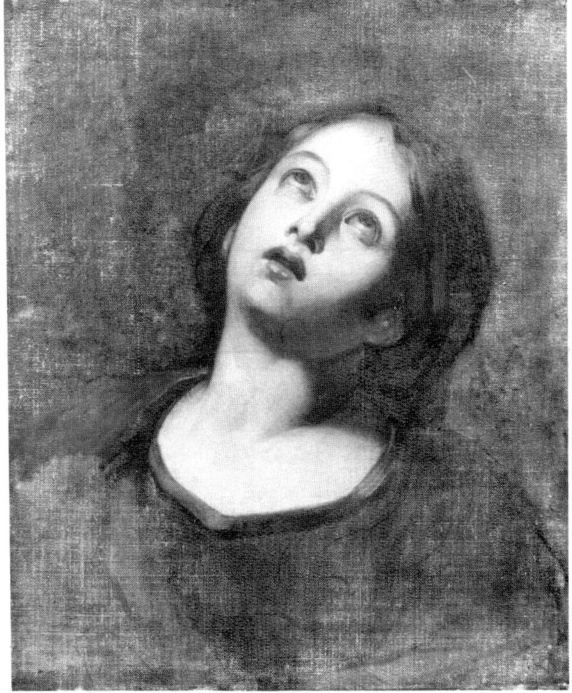

Fig. 78   Italian School, *circa* 1800,
Head of a saint (cat. no. 1239).

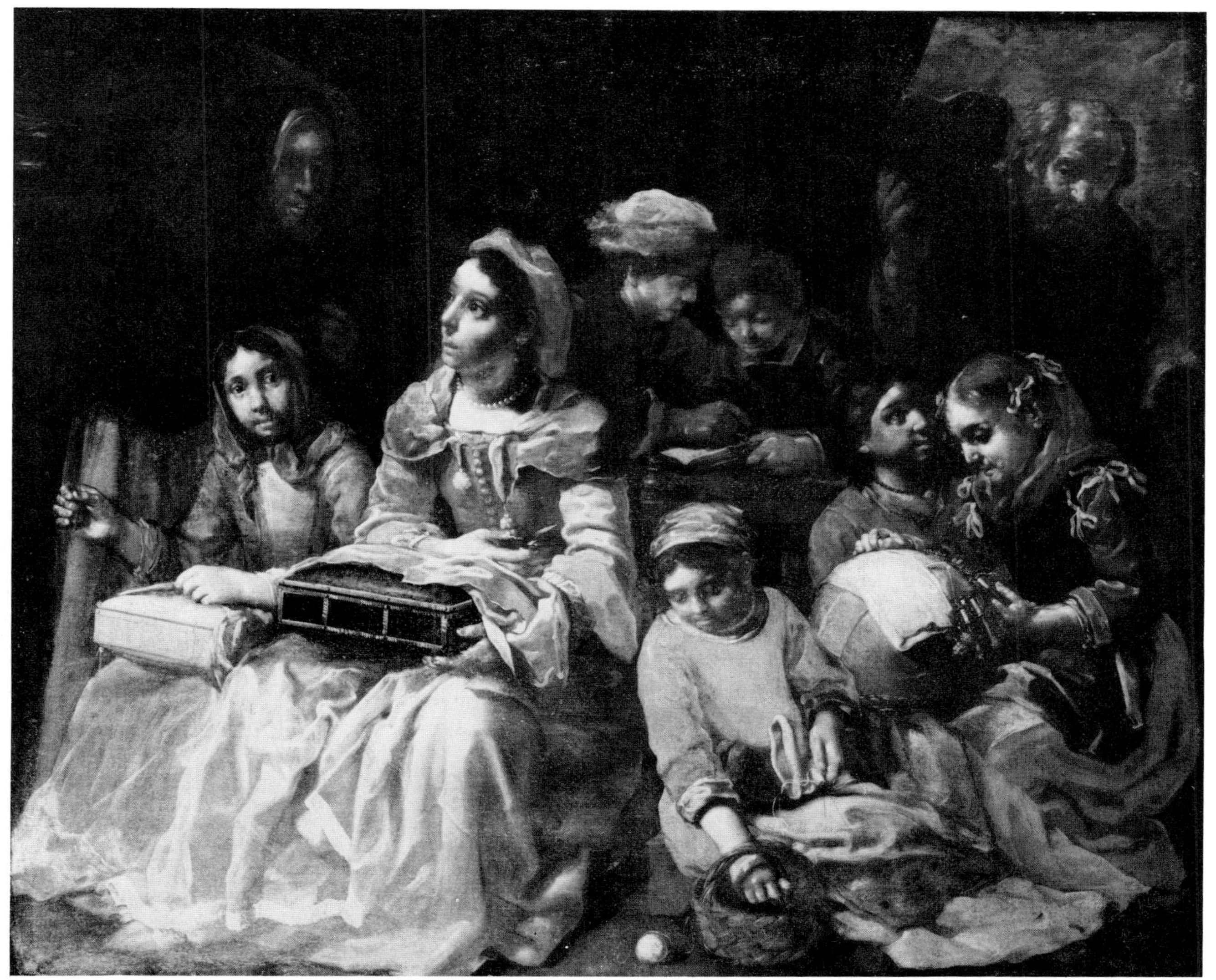

Fig. 79 Eberhard Keil, *The embroidery shop* (cat. no. 4092).

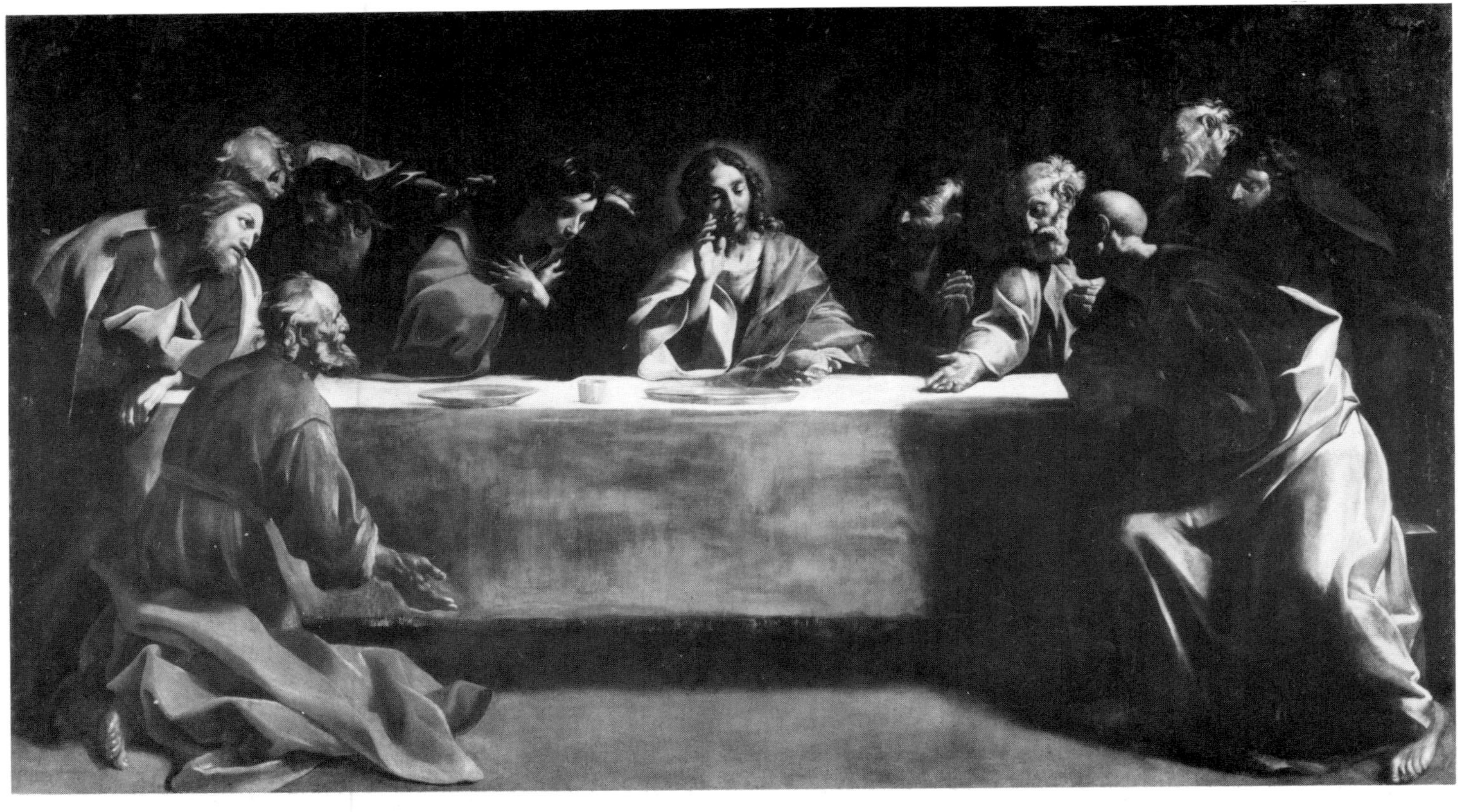

FIG. 80 Giovanni Lanfranco, *The Last Supper* (cat. no. 67).

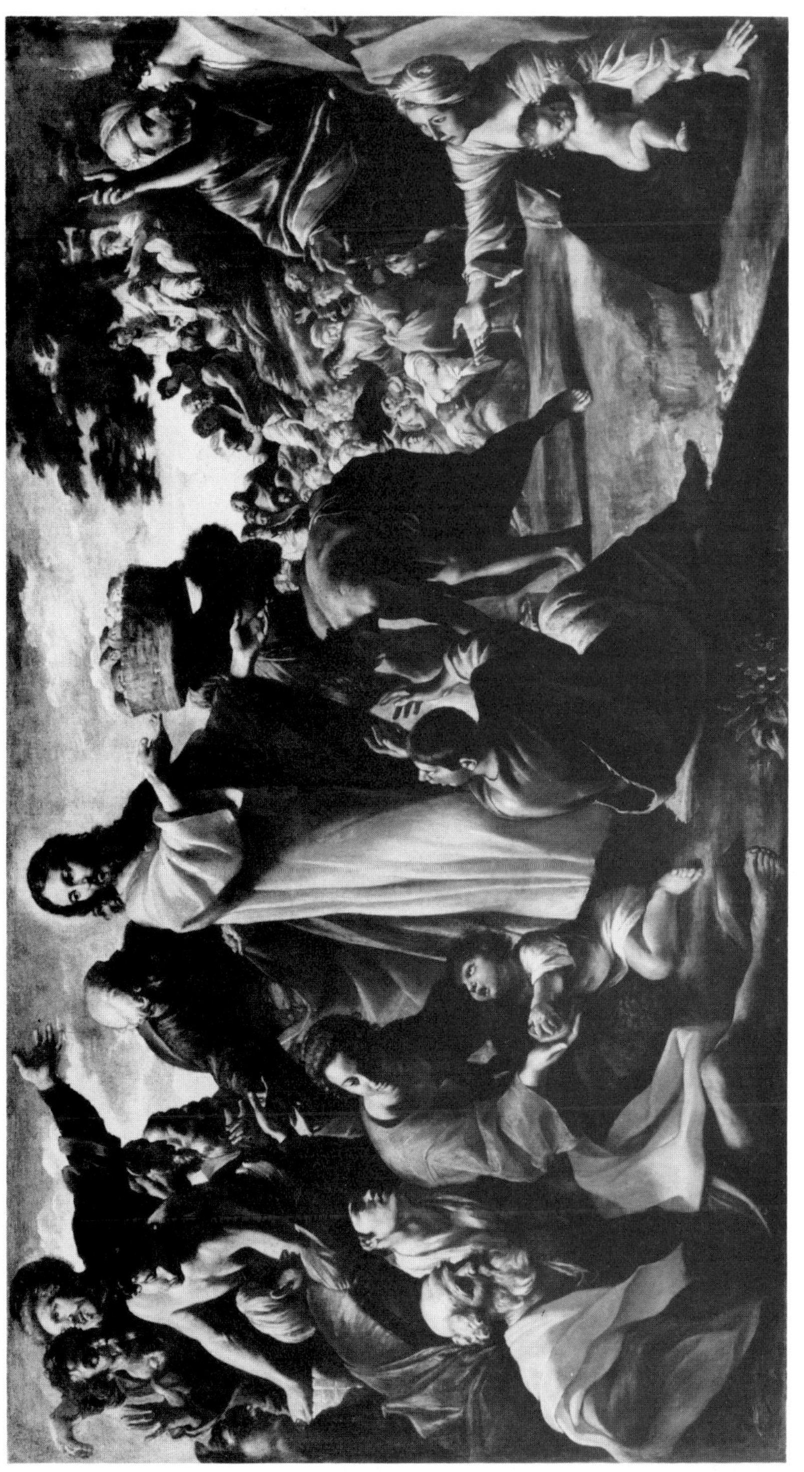

Fig. 81 Giovanni Lanfranco, *Multiplication of loaves and fishes* (cat. no. 72).

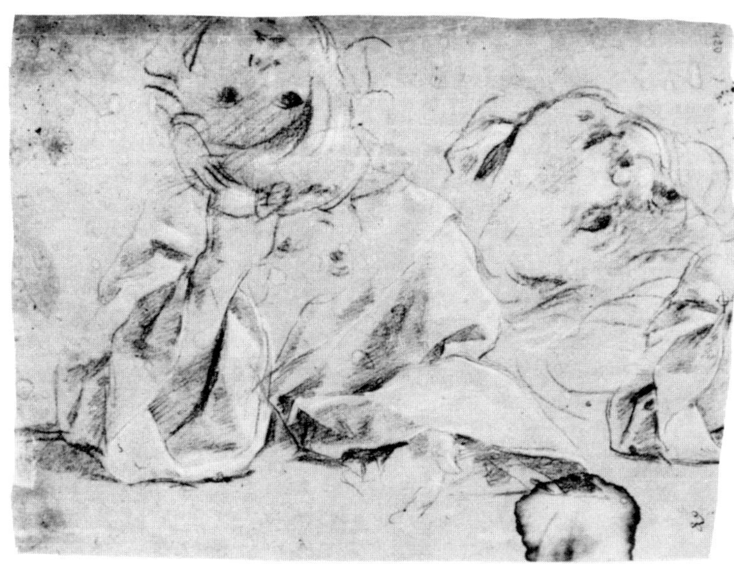

Fig. 82   Giovanni Lanfranco, *Hands, arms and draperies of Christ* (study for no. 67). Black and white chalk on paper, 233 × 307 mm. Museo di Capodimonte, Naples (inv. no. 420).

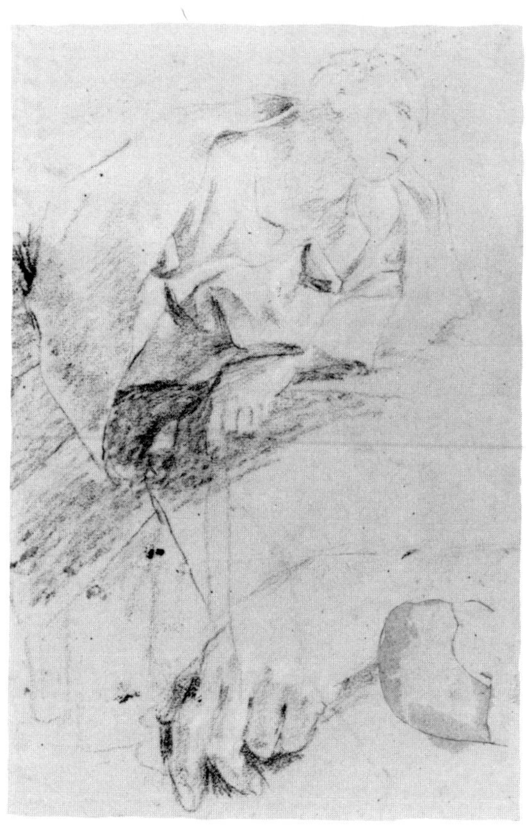

Fig. 83   Giovanni Lanfranco, *An apostle* (study for no. 67). Black and white chalk on grey-brown paper, 355 × 229 mm. The Royal Library, Windsor Castle (inv. no. 5692). Reproduced by gracious permission of Her Majesty Queen Elizabeth II.

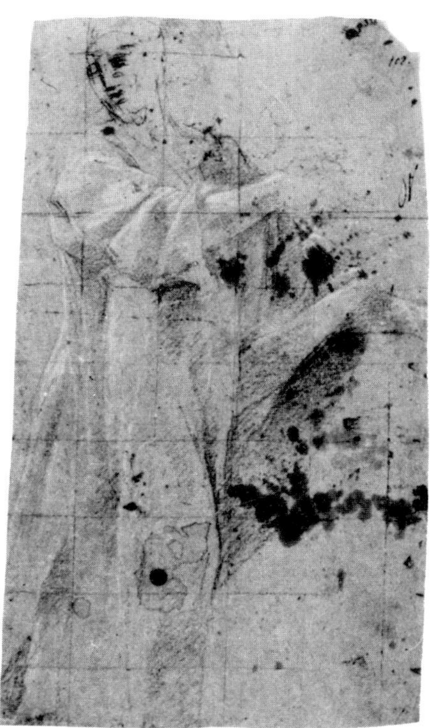 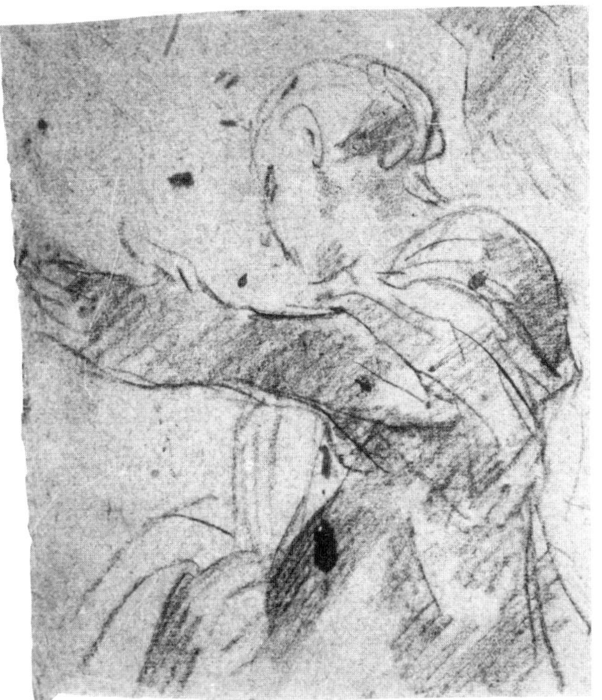

FIG. 84 Giovanni Lanfranco, *Figure of Christ* (study for no. 72). Black and white chalk on grey-green paper, 422 × 236 mm. Museo di Capodimonte, Naples (inv. no. 336 *recto*).

FIG. 86 Giovanni Lanfranco, *A figure on the hillock* (study for no. 72). Black and white chalk on blue paper, 272 × 220 mm. Museo di Capodimonte, Naples (inv. no. 493 *verso*), (detail).

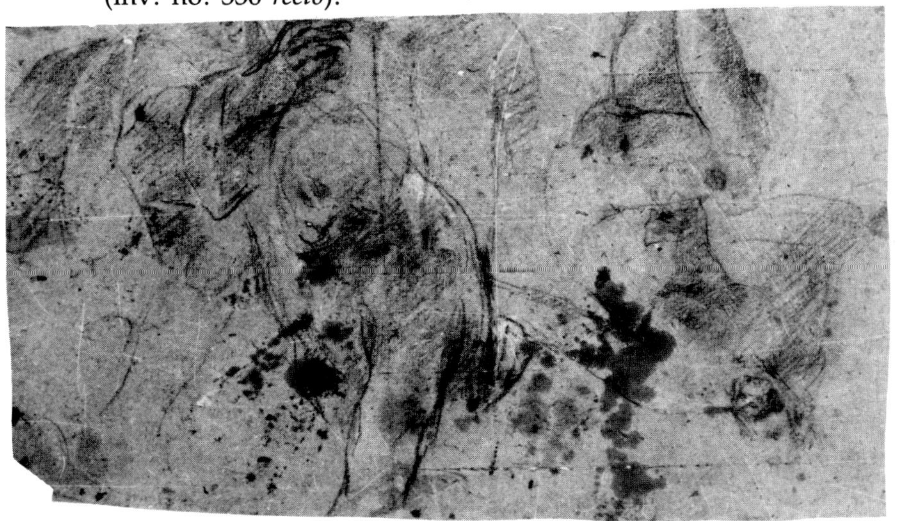

FIG. 85 Giovanni Lanfranco, *Young man bending down* (study for no. 72). Black and white chalk on grey-green paper, 422 × 236 mm. Museo di Capodimonte, Naples (inv. no. 336 *verso*).

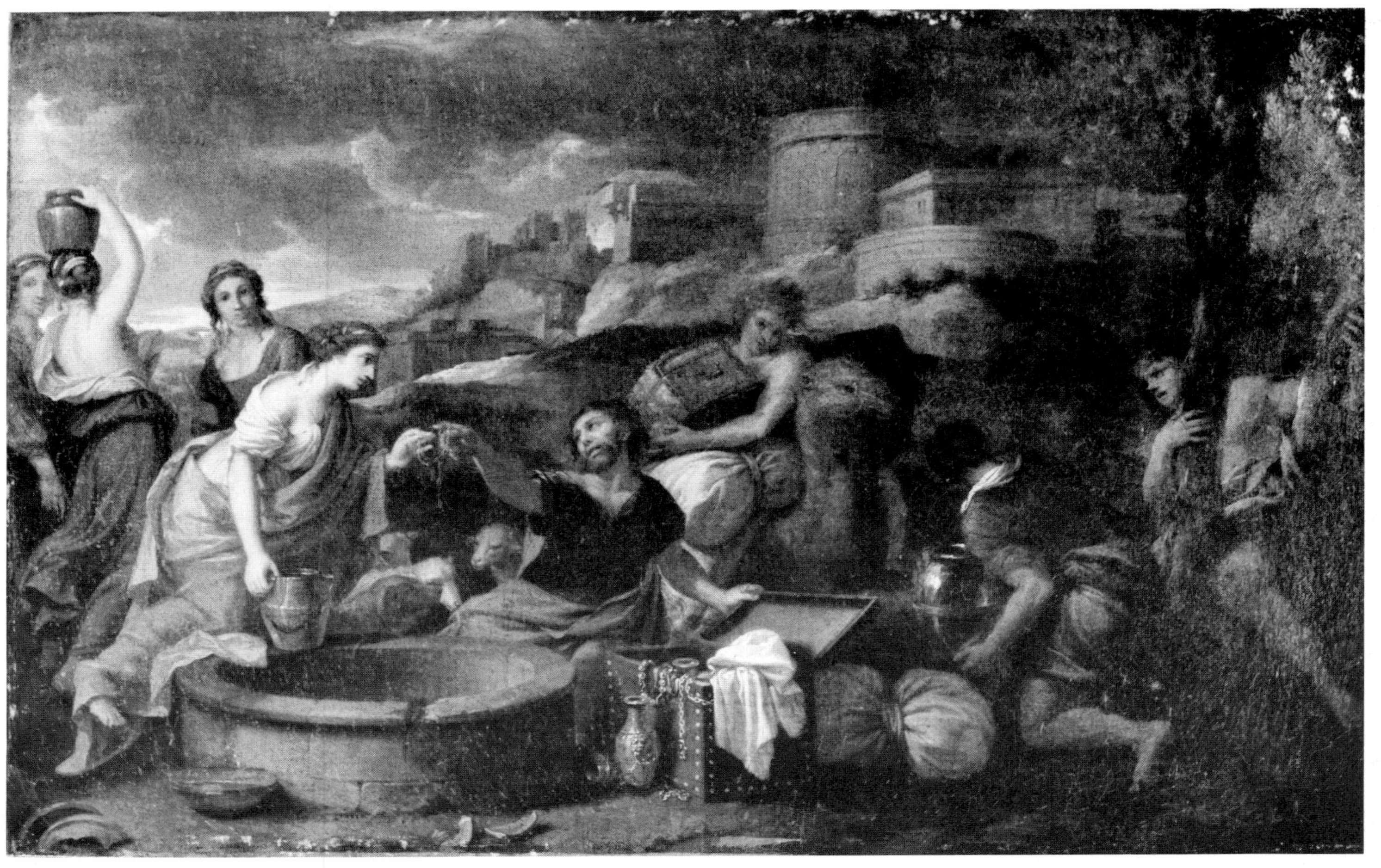

Fig. 87   Filippo Lauri, *Rebecca at the well* (cat. no. 989).

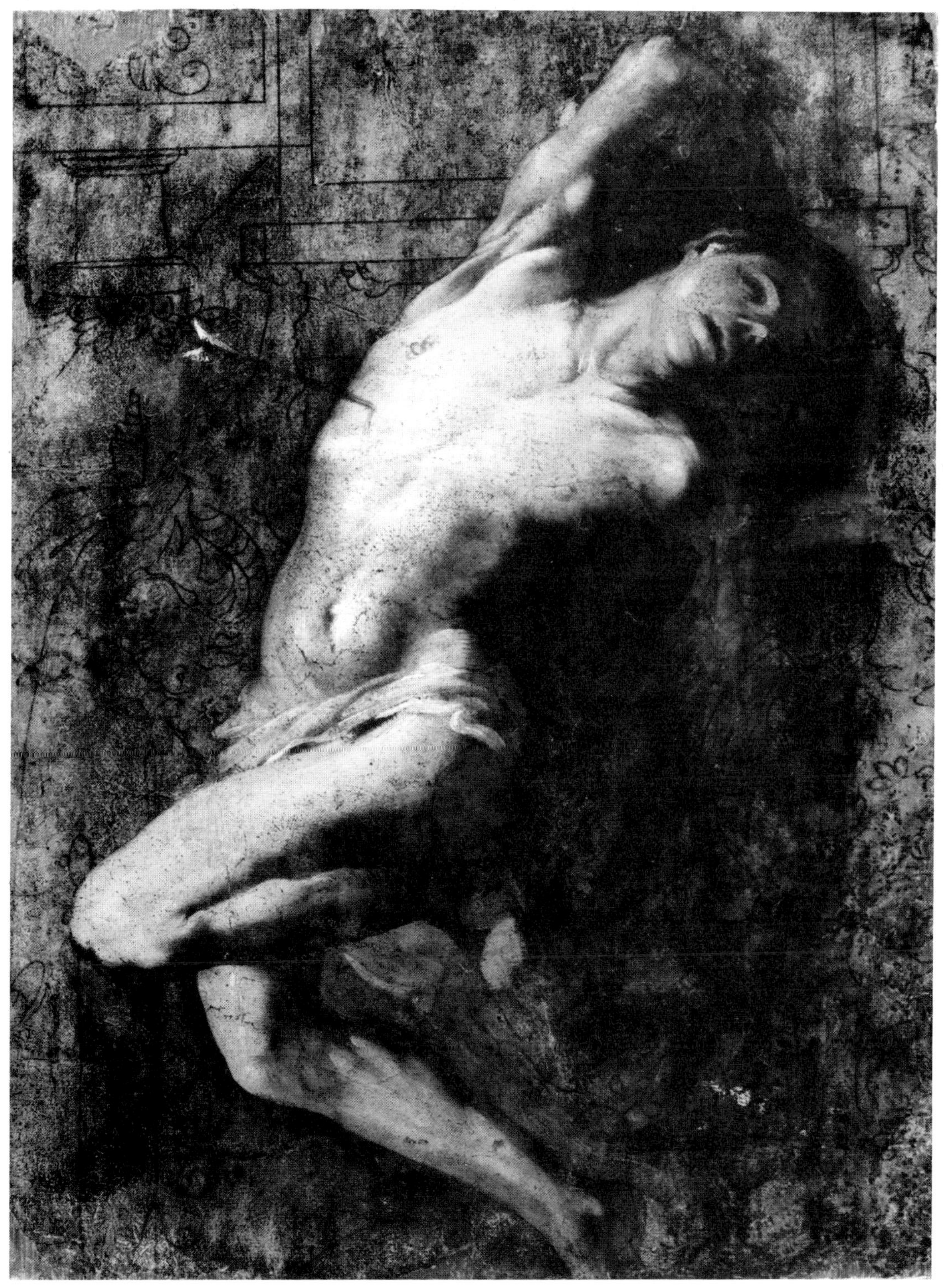

FIG. 88   Giovanni Battista Langetti, *St. Sebastian* (cat. no. 4002).

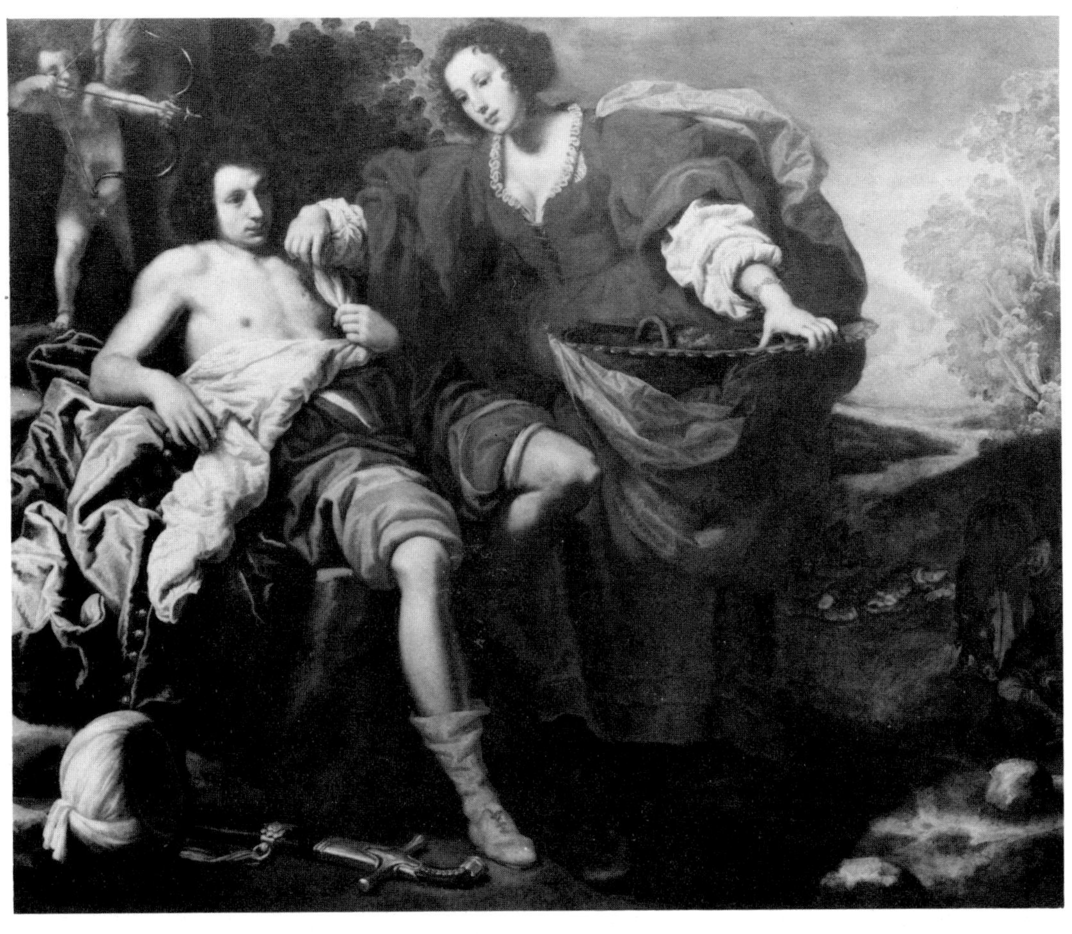

FIG. 89 Lorenzo Lippi, *Medoro and Angelica* (cat. no. 1747).

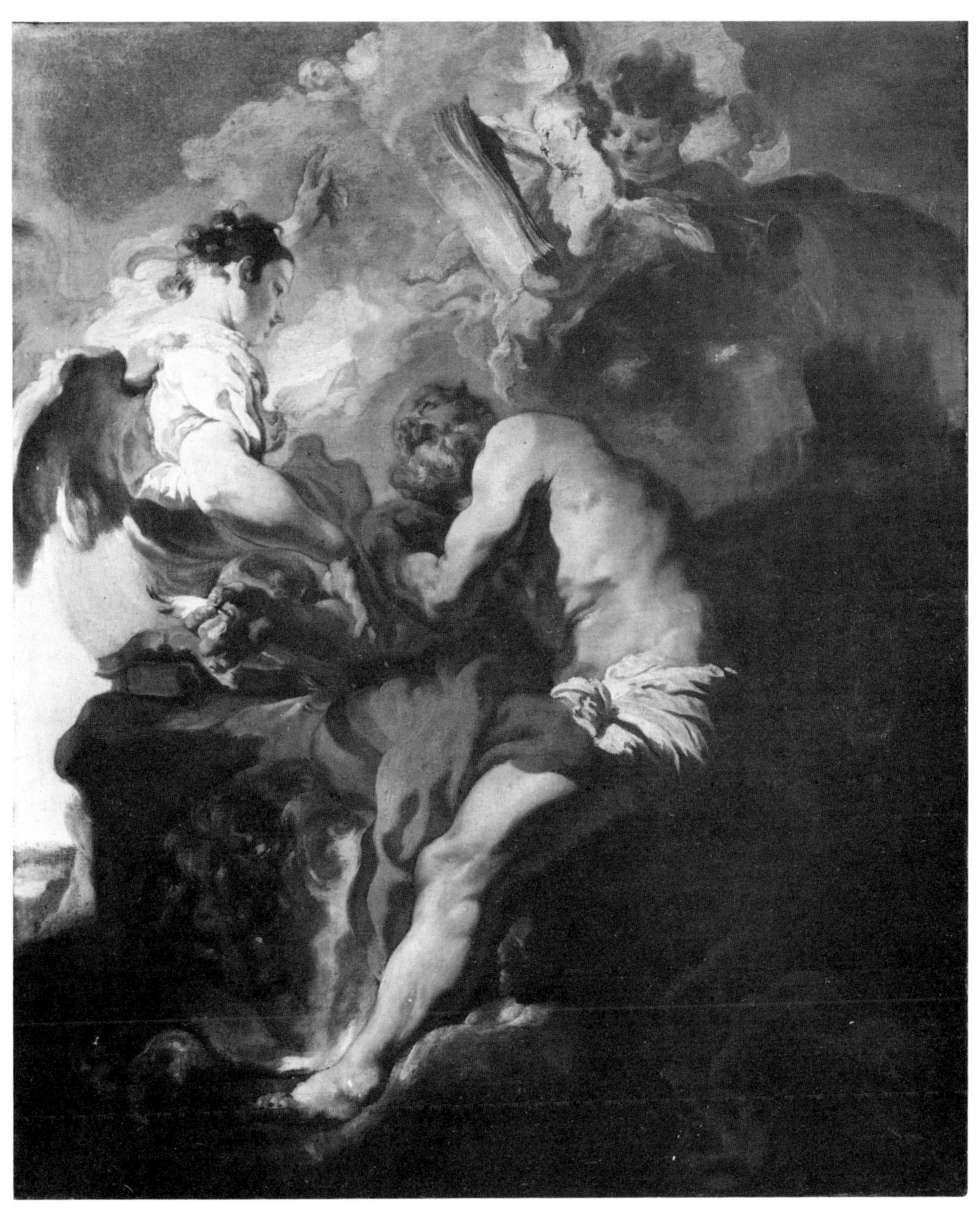

FIG. 90   After Liss, *The vision of St. Jerome* (cat. no. 981).

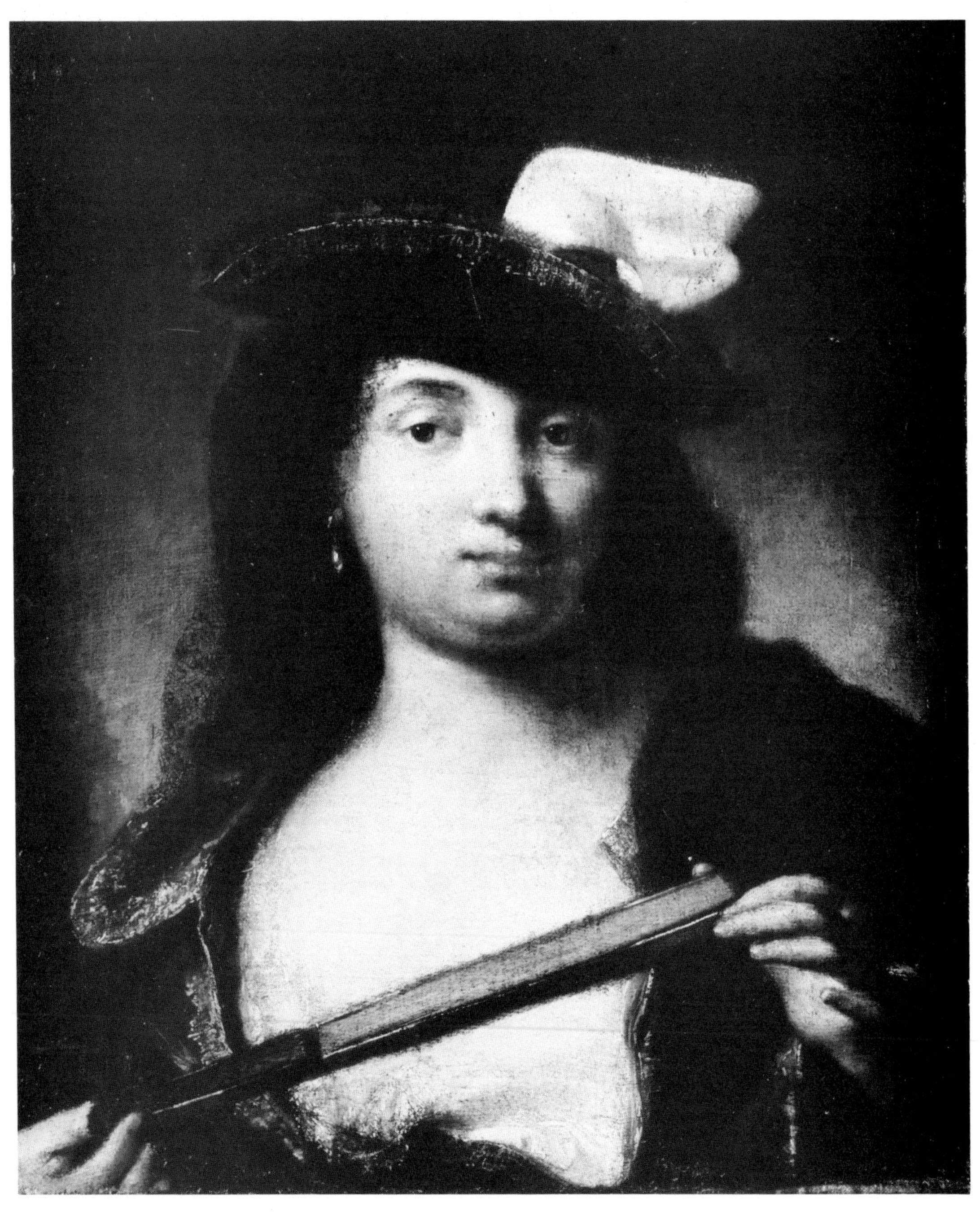

Fig. 91 Attributed to Alessandro Longhi, *Portrait of a lady holding a fan* (cat. no. 1814).

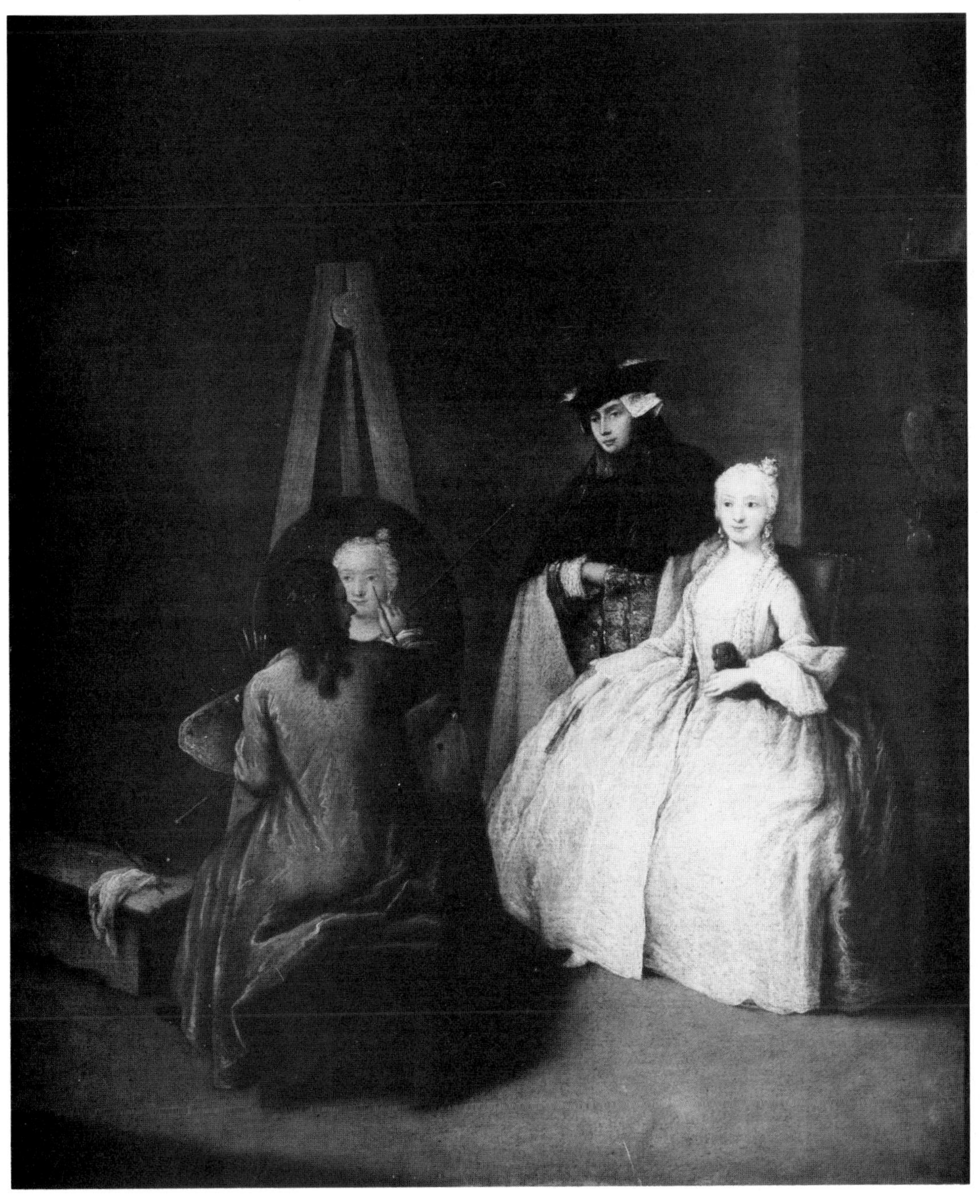

FIG. 92   Pietro Longhi, *The artist painting a lady's portrait* (cat. no. 952).

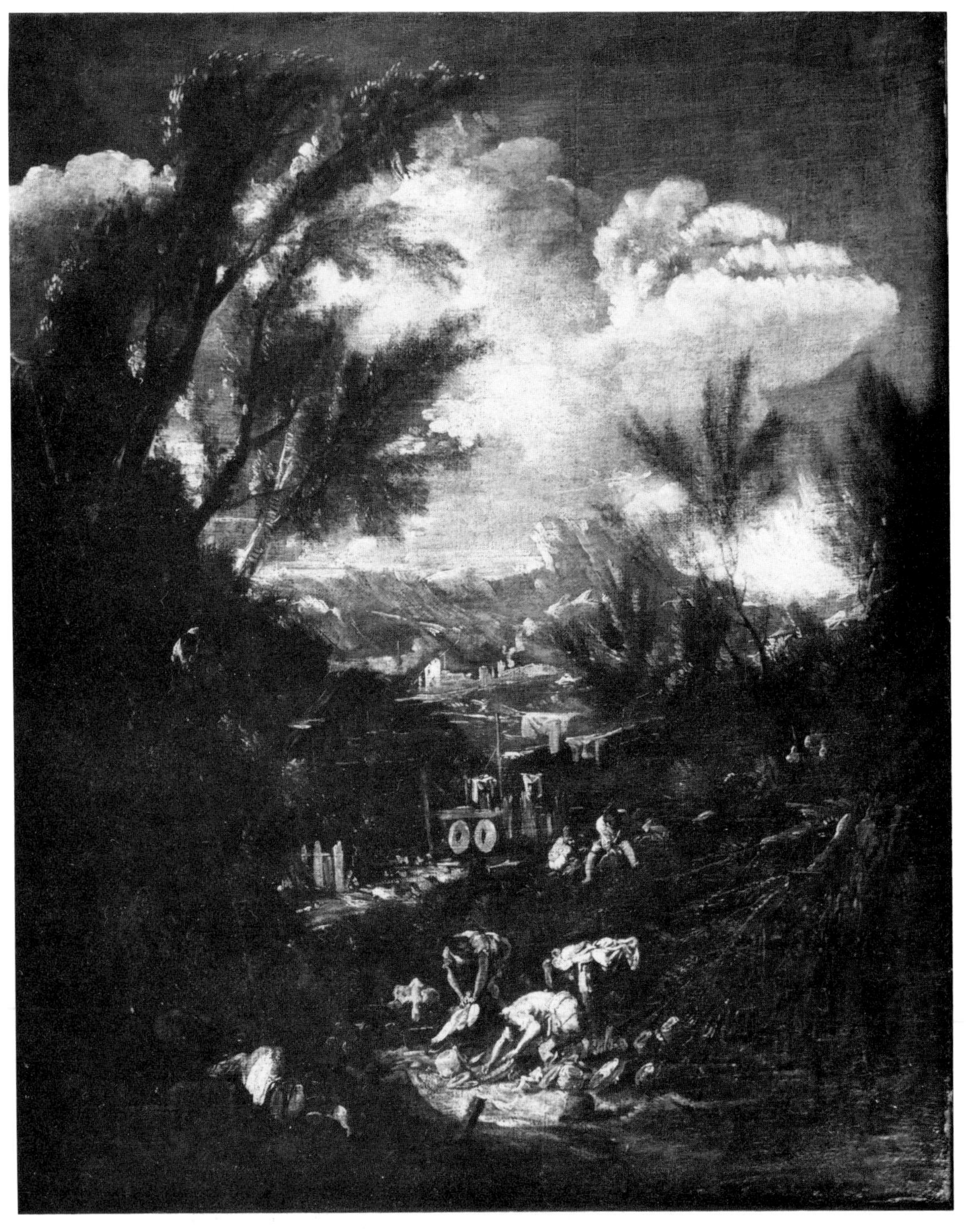

Fig. 93   Alessandro Magnasco, *Landscape with washerwomen* (cat. no. 678).

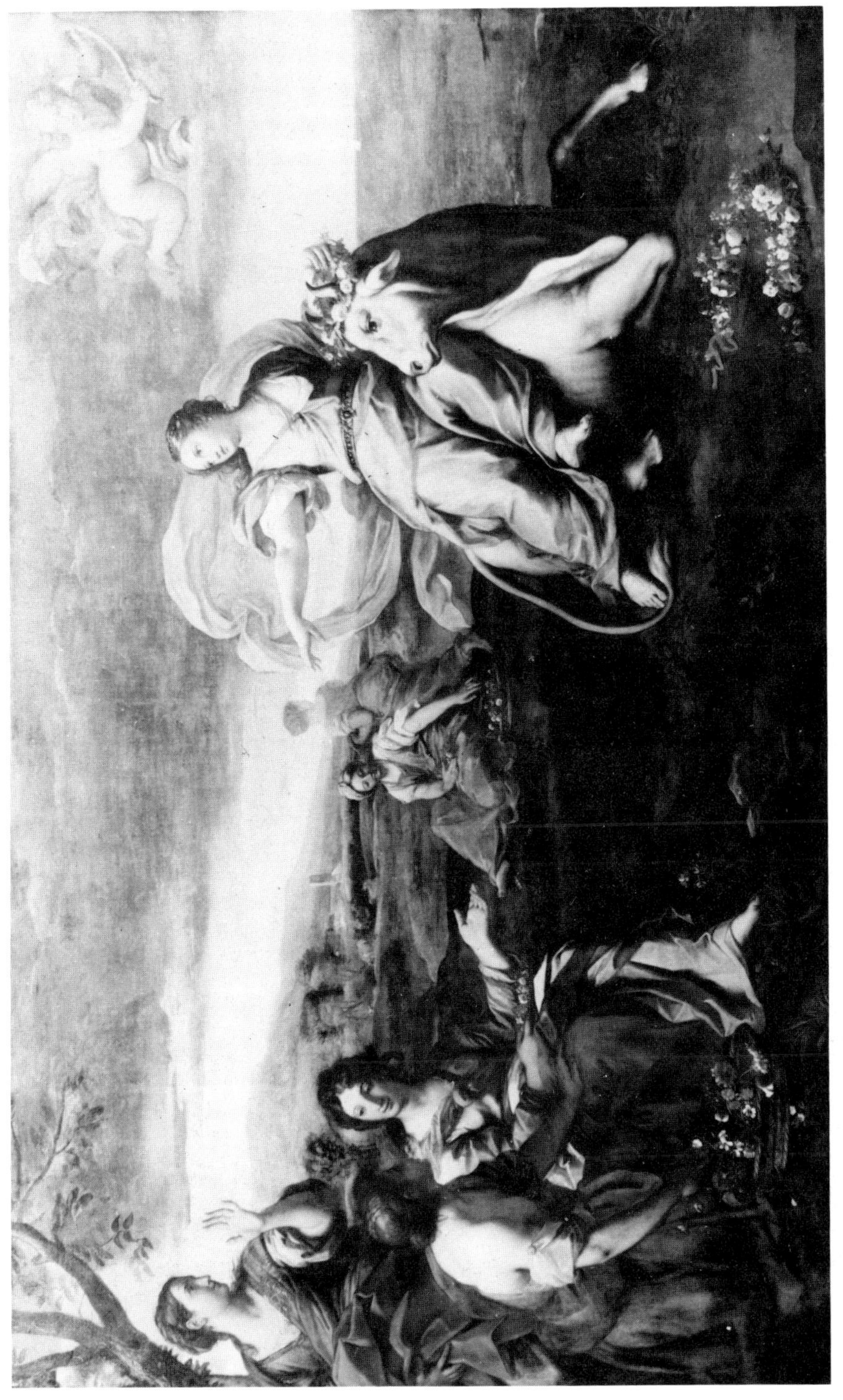

FIG. 94 Carlo Maratti, *Europa and the bull (Jupiter)* (cat. no. 81).

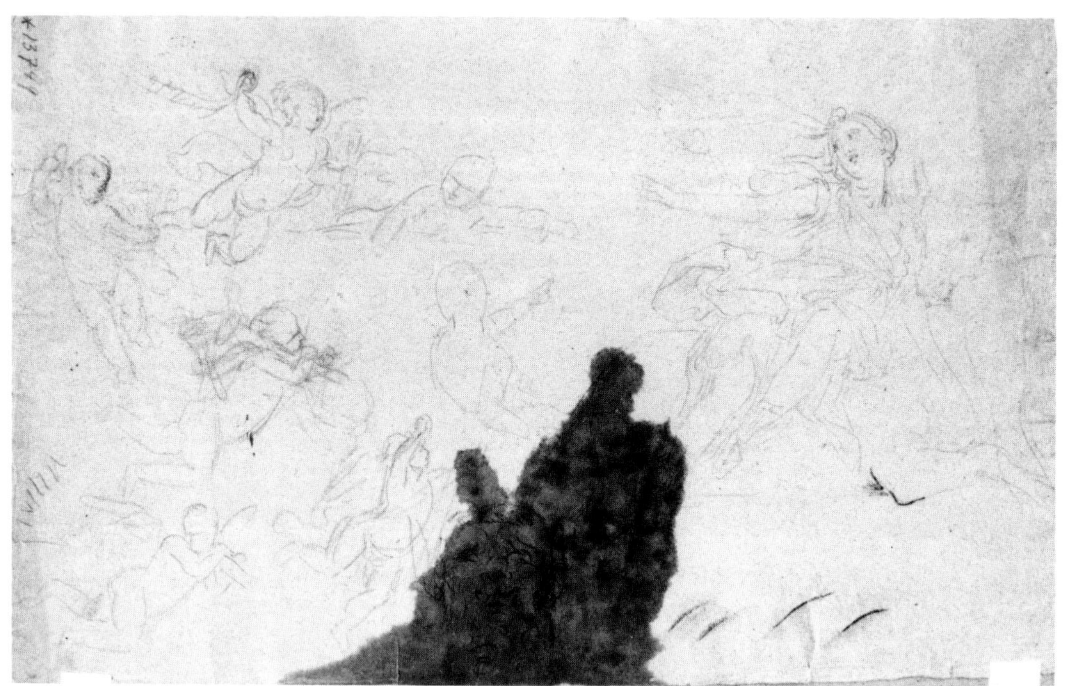

FIG. 95   Carlo Maratti, *Sketch for Europa*. Black chalk on grey paper, heightened with white, 267 × 423 mm. Kunstmuseum, Düsseldorf, (cat. no. FP 13749 *verso*).

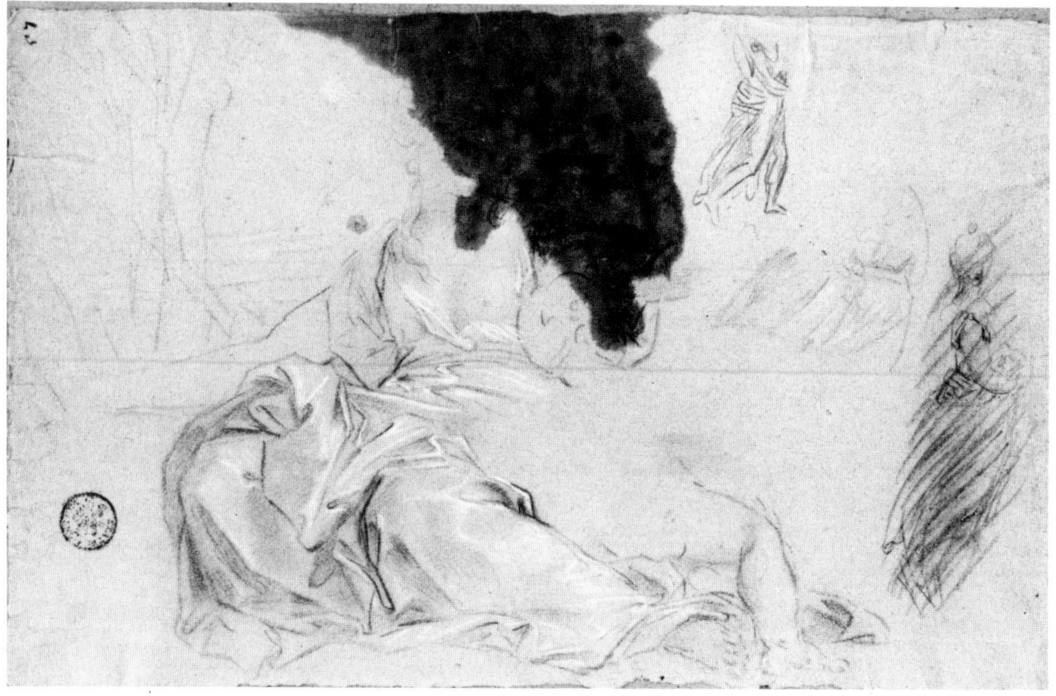

FIG. 96   Carlo Maratti, *Sketch for one of Europa's attendants*. Black chalk on grey paper, heightened with white, 267 × 423 mm. Kunstmuseum, Düsseldorf, (cat. no. FP 13749 *recto*).

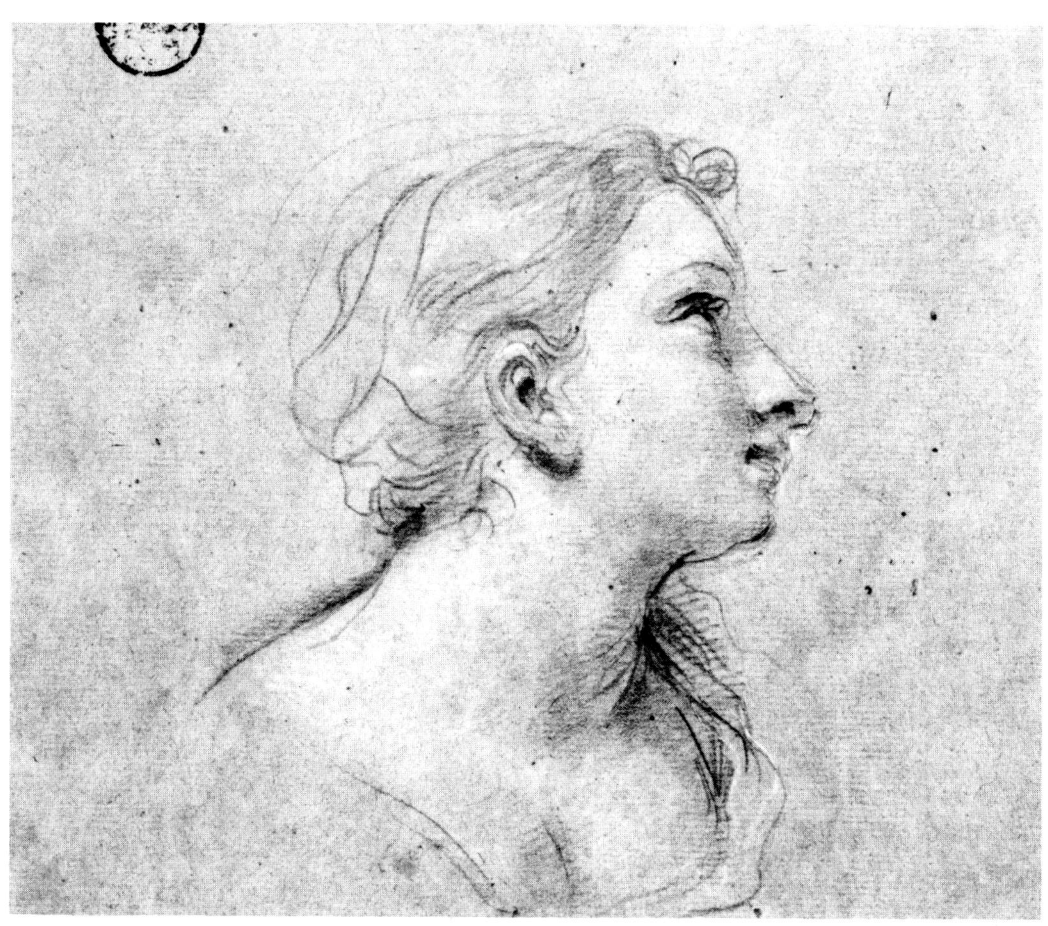

FIG. 97 Carlo Maratti, *Sketch for the head of one of Europa's attendants*. Black chalk on blue paper, heightened with white, 196 × 222 mm. Kunstmuseum, Düsseldorf, (cat. no. FP7545).

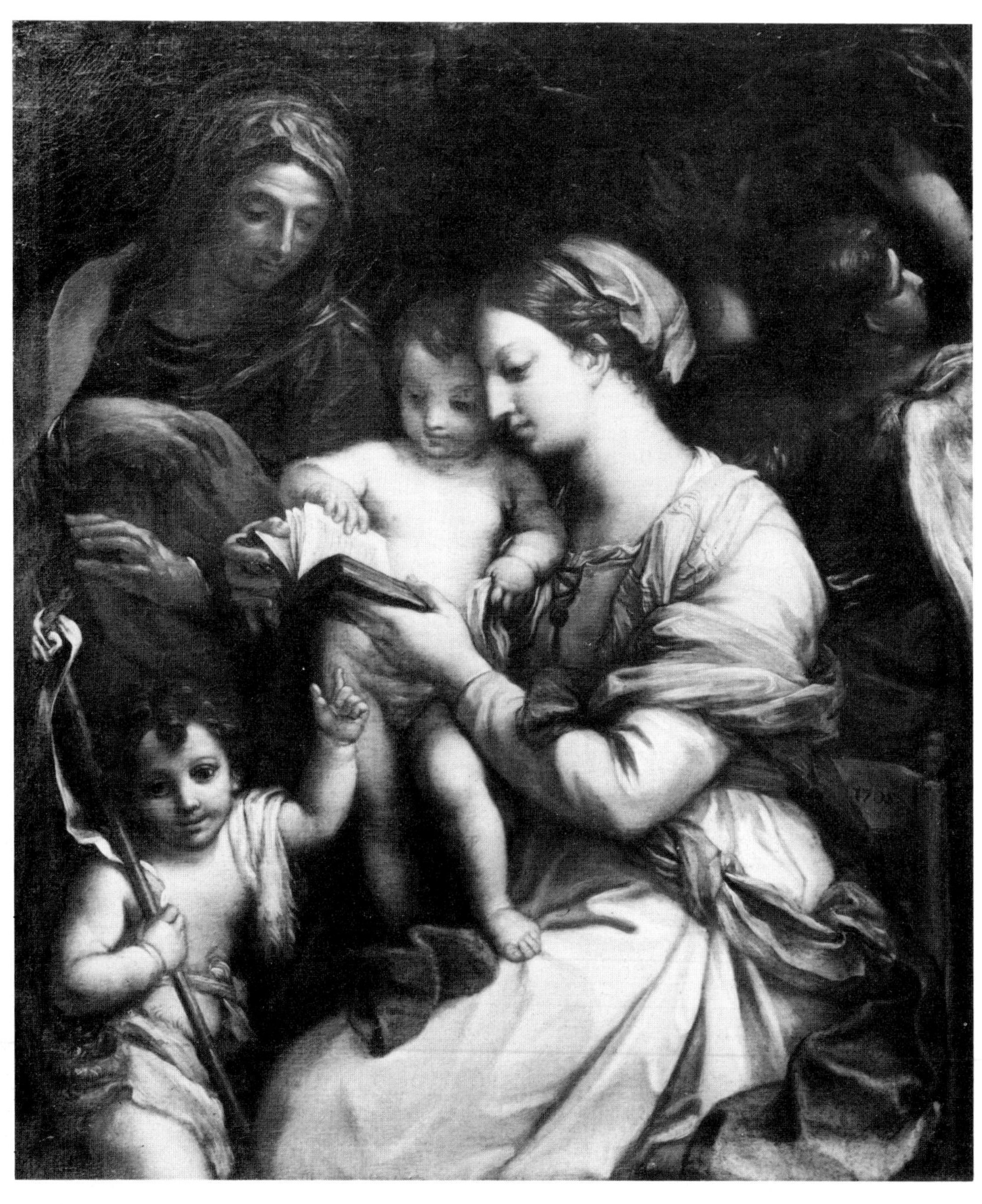

FIG. 98 Studio of Maratti, *The Virgin and Child, with St. Elizabeth, St. John the Baptist, and an angel* (cat. no. 1703).

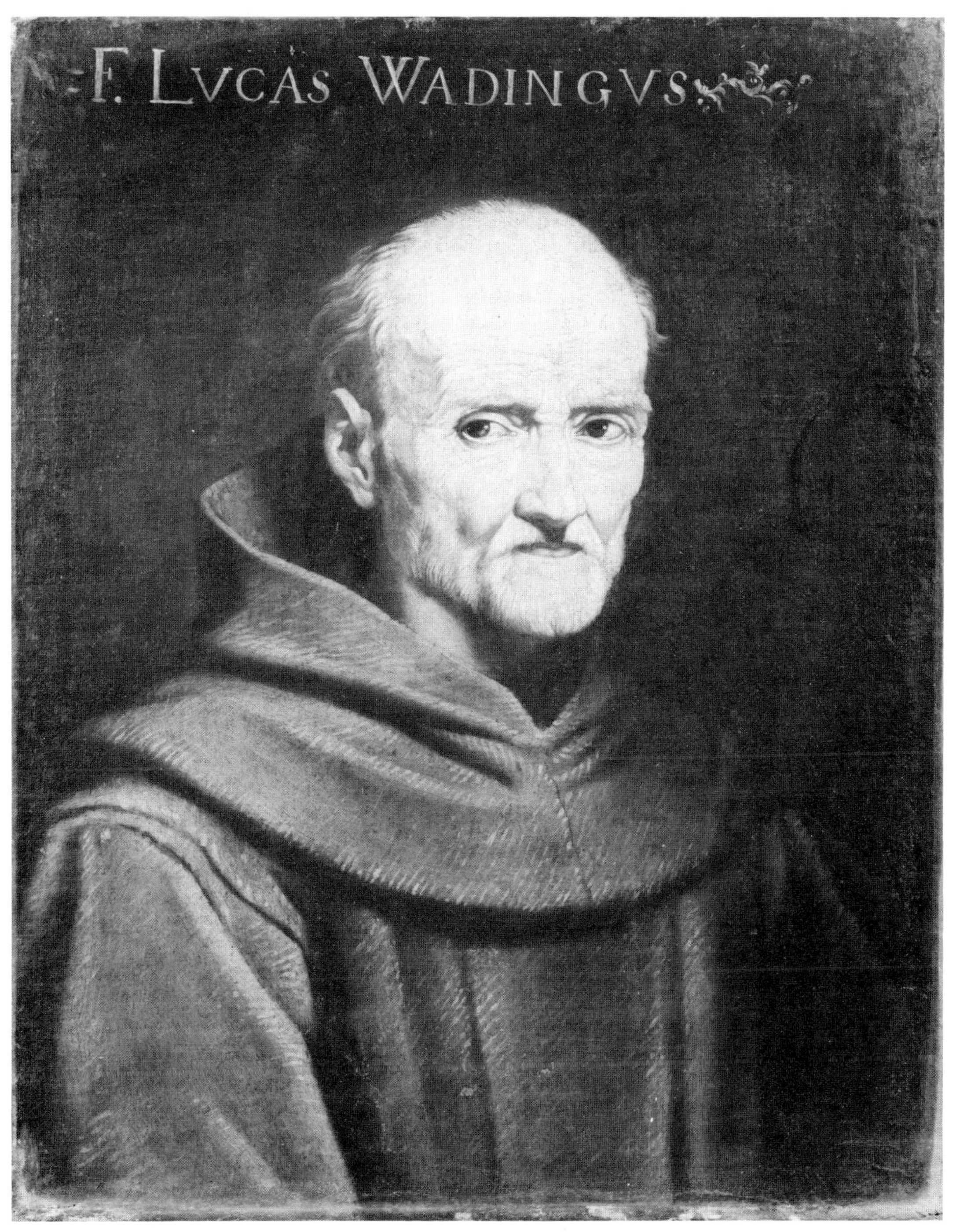

FIG. 99   After Maratti, *Father Luke Wadding, O.F.M., 1588-1657* (cat. no. 298).

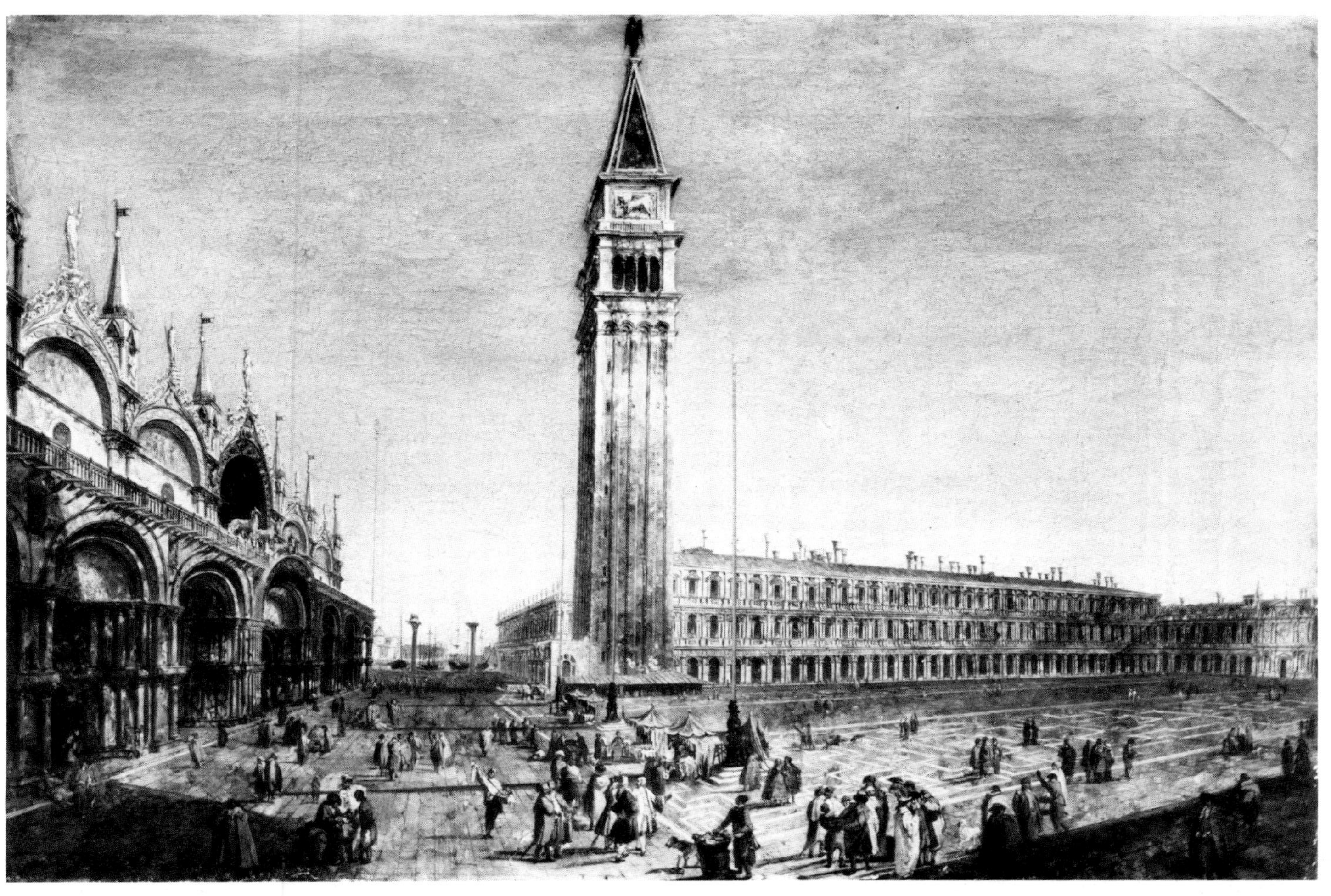

FIG. 100   Michele Marieschi, *Piazza San Marco, Venice* (cat. no. 473).

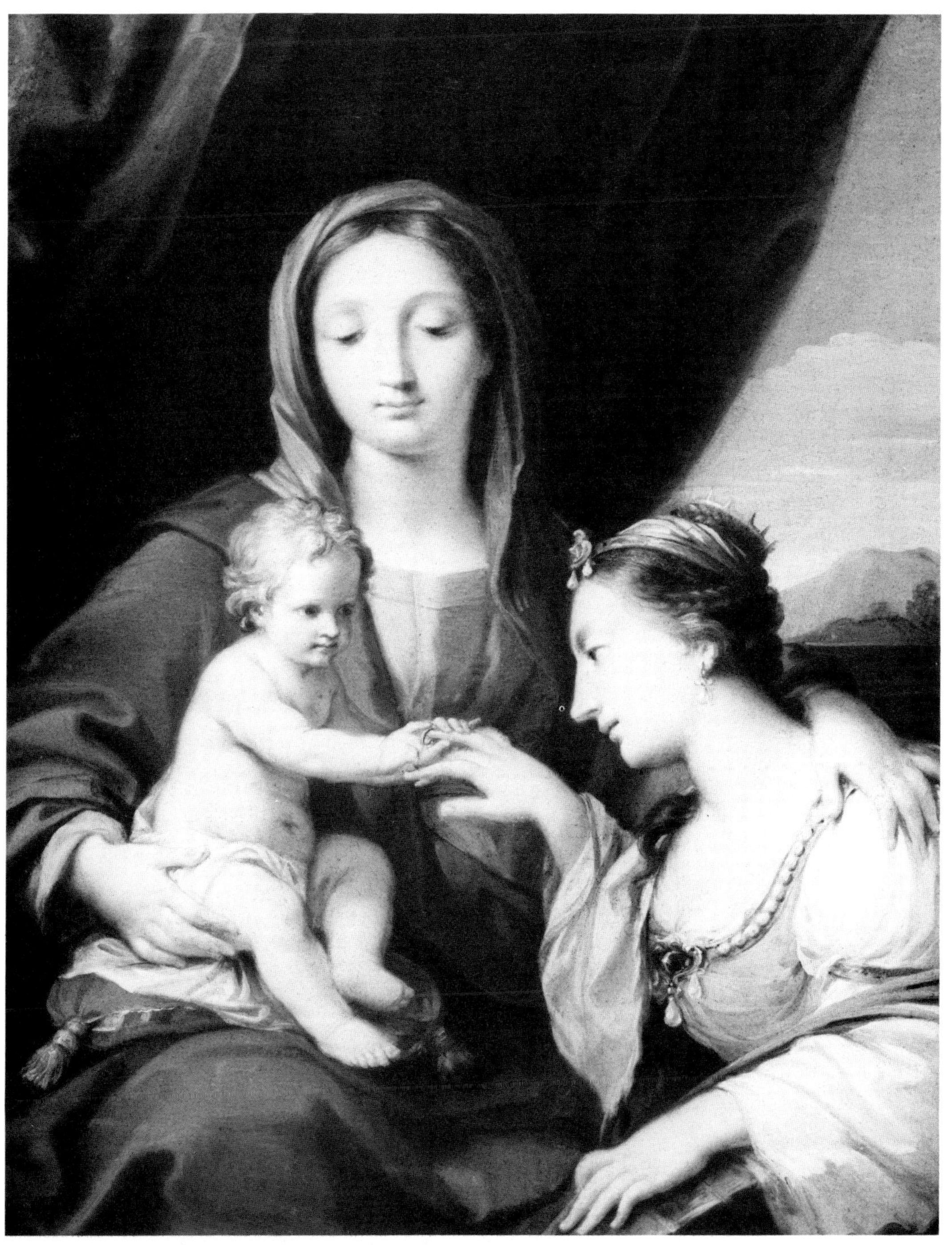

Fig. 101   Agostino Masucci, *Mystic marriage of St. Catherine* (cat. no. 1040).

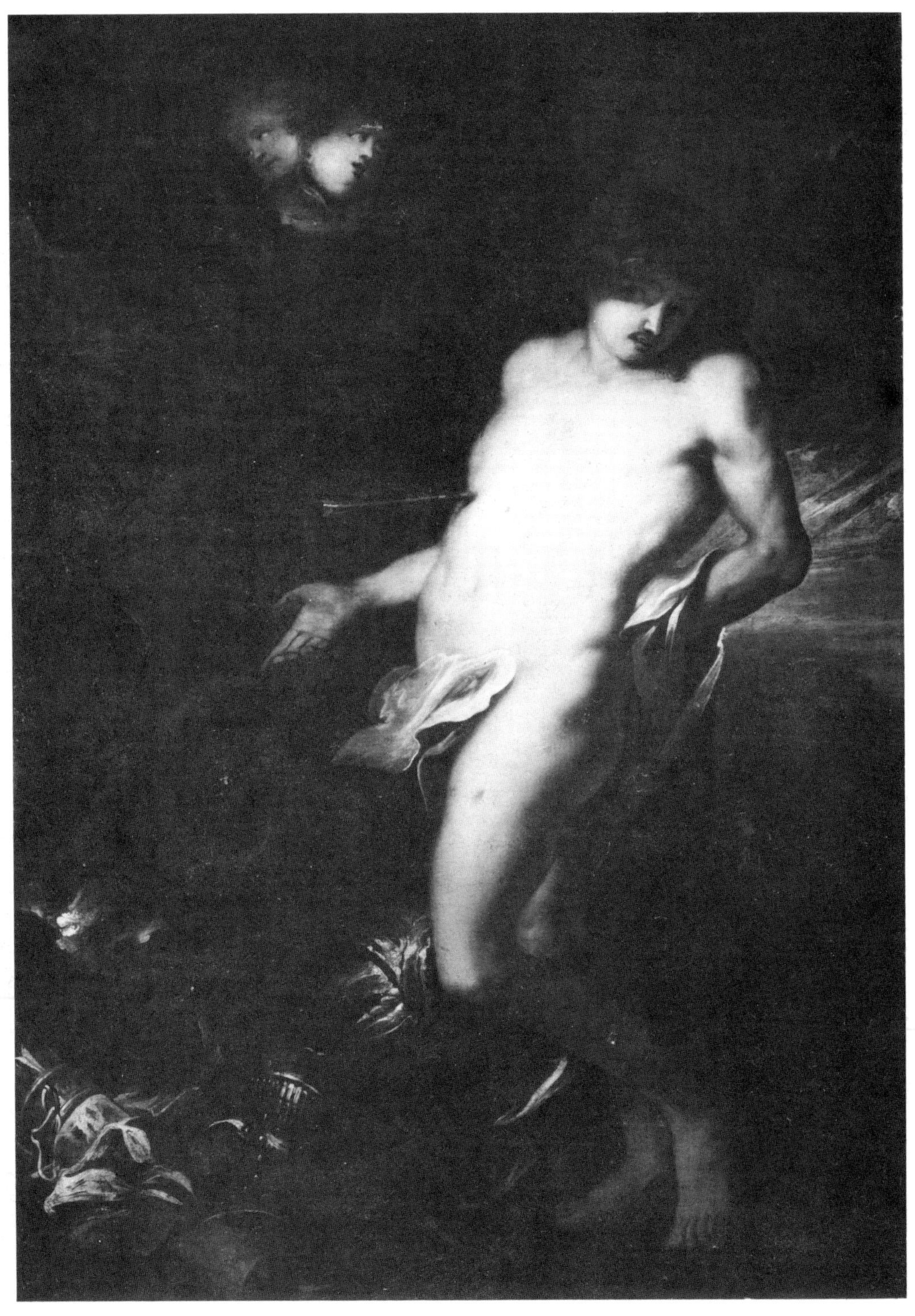

FIG. 102   Attributed to Mehus, *St. Sebastian* (cat. no. 1661).

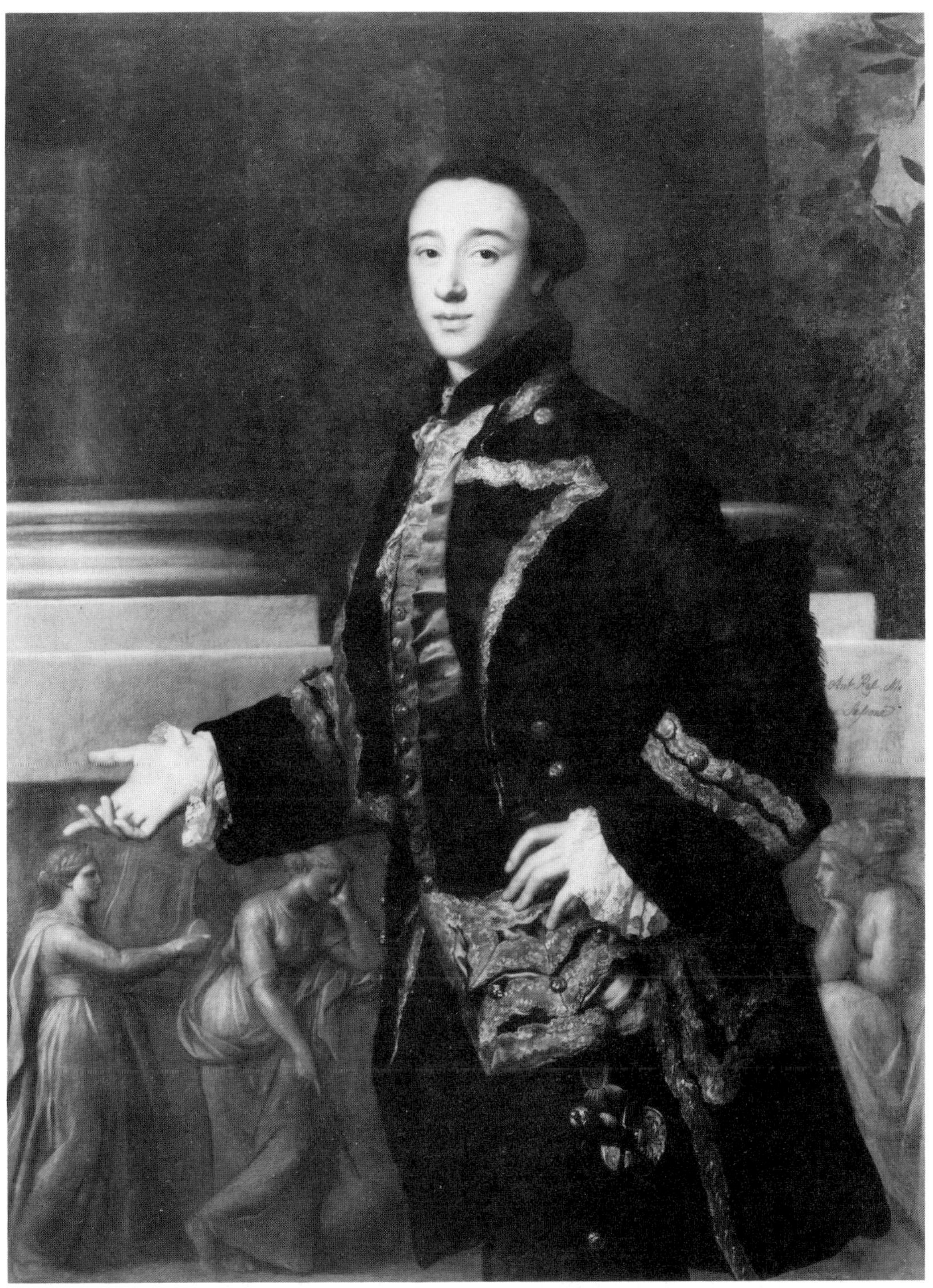

FIG. 103 Anton Raphaël Mengs, *Thomas Conolly, 1738-1803* (cat. no. 4458).

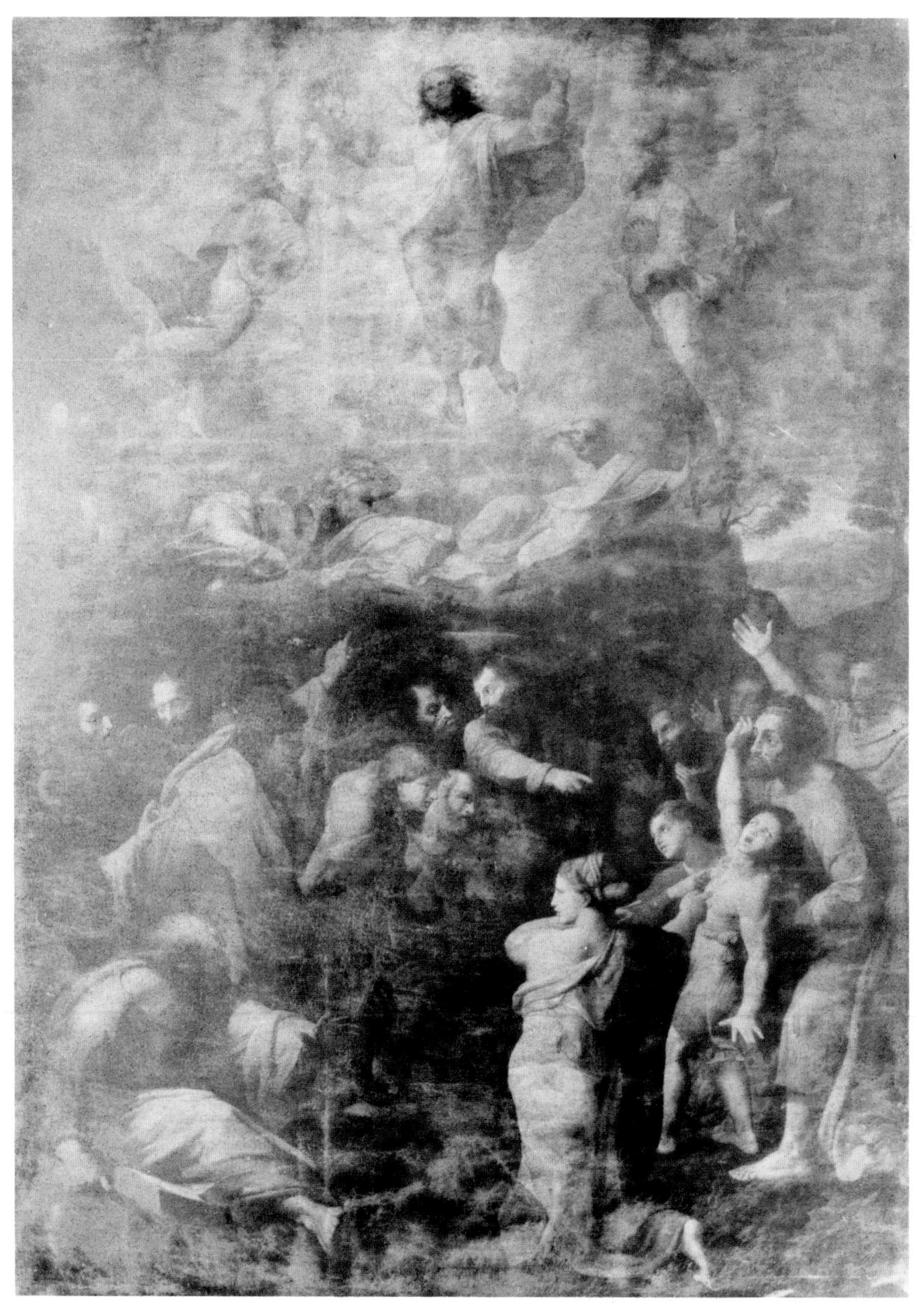

FIG. 104   Attributed to Mengs, *The Transfiguration* (after Raphael) (cat. no. 120).

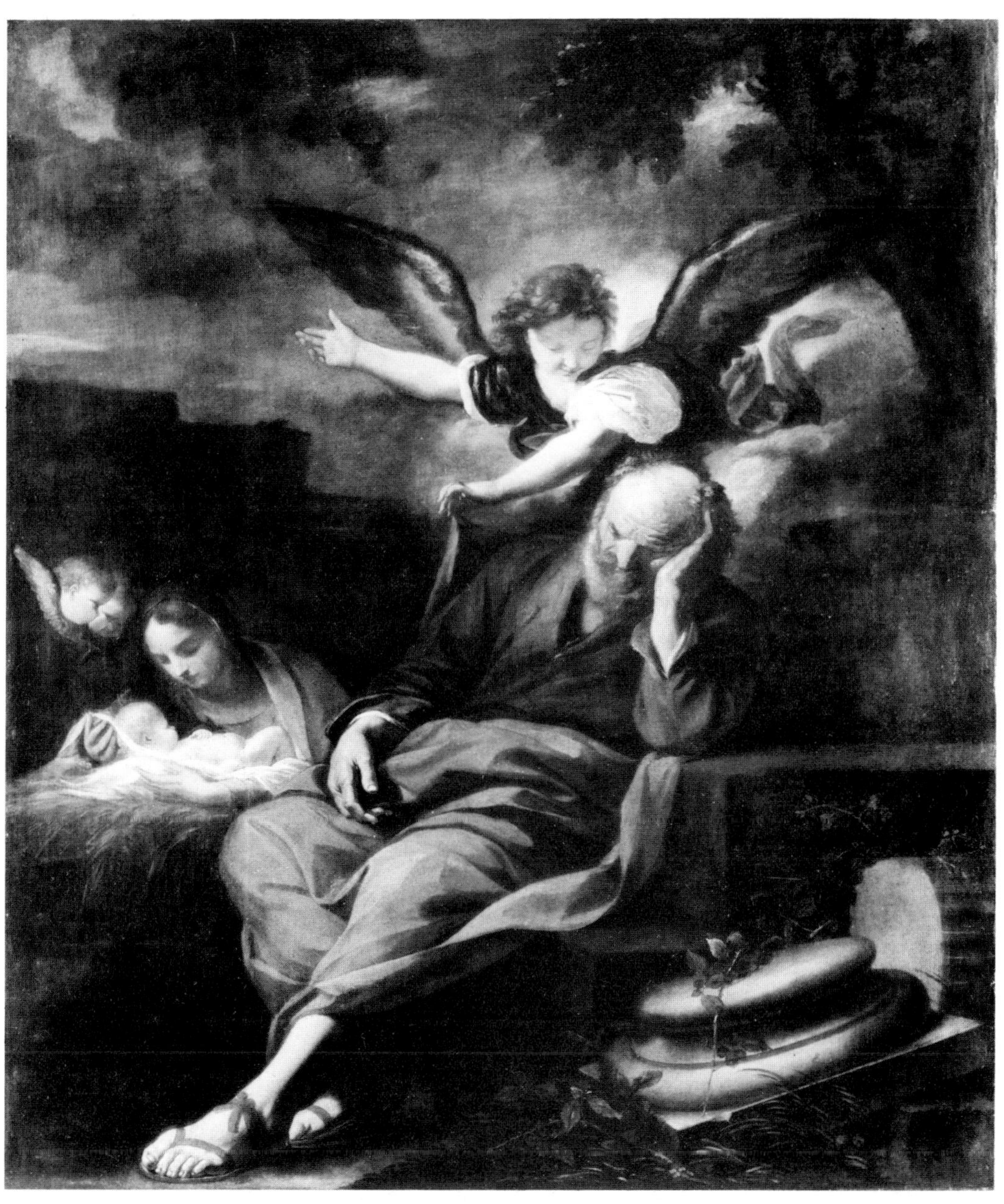

FIG. 105   Pier Francesco Mola, *St. Joseph's dream* (cat. no. 1893).

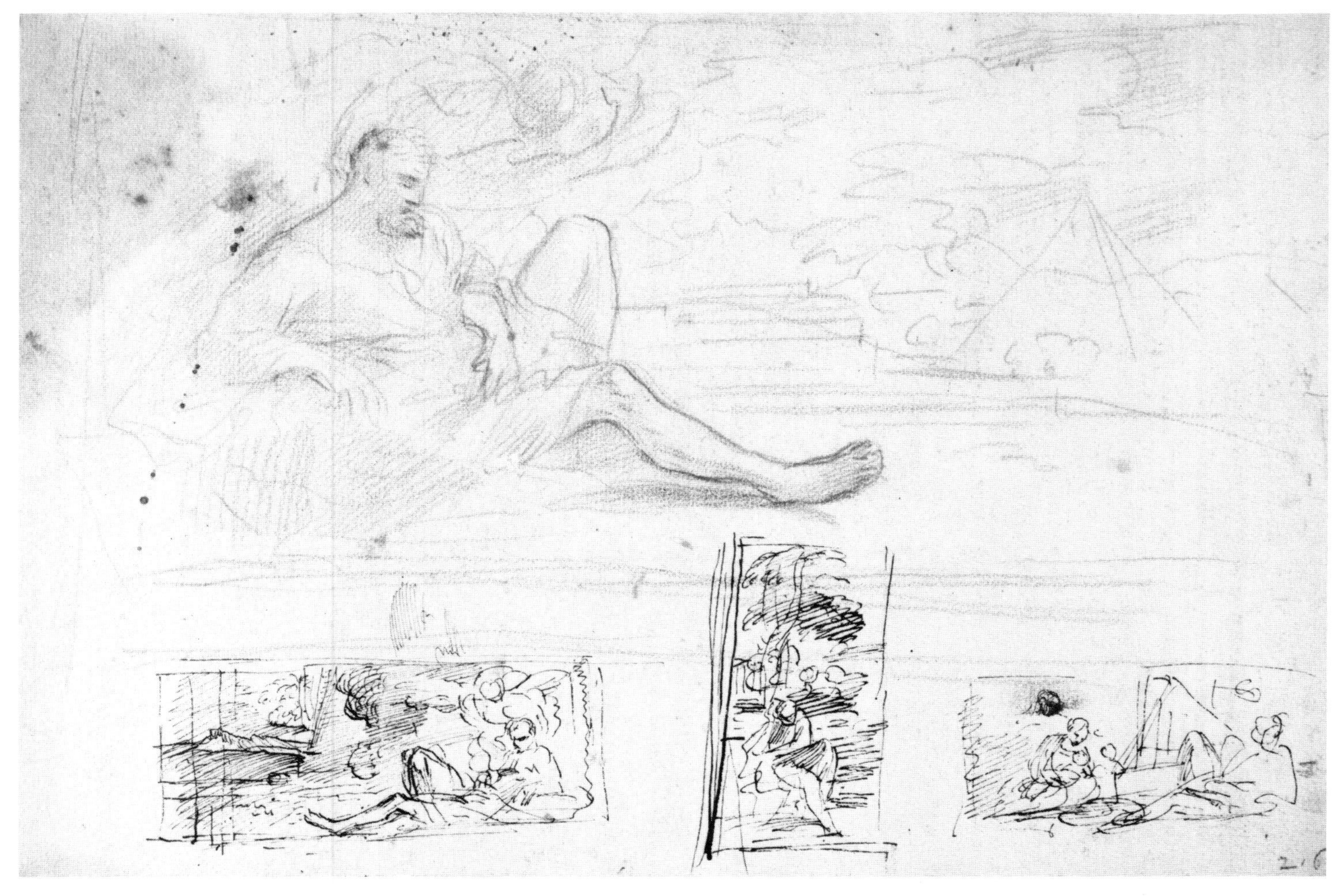

FIG. 106 Pier Francesco Mola, *St. Joseph's dream*, Red chalk, and pen and ink, 261 × 395 mm. The British Museum, (inv. no. 1946. 7. 13. 720). Reproduced by courtesy of the Trustees of the British Museum.

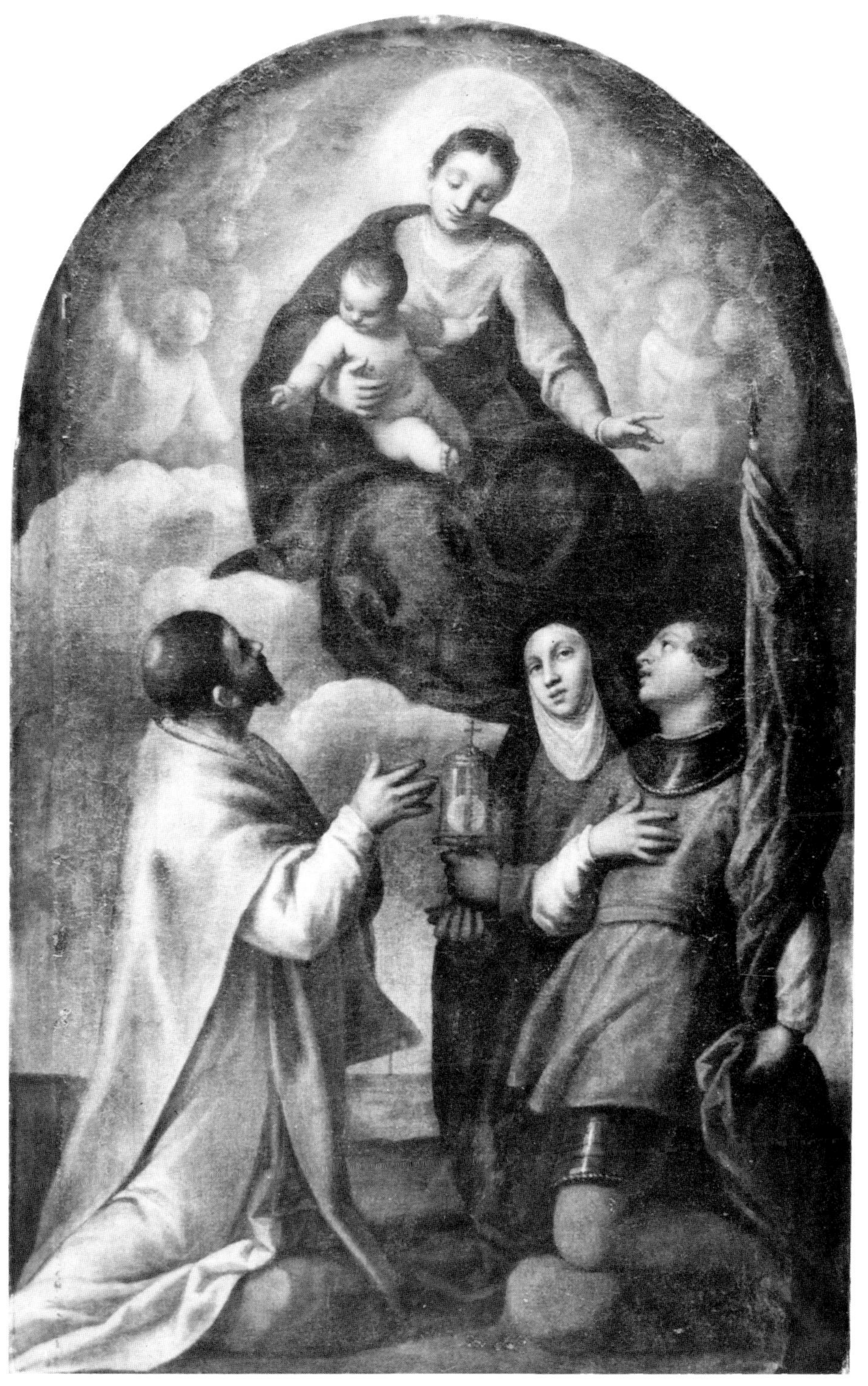

Fig. 107   Palma Giovane, *Madonna and Child with saints and angels* (cat. no. 68).

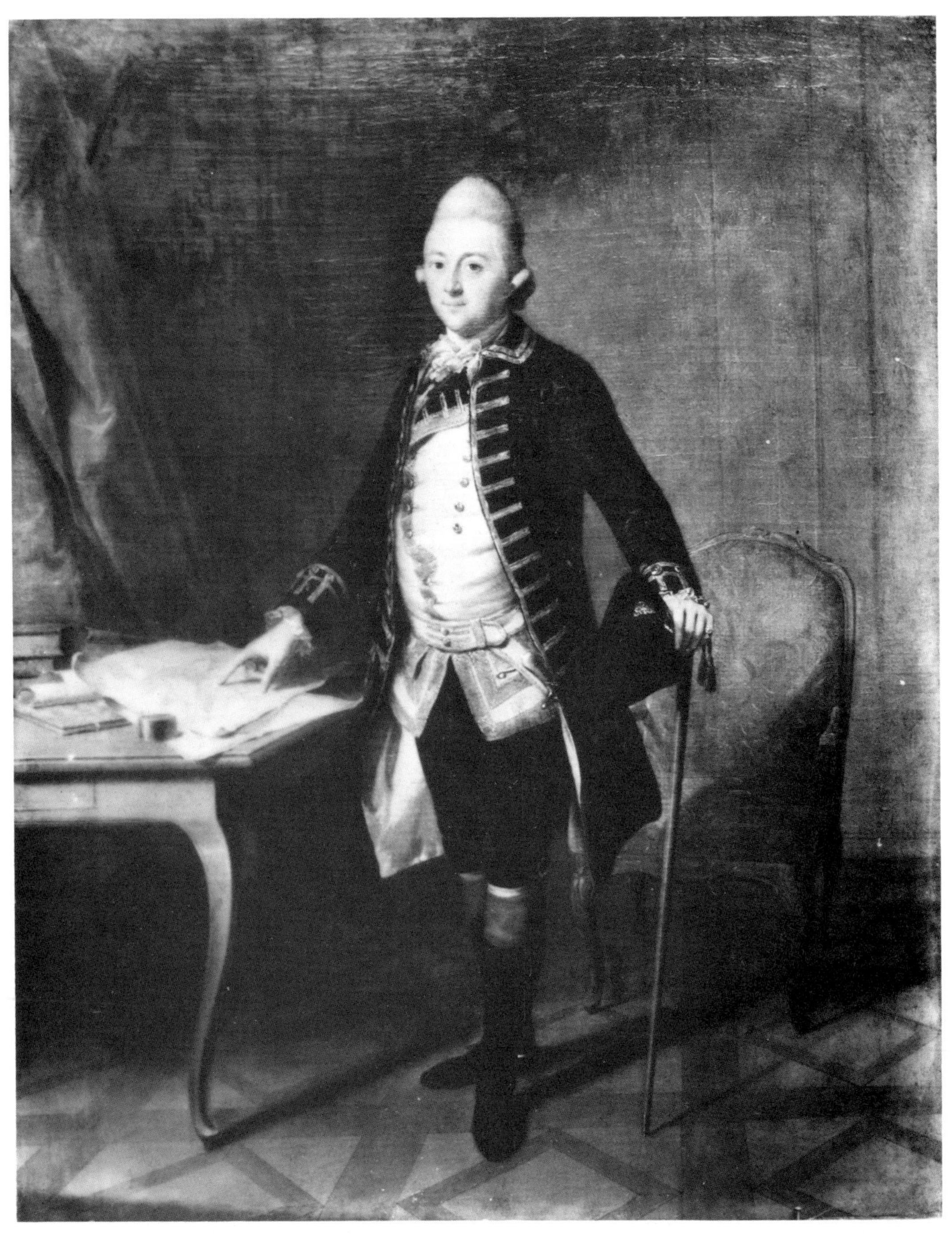

FIG. 108   Bartolomeo Nazari, *Major General Christopher Nugent, d.1742* (cat. no. 261).

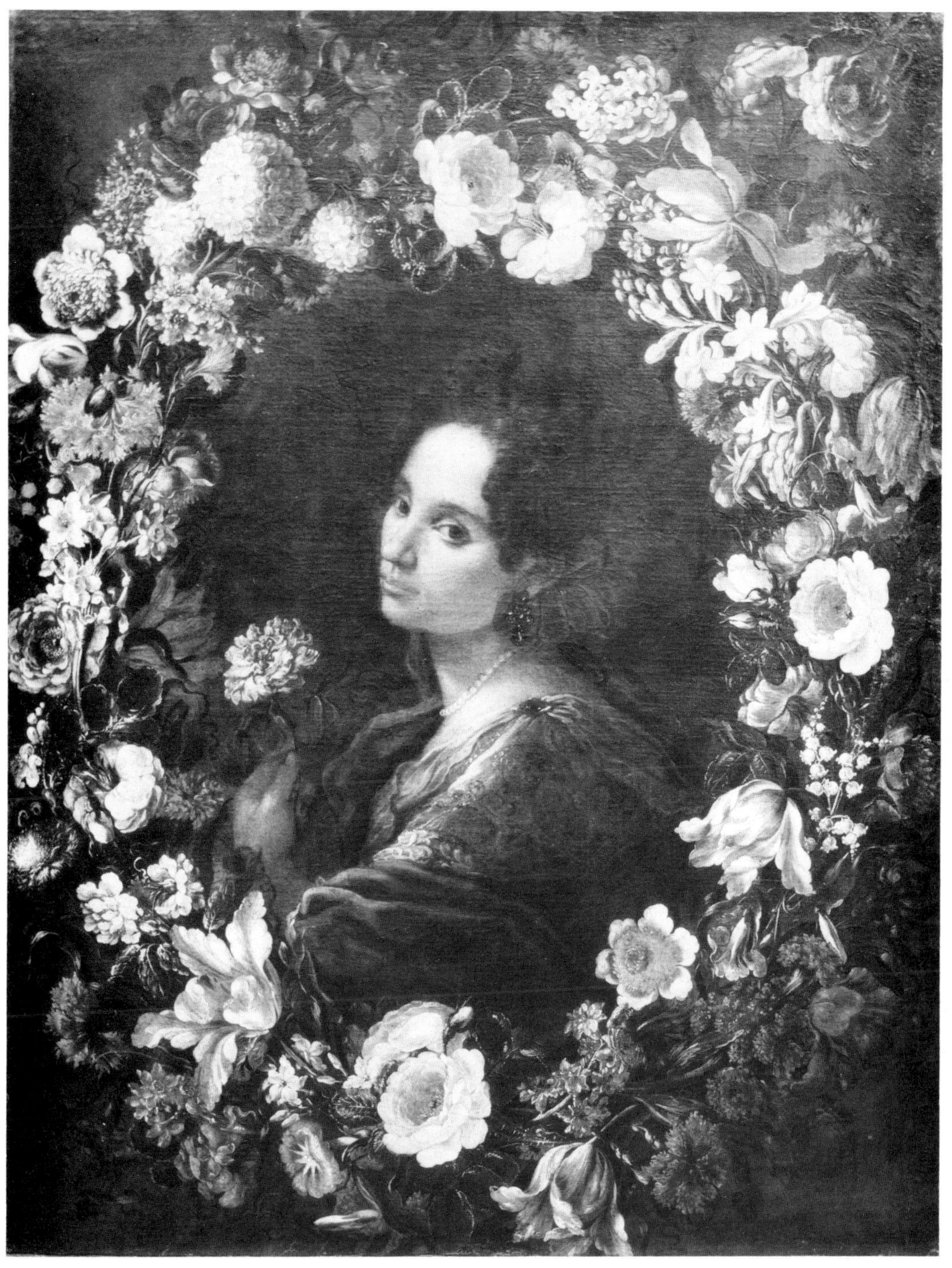

Fig. 109   Mario Nuzzi, *A lady, surrounded by a garland of flowers* (cat. no. 262).

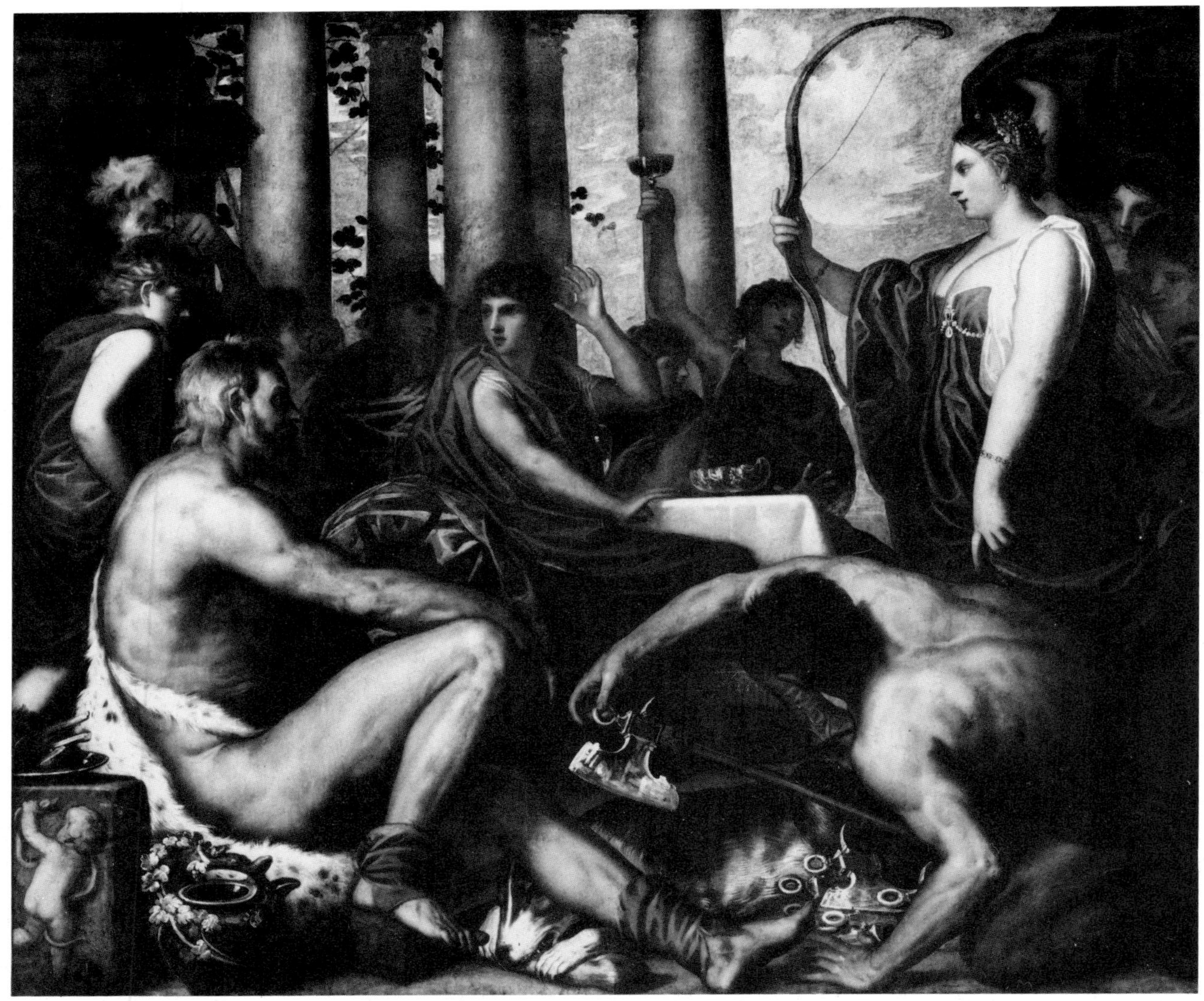

Fig. 110 Padovanino, *Penelope bringing the bow of Odysseus to her suitors* (cat. no. 87).

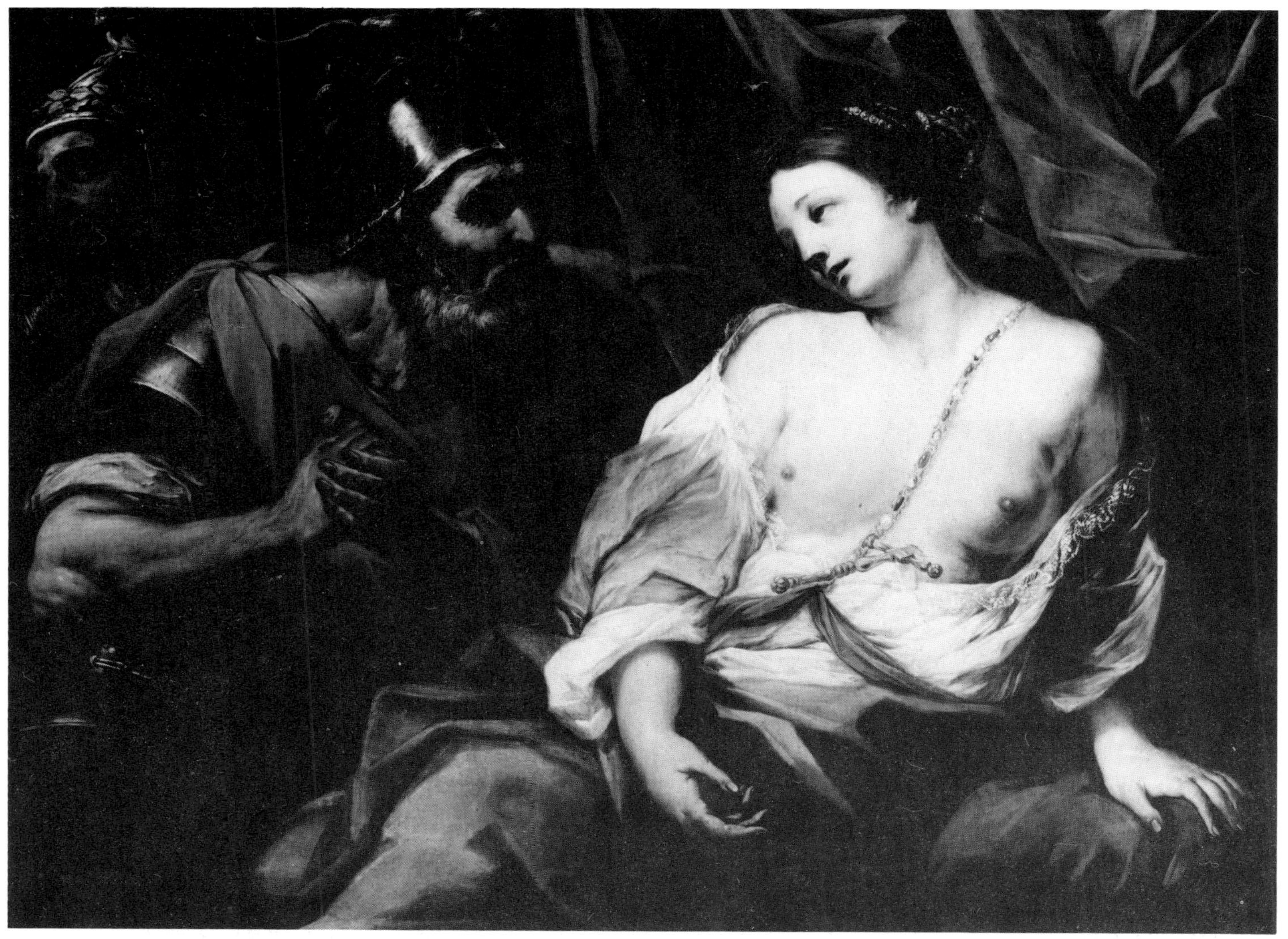

Fig. 111 Attributed to Paolo Pagani, *Death of Lucretia* (cat. no. 1086).

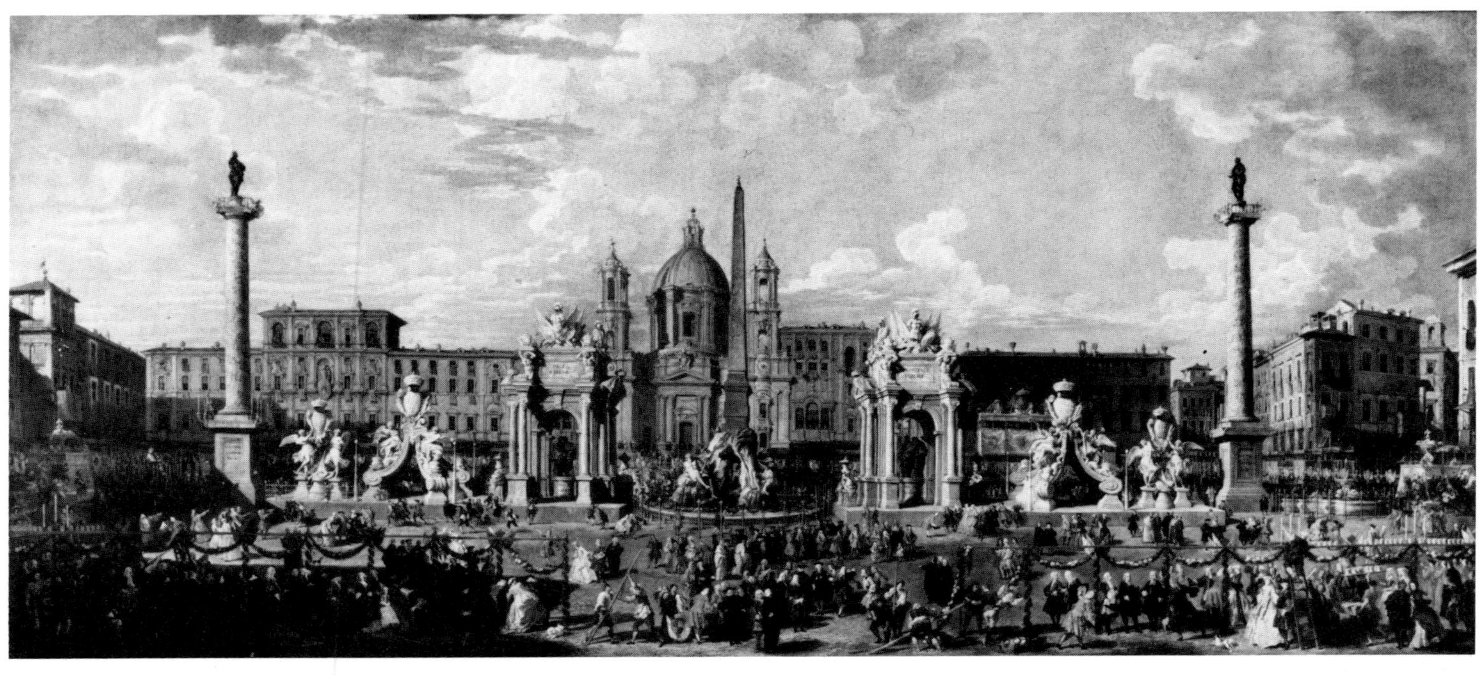

FIG. 112 Giovanni Paolo Panini, *Fête in the Piazza Navona, Rome, to celebrate the birth of a Dauphin in France, 1729* (cat. no. 95).

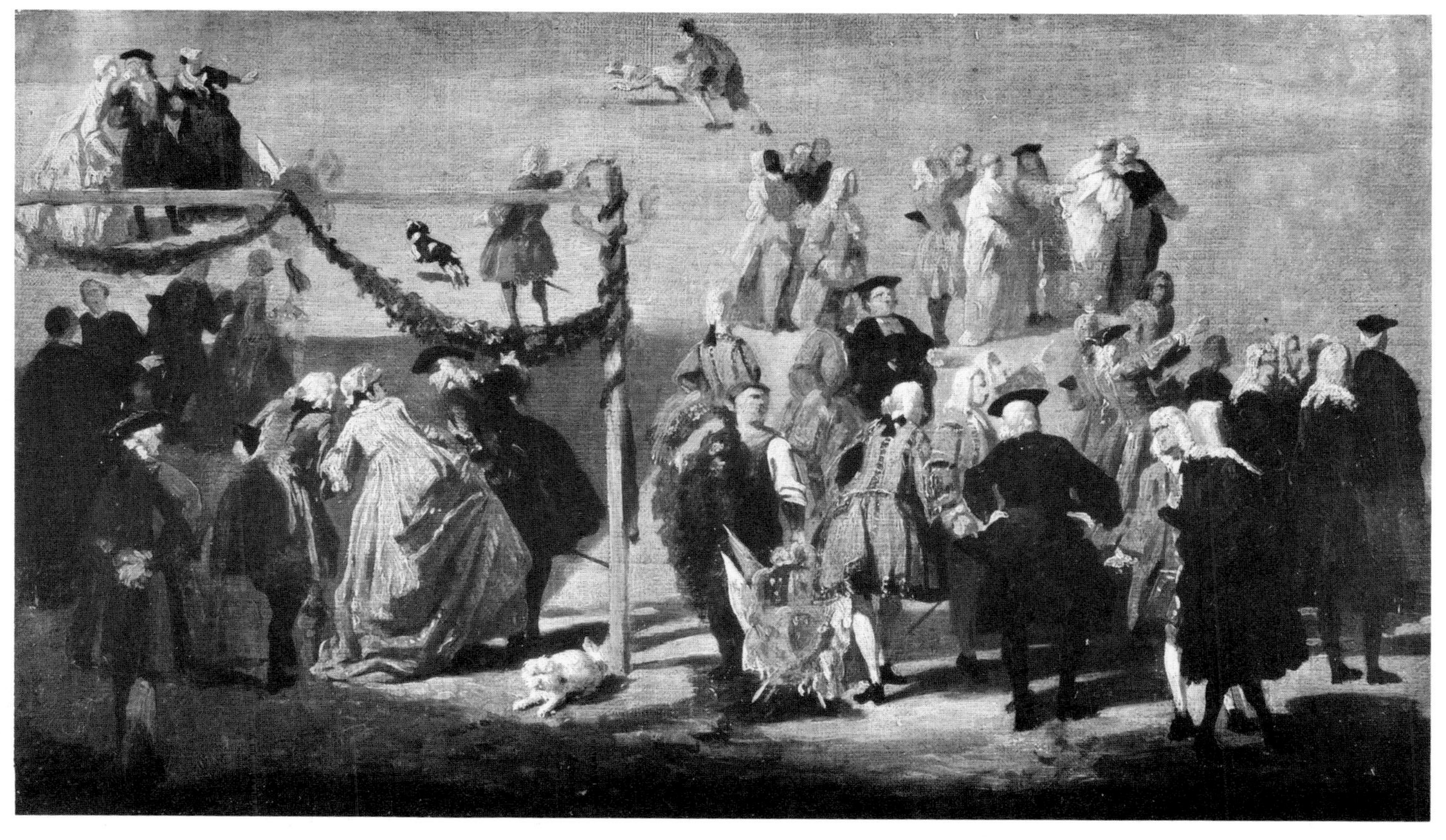

Fig. 113 Giovanni Paolo Panini, *Group of figures* (study for no. 95). Oil on canvas, 27.0 × 45.7 cm. The Art Institute of Chicago (inv. no. 33. 914). Reproduced by courtesy of the Art Institute of Chicago.

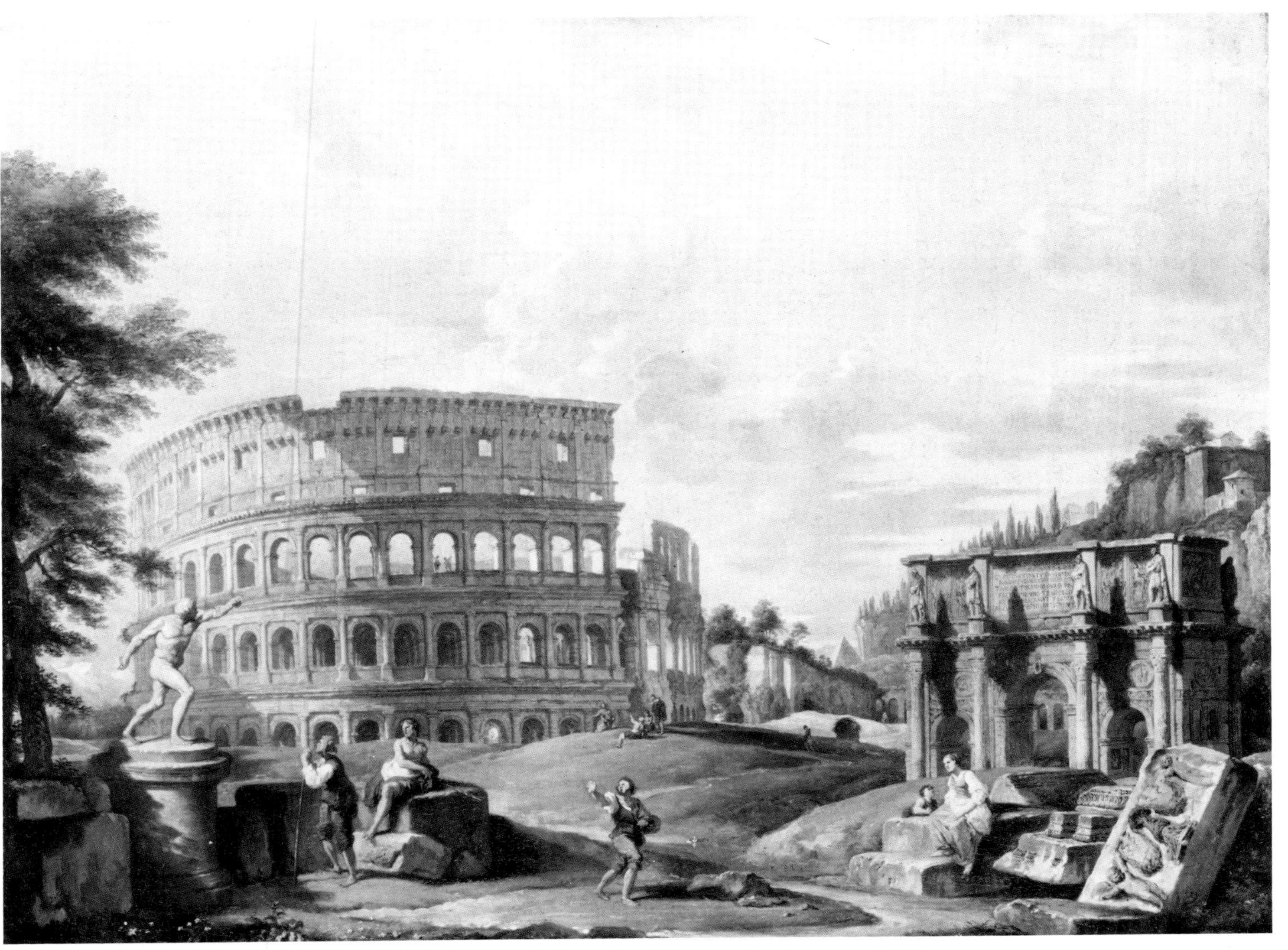

Fig. 114   Giovanni Paolo Panini, *The Colosseum and the arch of Constantine* (cat. no. 725).

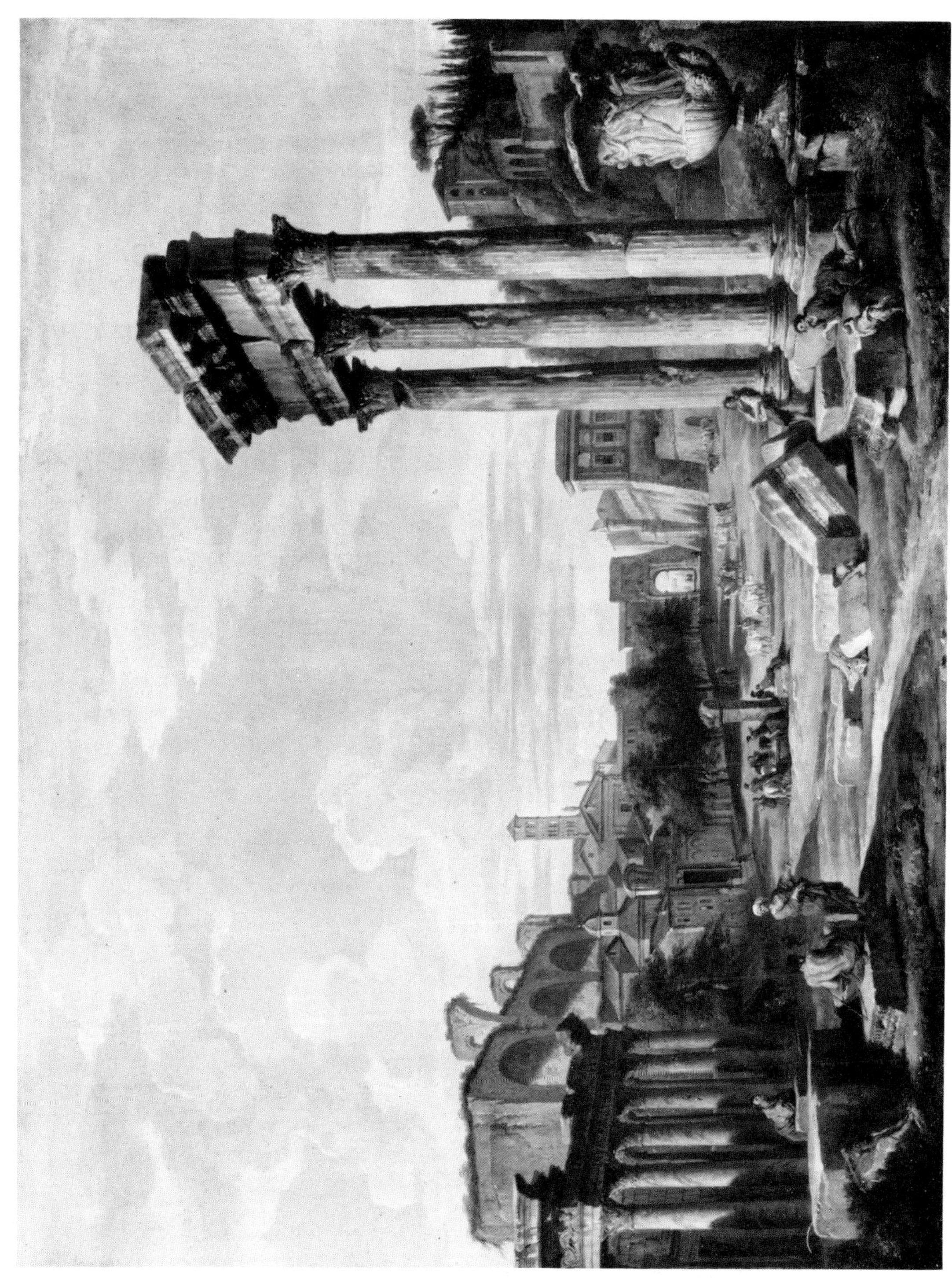

FIG. 115 Giovanni Paolo Panini, *The Roman Forum* (cat. no. 726).

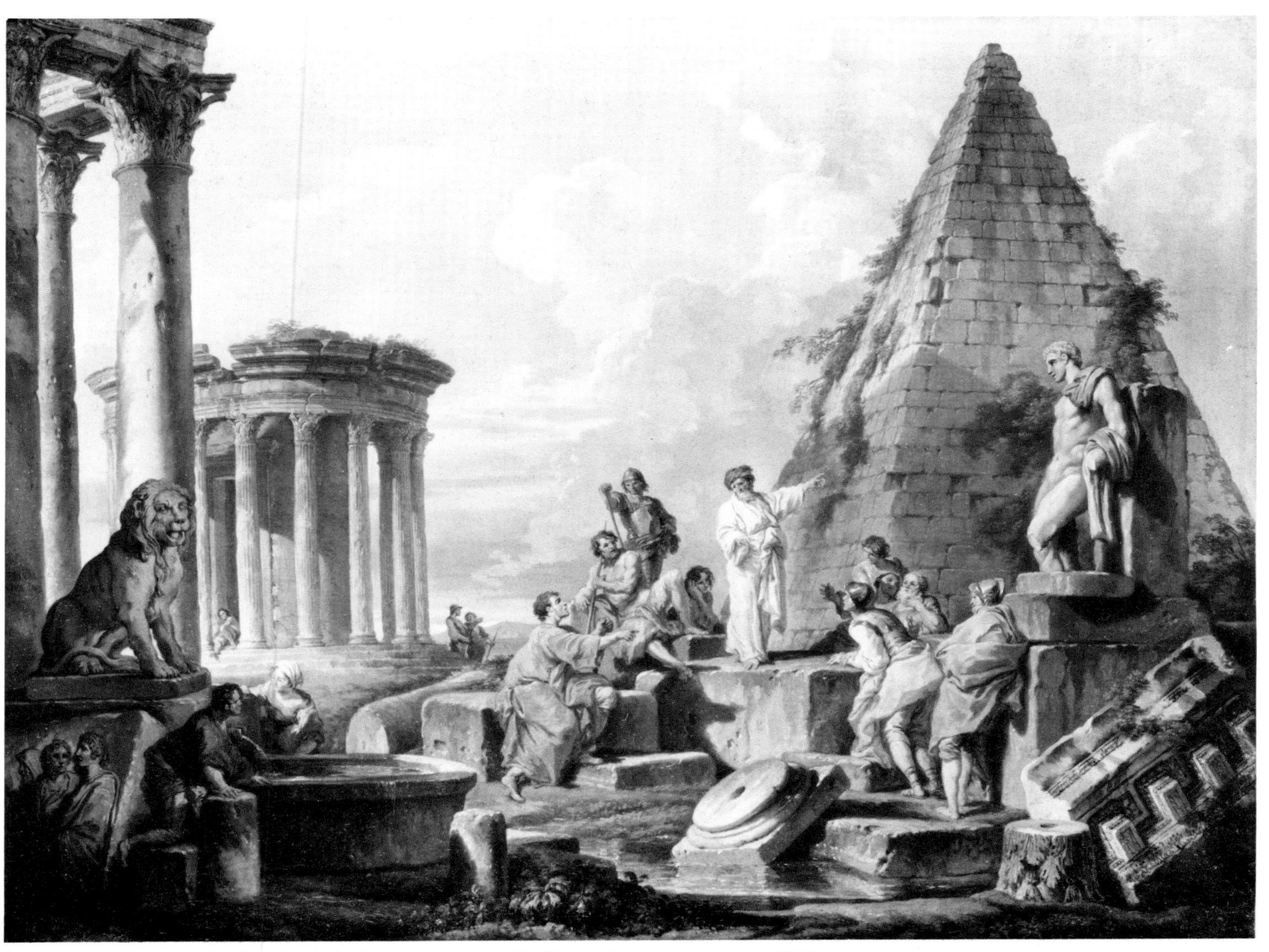

Fig. 116 Giovanni Paolo Panini, *Roman ruins with fifteen figures* (cat. no. 727).

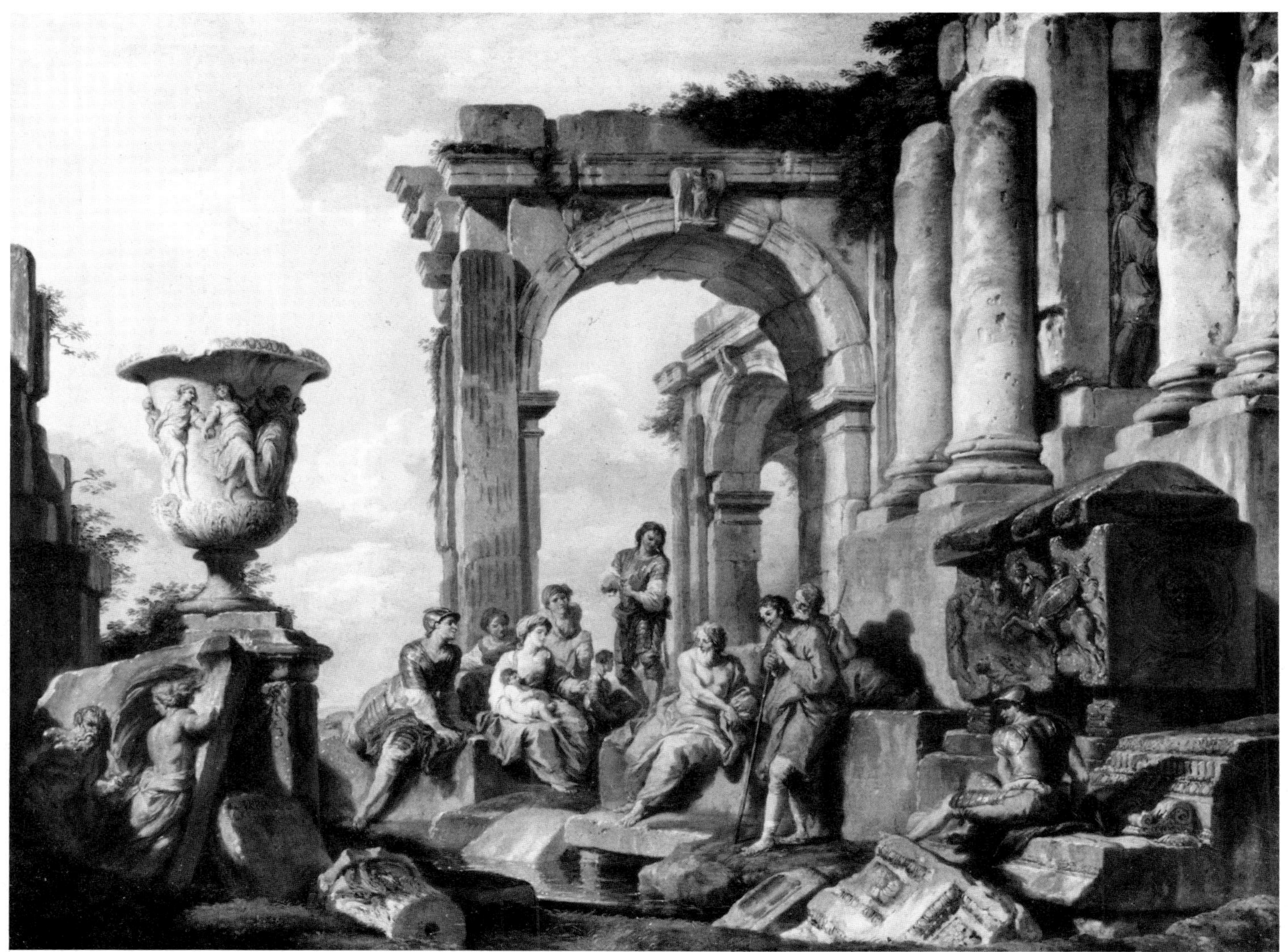

FIG. 117 Giovanni Paolo Panini, *Roman ruins with eleven figures* (cat. no. 728).

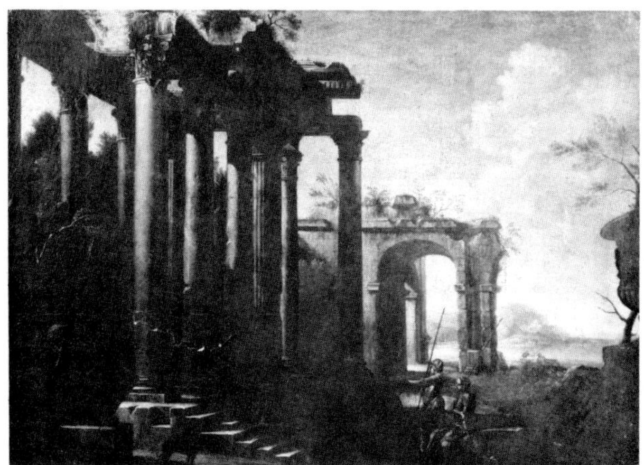

FIG. 118   Style of Panini, *Ruins with figures* (cat. no. 1531).

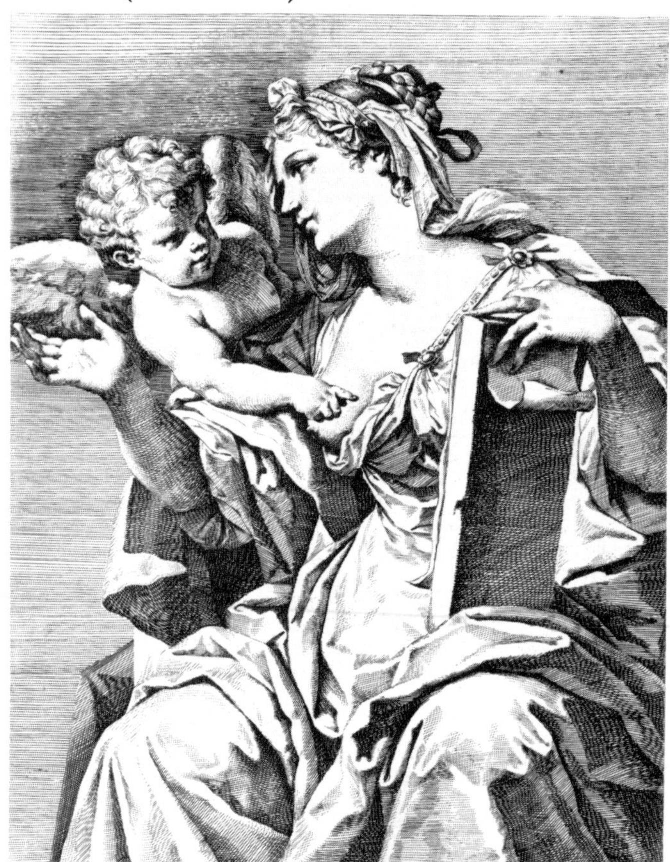

FIG. 119   Giuseppe Maria Rolli after Pasinelli, *(?) Pittura*. Engraving, 329 × 250 mm. The British Museum, (inv. no. 1874. 8. 8. 737). Reproduced by courtesy of the Trustees of the British Museum.

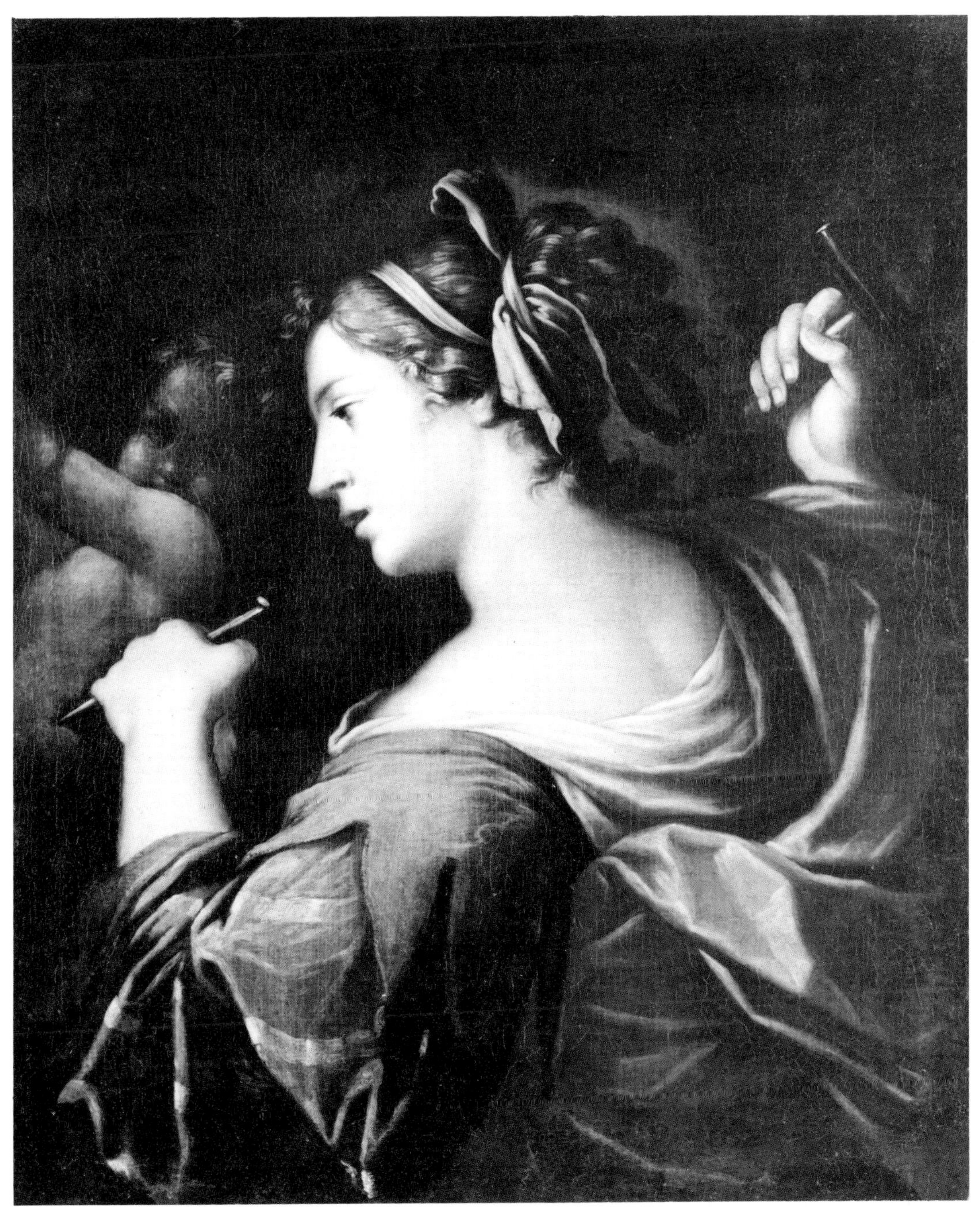

FIG. 120   Lorenzo Pasinelli, *The Muse of Sculpture* (cat. no. 1335).

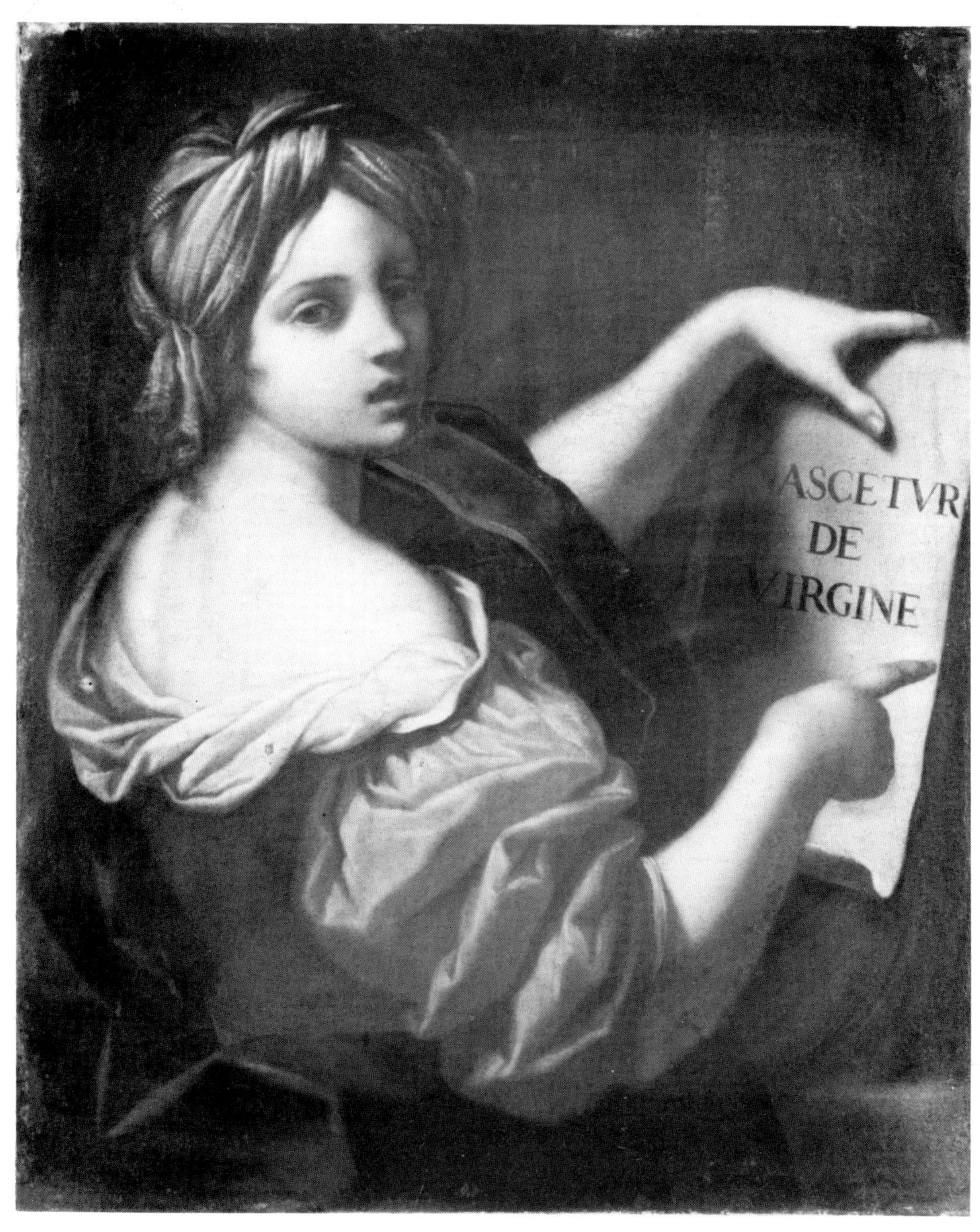

FIG. 121 Attributed to Pasinelli, *Albunea, the Tiburtine Sibyl* (cat. no. 1740).

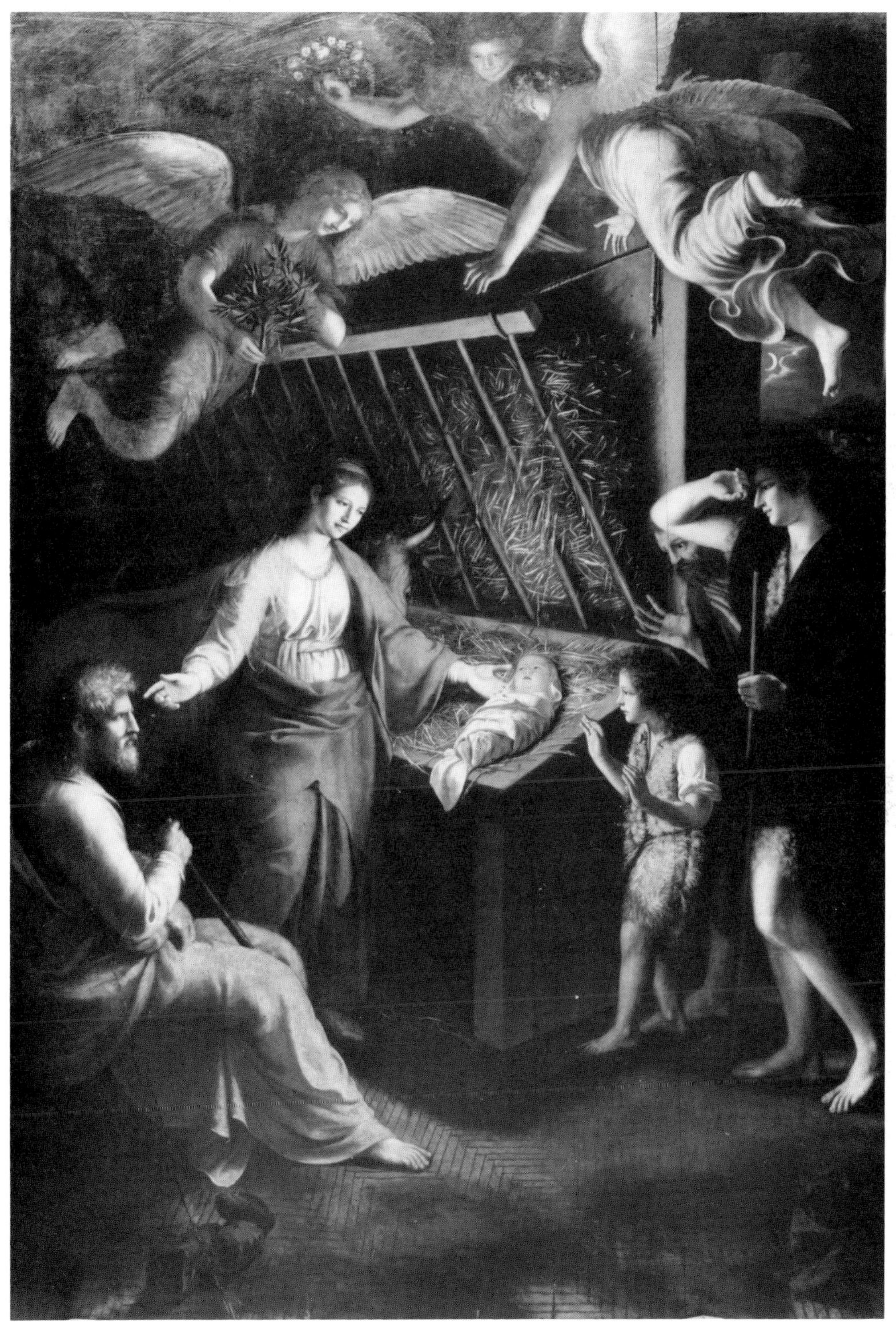

Fig. 122 Francesco Pascucci, *Adoration of the shepherds* (cat. no. 1918).

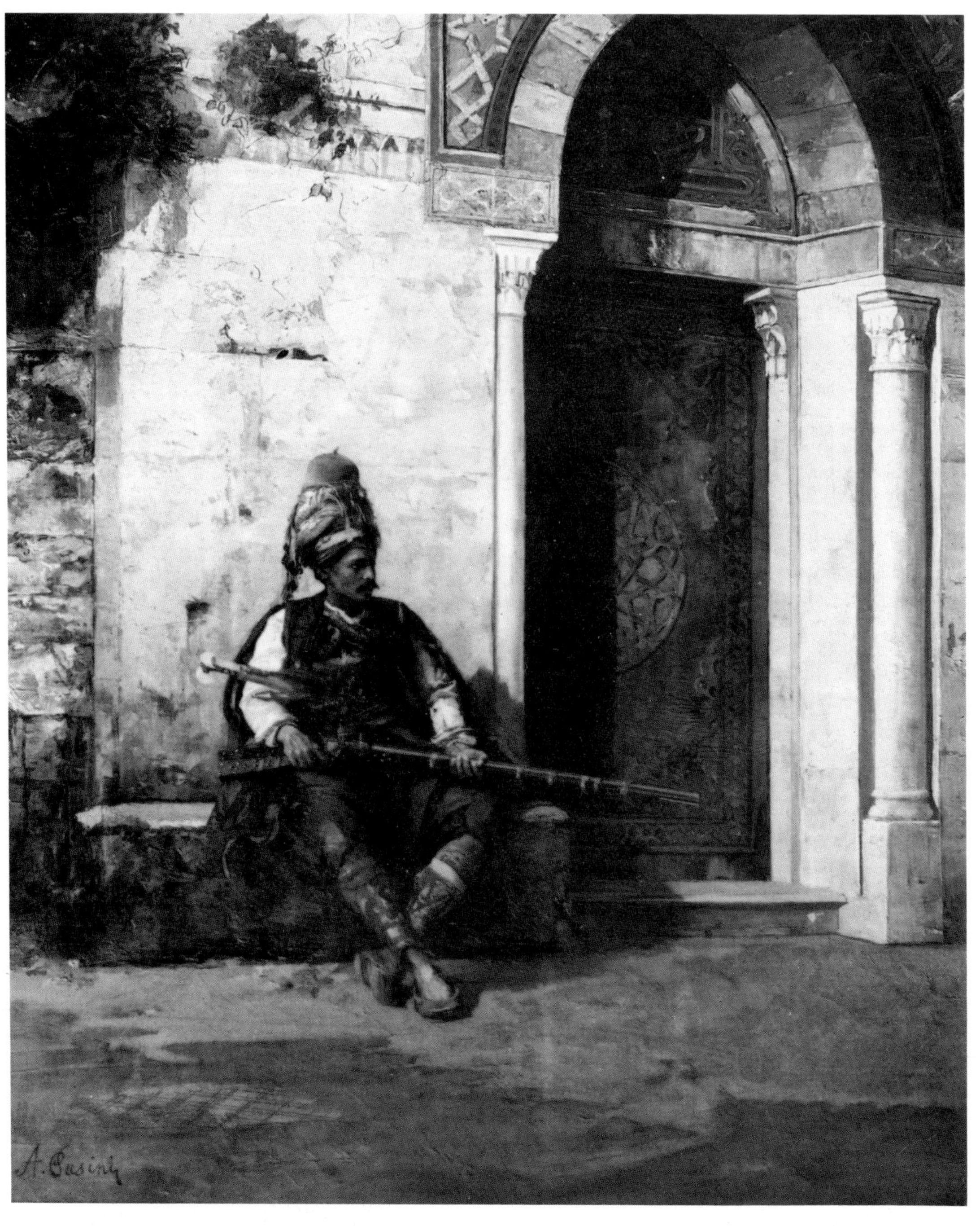

FIG. 123   Alberto Pasini, *An Arab soldier seated by a doorway* (cat. no. 4269CB).

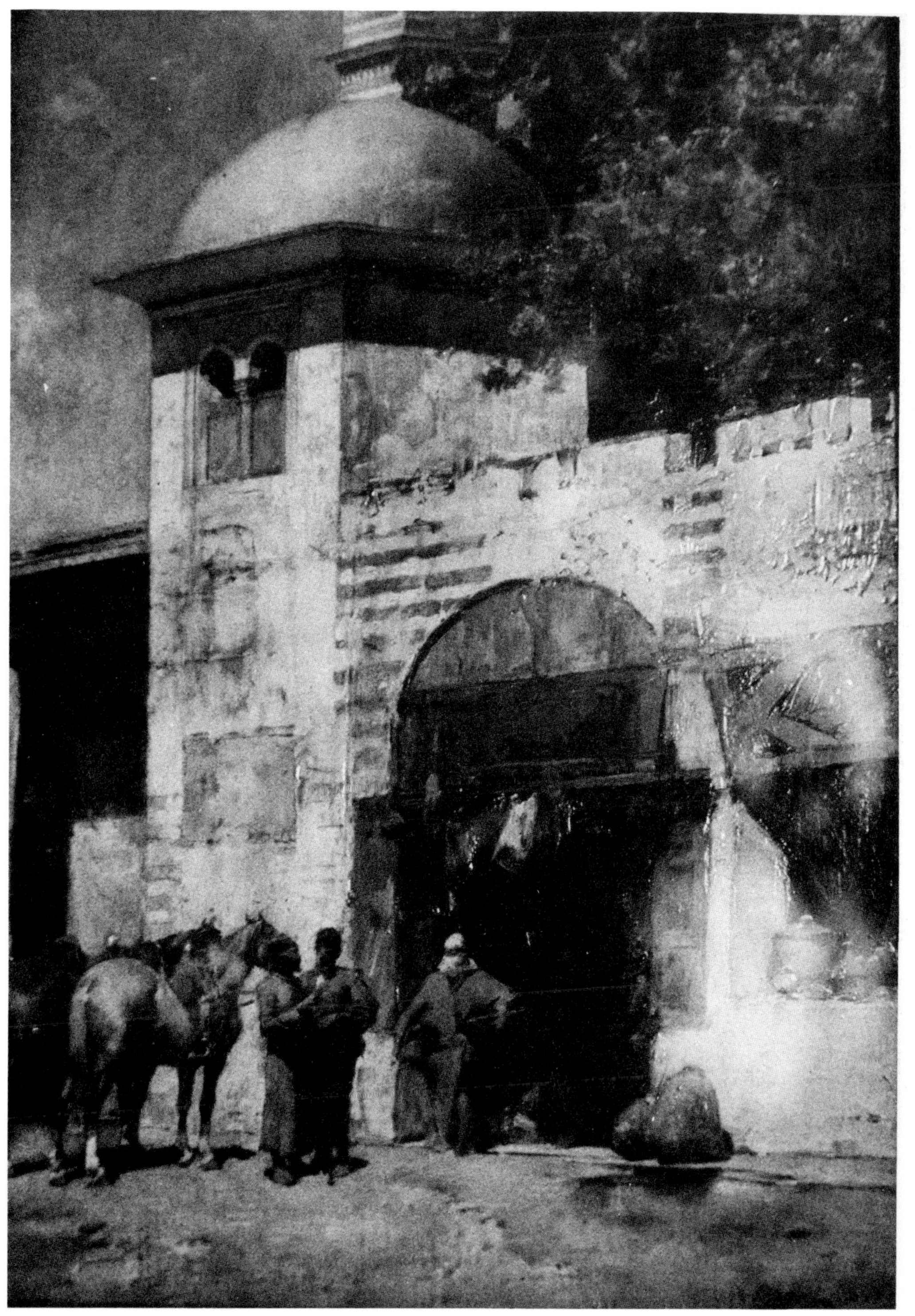

FIG. 124 Alberto Pasini, *An Eastern scene* (cat. no. 4271CB).

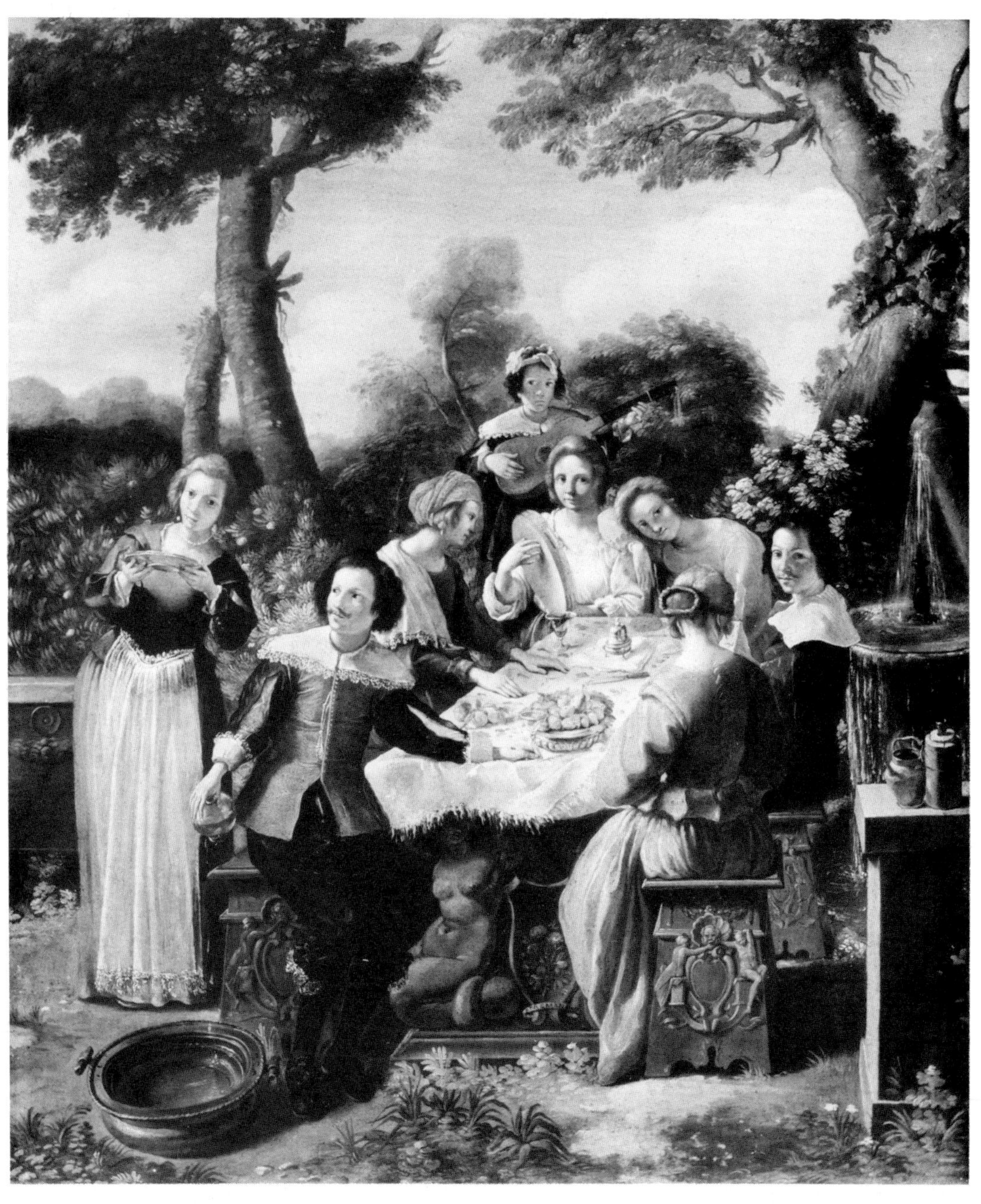

FIG. 125   Giovanni Battista Passeri, *Party feasting in a garden* (cat. no. 993), Prior to 1983 cleaning and restoration.

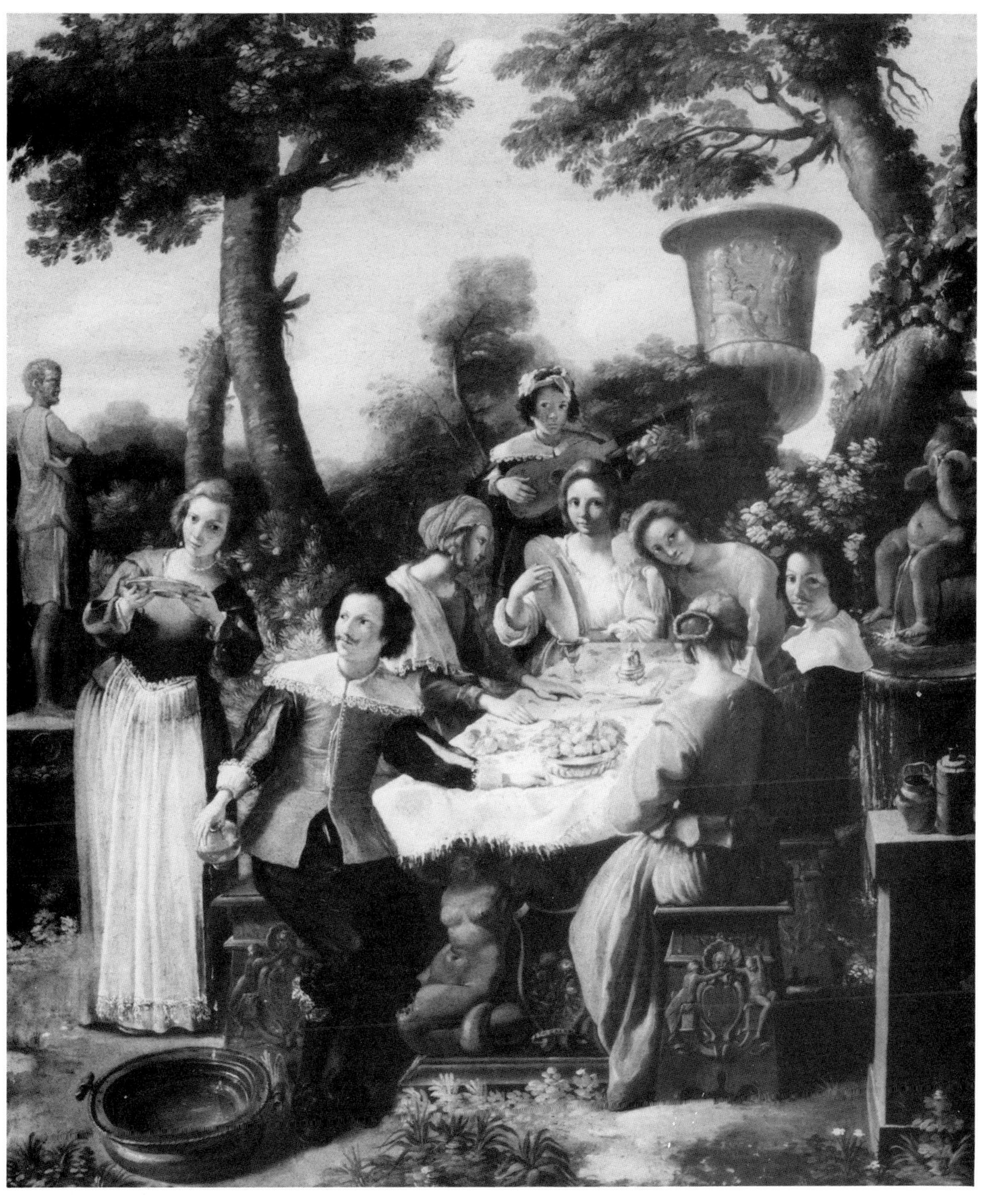

Fɪɢ. 126   Giovanni Battista Passeri, *Party feasting in a garden* (cat. no. 993).

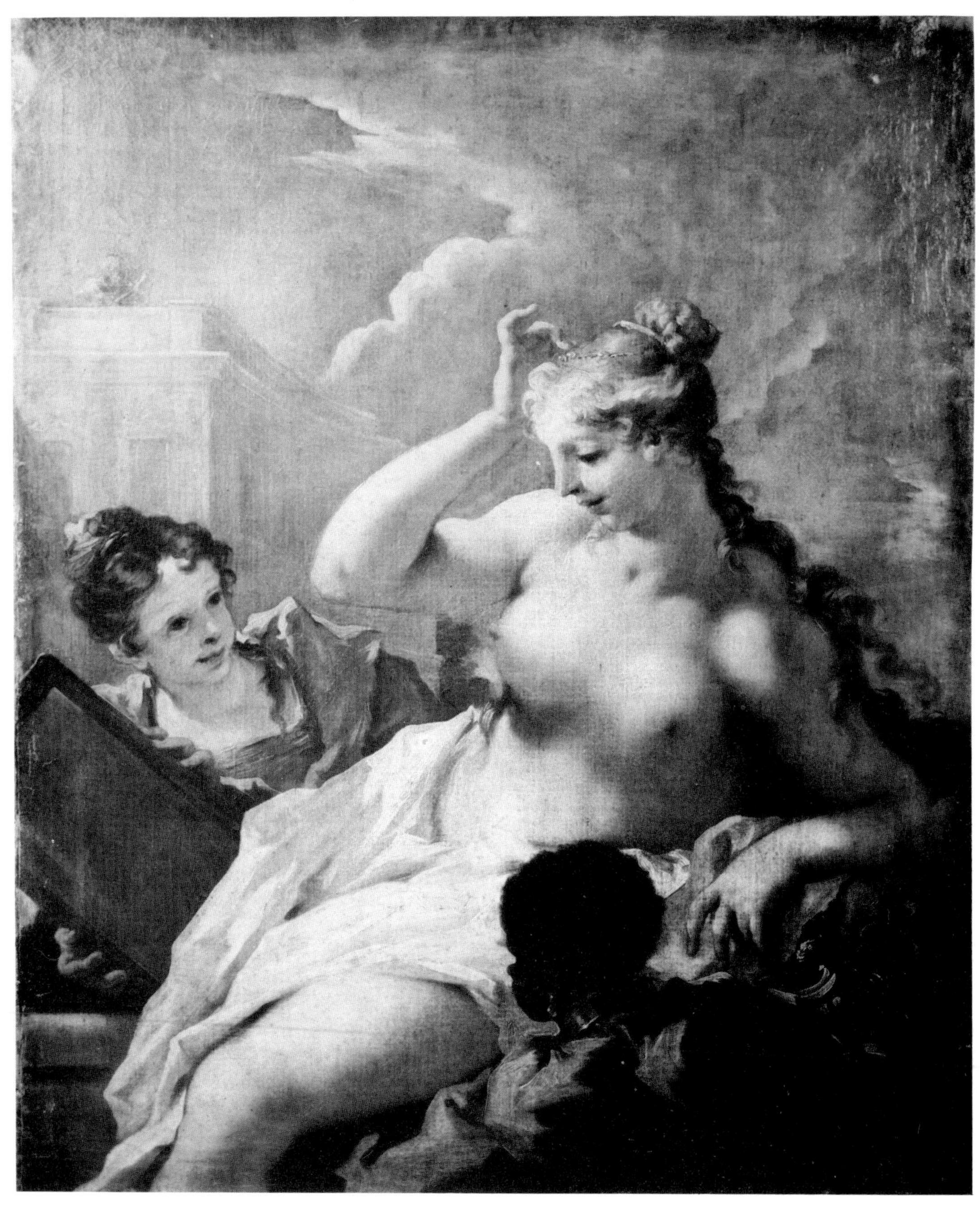

FIG. 127   Giovanni Antonio Pellegrini, *Bathsheba* (cat. no. 467).

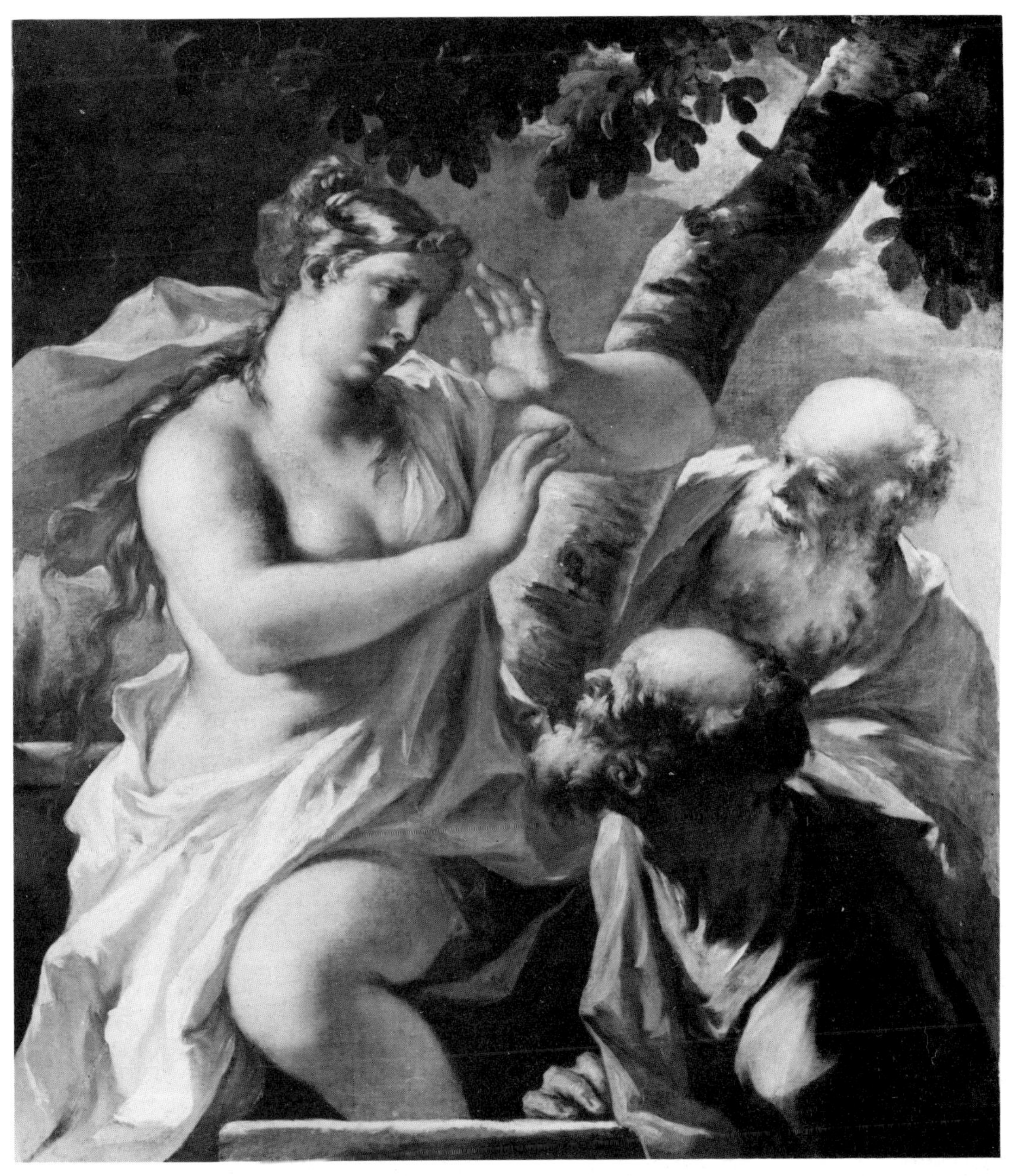

FIG. 128   Giovanni Antonio Pellegrini, *Susanna and the Elders* (cat. no. 1938).

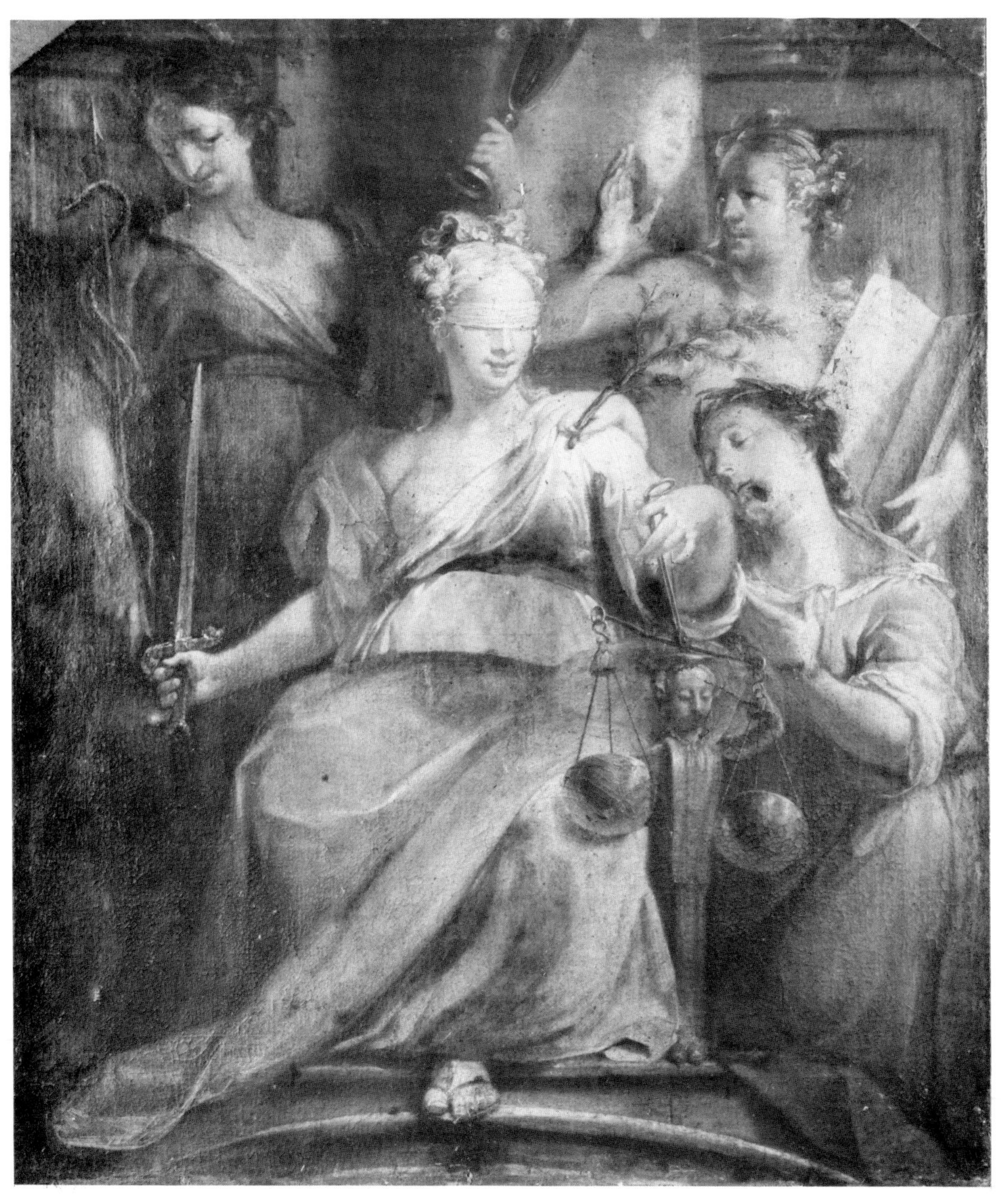

Fɪɢ. 129 Attributed to Pellegrini, *Allegory of Justice* (cat. no. 1999).

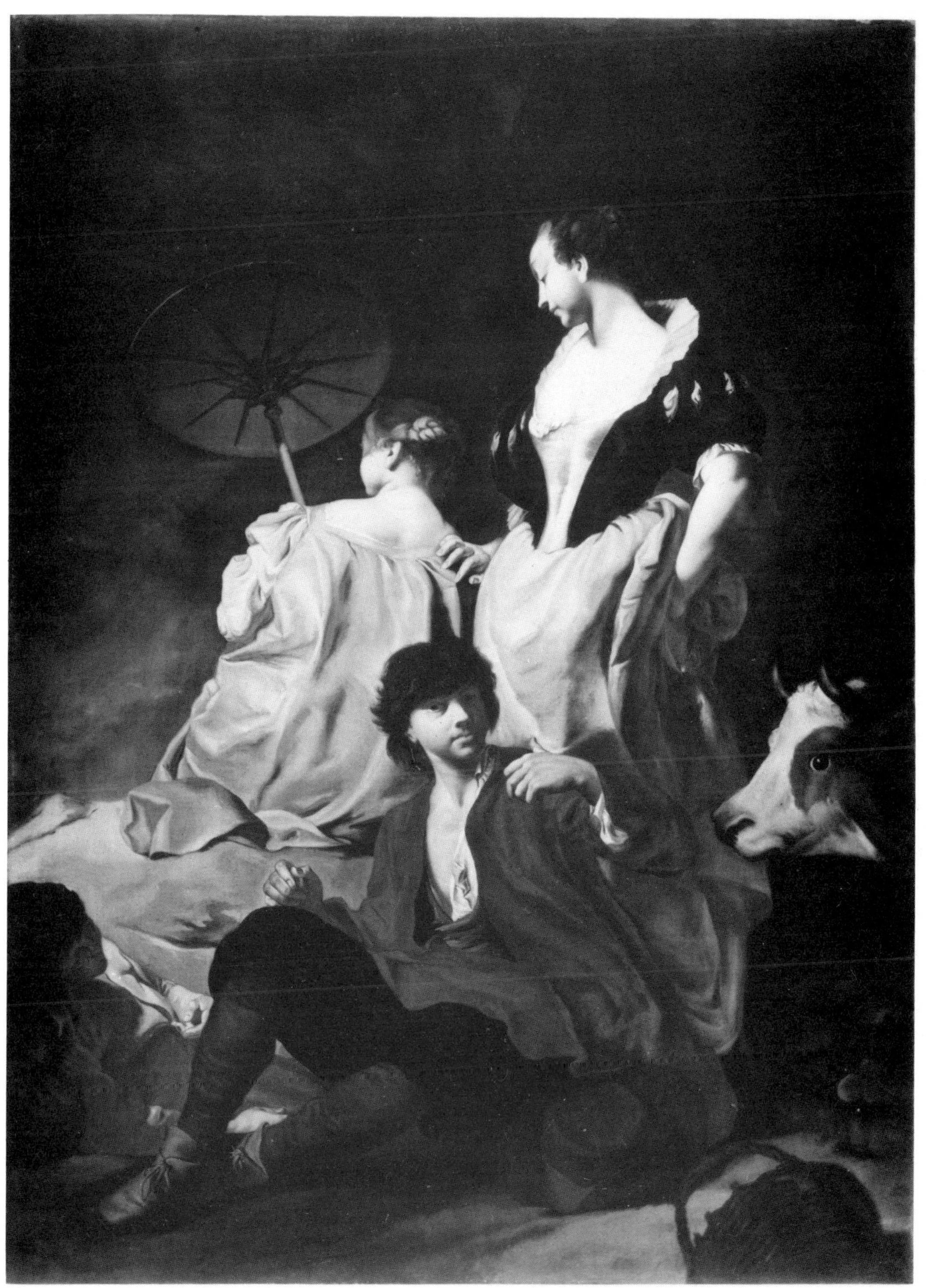

FIG. 130   Studio of Piazzetta, *A pastoral outing* (cat. no. 656).

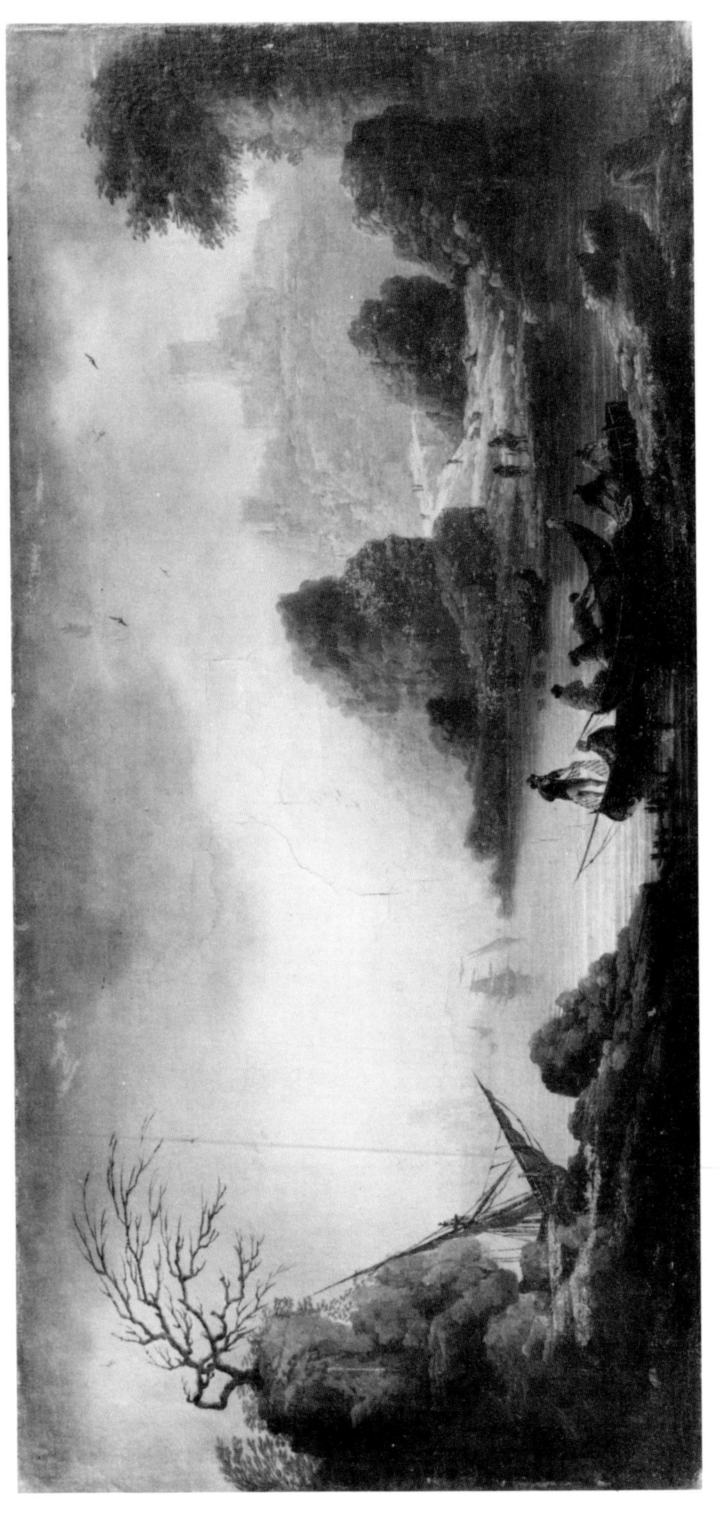

Fig. 131   Andrea Piscelli, *Lake scene with figures* (cat. no. 1093).

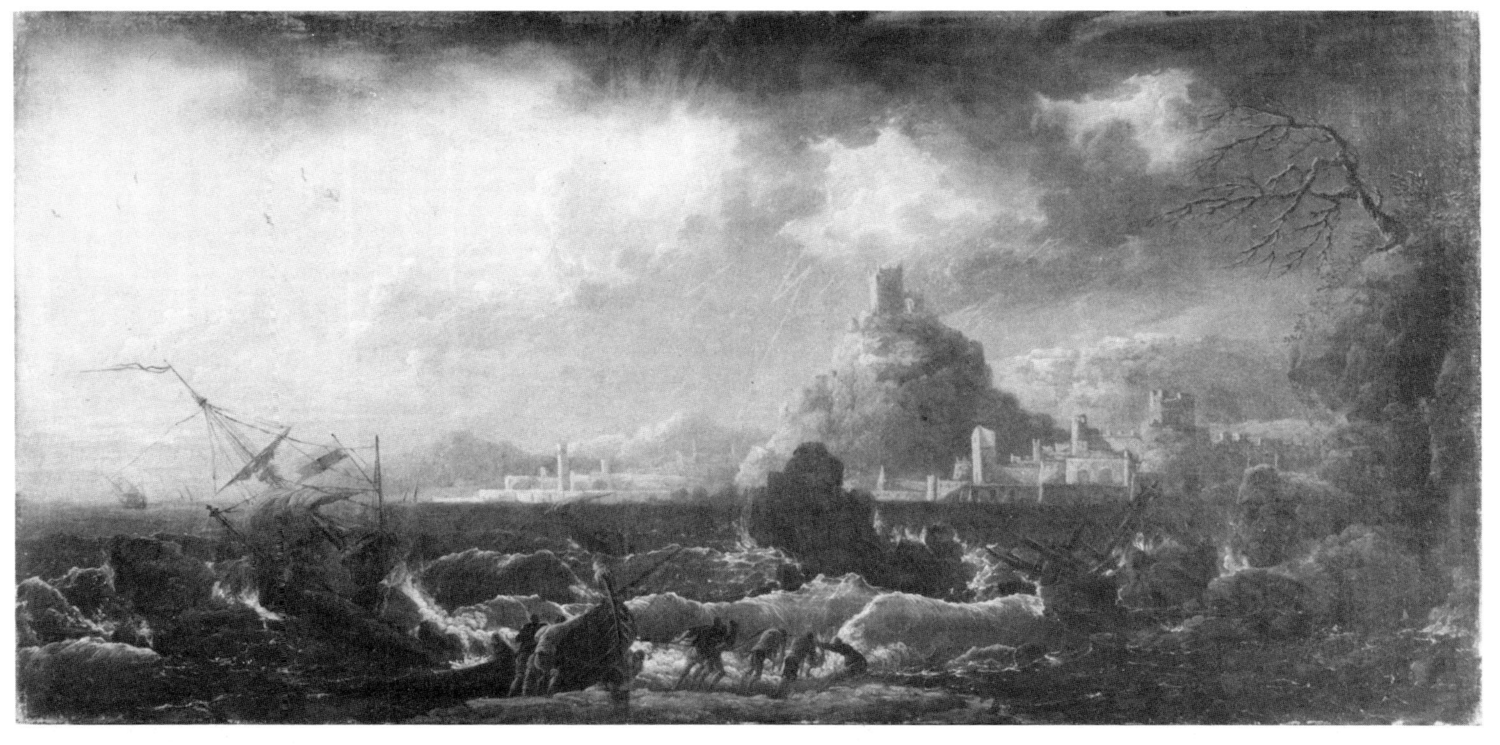

Fig. 132 Andrea Piscelli, *Coast scene with shipwreck* (cat. no. 1094).

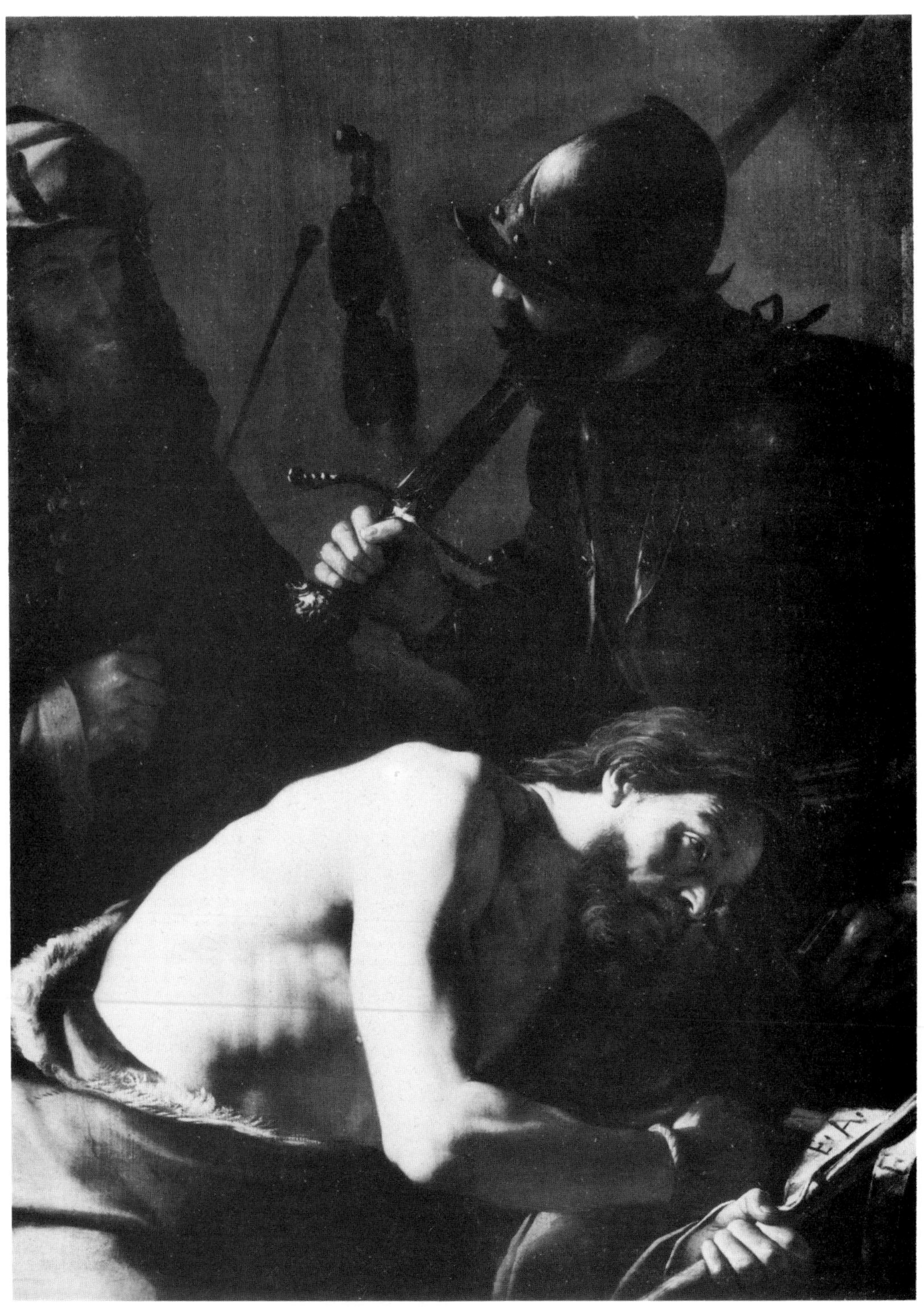

FIG. 133 Mattia Preti, *The beheading of St. John the Baptist* (cat. no. 366).

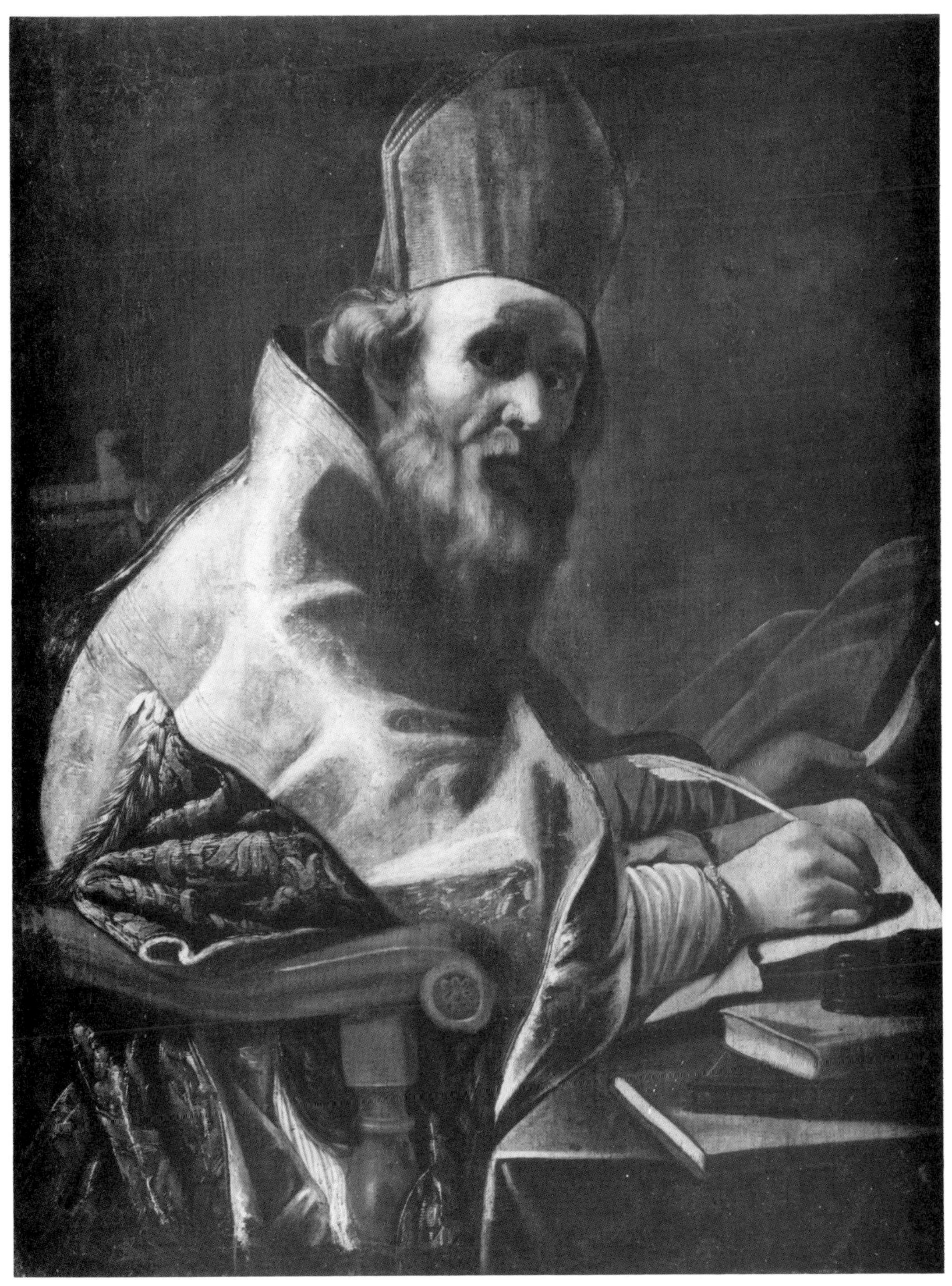

FIG. 134 Attributed to Preti, *St. Ambrose* (cat. no. 1912).

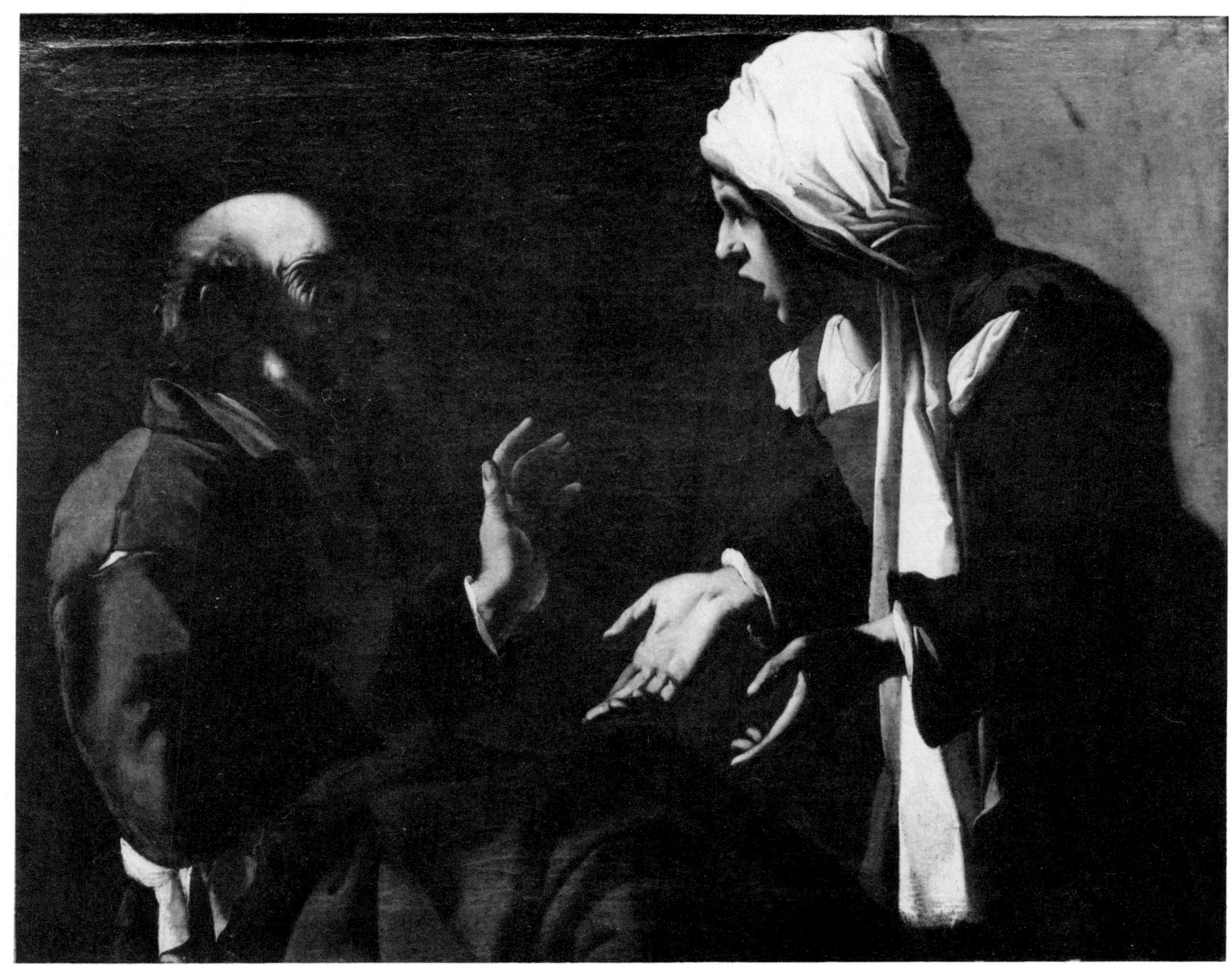

Fig. 135 Pensionante del Saraceni, *St. Peter denying Christ* (cat. no. 1178).

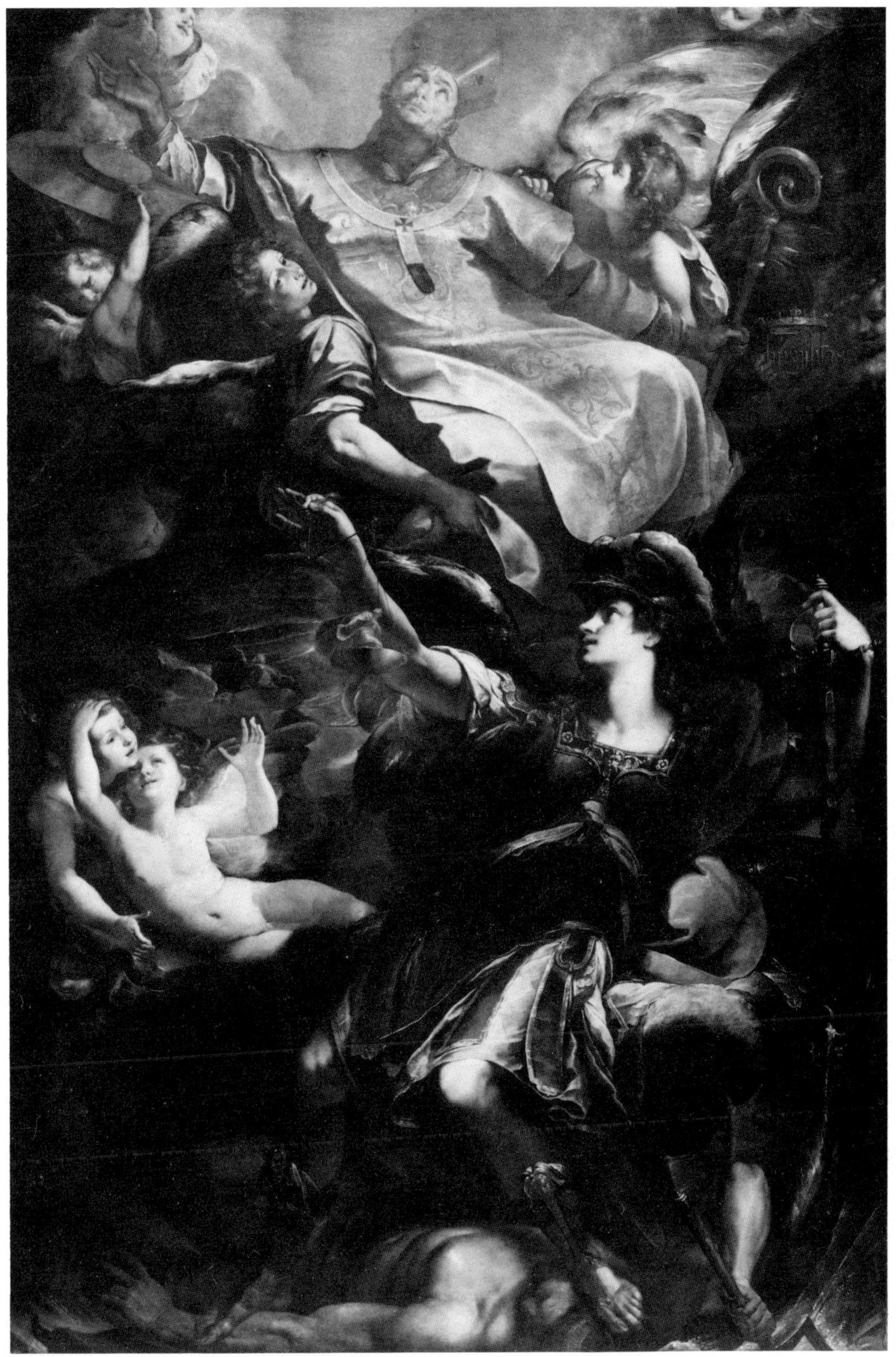

FIG. 136   Giulio Cesare Procaccini, *St. Charles Borromeo in glory with the Archangel Michael* (cat. no. 1820).

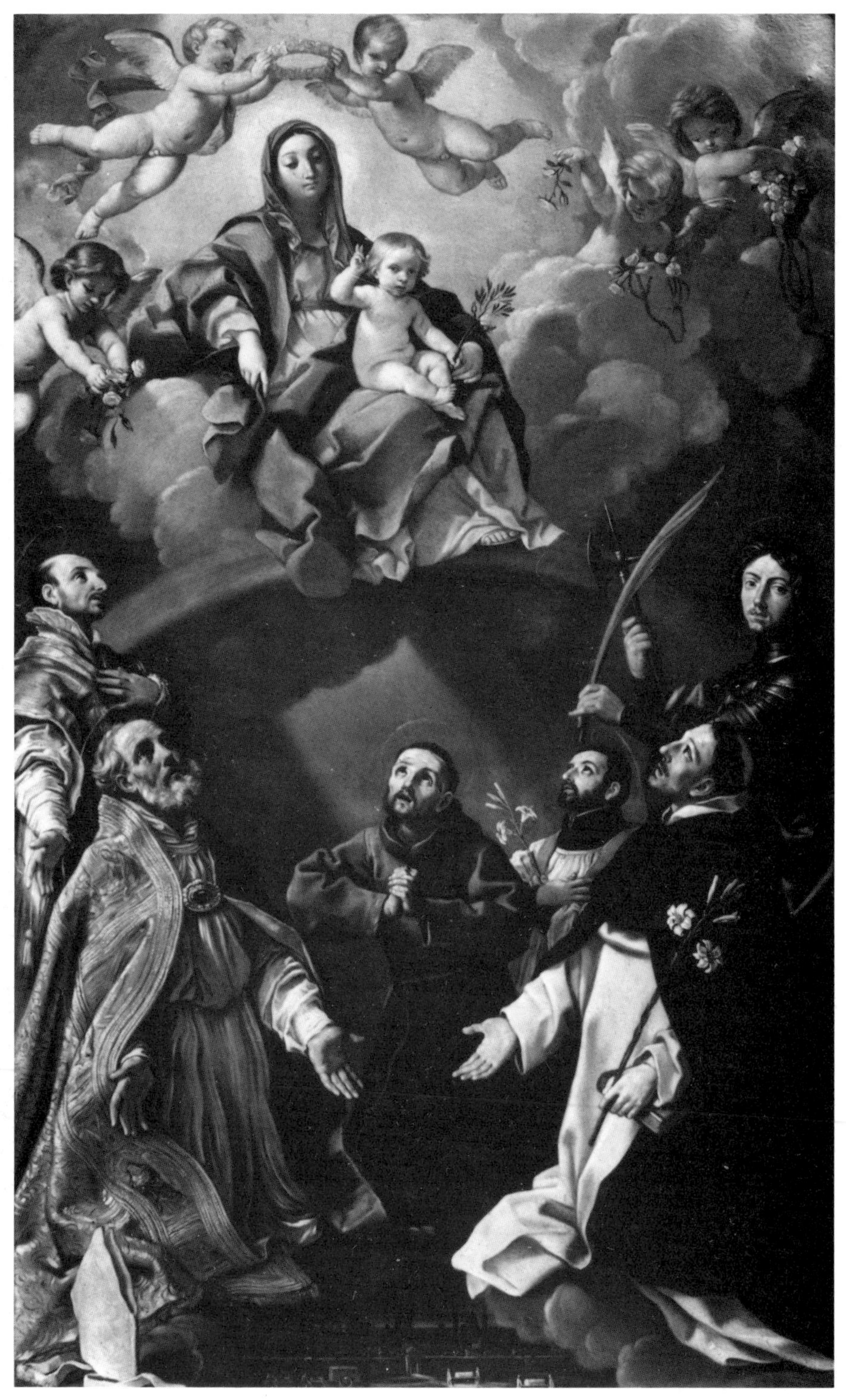

FIG. 137   After Reni, *Virgin and Child with the protector saints of the city of Bologna* (cat. no. 118).

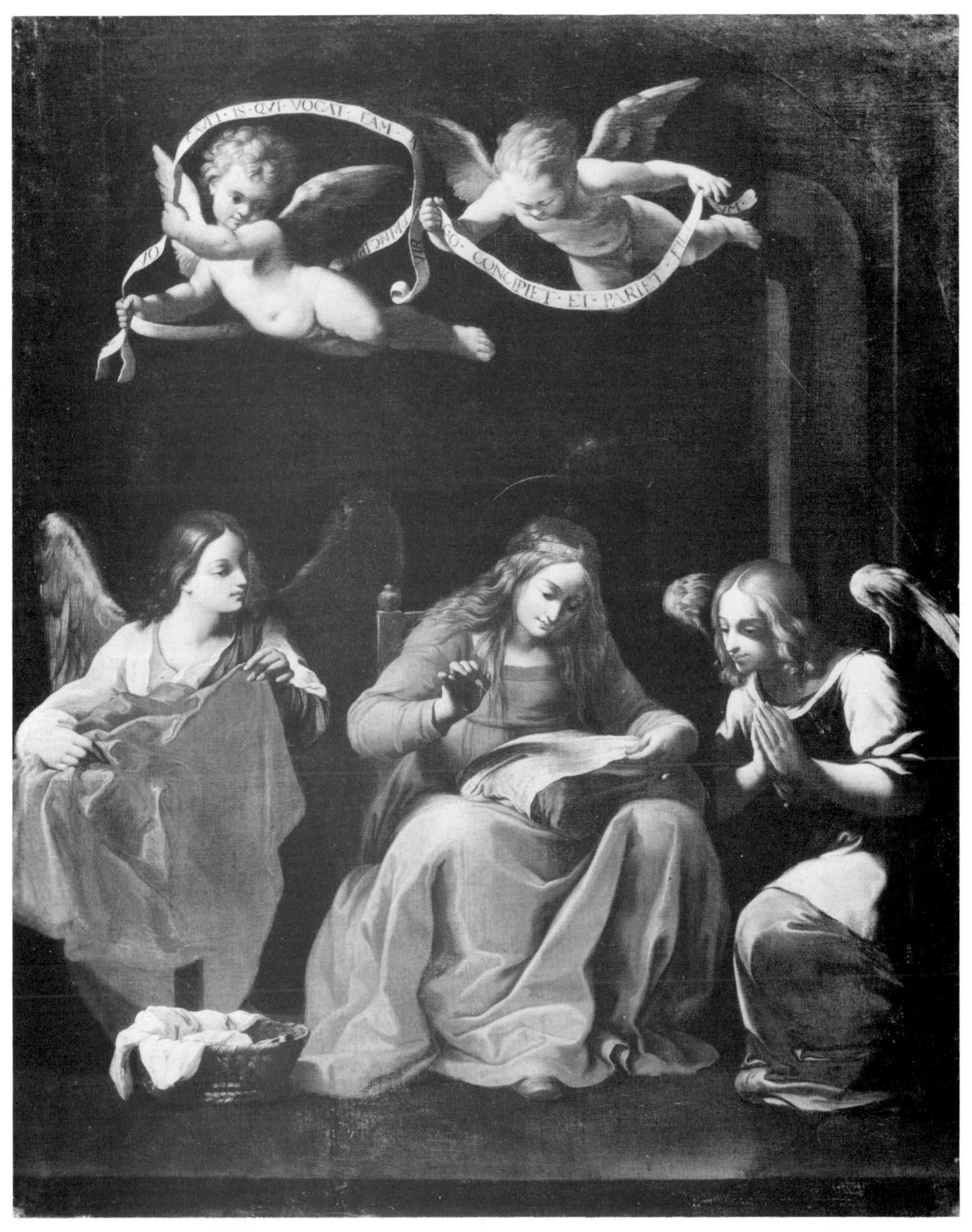

Fig. 138 After Reni, *The Virgin sewing* (cat. no. 1065).

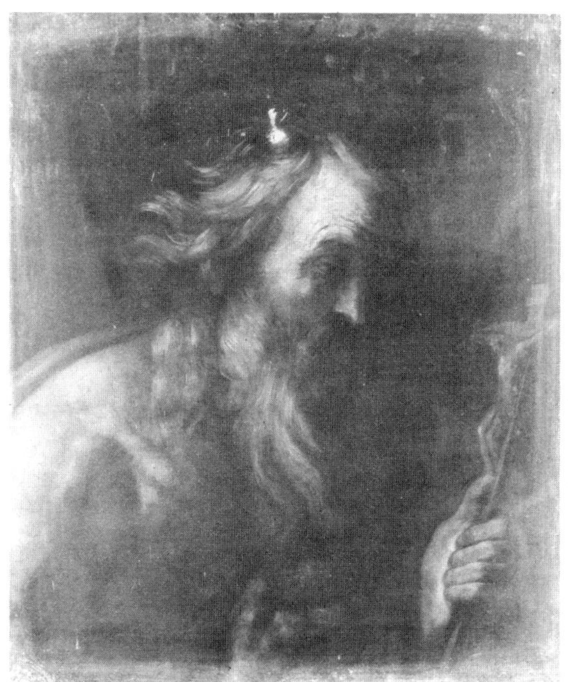

Fig. 139   After Reni, *St. Jerome* (cat. no. 1334).

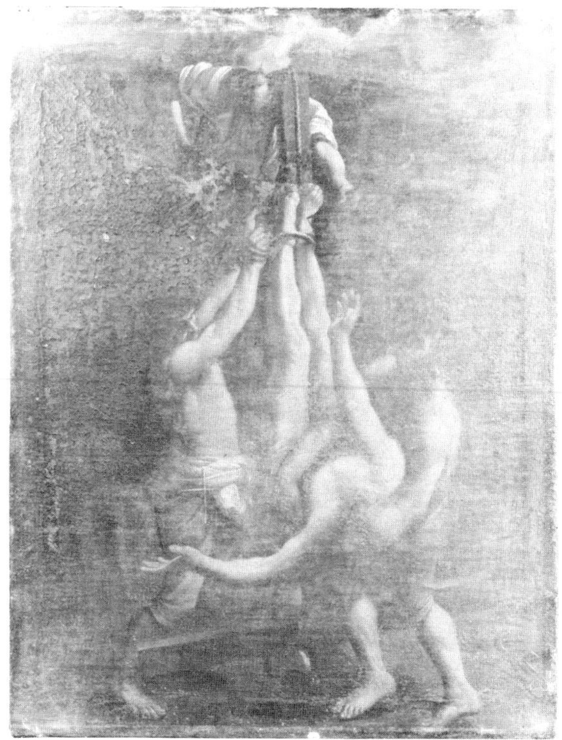

Fig. 140   After Reni, *The crucifixion of St. Peter*
(cat. no. 1695).

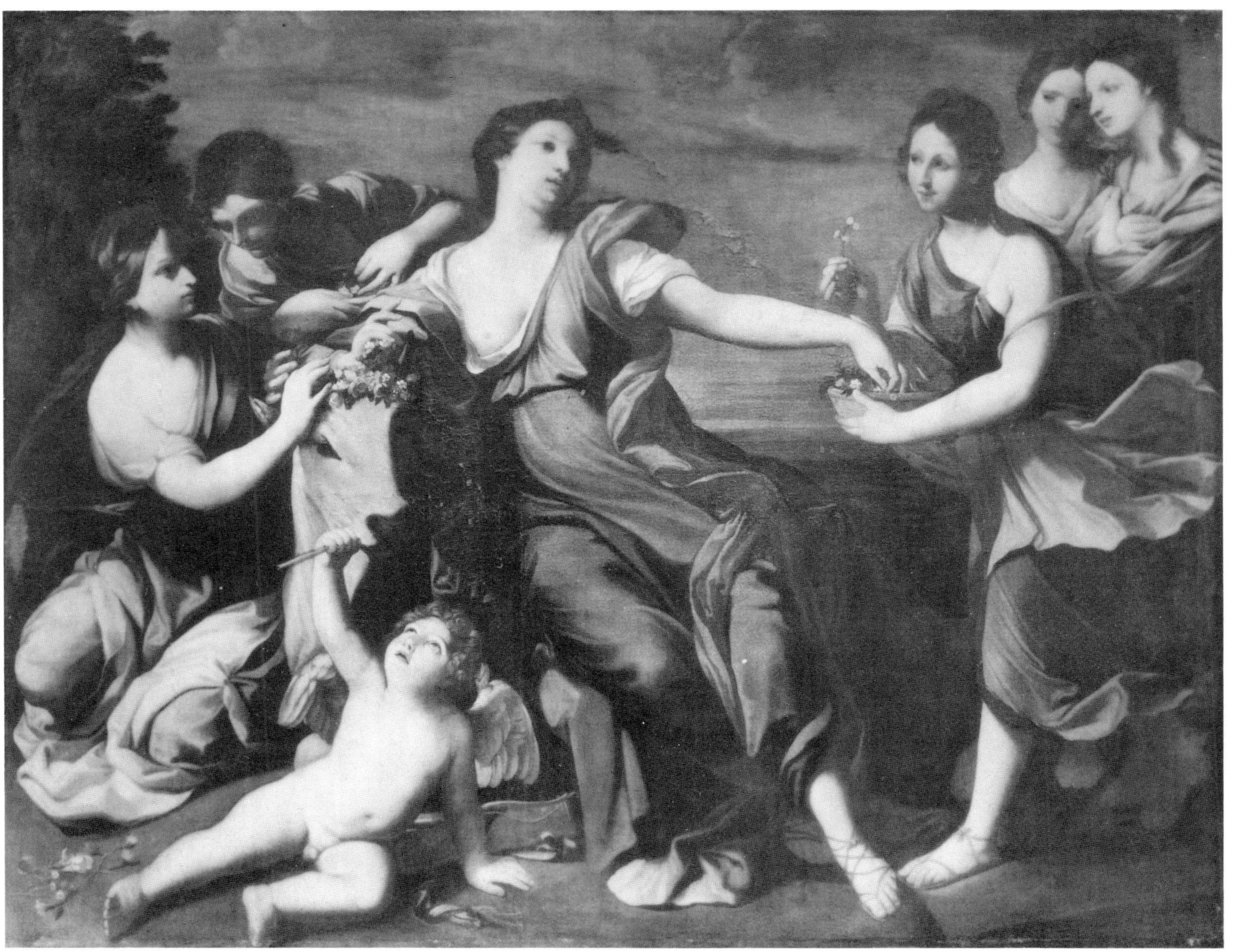

FIG. 141   After Reni, *Rape of Europa* (cat. no. 1908).

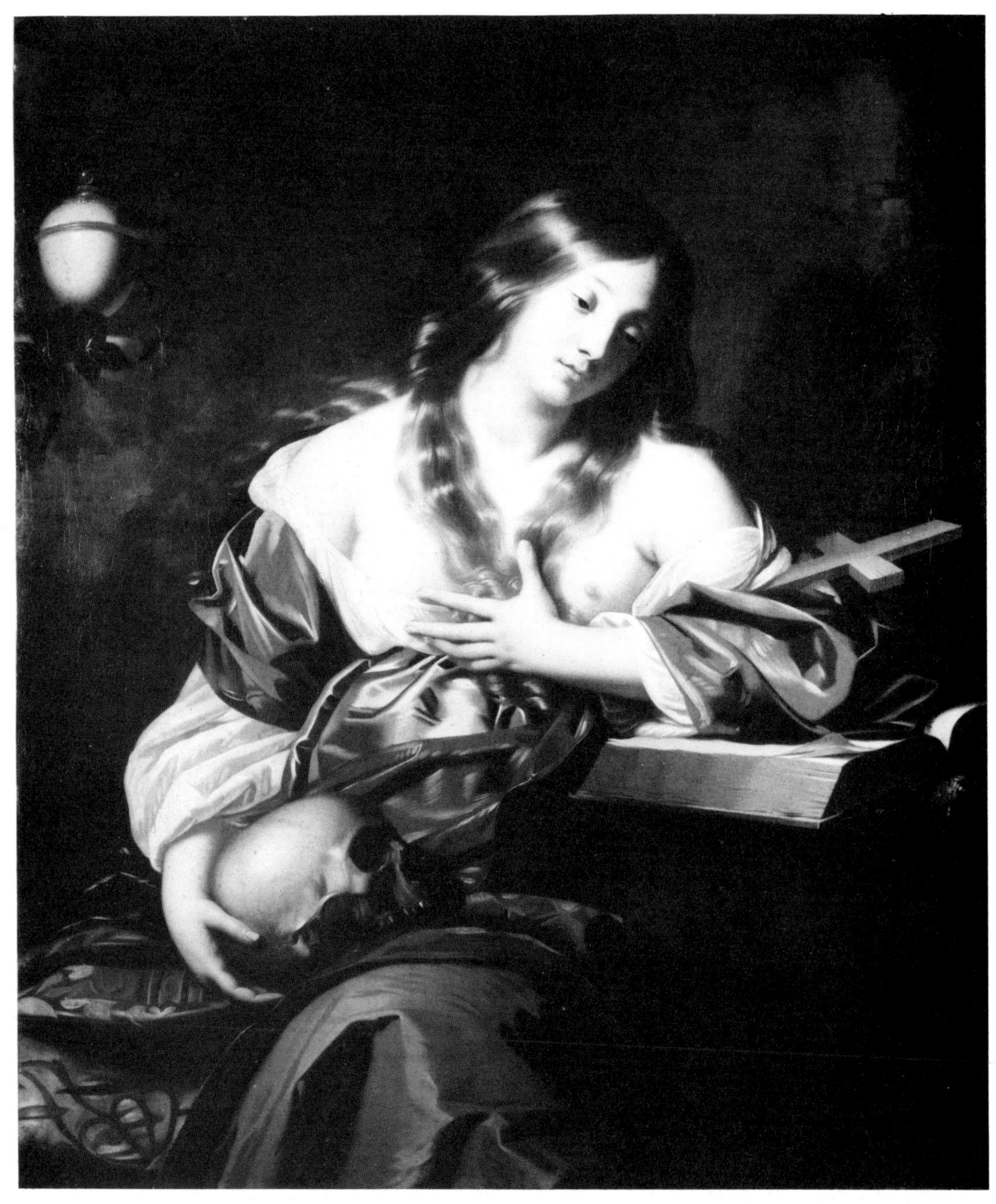

FIG. 142   Niccolo Renieri, *St. Mary Magdalen* (cat. no. 363).

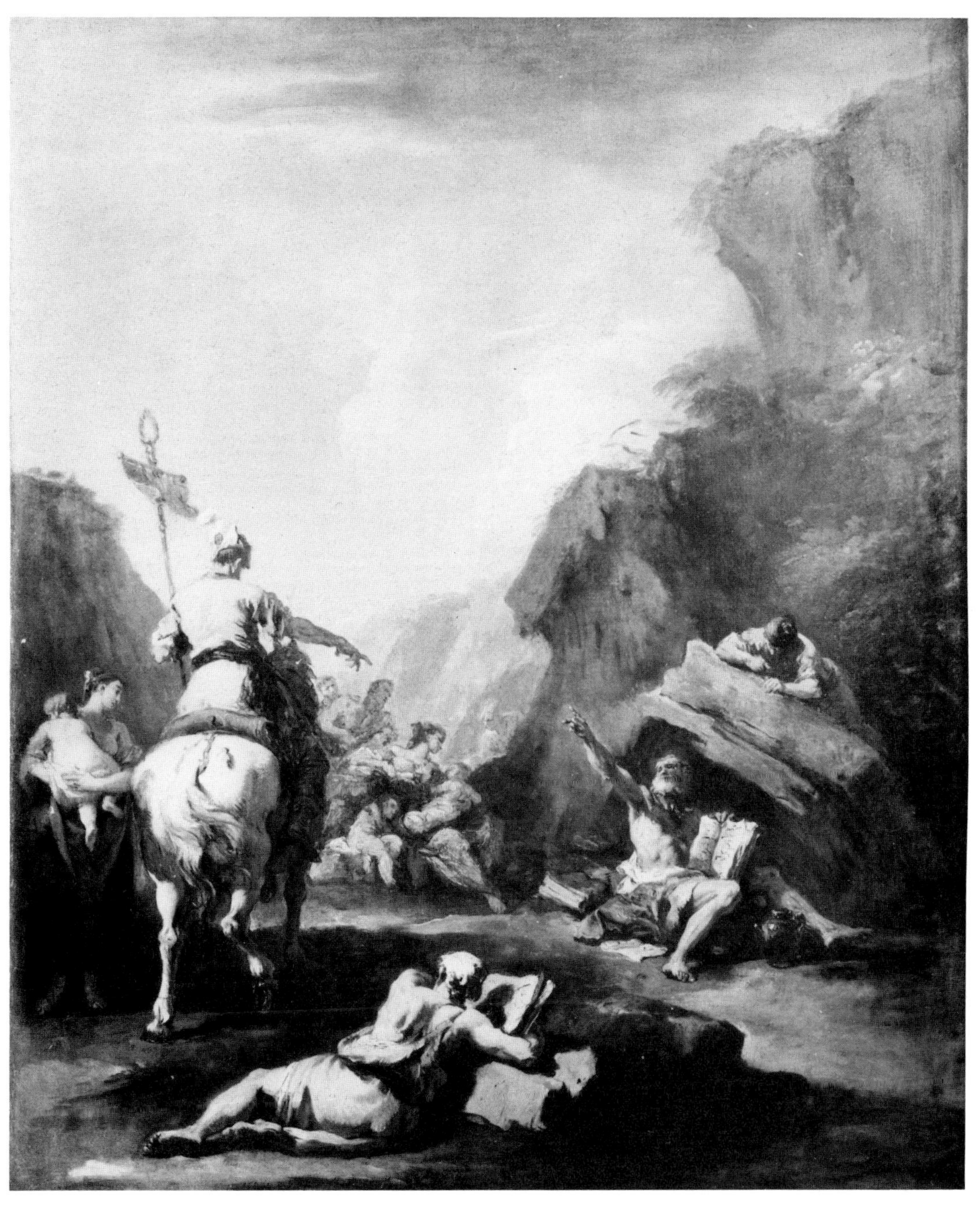

FIG. 143   Sebastiano Ricci, *King Hieron II of Syracuse calls on Archimedes to fortify the city* (cat. no. 1099).

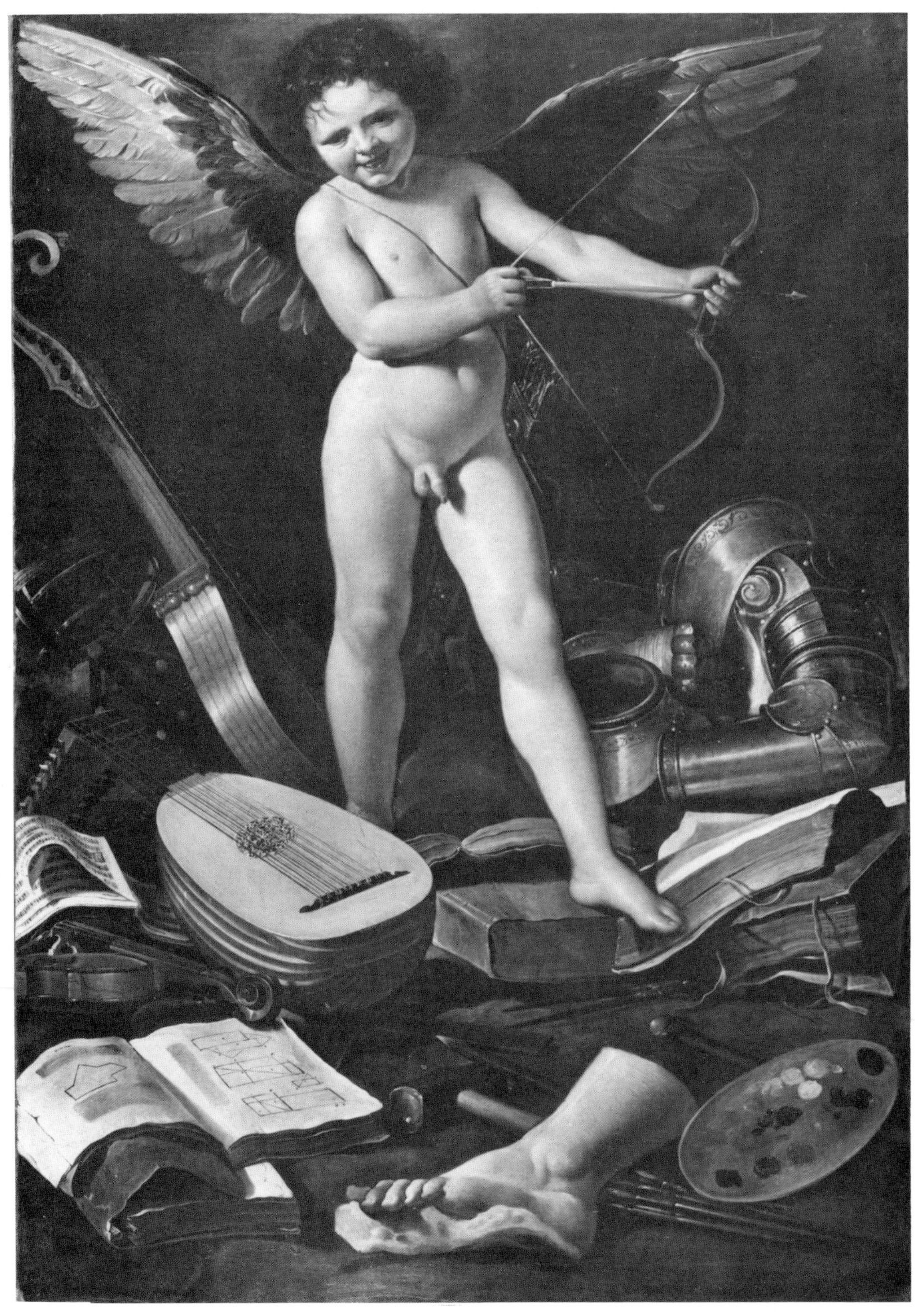

FIG. 144   Attributed to Riminaldi, *Victorious Earthly Love* (cat. no. 1235).

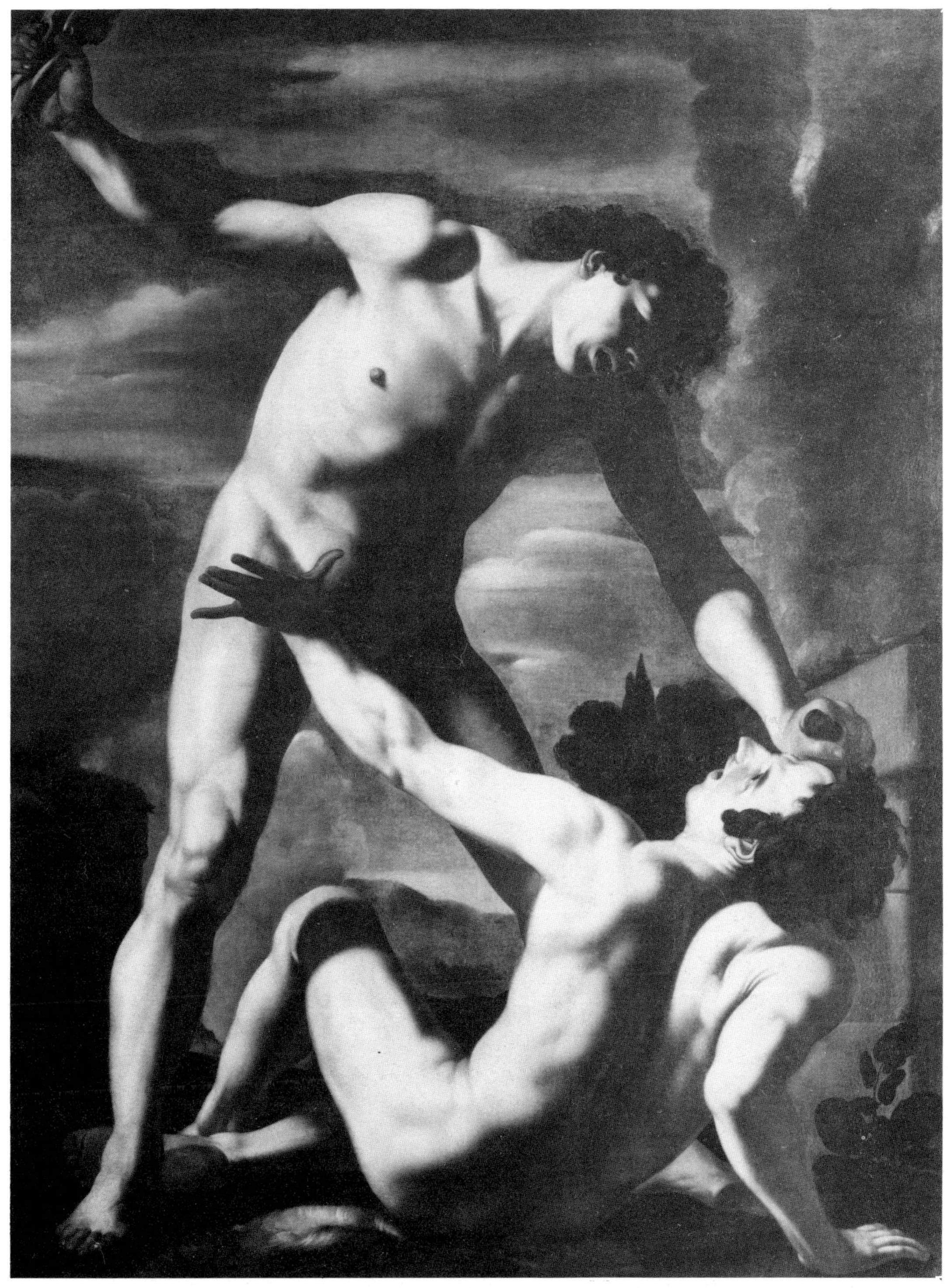

FIG. 145   Circle of Riminaldi, *Cain and Abel* (cat. no. 1667).

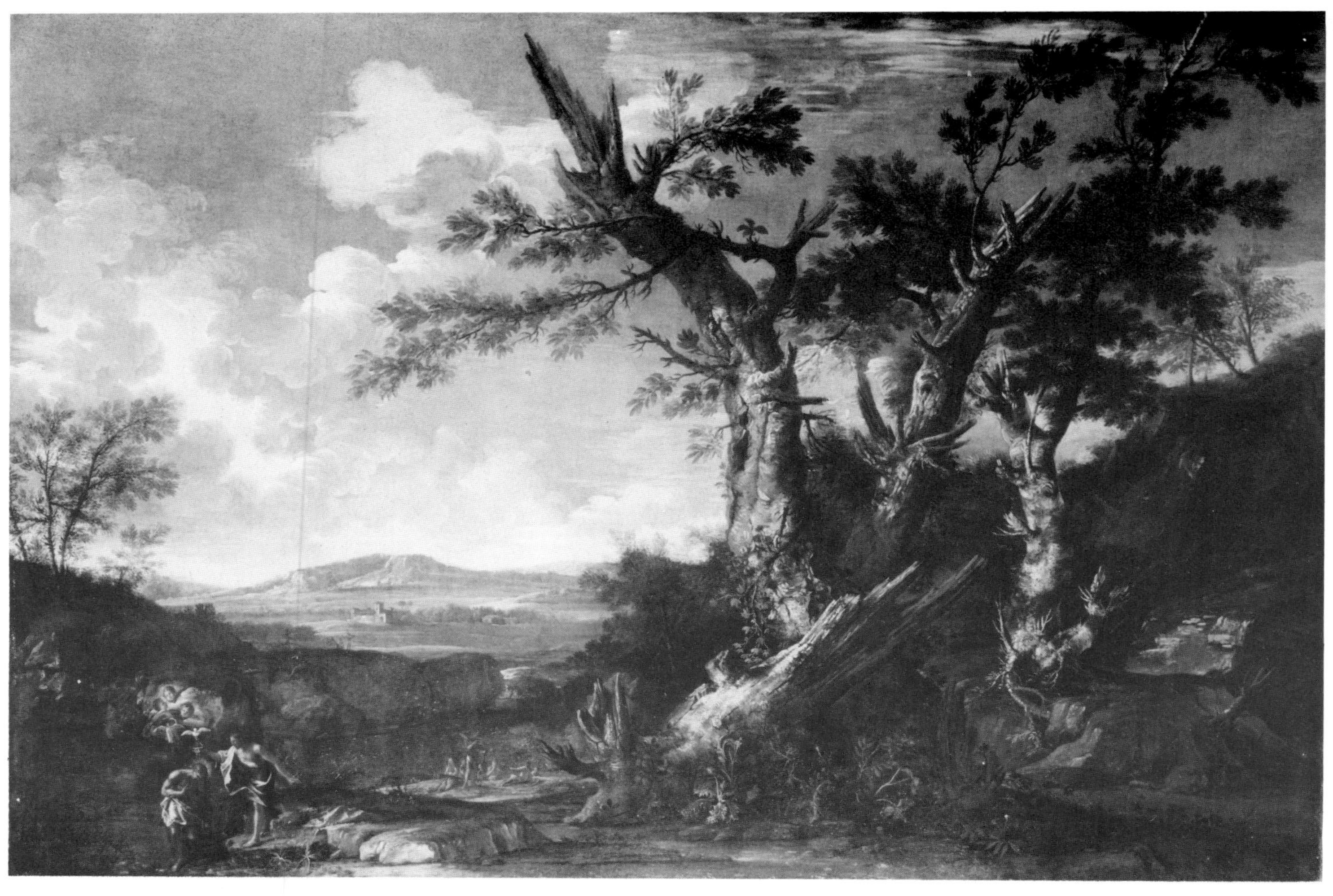

Fig. 146 Salvator Rosa, *Landscape with the baptism of Christ in the Jordan* (cat. no. 96).

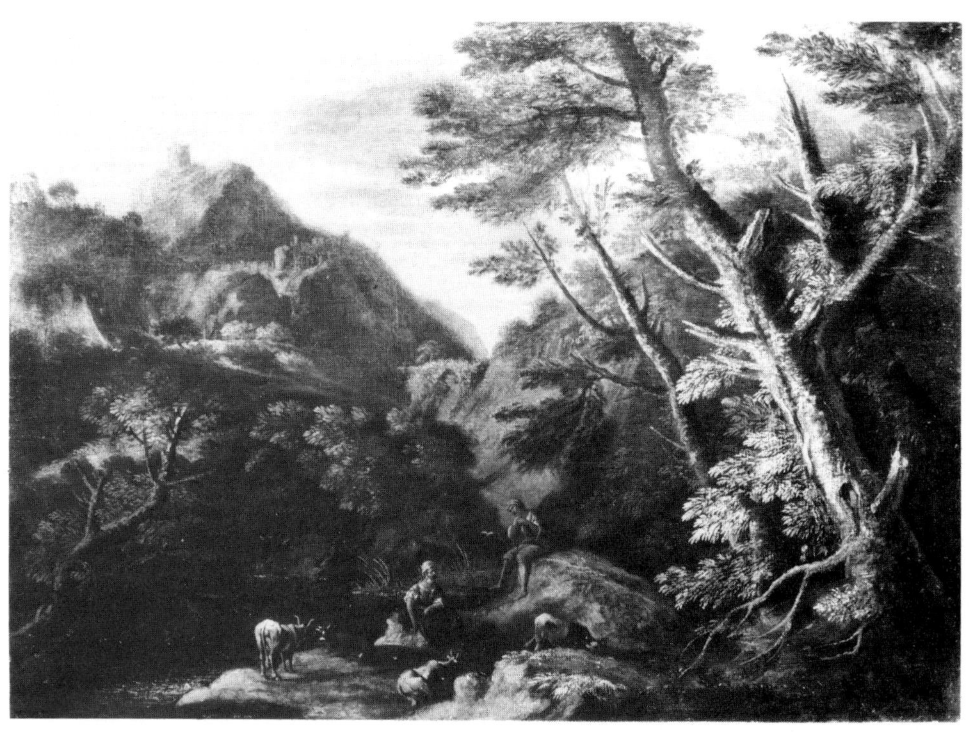

Fig. 147   School of Rosa, *Mountain landscape* (cat. no. 738).

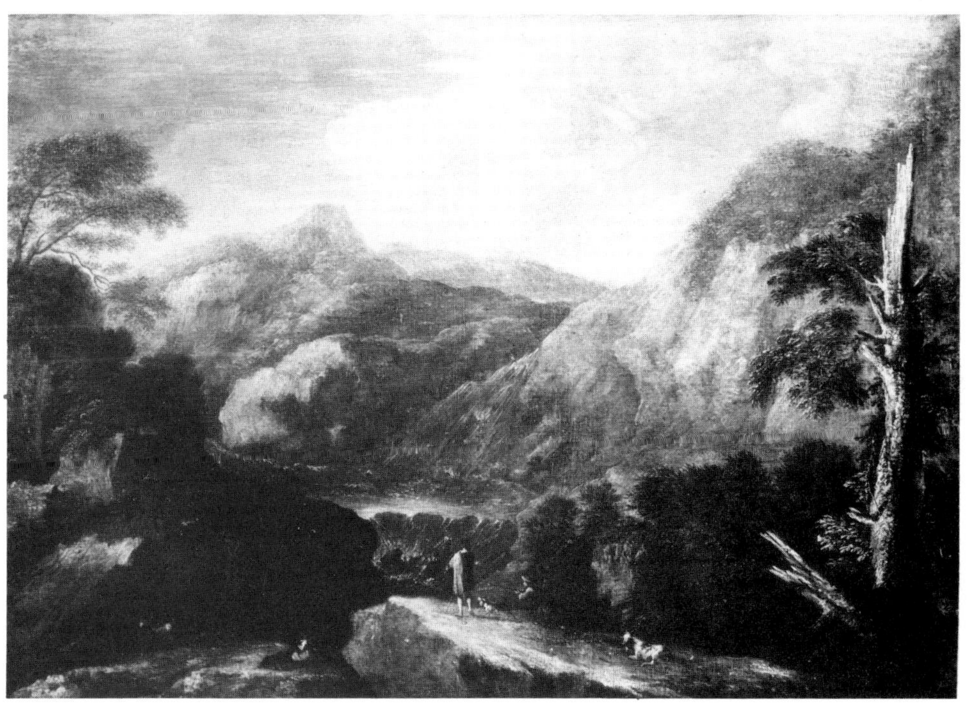

Fig. 148   School of Rosa, *Mountain landscape* (cat. no. 739).

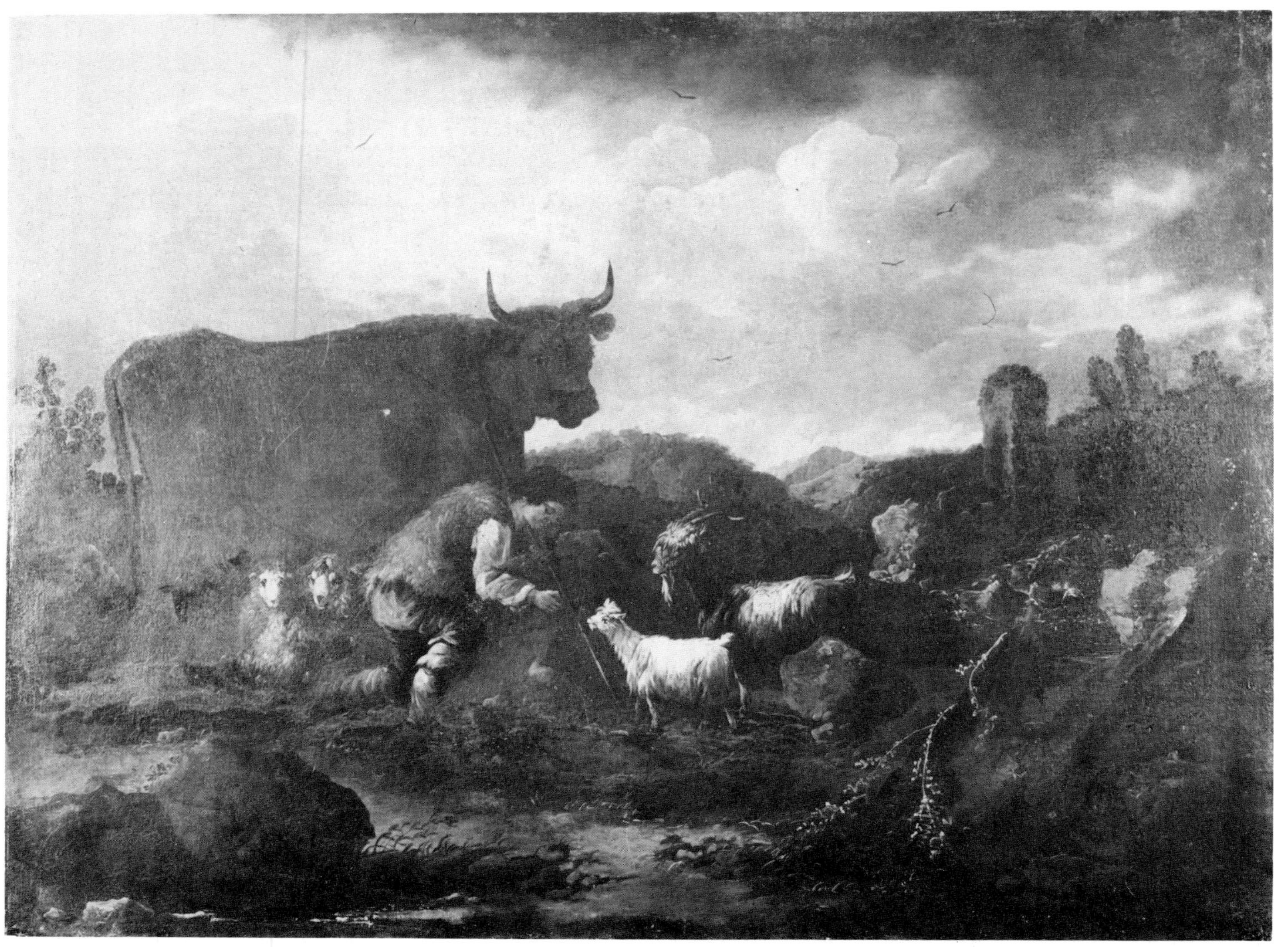

Fig. 149 Rosa da Tivoli, *Landscape with cattle* (cat. no. 1664).

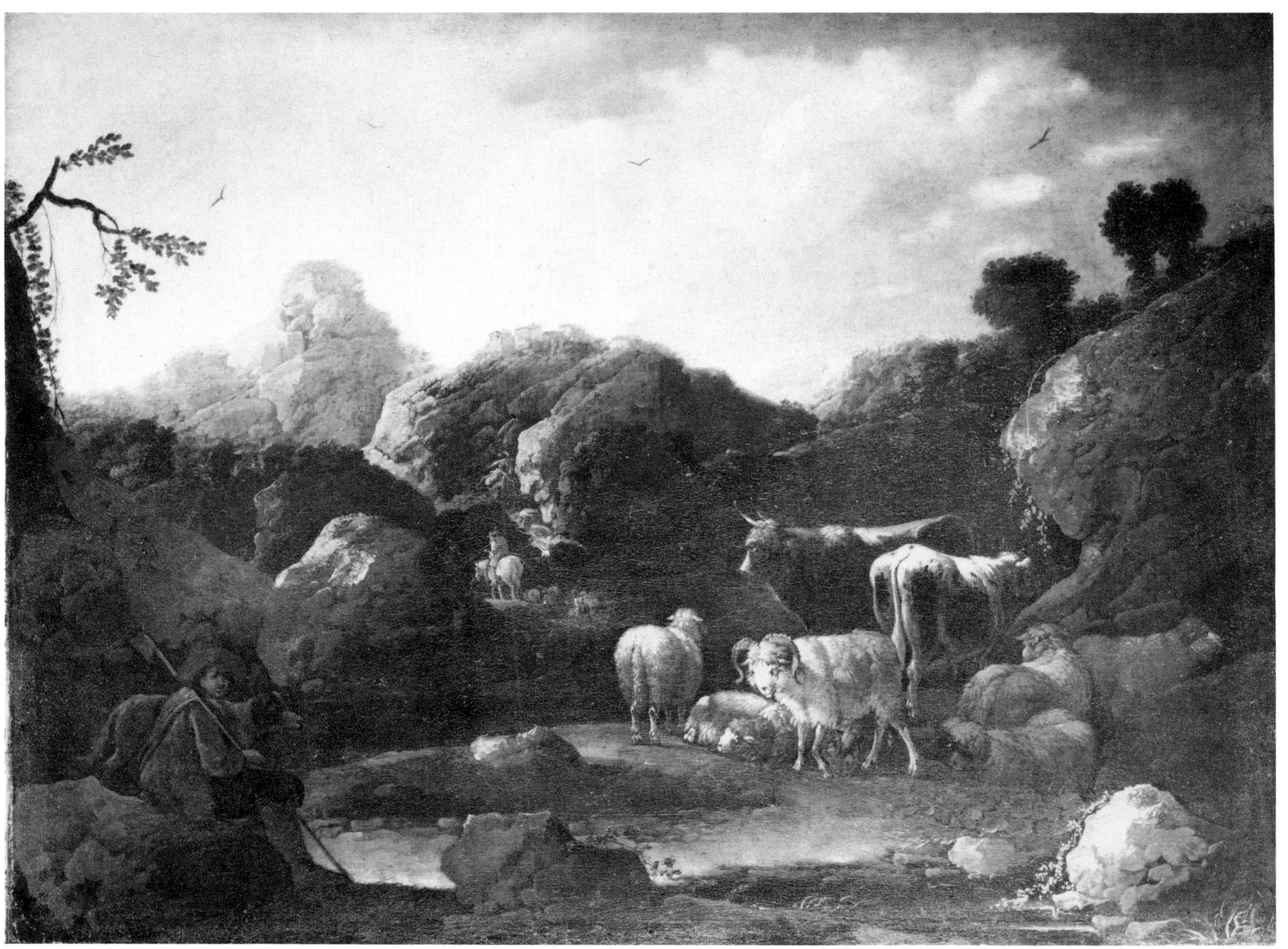

Fig. 150 Rosa da Tivoli, *Landscape with cattle and sheep* (cat. no. 1666).

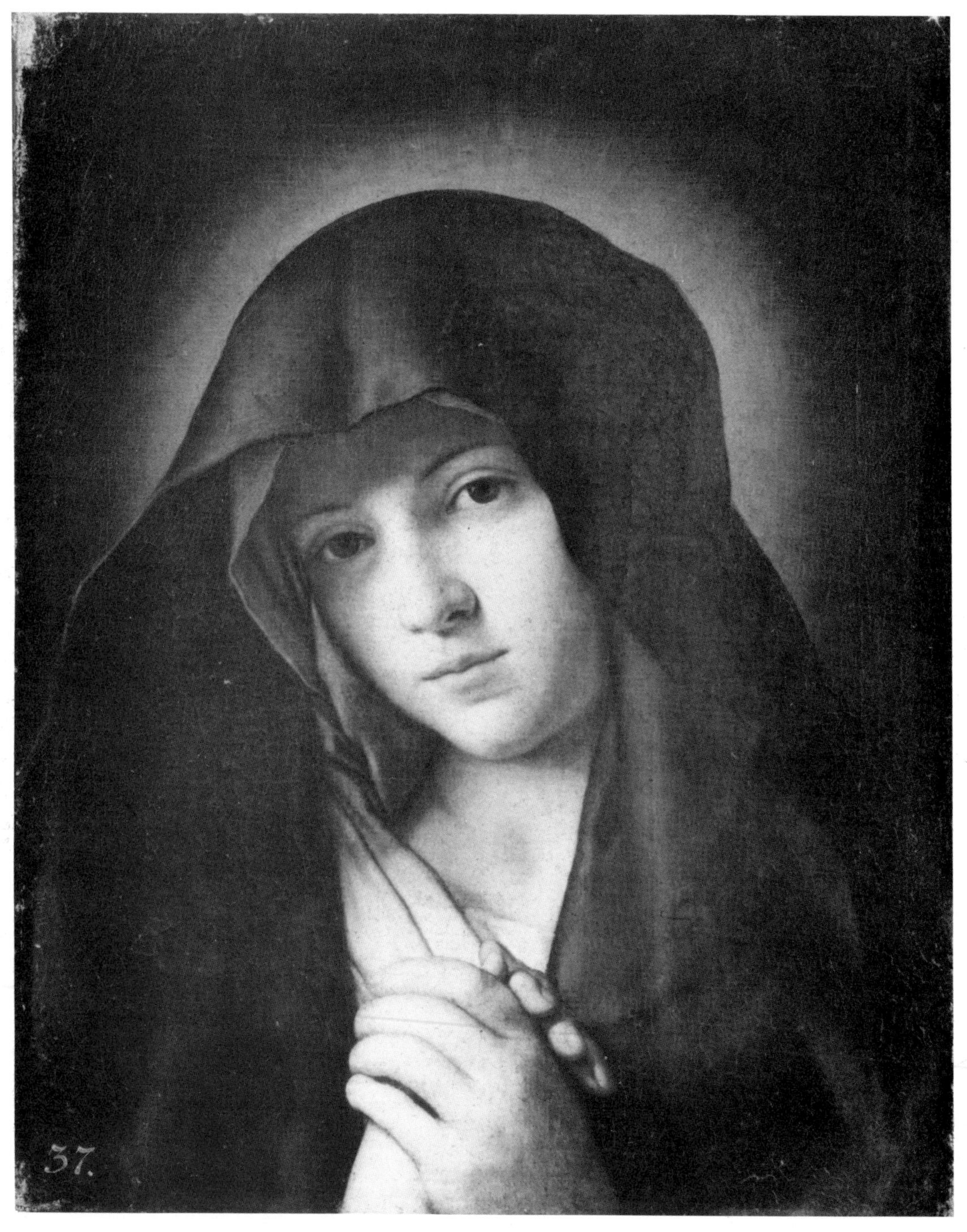

FIG. 151   After Sassoferrato, *Mater Dolorosa* (cat. no. 83).

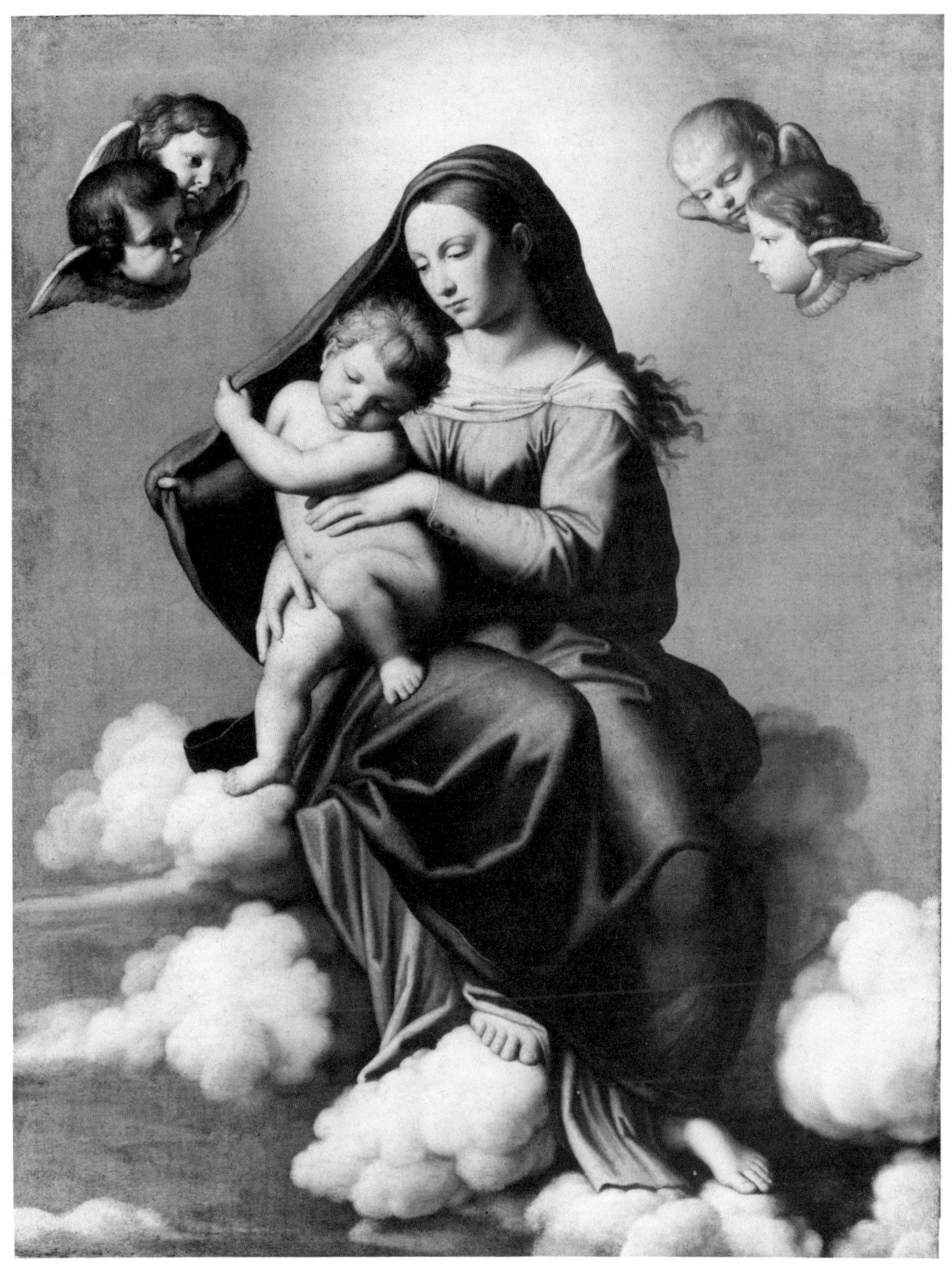

FIG. 152   Sassoferrato, *The Madonna and Child seated in clouds* (cat. no. 93).

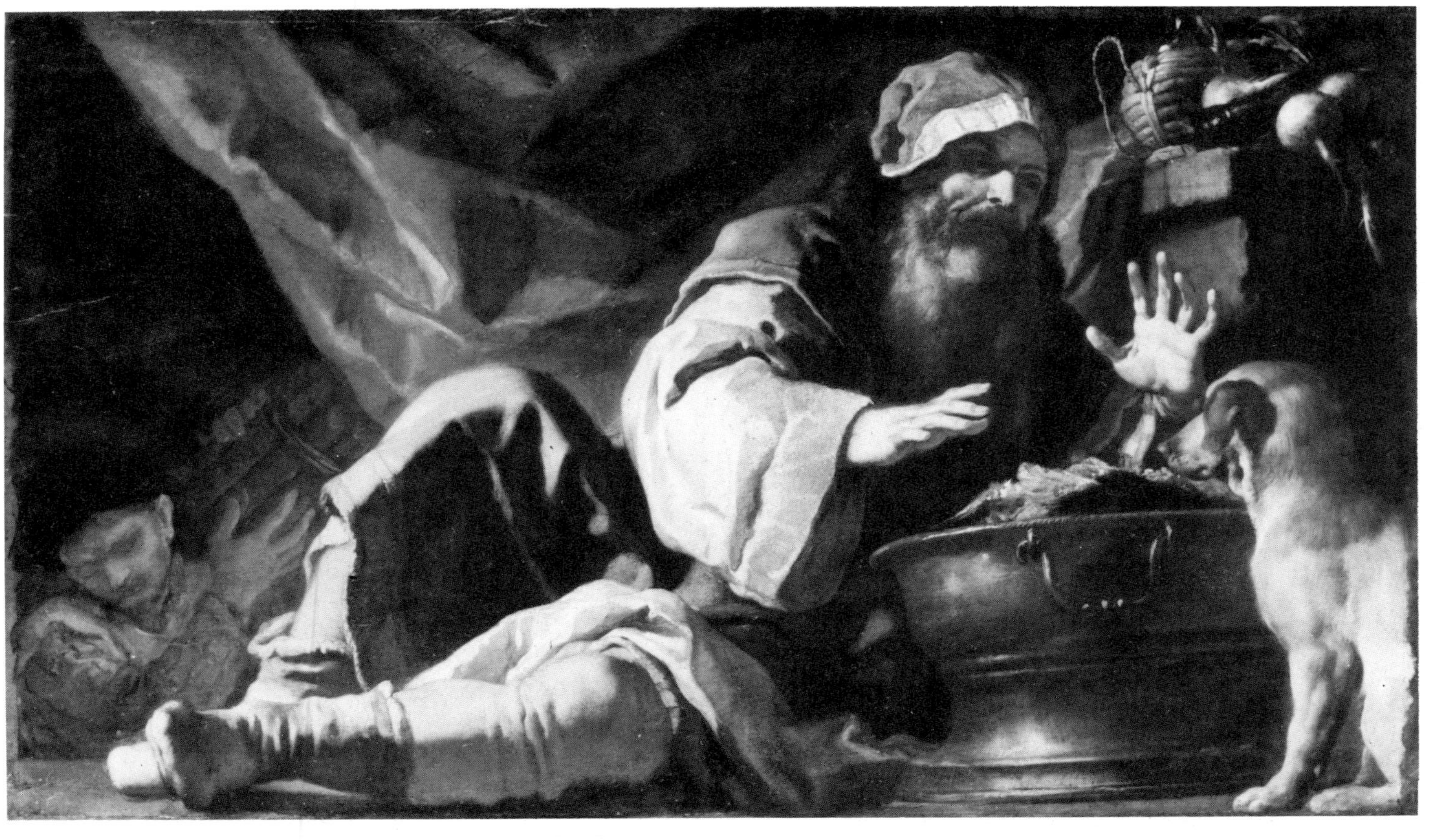

Fig. 153   Francesco Solimena, *Winter: A man warming his hands at a brazier* (cat. no. 626).

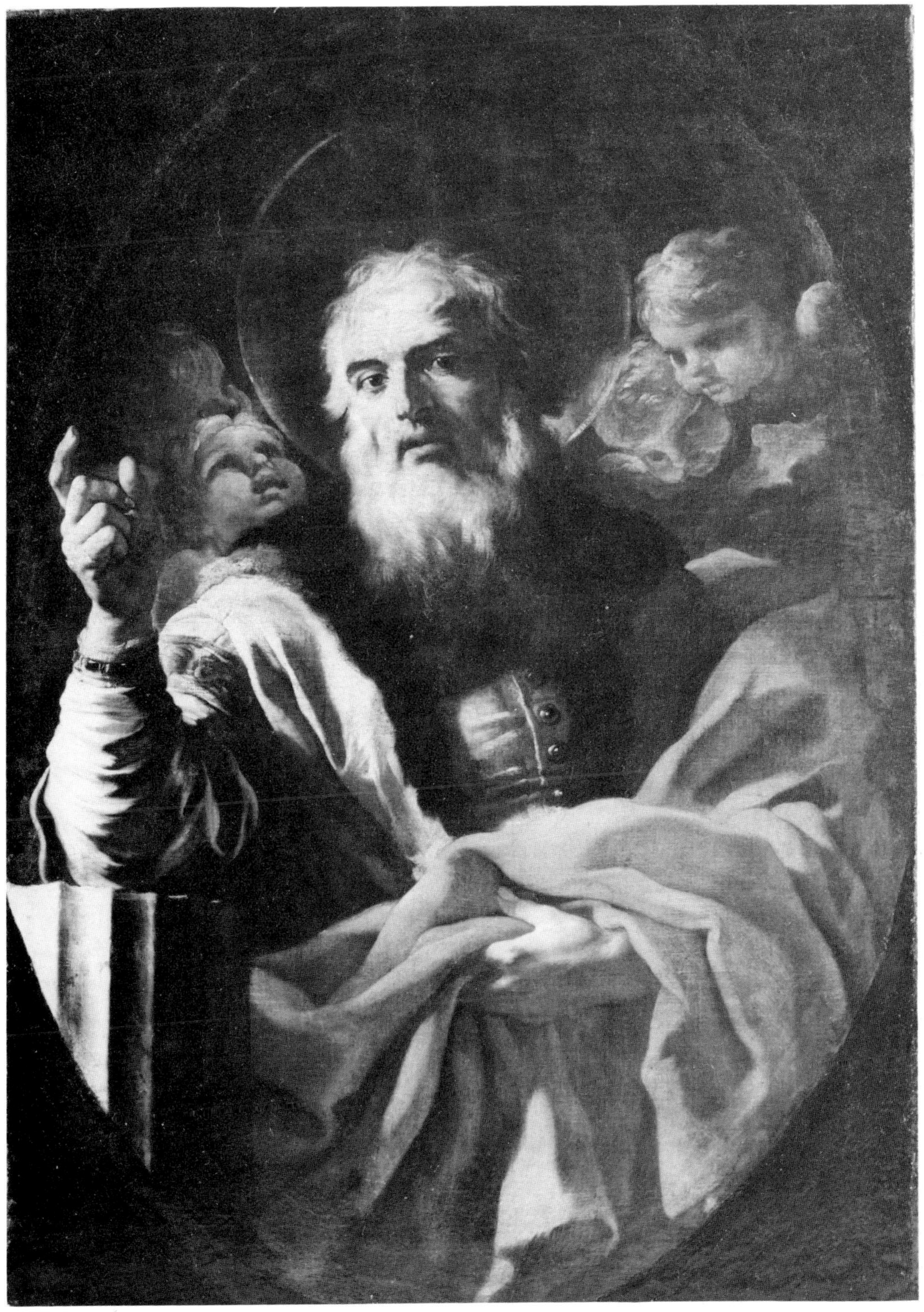

Fig. 154   Francesco Solimena, *St. Simplicius* (cat. no. 1107).

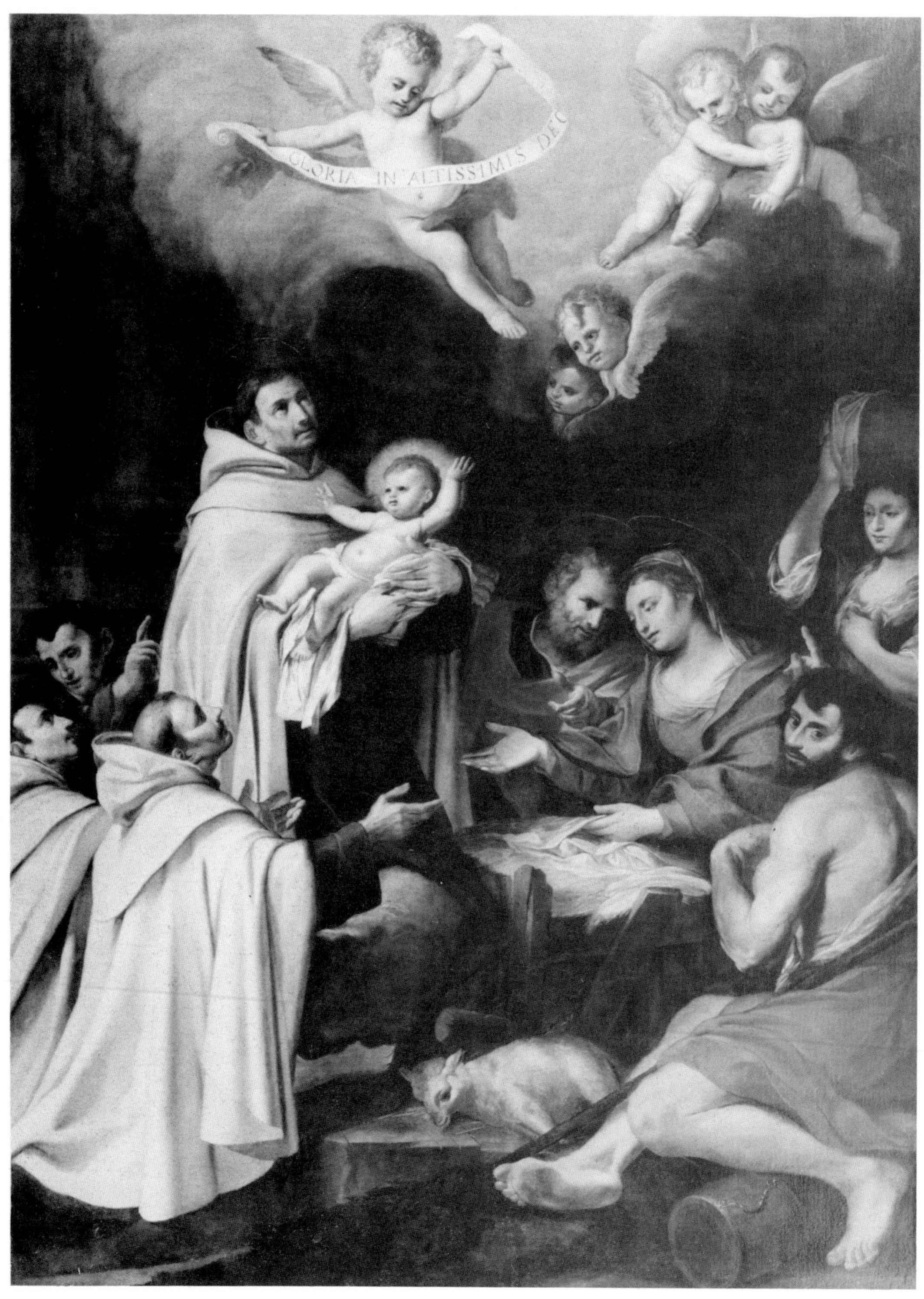

Fig. 155   Roman School, 2nd half of the 17th century, *The Holy Family with several Carmelite monks* (cat. no. 1911).

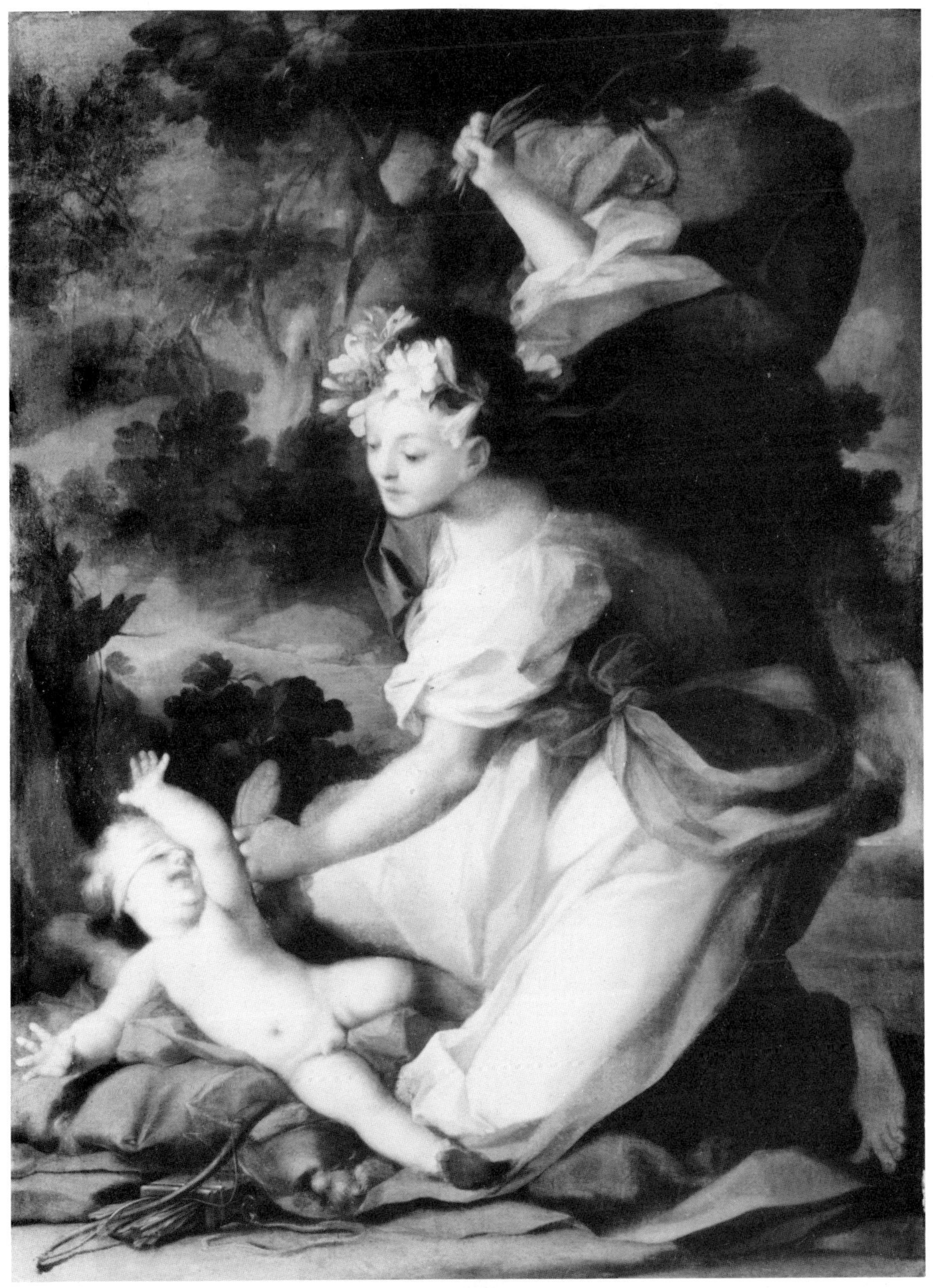

FIG. 156 Ignaz Stern, *Cupid chastised* (cat. no. 1739).

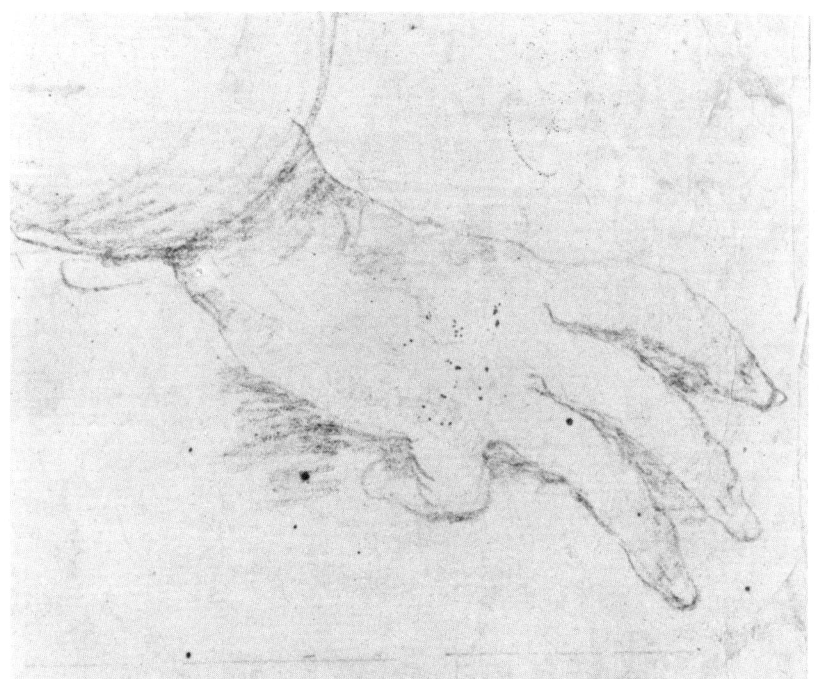

FɡG. 157 Bernardo Strozzi, *Study for right hand*. Pencil on paper,
        80 × 96 mm. Musée des Beaux-Arts, Rouen
        (Collection Baderou).

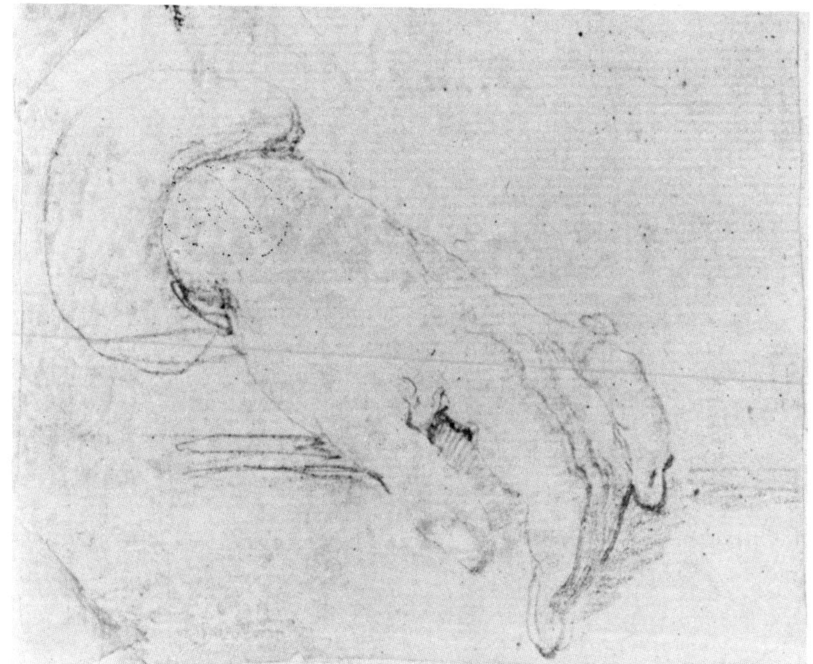

FɡG. 158 Bernardo Strozzi, *Study for left hand*. Pencil on paper,
        81 × 95 mm. Musée des Beaux-Arts, Rouen
        (Collection Baderou).

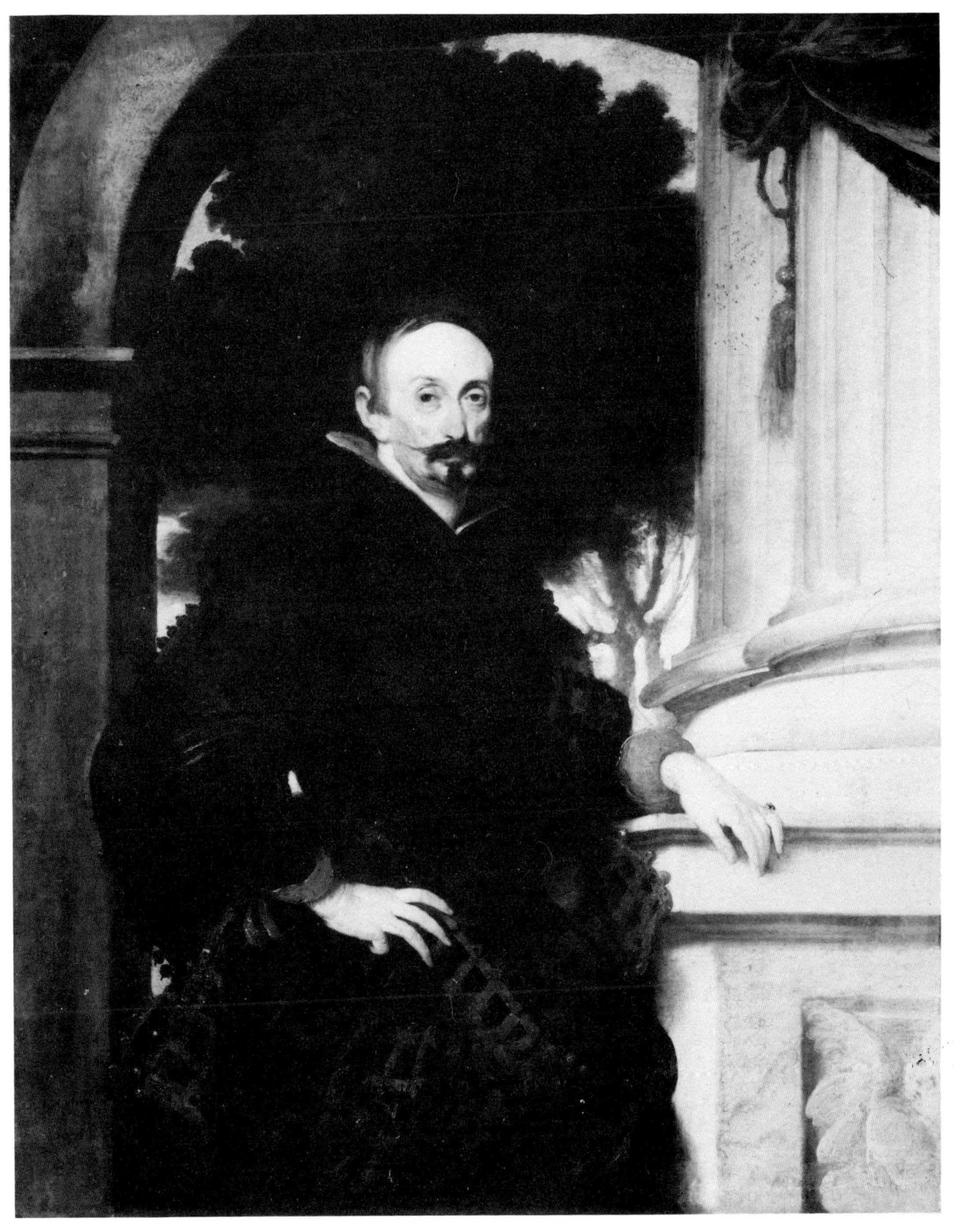

FIG. 159   Bernardo Strozzi, *Portrait of a gentleman* (cat. no. 781).

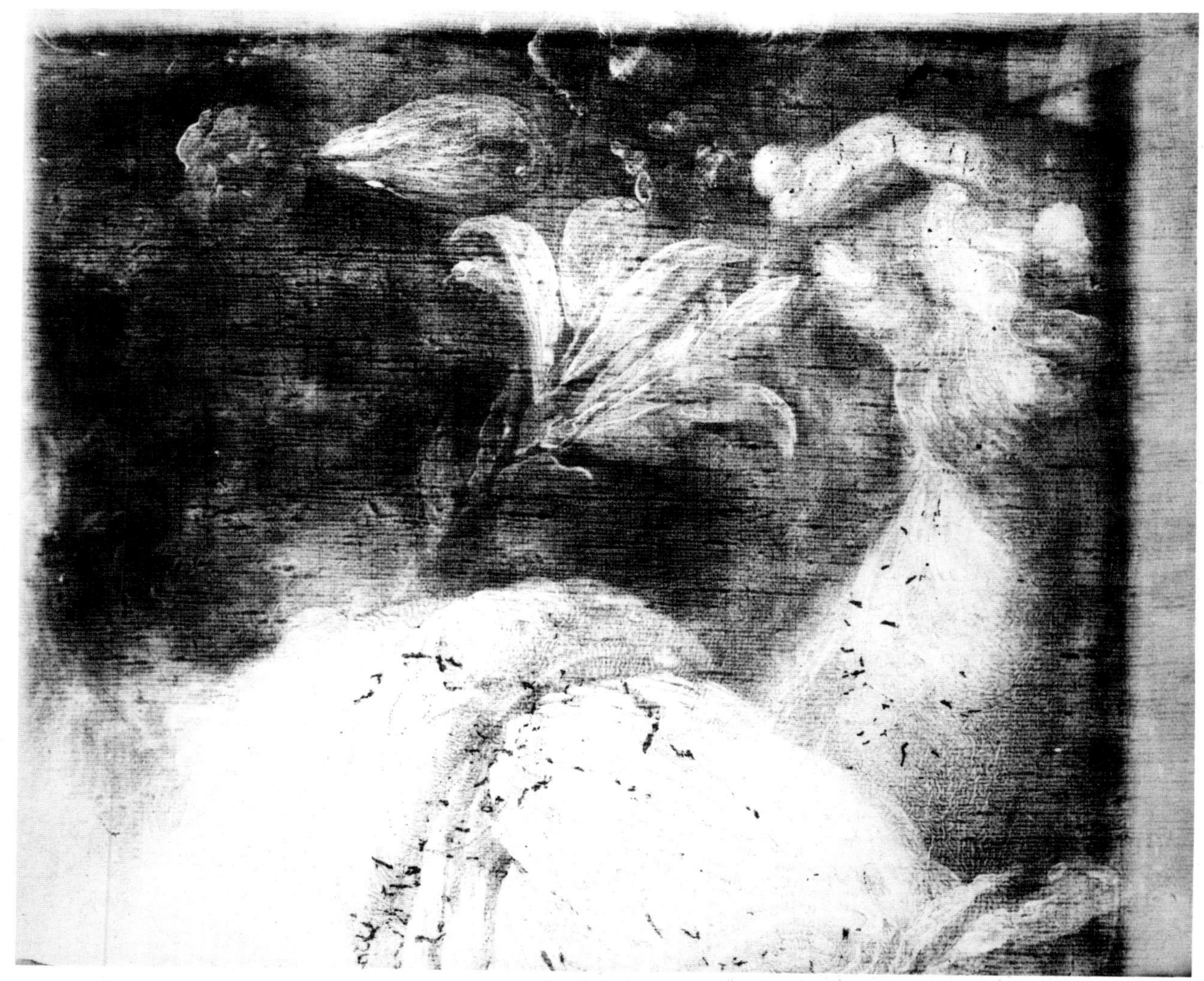

FIG. 160   Bernardo Strozzi, *Spring and summer* (cat. no. 856). X-radiograph of top right hand corner (taken in 1986).

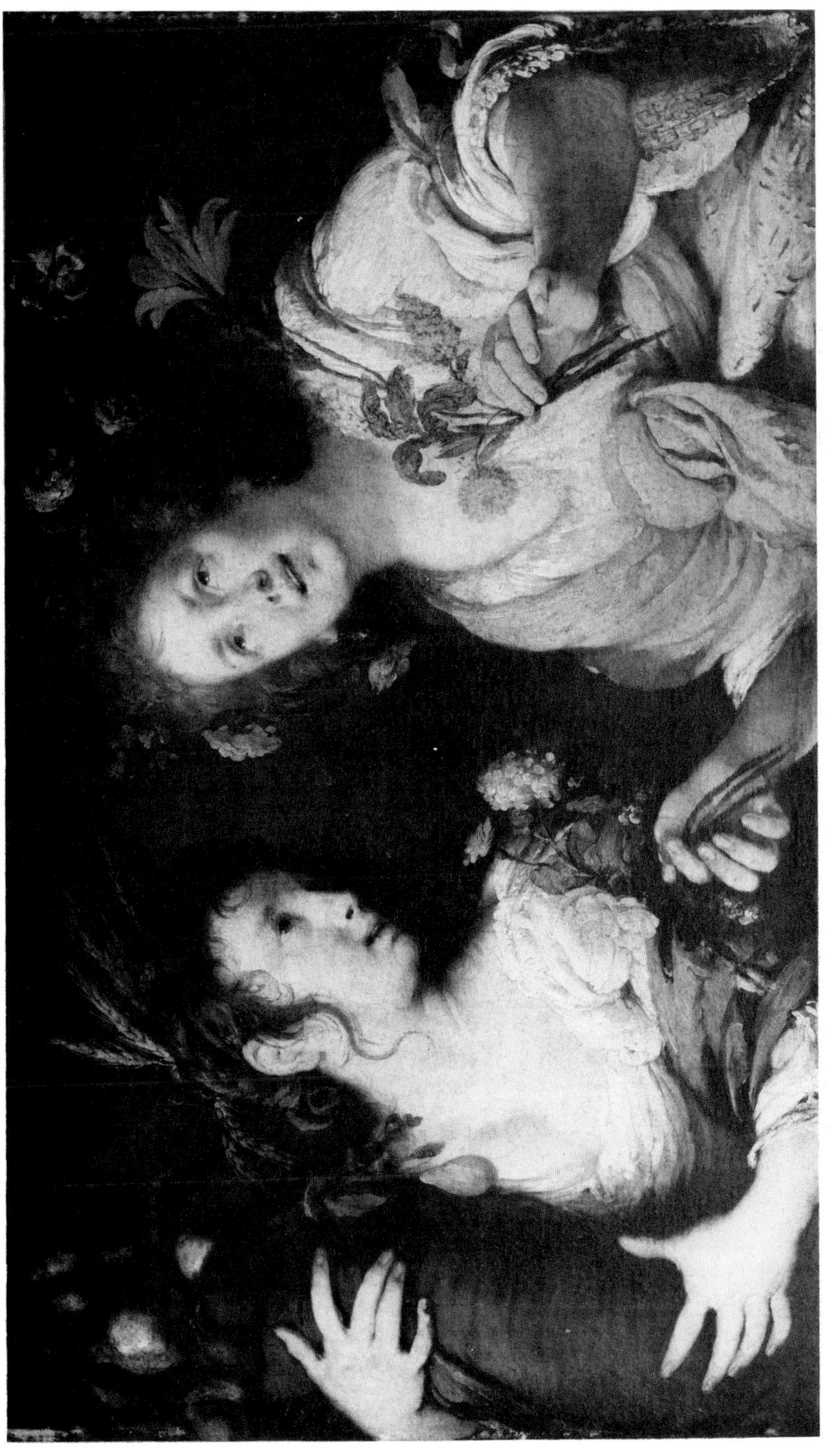

Fig. 161 Bernardo Strozzi, *Spring and summer* (cat. no. 856).

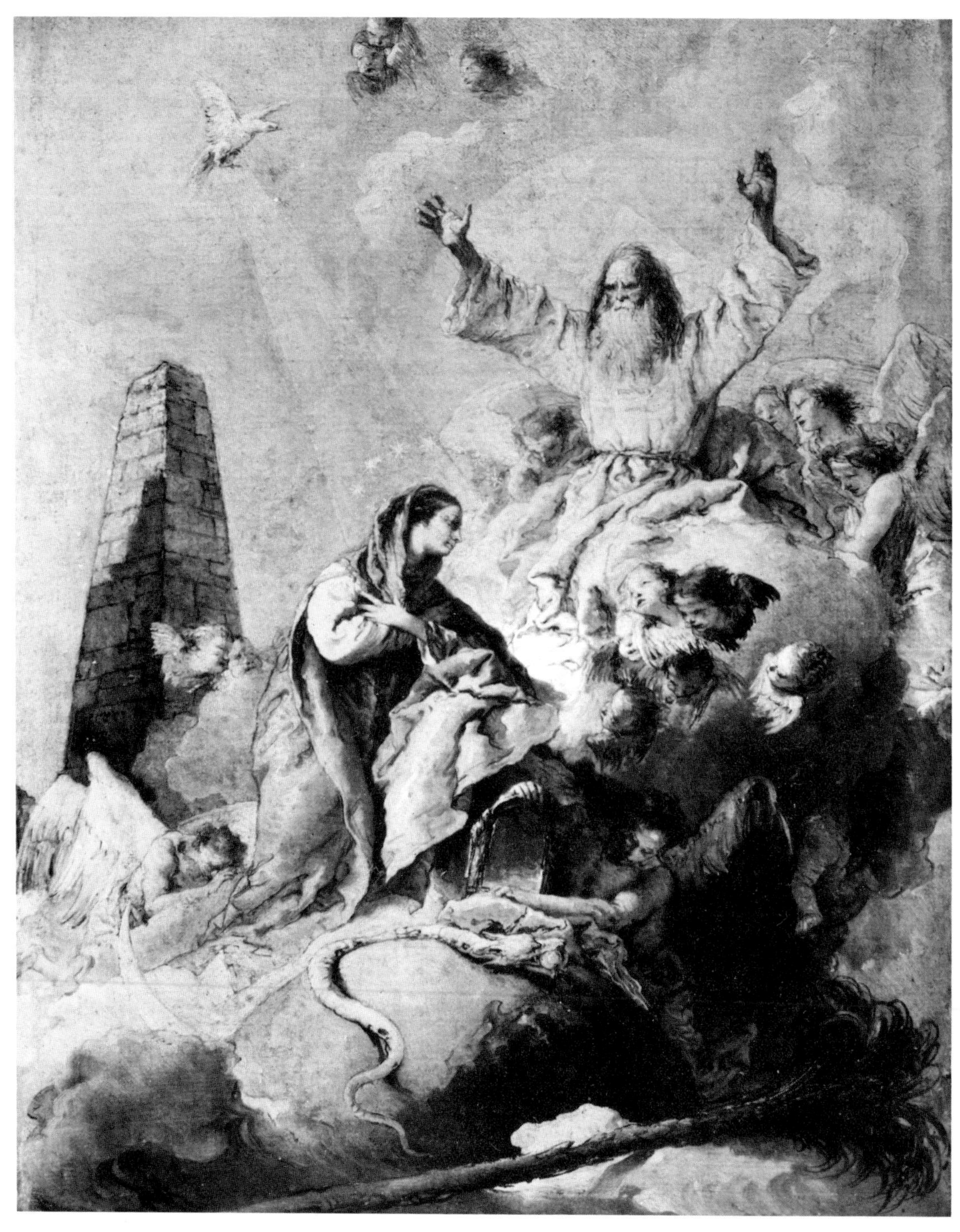

FIG. 162 Giovanni Battista Tiepolo, *Allegory of the Immaculate Conception and of Redemption* (cat. no. 353).

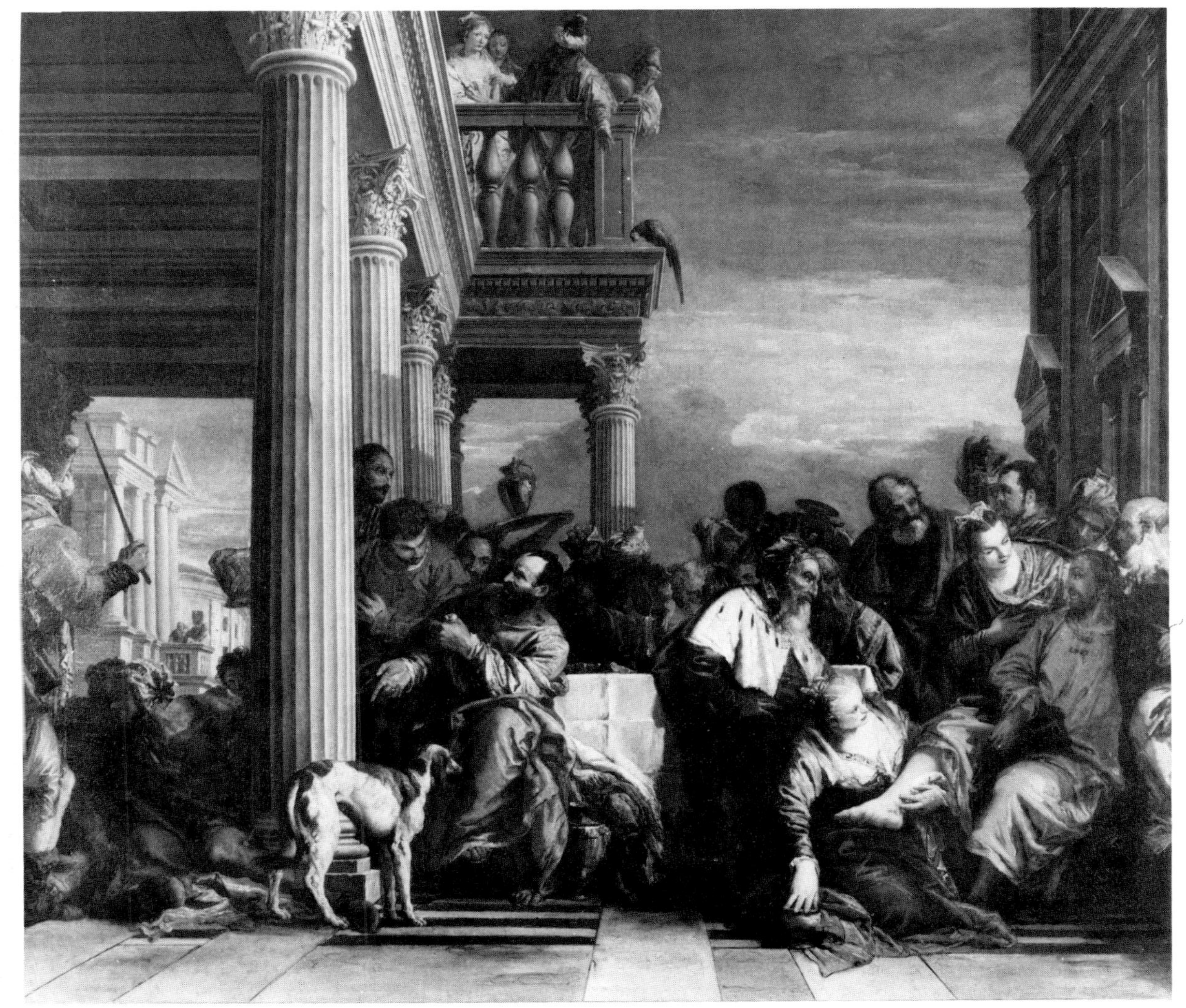

Fig. 163 Giovanni Battista Tiepolo, *Christ in the house of Simon the Pharisee* (after Veronese) (cat. no. 1111).

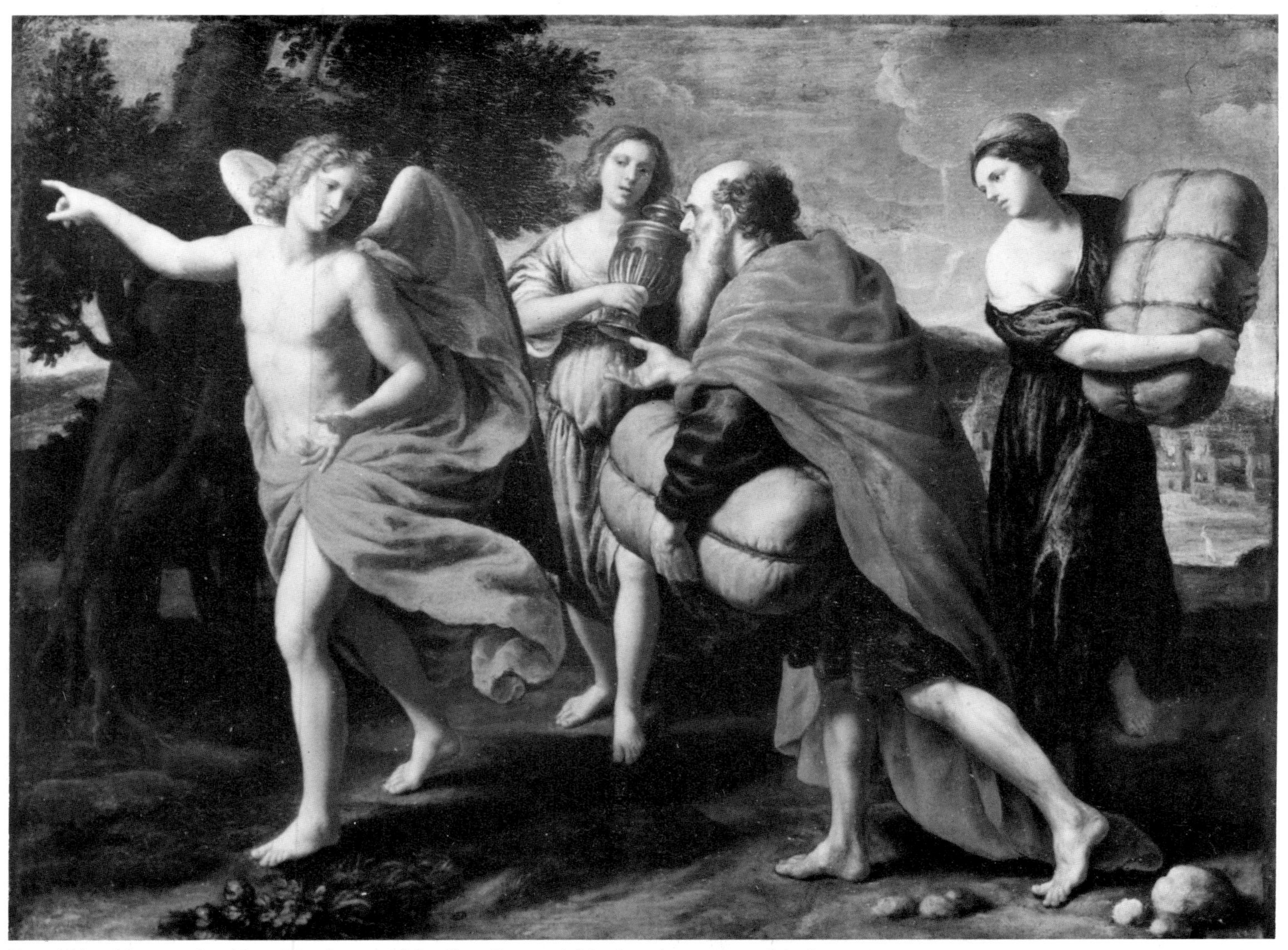

FIG. 164   Alessandro Turchi, *An angel leading Lot and his daughters out of Sodom* (cat. no. 1653).

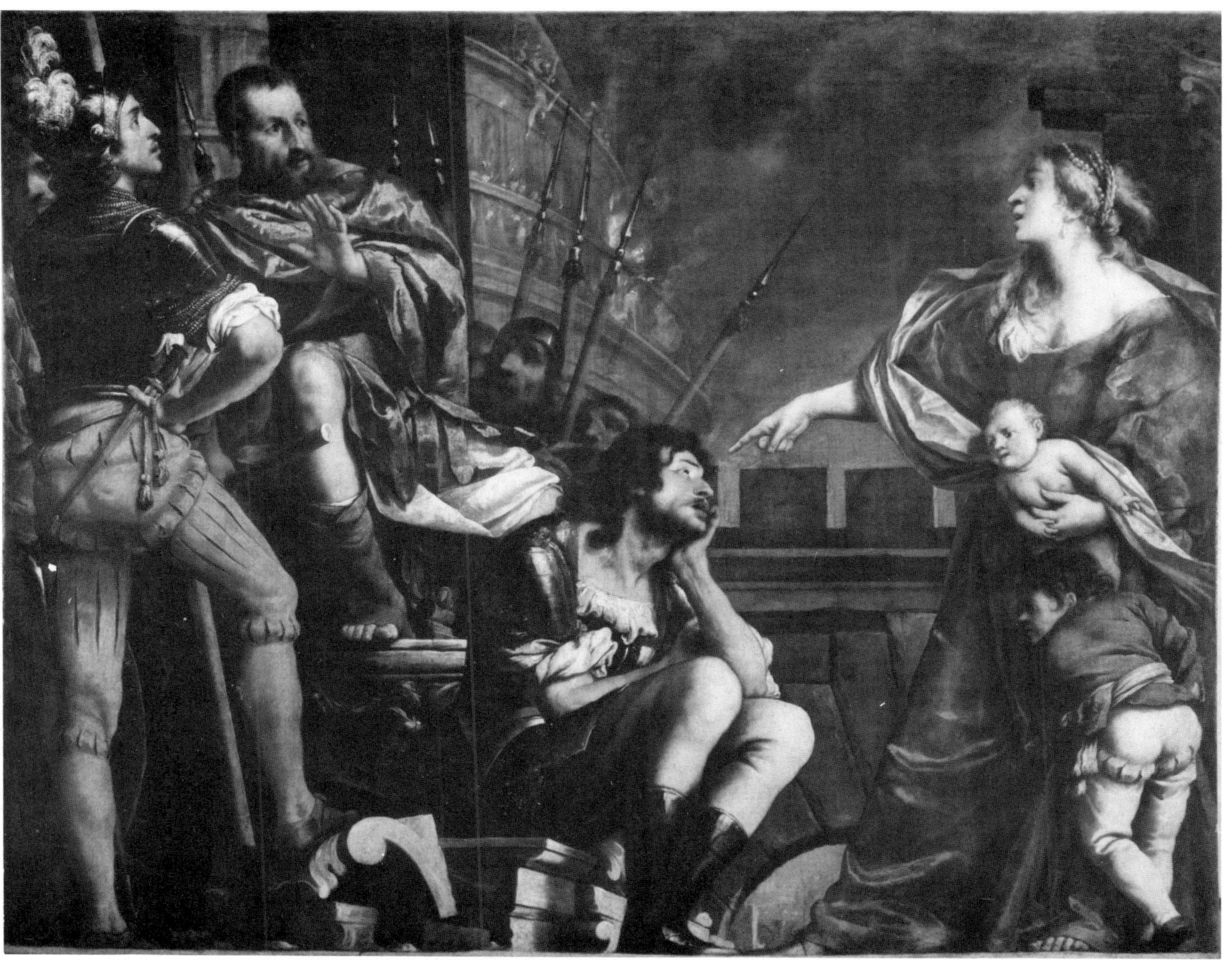

Fig. 165. Pietro della Vecchia, *"Timoclea brought before Alexander"* (cat. no. 94).

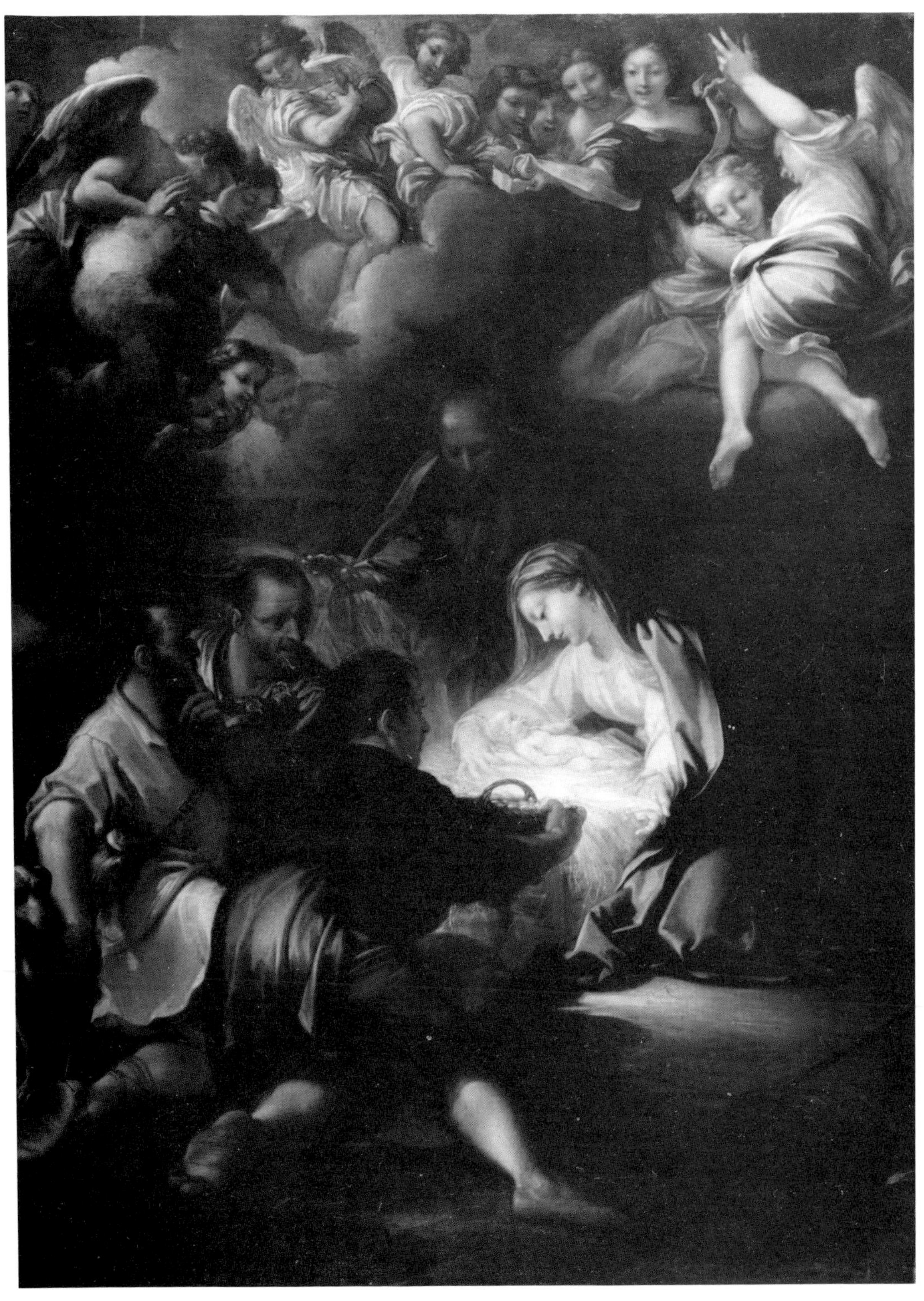

FIG. 166   Attributed to Girolamo Troppa, *The adoration of the shepherds* (cat. no. 1669)

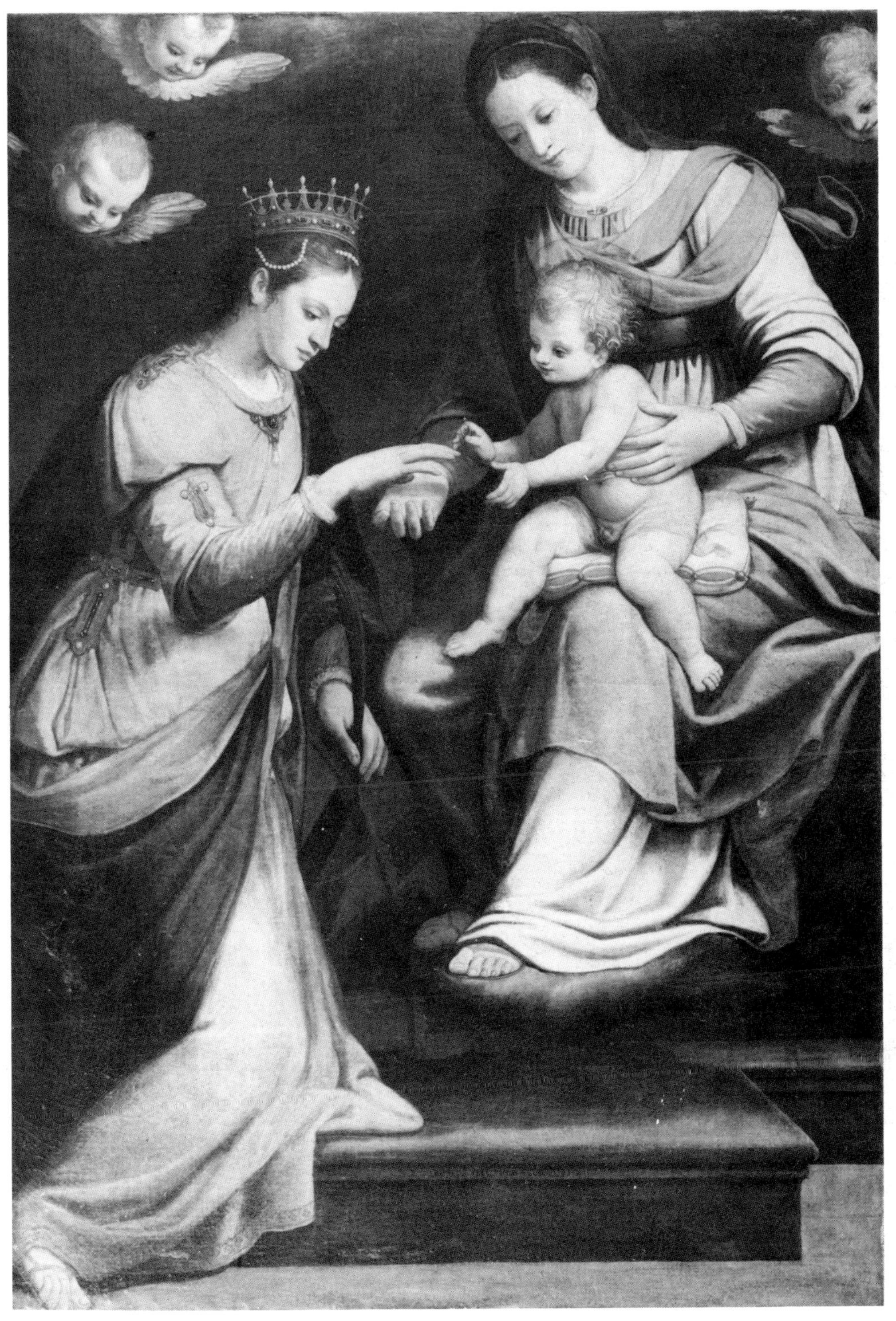

FIG. 167 Benedetto Veli, *The mystic marriage of St. Catherine* (cat. no. 1638).

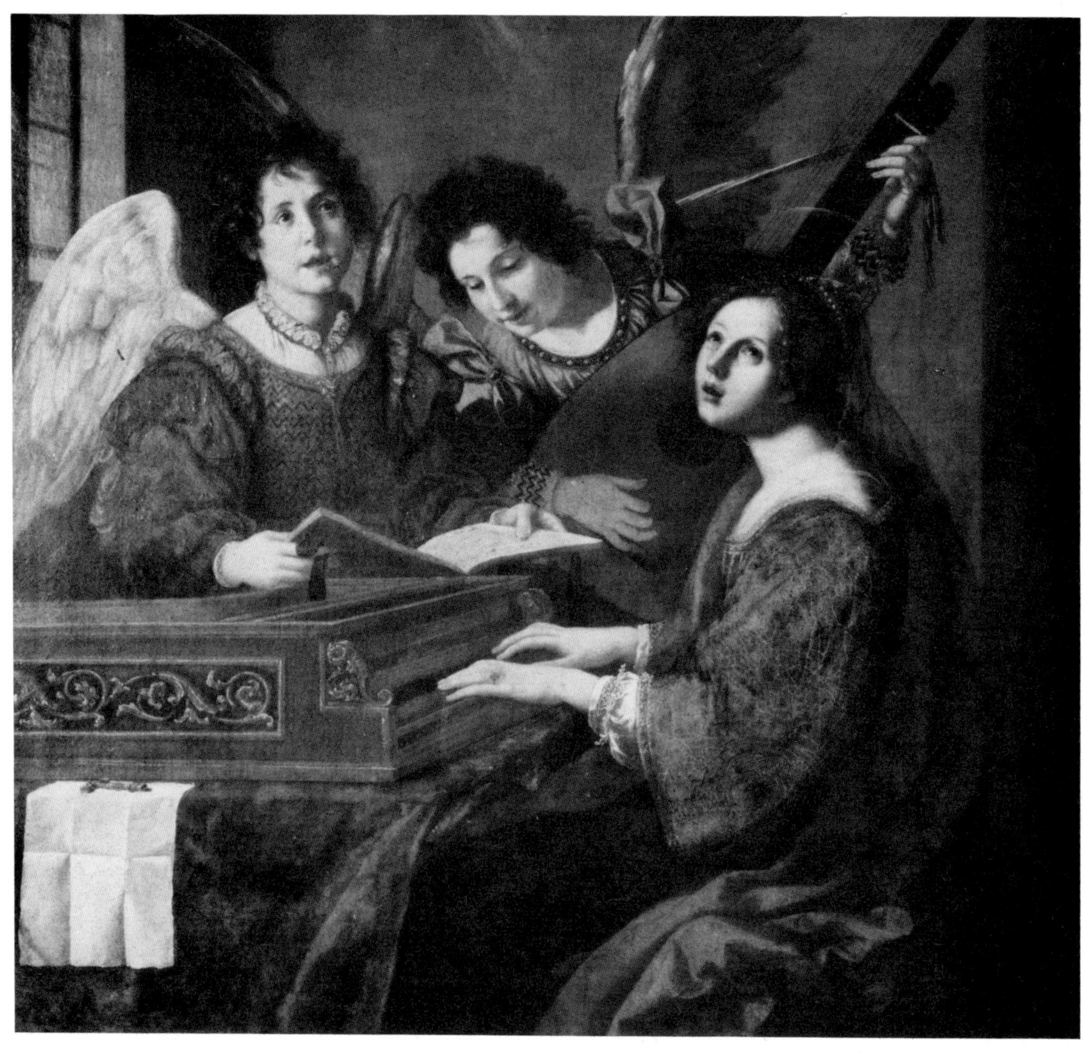

FIG. 168 Iacopo Vignali, *St. Cecilia* (cat. no. 183). Photograph taken prior to restoration in 1985.

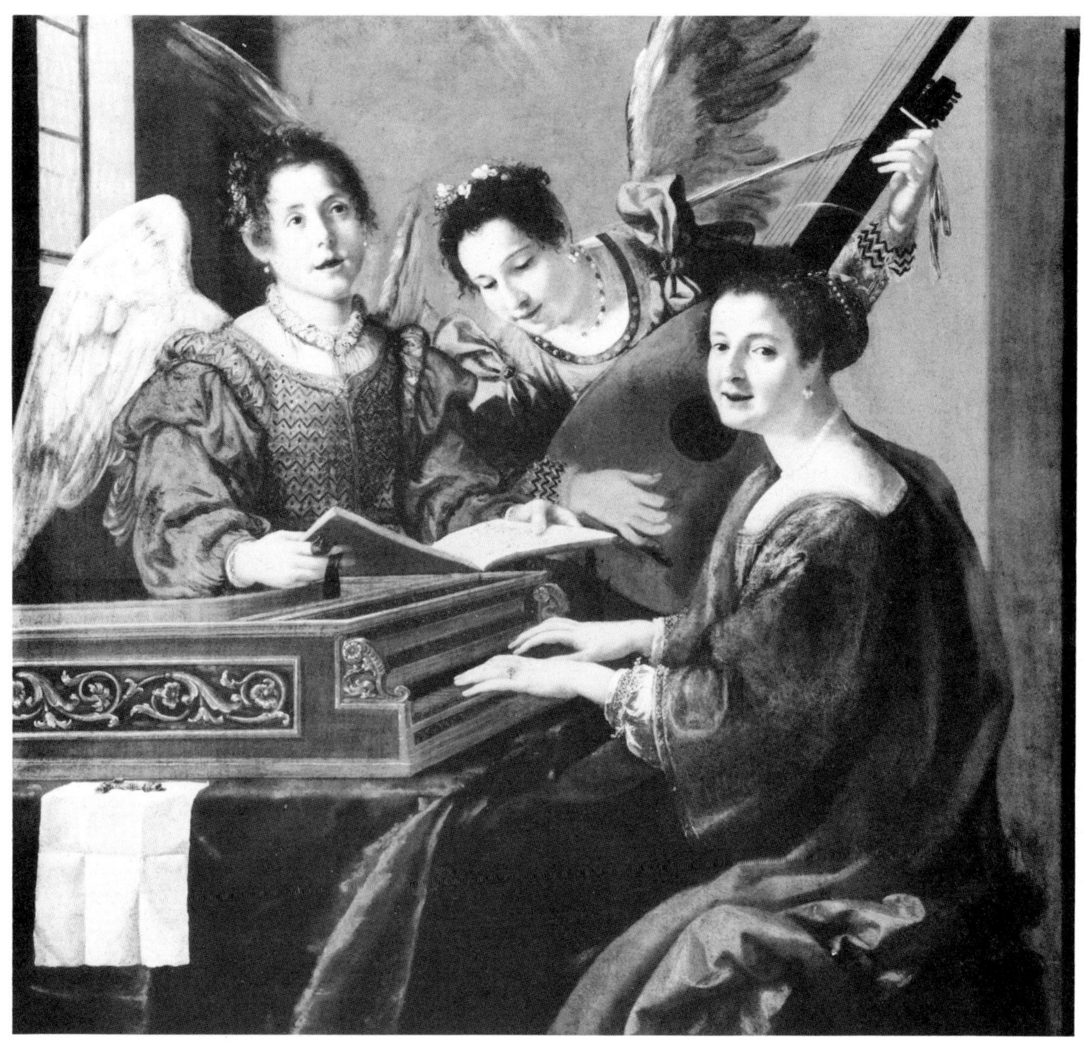

FIG. 169 Iacopo Vignali, *St. Cecilia* (cat. no. 183).

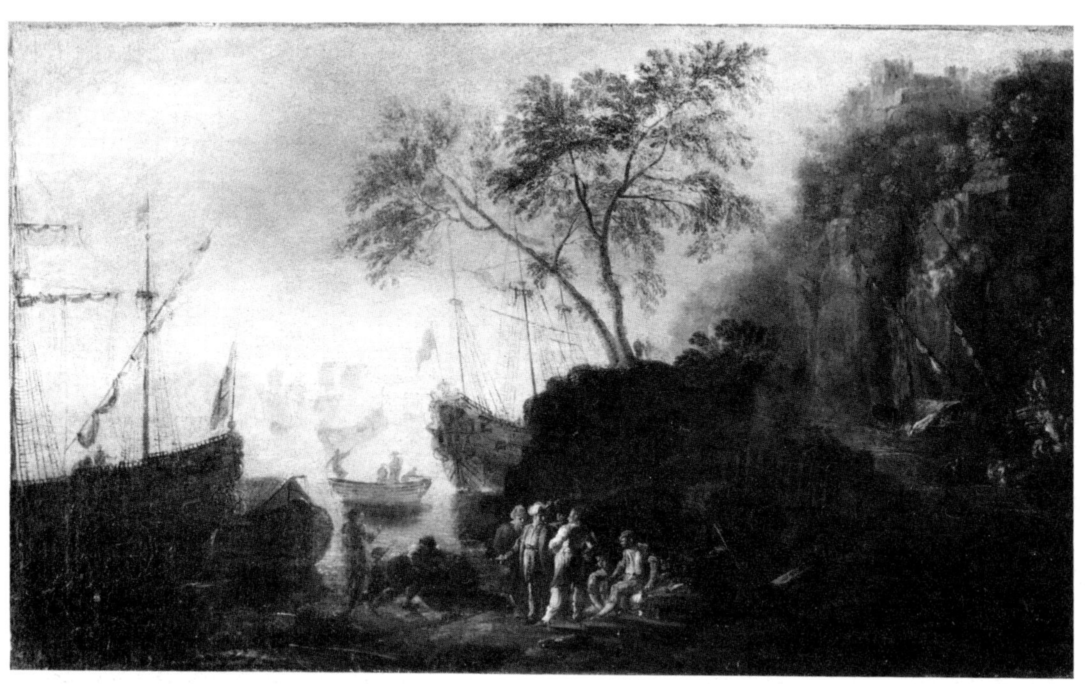

Fig. 170   School of Tassi, *Coast scene* (cat. no. 1751).

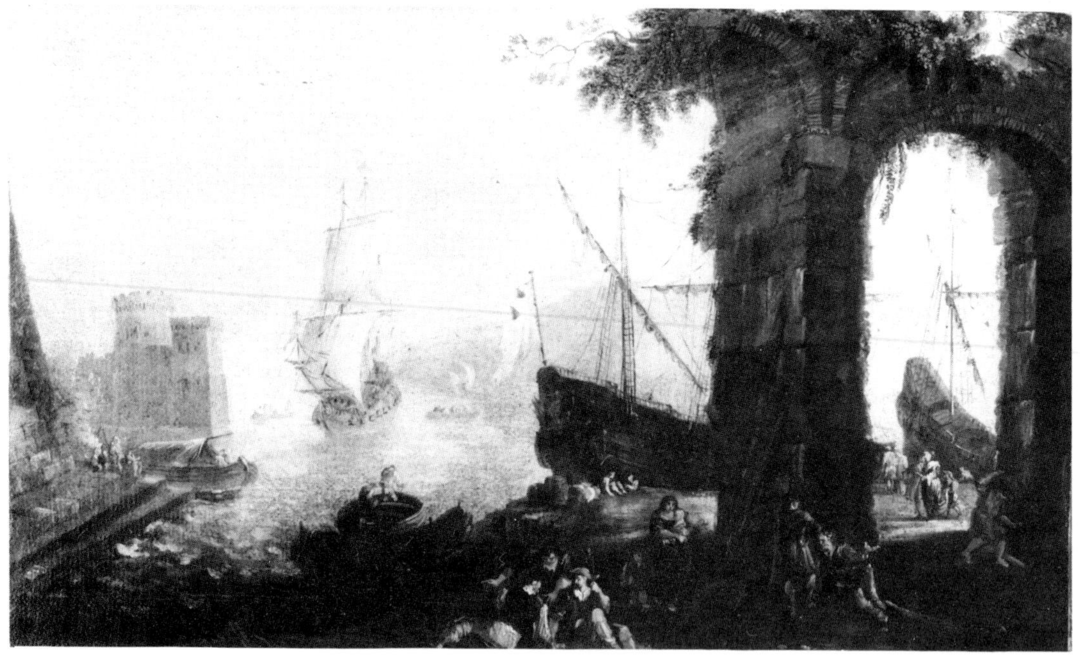

Fig. 171   School of Tassi, *Coast scene* (cat. no. 1752).

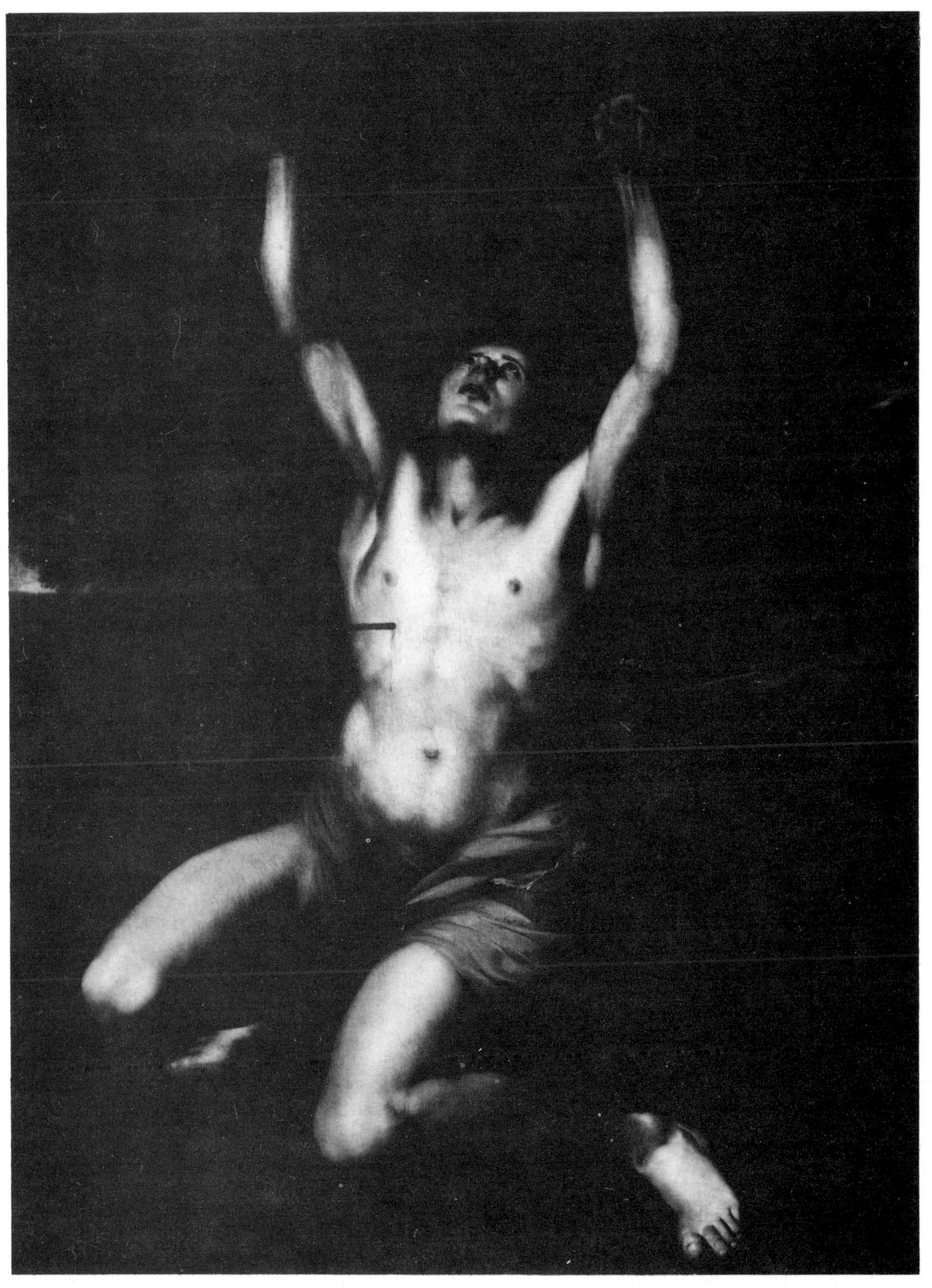

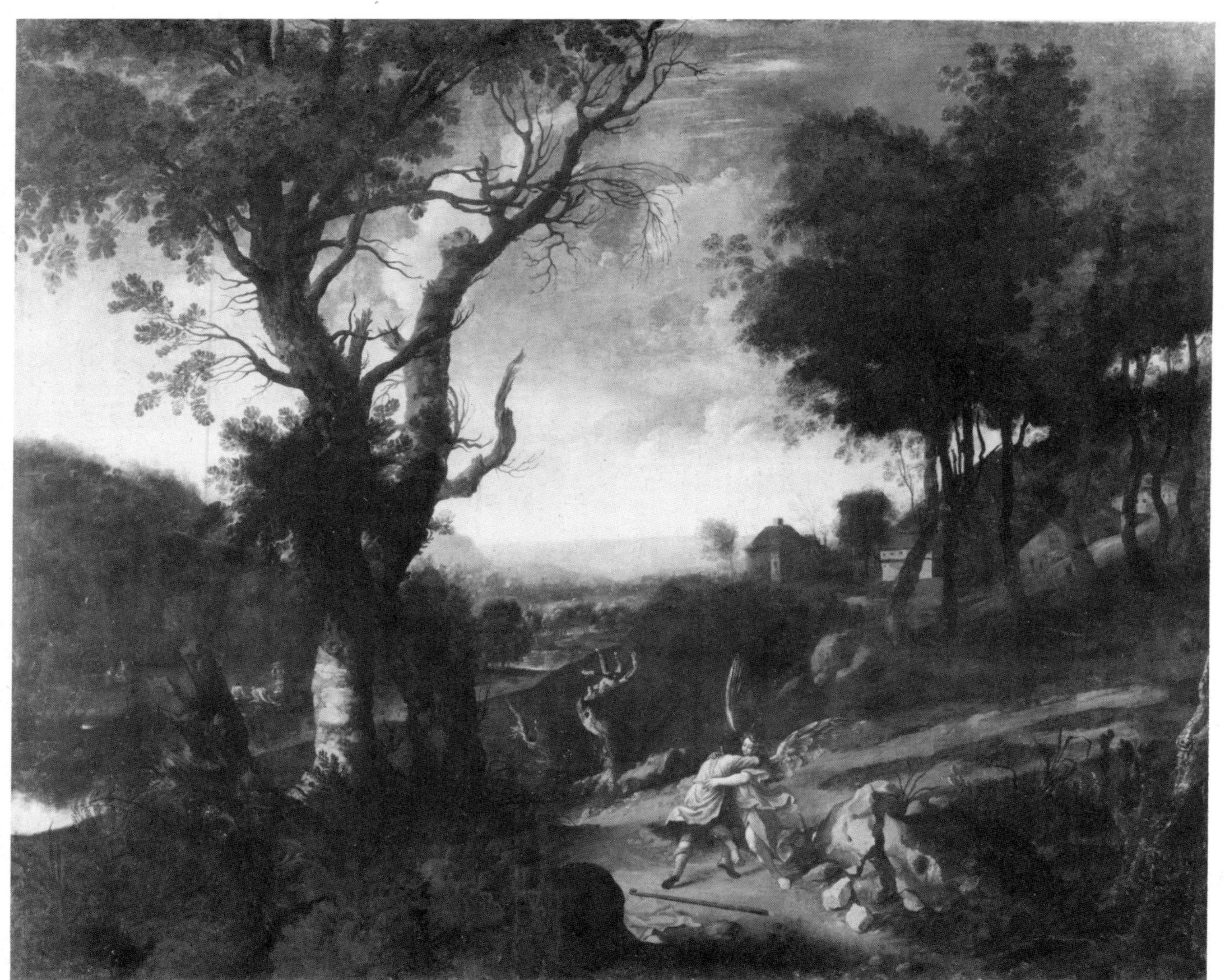

FIG. 173 Attributed to Viola, *Landscape with Jacob wrestling with the angel* (cat. no. 1977).